BUSINESS and SOCIETY
A Strategic Approach to Social Responsibility

BUSINESS and SOCIETY
A Strategic Approach to Social Responsibility

THIRD EDITION

Debbie M. Thorne
Texas State University–San Marcos

O. C. Ferrell
University of New Mexico

Linda Ferrell
University of New Mexico

Houghton Mifflin Company
Boston   New York

This book is dedicated to:

Catherine Thorne
– Debbie M. Thorne

Kathlene Ferrell
– O. C. Ferrell

Norlan and Phyllis Nafziger
– Linda Ferrell

Executive Publisher: George Hoffman
Executive Editor: Lisé Johnson
Sponsoring Editor: Mike Schenk
Associate Development Editor: Suzanna Smith
Associate Project Editor: Kristen Truncellito
Senior Art and Design Coordinator: Jill Haber
Cover Design Manager: Anne S. Katzeff
Senior Photo Editor: Jennifer Meyer Dare
Composition Buyer: Chuck Dutton
New Title Project Manager: Susan Brooks-Peltier
Editorial Assistant: John Powers
Marketing Coordinator: Erin Lane

Cover image: © Jean-Bernard Carillet/Lonely Planet Images

Printed in the U.S.A.

Library of Congress Control Number: 2006934903

ISBN-10: 0-618-82336-0
ISBN-13: 978-0-618-82336-9

123456789-MP-11 10 09 08 07

Contents

v

CHAPTER FOUR   Legal, Regulatory, and Political Issues   110

CHAPTER SEVEN **Employee Relations**   217

CHAPTER TEN   Environmental Issues   315

CHAPTER ELEVEN   Technology Issues   351

CHAPTER TWELVE The Social Audit 393

Preface

Business and its relationship to society have changed more over the last five years than the previous twenty years. Many activities considered socially responsible yet voluntary are now viewed as mandatory or are considered best practices. The institutionalization of social responsibility and business ethics is being felt and reflected on by businesses and public policy decision makers. The Sarbanes-Oxley Act of 2002 and the administrative rulings of the Securities and Exchange Commission have reformed corporate governance, internal controls, financial reporting, executive compensation, business ethics, and organizations' relations to stakeholders. The 2004 Amendments to the Federal Sentencing Commission emphasize development of an ethical leadership and an ethical corporate culture to avoid misconduct. Stakeholders have used public relations and legal means to express their concerns and influence the reputation of firms to create both positive and negative outcomes. Because of this transformation of corporate responsibility, the third edition of *Business and Society: A Strategic Approach to Social Responsibility* is designed to fully reflect on these changes. We have been diligent in this revision about discussing the most current knowledge and describing best practices related to social responsibility. The innovative text, cutting-edge cases, and comprehensive teaching and learning package for *Business and Society* ensure that business students understand and appreciate concerns about business ethics, social auditing, corporate governance, environmental responsibility, and a host of other factors for today's business leaders.

Business and Society is a highly readable and teachable text that focuses on the reality of social responsibility in the workplace. We have revised the third edition to be the most practical and applied business and society text available. A differentiating feature of this book is its focus on the role that social responsibility takes in strategic business decisions. We demonstrate that studying social responsibility provides knowledge and insights that positively contribute to organizational performance and professional success. This text prepares students for the social responsibility challenges and opportunities they will face throughout their careers. We provide the latest examples, stimulating cases, and unique learning tools that capture the reality and complexity of social responsibility. Students and instructors prefer this book because it presents examples, tools, and practices needed to develop and implement a socially responsible business strategy.

PHILOSOPHY OF THIS TEXT

Business and Society: A Strategic Approach to Social Responsibility introduces a strategic social responsibility framework for courses that address the role of business in society. Social responsibility is concerned with issues related to values and expectations as well as the rights of members of society. We view social responsibility as the extent to which a business adopts a strategic focus for fulfilling the economic, legal, ethical, and philanthropic responsibilities expected by all its stakeholders.

The compact format of this book provides twelve chapters on topics that professors view as essential in a course on business and society. We have developed manageable teaching materials that are flexible enough to incorporate current areas of interest. We provide a complete teaching and learning package that includes traditional resources for effectively using the book, diverse cases, role-play exercises, experiential exercises, "What Would You Do?" scenarios, videos, and student and instructor websites.

We demonstrate and help the instructor prove that social responsibility is a theoretically grounded, yet highly actionable and practical, field of interest. The relationship between business and society is inherently controversial and complex, but the intersection of its components, such as corporate governance, workplace ethics, the natural environment, government institutions, business objectives, community needs, and technology, is experienced in every organization. For this reason, we developed this text to effectively assist decision making and inspire the application of social responsibility principles to a variety of situations and organizations.

A RELEVANT AND ENGAGING APPROACH

Our book provides cutting-edge knowledge based on research, best practices, and the latest developments in social responsibility. Reviewers inform us that our book takes a fresh look at real-world issues in an engaging, readable way that connects students to reality. We integrate emerging developments in the field of corporate governance, business ethics, and information technology as well as environmental and social issues throughout the text. We balance our coverage by avoiding overemphasis of some topics and providing enough depth on key content areas so students receive the background they need to learn more about the relevant topics. For example, the internal and external environments of business changed tremendously with the corporate scandals of the early 2000s. These events shocked millions of Americans into reevaluating our economic system and their expectations of business. Today, organizational stakeholders are more concerned about business ethics, governance, and accountability—key concepts discussed throughout the book. This text was revised to incorporate both the subtle and obvious long-term ramifications of these and other recent events on social responsibility.

A business and society course provides the necessary grounding for discussing the interactions, effects, and changes to social responsibility that we experience every day as new events occur. For this reason, our goal is to make *Business and Society* as interesting, timely, thought provoking, and useful as possible. To accomplish this goal, we incorporate historical, current, and emerging concepts and theories, draw on current news and corporate events from around the world, and take an active and experiential learning perspective. We encourage our readers to contemplate their understanding of social responsibility and the challenges and opportunities it poses for executives, communities, employees, governments, consumers, and other constituents.

CONTENT AND ORGANIZATION

Professors who teach business and society courses come from diverse backgrounds, including law, management, marketing, philosophy, and many others. Such diversity affords great opportunities to the field of business and society and showcases the central role that social responsibility occupies within various academic, professional, work, and community circles. Because of the widespread interest and multiplicity of stakeholders, the philosophy and practice of social responsibility are both exciting and debatable; they are in a constant state of discussion and refinement—just like all important business concepts and practices.

The term *social responsibility* came into widespread use during the 1990s, but many other terms, like those mentioned at the beginning of the Preface, are also used. In Chapter 1, "Social Responsibility Framework," we define social responsibility as the adoption by a business of a strategic focus for fulfilling the economic, legal, ethical, and philanthropic responsibilities expected of it by its stakeholders. Social responsibility must be fully valued and championed by top managers and granted the same planning time, priority, and management attention as any company initiative. Our framework begins with the social responsibility philosophy, includes the four types of responsibilities, involves many types of stakeholders, and ultimately results in both short- and long-term performance gains. We take a strategic orientation to social responsibility, so students develop knowledge, skills, and attitudes for understanding how organizations achieve many benefits through social responsibility. This chapter also offers evidence that resources invested in social responsibility contribute to improved corporate reputation and financial performance. We explore the central role of trust in maintaining positive relationships with stakeholders, particularly employees, customers, and shareholders. By fostering a high level of trust in stakeholder relationships, companies receive a variety of benefits, including lower operating costs and positive long-term relationships. Misconduct can harm a firm's reputation, sales, and stock price, but addressing stakeholder concerns through a strategic responsibility program can improve a firm's bottom line.

To gain the benefits of social responsibility, effective and mutually beneficial relationships must be developed with customers, employees, investors, competitors, government, the community, and others who have a stake in the company. Chapter 2, "Strategic Management of Stakeholder Relationships," examines the types and attributes of stakeholders, how stakeholders become influential, and the processes for integrating and managing their influence on a firm. The chapter introduces the stakeholder interaction model and examines the impact of global business, corporate reputation, and crisis situations on stakeholder relationships.

Because both daily and strategic decisions affect a variety of stakeholders, companies must maintain a governance structure for ensuring proper control and responsibility for their actions. Chapter 3, "Corporate Governance," examines the rights of shareholders, the accountability of top management for corporate actions, executive compensation, and strategic-level processes for ensuring that economic, legal, ethical, and philanthropic responsibilities are satisfied. Corporate governance is an integral element for social responsibility, which, until the recent scandals, had not received the same level of emphasis as issues such as the environment and human rights.

Chapter 4, "Legal, Regulatory, and Political Issues," explores the complex relationship between business and government. Every business must be aware of and abide by the laws and regulations that dictate required business conduct. This chapter also examines how business can participate in the public policy process to influence government. A strategic approach for legal compliance, based on the Federal Sentencing Guidelines for Organizations, is also provided. Chapter 5, "Business Ethics and Ethical Decision Making," and Chapter 6, "Strategic Approaches to Improving Ethical Behavior," are devoted to exploring the role of ethics in business decision making. Business ethics relates to responsibilities and expectations that exist beyond legally prescribed levels. We examine the factors that influence ethical decision making and consider how companies can apply this understanding to improve ethical conduct. We fully describe the components of an organizational ethics program and detail the implementation plans needed for effectiveness.

Chapter 7, "Employee Relations," and Chapter 8, "Consumer Relations," explore relationships with two pivotal stakeholders. Employees and consumers, although different by definition, have similar expectations of the economic, legal, ethical, and philanthropic responsibilities that must be addressed by business. Chapter 9, "Community Relations and Strategic Philanthropy," examines companies' synergistic use of organizational core competencies and resources to address key stakeholders' interests and achieve both organizational and social benefits. While traditional benevolent philanthropy involves donating a percentage of sales to social causes, a strategic approach aligns employees and organizational resources and expertise with the needs and concerns of stakeholders. Strategic philanthropy involves both financial and nonfinancial contributions (employee time, goods and services, technology and equipment, as well as facilities) to stakeholders, but it also benefits the company.

Chapter 10, "Environmental Issues," explores the significant environmental issues business and society face today, including air pollution, global warming, water pollution and water quantity, land pollution, waste management, deforestation, urban sprawl, biodiversity, and genetically modified foods. This chapter also considers the impact of government environmental policy and regulation, and it examines how some companies are doing more than these laws require to address environmental issues and act in an environmentally responsible manner.

Thanks to the Internet and other technological advances, communication is faster than ever, information can be found about almost any topic, and people are living longer, healthier lives. Chapter 11, "Technology Issues," provides cutting-edge information on the unique issues that arise as a result of enhanced technology in the workplace and business environment, including its effects on privacy, intellectual property, and health. The strategic direction for technology depends on the government's and businesses' ability to plan, implement, and audit the influence of technology on society.

Regardless of an organization's particular situation, without reliable measurements of the achievement of objectives, a company has no concrete way to verify its importance, link it to organizational performance, justify expenditures, or adequately address stakeholder concerns. Chapter 12, "The Social Audit," describes an auditing procedure that can measure and improve the social responsibility effort. This chapter takes a complete strategic perspective on social responsibility, including stakeholder relations, legal and ethical issues, and philanthropy. This audit is important for demonstrating commitment and ensuring the continuous improvement of the social responsibility effort. An example of a company's social responsibility or social audit is included in the book's website. Since many instructors use the audit as a class project or organizing mechanism for the course, the chapter and website serve as important additions to instructor resources.

SPECIAL FEATURES

Business and Society has a highly visible practical orientation. This text provides a variety of features to aid students in understanding the relevance and seeing the real-world application of key concepts, in identifying key points and recalling important ideas, and in applying their knowledge to realistic situations. The purpose of all these tools is to take students through a complete strategic planning and implementation perspective on business and society concerns by incorporating an active and team-based learning perspective.

Examples from companies and circumstances all over the world appear throughout the text. Every chapter opens with a vignette and includes numerous examples that shed more light on how social responsibility works in today's business. In this edition, all boxed features focus on the global dimensions of social responsibility. Chapter opening objectives, a chapter summary, boldfaced key terms, and discussion questions at the end of the chapter help direct students' attention to key points.

Experiential exercises at the end of each chapter help students apply social responsibility concepts and ideas to business practice. Most of the exercises involve research on the activities, programs, and philosophies that companies and organizations are using to implement social responsibility today. These exercises are designed for higher level learning and require students to apply, analyze, synthesize, and evaluate knowledge, concepts, practices, and possibilities for social responsibility. At the same time, the instructor can generate rich and complex discussions from student responses to the exercises. For example, the experiential exercise for Chapter 1 asks students to examine *Fortune* magazine's annual list of most admired companies. This exercise sets the stage for a discussion on the broad context in which stakeholders, business objectives, and responsibilities converge. The experiential exercise for the technology chapter requires students to visit websites targeted at children. In visiting the site, students take on the perspective of a child and then assess the site for any persuasion, potentially worrisome content, privacy issues, and guidelines of the Children's Online Privacy Protection Act.

"What Would You Do?" exercises depict people in real-world scenarios who are faced with a decision about social responsibility in the workplace. The exercise in Chapter 9 discusses the dilemma of a newly named vice president of corporate philanthropy. His charge over the next year is to develop a stronger reputation for philanthropy and social responsibility with the company's stakeholders, including employees, customers, and the community. At the end of the scenario, students are asked to help the VP develop a plan for gaining internal support for the office and its philanthropic efforts. Another exercise describes ethical conflict that occurs when an employee discovers that a coworker is using company resources for personal consulting jobs. He confronts his coworker and learns that she is using the resources after normal work hours and on the weekends. He is also concerned that the intellectual capital generated by company projects is getting used in these consulting jobs. Students are asked to help the employee decide what to do with this information.

So that students learn more about specific practices, problems, and opportunities in social responsibility, fourteen cases are provided at the end of this book. The cases represent a comprehensive collection for examining social responsibility in a multidimensional way. Seven cases relate to the successful management of social responsibility, and seven examine the specific challenges of social responsibility. The recent travails and successes of high-profile companies and people, including Enron, Tyco, Coca-Cola, Martha Stewart, New Belgium Brewing, Home Depot, Global Crossing, Texas Instruments, PETCO, HCA, Nike, Wal-Mart, and Starbucks, allow students to consider the effects of stakeholders and responsibility expectations on larger and well-known businesses. These cases represent the most up-to-date and compelling issues in social responsibility. Students will find these cases pivotal to their understanding of the complexity of social responsibility in practice. Additional cases on the text website give professors more resources for testing and other course projects.

In addition to many examples, end-of-chapter exercises, and the cases, several role-play exercises are provided in the *Instructor's Resource Manual*. The role-play exercises are built around a fictitious yet plausible scenario or case, support higher level learning objectives, and require group decision-making skills. They can be used in classes of any size. Implementation of the exercises can be customized to the time frame, course objectives, student population, and other unique characteristics of a course. These exercises are aligned with trends in higher education toward teamwork, active learning, and student experiences in handling real-world business issues. For example, the National Farm & Garden exercise places students in a crisis situation that requires an immediate response and consideration of changes over the long term. The role-play simulations (1) give students the opportunity to practice making decisions that have consequences for social responsibility, (2) utilize a team-based approach, (3) re-create the pressures, power, information flows, and other factors that affect decision making in the workplace, and (4) incorporate a debriefing and feedback period for maximum learning and linkages to course objectives. We developed the role-play exercises to enhance more traditional learning tools and to complement the array of resources provided to users of this text. Few textbooks offer this level of teaching support and proprietary learning devices.

A COMPLETE SUPPLEMENTS PACKAGE

The comprehensive *Instructor's Resource Manual* includes chapter outlines, answers to the discussion questions at the end of each chapter, comments on the experiential exercises at the end of each chapter, comments on each case, and a sample syllabus. The role-play exercises are included in the manual along with specific suggestions for using and implementing them in class.

HM Testing, a computerized version of the Test Bank, provides multiple-choice and essay questions for each chapter and includes a mix of descriptive and application questions. When preparing a test, instructors are able to select, edit, and add questions or generate randomly selected questions to produce a test master for easy duplication. An Online Testing System and grade-book function allow instructors to administer tests through a network system, modem, or personal computer and to set up a new class, record grades from tests or assignments, analyze grades, and produce class and individual statistics. This program can be used on both PCs and Macintosh computers.

- The *Online Study Center*, the student website at college.hmco.com/pic/thorne3e, contains many helpful links and exercises to guide your students through the concepts within the text. Company links, glossary, role-play scenarios, and experiential exercises are available without a passkey. Much more information will be available to students behind the *Your Guide to an A* passkey.

- *Your Guide to an A* provides students with access to premium online study tools designed to help students get a better grade. These assets include:
  - ACE+
  - Flashcards
  - Social Responsibility Research Resources
  - Business and Society Challenges

  Please use the code in the *Your Guide to an A* passkey that came with new copies of your textbook. If you purchased a used textbook, the passkey is available for purchase through your bookstore or through Houghton Mifflin's eCommerce site (go to college.hmco.com/pic/thorne3e and click the "Purchase Product" link for *Your Guide to an A*).

- The password-protected *Instructor Website* includes, among other assets, PowerPoint slides and files from the *Instructor's Resource Manual,* which can be downloaded and customized to fit any instructor's specific needs.

- Finally, several *videos* are available for instructors wishing to bring real-world examples into the classroom. A video guide presents overviews and questions for discussion and suggested uses for the videos.

ACKNOWLEDGMENTS

A number of individuals provided reviews and suggestions that helped improve the text and related materials. We sincerely appreciate their time, expertise, and interest in the project.

We wish to acknowledge the many people who played an important role in the development of this book. Melanie Drever at the University of Wyoming assisted in writing timely and thought-provoking cases and also played a key role in research, editing, and project management. Kevin Kuhl and Randall Moshier assisted with research and provided support in revising several chapters. Finally, we express much appreciation to our colleagues and the administration at Colorado State University, Texas State University–San Marcos, the University of New Mexico, and the University of Wyoming.

Our goal is to provide materials and resources that enhance and strengthen both teaching and learning about social responsibility. We invite your comments, concerns, and questions. Your suggestions will be sincerely appreciated and utilized.

DEBBIE M. THORNE

O. C. FERRELL

LINDA FERRELL

CHAPTER 1

Social Responsibility Framework

CHAPTER OBJECTIVES

- To define the concept of social responsibility
- To trace the development of social responsibility
- To examine the global nature of social responsibility
- To discuss the benefits of social responsibility
- To discuss the framework for understanding social responsibility

CHAPTER OUTLINE

Social Responsibility Defined

Development of Social Responsibility

Global Nature of Social Responsibility

Benefits of Social Responsibility

Framework for Studying Social Responsibility

Huntsman is a global manufacturer and marketer of a wide variety of chemicals. Originally founded in 1970 as the Huntsman Container Corporation, this Salt Lake City–based corporation operates in twenty-two countries and generates annual revenues exceeding $13 billion. The firm employs 11,300 individuals in over 100 locations in places as diverse as São Paulo, Brazil, Cairo, Egypt, Chocolate Bayou, Texas, and Kobe, Japan. Huntsman has six business divisions: polyurethanes, advanced materials, performance products, pigments, polymers, and base chemicals. The company supplies chemicals and related materials to many different industries, including adhesives and inks, automotive, personal care, furniture, transportation, agriculture, health care, packaging, and construction. Huntsman recently launched its green chemistry business unit, which is devoted to the design of products and processes that reduce or eliminate the use or generation of hazardous substances. This new unit will be working closely with the other six divisions to ensure that Huntsman remains a leader in environmentally sound engineering and manufacturing processes.

The company still bears the name of its founder and chairman, Jon M. Huntsman, who firmly believes that companies must honor a range of economic, legal, ethical, and philanthropic responsibilities. The company's associates have developed a values statement that is fully aligned with his vision and mission:

Our associates

- *are proud that our Founder and Chairman, Jon M. Huntsman, and the Huntsman family choose to support cancer research, poverty relief, children, and the aged with profits from the business*
- *believe in the environmental benefits we offer through our products*
- *are convinced that working safely is the highest priority and that the safety and health of the general public, our customers, suppliers, and ourselves should never be compromised*
- *believe that we should work closely with all our neighbors so that we continue to enjoy our privilege to operate*
- *understand that we are on a journey and that we must work diligently to continuously improve our performance in the fields of environment, health, and safety*

Along with the traditional links to information about the company and its products, Huntsman's website includes a section on "social responsibility," which primarily addresses the company's philanthropic endeavors. Huntsman has been very active with causes that link to cancer research, domestic violence, world hunger, homelessness, and education. At one point in the early 2000s, the corporation hit financially rough times, so Huntsman took out loans to fulfill its charitable obligations. Most firms would not have gone this far, but Jon Huntsman concluded, "When the economy gets tough, that's when people need you most. And yet that's when most people renege on their charitable contributions because they have less money to give. It's a Catch-22 situation." This same type of generosity was rewarded by the company's suppliers, who worked with the company throughout the economic downturn. Jon Huntsman believes that the company's solid relationships and community involvement helped to stave off bankruptcy during this time.

Another part of the Huntsman website discloses the company's corporate governance standards, business conduct guidelines, and other ethics policies designed to meet and exceed legal standards. Jon Huntsman recently authored *Winners Never Cheat,* in which he discloses the practices, assumptions, and values that led to his company's success. This book clearly suggests that, in a time of numerous business scandals, honesty is more than right—it's the best competitive differentiator. Huntsman, which was a privately held firm until 2005, has taken a number of actions that demonstrate its commitment to economic, legal, ethical, and philanthropic responsibilities. Although some of these responsibilities are mandatory, others are discretionary and were built over time as the Huntsman business grew and profited and societal expectations changed.[1] ∎

Businesses today face increasingly complex, and often competing, motives and incentives in their decision making. In a recent *Business Week*–Harris Poll survey of the general population, 95 percent of respondents agreed with the following statement: "U.S. corporations should have more than one purpose. They also owe something to their workers and the communities in which they operate, and they should sometimes sacrifice some profit for the sake of making things better for their workers and communities."[2] In an era of intense global competition and increasing media scrutiny, consumer activism, and government regulation, all types of organizations need to become adept at fulfilling these expectations. Like Huntsman, many companies are trying, with varying results, to meet the many economic, legal, ethical, and philanthropic responsibilities they now face. Satisfying the expectations of social responsibility is a never-ending process of continuous improvement that requires leadership from top management, buy-in from employees, and good relationships across the community, industry, market, and government. Companies must properly plan, allocate, and use resources to satisfy the demands placed on them by investors, employees, customers, business partners, the government, the community, and others.

In this chapter, we examine the concept of social responsibility and how it relates to today's complex business environment. First, we define social responsibility. Next, we consider the development of social responsibility, its benefits to organizations, and the changing nature of expectations in our increasingly global economy. Finally, we introduce the framework for studying social responsibility used by this text, which includes such elements as strategic management for stakeholder relations; legal, regulatory, and political issues; business ethics; corporate governance; consumer relations; employee relations; philanthropy and community relations; environmental issues; technology issues; and the social audit.

SOCIAL RESPONSIBILITY DEFINED

Business ethics, corporate volunteerism, compliance, corporate citizenship, reputation management—these are terms you may have heard used, or even used yourself, to describe the various rights and responsibilities of business organizations. You may have thought about what these terms actually mean for business practice. You may also have wondered what expectations of business these phrases describe. In this chapter, we clarify some of the confusion that exists in the terminology that people use when they talk about expectations for business conduct. To this end, we begin by defining social responsibility.

In most societies, businesses are granted a license to operate and the right to exist through a combination of social and legal mechanisms. Businesses are expected to pay taxes, abide by laws and regulations, treat employees fairly, follow through on contracts, protect the natural environment, meet warranty obligations, and adhere to many other standards. Companies that continuously meet and exceed these standards are rewarded with customer satisfaction, employee dedication, investor loyalty, strong relationships in the community, and the time and energy to continue focusing on business-related concerns. Firms that fail to meet these responsibilities can face

GRANITE

Core Values

Granite's Core Values represent who we are and provide, without question, the standard of behavior by which we conduct business. These values are the heart, soul, and character of Granite. Our Code embodies the vision of our company founders and encompasses the values that have been and will continue to be vital to the future success of the Company. Our Core Values represent how we treat each other, how we deal with our customers, how we respond to our stake-holders, and how we hold each other and ourselves accountable. This is the legacy we will leave for generations to come.

The following eight ethical Core Values represent the cornerstone of our Code of Conduct. While achieving these high standards may be difficult to attain, we nonetheless aspire to live our lives and conduct our business with:

Honesty	Consideration of Others
Integrity	Pursuit of Excellence
Fairness	Reliability
Accountability	Citizenship

Honesty
- Be truthful, accurate and straightforward.
- Be candid and non-deceptive in communication and conduct.

Integrity
- Maintain consistency between your beliefs and your behavior – walk your talk!
- Have the courage to contend boldly for that which is right and reject firmly that which is wrong.

Fairness
- Endeavor to be reasonable, open-minded, impartial, even-handed, and non-discriminatory in all your dealings.
- Genuinely partner and actively collaborate within and outside the Company.
- Maintain, without deviation, an attitude of sincerity, tolerance, consideration, and assistance towards others, regardless of position.

We Build CHARACTER   Code of Conduct: Core Values | 2

GRANITE

Accountability
- Accept responsibility for your own actions or inactions and for those whom you supervise.
- Take prompt, constructive steps to correct mistakes or defects.
- Promote teamwork by holding each other accountable – rejecting behaviors inconsistent with this Code of Conduct.

Consideration of Others
- Practice the principles of the Golden Rule.
- Respect the dignity, rights, safety, and personal property of others.
- Be open to the ideas and opinions of others.
- Exercise patience and remain positive under all circumstances.
- Assure that those whom you supervise are not put in compromising situations.

Pursuit of Excellence
- Consistently apply diligence, perseverance, attention to detail, and good work habits to ensure quality projects, products and excellent customer service.
- Build capabilities throught continuous learning, coaching, mentoring and teaching.
- Never accept complacency or indifference.
- Remain flexible and open to possibilities.

Reliability
- Only make realistic commitments and follow-through on the commitments you make.
- Be prompt and responsive in business dealings within and outside the company.

Citizenship
- Comply with all governmental laws, rules and regulations.
- Show consideration for the safety and welfare of everyone, including our natural environment.
- Respond to the impact our work has on the natural environment by consistently evaluating and improving our efforts so that our projects and processes work in harmony with the environment.
- Cultivate an organization that actively encourages us to be the best of who we are and continuously strives to make a difference in our communities and the word.

We Build CHARACTER   Code of Conduct: Core Values | 3

Eight core values guide both day-to-day and strategic decision making at Granite Construction, which has been named to *Fortune* magazine's annual list of the 100 Best Companies to Work For.

penalties, both formal and informal, and may have their attention diverted away from core business issues. For example, a restaurant that delivers poor-quality food and shoddy service may be informally sanctioned by customers who decide to take their business elsewhere. These same customers often tell friends and family to avoid the restaurant, thus creating a spiral of effects that eventually shutters the restaurant's doors. On the other hand, a large multinational corporation may be faced with pro-testors who use physical means to destroy or deface one of its retail stores. In this case, the company is not permanently harmed, but it must allocate resources to remodel the store and answer criticism. Finally, a company engaged in deceptive practices may face formal investigation by a government agency. This investigation could lead to legal charges and penalties, perhaps severe enough to significantly alter the company's products and practices or close the business. For example, Conseco Inc., a large insurance and finance company, filed for Chapter 11 bankruptcy protection amid a federal investigation into its accounting practices and investor lawsuits. Before the filing, Conseco reported $52.3 billion in assets, making its bankruptcy one of the largest in U.S. history. Although the firm eventually emerged from bankruptcy, investors and analysts continue to be critical of Conseco's executive management and strategic direction.[3]

TABLE 1.1	Six Characterizations of Social Responsibility

Characterization	Description
1. License to operate	Social responsibility is a condition for doing business, and as with customer requirements, a firm should find the most efficient way to meet requirements from the government and other external groups.
2. Long-term business investment	Like research and development, social responsibility is designed to improve the business environment for future progress.
3. Vehicle for achieving goals and reputation	Companies that focus on social responsibility will have stronger customer loyalty, more committed employees, better government relations, and ultimately, stronger reputations.
4. Activity to avoid exposure and risk	Responsible activities help companies avoid being singled out or exposed to unnecessary outsider intrusion.
5. Economic and constructive	Companies should reinforce the economic foundation and viability of the communities in which they operate.
6. Oxymoron	Companies are designed to increase shareholder wealth.

Sources: Archie Carroll, "A Three-Dimensional Conceptual Model of Corporate Social Performance," *Academy of Management Review* 4 (1979): 497–505; Kim Davenport, "Corporate Citizenship: A Stakeholder Approach for Defining Corporate Social Performance and Identifying Measures for Assessing It," *Business and Society* 39 (June 2000): 210–219.

Businesses today are expected to look beyond self-interest and recognize that they belong to a larger group, or society, that expects responsible participation. Thus, if any group, society, or institution is to function, there must be a delicate interplay between rights (i.e., what people expect to get) and responsibilities (i.e., what people are expected to contribute) for the common good. The adage "no man is an island" describes the relational and integrative nature of society. Although businesses are not human beings, they plan, develop goals, allocate resources, and act and behave purposefully. Thus, society grants them both benefits and responsibilities.

The term *social responsibility* came into widespread use in the business world during the 1970s, but there remains some confusion over the term's exact meaning. Table 1.1 lists some of the different ways people commonly use the term to describe business responsibilities. Many of these characterizations have elements in common, such as focusing on the achievement of both corporate and social goals and recognizing the broad groups to which business has an obligation. Only the sixth characterization, which describes social responsibility as an oxymoron, is distinctly different from the others. This view of social responsibility, articulated in the famous economist Milton Friedman's 1962 *Capitalism and Freedom,* asserts that business has one purpose, satisfying its investors or stockholders, and that any other considerations are outside its scope.[4] Although this view still exists today, it has lost some credence as more and more companies have assumed the social responsibility orientation.[5] We define **social responsibility** as the adoption by a business of a strategic focus for fulfilling the economic, legal, ethical, and philanthropic responsibilities expected of it by its stakeholders. This definition encompasses a wide range of objectives and activities, including both historical views of business and perceptions that have emerged in the last decade. Let's take a closer look at the parts of this definition.

social responsibility the adoption by a business of a strategic focus for fulfilling the economic, legal, ethical, and philanthropic responsibilities expected of it by its stakeholders

Social Responsibility Applies to All Types of Businesses

It is important to recognize that all types of businesses—small and large, sole proprietorships and partnerships, as well as large corporations—implement social responsibility initiatives to further their relationships with their customers, their employees, and their community at large. For example, RunTex, a store in Austin, Texas, which sells athletic shoes, clothing, and accessories, donates used shoes (which customers have traded in for discounts on new shoes) to the community's poor and homeless. The company also cosponsors walk/run events that generate funds for local and national social causes. Thus, the ideas advanced in this book are equally relevant and applicable across a broad spectrum of business firms.

Although the social responsibility efforts of large corporations usually receive the most attention, the activities of small businesses may have a greater impact on local communities.[6] Owners of small businesses often serve as community leaders, provide goods and services for customers in smaller markets that larger corporations are not interested in serving, create jobs, and donate resources to local community causes. Medium-sized businesses and their employees have similar roles and functions on both a local and a regional level. Although larger firms produce a substantial portion of the gross national output of the United States, small businesses employ about half of the private sector workforce and produce roughly half of the private sector output. In addition to these economic outcomes, small business presents an entrepreneurial opportunity to many people, some of whom have been shut out of the traditional labor force. Women, minorities, and veterans are increasingly interested in self-employment and other forms of small business activity.[7] It is vital that all businesses consider the relationships and expectations that our definition of social responsibility suggests.

Social Responsibility Adopts a Strategic Focus

Social responsibility is not just an academic term; it involves action and measurement, or the "extent" to which a firm embraces the philosophy of social responsibility and then follows through with the implementation of initiatives. Our definition of social responsibility requires a formal commitment, or way of communicating the company's social responsibility philosophy and commitment. For example, Herman Miller, a multinational provider of office, residential, and health-care furniture and services, crafted a statement that it calls the Things That Matter (shown in Figure 1.1). This statement declares Herman Miller's philosophy and the way it will fulfill its responsibilities to its customers, its shareholders, its employees, the community, and the natural environment. Because this statement takes into account all of Herman Miller's constituents and applies directly to all of the company's operations, products, markets, and business relationships, it demonstrates the company's strategic focus on social responsibility. Other companies that embrace social responsibility have incorporated similar elements into their strategic communications, including mission and

FIGURE 1.1	Herman Miller, Inc.'s Things That Matter

- Curiosity and Exploration
- Performance
- Engagement
- Design
- Relationships
- Inclusiveness
- A Better World
- Transparency
- Foundations

Source: "The Basis of Our Community—Things That Matter," Herman Miller, Inc., www.hermanmiller.com/hm/content/audience/intro_pages/HMI_2005_BASIS_OF_OUR_COMMUNITY.pdf, accessed December 12, 2006. Courtesy of Herman Miller, Inc.

vision statements, annual reports, and websites. For example, the website and annual report of the Shimizu Corporation of Japan highlight a companywide commitment to constructing high-quality buildings that create social and cultural value and are in harmony with the environment. The company refers to this commitment as "Total Eco-Construction."[8]

In addition to a company's verbal and written commitment to social responsibility, our definition requires action and results. To implement its social responsibility philosophy, Herman Miller has developed and implemented several corporatewide strategic initiatives, including research on improving work furniture and environments, innovation in the area of ergonomically correct products, progressive employee development opportunities, and an environmental stewardship program. These efforts have earned the company many accolades, such as being named the "Most Admired" furniture manufacturer in America by *Fortune* magazine, and a place on numerous prestigious lists, including *Fortune* magazine's "100 Best Companies to Work for in America," *Forbes* magazine's "Platinum List" of America's 400 best-managed large companies, *Business Ethics* magazine's "100 Best Corporate Citizens," *Diversity Inc.* magazine's "Top 10 Corporations for Supplier Diversity," and *The Progressive Investor's* "Sustainable Business Top 20."[9] As this example demonstrates, effective social responsibility requires both words and action.

If any such initiative is to have strategic importance, it must be fully valued and championed by top management. Executives must believe in and support the integration of constituent interests and economic, legal, ethical, and philanthropic responsibilities into every corporate decision. For example, company objectives for brand awareness and loyalty can be developed and measured from both a marketing and a social responsibility standpoint because researchers have documented a relationship between consumers' perceptions of a firm's social responsibility and their intentions to purchase that company's brands.[10] Likewise, engineers can integrate consumers' desires for reduced negative environmental impact in product designs, and marketers can ensure that a brand's advertising campaign incorporates this product benefit. Finally, consumers' desires for an environmentally sound product may stimulate a stronger company interest in assuming environmental leadership in all aspects of its operations. Home Depot, for example, responded to demands by consumers and environmentalists for environmentally friendly wood products by launching a new initiative that gives preference to wood products certified as having been harvested responsibly over those taken from endangered forests.[11] With this action, the company, which has long touted its environmental principles, has chosen to take a leadership role in the campaign for environmental responsibility in the home-improvement industry. Although social responsibility depends on collaboration and coordination across many parts of the business and among its constituencies, it also produces effects throughout these same groups. We discuss some of these benefits in a later section of this chapter.

Because of the need for coordination, a large company that is committed to social responsibility often creates specific positions or departments to spearhead the various components of its program. For example, Target, the national retailer, uses a decentralized approach to manage employee volunteerism. Each Target store has a "good neighbor captain" who coordinates employees' efforts with a local charity or cause. The Sara Lee Corporation, whose brands include Bryan Meats, L'eggs, Coach, Kiwi, and Champion, has established an office of public responsibility to oversee its citizenship efforts.[12] The Japanese firm TOTO Ltd., the world's largest manufacturer of plumbing-related products, has created an explicit management structure for its social responsibility effort. TOTO's new president recently initiated a focus on becoming an excellent, more vibrant, and dynamic company. The major theme linking these three areas is corporate social responsibility, TOTO style. Upon opening a luxury showroom in New York, a TOTO executive commented, "It will provide an educational environment where they . . . may learn more about TOTO, its progressive social and environmental philosophies and innovative products." TOTO uses a variety of tools to communicate about its social responsibility efforts, including the following chart from a recent annual report (see Figure 1.2). On the first page of the company's annual report, the subtitle of "Corporate Social Responsibility Report" is also included.[13]

A smaller firm may give an executive, perhaps in human resources or corporate communications, the additional task of overseeing social responsibility. In a very small business, the owner is likely to make decisions regarding community involvement, ethical standards, philanthropy, and other areas. Regardless of the formal or informal nature of the structure, this department or executive should ensure that social responsibility initiatives are aligned with the company's corporate culture, integrated with companywide goals and plans, fully communicated within and outside the company, and measured to determine their effectiveness and strategic impact. In sum, social responsibility must be given the same planning time, priority, and management attention that is given to any other company initiative, such as continuous improvement, cost management, investor relations, research and development, human resources, or marketing research.

FIGURE 1.2   TOTO Corporate Social Responsibility Committee Structure

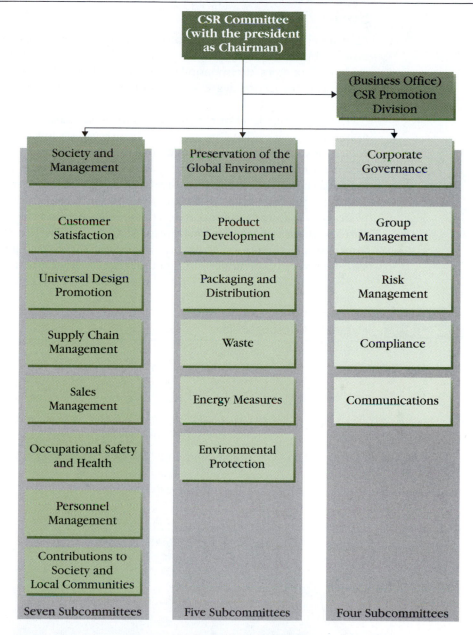

Social Responsibility Fulfills Society's Expectations

Another element of our definition of social responsibility involves society's expectations of business conduct. Many people believe that businesses should accept and abide by four types of responsibility: economic, legal, ethical, and philanthropic (see Figure 1.3). To varying degrees, the four types are required, expected, and/or desired by society.[14]

At the lowest level of the pyramid, businesses have a responsibility to be economically viable so that they can provide a return on investment for their owners, create jobs for the community, and contribute goods and services to the economy. The economy is influenced by the ways organizations relate to their stockholders, their customers, their employees, their suppliers, their competitors, their community, and even the natural environment. For example, in nations with corrupt businesses and industries, the negative effects often pervade the entire society. Transparency International, a German organization dedicated to curbing national and international corruption, conducts an annual survey on the effects of business and government corruption on a country's economic growth and prospects. The

| FIGURE 1.3 | Pyramid of Responsibility |

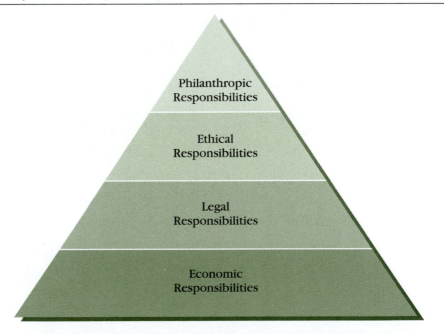

Source: Reprinted from *Business Horizons* 34 (July–August 1991): 42. Archie B. Carroll, "The Pyramid of Corporate Social Responsibility: Toward the Moral Management of Organizational Stakeholders." Copyright © 1991 by the Board of Trustees of Indiana State University, Kelley School of Business, with permission of Elsevier.

organization reports that corruption reduces economic growth, inhibits foreign investment, and often channels investment and funds into "pet projects" that may create little benefit other than high returns to the corrupt decision makers. For example, many of the countries with the highest levels of perceived corruption also report the highest levels of poverty in the world. These countries include Bangladesh, Chad, Haiti, and Myanmar. Transparency International also notes that some relatively poor counties, including Bulgaria, Colombia, and Estonia, have made positive strides in curbing corruption. However, Canada and Ireland have started to experience higher levels of perceived corruption, yet maintain relatively strong economies. Transparency International encourages governments, consumers, and nonprofit groups to take action in the fight against corruption (see Figure 1.4).[15] Although business and society may be theoretically distinct, there are a host of practical implications for the four levels of social responsibility, business, and its effects on society.

At the next level of the pyramid, companies are required to obey laws and regulations that specify the nature of responsible business conduct. Society enforces its expectations regarding the behavior of businesses through the legal system. If a business chooses to behave in a way that customers, special-interest groups, or other businesses perceive as irresponsible, these groups may ask their elected representatives to draft legislation to regulate the firm's behavior, or they may sue the firm in a court of law in an effort to force it to "play by the rules." For example, many businesses have

FIGURE 1.4	Recommendations for Countering Corruption

By lower income countries
- Increase resources and political will for anticorruption efforts.
- Enable greater public access to information about budgets, revenue, and expenditure.

By higher income countries
- Combine increased aid with support for recipient-led reforms.
- Reduce tied aid, which limits local opportunities and ownership of aid programs.

By all countries
- Promote strong coordination among governments, the private sector, and civil society to increase efficiency and sustainability in anticorruption and good governance efforts.
- Ratify, implement, and monitor existing anticorruption conventions in all countries to establish international norms. These include the UN Convention Against Corruption, the OECD Anti-Bribery Convention, and the regional conventions of the African Union and the Organization of American States.

Source: "Corruption Perceptions Index 2005," Transparency International, http://www.transparency.org/policy_research/surveys_indices/cpi/2005/media_pack, accessed May 31, 2006. Copyright © by the Institute for Policy Studies. Reprinted with permission.

complained that Microsoft Corporation effectively had a monopoly in the computer operating system and Web browser markets and that the company acted illegally to maintain this dominance. Their complaints were validated in 2000 when a U.S. district judge ruled in a federal lawsuit that Microsoft had indeed used anticompetitive tactics to maintain its Windows monopoly in operating-system software and to attempt to dominate the Web browser market by illegally bundling its Internet Explorer Web browser into its Windows operating system. Microsoft, which vehemently denied the charges, appealed that decision. The election of George W. Bush and a court of appeal's ruling to overturn the judge's decision shifted the focus to settlement talks, away from an earlier suggestion to break up the company. Microsoft began implementing the provisions of the antitrust settlement agreement in late 2002, including hiring a compliance officer.[16]

Beyond the economic and legal dimensions of social responsibility, companies must decide what they consider to be just, fair, and right—the realm of business ethics. Business ethics refers to the principles and standards that guide behavior in the world of business. These principles are determined and expected by the public, government regulators, special-interest groups, consumers, industry, and individual organizations. The most basic of these principles have been codified into laws and regulations to require that companies conduct themselves in ways that conform to society's expectations. Many firms and industries have chosen to go beyond these basic laws in an effort to act responsibly. The Direct Selling Association (DSA), for example, has established a code of ethics that applies to all individual and company members of the association. Because direct selling, such as door-to-door selling, involves personal contact with consumers, there are many ethical issues that can arise. For this reason, the DSA code directs the association's members to go beyond legal standards of conduct in areas such as product representation, appropriate ways of contacting consumers, and warranties and guarantees. In addition, the DSA actively works with government agencies and consumer groups to ensure that ethical standards are pervasive in the direct selling industry. The World Federation of Direct Selling Associations (WFDSA) also maintains two codes of conduct, one for dealing with consumers and the other for interactions within the industry, that provide guidance for direct sellers around the world in countries as diverse as Argentina, Canada, Finland, Taiwan, and Poland.[17]

At the top of the pyramid are philanthropic activities, which promote human welfare and goodwill. By making voluntary donations of money, time, and other resources, companies can contribute to their communities and society and improve the quality of life. For example, Hitachi, Ltd., of Tokyo, Japan, established the Hitachi Foundation, a nonprofit philanthropic organization that invests in increasing the well-being of underserved people and communities. With over two decades of existence and annual contributions of $4.0 million, the foundation is considered a pioneer of global social responsibility.[18] Although Hitachi is not required to support the community, similar corporate actions are increasingly desired and expected by people around the world.

When the pyramid was first introduced, many people assumed that there was a natural progression from economic to philanthropic responsibilities, meaning that a

FIGURE 1.5	Social Responsibility Continuum

Minimal ←──────────────────────────────────→ **Strategic**

Economic and
legal considerations
focusing on contractual
stakeholders

Economic, legal, ethical,
and philanthropic
considerations focusing
on all stakeholders

Source: Based on ideas presented in Malcolm McIntosh, Deborah Leipziger, Keith Jones, and Gill Coleman, *Corporate Citizenship: Successful Strategies for Responsible Companies* (London: Financial Times Management, 2000); Linda S. Munilla and Morgan P. Miles, "The Corporate Social Responsibility Continuum as a Component of Stakeholder Theory," *Business and Society Review* 110 (December 2005): 371–387.

firm had to be economically viable before it could properly consider the other three elements. Today, the pyramid is viewed in a more holistic fashion, with all four responsibilities seen as related and integrated, and this is the view we will use in this book.[19] In fact, companies demonstrate varying degrees of social responsibility at different points in time. Figure 1.5 depicts the social responsibility continuum. Companies' fulfillment of their economic, legal, ethical, and philanthropic responsibilities can range from minimal to strategic. Firms that focus only on the expectations required

Executives around the world are making corporate commitments to become more socially responsible, including Etisalat, a telecommunications firm based in the United Arab Emirates.

by laws and contracts demonstrate minimal responsibility or a compliance orientation. Firms that take minimal responsibility view such activities as a "cost of doing business." Some critics believe that pharmaceutical manufacturers take the minimal approach with respect to the advertising and sale of certain drugs. A recent situation involving two pain medicines known as Cox-2 inhibitors demonstrates this point. After safety concerns were expressed about Cox-2 inhibitors, Merck voluntarily withdrew Vioxx from the market while Pfizer began an advertising campaign focused on the safety record of Celebrex, a major competitor to Vioxx. The Food and Drug Administration soon advised Pfizer to discontinue the advertising. While Celebrex remains on the market, some critics have assessed Merck's decision to withdraw Vioxx as over-reactionary. Research on both drugs continues.[20]

Strategic responsibility is realized when a company has integrated a range of expectations, desires, and constituencies into its strategic direction and planning processes. In this case, an organization considers social responsibility an essential component of its vision, mission, values, and practices. BP, formerly known as British Petroleum, is communicating its commitment to strategic responsibility through an image campaign that profiles the multinational firm as "Beyond Petroleum" in its interests, stakeholders, and activities. BP considers climate change, responsible operations, and social and economic development as critical responsibilities in its business efforts. Finally, firms may operate outside the continuum by taking the approach that social responsibility is being forced by government, nongovernmental organizations, consumer groups, and other stakeholders. In this case, any expenditures are considered a "tax" that occurs outside the firm's strategic direction and resource allocation process. Executives with this philosophy often maintain that customers will be lost, employees will become dissatisfied, and other detrimental effects will occur because of forced social responsibility.[21]

In this book, we will give many examples of firms that are at different places along this continuum to show how the pursuit of social responsibility is never ending. For example, Coca-Cola, the world's largest beverage firm, dropped out of the top ten in *Fortune* magazine's annual list of "America's Most Admired Companies" in 2000 and out of the top 100 in *Business Ethics* magazine's annual list of "100 Best Corporate Citizens" in 2001. For a company that had spent years on both lists, this was disappointing, but perhaps it was not unexpected, as the company was planning to eliminate 6,000 jobs, was facing a racial discrimination lawsuit, was still recovering from a product contamination scare in Europe, and was trying to salvage its relationships with its bottlers. Then, in 2002, Coca-Cola scored highest in the beverage industry on *Fortune* magazine's measure of social responsibility, and the *Business Ethics* magazine survey highlighted Coca-Cola's relationships with stakeholders. Just a few years later, Coca-Cola lost most of the gains it had experienced in the U.S. rankings but upheld a top-twenty-five ranking in *Fortune* magazine's list of globally admired corporations. As with most multinational firms, Coca-Cola must continuously monitor a number of social responsibility issues and determine the most appropriate corporate response and action. Table 1.2 outlines the complexity of managing corporate citizenship in both host and home country environments.[22]

| **TABLE 1.2** | Managing Social Responsibility in Home and Host Markets |

		3 **Expansionists**	4 **Activists**
Level of citizenship expectations in the host market	High	Companies adopt citizenship profiles that are greater than in their home market.	Companies adopt citizenship profiles that are active both at home and abroad.
	Low	1 **Minimalists** Companies adopt citizenship profiles that are at a minimum at home and abroad.	2 **Reductionists** Companies adopt citizenship profiles that are lower than in their home market.
		Low	High

Level of citizenship expectations
in the home market

Source: Naomi Gardberg and Charles Fombrun, "Corporate Citizenship: Creating Intangible Assets Across Institutional Environments," *Academy of Management Review* 31 (April 2006): 329–336. Copyright © 2006 by Academy of Management Review. Reproduced with permission of Academy of Management Review.

Social Responsibility Requires a Stakeholder Orientation

The final element of our definition involves those to whom an organization is responsible, including customers, employees, investors and shareholders, suppliers, governments, communities, and many others. These constituents have a stake in, or claim on, some aspect of a company's products, operations, markets, industry, and outcomes and thus are known as **stakeholders**. We explore the roles and expectations of stakeholders in Chapter 2. Companies that consider the diverse perspectives of these constituents in their daily operations and strategic planning are said to have a stakeholder orientation, meaning that they are focused on stakeholders' concerns. Adopting this orientation is part of the social responsibility philosophy, which implies that business is fundamentally connected to other parts of society and must take responsibility for its effects in those areas. Table 1.3 examines the relationship between stakeholder perspectives and strategic, minimal/compliance, and forced responsibility.[23]

R. E. Freeman, one of the earliest writers on stakeholder theory, maintains that business and society are "interpenetrating systems," in that each affects and is affected by the other.[24] For example, Kingfisher, the operator of more than 600 home improvement retail stores in Europe and Asia, developed a formal process for securing stakeholder input on a variety of issues, including child labor, fair wages, environmental impact, and equal opportunity. To develop a vision and key objectives in these areas, Kingfisher confers with suppliers, store managers, employees, customers, government representatives, and other relevant stakeholders. For example, the firm recently met with seventy suppliers in China to discuss factory working conditions and conducted focus groups in the United Kingdom to discover customers' main social

stakeholders
constituents that have a stake in, or claim on, some aspect of a company's products, operations, markets, industry, and outcomes

TABLE 1.3	Stakeholder Perspectives Along the Social Responsibility Continuum		
Stakeholder Group	**Compliance CSR Perspective**	**Strategic CSR Perspective**	**Forced CSR Perspective**
Owners	Perceives CSR as a cost or tax to do business	Perceives CSR as a mechanism to potentially create value more effectively and efficiently, create competitive advantage, hence enhance the economic value of the firm	Result in lower returns to the owners due to the potentially higher cost structure and damage to the corporation's reputation
Creditors	No impact on cost of credit	Credit ratings are impacted by social and environmental risks and how the firm manages these risks Superior CSR management tends to lower levels of social and environmental risks and lowers the probability of default, therefore reducing the cost of capital	Cost of credit may be adversely impacted if creditors perceive that firm costs are increased or revenues reduced due to a "forced" CSR—may be associated with higher financial risk
Customers	No impact on target market, marketing mix, or marketing strategy	A superior environmental and social reputation could allow the firm to target more socially and/or environmentally oriented market segments, creating additional value for the customers and superior returns for the firm	May result in alienation of specific customer segments, loss of brand equity, and negative impact on corporate reputation
Regional/national community	No impact	May become a corporate citizen "role model"—may enhance regional/national reputation for social and environmental management. SA 8000, Emas, and ISO 14000 have become standards for global market access.	May result in an increase in regulatory scrutiny
Local community	No impact	Tends to result in a superior reputation in the community, with many positive consequences	Tends to result in a very negative reputation in the community, with many negative consequences

Source: Linda S. Munilla and Morgan P. Miles, "The Corporate Social Responsibility Continuum as a Component of Stakeholder Theory," *Business and Society Review* 110 (December 2005): 371–387.

responsibility concerns. Every quarter, Kingfisher's eleven operating companies complete a 165-point questionnaire over the firm's social responsibility focus areas, including product stewardship, energy management, sustainable operation, supply chain management, equality and diversity, and community investment. Health and safety issues are handled by a separate function. The survey results enable Kingfisher to rate its progress on the six issues from (1) minimum action to (3) leadership position in the industry and community.[25] Kingfisher largely strengthened its dedication and efforts in the 1990s, when social responsibility and the requisite stakeholder orientation became more popular and more generally accepted within the corporate community. Many events have led to this era of increasing accountability and responsibility.

DEVELOPMENT OF SOCIAL RESPONSIBILITY

In 1959, Harvard economist Edward Mason asserted that business corporations are "the most important economic institutions."[26] His declaration implied that companies probably affect the community and society as much, or perhaps more, in social terms as in monetary, or financial, terms. For example, most businesses use advertising to convey messages that have an economic impact but also have a social meaning. As an extreme example, when Benetton decided to use convicted felons who had been given death sentences in an advertising campaign, many people were outraged. The Italian clothier had a history of using cutting-edge advertising to comment on social ideas and political issues, but some people felt that this campaign went too far. Other controversies surrounded campaigns that included photographs of a dead soldier's bloody uniform, three human hearts, condoms, and victims of HIV/AIDS. Benetton's original goal was to open up a dialog on the controversial issue of the death penalty, but criticism of the campaign was rampant and at least one major retailer dropped its contract with Benetton as a result. While Benetton's sales have continued to be challenged by other European clothiers, the retailer has diminished the shock value of its advertising. However, the company continues to focus on cultural and social issues through its advertising, often partnering with nonprofit organizations. Benetton has promoted a wide variety of causes, including protecting endangered species and reducing world hunger and poverty.[27]

Although most companies do not go to the extremes that Benetton does, companies do influence many aspects of our lives, from the workplace to the natural environment. This influence has led many people to conclude that companies' actions should be designed to benefit employees, customers, business partners, and the community as well as shareholders. Social responsibility has become a benchmark for companies today.[28] However, these expectations have changed over time. For example, the first corporations in the United States were granted charters by various state governments because they were needed to serve an important function in society, such as transportation, insurance, water, or banking services. In addition to serving as a "license to operate," these charters specified the internal structure of these firms, allowing their actions to be more closely monitored.[29] During this period, corporate charters were often granted for a limited period of time because many people, including legislators, feared the power that corporations could potentially wield. It was not until the mid-1800s that profit and responsibility to stockholders became major corporate goals.[30]

After World War II, as many large U.S. firms came to dominate the global economy, their actions inspired imitation in other nations. The definitive external characteristic of these firms was their economic dominance. Internally, they were marked by the virtually unlimited autonomy afforded to their top managers. This total discretion meant that these firms' top managers had the luxury of not having to answer much for their actions.[31] In the current business mind-set, such total autonomy would be viewed as a hindrance to social responsibility because there is no effective system of checks and balances. In Chapter 3, we elaborate on corporate governance, the process of control and accountability in organizations that is necessary for social responsibility.

In the 1950s, the 130 or so largest companies in the United States provided more than half of the country's manufacturing output. The top 500 firms accounted for almost two-thirds of the country's nonagricultural economic activity.[32] U.S. productivity and technological advancements also dramatically outpaced those of global competitors, such as Japan and Western Europe. For example, the level of production in the United States was twice as high as that in Europe and quadruple that in Japan. The level of research and development carried out by U.S. corporations was also well ahead of overseas firms. For these reasons, the United States was perceived as setting a global standard for other nations to emulate.

The power of these large U.S. corporations was largely mirrored by the autonomy of their top managers.[33] This autonomy could be characterized as "largely unchecked," as most such managers had the authority to make whatever decisions they thought necessary. Because of the relative lack of global competition and shareholder input during the 1950s and 1960s, there were few formal governance procedures to restrain management's actions. However, this laxity permitted management to focus not just on profit margins but also on a wide variety of discretionary activities, including charitable giving. Thus, it is interesting to note that although top managers' actions were rarely questioned or scrutinized, these managers did use their company's resources to address broader concerns than self-interest. Although the general public was sometimes suspicious of the power held by top managers in large corporations, it also recognized the gains it received from these corporations, such as better products, more choices, good employee salaries, and other such benefits. During this period, many corporations put money into their communities. Although these firms had high executive pay, organizational inefficiencies, high overhead costs, and various other problems, they were quick to share their gains. Employees in the lower echelons of these large corporations received substantially higher wages and better benefits than the national average. This practice has continued into the present; for example, what major automobile manufacturers pay their workers is 50 percent above the national average and 40 percent above the manufacturing national average.[34]

During the 1950s and 1960s, these companies provided other benefits that are often overlooked. Their contributions to charities, the arts, culture, and other community activities were often quite generous. They spent considerable sums of money on research that was more beneficial to the industry or to society than to the companies' own profitability. For example, the lack of competition meant that companies had the profits to invest in higher quality products for consumer and industrial use. Although the government passed laws that required companies to take actions to protect the natural environment, make products safer, and promote equity and diversity in the workplace, many companies voluntarily adopted responsible practices and did not constantly fight government regulations and taxes. These corporations once provided many of the services that are now provided by the government in the United States. For example, during this period, the U.S. government spent less than the government of any other industrialized nation on such things as pensions and health benefits, as these were provided by companies rather than by the government.[35] In the 1960s and 1970s, however, the business landscape changed.

Economic turmoil during the 1970s and 1980s almost eliminated the old corporations. Venerable firms that had dominated the economy in the 1950s and 1960s became extinct or ineffective as a result of bankruptcies, takeovers, or other threats, including high energy prices and an influx of foreign competitors. The stability experienced by the U.S. firms of mid-century dissolved. During the 1960s and 1970s, the *Fortune* 500 had a relatively low turnover of about 4 percent. By 1990, however, one-third of the companies in the *Fortune* 500 of 1980 had disappeared, primarily as a result of takeovers and bankruptcies. The threats and instability led companies to protect themselves from business cycles by becoming more focused on their core competencies and reducing their product diversity. To combat takeovers, many companies adopted flatter organizational hierarchies. Flatter organizations meant workforce reduction but also entailed increasing empowerment of lower level employees.

Thus, the 1980s and 1990s brought a new focus on profitability and economies of scale. Efficiency and productivity became the primary objectives of business. This fostered a wave of downsizing and restructuring that left some people and communities without financial security. Before 1970, large corporations employed about one of every five Americans, but by the 1990s, they employed only one in ten. The familial relationship between employee and employer disappeared, and along with it went employee loyalty and company promises of lifetime employment. Companies slashed their payrolls to reduce costs, and employees changed jobs more often. Workforce reductions and "job hopping" were almost unheard of in the 1960s but had become commonplace two decades later. These trends made temporary employment and contract work the fastest growing forms of employment throughout the 1990s.[36]

Along with these changes, top managers were stripped of their former freedom. Competition heated up, and both consumers and stockholders grew more demanding. The increased competition led business managers to worry more and more about the bottom line and about protecting the company. Escalating use of the Internet provided unprecedented access to information about corporate decisions and conduct and fostered communication among once unconnected groups, furthering consumer awareness and shareholder activism. Consumer demands put more pressure on companies and their employees. The education and activism of stockholders had top management fearing for their jobs. Throughout the last two decades of the twentieth century, legislators and regulators initiated more and more regulatory requirements every year. These factors resulted in difficult trade-offs for management.

The benefits of the corporations of old were largely forgotten in the 1980s, but concern for corporate responsibilities was renewed in the 1990s. Partly as a result of business scandals and Wall Street excesses in the 1980s, many industries and companies decided to pursue and expect more responsible and respectable business practices.

Many of these practices focused on creating value for stakeholders through more effective processes and decreased the narrow and sole emphasis on corporate profitability. At the same time, consumers and employees became less interested in making money for its own sake and turned toward intrinsic rewards and a more holistic approach to life and work.[37] This resulted in increased interest in the development of human and intellectual capital; the installation of corporate ethics programs; the development of programs to promote employee volunteerism in the community, strategic philanthropy efforts, and trust in the workplace; and the initiation of a more open dialog between companies and their stakeholders.

Despite major advances in the 1990s, the sheer number of corporate scandals at the beginning of the twenty-first century prompted a new era of social responsibility. The downfall of Enron, WorldCom, and other corporate stalwarts caused regulators, former employees, investors, nongovernmental organizations, and ordinary citizens to question the role and integrity of big business and the underlying economic system. Federal legislators passed the Sarbanes-Oxley Act to overhaul securities laws and governance structures. The new Public Company Accounting Oversight Board was implemented to regulate the accounting and auditing profession. Harvey Pitt, the Securities and Exchange Commission chairman, resigned after a series of gaffes reduced his ability to lead in turbulent times. America's home decorating guru, Martha Stewart, was indicted on charges related to the sale of ImClone stock. The ImClone CEO, Sam Waksal, lost his job amid insider trading and securities fraud charges and began serving a seven-year sentence in mid-2003. Newspapers, business magazines, and news websites devoted entire sections—often labeled as Corporate Scandal, Year of the Apology, or Year of the Scandal—to the trials and tribulations of executives, their companies and auditors, and stock analysts.

Mark Lilla, a professor at the University of Chicago, notes that perceptions of business and society often represent the confluence of the ideas of two decades, the 1960s and 1980s. From the 1960s, we gained a stronger interest in social issues and in how all parts of society can help prevent these issues from arising and resolve them when they do. The economic upheaval and excess of the 1980s alerted many people to the influence that companies have on society when the desire to make money profoundly dominates their activities.[38] The economic growth and gains of the 1990s brought sharp reminders of the 1980s, involving both exorbitant executive salaries and exorbitant executive personal wealth, which eventually took their toll on markets and companies.[39] Events of the past and the scandalous start to the twenty-first century brought calls for a stronger balance between the global market economy and social responsibility, social justice, and cohesion. This is evident on a global scale as special-interest groups, companies, human rights activists, and governments strive to balance worldwide economic growth and spending with social, environmental, technological, and cultural issues.

GLOBAL NATURE OF SOCIAL RESPONSIBILITY

Although many forces have shaped the debate on social responsibility, the increasing globalization of business has made it an international concern. For example, as people around the world celebrated the year 2000, there was also a growing backlash against big business, particularly multinational corporations. A wide variety of protests were held around the globe, but their common theme was criticism of the increasing power and scope of business. The corporate scandals fortified this criticism and awoke even the staunchest of business advocates. Questions of corruption, environmental protection, fair wages, safe working conditions, and the income gap between rich and poor were posed. Many critics and protesters believe that global business involves exploitation of the working poor, destruction of the planet, and a rise in inequality.[40] Ruy Teixeira, a pollster from the Century Foundation, says, "There's a widespread sense of unfairness and distrust today, where people think companies are not quite playing by the rules." *Business Week* weighed in with a cover story entitled "Too Much Corporate Power?"[41] A Gallup poll in mid-2002 showed that Americans were highly distrustful of executives in large businesses. Thirty-eight percent felt that big business had become a threat to the U.S. future, and nearly 80 percent believed that executives would take improper actions to benefit themselves.[42] More recent polls indicate that trust is rebounding in certain countries, but companies are still vulnerable to the ramifications of distrust. In an environment where consumers distrust business, greater regulation and lower brand loyalty are likely results. We discuss more of the relationship between social responsibility and business outcomes later in this chapter.[43]

The globalization of business is fodder for many critics, who believe the movement is detrimental because it destroys the unique cultural elements of individual countries, concentrates power within developed nations and their corporations, abuses natural resources, and takes advantage of people in developing countries. Multinational corporations are perhaps most subject to criticism because of their size and scope. More than half of the world's top 100 economies are not national economies at all; they are corporations like Wal-Mart and Royal Dutch Shell. For example, General Motor's revenues are roughly the size of the combined revenues of Hungary, Ireland, and New Zealand. Table 1.4 lists the top fifty economies in the world, which includes a combination of countries and companies. Because of the economic and political power they potentially wield, the actions of large, multinational companies are under scrutiny by many stakeholders. For example, a victims' advocate group charged that Unocal, a large U.S.-based oil and gas exploration and production firm, knew that the government of Myanmar forced peasants to help build a pipeline for the company. Peasants who resisted the military government were tortured or killed. Unocal has denied knowing of the oppression but faced charges under a 1789 U.S. law called the Alien Tort Claims Act. The case was eventually settled for an undisclosed amount.[44] Most allegations by antiglobalization protestors are not this extreme, but the issues are still of consequence. For example, the pharmaceutical industry has long been criticized for excessive pricing, interference with clinical evaluations, some disregard for developing nations, and aggressive promotional practices. Critics have called on governments, as well as public health organizations, to influence the industry in changing some of its practices.[45]

Advocates of the global economy counter these allegations by pointing to increases in overall economic growth, new jobs, new and more effective products, and other positive effects of global business. Although these differences of opinion provide fuel for debate and discussion, the global economy probably, in the words of author John Dalla Costa, "holds much greater potential than its critics think, and much

TABLE 1.4	Top Fifty Economies in the World			
Country/Corporation	GDP/Sales ($mil)		Country/Corporation	GDP/Sales ($mil)
1. United States	8,708,870.0		26. *Exxon Mobil*	163,881.0
2. Japan	4,395,083.0		27. *Ford Motor*	162,558.0
3. Germany	2,081,202.0		28. *Daimler Chrysler*	159,985.7
4. France	1,410,262.0		29. Poland	154,146.0
5. United Kingdom	1,373,612.0		30. Norway	145,449.0
6. Italy	1,149,958.0		31. Indonesia	140,964.0
7. China	1,149,814.0		32. South Africa	131,127.0
8. Brazil	760,345.0		33. Saudi Arabia	128,892.0
9. Canada	612,049.0		34. Finland	126,130.0
10. Spain	562,245.0		35. Greece	123,934.0
11. Mexico	474,951.0		36. Thailand	123,887.0
12. India	459,765.0		37. *Mitsui*	118,555.2
13. Korea, Republic	406,940.0		38. *Mitsubishi*	117,765.6
14. Australia	389,691.0		39. *Toyota Motor*	115,670.9
15. Netherlands	384,766.0		40. *General Electric*	111,630.0
16. Russian Federation	375,345.0		41. *Itochu*	109,068.9
17. Argentina	281,942.0		42. Portugal	107,716.0
18. Switzerland	260,299.0		43. *Royal Dutch/Shell*	105,366.0
19. Belgium	245,706.0		44. Venezuela	103,918.0
20. Sweden	226,388.0		45. Iran, Islamic Republic	101,073.0
21. Austria	208,949.0		46. Israel	99,068.0
22. Turkey	188,374.0		47. *Sumitomo*	95,701.6
23. *General Motors*	176,558.0		48. *Nippon Tel & Tel*	93,591.7
24. Denmark	174,363.0		49. Egypt, Arab Republic	92,413.0
25. *Wal-Mart*	166,809.0		50. *Marubeni*	91,807.4

Source: Corporate Watch, "Top 200: The Rise of Corporate Global Power," http://www.corpwatch.org/downloads/top200.pdf, accessed June 10, 2006.

more disruption than its advocates admit. By definition, a global economy is as big as it can get. This means that the scale of both the opportunity and the consequences are at an apex."[46] In responding to this powerful situation, companies around the world are increasingly implementing programs and practices that strive to achieve a balance between economic responsibilities and other social responsibilities. The Nestlé Company, a global foods manufacturer and marketer, published the Nestlé Corporate Business Principles in 1998 and revised them in 2002 and 2004. These principles serve as a management tool for decision making at Nestlé and have been translated into over forty languages. The updated principles are consistent with the United Nations' Global Compact, an accord that covers environmental standards, human rights, and labor conditions.[47]

In most developed countries, social responsibility involves stakeholder accountability and the economic, legal, ethical, and philanthropic dimensions discussed earlier in the chapter. However, a key question for implementing social responsibility on a global scale is: "Who decides on these responsibilities?" Many executives and managers face the challenge of doing business in diverse countries while attempting to maintain their employers' corporate culture and satisfy their expectations. Some companies have adopted an approach in which broad corporate standards can be adapted at a local level. For example, a corporate goal of demonstrating environmental leadership could be met in a number of different ways depending on local conditions and needs. The Compaq Computer Corporation, which merged with Hewlett-Packard in 2002, implemented its goal of environmental responsibility in different ways depending on the needs in various regions of the world. In North America, Compaq focused on recycling and reducing waste. In Latin America, corporate resources were devoted to wastewater treatment and cleanup of contaminated soil. Efforts in the firm's Asia-Pacific division included the distribution of "green kits" to educate managers, employees, and other stakeholders about Compaq's commitment to environmental leadership.[48]

Global social responsibility also involves the confluence of government, business, trade associations, and other groups. For example, countries that belong to the Asia-Pacific Economic Cooperation (APEC) are responsible for half the world's annual production and trade volume. As APEC works to reduce trade barriers and tariffs, it has also developed meaningful projects in the areas of sustainable development, clean technologies, workplace safety, management of human resources, and the health of the marine environment. This powerful trade group has demonstrated that economic, social, and ethical concerns can be tackled simultaneously.[49] Like APEC, other trade groups are also exploring ways to enhance economic productivity within the context of legal, ethical, and philanthropic responsibilities.

In sum, progressive global businesses recognize the "shared bottom line" that results from the partnership among business, communities, government, customers, and the natural environment. In the Millennium Poll, a survey of more than 25,000 citizens in twenty-three countries, 66 percent of the respondents indicated that they want companies to go beyond their traditional role of making a profit, paying taxes, and providing jobs. More than half the respondents said that they believe their national government and companies should focus more on social and environmental goals than on economic goals in the first decade of the new millennium.[50] This survey reiterates our philosophy that business is accountable to a variety of stakeholders and has a number of responsibilities. Thus, our concept of social responsibility is applicable to businesses around the world, although adaptations of implementation and other details on the local level are definitely required. In companies around the world, there is also the recognition of the relationship between strategic social responsibility and benefits to society and organizational performance.

International Business and Poverty Reduction

The United Nations (UN) is a supraregional organization of nearly 200 nations and states from all parts of the world. The UN was originally established in 1945 with fifty-one member countries. Today, the organization is involved in hundreds of projects and established a set of goals, entitled the Millennium Development Goals, in the early twenty-first century. The first goal is to halve the number of people on earth whose income is less than $1 U.S. per day. Roughly 1 billion people fall into this category.

To respond to the first development goal, non-government organizations (NGOs) and business groups have been encouraged to work together in assessing the problems and providing solutions. Oxfam and Unilever recently collaborated on a research project to (1) investigate the impact of business on the lives of poor people and (2) explore potential links between international business and poverty reduction. Unilever is a global corporation that operates in the food, home-care, and personal-care categories. The company has many well-known brands, including Dove, Lipton, Knorr, Surf, and Vaseline.

Oxfam International is a leading NGO, comprised of twelve organizations and over 3,000 partners, who are working together on the fight against poverty, suffering, and injustice. Oxfam was formed in 1995 but already has a solid history of developing and implementing programs for change around the world. Examples of these projects include improving the production of rice in Laos, curbing violence against women in Guatemala, investigating poor labor conditions in Asia, providing emergency food relief in Niger, and teaching farmers in Georgia, once part of the Soviet Union, to grow tropical fruits.

Together, Oxfam and Unilever examined ways in which Unilever's employment, products, and value chain affect the poorest people of Indonesia. Specifically, they were looking for win-win scenarios that linked Unilever's economic development clout with sustainable poverty reduction. Ultimately, this information can be used to assist other companies in understanding how value chains create employment and income, both directly and indirectly. The insights and outcomes from this study include:

1. Cleaning up the Brantas River, so Unilever had clean water for its manufacturing facilities and local residents could begin new businesses using the clean water source.

2. Participating in value chains does not automatically guarantee improvements in the lives of people living in poverty.

3. Employing workers who are closely and more formally linked with Unilever's operations provides greater benefit to the employees and their families.

4. Contracting out employment may reduce a company's ability to monitor the situation and result in gaps between corporate policy and practice.

5. Learning that, in addition to business, other social institutions and resources are needed to create a long-term reduction in poverty.

Sources: "Exploring the Links Between International Business and Poverty Reduction: A Case Study of Unilever in Indonesia," Oxfam Great Britain, http://www.oxfam.org.uk/what_we_do/issues/livelihoods/unilever.htm, accessed May 30, 2006; Oxfam International, www.oxfam.org, accessed June 11, 2006; Unilever, "Creating and Sharing Wealth: Indonesia," http://www.unilever.com/ourvalues/environmentandsociety/env_social_report/creating_sharing_wealth/indonesia/default.asp, accessed May 30, 2006; United Nations, "The UN in Brief," http://www.un.org/Overview/brief.html, accessed June 13, 2006. ■

BENEFITS OF SOCIAL RESPONSIBILITY

The importance of social responsibility initiatives in enhancing stakeholder relationships, improving performance, and creating other benefits has been debated from many different perspectives.[51] Many business managers view such programs as costly activities that provide rewards only to society at the expense of the bottom line. Another view holds that some costs of social responsibility cannot be recovered through improved performance. Although it is true that some aspects of social responsibility may not accrue directly to the bottom line, we believe that organizations benefit indirectly over the long run from these activities. Moreover, ample research and anecdotal evidence demonstrate that there are many rewards for companies that implement such programs. Some of these rewards include increased efficiency in daily operations, greater employee commitment, higher product quality, improved decision making, increased customer loyalty, and improved financial performance. In short, companies that establish a reputation for trust, fairness, and integrity develop a valuable resource that fosters success, which then translates to greater financial performance (see Figure 1.6). This section provides evidence that resources invested in social responsibility programs reap positive outcomes for organizations and stakeholders.

Trust

Trust is the glue that holds organizations together and allows them to focus on efficiency, productivity, and profits. According to Stephen R. Covey, author of *The 7 Habits of Highly Effective People,* "Trust lies at the very core of effective human interactions. Compelling trust is the highest form of human motivation. It brings out the very best in people, but it takes time and patience, and it doesn't preclude the necessity to train and develop people so their competency can rise to that level of trust." When trust is low, organizations decay and relationships deteriorate, resulting in infighting, playing politics within the organization, and general inefficiency. Employee

| FIGURE 1.6 | The Role of Social Responsibility in Performance |

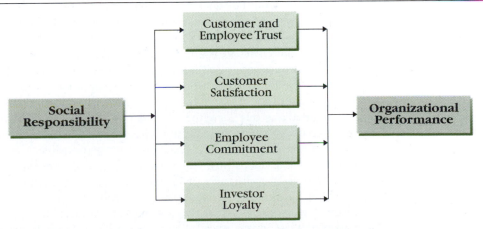

commitment to the organization declines, product quality suffers, employee turnover skyrockets, and customers turn to more trustworthy competitors.[52]

In a trusting work environment, however, employees can reasonably expect to be treated with respect and consideration by both their peers and their superiors. They are also more willing to rely and act on the decisions and actions of their coworkers. Thus, trusting relationships between managers and their subordinates and between peers contribute to greater decision-making efficiencies. Research by the Ethics Resource Center indicates that this trust is pivotal for supporting an ethical climate. Employees of an organization with a strong ethical culture are much more likely to report misconduct but are much less likely to observe misconduct than employees in firms with a weak ethical culture.[53]

Trust is also essential for a company to maintain positive long-term relationships with customers. A study by Cone-Roper reported that three of four consumers say they avoid or refuse to buy from certain businesses. Poor service was the number one reason cited for refusing to buy, but business conduct was the second reason that consumers gave for avoiding specific companies.[54] For example, after the *Exxon Valdez* oil spill in 1989, certain groups and individual citizens aggressively boycotted Exxon because of its response to the environmental disaster.

Customer Satisfaction

The prevailing business philosophy about customer relationships is that a company should strive to market products that satisfy customers' needs through a coordinated effort that also allows the company to achieve its own objectives. It is well accepted that customer satisfaction is one of the most important factors for business success. Although companies must continue to develop and adapt products to keep pace with consumers' changing desires, it is also crucial to develop long-term relationships with customers. Relationships built on mutual respect and cooperation facilitate the repeat purchases that are essential for success. By focusing on customer satisfaction, a business can continually strengthen its customers' trust in the company, and as their confidence grows, this in turn increases the firm's understanding of their requirements.

In a Cone-Roper national survey of consumer attitudes, 81 percent of consumers indicated they would be likely to switch to brands associated with a good cause if price and quality were equal. These results were up 11 percent from the same study in 1997 and show that consumers take for granted that they can buy high-quality products at low prices; therefore, companies need to stand out as doing something—something that demonstrates their commitment to society. The survey also indicated that consumers believed companies should continue supporting causes, even during an economic downturn.[55] A study by Harris Interactive Inc. and the Reputation Institute reported that one-quarter of the respondents had boycotted a firm's products or lobbied others to do so when they did not agree with the firm's policies or activities.[56] Another way of looking at these results is that irresponsible behavior could trigger disloyalty and refusals to buy, whereas good social responsibility initiatives could draw customers to a company's products. For example, many firms use cause-related marketing programs to donate part of a product's sales revenue to a charity that is meaningful to the product's target market. Among the best-known cause-related marketing programs is Avon's "pink ribbon," which we discuss in the Chapter 9.

Employee Commitment

Employee commitment stems from employees who believe their future is tied to that of the organization and are willing to make personal sacrifices for the organization.[57] Hershey Foods is an example of a business that historically drew substantial benefits from its long-lasting commitment to social responsibility. Every year, Hershey employees receive a booklet entitled *Key Corporate Policies,* which describes the values—fairness, integrity, honesty, respect—at the heart of the company's way of doing business. Employees are asked to sign the booklet and are made aware of procedures for reporting concerns about proper conduct or policies in the workplace. These efforts help employees understand the importance of developing and maintaining respectful relationships with both colleagues and customers. Because they support the idea that customers should receive full value for their money, employees are also committed to delivering the highest quality standards possible. Today, Hershey claims about 43 percent of the U.S. chocolate market.[58]

When companies fail to provide value for their employees, loyalty and commitment suffer. A survey by Walker Information Global Network found low levels of employee loyalty and commitment worldwide. The study, which surveyed thousands of employees in thirty-two countries, found that only one in three workers is "truly loyal" to the organization for which he or she works.[59] Employees spend many of their waking hours at work; thus, an organization's commitment to goodwill and respect of its employees usually results in increased employee loyalty and support of the company's objectives.

Investor Loyalty

Investors look at a corporation's bottom line for profits or the potential for increased stock prices. To be successful, relationships with stockholders and other investors must rest on dependability, trust, and commitment. But investors also look for potential cracks or flaws in a company's performance. Companies perceived by their employees as having a high degree of honesty and integrity had an average three-year total return to shareholders of 101 percent, whereas companies perceived as having a low degree of honesty and integrity had a three-year total return to shareholders of just 69 percent.[60] When the Securities and Exchange Commission investigated Sunbeam for improprieties in accounting procedures, the company's stock plummeted from a high of $54 to almost worthless. The negative publicity associated with the alleged misconduct had an enormous impact on investors' confidence in Sunbeam—a previously trusted and respected U.S. brand.[61]

Many shareholders are also concerned about the reputation of companies in which they invest. Investors have even been known to avoid buying the stock of firms they view as irresponsible. For example, fifteen mutual fund managers announced a boycott of Mitsubishi stock after the Japanese firm refused to cancel a plan to build a factory on a Mexican lagoon that is also a major breeding site for gray whales.[62] Many socially responsible mutual funds and asset management firms are available to help concerned investors purchase stock in responsible companies. These investors recognize that corporate responsibility is the foundation for efficiency, productivity, and profits. On the other hand, investors know that fines or negative publicity can decrease a company's stock price, customer loyalty, and long-term viability. Consequently, many chief executives spend a great deal of time communicating with investors about their firms' reputations and financial performance and trying to attract them to their stock.

The issue of drawing and retaining investors is a critical one for CEOs, as roughly 50 percent of investors sell their stock in companies within one year, and the average household replaces 80 percent of its common stock portfolio each year.[63] This focus on short-term gains subjects corporate managers to tremendous pressure to boost short-term earnings, often at the expense of long-term strategic plans. The resulting pressure for short-term gains deprives corporations of stable capital and forces decision makers into a "quarterly" mentality. Conversely, those shareholders willing to hold onto their investments are more willing to sacrifice short-term gains for long-term income. Attracting these long-term investors shields companies from the vagaries of the stock market and gives them flexibility and stability in long-term strategic planning. In the aftermath of the Enron scandal, however, trust and confidence in financial audits and published financial statements were severely shaken. Membership in grassroots investment clubs declined, retail stock investments declined, and investors called for increased transparency in company operations and reports.[64] Gaining investors' trust and confidence is vital for sustaining a firm's financial stability.

The Bottom Line: Profits

Social responsibility is positively associated with return on investment, return on assets, and sales growth.[65] A company cannot continuously be socially responsible and nurture and develop an ethical organizational culture unless it has achieved financial

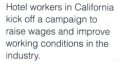

Hotel workers in California kick off a campaign to raise wages and improve working conditions in the industry.

performance in terms of profits. Businesses with greater resources—regardless of their staff size—have the ability to promote their social responsibility along with serving their customers, valuing their employees, and establishing trust with the public.

Many studies have identified a positive relationship between social responsibility and financial performance.[66] For example, a survey of the 500 largest public corporations in the United States found that those that commit to responsible behavior and emphasize compliance with codes of conduct show better financial performance.[67] A managerial focus on stakeholder interests can affect financial performance, although the relationships between stakeholders and financial performance vary and are very complex.[68] A meta-analysis of twenty-five years of research identified thirty-three studies (63 percent) demonstrating a positive relationship between corporate social performance and corporate financial performance, five studies (about 10 percent) indicating a negative relationship, and fourteen studies (27 percent) yielding an inconclusive result or no relationship.[69] Research on the effects of legal infractions suggests that the negative effect of misconduct does not appear until the third year following a conviction, with multiple convictions being more harmful than a single one.[70]

National Economy

An often-asked question is whether business conduct has any bearing on a nation's overall economic performance. Many economists have wondered why some market-based economies are productive and provide a high standard of living for their citizens, whereas other market-based economies lack the kinds of social institutions that foster productivity and economic growth. Perhaps a society's economic problems can be explained by a lack of social responsibility. Trust stems from principles of morality and serves as an important "lubricant of the social system."[71] Many descriptions of market economies fail to take into account the role of such institutions as family, education, and social systems in explaining standards of living and economic success. Perhaps some countries do a better job of developing economically and socially because of the social structure of their economic relationships.

Social institutions, particularly those that promote trust, are important for the economic well-being of a society.[72] Society has become economically successful over time "because of the underlying institutional framework persistently reinforcing incentives for organizations to engage in productive activity."[73] In some developing countries, opportunities for political and economic development have been stifled by activities that promote monopolies, graft, and corruption and by restrictions on opportunities to advance individual, as well as collective, well-being. Author L. E. Harrison offers four fundamental factors that promote economic well-being: "(1) The degree of identification with others in a society—the radius of trust, or the sense of community; (2) the rigor of the ethical system; (3) the way authority is exercised within the society; and (4) attitudes about work, innovation, saving, and profit."[74]

Countries with strong trust-based institutions foster a productivity-enhancing environment because they have ethical systems in place that reduce transaction costs and make competitive processes more efficient and effective. In market-based systems with a great degree of trust, such as Japan, Great Britain, Canada, the United States, and Sweden, highly successful enterprises can develop through a spirit of cooperation and the ease in conducting business.[75]

TABLE 1.5	Forms of Corruption in Private and Public Health-Care Systems

- **Embezzlement and theft** from the health budget or user-fee revenue. This can occur at central or local government level or at the point of allocation to a particular health authority or health centre. Medicines and medical supplies or equipment may be stolen for personal use, use in private practice or resale.

- **Corruption in procurement.** Engaging in collusion, bribes and kickbacks in procurement results in overpayment for goods and contracted services, or in failure to enforce contractual standards for quality. In addition, hospital spending may include large investments in building construction and purchase of expensive technologies, areas of procurement that are particularly vulnerable to corruption.

- **Corruption in payment systems.** Corrupt practices include waiving fees or falsifying insurance documents for particular patients or using hospital budgets to benefit particular favoured individuals; illegally billing insurance companies, government or patients for services that are not covered or services not actually provided, in order to maximise revenue; falsification of invoice records, receipt books or utilisation records, or creation of 'ghost' patients.

- **Corruption in the pharmaceutical supply chain.** Products can be diverted or stolen at various points in the distribution system; officials may demand 'fees' for approving products or facilities for clearing customs procedures or for setting prices; violations of industry marketing code practices may distort medical professionals' prescribing practices; demands for favours may be placed on suppliers as a condition for prescribing medicines; and counterfeit or other sub-standard medicines may be allowed to circulate.

- **Corruption at the point of health service delivery** can take many forms: extorting or accepting under-the-table payments for services that are supposed to be provided free of charge; soliciting payments in exchange for special privileges or treatment; and extorting or accepting bribes to influence hiring decisions and decisions on licensing, accreditation or certification.

Source: Transparency International, "Global Corruption Report 2006," http://www.transparency.org/publications/gcr, accessed June 12, 2006.

Superior financial performance at the firm level within a society is measured as profits, earnings per share, return on investment, and capital appreciation. Businesses must achieve a certain level of financial performance to survive and reinvest in the various institutions in society that provide support. On the other hand, at the institutional or societal level, a key factor distinguishing societies with high standards of living is trust-promoting institutions. The challenge is to articulate the process by which institutions that support social responsibility can contribute to firm-level superior financial performance.[76]

A comparison of countries that have high levels of corruption and underdeveloped social institutions with countries that have low levels of corruption reveals differences in the economic well-being of the country's citizens. Transparency International, an organization discussed earlier, publishes an annual report on global corruption that emphasizes the effects of corruption on the business and social sectors. This annual review recently focused on corruption in health-care systems and discovered five key types of corruption, which are listed in Table 1.5. Since health care is managed through a system of both public expenditures and private investment, the industry is especially interesting to examine. Transparency International concluded, "Corruption in the health sector deprives those most in need of essential medical care and helps spawn drug-resistant strains of deadly diseases." The organization recognizes that health care is largely affected by a country's economic well-being and social institutions that support ethics and responsibility. Countries with better access to and quality of health care are more likely to be economically and socially stable. As stated several times in this chapter, conducting business in an ethical and responsible manner generates trust and leads to relationships that promote higher productivity and a positive cycle of effects.[77]

FRAMEWORK FOR STUDYING SOCIAL RESPONSIBILITY

The framework we developed for this text is designed to help you understand how businesses fulfill social expectations. Figure 1.7 illustrates the concept that social responsibility is a process. It begins with the social responsibility philosophy, includes the four levels of social responsibilities, involves many types of stakeholders, and ultimately results in both short- and long-term performance benefits. As we discussed earlier, social responsibility must have the support of top management—both in

FIGURE 1.7   Social Responsibility Model

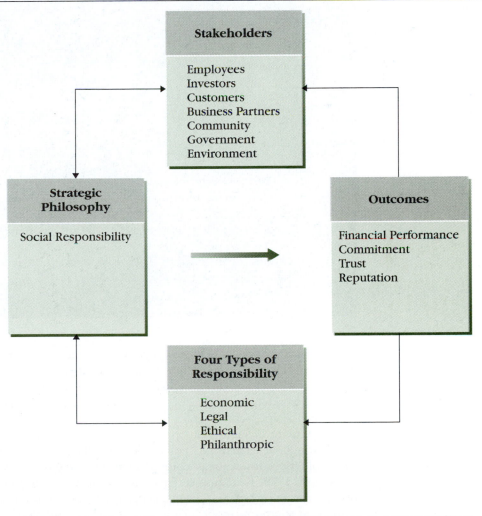

Source: Adapted from Charles J. Fombrun, "Three Pillars of Corporate Citizenship," in *Corporate Global Citizenship,* ed. Noel M. Tichy, Andrew R. McGill, and Lynda St. Clair (San Francisco: New Lexington Press, 1997), pp. 27–42.

One way Cummins demonstrates strategic social responsibility is through the publication and distribution of its sustainability report.

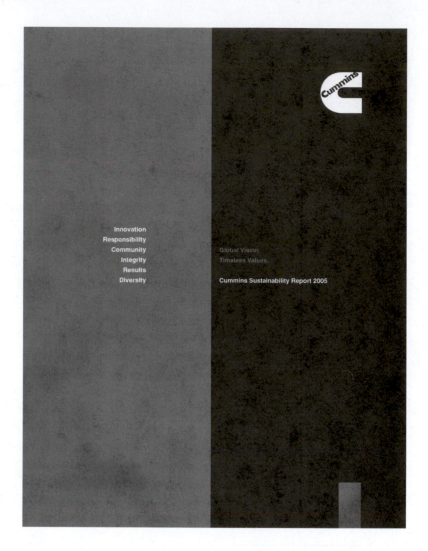

Innovation
Responsibility
Community
Integrity
Results
Diversity

Global Vision
Timeless Values.

Cummins Sustainability Report 2005

words and in deeds—before it can become an organizational reality. Like many organizations, Cummins Engine Company has faced a number of challenges over the past several decades. Cummins, founded in 1919 and based in Columbus, Indiana, is currently the world leader in the design and manufacture of diesel engines. Cummins was Columbus's largest employer for many years, and the firm provided many benefits to the community, including job opportunities and economic growth.

Throughout its first sixty years of business, Cummins also performed well for its shareholders. The company enjoyed increased profits for forty-three consecutive years, until 1979. Cummins suffered during the 1980s, however, and it had to fend off the threat of hostile takeovers. Its stock price plummeted and stock owners demanded short-run profits at the expense of the company's long-term goals. The founding family repelled one takeover attempt with a large infusion of capital and thwarted another attempt by expanding the firm's shareholder-rights program.

Despite its financial woes, Cummins remained focused on research and development, managed to produce a more environmentally friendly diesel engine, and even engaged in limited charitable giving. These actions were consistent with the personality and beliefs of Henry Schacht, Cummins's CEO for more than twenty years, who believed that the company should not aim solely at profit but rather should develop a balanced set of values.

Although Schacht's beliefs provided a strong foundation, Cummins did not always achieve its social and economic goals. In 1983, for the first time ever, the company was forced to lay off some employees. Later in the decade, the company closed plants and laid off even more people. To reverse these trends, Schacht adopted a new business plan that included cooperation with unions, former employees, and other firms to spur economic development. Expansion into Japan, India, and China soon followed.

Throughout this difficult period, Cummins still managed to donate to charities, participate in civic activities, and invest in employee programs and innovative benefits. For example, Cummins is one of several companies implementing steps to reduce workloads and improve work/life balance, which we discuss in Chapter 7. By the end of the twentieth century, Cummins was back on track financially, with sales topping $6.6 billion, up 6 percent from the prior year. Sales in 2005 nearly reached $10 billion. Cummins's drive to build positive relationships with its employees, its customers, and its community led *Business Ethics* to rank the firm on the magazine's list of the "100 Best Corporate Citizens."[78]

Once the social responsibility philosophy is accepted, the four aspects of corporate social responsibility are defined and implemented through programs that incorporate stakeholder input and feedback. Cummins, like other companies, is aware of the potential costs associated with addressing social responsibility issues and stakeholder requirements. When social responsibility programs are put into action, they have both immediate and delayed outcomes.

Figure 1.8 depicts how the chapters of this book fit into our framework. This framework begins with a look at the importance of working with stakeholders to achieve social responsibility objectives. The framework also includes an examination of the influence on business decisions and actions of the legal, regulatory, and political environment; business ethics; and corporate governance. The remaining chapters of the book explore the responsibilities associated with specific stakeholders and issues that confront business decision makers today, including the process of implementing a social responsibility audit.

Strategic Management of Stakeholder Relationships

Social responsibility is grounded in effective and mutually beneficial relationships with customers, employees, investors, competitors, government, the community, and others who have a stake in the company. Increasingly, companies are recognizing that these constituents both affect and are affected by their actions. For this reason, many companies attempt to address the concerns of stakeholder groups, recognizing that failure to do so can have serious long-term consequences. For example, the Connecticut Better Business Bureau revoked the membership of Priceline.com after the

FIGURE 1.8 An Overview of This Book

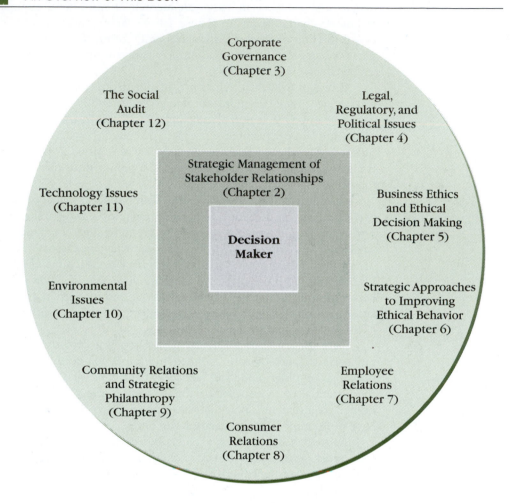

Internet company failed to address complaints related to misrepresentation of products, billing problems, and refunds.[79] Chapter 2 examines the types of stakeholders and their attributes, how stakeholders become influential, and the processes for integrating and managing stakeholders' influence on a firm. It also examines the impact of corporate reputation and crisis situations on stakeholder relationships.

Corporate Governance

Because both daily and strategic decisions affect a variety of stakeholders, companies must maintain a governance structure to ensure proper control of their actions and assign responsibility for those actions. In Chapter 3, we define corporate governance and discuss its role in achieving strategic social responsibility. Key governance issues addressed include the rights of shareholders, the accountability of top management for corporate actions, executive compensation, and strategic-level processes for ensuring that economic, legal, ethical, and philanthropic responsibilities are satisfied.

Legal, Regulatory, and Political Issues

In Chapter 4, we explore the complex relationship between business and government. Every business must be aware of and abide by the laws and regulations that dictate acceptable business conduct. This chapter also examines how business can influence government by participating in the public policy process. A strategic approach for legal compliance is also provided.

Business Ethics

Because individual values are a component of organizational conduct, these findings raise concerns about the ethics of future business leaders. Chapters 5 and 6 are devoted to exploring the role of ethics in business decision making. These chapters explore business responsibilities that go beyond the conduct that is legally prescribed. We also examine the factors that influence ethical decision making and consider how companies can apply this understanding to increase their ethical conduct.

Employee Relations

In today's business environment, most organizations want to build long-term relationships with a variety of stakeholders, but particularly with employees—the focus of Chapter 7. Employees today want fair treatment, excellent compensation and benefits, and assistance in balancing work and family obligations. Raytheon developed a computer program called SilentRunner that can detect patterns of data activity that may reflect employee fraud, insider trading, espionage, or other unauthorized activity.[80] Critics, however, question whether the use of such software contributes to an environment of trust and commitment. Research has shown that committed and satisfied employees are more productive, serve customers better, and are less likely to leave their employers. These benefits are important to successful business performance, but organizations must be proactive in their human resources programs if they are to receive them.

Consumer Relations

Chapter 8 explores companies' relationships with consumers. This constituency is part of a firm's primary stakeholder group, and there are a number of economic, legal, ethical, and philanthropic responsibilities that companies must address. Chapter 8 therefore considers the obligations that companies have toward their customers, including health and safety issues, honesty in marketing, consumer rights, and related responsibilities.

Community and Philanthropy

Chapter 9 examines community relations and strategic philanthropy, the synergistic use of organizational core competencies and resources to address key stakeholders' interests and to achieve both organizational and social benefits. Whereas traditional benevolent philanthropy involves donating a percentage of sales to social causes, a strategic approach aligns employees and organizational resources and expertise with the needs and concerns of stakeholders, especially the community. Strategic philan-thropy involves both financial and nonfinancial contributions (employee time, goods and services, technology and equipment, and facilities) to stakeholders and reaps ben-efits for the community and company.

Environmental Issues

In Chapter 10, we explore some of the significant environmental issues that business and society face today, including air pollution, global warming, water pollution and water quantity, land pollution, waste management, deforestation, urban sprawl, bio-diversity, and genetically modified foods. For example, consumers around the world have expressed fears about the safety of food products that contain genetically modi-fied crops. Although current research suggests that these products pose no threat to health or to the environment, the debate surrounding their use has grown increas-ingly bitter. Many companies are beginning to rethink their use of these crops in re-sponse to consumer concerns. Among them is J. R. Simplot Co., which has asked its farmers to stop growing genetically modified potatoes that may be used in the french fries it supplies to McDonald's.[81] This chapter also considers the impact of govern-ment environmental policy and regulation and examines how some companies are going beyond these laws to address environmental issues and act in an environmen-tally responsible manner.

Technology Issues

Thanks to the Internet and other technological advances, we can communicate faster than ever before, find information about just about anything, and live longer, health-ier lives. However, not all of the changes that occur as a result of new technologies are positive. For example, because shopping via the Internet does not require a signature to verify transactions, online credit-card fraud is significantly greater than credit-card fraud through mail-order catalogs and almost nine times higher than for traditional storefront retailers. A major identity theft ring in New York affected thousands of people with losses totaling nearly $3 million. Members of the theft ring illegally obtained the credit records of consumers and then sold them to criminals for about $60 per record. The criminals used the credit records to obtain loans, drain bank accounts, and perform other fraudulent activities.[82] In Chapter 11, we examine the issues that arise as a result of enhanced technology in the business environment, in-cluding the effects of new technology on privacy, intellectual property, and health. The strategic direction for technology depends on the ability of government and business to plan the implementation of new technology and to assess the influence of that tech-nology on society.

The Social Audit

Without reliable measurements of the achievement of social responsibility goals, a company has no concrete way to verify the importance of these objectives, link them to organizational performance, justify expenditures on them to stockholders and in-vestors, or address any stakeholder concerns involving them. Chapter 12 describes an auditing and assurance procedure that can be used to measure and improve the social responsibility effort. This chapter takes you through a complete strategic perspective on social responsibility, including stakeholder relations, legal and ethical issues, and philanthropy. Such an audit is important for demonstrating commitment and ensuring the continuous improvement of the social responsibility effort.

We hope this framework provides you with a way of understanding the range of concepts, ideas, and practices that are involved in an effective social responsibility initiative. So that you can learn more about the practices of specific companies, a number of cases are provided at the end of the book. In addition, every chapter includes an opening vignette and other examples that shed more light on how social responsibility works in today's businesses. Every chapter also includes a real-life scenario and experiential exercise to help you apply concepts and examine your own decision-making process. As you will soon see, the concept of social responsibility is both exciting and controversial; it is in a constant state of development—just like all important business concepts and practices. A recent survey of thought leaders in the area of social responsibility found that a majority believes social responsibility is making steady progress into conventional business thinking. Much like the social responsibility continuum introduced in this chapter, the thought leaders described several stages of commitment to corporate social responsibility. These stages range from light, where companies are concerned about responding to complaints, to deep, where companies are founded on a business model of improving social or environmental circumstances. Many companies fall somewhere in between, with a focus on complying with new standards and surviving in a climate of increasing social responsibility expectations.[83] We encourage you to draw on current news events and your own experiences to understand social responsibility and the challenges and opportunities it poses for your career, profession, leadership approach, and the business world.

SUMMARY

The term *social responsibility* came into widespread use during the last several decades, but there remains some confusion over the term's exact meaning. This text defines social responsibility as the adoption by a business of a strategic focus for fulfilling the economic, legal, ethical, and philanthropic responsibilities expected of it by its stakeholders.

All types of businesses can implement social responsibility initiatives to further their relationships with their customers, their employees, and the community at large. Although the efforts of large corporations usually receive the most attention, the actions of small businesses may have a greater impact on local communities.

The definition of social responsibility involves the extent to which a firm embraces the social responsibility philosophy and follows through with the implementation of initiatives. Social responsibility must be fully valued and championed by top managers and given the same planning time, priority, and management attention as is given to any other company initiative.

Many people believe that businesses should accept and abide by four types of responsibility: economic, legal, ethical, and philanthropic. Companies have a

responsibility to be economically viable so that they can provide a return on investment for their owners, create jobs for the community, and contribute goods and
services to the economy. They are also expected to obey laws and regulations that
specify what is responsible business conduct. Business ethics refers to the principles
and standards that guide behavior in the world of business. Philanthropic activities
promote human welfare or goodwill. These responsibilities can be viewed holistically,
with all four related and integrated into a comprehensive approach. Social responsibility can also be expressed as a continuum.

Because customers, employees, investors and shareholders, suppliers, governments, communities, and others have a stake in or claim on some aspect of a company's products, operations, markets, industry, and outcomes, they are known as
stakeholders. Adopting a stakeholder orientation is part of the social responsibility
philosophy.

The influence of business has led many people to conclude that corporations
should benefit their employees, their customers, their business partners, and their
community as well as their shareholders. However, these responsibilities and expectations have changed over time. After World War II, many large U.S. firms dominated
the global economy. Their power was largely mirrored by the autonomy of their top
managers. Because of the relative lack of global competition and stockholder input
during the 1950s and 1960s, there were few formal governance procedures to restrain
management's actions. The stability experienced by mid-century firms dissolved in
the economic turmoil of the 1970s and 1980s, leading companies to focus more on
their core competencies and reduce their product diversity. The 1980s and 1990s
brought a new focus on efficiency and productivity, which fostered a wave of downsizing and restructuring. Concern for corporate responsibilities was renewed in the
1990s. In the 1990s and beyond, the balance between the global market economy
and an interest in social justice and cohesion best characterizes the intent and need for
social responsibility. Despite major advances in the 1990s, the sheer number of corporate scandals at the beginning of the twenty-first century prompted a new era of
social responsibility.

The increasing globalization of business has made social responsibility an international concern. In most developed countries, social responsibility involves economic,
legal, ethical, and philanthropic responsibilities to a variety of stakeholders. Global
social responsibility also involves responsibilities to a confluence of governments,
businesses, trade associations, and other groups. Progressive global businesses recognize the "shared bottom line" that results from the partnership among businesses,
communities, governments, and other stakeholders.

The importance of social responsibility initiatives in enhancing stakeholder relationships, improving performance, and creating other benefits has been debated from
many different perspectives. Many business managers view such programs as costly activities that provide rewards only to society at the expense of the bottom line. Others
hold that some costs of social responsibility cannot be recovered through improved
performance. Although it is true that some aspects of social responsibility may not
accrue directly to the bottom line, we believe that organizations benefit indirectly
over the long run from these activities. Moreover, ample research and anecdotal

evidence demonstrate that there are many rewards for companies that implement such programs.

The process of social responsibility begins with the social responsibility philosophy, includes the four responsibilities, involves many types of stakeholders, and ultimately results in both short- and long-term performance benefits. Once the social responsibility philosophy is accepted, the four types of responsibility are defined and implemented through programs that incorporate stakeholder input and feedback.

KEY TERMS

social responsibility (p. 5)
stakeholders (p. 15)

DISCUSSION QUESTIONS

1. Define social responsibility. How does this view of the role of business differ from your previous perceptions? How is it consistent with your attitudes and beliefs about business?
2. If a company is named to one of the "best in social responsibility" lists, what positive effects can it potentially reap? What are the possible costs or negative outcomes that may be associated with being named to one of these lists?
3. What historical trends have affected the social responsibilities of business? How have recent scandals affected the business climate, including any changes in responsibilities and expectations?
4. How would you respond to the statement that this chapter presents only the positive side of the argument that social responsibility results in improved organizational performance?
5. On the basis of the social responsibility model presented in this chapter, describe the philosophy, responsibilities, and stakeholders that make up a company's approach to social responsibility. What are the short- and long-term outcomes of this effort?
6. Consider the role that various business disciplines, including marketing, finance, accounting, and human resources, have in social responsibility. What specific views and philosophies do these different disciplines bring to the implementation of social responsibility?

EXPERIENTIAL EXERCISE

Evaluate *Fortune* magazine's annual list of the most admired companies found on the magazine's website (www.fortune.com). These companies as a group have superior financial performance compared to other firms. Go to each company's website and try to assess its management commitment to the welfare of stakeholders. If any of the companies have experienced legal or ethical misconduct, explain how this may affect specific stakeholders. Rank the companies on the basis of the information available and your opinion on their fulfillment of social responsibility.

WHAT WOULD YOU DO?

Jamie Ramos looked out her window at the early morning sky and gazed at the small crowd below. The words and pictures on their posters were pretty tame this time, she thought. The last protest group used pictures of tarred lungs, corpses, and other graphic photos to show the effects of smoking on a person's internal organs. Their words were also hateful, so much so that employees at the Unified Tobacco headquarters were afraid to walk in and out of the main building. Those who normally took smoking breaks on the back patio decided to skip the break and eat something instead at the company-subsidized cafeteria. By midday, Unified hired extra security to escort employees in and out of the building and to ensure that protestors followed the state guideline of staying at least fifteen feet from the company's entrance. The media picked up on the story—and the photos—and it caused quite a stir in the national press.

At least this protest group seemed fairly reasonable. Late yesterday, a state court provided a reduced judgment to the family of a lifelong smoker, now deceased. This meant that Unified was going to owe millions less than originally expected. The length and stress of the lawsuit had taken its toll, especially on top management, although all employees were certainly affected. After two years of being battered in the media, learning of a huge settlement, and then continuing on with the appeals process, emotions were wearing thin with the continued criticism.

Jamie wondered what this day would bring. As the manager of community relations, her job was to represent Unified in the community, manage the employee volunteer program, create a quarterly newsletter, serve as a liaison to the company's philanthropic foundation, develop solid relationships, and serve on various boards related to social welfare and community needs. The company's foundation donated nearly $1.5 million a year to charities and causes. Over one-quarter of its employees volunteered ten hours a month in their communities.

Jamie reported to a vice president and was pleased with the career progress she had made since graduating from college eight years earlier. Although some of her friends wondered out loud how she could work for a tobacco company, Jamie was steadfast in her belief that even a tobacco firm could contribute something meaningful to society. She had the chance to effect some of those contributions in her community relations role.

Jamie's phone rang and she took a call from her vice president. The VP indicated that, although the protestors seemed relatively calm this time, he was not comfortable with their presence. Several employees had taped signs in office windows telling the protestors to "Go away." Other VPs had dropped by his office to discuss the protest and thought that the responsibility for handling these issues fell to his group. He went on to say that he needed Jamie's help, and the assistance of a few others, in formulating a plan to (1) deal with the protest today and (2) strengthen the strategy for communicating the company's message and goodwill in the future. Their meeting would begin in one hour, so Jamie had some time to sketch out her recommendations on both issues. What would you do?

CHAPTER 2

Strategic Management of Stakeholder Relationships

CHAPTER OBJECTIVES

- To define stakeholders and understand their importance
- To distinguish between primary and secondary stakeholders
- To discuss the global nature of stakeholder relationships
- To consider the impact of reputation and crisis situations on social responsibility performance
- To examine the development of stakeholder relationships
- To explore how stakeholder relationships are integral to social responsibility

CHAPTER OUTLINE

Stakeholders Defined

Stakeholder Issues and Interaction

Performance with Stakeholders

Crisis Management

Development of Stakeholder Relationships

Implementing a Stakeholder Perspective in Social Responsibility

Link Between Stakeholder Relationships and Social Responsibility

America's children are growing not in height or intellectual capacity but in weight. Advertising of highly processed, corn syrup–laced fast foods is at the heart of the controversy. While TV advertising of food and restaurants has dropped 34 percent from 1977 to 2004, the use of the Internet, promotions, school advertising and vending machines, sponsored sports stadiums, and licensing are on the rise. The Senate is investigating greater Federal Trade Commission (FTC) scrutiny of advertising tactics aimed at children. Regulators, government, parents, and our society in general are concerned with the health of our children.

A recent study found that black-oriented television (BET) runs far more ads for fast food and snacks than WB Network and the Disney Channel in the same time periods. A study in a pediatric medical journal found that children consume an extra 167 calories for every hour of TV that they watch. The American Academy of Pediatrics now suggests that parents not allow their children over the age of two to spend more than two hours per day with screen media. Obesity affects roughly 18 percent of black children compared with 14 percent of white children, and the rate is highest among the Hispanic population with 20 percent of children impacted.

Studies conducted by the Kaiser Family Foundation have found that the average child sees around 40,000 advertisements per year on television. Most of these encourage children to consume candy, cereal, fast food, and soft drinks. The Institute of Medicine released a report in December 2005 that compiled 123 research studies over the course of thirty years; there is "strong evidence" in the report that advertising is linked with obesity in young children. What seems to be particularly problematic is the use of popular licensed children's cartoon characters (e.g., SpongeBob SquarePants and Scooby Doo) to advertise these unhealthy foods. Therefore, one could make a case for the fact that many food manufacturers are operating outside what is socially responsible by encouraging children to eat food that is detrimental to their health. However, some companies are choosing to do something about this problem.

Obesity can greatly impact children's health. According to the Centers for Disease Control and Prevention, since 1980 the number of overweight children between the ages of six and eleven (the group most targeted by advertisements containing cartoon characters) has more than doubled. The Kaiser findings indicate that food advertisements may influence the food choices/requests children make and confuse them regarding what is nutritious and what is not. Companies have been using cartoon characters to market junk food since Mickey Mouse appeared on boxes of Post Toasties in 1935. The Institute of Medicine study recommended that food companies stop using licensed characters to advertise their high-sugar, high-calorie, low-nutrient foods and to only use these characters to market healthful food choices. The Kaiser study also indicated that companies can have a positive impact on children by using their favorite characters to advertise healthy foods.

Although the food industry has long denied the connection between advertising and obesity, the recent evidence is pretty clear in supporting the connection. Some companies, such as General Mills, are remaining silent on the issue, whereas others are making some positive changes. Kraft Foods has begun limiting its use of cartoon characters in a promise to promote better nutritional standards for children younger than twelve. Although Kellogg is using Chicken Little to advertise Froot Loops, the boxes of cereal do contain Chicken Little teaching children how to choose healthy breakfast foods through a baseball game. Viacom recently agreed to place SpongeBob SquarePants on spinach packages.

Although some companies are making efforts to promote healthier food choices for children, those in the food industry as a whole will need to agree on a definition of what makes a food healthy, but this is no easy task and something many would rather not do. The information is out there regarding this issue; the question is whether or not companies choose to be socially responsible in advertising to children or whether they keep the focus on the bottom line.

Responsible marketers are taking this concern as a wake-up call and an indication that the market desires healthier food options. Kraft Foods is introducing a line of 100 percent whole grain crackers, chocolate chip cookies, and Fig Newtons. Kraft CEO Roger Deromedi said, "We're taking steps that are responsible to societal concerns, while at the same time driving our business results by transforming our portfolio to better align with consumer trends." Mars, Inc. is rolling out a new line of cocoa-based snacks that significantly reduce bad cholesterol, promote healthy circulation, and protect against heart disease.

McDonald's has been one of the marketers under fire over the past several years for targeting children with their Happy Meals and play lands into consuming unhealthy menu alternatives. McDonald's has responded to stakeholders' health concerns by eliminating Super Size menu options, introducing salads and healthier snacks such as apple slices, and attractively repackaging their milk. It is introducing food wrappers and boxes that provide nutritional information for the menu selection. McDonald's "transparency" in providing calories and fat grams on its products shows a sensitivity and concern for consumer health and stakeholder interests.[1] ■

*A*s this example illustrates, most organizations have a number of constituents, who in turn have other stakeholders to consider. In this case, the food industry and its member companies are facing the complex task of balancing government, parent, children, and corporate concerns. These stakeholders are increasingly expressing opinions that have an effect on the industry's time, operations, member relationships, and products. Today, many organizations are learning to anticipate such issues and to address them in their plans and actions long before they become the subject of media stories or negative attention.

In this chapter, we examine the concept of stakeholders and explore why these groups are important for today's businesses. First, we define stakeholders and examine primary, secondary, and global stakeholders. Then, we examine the concept of a stakeholder orientation to enhance social responsibility. Next, we consider the impact of corporate reputation and crisis situations on stakeholder relationships. Finally, we examine the development of stakeholder relationships implementing a stakeholder perspective and the link between stakeholder relationships and social responsibility.

STAKEHOLDERS DEFINED

In Chapter 1, we defined stakeholders as those people and groups to whom an organization is responsible—including customers, investors and shareholders, employees, suppliers, governments, communities, and many others—because they have a "stake" or claim in some aspect of a company's products, operations, markets, industry, or outcomes. These groups not only are influenced by businesses, but they also have the ability to affect businesses.

Aramark's Just4U menu allows students at the University of Pennsylvania to customize their meal options with low-fat, low-carb, and other nutritional choices.

Responsibility issues, conflicts, and successes revolve around stakeholder relationships. Building effective relationships is considered one of the more important areas of business today. The stakeholder framework is recognized as a management theory that attempts to balance stakeholder interests. Issues related to indivisible resources and unequal levels of stakeholder salience constrain managers' efforts to balance stakeholder interests.[2] A business exists because of relationships among employees, customers, shareholders or investors, suppliers, and managers that develop strategies to attain success. In addition, an organization usually has a governing authority, often called a *board of directors*, that provides oversight and direction to make sure the organization stays focused on objectives in an ethical, legal, and socially responsible manner. When misconduct is discovered in organizations, it is often the case that there is knowing cooperation or compliance that facilitates the acceptance and perpetuation of unethical conduct.[3] Therefore, relationships are not only associated with organizational success but also with organizational failure to assume responsibility.

The historical assumption that the foremost objective of business is profit maximization led to the belief that business is accountable primarily to investors and others involved in the market and economic aspects of an organization. Because shareholders and other investors provide the financial foundation for business and expect something in return, managers and executives naturally strive to maintain positive relationships with them.[4]

In the latter half of the twentieth century, perceptions of business accountability evolved toward an expanded model of the role and responsibilities of business in society. The expansion included questions about the normative role of business: "What is the appropriate role for business to play in society?" and "Should profit be the sole objective of business?"[5] Many businesspeople and scholars have questioned the role of social responsibility in business. Legal and economic responsibilities are generally accepted as the most important determinants of performance: "If this is well done," say classical theorists, "profits are maximized more or less continuously and firms carry out their major responsibilities to society."[6] Some economists believe that if companies address economic and legal issues, they are satisfying the demands of society, and trying to anticipate and meet additional needs would be almost impossible. Milton Friedman has been quoted as saying that "the basic mission of business [is] thus to produce goods and services at a profit, and in doing this, business [is] making its maximum contribution to society and, in fact, being socially responsible."[7] Even with the business ethics scandals of the twenty-first century, Friedman suggests that, although individuals guilty of wrongdoing should be held accountable, the market is a better deterrent than new laws and regulations that discourage firms from wrongdoing.[8] Thus, Friedman would diminish the role of stakeholders such as the government and employees in requiring that businesses demonstrate responsible and ethical behavior.

This Darwinian form of capitalism has unfortunately been exported to many less developed and developing countries and is associated with a Wild West economy where anything goes in business. Friedman's capitalism is a far cry from Adam Smith's, one of the founders of capitalism. Smith created the concept of the invisible hand and spoke about self-interest; however, he went on to explain that this common good is associated with psychological motives and that each individual has to produce for the common good, "with values such as Propriety, Prudence, Reason, Sentiment and promoting the happiness of mankind."[9] These values could be associated with the needs and concerns of stakeholders.

In the twenty-first century, Friedman's form of capitalism is being replaced by Smith's original concept of capitalism (or what is now called enlightened capitalism), a notion of capitalism that reemphasizes stakeholder concerns and issues. This shift may be occurring faster in developed countries than in those still being developed. Theodore Levitt, a renowned business professor, once wrote that, although profits are required for business just like eating is required for living, profit is not the purpose of business any more than eating is the purpose of life.[10] Norman Bowie, a well-known philosopher, extended Levitt's sentiment by noting that focusing on profit alone can create an unfavorable paradox that causes a firm to fail to achieve its objectives. Bowie contends that when a business also cares about the well-being of stakeholders, it earns trust and cooperation which ultimately reduces costs and increases productivity.[11]

These perspectives take into account both market and nonmarket constituencies that may interact with a business and have some effect on the firm's policies and strategy.[12] Market constituencies are those who are directly involved and affected by the business purpose, including investors, employees, customers, and other business partners. Nonmarket groups include the general community, media, government, special-interest groups, and others who are not always directly tied to issues of profitability and performance.

There is much evidence that social responsibility is associated with increased profits. For example, one survey indicates that three of four consumers refuse to buy from certain businesses, and a business's poor conduct was an important reason to avoid a business.[13] An important academic study found that there is a direct relationship between social responsibility and profitability. The study also found that social responsibility contributes to employee commitment and customer loyalty—vital concerns of any firm trying to increase profits.[14]

STAKEHOLDER ISSUES AND INTERACTION

Stakeholders provide resources that are more or less critical to a firm's long-term success. These resources may be both tangible and intangible. Shareholders, for example, supply capital; suppliers offer material resources or intangible knowledge; employees and managers grant expertise, leadership, and commitment; customers generate revenue and provide loyalty and positive word-of-mouth promotion; local communities provide infrastructure; and the media transmits positive corporate images. When individual stakeholders share similar expectations about desirable business conduct, they may choose to establish or join formal communities that are dedicated to better defining and advocating these values and expectations. Stakeholders' ability to withdraw—or to threaten to withdraw—these needed resources gives them power over businesses.[15] For example, in the United Kingdom, the Office of Fair Trading Consumer Codes Approval Scheme recognizes businesses and organizations that successfully promote and safeguard consumer interests beyond the minimum requirements of consumer law. Consumers may look for this approval when choosing retailers to patronize.

New reforms to improve corporate accountability and transparency also suggest that other stakeholders—including banks, law firms, and public accounting firms—can play a major role in fostering responsible decision making.[16] Stakeholders apply their values and standards to many diverse issues, such as working conditions, consumer rights, environmental conservation, product safety, and proper information disclosure, issues that may or may not directly affect an individual stakeholder's own welfare. We can assess the level of social responsibility an organization bears by scrutinizing its effects on the issues of concern to its stakeholders. Table 2.1 provides examples of common stakeholder issues along with indicators of businesses' impacts on these issues.[17]

Identifying Stakeholders

We can identify two different types of stakeholders. **Primary stakeholders** are those whose continued association is absolutely necessary for a firm's survival; these include employees, customers, investors, and shareholders, as well as the governments and communities that provide necessary infrastructure. For example, General Motors diluted pensions of salaried employees and cut medical benefits to retired employees who are primary stakeholders. Figure 2.1 shows the national trend of firms with over 200 employees to offer fewer health benefits for retirees, dropping from a high of around 66 percent in 1988 to around 32 percent in 2005.

Secondary stakeholders do not typically engage in transactions with a company and thus are not essential for its survival; these include the media, trade associations, and special-interest groups. The American Association of Retired People (AARP), a special-interest group, works to support the rights of retirees in areas such as health-care benefits. Both primary and secondary stakeholders embrace specific values and standards that dictate what constitutes acceptable or unacceptable corporate behaviors. It is important for managers to recognize that primary groups may present more day-to-day concerns, but secondary groups cannot be ignored or given less consideration in the ethical decision-making process.

In Great Britain, the Office of Fair Trade issues this logo to companies that agree to treat customers fairly and honestly. Consumers look for the logo when shopping and selecting retailers.

primary stakeholders

those whose continued association is absolutely necessary for a firm's survival; these include employees, customers, investors, and shareholders, as well as the governments and communities that provide necessary infrastructure

secondary stakeholders

those who do not typically engage in transactions with a company and thus are not essential for its survival; these include the media, trade associations, and special-interest groups

| TABLE 2.1 | Examples of Stakeholder Issues and Associated Measures of Corporate Impacts |

Stakeholder Groups and Issues	Potential Indicators of Corporate Impact on These Issues
Employees	
1. Compensation and benefits	1. Ratio of lowest wage to national legal minimum or to local cost of living
2. Training and development	2. Changes in average years of training of employees
3. Employee diversity	3. Percentages of employees from different genders and races
4. Occupational health and safety	4. Standard injury rates and absentee rates
5. Communications with management	5. Availability of open-door policies or ombudsmen management
Customers	
1. Product safety and quality	1. Number of product recalls over time
2. Management of customer complaints	2. Number of customer complaints and availability of complaints procedures to answer them
3. Services to customers with disabilities	3. Availability and nature of measures taken to ensure services to customers with disabilities
Investors	
1. Transparency of shareholder processes	1. Availability of procedures to inform shareholders about corporate activities
2. Shareholder rights	2. Frequency and type of litigation involving violations of shareholder rights
Suppliers	
1. Encouraging suppliers in developing countries	1. Prices offered to suppliers in developed countries and developing countries in comparison to other suppliers
2. Encouraging minority suppliers	2. Percentage of minority suppliers
Community	
1. Public health and safety	1. Availability of emergency response plan protection
2. Conservation of energy and materials	2. Data on reduction of waste produced and materials in comparison to industry
3. Donations and support of local organizations	3. Annual employee time spent in community service organizations
Environmental Groups	
1. Minimizing the use of energy	1. Amount of electricity purchased; percentage of "green" electricity
2. Minimizing emissions and waste	2. Type, amount, and designation of waste generated
3. Minimizing adverse environmental effect of products	3. Percentage of product weight reclaimed after use/effects of goods and services

| FIGURE 2.1 | Declining Retiree Health Benefits |

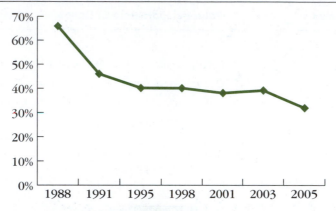

Source: Kaiser/HRET; KPMG; Health Insurance Association of America. As referenced by David Wessel, Ellen E. Schultz, and Laurie McGinley, "GM's Decision to Cut Pensions Accelerates Broad Corporate Shift," *Wall Street Journal*, February 8, 2006, p. A1.

stakeholder interaction model

a visual representation of interactions between the organization and stakeholders

Figure 2.2 offers a conceptualization of the relationship between businesses and stakeholders. In this **stakeholder interaction model**, there are two-way relationships between the firm and a host of stakeholders. In addition to the fundamental input of investors, employees, and suppliers, this approach recognizes other stakeholders and explicitly acknowledges the dialog that exists between a firm's internal and external environments.

A Stakeholder Orientation

stakeholder orientation

the degree to which a firm understands and addresses stakeholder demands

The degree to which a firm understands and addresses stakeholder demands can be referred to as a **stakeholder orientation**. This orientation comprises three sets of activities: (1) the organization-wide generation of data about stakeholder groups and assessment of the firm's effects on these groups, (2) the distribution of this information throughout the firm, and (3) the organization's responsiveness as a whole to this intelligence.[18]

Generating data about stakeholders begins with identifying the stakeholders that are relevant to the firm. Relevant stakeholder communities should be analyzed on the basis of the power each enjoys as well as by the ties between them. Next, the firm should characterize the concerns about the business's conduct that each relevant stakeholder group shares. This information can be derived from formal research, including surveys, focus groups, Internet searches, or press reviews. For example, Ford Motor Company obtains input on social and environmental responsibility issues from company representatives, suppliers, customers, and community leaders. Shell has an online discussion forum where website visitors are invited to express their opinions on the company's activities and their implications. This information can also be generated informally by employees and managers as they carry out their daily activities. For example, purchasing managers know about suppliers' demands, public relations executives about the media, legal counselors about the regulatory environment, financial executives about investors, sales representatives about customers, and human resources advisors

| **FIGURE 2.2** | Stakeholder Model for Implementing Social Responsibilities |

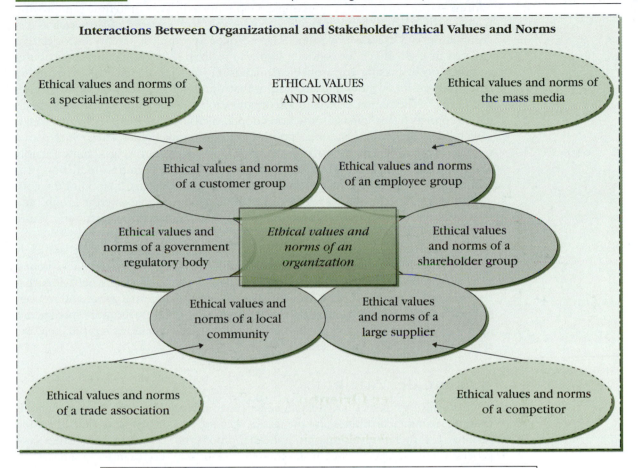

Source: Adapted from Isabelle Maignan, O. C. Ferrell, and Linda Ferrell. "A Stakeholder Model for Implementing Social Responsibility in Marketing," *European Journal of Marketing* 39 (Sep./Oct. 2005), pp. 956–977. Copyright © 2005 by Emerald Insight. Reprinted with permission.

about employees. Finally, the company should evaluate its impact on the issues that are important to the various stakeholders it has identified.[19] To develop effective stakeholder dialogs, management needs to appreciate how others perceive the risks of a specific decision. A multiple stakeholder perspective must take into account communication content and transparency when communicating with specific stakeholders.[20]

Given the variety of the employees involved in the generation of information about stakeholders, it is essential that this intelligence be circulated throughout the firm. This requires that the firm facilitate the communication of information about the nature of relevant stakeholder communities, stakeholder issues, and the current impact of the firm on these issues to all members of the organization. The dissemination of stakeholder intelligence can be organized formally through activities such as newsletters and internal information forums.[21]

A stakeholder orientation is not complete unless it includes activities that actually address stakeholder issues. For example, Gap reported that although it is improving factory inspections, it is still struggling to wipe out deep-seated problems such as discrimination and excessive overtime. Gap revoked approval of seventy factories that violated its code of vendor conduct. Gap also realized that it sometimes contributes to problems by making unreasonable demands on factories; therefore, it is becoming stricter about its own deadlines to ensure that dumping rush jobs on factories does not occur.[22] The responsiveness of the organization as a whole to stakeholder intelligence consists of the initiatives the firm adopts to ensure that it abides by or exceeds stakeholder expectations and has a positive impact on stakeholder issues. Such activities are likely to be specific to a particular stakeholder group (e.g., family-friendly work schedules) or to a particular stakeholder issue (e.g., pollution-reduction programs). These responsiveness processes typically involve the participation of the concerned stakeholder groups. Kraft, for example, includes special-interest groups and university representatives in its programs to become sensitized to present and future ethical issues.

A stakeholder orientation can be viewed as a continuum in that firms are likely to adopt the concept to varying degrees. To gauge a given firm's stakeholder orientation, it is necessary to evaluate the extent to which the firm adopts behaviors that typify both the generation and dissemination of stakeholder intelligence and responsiveness to it. A given organization may generate and disseminate more intelligence about certain stakeholder communities than about others and, as a result, may respond to that intelligence differently.[23]

Stakeholder Attributes[24]

Traditionally, companies have had an easier time understanding the issues stakeholders raise than their attributes and the tactics they use to affect organizational decision making. It is therefore necessary to understand both the content (specific issues) and process (actions, tactics) of each stakeholder relationship. For example, animal rights activists sometimes use an unreasonable process to communicate the content of their beliefs. Although they are controversial, animal rights issues do have solid support from a number of citizens. One mechanism for understanding stakeholders and their potential salience to a firm involves assessing three stakeholder attributes: power, legitimacy, and urgency. This assessment provides one analytical tool to help managers uncover the motivations and needs of stakeholders and how they relate to the company and its interests. In addition, stakeholder actions may also sensitize the firm to issues and viewpoints not previously considered.[25]

Power, legitimacy, and urgency are not constant, meaning stakeholder attributes can change over time and context. For example, there was a very strong "Buy American" sentiment in the United States in the 1980s, a time when Japanese manufacturers were making steady market share gains. Today, there is less consumer activism or retailer strategy on activism toward this nationalistic buying criterion. Thus, although these stakeholders may still have a legitimate claim for buying from U.S. firms, they are neither using their power nor creating a sense of urgency regarding this issue today. It seems that nationalism, as it relates to retail purchasing, is no longer a key buying criterion. The U.S. economy has been strong, so products from other countries have not been seen as threatening. In polls after September 11, 2001 30 percent of Americans said they preferred to buy American-made goods, but over 40 percent said they pay little attention to a good's origin.[26]

power

the extent to which a stakeholder can gain access to coercive, utilitarian, or symbolic means to impose or communicate its views to the organization; power may be coercive, utilitarian, or symbolic

POWER A stakeholder has power to the extent that it can gain access to coercive, utilitarian, or symbolic means to impose or communicate its views to an organization.[27] *Coercive power* involves the use of physical force, violence, or some type of restraint. *Utilitarian power* involves financial or material control, such as boycotts that affect a company's bottom line. Finally, *symbolic power* relies on the use of symbols that connote social acceptance, prestige, or some other attribute. Symbolism contained in letter-writing campaigns, advertising messages, and websites can be used to generate awareness and enthusiasm for more responsible business actions. In fact, the Internet has conferred tremendous power on stakeholder groups in recent years. A number of "hate sites" have been placed on the Internet by disgruntled stakeholders, especially customers and former employees, to share concerns about certain corporate behaviors. Richard B. Freeman, a Harvard labor economist, says, "With the Internet, information flows instantly, so even if we don't have more people concerned about companies, those who are can do more about it."[28] Symbolic power is the least threatening of the three types.

Utilitarian measures, including boycotts and lawsuits, are also fairly prevalent, although they often come about after symbolic strategies fail to yield the desired response. For example, the U.S. government, an important stakeholder for most firms, recently banned the importation of goods made by children under the age of fifteen through indentured or forced labor.[29] This action came about after the media and activist groups exposed widespread abuses in the apparel industry. This law carries financial—utilitarian—repercussions for firms that purchase products manufactured under unacceptable labor conditions.

Finally, some stakeholders use coercive power to communicate their message. During a rally to protest McDonald's as a symbol of global capitalism, worker exploitation, and environmental insensitivity, a handful of protesters stormed a McDonald's restaurant in London, eventually tearing down the hamburger chain's famous "golden arches." A company spokesperson said that although the company abhors violence and destruction, it planned to reopen the damaged restaurant and start a dialog with activists to counter false allegations and accusations. The spokesperson emphasized the local, not global, nature of McDonald's in the United Kingdom, where the company employs 70,000 people and has over 1,235 restaurants.[30]

legitimacy

the perception or belief that a stakeholder's actions are proper, desirable, or appropriate within a given context

LEGITIMACY The second stakeholder attribute is legitimacy, which is the perception or belief that a stakeholder's actions are proper, desirable, or appropriate within a given context.[31] This definition suggests that stakeholder actions are considered legitimate when claims are judged to be reasonable by other stakeholders and by society in general. Legitimacy is gained through the stakeholder's ability and willingness to explore the issue from a variety of perspectives and then to communicate in an effective and respectful manner on the desire for change. Thus, extremist views are less likely to be considered legitimate because these groups often use covert and inflammatory measures that overshadow the issues and create animosity. For example, extreme groups have destroyed property, threatened customers, and committed other acts of violence that ultimately discredit their legitimacy.[32] McDonald's remained open to stakeholder dialog after the London restaurant was destroyed, although other companies might have shunned further communication with the protesters, citing their irrational and dangerous behavior. McDonald's also faced criticism for its unhealthy food, which was linked to obesity; in the UK, the health lobby claimed McDonald's food was bad for consumers. McDonald's took the claims to heart and decided to change their image. They intensified efforts to include healthy options on their menus. One issue arose concerning their Chicken Caesar salad, which had more fat and calories than McDonald's world-famous hamburger. However, management listened to consumers and, within three months, introduced a new low-fat dressing option. McDonald's has recovered well from its negative publicity and, by listening to its customers, has been able to change not only its image, through makeovers of its restaurants and sponsorship deals with Justin Timberlake and Destiny's Child, but also its focus. In the UK, McDonald's launched an "It's What I Eat and What I Do" initiative to increase activity among young children and try to counteract the obesity epidemic.[33] Although an issue may be legitimate, such as environmental sensitivity, it is difficult for the claim to be evaluated independently of the way the stakeholder group communicates about it.

urgency
the time sensitivity and the importance of the claim to the stakeholder

URGENCY Stakeholders exercise greater pressures on managers and organizations when they stress the urgency of their claims. Urgency is based on two characteristics: time sensitivity and the importance of the claim to the stakeholder. Time sensitivity usually heightens the stakeholder's effort and may compress an organization's ability to research and react to a claim. For example, protesters in Thailand formed a human chain around a hotel hosting the Asian Development Bank's annual meeting. The protest was aimed at increasing the bank's efforts to revitalize the regional economy and create more economic equity for the working poor. The protest was timed to occur during the bank's annual meeting, when officials would be developing new policies. Although bank officials did not formally meet with the protesters, the Asian Development Bank committed monies and backed projects to reduce poverty and other socioeconomic ills.[34]

In another example, labor and human rights are widely recognized as critical issues because they are fundamental to the well-being of people around the world. These rights have become a focal point for college student associations that criticized Nike, the world's leading shoe company, for its failure to improve the working conditions of employees of suppliers and for not making information available to interested stakeholders. Nike experienced a public backlash from its use of offshore subcontractors to manufacture its shoes and clothing. When Nike claimed no responsibility for the subcontractors' poor working conditions and extremely low wages, some consumers demanded greater accountability and responsibility by engaging in boycotts, letter-writing campaigns, public-service announcements, and so forth. Nike ultimately responded to the growing negative publicity by changing its practices and becoming a model company in managing offshore manufacturing.

Overall, stakeholders are considered more important to an organization when their issues are legitimate, their claims are urgent, and they can make use of their power on the organization. These attributes assist the firm and employees in determining the relative importance of specific stakeholders and making resource allocations for developing and managing the stakeholder relationship.

PERFORMANCE WITH STAKEHOLDERS

Managing stakeholder relationships effectively requires careful attention to a firm's reputation and the effective handling of crisis situations. Motorola, a large telecommunications company, was not aware that one of its European distributors sold Motorola semiconductor chips to a manufacturer of landmine component parts. When Motorola, the recipient of numerous social responsibility accolades, learned of the situation, it investigated, stopped selling to the distributor, and created better oversight for its distribution channels. In the process, Motorola was mindful of potential effects on its reputation with stakeholders. In a similar turn, De Beers, the world's largest diamond producer, announced it would stop buying diamonds from Angola, after a group of European organizations launched a campaign to alert the public to the fact that an Angolan rebel group, Unita, funded wars and casualties through diamond sales.[35]

Reputation Management

There are short- and long-term outcomes associated with positive stakeholder relationships. One of the most significant of these is a positive reputation. Because a company's reputation has the power to attract or repel stakeholders, it can be either an asset or a liability in developing and implementing strategic plans and social responsibility initiatives.[36] Reputations take a long time to build or change, and it is far more important to monitor reputation than many companies believe. Whereas a strong reputation may take years to build, it can be destroyed seemingly overnight if a company does not handle crisis situations to the satisfaction of the various stakeholders involved.

Corporate reputation, image, and brands are more important than ever and are among the most critical aspects of sustaining relationships with constituents, including investors, customers, financial analysts, media, and government watchdogs. It takes companies decades to build a great reputation, yet just one slip can cost a company dearly. Although an organization does not control its reputation in a direct sense, its actions, choices, behaviors, and consequences do influence the reputation that exists in the perceptions of stakeholders. Companies such as Exxon Mobil, Chevron Corp., and Royal Dutch Shell Plc. received low ratings from the public in a corporate reputation survey for what the public perceived as the "heartless" spike in prices at the pump, while at the same time the companies were enjoying record profits. In the same survey, despite corporate-governance reforms and a growing commitment to ethics and social responsibility, the overall reputation of American corporations continued to slip. In 2005, 71 percent of respondents rated American businesses' reputation as "not good" or terrible compared to 68 percent in 2004.[37]

reputation management
the process of building and sustaining a company's good name and generating positive feedback from stakeholders

Reputation management is the process of building and sustaining a company's good name and generating positive feedback from stakeholders. A company's reputation is affected by every contact with a stakeholder.[38] Various trends may affect how companies manage their reputations. These trends include market factors, such as increased consumer knowledge and community access to information, and workplace factors, including technological advances, closer vendor relationships, and more inquisitive employees. These factors make companies more cautious about their actions because increased scrutiny in this area requires more attention from management. A company needs to understand these factors and how to properly address them to achieve a strong reputation. These factors have also helped companies recognize a link between reputation and competitive advantage. If these trends are dealt with wisely and if internal and external communication strategies are used effectively, a firm can position itself positively in stakeholders' minds and thus create a competitive advantage. Intangible factors related to reputation can account for as much as 50 percent of a firm's market valuation.[39]

The importance of corporate reputation has created a need for accurate reputation measures. As indicated in Table 2.2, business publications, research firms, consultants, and public relations agencies have established a foothold in the new field of

TABLE 2.2	Reputation Measures		
Reputation List	**Conducted By**	**Groups Surveyed**	**Primary Purpose**
100 Best Companies to Work for in America	Robert Lebering & Milton Moskowitz and Hewitt Associates	*Fortune* companies' employees and top managers	Publication
100 Best Corporate Citizens	*Business Ethics* magazine, KLD Research & Analytics, and Sandra Waddock and Samuel Graves, Boston College.	Drawn from 650 firms used in the socially screened Domini Index: the S&P 500, plus 150 other firms selected for industry balance and social excellence	Publication
America's Most Admired Companies	*Fortune* magazine and Clark, Martire & Bartolomeo	Company officers, directors, and analysts of *Fortune* 500 companies	Publication
Best and Worst: Social Responsibility	*Fortune* magazine and Clark, Martire & Bartolomeo	Company officers, directors, and analysts of *Fortune* 500 companies	Publication
Corporate Branding Index	Corporate Branding LLC	Vice president–level executives and above in the top 20 percent of U.S. businesses	Customized for clients
Corporate Reputation Index	Delahaye Medialink	Print and broadcast media	Sold as syndicated research
Maximizing Corporate Reputation	Burston-Marsteller	CEOs, executives, board members, financial community, government officials, business media, and consumers	Customized for clients
Reputation Quotient	Reputation Institute and Harris Interactive	General public	Customized for clients
World's Most-Respected Companies	Pricewaterhouse Coopers	CEOs from 75 countries	Publication

Sources: Christy Eidson and Melissa Master, "Who Makes the Call?" *Across the Board* 27 (March 2000): 16; Pamela Klein, "Measure What Matters," *Communication World* 16 (October–November 1999): 32; Prema Nakra, "Corporate Reputation Management: 'CRM' with a Strategic Twist," *Public Relations Quarterly* 45 (Summer 2000): 35.

reputation management through research and lists of "the most reputable" firms. However, some questions have arisen as to who can best determine corporate reputation. For example, some measures survey only chief executives, whereas others also elicit perceptions from the general public. Although executives may be biased toward a firm's financial performance, the general public may lack experience or data on which to evaluate a company's reputation. Regardless of how it is measured, reputation is the result of a process involving an organization and various constituents.[40]

The process of reputation management involves four components that work together: organizational identity, image, performance, and ultimately, reputation.[41] Organizational identity refers to how an organization wants to be viewed by its stakeholders, whereas organizational image is how stakeholders interpret the various aspects of a company to form an overall impression of it. Organizational performance involves the actual interaction between the company and its stakeholders. The interaction of organizational image and performance results in organizational reputation, the collective view of all stakeholders after their image of the firm is shaped through interactions with the company.

To build and manage a good reputation, these four areas must be aligned. Companies must manage identity and culture by pinpointing those standards and responsibilities that will allow them to achieve their objectives, work with stakeholders effectively, and continuously monitor and change for effectiveness.[42] The top corporate citizens selected by Sandra Waddock and Samuel Graves of Boston College, in the Business Ethics 100 Best Corporate Citizens list, provide recognition and publicity for outstanding performance using corporate responsibility criteria. Green Mountain Coffee ranked number two in 2005 and number one in 2006 as shown in Table 2.3. Green Mountain Coffee roasts high-quality Arabica coffees and offers over 100 coffee selections, including single-origins, estates, certified organics, Fair Trade Certified™, proprietary blends, and flavored coffees. They carefully select their coffee beans and then

Green Mountain Coffee Roasters sells coffee that meets standards for fair trade and organic farming.

TABLE 2.3   The Twenty Best Corporate Citizens

Rank	Company	Rank	Company
1.	Green Mountain Coffee Roasters	11.	Intel Corporation
2.	Hewlett-Packard Company	12.	Johnson & Johnson
3.	Advanced Micro Devices, Inc.	13.	Nike, Inc.
4.	Motorola, Inc.	14.	General Mills Inc.
5.	Agilent Technologies, Inc.	15.	Pitney Bowes, Inc.
6.	Timberland Company (The)	16.	Wells Fargo & Company
7.	Salesforce.com, Inc	17.	Starbucks Corporation
8.	Cisco Systems, Inc.	18.	Wainwright Bank & Trust Company
9.	Dell Inc.	19.	St. Paul Travelers Companies, Inc. (The)
10.	Texas Instruments Incorporated	20.	Ecolab Inc.

Source: David Raths, with Sandra Waddock and Samuel Graves, "100 Best Corporate Citizens of 2006,"
Business Ethics, Spring 2006, p. 24. Reprinted with permission from Business Ethics, P.O. Box 8439, Minneapolis,
MN 55408, 612/879-0695.

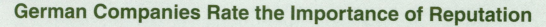

GLOBAL INITIATIVES

German Companies Rate the Importance of Reputation

Reputation management is becoming a key consideration for corporations around the world. A reputation is built over many years and through multiple interactions with customers, employees, suppliers, and other stakeholders. However, a reputation can be quickly harmed by a legal probe, ethics scandal, environmental disaster, employee layoffs, or some other social responsibility issue. Many businesspeople believe there is a relationship between a firm's reputation and its long-term performance. A recent study delved into the reasons that German firms invest resources into building, maintaining, and strengthening their reputations.

Executives at medium-sized and large German companies were asked a series of questions about corporate objectives and strategies related to reputation management. Roughly two-thirds of the respondents felt that reputation management was of "very high" or "high" importance to their companies. However, 30 percent considered reputation management to be of "low" or "very low" relevance to their organizations.

Firms operating in the food and services industries attached the most importance to reputation, whereas those in the automotive, retail, and manufacturing sectors indicated the least importance. Companies operating in agriculture, food, energy, and construction industries indicated that reputation management is fully integrated into corporate strategy. Top management has the responsibility for ensuring that reputation objectives were an explicit part of corporate strategy in 77 percent of the firms.

The following table lists a number of reputation objectives, with the percentage of respondents who believed the objective was of high importance to the organization. Developing a positive image and improving relationships with employees and customers were key considerations for the majority of companies. Other stakeholders, such as investors, suppliers, and the media, were seen as less relevant to reputation objectives and strategies. Only 15 percent of the respondents indicated

that reputation management was helpful with improving supplier relations; just over 20 percent believed the same for improving investor relations. Nearly 50 percent of the companies, however, believed that reputation objectives were very important to increasing profits.

TABLE Reputation Objectives of German Companies

Reputation Objectives	Percent Indicating Very Important
Development of a positive image	76.3
Heightening of customer satisfaction and loyalty	72.5
Improvement of customer relationships	66.4
Increase of corporate identity	60.3
Acquiring new customers	57.3
Heightening of employee motivation	56.5
Heightening of employee satisfaction	53.4
Increase in profits	48.4
Simplification of launching products on the market	37.2
Positive support by media	35.1
Improvement of corporate public image	31.3
Improvement of investor relations	25.8
Lowering the cost of capital	23.8
Improvement of investor relations	21.0
Improvement of supplier relations	15.3
Easier high-potential recruiting	13.7

Source: K. P. Wiedmann and H. Buxel, "Corporate Reputation Management in Germany: Results of an Empirical Study," *Corporate Reputation Review* 8, no. 2 (2005): 145–163, reproduced with permission of Palgrave Macmillan.

appropriately roast the coffees to maximize their taste and flavor differences. Green Mountain Coffee Roasters has consistently appeared on Forbes Magazine 200 Best Small Companies in America. It has been on the list for six years, and in 2004, it ranked sixty-eight compared to its 2003 position of seventy. There is openness in all aspects of communication that allows employees to have regular access to all levels of the organization, including CEO Bob Stiller. This encourages passion and commitment so that employees get to the crux of issues rather than play politics. The company uses technology such as voicemail or e-mail to inform the group of decisions and allows individual employees to voice their opinions and ideas. In this way, they have achieved a culture of involving people in ideas and issues, to come up with better solutions together, rather than allowing just one individual to come up with solutions that might not necessarily be the best. The empowerment of employees means that the company may seem chaotic at times. However, the communication across channels, in what is sometimes termed a "constellation of communication," ensures that the collaborative nature of getting things done spreads the word across the company and anyone can express their ideas and opinions. Although there are many meetings where employees are encouraged to share their views, the information is shared by following an agenda, which ensures that efficient decision making occurs seamlessly across the company.[43]

Thus, all these elements must be continually implemented to ensure that the company's reputation is maximized through community relations. However, most firms will, at one time or another, experience crisis situations that threaten or harm this reputation. How a company reacts, responds, and learns from the situation is indicative of its commitment and implementation of social responsibility.

CRISIS MANAGEMENT[44]

Organizational crises are far-reaching events that can have dramatic effects on both the organization and its stakeholders. Along with the industrialization of society, companies and their products have become ever more complex and therefore more susceptible to crisis. As a result, disasters and crisis situations are increasingly common events from which few organizations are exempt. For example, the size and geographic diversity of IBM's workforce and operations required the firm to develop a worldwide network of crisis management personnel. This group is trained to implement the company's crisis management team model in the event of natural disaster, product recall, major lawsuit, violence, or other misfortune. IBM put its plan into motion on September 11, 2001, and was able to restore core services within three days, lend its extra office space to house displaced customers and noncustomers, assist employees and communities affected by the tragedy, and use its technology and call centers to aid government agencies.[45]

An *ethical misconduct disaster* (EMD) can be an unexpected organizational crisis that results from employee misconduct, illegal activities such as fraud, or unethical decisions that significantly disrupts operations and threatens or is perceived to threaten the firm's continuity of operations. An EMD can be even more devastating than a natural disaster such as a hurricane or technology disruptions.[46]

As organizations plan for natural disasters and insure against traditional risks, so too should they prepare for ethical crises. An EMD can be managed by organizational initiatives to recognize, avoid, discover, answer, and recover from the misconduct. The potential damage of an ethical disaster can affect both business and society. The costs of an EMD from both a financial and reputation perspective can be assessed, as well as the need for planning to avoid an EMD. The role of leadership in preventing a crisis relates to a contingency plan to develop effective crisis management programs.

The risks facing organizations today are significant, and the reputational damage caused can be far greater for companies that find themselves unprepared. The key is to recognize that the risks associated with misconduct are real and that, if insufficient controls are in place, the company can suddenly find itself the subject of an EMD. Although it is hard to predict an ethical disaster, companies can and must prepare for one.

According to HealthSouth, they have spent "approximately $440 million in, among other things, stabilizing [their] operations, reconstructing [their] accounting records, producing restated and other financial statements, restructuring the Company finances and restoring HealthSouth's credibility—all responses to the crises created as a direct result of the fraud perpetrated while Richard Scrushy was CEO and Chairman." The result was "a cumulative net reduction in shareholders' equity of $3.9 billion."[47] In addition, the company agreed to pay "$100 million to settle a lawsuit claiming violations of federal securities laws" and "$325 million plus interest as part of a global settlement regarding certain alleged inappropriate Medicare billing practices."

Although HealthSouth Corporation's CEO Richard Scrushy was acquitted of participating in a $27 billion accounting fraud, many of his executives plea-bargained deals with the government for more lenient sentences.[48] In 2006, Scrushy was found guilty of paying a half million dollars in bribes to a former Alabama governor in exchange for a seat on a state health-care board. Moreover, the resulting damage to the firm's reputation was a disaster, and their only means of distancing themselves from their former leader was to provide the following comment on the company's website:

> As HealthSouth continues its unprecedented recovery from a massive fraud that occurred during the tenure of Richard Scrushy as CEO and Chairman, it is astonishing that he would have the audacity and shamelessness to comment on the current operations or the dedication of our approximately 40,000 employees. As we have stated in the past, Scrushy will not be offered any position within the Company by this management team or this Board of Directors. Under no circumstances would we reach out to Scrushy, who by his own defense has claimed a complete lack of knowledge as to the financial workings of the Company during his tenure as CEO and Chairman, despite his claims of possessing valuable expertise.[49]

Of course, not every unethical decision relates to accounting fraud. Many often begin as a marketing effort, and only in retrospect is it revealed to be unethical. And clearly not every decision becomes a crisis. When Blockbuster introduced its "The End of Late Fees" policy and promotion, a lawsuit brought by the New Jersey attorney general's office over possible deceptive pricing did not seem to dampen Blockbuster's reputation and stakeholder confidence. The attorney general's office was concerned that some consumers did not understand that they would have to pay the cost of the videocassette or DVD if they failed to return movies to Blockbuster within a stated period of time.[50]

It is critical for companies to manage crises effectively because research suggests that these events are a leading cause of organizational mortality. What follows are some key issues to consider in **crisis management**, the process of handling a high-impact event characterized by ambiguity and the need for swift action. In most cases, the crisis situation will not be handled in a completely effective or ineffective manner. Thus, a crisis usually leads to both success and failure outcomes for a business and its stakeholders and provides information for making improvements to future crisis management and social responsibility efforts.[51] Chapter 12 discusses the importance of social auditing in detecting and preventing crisis situations.

Organizational crises are characterized by a threat to a company's high-priority goals, surprise to its membership, and stakeholder demands for a short response time. The nature of crises requires a firm's leadership to communicate in an often stressful, emotional, uncertain, and demanding context. Crises are very difficult on a company's stakeholders as well. For this reason, the firm's stakeholders, especially its employees, shareholders, customers, government regulators, competitors, creditors, and the media, will closely scrutinize communication after a crisis. Hence, crises have widespread implications not only for the organization but also for each group affected by the crisis.

To better understand how crises develop and move toward resolution, some researchers use a medical analogy. Using the analogy, the organization proceeds through chronological stages similar to a person with an illness. The prodromal stage is a precrisis period during which warning signs may exist. Next is the acute stage, in which the actual crisis occurs. During the third (or chronic) stage, the business is required to sufficiently explain its actions to move to the final stage, crisis resolution. Figure 2.3 illustrates these stages. Although the stages are conceptually distinct, some crises happen so quickly and without warning that the organization may move from the prodromal to acute stage within minutes. Many organizations faced this situation after Hurricane Katrina crashed into New Orleans and the Mississippi Gulf Coast, disrupting all business and social activity for years.

One of the fundamental difficulties that a company faces is how to communicate effectively to stakeholders during and after a disaster. Once a crisis strikes, the firm's stakeholders need a quick response in the midst of the duress and confusion. They need information about how the company plans to resolve the crisis as well as what

crisis management
the process of handling a high-impact event characterized by ambiguity and the need for swift action

---

FIGURE 2.3   Crisis Management Process

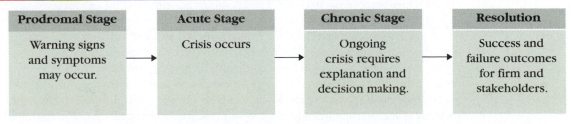

Prodromal Stage	**Acute Stage**	**Chronic Stage**	**Resolution**
Warning signs and symptoms may occur.	Crisis occurs	Ongoing crisis requires explanation and decision making.	Success and failure outcomes for firm and stakeholders.

each constituent can do to mitigate its own negative effects. If a company is slow to respond, stakeholders may feel that the company does not care about their needs or is not concerned or remorseful, if the company is at fault, about the crisis. Furthermore, a delayed response may in fact increase the suffering of particular stakeholder groups. For instance, some stakeholders may take on considerable debt due to medical expenses as a result of the crisis. Therefore, a rapid response to stakeholders is central to any crisis resolution strategy so that these groups can plan their recovery.

Ironically, crisis events are often so chaotic that a company's leadership may not be certain of the cause of the situation before the media and other relevant groups demand a statement. Thus, it is not surprising for organizations to begin their crisis response with some degree of ambiguity in their statements. In fact, some crisis theorists advise companies to avoid too much detail in their initial response due to the embarrassment that results from changing positions later in the crisis when more information is available. Still, stakeholder groups want and, as a matter of safety in some cases, need access to whatever information the firm can share. Although tensions between the public's needs and the organization's fear of litigation can hamper an organization's willingness to communicate, the demand for information in such situations is unyielding.

Not only should the firm's leadership make a public statement quickly, but it is also necessary for the organization to communicate about specific issues to stakeholder groups. First, leadership should express concern and/or remorse for the event. Second, the organization should delineate guidelines regarding how it intends to address the crisis so that stakeholders can be confident that the situation will not escalate or recur. Finally, the company should provide explicit criteria to stakeholders regarding how each group will be compensated for any negative effects it experiences as a result of the crisis. Many companies, however, overlook these three essential conditions of crisis management. More often, they focus on minimizing harm to the organization's image, denying responsibility for the crisis, and shifting blame away from the organization and toward other stakeholder groups. Although this may be an appropriate strategy when the firm is not actually responsible, too often companies choose this course of action under the stress of the crisis when they are responsible or partially responsible for the crisis without expressing sufficient remorse for their involvement or concern for their stakeholders.

The varying communication needs and levels of concern of stakeholders during and after a crisis often hamper effective communication. The firm's leadership should try to communicate as much accurate information to these groups as possible to minimize their uncertainty. When a firm fails to do so, its credibility, legitimacy, and reputation in the eyes of stakeholders often suffer. Adding to the complexity of communication challenges, the needs of various stakeholder groups may conflict. For instance, the needs of customers who become ill as a result of a contaminated product and their desire to have medical bills paid may be at odds with the company's ability to bolster its stock price to satisfy shareholders. Some stakeholders will obviously have more opportunities than others to voice their concerns after a crisis. Victims and the general public rarely have an opportunity to meet with the organization's leadership after a crisis. Conversely, the organization's stockholders and employees will likely have a greater opportunity to express their views about the crisis and therefore may have their ideas accepted by management. Some researchers suggest that, due to this ability to communicate directly with leadership, internal stakeholder needs often take precedence over those of external stakeholders. Organizations have a responsibility to manage the competing interests of stakeholders to ensure that all stakeholder groups are treated fairly in the aftermath of a crisis. Responsible companies try to balance the needs of their stakeholders rather than favoring some groups over others. The Walt Disney Corporation experienced a potential crisis of public concern after an elderly woman died riding the Magic Kingdom's Pirates of the Caribbean and a four year old died after riding the EPCOT Resort's Mission: Space as well as a series of other incidents.[52] Since Disney is not directly regulated by the state of Florida, it released a written statement to the press and various stakeholders stating that its own engineers deemed the rides safe. At a very small cost, Disney's invitation to state inspectors to inspect its rides sent a message that the company was going beyond the minimum (legal) requirement in its response to recover ground in the perception crisis over ride safety.[53] Organizations that fail to accomplish this communication function risk alienating stakeholder groups and intensifying the negative media attention toward the company. For many reasons, including effective crisis management, organizations need to understand and pursue solid and mutually beneficial relationships with stakeholders.

DEVELOPMENT OF STAKEHOLDER RELATIONSHIPS

Relationships of any type, whether they involve family, friends, coworkers, or companies, are founded on principles of trust, commitment, and communication. They also are associated with a certain degree of time, interaction, and shared expectations. For instance, we do not normally speak of "having a relationship" with someone we have just met. We even differentiate between casual acquaintances, work colleagues, and close friends.

In business, the concept of relationships has gained much acceptance. Instead of just pursuing one-time transactions, companies are now searching for ways to develop long-term and collaborative relationships with their customers and business partners.[54] Many companies focus on relationships with suppliers, buyers, employees, and others directly involved in economic exchange. These relationships involve investments of several types. Some investments are tangible, such as buildings, equipment, new tools, and other elements dedicated to a particular relationship. For example, Hormel Foods implemented an Internet-based procurement system that allowed its suppliers to view the firm's production schedules and revise their own business operations accordingly.[55] Other investments are less tangible, such as the time, effort, trust, and commitment required to develop a relationship. Although Hormel's suppliers need the electronic infrastructure and employee knowledge to use the new procurement process, these suppliers must also trust that their relationship with Hormel is solid and will be worth these investments. Some suppliers may have concerns that their investment in Hormel's system may not be transferable to other business opportunities and partnerships. They may also have concerns about information privacy.

Whereas tangible investments are often customized for a specific business relationship, intangible efforts have a more lucid and permeable quality. Although social responsibility involves tangible activities and other communication signals, the key to good stakeholder relationships resides in trust, communication quality, and mutual respect. As a company strives to develop a dialog and a solid relationship with one stakeholder, investments and lessons learned through the process should add value to other stakeholder relationships. For example, Starbucks provides excellent benefits, including health care for part-time employees, and supports fair trade or a fair income for farmers growing its coffee.

social capital

an asset that resides in relationships and is characterized by mutual goals and trust

These efforts result in **social capital**, an asset that resides in relationships and is characterized by mutual goals and trust.[56] Like financial and intellectual capital, social capital facilitates and smoothes internal and external transactions and processes. For example, social capital among companies in the chemical industry led to the development of Responsible Care, a progressive and voluntary program of environmental, health, and safety (EHS) standards. Several high-profile accidents had eroded chemical companies' social capital with their communities, the government, and other stakeholder groups. The Chemical Manufacturers Association implemented the program to promote stronger EHS performance and to "improve the legislative, regulatory, market, and public interest climate for the industry." Thus, Responsible Care was aimed at advancing internal company operations as well as various stakeholder relationships. The industry continues to update and refine the initiative.[57] Unlike financial and intellectual capital, however, social capital is not tangible or the obvious property of one organization. In this same regard, social responsibility is not compartmentalized or reserved for a few issues or stakeholders but should have the companywide strategic focus discussed in Chapter 1.

IMPLEMENTING A STAKEHOLDER PERSPECTIVE IN SOCIAL RESPONSIBILITY[58]

An organization that develops effective corporate governance and understands the importance of business ethics and social responsibility in achieving success should develop some processes for managing these important concerns. Although there are many different approaches, we provide some steps that have been found effective to utilize the stakeholder framework in managing responsibility and business ethics. The steps include (1) assessing the corporate culture, (2) identifying stakeholder groups, (3) identifying stakeholder issues, (4) assessing the organization's commitment to social responsibility, (5) identifying resources and determining urgency, and (6) gaining stakeholder feedback. The importance of these steps is to include feedback from relevant stakeholders in formulating organizational strategy and implementation.

Step 1: Assessing the Corporate Culture

To enhance organizational fit, a social responsibility program must align with the corporate culture of the organization. The purpose of this first step is to identify the organizational mission, values, and norms that are likely to have implications for social responsibility. In particular, relevant existing values and norms are those that specify the stakeholder groups and stakeholder issues that are deemed most important by the organization. Very often, relevant organizational values and norms can be found in corporate documents such as the mission statement, annual reports, sales brochures, or websites. For example, Green Mountain Coffee is a pioneer in helping struggling coffee growers by paying them fair trade prices. The company also offers microloans to coffee-growing families to underwrite business ventures that diversify agricultural economies. It has been on the *Business Ethics* 100 Best Corporate Citizens since 2003 and climbed to the number one position in 2006.[59]

Step 2: Identifying Stakeholder Groups

In managing this stage, it is important to recognize stakeholder needs, wants, and desires. There are many important issues that gain visibility because key constituencies such as consumer groups, regulators, or the media express an interest. When agreement, collaboration, or even confrontations exist on an issue, there is a need for a decision-making process. A model of collaboration to overcome the adversarial approaches to problem solving has been suggested. Managers can identify relevant stakeholders that may be affected by or may influence the development of organizational policy.

At an annual shareholder meeting, activist Laura Cayford and others questioned Coca-Cola's executives on several shareholder issues, including human rights abuses and water depletion.

Stakeholders have some level of power over a business because they are in the position to withhold, or at least threaten to withhold, organizational resources. Stakeholders have most power when their own survival is not really affected by the success of the organization and when they have access to vital organizational resources. For example, most consumers of shoes do not have a specific need to buy Nike shoes. Therefore, if they decide to boycott Nike, they have to endure only minor inconveniences. Nevertheless, their loyalty to Nike is vital to the continued success of the sport apparel giant. The proper assessment of the power held by a given stakeholder community also requires an evaluation of the extent to which that community can collaborate with others to pressure the firm.

Step 3: Identifying Stakeholder Issues

Together, steps 1 and 2 lead to the identification of the stakeholders who are both the most powerful and legitimate. The level of power and legitimacy determines the degree of urgency in addressing their needs. Step 3 consists then in understanding the nature of the main issues of concern to these stakeholders. Conditions for collaboration exist when problems are so complex that multiple stakeholders are required to resolve the issue and the weaknesses of adversarial approaches are understood.

For example, obesity in children is a major concern in our society with many stakeholders exerting pressure on food companies and Congress to address and resolve healthy food options for children. The average ten year old weighs ten pounds more today than a ten year old in the 1960s. There are concerns that today's children, facing obesity problems, may not live as long as their parents. The health care costs facing our society from childhood obesity could become a major tax and economic burden. Companies, such as Kraft Foods, Kelloggs, and Post are responding to these stakeholder concerns and using more whole grains and eliminating transfats.

Step 4: Assessing the Organization's Commitment to Social Responsibility

Steps 1 through 3 consist of generating information about social responsibility among a variety of influencers in and around the organization. Step 4 brings these three first stages together to arrive at an understanding of social responsibility that specifically matches the organization of interest. This general definition will then be used to evaluate current practices and to select concrete social responsibility initiatives. Firms such as Starbucks have selected activities that address stakeholder concerns. Starbucks has formalized its initiatives in official documents such as annual reports, webpages, and company brochures. They have a website devoted to social responsibility. Starbucks is concerned with the environment and integrates policies and programs throughout all aspects of operations to minimize their environmental impact. They also have many community building programs that help them be good neighbors and contribute positively to the communities where their partners and customers live, work, and play.[61]

Step 5: Identifying Resources and Determining Urgency

The prioritization of stakeholders and issues along with the assessment of past performance provides for allocating resources. Two main criteria can be considered. First, the levels of financial and organizational investments required by different actions should be determined. A second criterion when prioritizing social responsibility challenges is urgency. When the challenge under consideration is viewed as significant and when stakeholder pressures on the issue could be expected, then the challenge can be treated as urgent. For example, Wal-Mart has been the focus of legislation in Maryland that forced the retailer to pay more for its employee health care. The legislation requires employers with more than 10,000 workers to spend at least 8 percent of their payroll on employee health care.[62] The legislation is now being considered by twenty-two other states. Wal-Mart recently offered to improve health-care benefits for its employees as a direct result of the pressure.[63]

Step 6: Gaining Stakeholder Feedback

Stakeholder feedback can be generated through a variety of means. First, stakeholders' general assessment of the firm and its practices can be obtained through satisfaction or reputation surveys. Second, to gauge stakeholders' perceptions of the firm's contributions to specific issues, stakeholder-generated media such as blogs, websites, podcasts, and newsletters can be assessed. Third, more formal research may be conducted using focus groups, observation, and surveys. Websites can be both positive and negative; for example, www.wakeupwalmart.com launched by the United Food and Commercial Workers union has over 115,000 members, and another group called Wal-Mart Watch is also gaining members. Both groups have articles and stories about the retail giant on their websites that do not flatter Wal-Mart. The pressure has forced the retailer to listen to its consumers and change its ways. To counter the claims by these groups, Wal-Mart launched its own site, www.walmartfacts.com, to tell its side of the story.

LINK BETWEEN STAKEHOLDER RELATIONSHIPS AND SOCIAL RESPONSIBILITY

You may be wondering what motivations companies have for pursuing stakeholder relationships. As the previous section indicates, a great deal of time, effort, and commitment goes into the process of developing and implementing a stakeholder perspective. Some companies have been accused of "window dressing," or publicizing their stakeholder efforts without having a true commitment behind them. For example, The Body Shop, which has received much positive attention for its social responsibility efforts, has also been accused of selectively communicating information and hiding less favorable company issues.[64] Its latest values report communicates strongly held values that go to the core of the organization and permeate all of its practices. Previously, The Body Shop crafted reports for specific stakeholder groups, and The Body Shop was criticized in 2005 for returning to an all-in-one format no longer crafted for specific stakeholder groups.[65] As was discussed in Chapter 1, social responsibility is a relational approach and involves the views and stakes of a number of groups. Stakeholders are engaged in the relationships that both challenge and support a company's efforts. Thus, without a solid understanding of stakeholders and their interests, a firm may miss important trends and changes in its environment and not achieve strategic social responsibility.

Rather than holding all companies to one standard, our approach to evaluating performance and effectiveness resides in the specific expectations and actual results that develop between each organization and its stakeholders. Max Clarkson, an influential contributor to our understanding of stakeholders, sums up this view:

> Performance is what counts. Performance can be measured and evaluated. Whether a corporation and its management are motivated by enlightened self-interest, common sense or high standards of ethical behavior cannot be determined by empirical methodologies available today. These are not questions that can be answered by economists, sociologists, psychologists, or any other kind of social scientist. They are interesting questions, but they are not relevant when it comes to evaluating a company's performance in managing its relationships with its stakeholder groups.[66]

Although critics and some researchers may seek answers and evidence as to the motivations of business for social responsibility, we are interested in what companies are actually doing that is positive, negative, or neutral for their stakeholders and their stakeholders' interests. The Reactive-Defensive-Accommodative-Proactive Scale (see Table 2.4) provides a method for assessing a company's strategy and performance with each stakeholder. This scale is based on a continuum of strategy options and performance outcomes with respect to stakeholders.[67] This evaluation can take place as stakeholder issues arise or are identified. Therefore, it is possible for one company to be rated at several different levels because of varying performance and transitions over time. For example, a poorly handled crisis situation may provide feedback for continuous improvement that creates more satisfactory performance in the future. Or a company may demonstrate a proactive stance toward employees yet be defensive with consumer activists.

The reactive approach involves denying responsibility and doing less than is required. This approach can be characterized as "fighting it all the way."[68] A firm that fails to invest in safety and health measures for employees is denying its responsibilities. An organization with a defensive strategy acknowledges reluctantly and

TABLE 2.4	The Reactive-Defensive-Accommodative-Proactive Scale	
Rating	**Strategy**	**Performance**
Reactive	Deny responsibility	Doing less than required
Defensive	Admit responsibility, but fight it	Doing the least that is required
Accommodative	Accept responsibility	Doing all that is required
Proactive	Anticipate responsibility	Doing more than is required

Source: Max B. E. Clarkson, "A Stakeholder Framework for Analyzing and Evaluating Corporate Social Performance," *Academy of Management Review* 20 (January 1995): 92–117.

partially the responsibility issues that may be raised by its stakeholders. A firm in this category fulfills basic legal obligations and demonstrates the minimal responsibility discussed in Chapter 1. With an accommodative strategy, a company attempts to satisfy stakeholder demands by doing all that is required and may be seen as progressive because it is obviously open to this expanded model of business relationships.[69] Today, many organizations are giving money and other resources to community organizations as a way of demonstrating social responsibility. Finally, the proactive approach not only accepts but also anticipates stakeholder interests. In this case, a company sincerely aligns legitimate stakeholder views with its responsibilities and will do more than is required to meet them.[70] Hoechst, a German life sciences company now part of Aventis, gradually assumed the proactive orientation with communities in which it operates. The initiation of a community discussion group led to information sharing and trust building and helped transform Hoechst into a society-driven company.[71]

The Reactive-Defensive-Accommodative-Proactive Scale is useful because it evaluates real practice and allows an organization to see its strengths and weaknesses within each stakeholder relationship. SABMiller, the second largest brewer in the world, uses a risk assessment program to understand the stakeholders and issues that may pose a potential risk to its reputation. These risks are prioritized, planned for, monitored, and if necessary, responded to if SABMiller cannot predict, preempt, or avoid the concern.[72] Results from a stakeholder assessment like the one at SABMiller should be included in the **social audit**, which assesses and reports a firm's performance in adopting a strategic focus for fulfilling the economic, legal, ethical, and philanthropic social responsibilities expected of it by its stakeholders. Chapter 12 takes an extensive look at this audit. Because stakeholders are so important to the concept of social responsibility, as well as to business success, Chapters 3–10 are devoted to exploring significant stakeholder relationships and issues.

social audit

the process of assessing and reporting a firm's performance in adopting a strategic focus for fulfilling the economic, legal, ethical, and philanthropic social responsibilities expected of it by its stakeholders

SUMMARY

Stakeholders refer to those people and groups who have a "stake" in some aspect of a company's products, operations, markets, industry, or outcomes. The relationship between organizations and their stakeholders is a two-way street.

The historical assumption that the key objective of business is profit maximization led to the belief that business is accountable primarily to investors and others involved in the market and economic aspects of the organization. In the latter half of the twentieth century, perceptions of business accountability evolved to include both market constituencies that are directly involved and affected by the business purpose (e.g., investors, employees, customers, and other business partners) and nonmarket constituencies that are not always directly tied to issues of profitability and performance (e.g., the general community, media, government, and special-interest groups).

In the stakeholder model, relationships, investors, employees, and suppliers provide inputs for a company to benefit stakeholders. This approach assumes a relatively mechanistic, simplistic, and nonstakeholder view of business. The stakeholder model assumes a two-way relationship between the firm and a host of stakeholders. This approach recognizes additional stakeholders and acknowledges the two-way dialog and effects that exist with a firm's internal and external environment.

Primary stakeholders are fundamental to a company's operations and survival and include shareholders and investors, employees, customers, suppliers, and public stakeholders, such as government and the community. Secondary stakeholders influence and/or are affected by the company but are neither engaged in transactions with the firm nor essential for its survival.

As more firms conduct business overseas, they encounter the complexity of stakeholder issues and relationships in tandem with other business operations and decisions. Although general awareness of the concept of stakeholders is relatively high around the world, the importance of stakeholders varies from country to country.

A stakeholder has power to the extent that it can gain access to coercive, utilitarian, or symbolic means to impose or communicate its views to the organization. Legitimacy is the perception or belief that a stakeholder's actions are proper, desirable, or appropriate within a given context. Stakeholders exercise greater pressures on managers and organizations when they stress the urgency of their claims. These attributes can change over time and context.

The degree to which a firm understands and addresses stakeholder demands can be referred to as a stakeholder orientation. This orientation comprises three sets of activities: (1) the organization-wide generation of data about stakeholder groups and assessment of the firm's effects on these groups, (2) the distribution of this information throughout the firm, and (3) the organization's responsiveness as a whole to this intelligence.

Reputation management is the process of building and sustaining a company's good name and generating positive feedback from stakeholders. The process of reputation management involves the interaction of organizational identity (how the firm wants to be viewed), organizational image (how stakeholders initially perceive the firm), organizational performance (actual interaction between the company and stakeholders), and organizational reputation (the collective view of stakeholders after interactions with the company). Stakeholders will reassess their views of the company on the basis of how the company has actually performed.

Crisis management is the process of handling a high-impact event characterized by ambiguity and the need for swift action. Some researchers describe an organization's progress through a prodromal, or precrisis, stage to the acute stage, chronic stage, and finally, crisis resolution. Stakeholders need a quick response with information about how the company plans to resolve the crisis, as well as what they can do to mitigate negative effects to themselves. It is also necessary to communicate specific issues to stakeholder groups, including remorse for the event, guidelines as to how the organization is going to address the crisis, and criteria regarding how stakeholder groups will be compensated for negative effects.

Companies are searching for ways to develop long-term, collaborative relationships with their stakeholders. These relationships involve both tangible and intangible investments. Investments and lessons learned through the process of developing a dialog and relationship with one stakeholder should add value to other stakeholder relationships. These efforts result in social capital, an asset that resides in relationships and is characterized by mutual goals and trust.

The first step in developing stakeholder relationships is to acknowledge and actively monitor the concerns of all legitimate stakeholders. A firm should adopt processes and modes of behavior that are sensitive to the concerns and capabilities of each stakeholder. Information should be communicated consistently across all stakeholders. A firm should be willing to acknowledge and openly address potential conflicts. Investments in education, training, and information will improve employees' understanding of and relationships with stakeholders. Relationships with stakeholders need to be periodically assessed through both formal and informal means. Sharing feedback with stakeholders helps establish the two-way dialog that characterizes the stakeholder model.

An organization that develops effective corporate governance and understands the importance of business ethics and social responsibility in achieving success should develop some processes for managing these important concerns. Although there are many different approaches, we provide some steps that have been found effective to utilize the stakeholder framework in managing responsibility and business ethics. The steps include (1) assessing the corporate culture, (2) identifying stakeholder groups, (3) identifying stakeholder issues, (4) assessing the organization's commitment to social responsibility, (5) identifying resources and determining urgency, and (6) gaining stakeholder feedback. The importance of these steps is to include feedback from relevant stakeholders in formulating organizational strategy and implementation.

The Reactive-Defensive-Accommodative-Proactive Scale provides a method for assessing a company's strategy and performance with one stakeholder. The reactive approach involves denying responsibility and doing less than is required. The defensive approach acknowledges only reluctantly and partially the responsibility issues that may be raised by the firm's stakeholders. The accommodative strategy attempts to satisfy stakeholder demands. The proactive approach accepts and anticipates stakeholder interests. Results from this stakeholder assessment should be included in the social audit, which assesses and reports a firm's performance in fulfilling the economic, legal, ethical, and philanthropic social responsibilities expected of it by its stakeholders.

KEY TERMS

primary stakeholders (p. 46)
secondary stakeholders (p. 46)
stakeholder interaction model (p. 48)
stakeholder orientation (p. 48)
power (p. 51)
legitimacy (p. 51)
urgency (p. 52)
reputation management (p. 53)
crisis management (p. 59)
social capital (p. 62)
social audit (p. 67)

DISCUSSION QUESTIONS

1. Define *stakeholder* in your own terms. Compare your definition with the definition used in this chapter.
2. What is the difference between primary and secondary stakeholders? Why is it important for companies to make this distinction?
3. How do legitimacy, urgency, and power attributes positively and negatively affect a stakeholder's ability to develop relationships with organizations?
4. What is reputation management? Explain why companies are concerned about their reputation and its

effects on stakeholders. What are the four elements of reputation management? Why is it important to manage these elements?

5. Define *crisis management*. What should a company facing a crisis do to satisfy its stakeholders and protect its reputation?

6. Describe the process of developing stakeholder relationships. What parts of the process seem most important? What parts seem most difficult?

7. How can a stakeholder orientation be implemented to improve social responsibility?

8. What are the differences between the reactive, defensive, accommodative, and proactive approaches to stakeholder relationships?

EXPERIENTIAL EXERCISE

Choose two companies in different industries and visit their respective websites. Peruse these sites for information that is directed at three company stakeholders: employees, customers, and the media. For example, a company that places its annual reports online may be appealing primarily to the interests of investors. Make a list of the types of information that are on the site and indicate how the information might be used and perceived by these three stakeholder groups. What differences and similarities did you find between the two companies?

WHAT WOULD YOU DO?

Literally hundreds of buildings dotted the ground below, and the thousands of cars on highways looked like ants on a mission. The jet airliner made its way to the Bangkok International Airport and eased into the humid afternoon. The group of four passed through customs control and looked for the limousine provided by Suvar Corporation, their Thai liaison in this new business venture. Representing Global Amusements were the vice president of corporate development, director of Asian operations, vice president of global relations, and director of governmental relations for Southeast Asia.

Global Amusements, headquartered in London, was considering the development of a Thai cultural amusement center on the island of Phuket. Phuket is a tourist destination known for its stunning beaches, fine resorts, and famous Thai hospitality. Both Global Amusements and Suvar Corporation believed Phuket was a great candidate for a new project. The amusement center would focus on the history of Thailand and include a variety of live performances, rides, exhibits, and restaurants. Domestic and international travelers who visited Phuket would be the primary target market.

Global Amusements had been in business for nearly twenty years and currently used a joint venture approach in establishing new properties. Suvar was its Thai partner, and the two firms had been successful two years ago in developing a water amusement park outside Bangkok. Phuket could hold much promise, but there were likely to be concerns about the potential destruction of its beauty and the exploitation of this well-preserved island and cultural reserve.

Following a day to adjust to the time zone and refine the strategy for the visit, the next three days would be spent in Bangkok, meeting with various company and governmental officials who had a stake in the proposed amusement facility. After a short flight to Phuket, the group would be the guest of the Southern Office of the Tourism Authority of Thailand for nearly a week. This part of the trip would involve visits to possible sites as well as meetings with island government officials and local interest groups.

After arriving at the hotel, the four employees of Global Amusement agreed to meet later that evening to discuss their strategy for the visit. One of their main concerns was the development of an effective stakeholder analysis. Each member of the group was asked to bring a list of primary and secondary stakeholders and indicate the various concerns or "stakes" that each might have with the proposed project. What would you do?

CHAPTER 3

Corporate Governance

CHAPTER OBJECTIVES

- To define corporate governance
- To describe the history and practice of corporate governance
- To examine key issues to consider in designing corporate governance systems
- To describe the application of corporate governance principles around the world
- To provide information on the future of corporate governance

CHAPTER OUTLINE

Corporate Governance Defined

History of Corporate Governance

Corporate Governance and Social Responsibility

Issues in Corporate Governance Systems

Corporate Governance Around the World

Future of Corporate Governance

In the early 2000s, Adelphia Communications Corporation was the sixth largest cable television company in the United States. It was the dominant cable provider for southern Florida, western New York, and Los Angeles. In addition to cable entertainment, Adelphia offered digital cable, high-speed Internet access, long-distance telephone service, home security, and paging. Adelphia was founded by the brothers John and Gus Rigas in 1952 and was part of the pioneering effort to encourage customers to throw away the "rabbit ears" on their televisions sets. In 2001, John was inducted into the Cable Television Hall of Fame. John's sons, Michael, Tim, and James, were executives at Adelphia and, along with their father, sat on the board of directors. The company was admired for its aggressive growth.

Adelphia filed for Chapter 11 of the U.S. Bankruptcy Code in June 2002. The events leading to the bankruptcy highlight the misconduct that can occur when a firm's corporate governance system is weak or barely existent. Consider these actions and their effect on stakeholders, such as employees, shareholders, and others. A Rigas relative was paid nearly $13 million for furniture and design services in 2001. In addition to the use of corporate jets for personal business, off-balance-sheet loans were made to family members. For example, Adelphia helped fund the family purchase of a golf course and the Buffalo Sabres. The hockey team filed for bankruptcy in 2003 after the National Hockey League assumed control of the franchise amid the Adelphia downfall. The cable company was listed as one of the Sabres' largest creditors, as Adelphia attempted to reclaim $130 million that the Rigas family illegally used to purchase and run the sports team. John Rigas's daughter, Ellen, and her husband lived rent-free in a Manhattan apartment owned by Adelphia. Ellen's husband served on Adelphia's board of directors. A Rigas-owned farm made most of its revenue by performing snow removal, landscaping, and related services for Adelphia.

In late 2002, John Rigas, Michael Rigas, Tim Rigas, the former Vice President of Finance James R. Brown, and the former Assistant Treasurer Michael Mulcahey were indicted on twenty-three counts of conspiracy, bank fraud, securities fraud, and wire fraud. All executives originally pleaded innocent, but Brown later pleaded guilty to three charges in exchange for his testimony against the Rigases. Adelphia is pursuing its own civil lawsuit in federal court that charges Rigas family members and twenty companies controlled by the family with violation of the Racketeer Influenced and Corrupt Organizations Act (RICO), including a breach of fiduciary duty, abuse of control, waste of corporate assets, and substantial self-dealing. Adelphia is seeking billions of dollars in damages. The Securities and Exchange Commission also has a civil lawsuit pending against the Rigases. The SEC also sued Adelphia as a company.

Adelphia sued its external auditor, Deloitte & Touche, for fraud and negligence in failing to uncover the personal gain afforded to the Rigas family. The auditing firm countered that Adelphia's board of directors knew of and approved some of the transactions under complaint. At the time, the board was stacked with family members and insiders, and there were few internal control systems in place. Adelphia's new board revoked the $4.2 million severance package offered to the former Chief Executive John Rigas. Three insurers that provided liability coverage for Adelphia's directors and officers of the firm sued to rescind the contract on the basis that these leaders were aware of the fraud when they applied for coverage.

Other stakeholders potentially harmed by Adelphia's bankruptcy are Scientific-Atlanta Inc., Fox News, In Demand, FX, and other channels. These companies are waiting for collections from Adelphia. Scientific-Atlanta advanced $83.8 million to Adelphia to promote a box to help market digital service; however, Adelphia used that money to pay off reported expenses. Not only were the suppliers affected but so were rival cable companies and the entire industry. Share prices of leading cable firms fell as a result of the Adelphia scandal. The cable industry became wary of the misconduct's effect on its reputation and worried that investors might lose faith or confidence because of situations at Adelphia and other companies like WorldCom. Investors were guarded because there are still founding families operating cable companies. The central problem is that several executives acted in their own self-interest at a company with an ineffectual control, risk, and governance system to detect and prevent such misconduct.

In 2004, John and Timothy Rigas were convicted on eighteen of the twenty-three counts against them. They were convicted of all fifteen securities fraud charges as well as one count of conspiracy and two counts of bank fraud. One year later, John Rigas was sentenced to fifteen years in prison, and his son Timothy was sentenced to twenty years. Michael Rigas was sentenced to ten months of home confinement and two years of probation after pleading guilty to one count of making a false entry in a financial record. Mike Mulcahey was found not guilty on all counts against him. John and Timothy Rigas remain free on bail pending their appeals.

Today, Adelphia has 14,000 employees and is on the path to recovery. It has new leadership in place and has relocated its corporate offices to Denver, Colorado. It is working hard to restore its reputation and is strengthening its business operations and financial performance. According to the company website, it is now guided by strong, well-defined values and a code of ethical conduct. Upgrades of the company's network are proceeding rapidly, allowing Adelphia to introduce advanced products like high-definition television and video on demand and to extend the reach of its popular high-speed Internet service. The company remains focused on improving its corporate governance and strengthening customer service.[1] ■

The Adelphia story spotlights the increasing accountability that accompanies business decisions today, especially those made by high-level personnel in publicly held corporations. Stakeholders are demanding greater transparency in business, meaning that company motives and actions must be clear, open for discussion, and subject to scrutiny. Although some organizations have operated fairly independently in the past, recent scandals and the associated focus on the role of business in society have highlighted a need for systems that take into account the goals and expectations of various stakeholders. To respond to these pressures, businesses must effectively implement policies that provide strategic guidance on appropriate courses of action. This focus is part of corporate governance, the system of checks and balances that ensures that organizations are fulfilling the goals of social responsibility.

Governance procedures and policies are typically discussed in the context of publicly traded firms, especially as they relate to corporations' responsibilities to investors.[2] However, the trend is toward discussing governance within many industry sectors, including nonprofits, small businesses, and family-owned enterprises. We believe governance deserves broader consideration because there is evidence of a link between good governance and strong social responsibility. Before the governance crises of Enron, Tyco, and other firms, James McRitchie, editor of Corporate Governance.Net, commented on corporate governance: "Despite its still relatively low profile, it's where much of the real action is going on when it comes to positively changing corporate behavior."[3] Corporate governance and accountability are key drivers of change for business in the twenty-first century.[4] It is abundantly clear, to experts and nonexperts alike, that corporate governance is in need of immediate attention by a wide range of firms and stakeholders. The corporate scandals at Adelphia, WorldCom, Tyco, Global Crossing, and other firms in the early 2000s represented a fundamental breakdown in basic principles of the capitalist system. Investors and other stakeholders must be able to trust management while boards of directors oversee managerial decisions. The egregious oversights that left thousands without jobs or retirement savings, saw executives being led away to court, prompted federal legislation, and sparked major reform in the accounting and auditing fields challenged the tenets of our economic system.[5]

In this chapter, we define corporate governance and integrate the concept with the other elements of social responsibility. Then, we examine the corporate governance framework used in this book. Next, we trace the evolution of corporate governance and provide information on the status of corporate governance systems in several countries. We look at the history of corporate governance and the relationship of corporate governance to social responsibility. We also examine primary issues that should be considered in the development and improvement of corporate governance systems, including the roles of boards of directors, shareholders and investors, internal control and risk management, and executive compensation. Finally, we consider the future of corporate governance and indicate how strong governance is tied to corporate performance and economic growth. Our approach in this chapter is to demonstrate that corporate governance is a fundamental aspect of social responsibility.

CORPORATE GOVERNANCE DEFINED

In a general sense, the term *governance* relates to the exercise of oversight, control, and authority. For example, most institutions, governments, and businesses are organized so that oversight, control, and authority are clearly delineated. These organizations usually have an owner, president, chief executive officer, or board of directors that serves as the ultimate authority on decisions and actions. Nonprofit organizations, such as homeowners associations, have a president and board of directors to make decisions in the interest of a community of homeowners. A clear delineation of power and accountability helps stakeholders understand why and how the organization chooses and achieves its goals. This delineation also demonstrates who bears the ultimate risk for organizational decisions. Sarbanes-Oxley and the Federal Sentencing Guidelines put responsibility on top officers and the board of directors. Although many companies have adopted decentralized decision making, empowerment, team projects, and less hierarchical structures, governance remains a required mechanism for ensuring continued growth, change, and accountability to regulatory authorities. Even if a company has adopted a consensus approach for its operations, there has to be authority for delegating tasks, making tough and controversial decisions, and balancing power throughout the organization. Governance also provides oversight to uncover and address mistakes, risks, and misconduct. Consider the failure of boards at Enron, WorldCom, Adelphia, and Tyco to address risks and provide internal controls to prevent misconduct.

We define **corporate governance** as the formal system of oversight, accountability, and control for organizational decisions and resources. Oversight relates to a system of checks and balances that limits employees' and managers' opportunities to deviate from policies and codes of conduct. Accountability relates to how well the content of workplace decisions is aligned with a firm's stated strategic direction. Control involves the process of auditing and improving organizational decisions and actions. The philosophy that a board or firm holds regarding oversight, accountability, and control directly affects how corporate governance works.

Corporate Governance Framework

Most businesses and many courses taught in colleges of business operate under the belief that the purpose of business is to maximize profits for shareholders. In 1919, the Michigan Supreme Court in the case of *Dodge v. Ford Motor Co.*[6] ruled that a business exists for the profit of shareholders, and the board of directors should focus on that objective. On the other hand, the stakeholder model places the board of directors in the central position to balance the interests and conflicts of the various constituencies. External control of the corporation includes government regulation but also includes key stakeholders such as employees, consumers, and communities, who exert pressures for responsible conduct. Many of the obligations to balance stakeholder interest have been institutionalized in legislation that provides incentives for responsible conduct. The Federal Sentencing Guidelines for Organizations provides incentives for developing an ethical culture and efforts to prevent misconduct. Sarbanes-Oxley legislation holds top officers and boards of directors legally responsible for accurate financial reporting.

Today, the failure to balance stakeholder interests can result in a failure to maximize shareholders' wealth. Wal-Mart may be failing to maximize the growth of its market value because investors are concerned about its ability to manage stakeholder interests. Wal-Mart's shareholders have seen almost no growth over the past few years as it battles employees, communities, and special-interest groups over ethical issues. Most firms are moving more toward a balanced stakeholder model, as they see that this approach will sustain the relationships necessary for long-run success.

Both directors and officers of corporations are fiduciaries for the shareholders. Fiduciaries are persons placed in positions of trust who use due care and loyalty in acting on behalf of the best interests of the organization. There is a duty of care, also called a *duty of diligence,* to make informed and prudent decisions.[7] Directors have a duty to avoid ethical misconduct in their director role and to provide leadership in decisions to prevent ethical misconduct in the organization. Directors are not held responsible for negative outcomes if they are informed and diligent in their decision making. General Motors' directors can be held responsible for the accuracy of financial reporting; however, manufacturing cars that lose market share is a serious concern, although it is not a legal issue. This means directors have an obligation to request information, research, and use accountants, attorneys, and obtain the services of consultants in matters where they need assistance or advice.

The duty of loyalty means that all decisions should be in the interests of the corporation and its stakeholders. Conflicts of interest exist when a director uses the position to obtain personal gain, usually at the expense of the organization. For example, before the Sarbanes-Oxley Act, directors could give themselves and officers interest-free loans. Scandals at Tyco, Kmart, and WorldCom are all associated with officers receiving personal loans that damaged the corporation.

Officer compensation packages challenge directors, especially those on the board and not independent. Directors have an opportunity to vote for others' compensation in return for their own increased compensation. Opportunities to know about the investments, business ventures, and stock market information create issues that could violate the duty of loyalty. Insider trading of a firm's stock has very specific rules, and violations can result in serious punishment. The obligations of directors and officers for legal and ethical responsibility interface and fit together based on their fiduciary relationships. Ethical values should guide decisions and buffer the possibility of illegal conduct. With increased pressure on directors to provide oversight for organizational ethics, there is a trend toward director training to increase their competence in ethics program development as well as other areas, such as accounting.

Corporate governance establishes fundamental systems and processes for oversight, accountability, and control. This requires investigating, disciplining, and planning for recovery and continuous improvement. Effective corporate governance creates compliance and values so that employees feel that integrity is at the core of competitiveness.[8] Even if a company has adopted a consensus approach to decision making, there should be oversight and authority for delegating tasks, making difficult and sometimes controversial decisions, balancing power throughout the firm, and maintaining social responsibility. Governance also provides mechanisms for identifying risks and planning for recovery when mistakes or problems occur.

Stora Enso, an integrated packaging, forest products, and paper company based in Finland, recently developed a statement about its commitment to corporate governance.

TABLE 3.1	Corporate Governance Issues

Shareholder rights

Executive compensation

Composition and structure of the board of directors

Auditing and control

Risk management

CEO selection and termination decisions

Integrity of financial reporting

Stakeholder participation and input into decisions

Compliance with corporate governance reform

Role of the CEO in board decisions

Organizational ethics programs

The development of stakeholder orientation should interface with the corporation's governance structure. Corporate governance is also part of a firm's corporate culture that establishes the integrity of all relationships. A governance system that does not provide checks and balances creates opportunities for top managers to put their own self-interests before those of important stakeholders. Consider the accounting scandal at Adelphia Communications presented earlier. Company founders were able to defraud Adelphia's stockholders out of billions of dollars by falsifying the firm's financial reports because its corporate governance systems failed to prevent this type of fraud.[9]

Concerns about the need for greater corporate governance are not limited to the United States. Reforms in governance structures and issues are occurring all over the world.[10] In many nations, companies are being pressured to implement stronger corporate governance mechanisms by international investors, by the process of becoming privatized after years of unaccountability as state companies, or by the desire to imitate successful governance movements in the United States, Japan, and the European Union.[11]

Table 3.1 lists examples of major corporate governance issues. These issues normally involve strategic-level decisions and actions taken by boards of directors, business owners, top executives, and other managers with high levels of authority and accountability. Although these people have often been relatively free from scrutiny, changes in technology, consumer activism, government attention, recent ethical scandals, and other factors have brought new attention to such issues as transparency, executive pay, risk and control, resource accountability, strategic direction, stockholder rights, and other decisions made for the organization.

HISTORY OF CORPORATE GOVERNANCE

In the United States, a discussion of corporate governance draws on many parallels with the goals and values held by the U.S. founding fathers.[12] As we mentioned earlier in the chapter, governance involves a system of checks and balances, a concept associated with the distribution of power within the executive, judiciary, and legislative branches of the U.S. government. The U.S. Constitution and other documents have a strong focus on accountability, individual rights, and the representation of broad interests in decision making and resource allocation.

In the late 1800s and early 1900s, corporations were headed by such familiar names as Carnegie, DuPont, and Rockefeller. These "captains of industry" had ownership investment and managerial control over their businesses. Thus, there was less reason to talk about corporate governance because the owner of the firm was the same individual who made strategic decisions about the business. The owner primarily bore the consequences—positive or negative—of decisions made. During the twentieth century, however, an increasing number of public companies and investors brought about a gradual shift in the separation of ownership and control. By the 1930s, corporate ownership was dispersed across a large number of individuals. This raised new questions about control and accountability for organizational resources and decisions.

One of the first known anecdotes that helped shape our current understanding of accountability and control in business occurred in the 1930s. In 1932, Lewis Gilbert, a stockholder in New York's Consolidated Gas Company, found his questions repeatedly ignored at the firm's annual shareholders' meeting. With his brother, Gilbert pushed for reform, which led the brand-new U.S. Securities and Exchange Commission (SEC) to require corporations to allow shareholder resolutions to be brought to a vote of all stockholders. Because of the Gilbert brothers' activism, the SEC formalized the process by which executives and boards of directors respond to the concerns and questions of investors.[13]

Since the mid-1900s, the approach to corporate governance has involved a legal discussion of principals and agents in the business relationship. Essentially, owners are "principals" who hire "agents," the executives, to run the business. A key goal of businesses is to align the interests of principals and agents so that organizational value and viability are maintained. Achieving this balance has been difficult, as evidenced by these terms coined about business in the media—*junk bonds, empire building, golden parachute,* and *merger madness.* In these cases, the long-term value and competitive stance of organizations were traded for short-term financial gains or rewards. The results of this short-term view included workforce reduction, closed manufacturing plants, struggling communities, and a generally negative perception of corporate leadership. In our philosophy of social responsibility, these long-term effects should be considered alongside decisions designed to generate short-run gains in financial performance.

The Sarbanes-Oxley Act provided the most significant piece of corporate governance reform in over sixty years. Under these rules, both CEOs and CFOs are required to certify that their quarterly and annual reports accurately reflect performance and comply with requirements of the SEC. Among other changes, the act also requires more independence of boards of directors, protects whistle-blowers, and establishes a Public Company Accounting Oversight Board. The New York Stock Exchange (NYSE) and NASDAQ overhauled the governance standards required for listed firms and submitted the changes for review, comment, and approval by the SEC. Business ethics, director qualifications, unique concerns of foreign firms, loans to officers and directors, internal auditing, and many other issues are part of the NYSE and NASDAQ reforms.[14]

TABLE 3.2	*Fortune*'s Best and Worst Companies for Social Responsibility

Best Companies	Worst Companies
United Parcel Service	Tenet Healthcare
International Paper	AK Steel Holding
Exelon	MCI
ChevronTexaco	US Airways Group
Publix Super Markets	Federal-Mogul
Weyerhaeuser	Siebel Systems
Starbucks	UTStarcom
Walt Disney	Paccar
Herman Miller	Stanley Works
Altria Group	Canadaigua Brands

Source: "America's Most Admired Companies 2006: The Best and Worst Companies for Social Responsibility," *Fortune*, March 6, 2006. © 2006 Time Inc. All rights reserved.

Thus, the lack of effective control and accountability mechanisms has prompted the current interest in corporate governance. Beyond the legal issues associated with governance, there has also been interest in the board's role in social responsibility and stakeholder engagement. Table 3.2 provides *Fortune*'s assessment of the best and worst companies for social responsibility. The board of directors should provide leadership for social responsibility initiatives. The ten worst firms should examine their corporate governance, board of directors' leadership, and the cause of their low rating. It is apparent that some boards have been assuming greater responsibility for strategic decisions and have decided to focus on building more effective social responsibility, as indicated by the ten best companies in Table 3.2.

CORPORATE GOVERNANCE AND SOCIAL RESPONSIBILITY

Although most executives and board members do not deal with issues as complex as mergers on a daily basis, they are accountable for strategic-level decisions and their effects throughout the organization and society. However, there is variability in how individuals, industries, and even nations approach business accountability and control. To understand the role of corporate governance in business today, it is also important to consider how it relates to fundamental beliefs about the purpose of business organizations. Some people believe that as long as a company is maximizing shareholder wealth and profitability, it is fulfilling its core responsibility. Although this must be accomplished in accordance with legal and ethical standards, the primary focus is on the economic dimension of social responsibility. Thus, this belief places the philanthropic dimension beyond the scope of business. Other people, however, take the view that a business is an important member, or citizen, of society and must assume broad responsibilities. This view assumes that business performance is reflexive, meaning it both affects and is influenced by internal and external factors. In this case, performance is often considered from a financial, social, and ethical perspective. From these assumptions, we can derive two major conceptualizations of corporate governance: the shareholder model and the stakeholder model.[15]

shareholder model of corporate governance

model that bases management decisions toward what is in the best interests of investors; founded in classic economic precepts, including the maximization of wealth for investors and owners

The **shareholder model of corporate governance** is founded in classic economic precepts, including the maximization of wealth for investors and owners. For publicly traded firms, corporate governance focuses on developing and improving the formal system of performance accountability between top management and the firms' shareholders.[16] Thus, the shareholder orientation should drive management decisions toward what is in the best interests of investors. Underlying these decisions is a classic agency problem, where ownership (i.e., investors) and control (i.e., managers) are separate. Managers act as agents for investors, whose primary goal is shareholder value. However, investors and managers are distinct parties with unique insights, goals, and values with respect to the business. Managers, for example, may have motivations beyond shareholder value, such as market share, personal compensation, or attachment to particular products and projects. Because of these potential differences, corporate governance mechanisms are needed to ensure an alignment between investor and management interests.

For example, a former Qwest Communications International Inc. chief financial officer, Robin Szeliga, pleaded guilty to one count of insider trading. She was accused of improperly selling 10,000 shares of Qwest stock, earning a net profit of $125,000, in 2001 when she knew that some business units would fail to meet revenue targets and that the company had improperly used nonrecurring revenue to meet those goals. Szeliga, former CEO Joseph Nacchio, and five other former executives were accused of orchestrating a massive financial fraud that forced Qwest Communications to restate billions of dollars in revenue. The SEC wants repayment and civil penalties from all of the accused.[17] Because of these potential differences, corporate governance mechanisms are needed to align investor and management interests. The shareholder model has been criticized for its somewhat singular purpose and focus because there are other ways of "investing" in a business. Suppliers, creditors, customers, employees, business partners, the community, and others also invest their resources in the success of the firm.[18]

stakeholder model of corporate governance

model that sees management as having a responsibility to its stakeholders in addition to its responsibility for economic success; based on a collaborative and relational approach to business and its constituents

In the **stakeholder model of corporate governance**, the purpose of business is conceived in a broader fashion. Although a company has a responsibility for economic success and viability, it must also answer to other parties, including employees, suppliers, government agencies, communities, and groups with which it interacts. This model presumes a collaborative and relational approach to business and its constituents. Because management time and resources are limited, a key decision within the stakeholder model is to determine which stakeholders are primary. Once primary groups have been identified, appropriate corporate governance mechanisms are implemented to promote the development of long-term relationships.[19] As we discussed in Chapter 2, primary stakeholders include stockholders, suppliers, customers, employees, the government, and the community. Governance systems that consider stakeholder welfare in tandem with corporate needs and interests characterize this approach. Occidental Petroleum Corporation experienced the complexity of the stakeholder model when it began drilling for oil in Colombia. The Colombian government hired Occidental, but the native U'wa tribe opposed the drilling on religious and historical grounds. The clash of interests placed Occidental in the difficult position of balancing consumer, investor, government, and other stakeholder concerns. Occidental eventually exited Colombia.

Although these two approaches seem to represent ends of a continuum, the reality is that the shareholder model is a more restrictive precursor to the stakeholder model. Many businesses have evolved into the stakeholder model as a result of government initiatives, consumer activism, industry activity, and other external forces. In the aftermath of corporate scandals, the polarity between the two views narrowed, as it became clear how the economic accountability of corporations could not be detached from other responsibilities and stakeholder concerns. Although this trend began with large, publicly held firms, its aftereffects are being felt in many types of organizations and industries. Public hospitals, for example, have recently experienced a transition to the more holistic approach to corporate governance. Although public hospitals serve as a "safety net" for local governments' ability to provide health care, some experts object to the influence of government officials on these hospitals' boards of directors and operations. A new model of governance has emerged that calls for fewer government controls, more management autonomy and accountability, formal CEO and board evaluation systems, and more effective community involvement.[20]

The shareholder model focuses on a primary stakeholder—the investor—whereas the stakeholder model incorporates a broader philosophy toward internal and external constituents. According to the World Bank, a development institution whose goal is to reduce poverty by promoting sustainable economic growth around the world, corporate governance is defined by both internal (i.e., long-term value and efficient operations) and external (i.e., public policy and economic development) factors.[21] We are concerned with the broader conceptualization of corporate governance in this chapter.

In the social responsibility model that we propose, governance is the organizing dimension for keeping a firm focused on continuous improvement, accountability, and engagement with stakeholders. Although financial return, or economic viability, is an important measure of success for all firms, the legal dimension of social responsibility is also a compulsory consideration. The ethical and philanthropic dimensions, however, have not been traditionally mandated through regulation or contracts. This represents a critical divide in our social responsibility model and associated governance goals and systems because there are some critics who challenge the use of organizational resources for concerns beyond financial performance and legalities. This view was summarized in an editorial in *National Journal,* a nonpartisan magazine on politics and government: "Corporations are not governments. In the everyday course of their business, they are not accountable to society or to the citizenry at large. . . . Corporations are bound by the law, and by the rules of what you might call ordinary decency. Beyond this, however, they have no duty to pursue the collective goals of society."[22] This type of philosophy, long associated with the shareholder model of corporate governance, prevailed throughout the twentieth century. However, the revolution in corporate governance in the twenty-first century somewhat quieted proponents of this editorial's perspective.

The Social Responsibility Issues in Outsourcing

The use of outsourcing by companies has been an issue for debate over the last decade. Outsourcing offers a company many advantages as well as some social responsibility concerns. Each company should individually assess its unique situation before making the choice to outsource. In the United States, some critics believe that outsourcing shifts jobs to less developed nations and harms the economy.

An improved focus and cost savings are typical advantages that many companies realize from outsourcing. The cost savings generated from outsourcing can have many positive effects for a company. The money saved is sometimes used to add personnel to the payroll. This is actually contradictory to the belief that outsourcing reduces jobs domestically. Microsoft and Oracle are two examples of companies that have increased outsourcing abroad as well as jobs domestically. Some companies outsource because of the extremely competitive international marketplace. If they don't outsource, they aren't competitive and will have to cease operations.

Outsourcing basic activities allows a company to focus on key tasks. Many functions like payroll and data entry can be outsourced, enabling an organization to spend time on other activities more beneficial to its success. Outsourcing operations also comes with challenges. A big problem is that foreign management lacks knowledge of the U.S. business environment. The foreign manager and employees have difficulty understanding customers, language, and business practices. This can cause problems for the organization as well as for customers who interact with outsourced operations.

Another concern is extra cost associated with infrastructure of the foreign country. Many companies must invest in upgrading the poor infrastructure. Without these upgrades, operations in the foreign country would be unlikely. This can be a major cost to the outsourcing project.

Many American companies outsource professional services to India. Intel hired 600 Indian engineers to help secure an Apple computer account. No longer limited to credit-card call centers and order-fulfillment operations, India is offering increasingly sophisticated services to business customers around the globe, including consulting, financial analysis, and cutting-edge scientific research. Many American companies have chosen to relocate their operations to India to take advantage of cheaper labor, and Indians are performing many jobs once done by Americans. Companies like PeopleSoft, Intel, Microsoft, and General Electric have established operations in India, as have many leading pharmaceutical manufacturers, such as Pfizer, Merck, and GlaxoSmithKline.[23] ■

ISSUES IN CORPORATE GOVERNANCE SYSTEMS

Organizations that strive to develop effective corporate governance systems consider a number of internal and external issues. In this section, we look at four areas that need to be addressed in the design and improvement of governance mechanisms. We begin with boards of directors, which have the ultimate responsibility for ensuring a governance focus. Then, we discuss the role of shareholders and investors, internal control and risk management, and executive compensation within the governance system. These issues affect most organizations, although individual businesses may face unique factors that create additional governance questions. For example, a company operating in several countries will need to resolve issues related to international governance policy.

Publicly held corporations hold annual shareholders meetings that may include hundreds of attendees, like this one for Daimler-Chrysler.

Publicly held corporations hold annual shareholders meetings that may include hundreds of attendees, like this one for Daimler-Chrysler.

Boards of Directors

Members of a company's board of directors assume responsibility for the firm's resources and legal and ethical compliance. The board appoints top executive officers and is responsible for providing oversight of their performance. This is also true of a university's board of trustees, and there are similar arrangements in the nonprofit sector. In each of these cases, board members have a fiduciary duty, which was discussed earlier in this chapter. These responsibilities include acting in the best interests of those they serve. Thus, board membership is not designed as a vehicle for personal financial gain; rather, it provides the intangible benefit of ensuring the success of the organization and the stakeholders affected and involved in the fiduciary arrangement.

For public corporations, boards of directors hold the ultimate responsibility for their firms' ethical culture and legal compliance. This governing authority is held responsible by the 2004 amendments to the Federal Sentencing Guidelines for creating an ethical culture that provides leadership, values, and compliance. The members of a company's board of directors assume legal responsibility for the firm's resources and decisions, and they appoint its top executive officers. For example, after $9 billion in accounting irregularities led WorldCom to declare the largest bankruptcy ever, the company replaced the board members who had failed to prevent the accounting scandal. In addition, there were lawsuits brought against board members for failure to carry out their fiduciary duties. The firm also fired many managers.[24]

The traditional approach to directorship assumed that board members managed the corporation's business. Research and practical observation have shown that boards of directors rarely, if ever, perform the management function.[25] Because boards meet usually four to six times a year, there is no way that time allocation would allow for effective management. In small nonprofit organizations, the board may manage most resources and decisions. The complexity of large organizations requires full attention on a daily basis. Today, boards of directors are concerned primarily with monitoring the decisions made by managers on behalf of the company. This includes choosing top executives, assessing their performance, helping to set strategic direction, evaluating company performance, developing CEO succession plans, communicating with stakeholders, maintaining legal and ethical practices, ensuring that control and accountability mechanisms are in place, and evaluating the board's own performance. In sum, board members assume the ultimate authority for organizational effectiveness and subsequent performance.

INDEPENDENCE Just as social responsibility objectives require more of employees and executives, boards of directors are also experiencing increasing accountability and disclosure mandates. The desire for independence is one reason that a few firms have chosen to split the powerful roles of chair of the board and CEO. Although the practice is common in the United Kingdom and activists have called for this move for years, the idea has only recently been considered by U.S. and Canadian firms. Chubb Corporation, Midas, Pathmark Stores, Toronto Dominion Bank, and Closure Medical have already made the transition. In addition to independence concerns, it is unlikely that one person can devote the time and energy it takes to be effective in both roles. The National Association of Corporate Directors is in favor of splitting the roles, whereas other experts suggest that a "presiding" chair take over most of the chair's and CEO's duties with respect to the board. Finally, opponents believe the new rules and practices emerging from governance reform may negate the role-split debate by improving other aspects of the board's membership and impact.[26]

Traditionally, board members were often retired company executives or friends of current executives, but the trend after the corporate scandals associated with Enron and WorldCom was toward "outside directors," who had valuable expertise yet little vested interest in the firm before assuming the director role. Thus, directors today are more likely chosen for their competence, motivation, and ability to bring enlightened and diverse perspectives to strategic discussions. Outside directors are thought to bring more independence to the monitoring function because they are not bound by past allegiances, friendships, a current role in the company, or some other matter that may create a conflict of interest. However, independent directors who sit on a board for a long time may eventually lose some of the outsider perspective.

Although insiders traditionally represented approximately 20 percent of members on most boards of directors, many high-technology companies filled their boards with insiders who were heavily invested in the firm. In addition to higher percentages of inside directors, these boards were often smaller than those found in large, traditional businesses. Yahoo!, for example, once had a board of six, including three company executives. Directors of new high-tech firms were usually brought in to add management and strategic expertise to the business, whereas traditional firms tended to choose board members who understood governance, succession planning, and other oversight roles. Norfolk Southern Corporation, a 175-year-old rail carrier highly rated for logistics excellence, had ten of twelve independent directors in 2006.[27]

QUALITY Finding board members who have some expertise in the firm's industry or who have served as chief executives at similar-sized organizations is a good strategy for improving the board's overall quality. Directors with competence and experiences that reflect some of the firm's core issues should bring valuable insights to bear on discussions and decisions. Directors without direct industry or comparable executive experience may bring expertise on important issues, such as auditing, executive compensation, succession planning, and risk management, to improve decision making. Board members must understand the company's strategy and operations; this suggests that members should limit the number of boards on which they serve. Directors need time to read reports, attend board and committee meetings, and participate in continuing education that promotes strong understanding and quality guidance. For example, directors on the board's audit committee may need to be educated on new accounting and auditing standards. Experts recommend that fully employed board members sit on no more than four boards, whereas retired members should limit their memberships to seven boards. Directors should be able to attend at least 75 percent of the meetings. Thus, many of the factors that promote board quality are within the control of directors.[28]

PERFORMANCE An effective board of directors can serve as a type of insurance against the business cycle and the natural highs and lows of the economy. A study by *Business Week* showed that during robust economic times, the stocks of firms with strong governance and boards outperformed companies with weaker governance by a two-to-one margin. During the economic slowdown in 2000 and 2001, however, the stocks of companies with strong governance bested weakly governed firms by four to one. A similar study by GovernanceMetrics International demonstrated that firms with strong governance greatly outperform Standard & Poor's 500-stock index, while those with weak governance significantly underperform the index.[29] Strong boards ask the tough, yet strategic, questions of management to ensure long-term performance.

Board independence, along with board quality, stock ownership, and corporate performance, are often used to assess the quality of corporate boards of directors. Many CEOs have lost their jobs because the board of directors is concerned about performance, ethics, and social responsibility. Notable examples include Michael Eisner from Disney, Carly Fiorina from Hewlett-Packard, and Scott Livengood from Krispy Kreme. The main reason for this is the boards' fear of losing their personal assets. This fear comes from two recent lawsuits by shareholders who sued the directors of Enron and WorldCom over their roles in the collapse of those firms. Both settlements called for the directors to pay large sums from their own pockets.[30] These events make it clear that board members are accountable for oversight.

Just as improved ethical decision making requires more of employees and executives, so too are boards of directors feeling greater demands for ethics and transparency. Directors today are increasingly chosen for their expertise, competence, and ability to bring diverse perspectives to strategic discussions. Outside directors are also thought to bring more independence to the monitoring function because they are not bound by past allegiances, friendships, a current role in the company, or some other issue that may create a conflict of interest. The chair of the board audit committee must be an outside independent director with financial expertise.

Many of the corporate scandals uncovered in recent years might have been prevented if each of the companies' boards of directors had been better qualified, more knowledgeable, and less biased. Warren Buffett did not stand for reelection to Coca-Cola's board of directors in 2006 after serving for seventeen years. Buffett cited the need to focus his attention on Berkshire Hathaway and its subsidiaries.[31] Coca-Cola has struggled over the past ten years with involvement in ethical misconduct and high turnover of top managers. A survey by *USA Today* found that corporate boards have considerable overlap. More than 1,000 corporate board members sit on four or more company boards, and of the nearly 2,000 boards of directors in the United States, more than 22,000 of their members are linked to boards of more than one company. For example, of the 1,000 largest companies, one-fifth share at least one board member with another top 1,000 firm.[32] This overlap creates the opportunity for conflicts of interest in decision making and limits the independence of individual boards of directors.

At Wal-Mart, questions have been raised by shareholders, who believe that recent reports of legal and regulatory issues raise serious concerns about the adequacy of the company's internal controls. There are cases such as the former Wal-Mart Vice Chairman Thomas Coughlin, who pleaded guilty to fraud and tax charges, and the charges that Wal-Mart knowingly hired contractors that furnished illegal immigrants to clean its floors. A group of institutional shareholders have called for Wal-Mart's board to form a special committee to conduct a "comprehensive review of the company's legal and regulatory controls, as well as its internal system for ensuring compliance with its own policies and standards."[33] In some cases, individuals have earned placement on multiple boards of directors because they have gained a reputation for going along with top management. This may foster a corporate culture that limits outside oversight of top managers' decisions.

Rules promulgated by the Sarbanes-Oxley Act and various stock exchanges now require a majority of independent directors on the board; regular meetings between nonmanagement board members; audit, compensation, governance, and nominating committees either fully made up of or with a majority of independent directors; and a financial expert on the audit committee. The governance area will continue to evolve as corporate scandals are resolved and the government and companies begin to implement and test new policies and practices. Regardless of the size and type of business for which boards are responsible, a system of governance is needed to ensure effective control and accountability. As a corporation grows, matures, enters international markets, and takes other strategic directions, it is likely that the board of directors will evolve to meet its new demands. Sir Adrian Cadbury, president of the Centre for Board Effectiveness in the United Kingdom and an architect of corporate governance changes around the world, has detailed responsibilities of boards in the future:

- Boards will be responsible for developing company purpose statements that cover a range of aims and stakeholder concerns.

- Annual reports and other documents will include more nonfinancial information.
- Boards will be required to define their role and implement self-assessment processes better.
- Selection of board members will become increasingly formalized, with less emphasis on personal networks and word of mouth.
- Boards will need to work more effectively as teams.
- Serving on boards will require more time and commitment than in the past.[34]

These trends are consistent with our previous discussion of social responsibility. In all facets of organizational life, greater demands are being placed on business decisions and people. Many of these expectations emanate from those who provide substantial resources in the organization—namely, shareholders and other investors.

Shareholders and Investors

Because they have allocated scarce resources to the organization, shareholders and investors expect to grow and reap rewards from their investments. This type of financial exchange represents a formal contractual arrangement and provides the capital necessary to fund all types of organizational initiatives, such as new product development and facilities construction. A *shareholder* is concerned with his or her ownership investment in publicly traded firms, whereas *investor* is a more general term for any individual or organization that provides capital to a firm. Investments include financial, human, and intellectual capital.

A shareholder of Samsung Electronics is stopped from using a bullhorn during a recent shareholders meeting in Seoul, Korea.

TABLE 3.3	Characteristics of a Successful Shareholder Activism Campaign

Alliances with social movements or public interest groups, where shareholder concerns and activity mesh with and play a part in a larger, multifaceted campaign

Grass-roots pressure, such as letter writings or phone-ins to public investors to generate support for the resolution

Communications: media outreach, public and shareholder education, etc.

High-level negotiations with senior decision makers

Support and active involvement from large institutional investors

A climate that makes it difficult for the company not to make the "right decision." For example, if you have a plainly compelling financial argument, you have a better chance of getting company management and other shareholders on board with your proposal.

Persistence. Shareholders don't go away. They own the company and have a right to be heard. Often shareholder activists stick with issues for years.

Source: "Characteristics of a Successful Shareholder Activism Campaign," Friends of the Earth, http://www.foe.org/international/shareholder/characteristics.html, accessed April 25, 2006. Courtesy Friends of the Earth © 2006.

SHAREHOLDER ACTIVISM Shareholders, including large institutional ones, have become more active in articulating their positions with respect to company strategy and executive decision making. *Activism* is a broad term that can encompass engaging in dialog with management, attending annual meetings, submitting shareholder resolutions, bringing lawsuits, and other mechanisms designed to communicate shareholder interests to the corporation. Table 3.3 lists characteristics of effective shareholder activism campaigns.

Shareholder resolutions are nonbinding, yet important, statements about shareholder concerns. A shareholder that meets certain guidelines may bring one resolution per year to a proxy vote of all shareholders at a corporation's annual meeting. Recent resolutions brought forward relate to auditor independence, executive compensation, independent directors, environmental impact, human rights, and other social responsibility issues. In some cases, the company will modify its policies or practices before the resolution is ever brought to a vote. In other situations, a resolution will receive less than a majority vote, but the media attention, educational value, and other stakeholder effects will cause a firm to reconsider, if not change, its original position to meet the resolution's proposal. The accounting scandals prompted many resolutions about executive compensation among shareholders who believe that improper compensation structures are often a precursor to accounting mismanagement.[35] The resolution process is regulated by the SEC in the United States and by complementary offices in other countries; some claim this is more favorable to the corporation than to shareholders.

Although labor and public pension fund activities have waged hundreds of proxy battles in recent years, they rarely have much effect on the target companies. Now shareholder activists are attacking the process by which directors themselves are elected. Shareholder resolutions at about 140 companies would require directors to gain a majority of votes cast to join the board. Ideally, this new practice will make

This Citizens Fund executive helps people invest in socially responsible ways.

boards of directors more attentive.[36] This example illustrates that although shareholders and investors want their resources used efficiently and effectively, they are increasingly willing to take a stand to encourage companies to change for reasons beyond financial return.

SOCIAL INVESTING Many investors assume the stakeholder model of corporate governance, which carries into a strategy of social investing, "the integration of social and ethical criteria into the investment decision-making process."[37] Roughly three-quarters of U.S. investors take social responsibility issues into account when choosing investment opportunities. Twelve percent indicate they are willing to take a lower rate of return if the company is a strong performer in the social responsibility area.[38] However, most social investors do not have to worry about a poor return on their investments. Socially conscious firms are strong performers for many of the reasons we discussed in Chapter 1. While social investing has traditionally been conducted through managed mutual funds, like those with Domini Social Investments, TIAA-CREF, Vanguard, and Calvert Group, some individual investors are using Web-based research to venture on their own. Websites such as FOLIOfn, SocialFunds.com, Morningstar, Inc., and others provide information and services to help the socially conscious investor in decision making.[39] Thus, there are a number of opportunities for individuals to demonstrate an active strategy with respect to investing and social responsibility. Whereas a passive investor is mainly concerned with buying and selling stock and receiving dividends, social investors are taking a variety of stakeholder issues into account when making investment decisions. A social investor takes the social responsibility of "ownership" seriously because a firm in which he or she invests implements plans and strategies on behalf of its owners. It could be argued that the dishonest actions of a firm were carried out on behalf of shareholders; thus, an investor in the firm would also be responsible. Conversely, it could be argued that a firm implementing a strong social responsibility strategy and agenda is doing so on behalf of its owners.[40] Shareholder activism is the strategy for ensuring that owners' perspectives on social responsibility are included on the corporate agenda.

Although social investing has received strong media attention over the last few years, the Quakers, a religious group, applied social investment criteria in the seventeenth century when they refused to invest, patronize, or partner with any business involved in the slave trade or military concerns.[41] Investors today use similar screening criteria in determining where to place their funds and resources. Table 3.4 provides an example of the screening criteria used to exclude or include companies in the social investment funds at Calvert Group, Ltd. Several other mutual funds and investors have similar standards. These criteria are used to screen for elimination or inclusion into a particular investment strategy. For example, one strategy may focus on the environmental records of firms, whereas another strategy may examine several social responsibility issues in tandem when including and excluding companies. The process used to evaluate a firm's record is another consideration for investors. For example, Calvert assesses policies and performance, whereas Oekom Research primarily reviews policies and company disclosure. Although Oekom considers performance, it can be difficult for a firm to be rated highly if it does not publish the information. Whereas Calvert takes the stance that a firm can perform well without disclosing its outcomes, Oekom focuses on the possibility for reputation problems if the company is not fully transparent in its activities.[42] Despite its subjective nature, professionally managed social investments total more than $2.29 trillion in the United States.[43] Not only do these social investments help individuals and institutions meet their social responsibility goals, but they also provide strong financial returns.

Shareholder activism and social investing are especially prevalent in the United States and United Kingdom, two countries that score relatively high on various corporate governance indexes. Several other European countries are also experiencing increasing rates of activism and social investing. Most activism and investing take place on an organizational level through mutual funds and other institutional arrangements, but some individual investors have affected company strategy and policy. Robert Monks, a leading corporate governance activist, once described Warren Buffett, the legendary investor from Omaha, Nebraska, as "epitomizing the kind of monitoring shareholder whose involvement enhances the value of the whole enterprise. Mr. Buffett personally salvaged the rogue Salomon Brothers [now Salomon Smith Barney] from the bankrupting implications of its illegal activities."[44] Although few investors have Buffett's financial clout and respect, he serves as a role model by paying attention to the control and accountability mechanisms of the companies in which he invests. After the series of crises in the early 2000s, investors started to become more interested, educated, and vigilant about companies in which they invest.

Colleges and universities are also becoming active in social investing. For example, most colleges have endowment funds, or monies that are invested for the long-term

TABLE 3.4	Social Analysis Criteria

1. Governance and ethics

Align the interests of management and boards with those of shareholders.

Have diverse, independent boards.

Publish sustainability reports in accordance with the Global Reporting Initiative.

Nurture a culture of ethics and compliance.

2. Environment

Maintain at least an average record in industry.

Develop products or processes that reduce or minimize environmental impact.

Implement innovative pollution prevention programs.

3. Workplace

Actively hire and promote minorities/women.

Provide safe and healthy workplace.

Provide work-family programs.

4. Product safety and impact

Do not allow major manufacturers of alcohol or tobacco or business in gambling establishments.

Produce or market products that enhance health or quality of life.

Respond promptly to product problems.

5. International operations and human rights

Have adopted specific human rights standards to govern international operations.

Use more stringent environmental and workplace standards than required by local law.

6. Indigenous people's rights

Respect land, sovereignty, and natural resources of indigenous communities.

Contribute to community-drive development and environmental management plans.

7. Community relations

Develop programs that target neglected communities, including low-income and minority populations.

Have a strong working relationship with local and community development organizations.

Source: "Social Analysis Criteria," adapted from Calvert Group, Ltd., www.calvertgroup.com/sri_647.html, accessed April 25, 2006.

future of the university. Because of these investments, stakeholders of higher education institutions are drawing attention to social responsibility issues. Harvard University, with an estimated endowment of nearly $13 billion, solicits input from the university community when deciding how to vote in a socially responsible manner on shareholder resolutions. A committee of faculty, students, and alumni advises the endowment fund's governing board, which ultimately votes on the resolutions.

The Student Transforming and Resisting Organizations (STARC) has student contacts at 120 colleges and universities who are dedicated to implementing socially responsible investment policies. Such student pressure has led colleges to sell stocks that are deemed counter to socially responsible investment goals. For example, the University of Wisconsin and the University of Minnesota divested shares of corporations with operations that support the military regime in Myanmar. Stanford, Tufts, Haverford, and the University of Washington no longer invest in tobacco companies.

STARC campaigns are committed to the following principles for investor responsibility at universities and colleges:

- Challenge corporate conduct that harms humans, animals, and the environment.

- Disclose to the university community all actions affecting corporate conduct that the institution takes as an investor or shareholder, including votes on shareholder resolutions.

- Empower a democratically selected committee to review the social implications of institutional investment decisions and policy.

- Commit to following the recommendations of this investor responsibility advisory committee in order to fulfill the institution's aim of advancing the public interest.

- Adopt guidelines for investment and shareholder activity that support responsible corporate conduct promoting human rights, indigenous rights, equity and diversity, animal rights, environmental quality, labor rights, and the production of safe and beneficial products; guidelines should also include requirements for corporate disclosure of records of corporate performance in these areas.[45]

INVESTOR CONFIDENCE Shareholders and other investors must have assurance that their money is being placed in the care of capable and trustworthy organizations. These primary stakeholders are expecting a solid return for their investment, but as illustrated earlier, they have additional concerns about social responsibility. When these fundamental expectations are not met, the confidence that investors and shareholders have in corporations, market analysts, investment houses, stockbrokers, mutual fund managers, financial planners, and other economic players and institutions can be severely tested. In Chapter 1, we discussed the importance of investor trust and loyalty to organizational and societal performance. Part of this trust relates to the perceived efficacy of corporate governance. Figures 3.1 and 3.2 demonstrate the extent to which strong governance is now considered an investment criterion and reason for a premium price.

Bankruptcies and financial misconduct in the early 2000s shook investor confidence. In the days after each major scandal broke, volatile, intraday stock market swings of 200 to 300 points were common. Mutual fund managers with sizable investments in firms accused of misconduct were questioned about their aptitude in choosing and selling stocks. Consumers, becoming financially uneasy and more cautious about spending, saw their portfolios and retirement accounts dwindle. At Charles Schwab, the largest discount brokerage in the United States, annual trades per account dropped to an average 3.6 compared to more than 8 per account the

FIGURE 3.1   Corporate Governance as an Investment Criterion

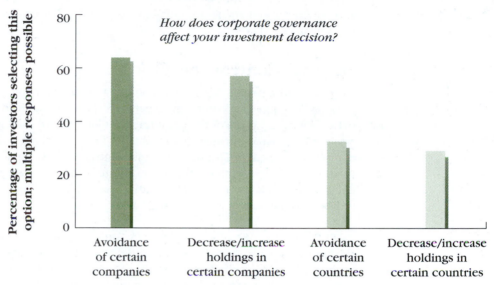

Corporate governance is now an established investment criterion.

How does corporate governance affect your investment decision?

Source: From McKinsey & Company, *McKinsey Global Investor Opinion Survey on Corporate Governance,* Copyright © 2002 by McKinsey & Company. http://www.mckinsey.com/practices/corporategovernance/PDF/ GlobalInvestorOpinionSurvey2002.pdf, accessed November 10, 2003. Copyright © 2002 by McKinsey & Company. Reprinted with permission.

FIGURE 3.2   Investor Willingness to Pay a Premium for Well-Governed Firms

A significant majority of investors say they are willing to pay a premium for a well-governed company.

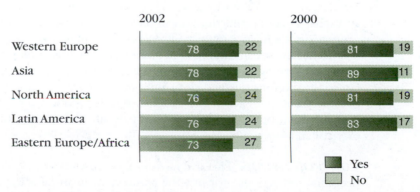

Percentage of Investors

	2002		2000	
	Yes	No	Yes	No
Western Europe	78	22	81	19
Asia	78	22	89	11
North America	76	24	81	19
Latin America	76	24	83	17
Eastern Europe/Africa	73	27		

Source: From McKinsey & Company, *McKinsey Global Investor Opinion Survey on Corporate Governance,* Copyright © 2002 by McKinsey & Company. http://www.mckinsey.com/clientservice/organizationleadership/ service/corpgovernance/research.asp, accessed October 1, 2006. Copyright © 2002 by McKinsey & Company. Reprinted with permission.

previous year. A group of finance ministers from twenty-four countries, known as G24, asked the United States to take quick action to restore investor confidence and ensure the continuation of global growth. The malfeasance at Global Crossing, Tyco, and other firms had effects throughout the global economic system. Essentially, stake-holders were calling for boards of directors and others with access to financial records and the power to demand accountability to tighten the control and risk environment in companies today.[46]

Internal Control and Risk Management

Controls and a strong risk management system are fundamental to effective opera-tions, as they allow for comparisons between the actual performance and the planned performance and goals of the organization. Controls are used to safeguard corporate assets and resources, protect the reliability of organizational information, and ensure compliance with regulations, laws, and contracts. Risk management is the process used to anticipate and shield the organization from unnecessary or overwhelming cir-cumstances, while ensuring that executive leadership is taking the appropriate steps to move the organization and its strategy forward.

INTERNAL AND EXTERNAL AUDITS Auditing, both internal and external, is the linchpin between risk and controls and corporate governance. Boards of directors must ensure that the internal auditing function of the company is provided with adequate funding, up-to-date technology, unrestricted access, independence, and authority to carry out its audit plan. To ensure these characteristics, the internal audit executive should report to the board's audit committee and, in most cases, the chief executive officer.[47]

The external auditor should be chosen by the board and must clearly identify its client as the board, not the company's chief financial officer. Under Sarbanes-Oxley, the board audit committee should be directly responsible for the selection, payment, and supervision of the company's external auditor. The act also prohibits an external auditing firm from performing some nonaudit work for the same public company, in-cluding bookkeeping, human resources, actuarial services, valuation services, legal services, and investment banking. The friendly relationship that can develop between an external auditor and the firm's financial team may affect the auditor's ability to maintain independence in the auditing process and report. For example, in more than half of the largest bankruptcies since 1996, the external audit report provided no hint of the pending financial downfall. The external audits conducted on K-mart, Global Crossing, and Enron issued clean audit perspectives just months before their respec-tive bankruptcies. Part of the problem relates to the sheer size and complexity of organizations, but these factors do not negate the tremendous responsibility that external auditors assume.

CONTROL SYSTEMS The area of internal control covers a wide range of company decisions and actions, not just the accuracy of financial statements and accounting records. Controls also foster understanding when discrepancies exist between corpo-rate expectations and stakeholder interests and issues. Internal controls effectively

| FIGURE 3.3 | Leadership on Key Issues That Affect Shareholder Value |

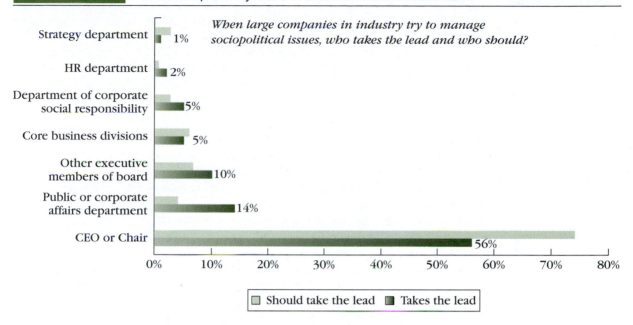

When large companies in industry try to manage sociopolitical issues, who takes the lead and who should?

Strategy department — 1%
HR department — 2%
Department of corporate social responsibility — 5%
Core business divisions — 5%
Other executive members of board — 10%
Public or corporate affairs department — 14%
CEO or Chair — 56%

☐ Should take the lead ■ Takes the lead

Source: The McKinsey Global Survey of Business Executives: Business and Society. *The McKinsey Quarterly,* The Online Journal of McKinsey & Co., January 2006.

limit employee or management opportunism or the use of corporate assets for individualistic or nonstrategic purposes. Controls also ensure the board of directors has access to timely and quality information that can be used to determine strategic options and effectiveness. For these reasons, the board of directors should have ultimate oversight for the integrity of the internal control system.[48] Although board members do not develop or administer the control system, they are responsible for ensuring that an effective system exists. The need for internal controls is rarely disputed, but implementation can vary. As Figure 3.3 shows, the CEO or chair appears to be the key decision maker relating to public and political debates that have an impact on shareholder value. Thus, internal control represents a set of tasks and resource commitments that require high-level attention.

Although most large corporations have designed internal controls, smaller companies and nonprofit organizations are less likely to have invested in a complete system. For example, a small computer shop in Columbus, Ohio, lost thousands of dollars due to embezzlement by the accounts receivable clerk. Because of the clerk's position and role in the company, she was able to post credit-card payments due her employer to her own account and later withdraw the income. Although she faced felony theft charges, her previous employer admitted feeling ashamed and did not want his business associated with a story on employee theft.[49] Such crime is common in small businesses because they often lack effective internal controls. Simple, yet proven, control mechanisms that can be used in all types of organizations are listed in

| **TABLE 3.5** | Internal Control Mechanisms for Small Businesses and Nonprofits |

Develop and disseminate a code of conduct that explicitly addresses ethical and legal issues in the workplace.

Rotate and segregate job functions to reduce the opportunity for opportunism (e.g., the person reconciling bank statements does not make deposits or pay invoices).

Screen employment applicants thoroughly, especially those who would assume much responsibility if hired.

Watch new employees especially carefully until they have gained knowledge and your trust.

Require all employees to take at least one week of vacation on an annual basis.

Limit access to valuable inventory and financial records. Use technology to track inventory, costs, human resources, finances, and other valuable business processes.

Implement unannounced inspections, spot checks, or "tests" of departments, systems, and outcomes.

Keep keys and pass codes secure and limit their duplication and distribution.

Insist that operating statements are produced on at least a monthly basis.

Ask questions about confusing financial statements and other records.

Sources: *Curtailing Crime: Inside and Out,* Crime Prevention Series, U.S. Small Business Administration, http://www.sba.gov/library/pubs/cp-2.doc, accessed May 9, 2006; "Protecting Against Employee Fraud," *Business First–Western New York,* June 14, 1999, p. 31; Kathy Hoke, "Eyes Wide Open," *Business First–Columbus,* August 27, 1999, pp. 27–28.

Table 3.5. These techniques are not always costly, and they conform to best practices in the prevention of ethical and legal problems that threaten the efficacy of governance mechanisms.

The 2004 amendments to the Federal Sentencing Guidelines for Organizations make it clear that a corporation's governing authority must be well informed about its control systems with respect to implementation and effectiveness. This places the responsibility squarely on the shoulders of the firm's leadership, usually the board of directors. The board must ensure that there is a high-ranking officer accountable for the day-to-day operational responsibility of the control systems. The board must also provide for adequate authority, resources, and access to the board or an appropriate subcommittee of the board. The guidelines further call for confidential mechanisms whereby the organization's employees and agents may report or seek guidance about potential or actual misconduct without fear of retaliation. Finally, the board is required to oversee the discovery of risks and to design, implement, and modify approaches to deal with those risks. Thus, the board of directors is clearly accountable for discovering risks associated with a firm's specific industry and assessing the firm's ethics program to ensure that it is capable of uncovering misconduct.[50]

RISK MANAGEMENT A strong internal control system should alert decision makers to possible problems, or risks, that may threaten business operations, including worker safety, company solvency, vendor relationships, proprietary information, environmental impact, and other concerns. As we discussed in Chapter 2, having a strong crisis management plan is part of the process for managing risk. The term *risk management* is normally used in a narrow sense to indicate responsibilities associated with insurance, liability, financial decisions, and related issues. Kraft General Foods, for example, has a risk management policy for understanding how prices of commodities, such as coffee, sugar, wheat, and cocoa, will affect its relationships throughout the supply chain.[51]

Most corporate leaders' greatest fear is discovering serious misconduct or illegal activity somewhere in their organization. The fear is that a public discovery can immediately be used by critics in the mass media, competitors, and skeptical stakeholders to undermine a firm's reputation. Corporate leaders worry that something will be uncovered outside their control that will jeopardize their careers and their organizations. Fear is a paralyzing emotion. Of course there are executives such as Bernard Ebbers, Dennis Kozlowski, and John Rigas who may have experienced fear because they knew about and perhaps even participated in serious misconduct that debilitated their companies and hurt many groups of stakeholders. These leaders were the captains of their respective ships, and they made a conscious decision to steer their firms into treacherous waters with a high probability of striking an iceberg.[52]

Corporate leaders do fear the possibility of reputation harm, financial loss, or a regulatory event that could potentially end their careers and even threaten their personal lives through fines or prison sentences. Indeed, the whole concept of risk management involves recognizing the possibility of a possible misfortune that could jeopardize or even destroy the corporation.[53]

Risk is always present within organizations, so executives must develop processes for remedying or managing its effects. A board of directors will expect the top management team to have risk management skills and plans in place. There are at least three ways to consider how risk poses either a potentially negative or positive concern for organizations.[54] First, risk can be categorized as a hazard. In this view, risk management is focused on minimizing negative situations, such as fraud, injury, or financial loss. Second, risk may be considered an uncertainty that needs to be hedged through quantitative plans and models. This type of risk is best associated with the term *risk management,* which is used in financial and business literature. Third, risk also creates the opportunity for innovation and entrepreneurship. Just as management can be criticized for taking too much risk, it can also be subject to concerns about not taking enough risk. For example, the merger between Daimler Benz and Chrysler represented risk taking for the potential benefit of both firms and their stakeholders. All three types of risk are implicitly covered by our definition of corporate governance because there are risks for both control (i.e., preventing fraud and ensuring accuracy of financial statements) and accountability (i.e., innovation to develop new products and markets). For example, the Internet and electronic commerce capabilities have introduced new risks of all types for organizations. Privacy, as we discuss in Chapter 10, is a major concern for many stakeholders and has created the need for policies and certification procedures. A board of directors may ensure that the company has established privacy policies that are not only effective but can also be properly monitored and improved as new technology risks and opportunities emerge in the business environment.[55]

Executive Compensation

How executives are compensated for their leadership, organizational service, and performance has become an extremely troublesome topic. Leading business publications, including the *Harvard Business Review* and *The Economist*, have weighed in on problems with compensation, perhaps the most controversial aspect of corporate governance in recent memory.[56]

Executive compensation is controversial. In fact, most boards spend more time deciding how much to compensate top executives than they do ensuring the integrity of the company's financial reporting systems.[57] Indeed, 73 percent of respondents in a *Business Week*/Harris poll indicated they believe that top officers of large U.S. companies receive too much compensation, while only 21 percent report executive compensation as "just about the right amount."[58] Many executives have received large compensation and bonus packages regardless of the success of their companies. For example, Carly Fiorina, former CEO of Hewlett-Packard, received at least $14 million when she was terminated in early 2005, which represented 2.5 times her base salary and cash bonus but not enough to require shareholder approval. However, two institutional shareholders are suing HP over her severance package; they believe that she received at least $21 million, more than 2.99 times her 2004 base salary and a cash bonus of about $5.6 million. Stock options and other benefits raised her total exit package further to $42 million, which means it should have received shareholder approval. It seems to be a growing trend by investors to sue over executive compensation.[59]

The Delaware Chancery Court issued its long-awaited and important opinion in the Disney litigation related to executive compensation and absolved the defendant directors of any liability. The decision makes it clear that investors cannot look to

During an era of rising executive compensation, critics and cartoonists question the extent to which executives are stakeholder-driven.

"Well, for $100 million, I <u>know</u> I'd focus only on the shareholders. For less than that, I'd be afraid my eyes might tend to wander."

judicially imposed liability for protection from disastrous compensation decisions and other governance failures. What the decision leaves unclear, however, is where shareholders can look for such protection under existing corporate arrangements. The court's opinion sends a reassuring message to directors: Directors have little to fear from liability. It also signals to investors that they should not look to the courts for protection from governance failures. In addition, other existing legal arrangements make it difficult for investors to use the other mechanisms suggested for redressing governance failures.[60]

On the other hand, SEC Chairman Christopher Cox says "in the agency's 72 year history no issue has generated such interest" as requiring the disclosure of corporate pay. Because of this, a 2006 rule now requires deferred pay and retirement benefits to be factored into annual compensation totals for companies' top five executives in reports to regulators and shareholders. Executives are going to be more under the microscope with compensation totals expected to shock many stakeholders. Many experts believe the new rule will not rein in executive pay.[61]

Unease over executive compensation often centers on the relationship between the highest paid executives and median employee wages in the company. If this ratio is perceived as too large, then critics believe that either rank-and-file employees are not being compensated fairly or high executive salaries represent an improper use of company resources. The average executive now earns nearly 400 times the average worker's salary, up from 40 times the average salary in the 1960s. Critics have asked whether business executives are generating such strong performance that they deserve this striking movement in pay over the last forty years. The usual answer is a resounding no.[62] Because of the enormous difference between CEO and employee pay, the business press is careful to support high levels of executive compensation only when it is directly linked to strong company performance. Most of the business press has criticized compensation packages over the last few years. Although the issue of executive compensation has received much attention in the media, some business owners have long recognized its potentially ill effects. In the early twentieth century, for example, the capitalist J. P. Morgan implemented a policy that limited the pay of top managers in businesses he owned to no more than twenty times the pay of any other employee.[63] According to a report by United for a Fair Economy, the average executive now earns 431 times the average blue-collar worker. The average CEO pay is now $11.8 million compared to average worker pay, which is now $27,460.[64] According to the report, if the minimum wage had risen as fast as CEO pay since 1990, the lowest paid workers in the United States would be earning $23.03 an hour today, not $5.15 an hour.[65]

Other people argue that because executives assume so much risk on behalf of the company, they deserve the rewards that follow from strong company performance. In addition, many executives' personal and professional lives meld to the point that they are "on call" twenty-four hours a day. Because not everyone has the skill, experience, and desire to become an executive and assume so much pressure and responsibility, market forces dictate a high level of compensation. When the pool of qualified individuals is limited, many corporate board members feel that offering a large compensation package is the only way to attract and retain a top executive to ensure their firm is not left without strong leadership. In an era when top executives are increasingly

TABLE 3.6	Chief Executive Officer Compensation	
Company	**Executive**	**Total Compensation**
Cendant	Henry Silverman	$133,261,147
Lehman Bros.	Richard Fuld Jr.	$119,539,850
Occidental Petroleum	Ray Irani	$106,524,159
Valero Energy	William Greehey	$89,450,243
Cisco Systems	John Chambers	$80,707,753
Morgan Stanley	John Mack	$68,187,675
Dell	Kevin Rollins	$67,168,843
United Technologies	George David	$55,866,941
Aetna	John Rowe	$51,531,256
Sunoco	John Drosdick	$49,075,736

Source: Gary Strauss and Barbara Hansen, "Companies Think They're Worth $100,000,000. Median Pay for CEOs of 100 Largest Companies Rose 25%," *USA Today*, April 10, 2006, p. B3.

willing to "jump ship" to other firms that offer higher pay, potentially lucrative stock options, bonuses, and other benefits, such thinking is not without merit.[66] Table 3.6 lists the total compensation of the top ten chief executives in U.S. industries. The heads of America's 500 biggest companies received an aggregate 54 percent pay raise in 2005. As a group, their total compensation amounted to $5.1 billion versus $3.3 billion in fiscal 2005.[67] The median pay for CEOs of the 100 largest companies rose 25 percent in 2005 to $17.9 million, which dwarfed the 3.1 percent average gain by typical American workers.[68]

Executive compensation is a difficult but important issue for boards of directors and other stakeholders to consider because it receives much attention in the media, sparks shareholder concern, and is hotly debated in discussions of corporate governance. One area for board members to consider is the extent to which executive compensation is linked to company performance. Plans that base compensation on the achievement of several performance goals, including profits and revenues, are intended to align the interests of owners with management. Amid rising complaints about excessive executive compensation, an increasing number of corporate boards are imposing performance targets on the stock and stock options they include in their CEOs' pay package. Many companies are now basing a portion of the equity granted to their CEOs on performance targets.[69] The expanded emphasis on performance targets is designed to keep executives from reaping rich rewards for reasons unrelated to their leadership skills. Stock options, which became a popular form of compensation in the 1990s, can gain value in a rising stock market, enabling executives to pocket windfalls even if their own companies' earnings growth is modest.[70] Another issue is whether performance-linked compensation encourages executives to focus on short-term performance at the expense of long-term growth.[71]

These examples show that executive compensation is an important, yet potentially explosive, issue for boards of directors and other stakeholders to consider. Under new NYSE rules, the compensation committee must be entirely made up of independent directors and must establish goals and responsibilities, member qualifications, and a process of self-evaluation. The NASDAQ revisions require independent directors' approval of CEO compensation, either through an independent compensation committee or through a majority of independent directors meeting in a closed session. Regardless of the structure, an integral matter for boards and compensation committees to consider is the extent to which executive compensation is linked to long-term company performance. Plans that base compensation on the achievement of several performance goals are intended to align the interests of owners with management. However, many executives are rewarded through stock options and other programs that provide an incentive for managing stock price and short-run gains. When executive wealth is heavily tied to the short-term performance of the company's stock, it can drive aggressive and misrepresentative accounting and related practices revealed in recent corporate scandals. Other points for review include the evaluation criteria for executive performance, use of compensation consultants to help determine appropriate pay, disclosure of executive compensation, industry standards for remuneration, the ability to attract top talent, and incentives for superior performance.[72] Questions like these are being asked around the world, with many constituents calling for more formalization and professionalism in corporate control systems and accountability to stakeholders.[73]

CORPORATE GOVERNANCE AROUND THE WORLD

Increased globalization, enhanced electronic communications, economic agreements and zones, and the reduction of trade barriers have created opportunities for firms around the world to conduct business with both international consumers and industrial partners. These factors are propelling the need for greater homogenization in corporate governance principles. Standard & Poor's recently launched a new service, Corporate Governance Scores, which analyzes four macroforces that affect the general governance climate of a country, including legal infrastructure, regulation, information infrastructure, and market infrastructure. On the basis of these factors, a country can be categorized as having strong, moderate, or weak support for effective governance practices at the company level. Institutional investors are very interested in this measure, as it helps determine possible risk.[74] As financial, human, and intellectual capital crosses borders, a number of business, social, and cultural concerns arise.

Institutional investors in companies based in emerging markets claim to be willing to pay as much as 30 percent more for shares in companies that are well governed. Global shareholders also would like companies in their countries to disclose more financial data, to adopt CEO pay plans that reward only strong performance, and to use independent boards with no ties to management. Institutional Shareholder Services, a research and consulting firm, surveyed 320 large investors overseeing $10.5 trillion in assets in nineteen countries, including the United States, Canada,

Great Britain, Australia, New Zealand, Japan, and China. Their report disclosed that:

1. Some 90 percent of Chinese investors think corporate governance is "a necessary building block for successful capital markets" in China.

2. Some 67 percent of shareholders say corporate governance "offers value, but it's hard to quantify" in earnings results, investment returns, and other traditional business measures.

3. Among the biggest obstacles to stronger worldwide governance are clashing business laws and practices, with no international body to police corporate governance issues; and lack of regulation and poor financial disclosure in countries such as China, where state-run companies dominate the business landscape.[75]

In response to this business climate, the Organisation for Economic Co-operation and Development (OECD), a forum for governments to discuss, develop, and enhance economic and social policy, issued a set of principles intended to serve as a global model for corporate governance.[76] After years of discussion and debate among institutional investors, business executives, government representatives, trade unions, and nongovernmental organizations, thirty OECD member governments signaled their agreement with the principles by signing a declaration to integrate them within their countries' economic systems and institutions. The purpose of the OECD Corporate Governance Principles (see Table 3.7) is to formulate minimum standards of fairness, transparency, accountability, disclosure, and responsibility for business

TABLE 3.7	OECD Principles of Corporate Governance
Principle	**Explanation**
1. Ensuring the basis for an effective corporate governance framework	The corporate governance framework should promote transparent and efficient markets, be consistent with the rule of law and clearly articulate the division of responsibilities among different supervisory, regulatory and enforcement authorities.
2. The rights of shareholders and key ownership functions	The corporate governance framework should protect and facilitate the exercise of shareholders' rights.
3. The equitable treatment of shareholders	The corporate governance framework should ensure the equitable treatment of all shareholders, including minority and foreign shareholders. All shareholders should have the opportunity to obtain effective redress for violation of their rights.
4. The role of stakeholders in corporate governance	The corporate governance framework should recognize the rights of stakeholders as established by law and encourage active cooperation between corporations and stakeholders in creating wealth, jobs, and the sustainability of financially sound enterprises.
5. Disclosure and transparency	The corporate governance framework should ensure that timely and accurate disclosure is made on all material matters regarding the corporation, including the financial situation, performance, ownership, and governance of the company.
6. The responsibilities of the board	The corporate governance framework should ensure the strategic guidance of the company, the effective monitoring of management by the board, and the board's accountability to the company and the shareholders.

Source: "OECD Principles for Corporate Governance," Organisation for Economic Co-operation and Development, http://www.oecd.org/document/49/0,2340,en_2649_201185_31530865_1_1_1_1,00.html, accessed April 25, 2006.

practice. The principles focus on the board of directors, which the OECD says should recognize the impact of governance on the firm's competitiveness. In addition, the OECD charges boards, executives, and corporations with maximizing shareholder value while responding to the demands and expectations of their key stakeholders.

The OECD Corporate Governance Principles cover many specific best practices, including (1) ensuring the basis for an effective corporate governance framework; (2) rights of shareholders to vote and influence corporate strategy; (3) greater numbers of skilled, independent members on boards of directors; (4) fewer techniques to protect failing management and strategy; (5) wider use of international accounting standards; and (6) better disclosure of executive pay and remuneration. Although member governments of the OECD are expected to uphold the governance principles, there is some room for cultural adaptation.

Best practices may vary slightly from country to country because of unique factors such as market structure, government control, role of banks and lending institutions, labor unions, and other economic, legal, and historical factors. Both industry groups and government regulators moved quickly in the United Kingdom after the Enron crisis was revealed. Because some British bankers were indicted in the scandal, corporate governance concerns increased in that country. Several British reforms are under way, including annual shareowners' votes on board remuneration policies and greater supervision of investment analysts and the accounting profession. Portugal is at the beginning stages of its capitalist market, with many companies still family controlled. The country's government issued a best practices code modeled after the OECD principles, but most companies are not yet in compliance. For example, 96 percent of listed companies do not offer proxy voting, which is one of the seventeen best practices.[77] Reasons for the financial crisis that occurred in Southeast Asia in the late 1990s partly involved corporate governance. For example, the government structure of some Asian countries created greater opportunities for corruption and nepotism. Banks were encouraged to extend credit to companies favored by the government. In many cases, these companies were in the export business, which created an imbalance in financing for other types of businesses. The concentration of business power within a few families and tycoons reduced overall competitiveness and transparency. Many of these businesses were more focused on size and expanded operations than profitability. Foreign investors recognized the weakening economies and pulled their money out of investments. The U.S. dollar appreciated sharply, and Asian currencies were largely devalued. Finally, the crisis brought to light the necessity of stronger governance mechanisms and regulatory reform in the region.[78]

FUTURE OF CORPORATE GOVERNANCE

As the issues discussed in the previous section demonstrate, corporate governance is primarily focused on strategic-level concerns for accountability and control. Although many discussions of corporate governance still revolve around responsibility in investor-owned companies, good governance is fundamental to effective performance in all types of organizations. As you have gleaned from history and government classes, a system of checks and balances is important for ensuring a focus on multiple perspectives and constituencies; proper distribution of resources, power, and decision authority; and the responsibility for making changes and setting direction.

To pursue social responsibility successfully, organizations must consider issues of control and accountability. As we learned earlier, the concept of corporate governance is in transition from the shareholder model to one that considers broader stakeholder concerns and inputs to financial performance. A number of market and environmental forces, such as the OECD and shareholder activism, have created pressures in this direction. This evolution is consistent with our view of social responsibility. Although some critics deride this expanded focus, a number of external and internal forces are driving business toward the stakeholder orientation and the formalization of governance mechanisms. One concern centers on the cost of governance. For example, the combined cost of meeting regulations for safety, health, labor standards, employee benefits, and civil rights is estimated at $91.9 million for all companies operating in the United States.[79]

Most businesspeople and academicians agree that the benefits of a strong approach to corporate governance outweigh its costs. However, the positive return on governance goes beyond organizational performance to benefit the industrial competitiveness of entire nations, something we discussed in Chapter 1. For example, corrupt organizations often fail to develop competitiveness on a global scale and can leave behind financial ruin, thus negating the overall economic growth of the entire region or nation. At the same time, corrupt governments usually have difficulty sustaining and supporting the types of organizations that can succeed in global markets. Thus, a lack of good governance can lead to insular and selfish motives because there is no effective system of checks and balances. In today's interactive and interdependent business environment, most organizations are learning the benefits of a more cooperative approach to commerce. It is possible for a company to retain its competitive nature while seeking a "win-win" solution for all parties to the exchange.[80] Further, as nations with large economies embrace responsible governance principles, it becomes even more difficult for nations and organizations that do not abide by such principles to compete in these lucrative and rich markets. There is a contagion effect toward corporate governance among members of the global economy, much like peer pressure influences the actions and decisions of individuals. Portugal is a good example of this effect.

Because governance is concerned with the decisions made by boards of directors and executives, it has the potential for far-reaching positive—and negative—effects. A recent study by the OECD found that stronger financial performance is the result of several governance factors and practices, including (1) large institutional shareholders that are active monitors of company decisions and boards, (2) owner-controlled firms, (3) fewer mergers, especially between firms with disparate corporate values and business lines, and (4) shareholders', not board of directors', decisions on executive remuneration.[81] The authors of the study note that these practices may not hold true for strong performance in all countries and economic systems. However, they also point out that a consensus view is emerging, with fewer differences among OECD countries than among all other nations. Similarities in organizational-level accountability and control should lead to smoother operations between different companies and countries, thereby bolstering competitiveness on many levels.

The future of corporate governance is directly linked to the future of social responsibility. Because governance is the control and accountability process for achieving social responsibility, it is important to consider who should be involved in the future. First and most obviously, business leaders and managers will need to embrace governance as an essential part of effective performance. Some of the elements of corporate governance, particularly executive pay, board composition, and shareholder rights, are likely to stir debate for many years. However, business leaders must recognize the forces that have brought governance to the forefront as a precondition of management responsibility. Thus, they may need to accept the "creative tension" that exists among managers, owners, and other primary stakeholders as the preferable route to mutual success.[82]

Second, governments have a key role to play in corporate governance. National competitiveness depends on the strength of various institutions, with primacy on the effective performance of business and capital markets. Strong corporate governance is essential to this performance, and thus, governments will need to be actively engaged in both affording protection and promoting accountability for corporate power and decisions. Just like the corporate crises in the United States, the Asian economic crisis discussed earlier prompted companies and governments around the world to consider tighter governance procedures. Finally, other stakeholders may become more willing to use governance mechanisms to influence corporate strategy or decision making. Investors, whether shareholders, employees, or business partners, have a stake in decisions and should be willing to take steps to align various interests for long-term benefits. There are many investors and stakeholders willing to exert great influence on underperforming companies.

Until recently, governance was one area in the business literature that had not received the same level of attention as other issues, such as environmental impact, diversity, and sexual harassment. Over the next few years, however, corporate governance will emerge as the operational centerpiece to the social responsibility effort. The future will require that business leaders have a different set of skills and attitudes, including the ability to balance multiple interests, handle ambiguity, manage complex systems and networks, create trust among stakeholders, and improve processes so leadership is pervasive throughout the organization.[83]

In the past, the primary emphasis of governance systems and theory was on the conflict of interests between management and investors.[84] Governance today holds people at the highest organizational levels accountable and responsible to a broad and diverse set of stakeholders. Although top managers and boards of directors have always assumed responsibility, their actions are now subject to greater accountability and transparency. A *Wall Street Journal* writer put the shift succinctly, indicating, "Boards of directors have been put on notice." An article on the need for change in corporate governance in *The Economist* provided an equally concise rationale, stating, "Too many boards are stuffed with yes men who question little that their chief executive suggests." In the aftermath of crises in the early 2000s, both publications devoted significant space to various reform mechanisms and their likelihood of success. Perhaps the greatest challenge is the power shift taking place between executives and board members. A key issue going forward will be the board's ability to align corporate decisions with various stakeholder interests.[85] Robert Monks, the activist money manager and leader on corporate governance issues, wrote that effective corporate governance requires understanding that the "indispensable link between the corporate constituents is the creation of a credible structure (with incentives and disincentives) that enables people with overlapping but not entirely congruent interests to have a sufficient level of confidence in each other and the viability of the enterprise as a whole."[86] We will take a closer look at some of these constituents and their concerns in the next few chapters.

SUMMARY

To respond to stakeholder pressures to answer for organizational decisions and policies, organizations must effectively implement policies that provide strategic guidance on appropriate courses of action. Such policies are often known as corporate governance, the formal system of accountability and control for organizational decisions and resources. Accountability relates to how well the content of workplace decisions is aligned with the firm's stated strategic direction, whereas control involves the process of auditing and improving organizational decisions and actions.

Both directors and officers of corporations are fiduciaries for the shareholders. Fiduciaries are persons placed in positions of trust who use due care and loyalty in acting on behalf of the best interests of the organization. There is a duty of care, also called a duty of diligence, to make informed and prudent decisions. Directors have a duty to avoid ethical misconduct in their director role and to provide leadership in decisions to prevent ethical misconduct in the organization. Directors are not held responsible for negative outcomes if they are informed and diligent in their decision making. The duty of loyalty means that all decisions should be in the interests of the corporation and its stakeholders. Conflicts of interest exist when a director uses the position to obtain personal gain, usually at the expense of the organization.

There are two major conceptualizations of corporate governance. The shareholder model of corporate governance focuses on developing and improving the formal system of performance accountability between top management and the firm's shareholders. The stakeholder model of corporate governance views the purpose of business in a broader fashion in which the organization not only has a responsibility for economic success and viability but also must answer to other stakeholders. The shareholder model focuses on a primary stakeholder—the investor—whereas the stakeholder model incorporates a broader philosophy that focuses on internal and external constituents.

Governance is the organizing dimension for keeping a firm focused on continuous improvement, accountability, and engagement with stakeholders. Although financial return, or economic viability, is an important measure of success for all firms, the legal dimension of social responsibility is also a compulsory consideration. The ethical and philanthropic dimensions, however, have not been traditionally mandated through regulation or contracts. This represents a critical divide in our social responsibility model and associated governance goals and systems because there are some critics who challenge the use of organizational resources for concerns beyond financial performance and legalities.

In the late 1800s and early 1900s, corporate governance was not a major issue because company owners made strategic decisions about their businesses. By the 1930s, ownership was dispersed across many individuals, raising questions about control and accountability. In response to shareholder activism, the Securities and Exchange Commission required corporations to allow shareholder resolutions to be brought to a vote of all shareholders. Since the mid-1900s, the approach to corporate governance has involved a legal discussion of principals (owners) and agents (managers) in the business relationship. The lack of effective control and accountability mechanisms in years past has prompted a current trend toward boards of directors playing a greater role in strategy formulation than they did in the early 1990s. Members of a company's board of directors assume legal responsibility and a fiduciary duty for organizational resources and decisions. Boards today are concerned primarily with monitoring the decisions made by managers on behalf of the company. The trend today is toward boards composed of outside directors who have little vested interest in the firm.

Shareholders have become more active in articulating their positions with respect to company strategy and executive decision making. Many investors assume the stakeholder model of corporate governance, which implies a strategy of integrating social and ethical criteria into the investment decision-making process. Although most activism and investing take place on an organizational level through mutual funds and other institutional arrangements, some individual investors have affected company strategy and policy.

Another significant governance issue is internal control and risk management. Controls allow for comparisons between actual performance and the planned performance and goals of the organization. They are used to safeguard corporate assets and resources, protect the reliability of organizational information, and ensure compliance with regulations, laws, and contracts. Controls foster understanding when discrepancies exist between corporate expectations and stakeholder interests and issues. A strong internal control system should alert decision makers to possible problems or risks that may threaten business operations. Risk can be categorized (1) as a hazard, in which case risk management focuses on minimizing negative situations, such as fraud, injury, or financial loss; (2) as an uncertainty that needs to be hedged through quantitative plans and models; or (3) as an opportunity for innovation and entrepreneurship.

How executives are compensated for their leadership, service, and performance is another governance issue. Many people believe the ratio between the highest paid executives and median employee wages in the company should be reasonable. Others argue that because executives assume so much risk on behalf of the organization, they deserve the rewards that follow from strong company performance. One area for board members to consider is the extent to which executive compensation is linked to company performance.

The Organisation for Economic Co-operation and Development has issued a set of principles from which to formulate minimum standards of fairness, transparency, accountability, disclosure, and responsibility for business practice. These principles help guide companies around the world and are part of the convergence that is occurring with respect to corporate governance.

Most businesspeople and academicians agree that the benefits of a strong approach to corporate governance outweigh its costs. Because governance is concerned with the decisions taken by boards of directors and executives, it has the potential for far-reaching positive, and negative, effects. The future of corporate governance is directly linked to the future of social responsibility. Business leaders and managers will need to embrace governance as an essential part of effective performance. Governments also have a role to play in corporate governance. National competitiveness depends on the strength of various institutions, with primacy on the effective performance of business and capital markets. Other stakeholders may become more willing to use governance mechanisms to affect corporate strategy or decision making.

KEY TERMS

corporate governance (p. 75)
shareholder model of corporate governance (p. 80)
stakeholder model of corporate governance (p. 80)

DISCUSSION QUESTIONS

1. What is corporate governance? Why is corporate governance an important concern for companies that are pursuing the social responsibility approach? How does it improve or change the nature of executive and managerial decision making?
2. Compare the shareholder and stakeholder models of corporate governance. Which one seems to predominate today? What implications does this have for businesses in today's complex environment?
3. How have economic circumstances contributed to the growing trend toward increasing corporate governance? Why are accountability and control so important in the twenty-first century?
4. What is the role of the board of directors in corporate governance? What responsibilities does the board have?
5. What role do shareholders and other investors play in corporate governance? How can investors effect change?
6. Why are internal control and risk management important in corporate governance? Describe three approaches organizations may take to managing risk.

7. Why is the issue of executive compensation controversial? Are today's corporate executives worth the compensation packages they receive?
8. In what ways are corporate governance practices becoming standardized around the world? What differences exist?
9. As corporate governance becomes a more important aspect of social responsibility, what new skills and characteristics will managers and executives need? Consider how pressures for governance require managers and executives to relate and interact with stakeholders in new ways.

EXPERIENTIAL EXERCISE

Visit the website of the Organisation for Economic Co-operation and Development (http://www.oecd.org). Examine the origins of the organization and its unique role in the global economy. After visiting the site, answer the following questions:

1. What are the primary reasons that OECD exists?
2. How would you describe OECD's current areas of concern and focus?
3. What role do you think OECD will play in the future with respect to corporate governance and related issues?

WHAT WOULD YOU DO?

The statewide news carried a story about Core-Tex that evening. There were rumors swirling that one of the largest manufacturers in the state was facing serious questions about its social responsibility. A former accountant for Core-Tex, whose identity was not revealed, made allegations about aggressive accounting methods and practices that overstated company earnings. He said he left Core-Tex after his supervisor and colleagues did not take his concerns seriously. The former accountant hinted that the company's relationship with its external auditor was quite close, since Core-Tex's new CFO had once been on the external auditing team. Core-Tex had recently laid off 270 employees—a move that was not unexpected in these turbulent financial times. However, the layoff hit some parts of the work site's community pretty hard. Finally, inspectors from the state environmental protection agency had just issued a series of citations to Core-Tex for improper disposal and high emissions at one of its larger manufacturing plants. A television station had run an exposé on the environmental citations a week ago.

CEO Kelly Buscio clicked off the television set and thought about the company's next steps. Core-Tex's attorney had cautioned the executive group earlier that week about communicating too much with the media and other constituents. The firm's vice president for marketing countered the attorney by insisting that Core-Tex needed to stay ahead of the rumors and assumptions that were being made about the company. The vice president of marketing said that suppliers and business partners were starting to question Core-Tex's financial viability. The vice president of information technology and the vice president of operations were undecided on the proper next steps. The vice president of manufacturing had not been at the meeting. Buscio rubbed her eyes and wondered what tomorrow could bring.

To her surprise, the newspapers were pretty gentle on Core-Tex the next day. There had been a major oil spill, the retirement of a *Fortune* 500 CEO, and a major league baseball championship game the night before, so the reporters were focused on those stories. The company's stock price, which averaged around $11.15, was down $0.35 by midmorning. Her VP of marketing suggested that employees needed to hear from the CEO and be reassured about Core-Tex's strong future. Her first call after lunch came from a member of the firm's board of directors. The director asked Buscio what the board could do to help the situation. What would you do?

CHAPTER 4

Legal, Regulatory, and Political Issues

CHAPTER OBJECTIVES

- To understand the rationale for government regulation of business

- To examine the key legislation that structures the legal environment for business

- To analyze the role of regulatory agencies in the enforcement of public policy

- To compare the costs and benefits of regulation

- To examine how business participates in and influences public policy

- To describe the government's approach for legal and ethical compliance

CHAPTER OUTLINE

Government's Influence on Business

Business's Influence on Government and Politics

The Government's Strategic Approach for Legal and Ethical Compliance

The Better Business Bureau (BBB) is one of the best-known self-regulatory associations in the United States. The BBB works to promote good business practices within communities and is supported by local member businesses. When a company violates bureau standards for good practice, the BBB warns consumers through the media. A recent nationwide alert was issued to advise college students, high school students, and other young people to beware of potentially fraudulent offers from modeling/talent agencies. Students are being approached on college campuses and targeted at sporting events and shopping venues. Some have responded to enticing ads that promise a glamorous career as a model or actor. The BBB is hoping to educate young people about the potential pitfalls of such offers.

Requests to local BBBs for reliability reports on various modeling/talent agencies have more than tripled during the past two years—an indication that more and more people are being approached by such agencies. Many of the 200,000 people who check with the BBB this year will find that the modeling/talent agency about which they are requesting information has an unsatisfactory record, and some of these will have already signed a contract or paid an upfront fee of $1,000 or more. The number of such complaints processed by the BBB rose by 50 percent in one year alone.

The BBB recommends that anyone considering an offer or advertisement to be a model or be in movies take the time to research the business, check its references, and come to a careful and well-examined decision. High-pressure sales tactics usually mean a scam artist is on the prowl. A reputable agency will give interested parties plenty of time to make an informed decision. Before paying any fees, the BBB suggests that potential signees (1) obtain all verbal promises, claims, and agency information in writing; (2) check the complaint history of the agency with the local BBB office, as well as the Consumer Protection Agency, and the state attorney general; (3) research state laws regarding such agencies and verify any licensing/bonding information;

(4) ask for a blank copy of any contract to review before signing; (5) be wary of claims about high salaries, especially in smaller cities or towns; (6) use common sense; (7) do not give in to demands for cash; and (8) do not be swayed by promises that a deposit is totally refundable. BBB records show that fewer than half of all complaints against modeling/talent agencies are ever resolved to the customer's satisfaction, indicating that the industry has many bogus operators who rely on misleading claims and promises to entice unsuspecting consumers. According to the BBB, the quickest way to verify an agency's reliability is to ask for proof of its success. A reputable agency will be willing to provide contact information for models or actors who have secured successful work based on the agency's efforts, as well as information for companies that have hired models or actors trained by the agency. Use this information to research the agency and determine whether a successful experience is likely. In addition to advice on specific industries, the BBB also works to dispel myths that many consumers have about the marketplace. Common myths include:

Myth 1: Consumers have a three-day right to cancel any purchase or contract.
Myth 2: Retailers are required to give refunds.
Myth 3: Sometimes you have to pay something when you win a prize.
Myth 4: There is a "lemon law" on all big-ticket items, including used cars.
Myth 5: Sometimes you have to pay before you can get a loan or credit card.
Myth 6: It is safe to give your credit-card number over the phone.
Myth 7: You have a better chance of winning a sweepstakes when you make a purchase.
Myth 8: Personal information you provide is always kept confidential.
Myth 9: Your credit report is private unless you authorize someone to see it.
Myth 10: Advertising that appears in respected media is legitimate.[1] ■

*A*lthough self-regulatory associations such as the Better Business Bureau provide an important service, especially to consumers, they generally lack the tools or authority to enforce their guidelines for good business practices. The government, however, has the power through laws and regulations to structure how businesses and individuals achieve their goals. The purpose of regulating firms is to create a fair competitive environment for businesses, consumers, and society. All stakeholders need to demonstrate a commitment to social responsibility through compliance with relevant laws and proactive consideration of social needs. Indeed, a recent study of 900 senior managers found that law ranks as one of the most important business subjects in terms of its effect on organizational practices and activities.[2] Thus, compliance with the law is an important foundation of social responsibility.

This chapter explores the complex relationship between business and government. First, we discuss some of the laws that structure the environment for the regulation of business. Major legislation relating to competition and regulatory agencies is reviewed to provide an overview of the regulatory environment. Next, we consider how businesses can participate in the public policy process through lobbying, political contributions, and political action committees. Finally, we offer a framework for a strategic approach to managing the legal and regulatory environment.

GOVERNMENT'S INFLUENCE ON BUSINESS

The government has a profound influence on business. In most Western countries, there is a history of elected representatives working through democratic institutions to provide the structure for the regulation of business conduct. For example, one of the differences that has long characterized the two major parties of the U.S. political system involves the government's role with respect to business. In general terms, the Republican Party favors less federal regulation of business, whereas the Democratic Party is more open to such initiatives.[3] Third-party and independent candidates more often focus on specific business issues or proclaim their distance from the two major political parties. However, the power and freedom of big business have resulted in conflicts among private businesses, government, private interest groups, and even individuals.

In the United States, the role that society delegates to government is to provide laws that are logically deduced from the Constitution and the Bill of Rights and to enforce these laws through the judicial system. Individuals and businesses, therefore, live under a rule of law that protects society and supports an acceptable quality of life. Ideally, by controlling the limitation of force by some parties, the overall welfare and freedom of all participants in the social system will be protected.

The provision of a court system to settle disputes and punish criminals, both organizational and individual, provides for justice and order in society. For example, Columbia/HCA, the world's largest hospital chain, was fined $745 million for defrauding Medicare through overbilling for home health care and laboratory services. In the same industry, HealthSouth faced a probe by the Department of Justice as well as class action lawsuits for both federal securities claims and fraud allegations. Despite being one of the leading providers of outpatient surgery, diagnostic imaging, and rehabilitative health-care services in the United States, HealthSouth was delisted from the New York Stock Exchange and remains on probation until 2009.[4] These examples illustrate how the judicial system can punish businesses that fail to comply with laws and regulatory requirements.

The legal system is not always accepted in some countries as insurance that business will be conducted in a legitimate way. A survey of Russian executives indicated that tax evasion methods, as well as other varieties of illegal corporate behavior, are presented in corporate training. Executives believe that business could not be successful in a completely legal way under Russia's existing conditions where illegal activities are viewed as socially acceptable. Since the former Soviet bloc was disbanded, some writers have argued that newfound freedoms in Russia have actually promoted a culture of unbridled capitalism and the opportunity to participate in new illegal deals and perpetuate scams.[5]

The existence of businesses, however, is based on laws permitting their creation, organization, and dissolution. From a social perspective, it is significant that a corporation has the same legal status as a "person" who can sue, be sued, and be held liable for debts. Laws may protect managers and stockholders from being personally liable for a company's debts, but individuals as well as organizations are still responsible for their conduct. Because corporations have a perpetual life, larger companies like ExxonMobil, General Motors, and Sony take on an organizational culture, including social responsibility values, that extends beyond a specific time period, management team, or geographical region.

Most companies are owned by individual proprietors or operated as partnerships. However, large incorporated firms like those just mentioned often receive the most attention because of their size, visibility, and impact on so many aspects of the economy and society. In a pluralistic society, diverse stakeholder groups such as business, labor, consumers, environmentalists, privacy advocates, and others attempt to influence public officials who legislate, interpret laws, and regulate business. The public interest is served though open participation and debate that result in effective public policy. Because no system of government is perfect, legal and regulatory systems are constantly evolving and changing in response to social institutions, including the business environment. For example, increasing use of the Internet for information and business has created a need for legislation and regulations to protect the owners of creative materials from unauthorized use and consumers from fraud and invasions of privacy. The line between acceptable and illegal activity on the Internet is increasingly difficult to discern and is often determined by judges and juries.

In response, the Better Business Bureau developed an online seal to certify reliability of organizations on the Internet. Nearly 30,000 businesses have met the program requirements in Figure 4.1 to earn the reliability seal. A recent survey indicates that 90 percent of the respondents had greater confidence when making a purchase from a company displaying the BBB's online seal.[6] Companies that adopt a strategic approach to the legal and regulatory system develop proactive organizational values and compliance programs that identify areas of risks and include formal communication, training, and continuous improvement of responses to the legal and regulatory environment. Companies that apply for and receive the Better Business Bureau seal for reliability, privacy, or children's privacy are examples of such companies. MisterArt,

FIGURE 4.1   Better Business Bureau's Reliability Program Requirements

Better Business Bureau's Reliability Program Requirements
- Become a member of the Better Business Bureau where company is headquartered;
- Provide the BBB with information regarding company ownership and management and the street address and telephone number at which they do business, which may be verified by the BBB in a visit to the company's physical premises;
- Be in business a minimum of one year (an exception can be made if a new business is a spinoff or a division of an existing business, which has a positive track record with the BBB);
- Have a satisfactory complaint handling record with the BBB;
- Agree to participate in the BBB's advertising self-regulation program, comply with the BBB Code of Advertising, and correct or withdraw online advertising when challenged by the BBB and found not to be substantiated or not in compliance with our children's advertising guidelines;
- Agree to abide by the BBB Code of Online Business Practices, and to cooperate with any BBB request for modification of a website to bring it into accordance with the Code;
- Respond promptly to all consumer complaints;
- Agree to dispute resolution, at the consumer's request, for unresolved disputes involving consumer products or services.

Source: Better Business Bureau, BBBOnLine: Reliability Program Requirements, http://www.bbbonline.org/ reliability/requirement.asp, accessed June 16, 2006. Copyright 2003, Reprinted with permission of the Council of Better Business Bureaus, Inc. 4200 Wilson Blvd., Arlington, VA 22203.

the largest online dealer of art and craft supplies, earned the seal a few years ago. A marketing executive at the online firm noted, "The BBBOnLine seal gives comfort to all Internet shoppers and shows them we care about our customers and our business." Multinational firms use the BBBOnLine seal program to meet the requirements of the European Commission's Directive on Data Protection and Japanese Privacy Seal program.[7]

In this section, we take a closer look at why and how the government affects businesses through laws and regulation, the costs and benefits of regulation, and how regulation may affect companies doing business in foreign countries.

The Rationale for Regulation

Although the United States was established as a capitalist system in which capitalist theory says "the invisible hand of competition" would regulate the economy, this system has not always worked effectively or in the best interest of consumers, business, or society as a whole. Since the days of Adam Smith, the federal and state governments have stepped in to enact legislation and create regulations to address particular issues and restrict the behavior of business in accordance with society's wishes. Many of the issues used to justify business regulation can be categorized as economic or social.

ECONOMIC AND COMPETITIVE REASONS FOR REGULATION A great number of regulations have been passed by legislatures over the last 100 years in an effort "to level the playing field" on which businesses operate. When the United States became an independent nation in the eighteenth century, the business environment consisted of many small farms, manufacturers, and cottage industries operating on a primarily local scale. With the increasing industrialization of the United States after the Civil War, "captains of industry" like John D. Rockefeller (oil), Andrew Carnegie (railroads and steel), Andrew Mellon (aluminum), and J. P. Morgan (banking) began to consolidate their business holdings into large national trusts. **Trusts** are organizations generally established to gain control of a product market or industry by eliminating competition. Such organizations are often considered detrimental because, without serious competition, they can potentially charge higher prices and provide lower quality products to consumers. Thus, as these firms grew in size and power, public distrust of them likewise grew because of often-legitimate concerns about unfair competition. This suspicion and the public's desire to require these increasingly powerful companies to act responsibly spurred the first antitrust legislation. If trusts are successful in eliminating competition, a monopoly can result.

trust
organizations established to gain control of a product market or industry by eliminating competition

A **monopoly** occurs when just one business provides a good or service in a given market. Utility companies that supply electricity, natural gas, water, or cable television are examples of monopolies. The government tolerates these monopolies because the cost of supplying the good or providing the service is so great that few companies would be willing to invest in new markets without some protection from competition. Monopolies may also be allowed by patent laws that grant the developer of a new technology a period of time (usually seventeen years) during which no other firm can use the same technology without the patent holder's consent. These relatively short-term monopolies are permitted to encourage businesses to engage in riskier research and development by allowing them time to recoup their research, development, and production expenses and to earn a reasonable profit.

monopoly
the situation where one business provides a good or service in a given market

Because trusts and monopolies lack serious competition, there are concerns that they may either exploit their market dominance to restrict their output and raise prices or lower quality to gain greater profits. This concern is the primary rationalization for their regulation by the government. Public utilities, for example, are regulated by state public utility commissions and, where they involve interstate commerce, are subject to federal regulation as well. In recent years, some of these industries have been "deregulated" with the idea that greater competition will police the behavior of individual firms.

Related to the issue of regulation of trusts and monopolies is society's desire to restrict destructive or unfair competition. What is considered unfair varies with the standard practice of the industry, the impact of specific conduct, and the individual case. When one company dominates a particular industry, it may engage in destructive competition or employ anticompetitive tactics. For example, it may slash prices in an effort to drive competitors out of the market and then raise prices later. It may conspire with other competitors to set, or "fix," prices so that each firm can ensure a certain level of profit. Other examples of unfair competitive trade practices are stealing trade secrets or obtaining other confidential information from a competitor's employees, trademark and copyright infringement, false advertising, and deceptive selling methods such as "bait and switch" and false representation of products. The Canadian Competition Bureau recently warned citizens about a scam originating from the United Kingdom. Many consumers received letters encouraging them to send money to enter a contest or pay some type of fee to claim a prize. In conjunction with several other government agencies, the Competition Bureau was able to confiscate checks, credit-card numbers, and money orders addressed to the fraudulent companies. In Canada, the Competition Act makes it a criminal offense to require consumers to pay before collecting their winnings, unless adequate and fair disclosure is made and the recipient actually wins the prize.[8]

Antitrust regulations also allow the government to punish firms that engage in anticompetitive practices. For example, two drug companies, Aventis SA and Andrx Corp., agreed to pay $80 million to settle allegations that they conspired to keep a cheaper, generic version of a blood-pressure medication off the market. Aventis paid Andrx almost $100 million not to market a generic form of Cardizem CD for eleven months. New York's attorney general said that consumers paid too much for Cardizem CD and its generic equivalents because the companies' conspiracy delayed the option of cheaper competitors.[9] We will take a closer look at specific antitrust regulations later in this chapter.

SOCIAL REASONS FOR REGULATION Regulation may also occur when marketing activities result in undesirable consequences for society. Many manufacturing processes, for example, create air, water, or land pollution. Such consequences create "costs" in the form of contamination of natural resources, illness, and so on that neither the manufacturer nor the consumer "pays" for directly. Because few companies are willing to shoulder these costs voluntarily, regulation is necessary to ensure that all firms within an industry do their part to minimize these costs and pay their fair share. Likewise, regulations have proven necessary to protect natural (e.g., forests, fishing grounds, and other habitats) and social resources (e.g., historical and architecturally or archeologically significant structures). We will take a closer look at some of these environmental protection regulations and related issues in Chapter 10.

Other regulations have come about in response to social demands for equality in the workplace, especially after the 1960s. Such laws and regulations require that companies ignore race, ethnicity, gender, religion, and disabilities in favor of qualifications that more accurately reflect an individual's capacity for performing a particular job. Likewise, deaths and injuries because of employer negligence resulted in regulations designed to ensure that people can enjoy a safe working environment. Executives from ACS Environmental and Air Power, Inc. were sentenced to jail time for falsifying safety and training records of employees working with asbestos, lead abatement, and other hazardous materials projects. Both companies were ordered to pay substantial fines and lost the right to government contracts.[10] We will take a closer look at laws and regulations related to the workplace in Chapter 7.

Still other regulations have resulted from special-interest group crusades for safer products. For example, Ralph Nader's *Unsafe at Any Speed,* published in 1965, criticized the automobile industry as a whole, and General Motors specifically, for putting profit and style ahead of lives and safety. Nader's consumer protection organization, popularly known as Nader's Raiders, successfully campaigned for legislation that required automakers to provide safety belts, padded dashboards, stronger door latches, head restraints, shatterproof windshields, and collapsible steering columns in automobiles. As we will see in Chapter 8, consumer activists also helped secure passage of several other consumer protection laws, such as the Wholesome Meat Act of 1967, the Clean Water Act of 1972, and the Toxic Substance Act of 1976.

Issues arising from the increasing use of the Internet have led to demands for new laws protecting consumers and business. According to a recent study, Internet users receive an average of 110 unwanted e-mails (spam) each week, and although 39 percent of online consumers use blocking software to avoid such unwanted e-mail, only about one-third of them are satisfied with the software's performance. Since spam-blocking technology is failing to keep up with unwanted electronic sales pitches for everything from lower interest rates to increased sexual drive, two Internet access services, America Online and Microsoft's MSN, joined forces to press for tough federal legislation to stop illicit commercial e-mail. The two companies want stiff jail terms for spammers who commit fraud by misrepresenting themselves online, the power to seek injunctions against the theft and use of proprietary e-mail addresses, and large fines to put spammers out of business. Legislation must block deceptive spammers without violating their First Amendment rights.[11]

As we shall see in Chapter 10, the technology associated with the Internet has generated a number of issues related to privacy, fraud, and copyrights. For instance, creators of copyrighted works such as movies, books, and music are calling for new laws and regulations to safeguard their ownership of these works. In response to these concerns, Congress enacted the Digital Millennium Copyright Act in 1998, which extended existing copyright laws to better protect "digital" recordings of music, movies, and the like. Many other countries have implemented similar measures. Copyright violations continue to plague many global industries, which to some critics calls into question the effectiveness of threatened legal action. A team of security specialists recommends technological, not legal, solutions as most effective in the fight against piracy and copyright infringement.[12] Concerns about the collection and use of personal information, especially regarding children, resulted in the passage of the Children's Online Privacy Protection Act of 2000 (COPPA). According to a recent study, many companies are not complying with COPPA. However, the Federal Trade Commission (FTC) enforces the act by levying fines against noncomplying website operators. For example, the FTC imposed $100,000 in fines against girlslife.com, bigmailbox.com, and insidetheweb.com, finding that the sites collected more information than was necessary for the activities involved and encouraged age falsification.[13] With good reason, consumers are also worried about becoming victims of online fraud. The U.S. Federal Trade Commission receives approximately 82,000 complaints a year about fraudulent activity related to online auctions. The use of fraudulent wire transfers in many of these auctions is becoming more prevalent, as the complaints about wire transfers have tripled in the last two years alone.[14] With online auctions

TABLE 4.1	Consumer Risk in Auctions		
Type of Risk	**In-person Auction**	**Online Auction**
Price information risk	High	Low
Time risk	Low	High
Vendor risk	Low	High
Security risk	Low	High
Privacy risk	Low	High
Performance risk	Low	High

Source: Dylan Cameron and Alison Galloway, "Consumer Motivations and Concerns in Online Auctions: An Exploratory Study," *International Journal of Consumer Studies* 29 (May 2005): 181–192.

generating an estimated $6.1 billion per year, consumers and businesses alike are exploring options, including regulation, to protect the security of online transactions.[15] Table 4.1 describes the types of risk that consumers encounter in both in-person and online auctions. It is clear that online auctions present significantly greater risk than in-person transactions, which is linked to the degree of protection that consumers demand or require from the government.

Laws and Regulations

As a result of business abuses and social demands for reform, the federal government began to pass legislation to regulate business conduct in the late nineteenth century. In this section, we will look at a few of the most significant of these laws. Table 4.2 summarizes many more laws that affect business operations.

SHERMAN ANTITRUST ACT The Sherman Antitrust Act, passed in 1890, is the principal tool employed by the federal government to prevent businesses from restraining trade and monopolizing markets. Congress passed the law, almost unanimously, in response to public demands to curtail the growing power and abuses of trusts in the late nineteenth century. The law outlaws "every contract, combination in the form of trust or otherwise, or conspiracy, in restraint of trade or commerce."[16] It also makes a violation of the law a felony crime, punishable by a fine of up to $10 million for corporate violators and $350,000 and/or three years in prison for individual offenders.[17]

The Sherman Antitrust Act applies to all firms operating in interstate commerce as well as to U.S. firms engaged in foreign commerce. The law has been used to break up some of the most powerful companies in the United States, including the Standard Oil Company (1911), the American Tobacco Company (1911), and AT&T (1984), and there was an attempt to break up Microsoft. In the Microsoft case, a U.S. district court judge ruled that the software giant inhibited competition by using unlawful tactics to protect its Windows monopoly in computer operating systems and by illegally expanding its dominance into the market for Internet Web-browsing software. In

TABLE 4.2	Major Business Laws

Act (Date Enacted)	Purpose
Sherman Antitrust Act (1890)	Prohibits contracts, combinations, or conspiracies to restrain trade; establishes as a misdemeanor monopolizing or attempting to monopolize
Clayton Act (1914)	Prohibits specific practices such as price discrimination, exclusive dealer arrangements, and stock acquisitions in which the effect may notably lessen competition or tend to create a monopoly
Federal Trade Commission Act (1914)	Created the Federal Trade Commission; also gives the FTC investigatory powers to be used in preventing unfair methods of competition
Robinson-Patman Act (1936)	Prohibits price discrimination that lessens competition among wholesalers or retailers; prohibits producers from giving disproportionate services or facilities to large buyers
Wheeler-Lea Act (1938)	Prohibits unfair and deceptive acts and practices regardless of whether competition is injured; places advertising of foods and drugs under the jurisdiction of the FTC
Lanham Act (1946)	Provides protections and regulation of brand names, brand marks, trade names, and trademarks
Celler-Kefauver Act (1950)	Prohibits any corporation engaged in commerce from acquiring the whole or any part of the stock or other share of the capital assets of another corporation when the effect substantially lessens competition or tends to create a monopoly
Fair Packaging and Labeling Act (1966)	Makes illegal the unfair or deceptive packaging or labeling of consumer products
Magnuson-Moss Warranty (FTC) Act (1975)	Provides for minimum disclosure standards for written consumer product warranties; defines minimum consent standards for written warranties; allows the FTC to prescribe interpretive rules in policy statements regarding unfair or deceptive practices
Consumer Goods Pricing Act (1975)	Prohibits the use of price maintenance agreements among manufacturers and resellers in interstate commerce
Antitrust Improvements Act (1976)	Requires large corporations to inform federal regulators of prospective mergers or acquisitions so that they can be studied for any possible violations of the law
Trademark Counterfeiting Act (1988)	Provides civil and criminal penalties against those who deal in counterfeit consumer goods or any counterfeit goods that can threaten health or safety
Trademark Law Revision Act (1988)	Amends the Lanham Act to allow brands not yet introduced to be protected through registration with the Patent and Trademark Office
Nutrition Labeling and Education Act (1990)	Prohibits exaggerated health claims and requires all processed foods to contain labels with nutritional information
Telephone Consumer Protection Act (1991)	Establishes procedures to avoid unwanted telephone solicitations; prohibits marketers from using automated telephone dialing system or an artificial or prerecorded voice to certain telephone lines
Federal Trademark Dilution Act (1995)	Provides trademark owners the right to protect trademarks and requires relinquishment of names that match or parallel existing trademarks
Digital Millennium Copyright Act (1998)	Refines copyright laws to protect digital versions of copyrighted materials, including music and movies
Children's Online Privacy Act (2000)	Regulates the collection of personally identifiable information (name, address, e-mail address, hobbies, interests, or information collected through cookies) online from children under age 13
Sarbanes-Oxley Act (2002)	Requires corporations to take responsibility to provide principles-based ethical leadership and holds CEOs and CFOs personally accountable for the credibility and accuracy of their company's financial statements

ordering that the company be split into two independent firms, Judge Thomas Penfield Jackson said that Microsoft had placed "an oppressive thumb on the scale of competitive fortune" by targeting competitors that threatened its Windows software monopoly. However, the ruling to break up Microsoft was appealed, and the order by Judge Jackson was overturned. The Supreme Court refused to hear an appeal by Microsoft that other aspects of its conviction should be overturned. Microsoft has provided regular updates on its progress in complying with the final antitrust judgment. In some cases, the government has decided to extend the time frame for the completion of certain provisions of the judgment, including the provision to rewrite technical documentation made available to software licensees.[18] The Sherman Act remains the primary source of antitrust law in the United States, although it has been supplemented by several amendments and additional legislation.

CLAYTON ANTITRUST ACT Because the provisions of the Sherman Antitrust Act were rather vague, the courts have not always interpreted the law as its creators intended. To rectify this situation, Congress enacted the Clayton Antitrust Act in 1914 to limit mergers and acquisitions that have the potential to stifle competition.[19] The Clayton Act also specifically prohibits price discrimination, tying agreements (when a supplier furnishes a product to a buyer with the stipulation that the buyer must purchase other products as well), exclusive agreements (when a supplier forbids an intermediary to carry products of competing manufacturers), and the acquisition of stock in another corporation where the effect may be to substantially lessen competition or tend to create a monopoly. In addition, the Clayton Act prohibits members of one company's board of directors from holding seats on the boards of competing corporations. The law also exempts farm corporations and labor organizations from antitrust laws.

FEDERAL TRADE COMMISSION ACT In the same year the Clayton Act was passed, Congress also enacted the Federal Trade Commission Act to further strengthen the antitrust provisions of the Sherman Act. Unlike the Clayton Act, which prohibits specific practices, the Federal Trade Commission Act more broadly prohibits unfair methods of competition. More significantly, this law created the Federal Trade Commission (FTC) to protect consumers and businesses from unfair competition. Of all the federal regulatory agencies, the FTC has the greatest influence on business activities.

When the FTC receives a complaint about a business or finds reason to believe that a company is engaging in illegal conduct, it issues a formal complaint stating that the firm is in violation of the law. If the company continues the unlawful practice, the FTC can issue a cease-and-desist order, which requires the offender to stop the specified behavior. Stanley Works, the maker of tools and equipment, was ordered to cease advertising practices that the FTC deemed as misleading with respect to the origin of its products. Stanley was accused of misrepresenting the foreign origin of some of its products. Several years later, the FTC relaunched its probe of Stanley Works and found that the company was not fully compliant with the cease-and-desist order. At this point, Stanley agreed to pay a $205,000 civil penalty for failing to provide accurate country-of-origin information on product labels.[20]

Thus, although a firm can appeal to the federal courts to have an order rescinded, the FTC can seek civil penalties in court, up to a maximum penalty of $10,000 a day for each infraction, if a cease-and-desist order is ignored. The commission can also require businesses to air corrective advertising to counter previous ads the commission considers misleading. For example, the maker of Doan's pills was required by the FTC to run corrective advertising to counter its unproven claim that its product is more effective than other pain relievers at alleviating back pain.[21]

In addition, the FTC helps to resolve disputes and makes rulings on business decisions, especially in emerging areas such as Internet privacy. For example, the commission approved a settlement that would permit the bankrupt Internet retailer Toysmart.com to sell its customer list as long as the buyer of the list agrees to abide by Toysmart's privacy guarantees.[22] In this case, the FTC helped to reinforce corporate guarantees of consumer privacy on the Internet.

ENFORCEMENT OF THE LAWS Because violations of the Sherman Antitrust Act are felony crimes, the Antitrust Division of the U.S. Department of Justice enforces it. The FTC enforces antitrust regulations of a civil, rather than criminal, nature. There are many additional federal regulatory agencies (see Table 4.3) that oversee the

| **TABLE 4.3** | Business Regulatory Agencies |

Agency (Date Established)	Major Areas of Responsibility
Food and Drug Administration (1906)	Enforces laws and regulations to prevent distribution of adulterated or misbranded foods, drugs, medical devices, cosmetics, veterinary products, and potentially hazardous consumer products
Federal Reserve Board (1913)	Regulates banking institutions; protects the credit rights of consumers; maintains the stability of the financial system; conducts the nation's monetary policy; and serves as the nation's central bank
Federal Trade Commission (1914)	Enforces laws and guidelines regarding business practices; takes action to stop false and deceptive advertising and labeling
Federal Communications Commission (1934)	Regulates communication by wire, radio, and television in interstate and foreign commerce
Securities and Exchange Commission (1934)	Regulates the offering and trading of securities, including stocks and bonds
National Labor Relations Board (1935)	Enforces the National Labor Relations Act; investigates and rectifies unfair labor practices by employers and unions
Equal Employment Opportunity Commission (1970)	Promotes equal opportunity in employment through administrative and judicial enforcement of civil rights laws and through education and technical assistance
Environmental Protection Agency (1970)	Develops and enforces environmental protection standards and conducts research into the adverse effects of pollution
Occupational Safety and Health Administration (1971)	Enforces the Occupational Safety and Health Act and other workplace health and safety laws and regulations; makes surprise inspections of facilities to ensure safe workplaces
Consumer Product Safety Commission (1972)	Ensures compliance with the Consumer Product Safety Act; protects the public from unreasonable risk of injury from any consumer product not covered by other regulatory agencies

enforcement of other laws and regulations. Most states also have regulatory agencies that make and enforce laws for individuals and businesses. In recent years, cooperation among state attorneys general, regulatory agencies, and the federal government has increased, particularly in efforts related to the control of drugs, organized crime, and pollution. Such cooperation among state attorneys general and the FTC resulted in a $34 million settlement with Nine West Group, one of the nation's largest manufacturers of women's shoes, on price-fixing charges. Authorities said that Nine West violated federal and state antitrust laws by making agreements with retailers to fix the prices of its shoes and to limit sales promotion periods to maintain the prices of its shoes and restrict competition among retailers who sold Nine West brands. In addition to the $34 million payment, the settlement requires that Nine West not fix dealer prices, not pressure dealers to adopt any resale price, not threaten to limit supplies to dealers that adopt their own resale prices, and satisfy recordkeeping provisions so the FTC can continue to monitor its compliance.[23]

In addition to enforcement by state and federal authorities, lawsuits by private citizens, competitors, and special-interest groups are used to enforce legal and regulatory policy. Through private civil actions, an individual or organization can file a lawsuit related to issues such as antitrust, price fixing, or unfair advertising. For example, one of the largest antitrust settlements to date occurred when several corporations brought a lawsuit against six of the world's largest manufacturers of vitamins. The suit accused the manufacturers, which accounted for 80 percent of the bulk sales of many popular vitamins, of colluding to fix prices with wholesale customers (large food and drug companies) over a nine-year period. The vitamin companies agreed to

After Natural Selections Foods recalled all of their spinach products because they may have been contaminated with *E. coli*, the U.S. Food and Drug Administration issued daily updates to consumers.

settle the case for $1.1 billion. Prior to this settlement, three of the manufacturers (F. Hoffman La Roche, BASF, and Rhone-Poulene) had been assessed a $750 million criminal fine for price fixing and market allocation.[24] An organization can also ask for assistance from a federal agency to address a concern. For example, American Express gained the assistance of the Department of Justice's Antitrust Division in accusing Visa and MasterCard of antitrust violations.[25]

Global Regulation

A company that engages in commerce beyond its own country's borders must contend with the potentially complex relationship among the laws of its own nation, international laws, and the laws of the nation in which it will be trading, as well as various trade restrictions imposed on international trade. International business activities are affected to varying degrees by each nation's laws, regulatory agencies, courts, the political environment, and special-interest groups. Some countries have established import barriers, including tariffs, quotas, minimum price levels, and port-of-entry taxes that affect the importation of products. The European Union and other countries, for example, banned cattle feed containing recycled cattle carcasses to prevent "mad cow" disease from which more than 100 people have died. France, for example, banned the importation of some cuts of beef and all livestock feed containing meat to curtail the spread of mad cow disease in that country.[26] Additionally, other laws may govern product quality and safety, distribution methods, and sales and advertising practices.

Although there is considerable variation and focus among different nations' laws, many countries have antitrust laws that are quite similar to those in the United States. Indeed, the Sherman Act has been copied throughout the world as the basis for regulating fair competition. German authorities, for example, accused Wal-Mart of exploiting its size to sell basic food items, such as milk, sugar, and flour, below cost on a regular basis in violation of German antitrust laws. Authorities feared the practice would harm small and medium-sized businesses that could not match the retail giant's lower prices. Wal-Mart now offers its own private brand in many product categories, a strategy that allows the retailer to be price competitive without crossing into antitrust territory.[27] Antitrust issues, such as price fixing and market allocation, have become a major area of international cooperation in the regulation of business.[28] Table 4.4 provides a list of situations and signs that antitrust may become a concern.

The North American Free Trade Agreement (NAFTA), which eliminates virtually all tariffs on goods produced and traded between the United States, Canada, and Mexico, makes it easier for businesses of each country to invest in the other member countries. The agreement also provides some coordination of legal standards governing business transactions among the three countries. NAFTA promotes cooperation among various regulatory agencies to encourage effective law enforcement in the free trade area. Within the framework of NAFTA, the United States and Canada have developed many agreements to enforce each other's antitrust laws. The agreement provides for cooperation in investigations, including requests for information and the opportunity to visit the territory of the other nation in the course of conducting investigations.[29]

TABLE 4.4	Signs of Possible Antitrust Violation

- any evidence that two or more competing sellers of similar products have agreed to price their products a certain way, to sell only a certain amount of their product, or to sell only in certain areas or to certain customers;

- large price changes involving more than one seller of very similar products of different brands, particularly if the price changes are of an equal amount and occur at about the same time;

- suspicious statements from a seller suggesting that only one firm can sell to a particular customer or type of customer;

- fewer competitors than normal submit bids on a project;

- competitors submit identical bids;

- the same company repeatedly has been the low bidder on contracts for a certain product or service or in a particular area;

- bidders seem to win bids on a fixed rotation;

- there is an unusual and unexplainable large dollar difference between the winning bid and all other bids; or

- the same bidder bids substantially higher on some bids than on others, and there is no logical cost reason to explain the difference.

Source: U.S. Department of Justice, "Antitrust Enforcement and the Consumer," http://www.usdoj.gov/atr/public/div_stats/211491.pdf, accessed June 15, 2006.

The European Union (EU) was established in 1958 to promote free trade among its members and now includes twenty-five European nations, with more expected to be admitted over the next several years.[30] To facilitate trade among its members, the EU is working to standardize business laws and trade barriers, to eliminate customs checks among its members, and to create the use of a standard currency (the euro) for use by all members. Moreover, the Commission of the European Communities has entered into an agreement with the United States, similar to NAFTA, regarding joint antitrust laws.[31] A new offensive in the battle against Microsoft has been mounted by a coalition of computer, telephone, and Internet companies. The Computer and Communications Association filed a formal complaint with the European Commission, which enforces EU competition laws. The association has accused Microsoft of violating European antitrust law with its Windows XP operating system.[32] Another collaborative law enforcement effort, this one between the Council of Europe and the United States, is the crafting of a treaty covering computer crimes.[33]

Costs and Benefits of Regulation

COSTS OF REGULATION Regulation results in numerous costs for businesses, consumers, and society at large. Although many experts have attempted to quantify these costs, it is quite difficult to find an accurate measurement tool. To generate such measurements, economists often classify regulations as economic (applicable to specific industries or businesses) or social (broad regulations pertaining to health, safety, and the environment). One yardstick for the direct costs of regulation is the administrative spending patterns of federal regulatory agencies. According to one estimate, the

| **FIGURE 4.2** | Federal Regulatory Spending Activity, 1960–2006 (fiscal years, billions of dollars) |

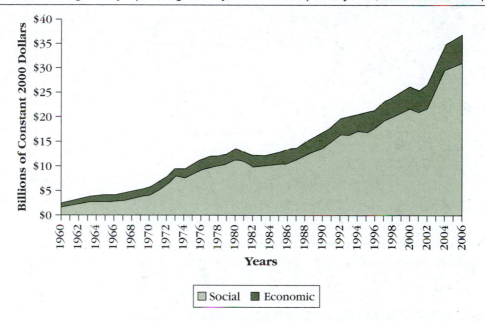

Source: "Administrative Costs of Federal Regulation," via http://wc.wustl.edu/Reg_Report/Press_Release2005.pdf, accessed June 15, 2006; Susan Dudley and Melinda Warren, "Upward Trend in Regulation Continues: An Analysis of the U.S. Budget for Fiscal Years 2005 and 2006," Regulatory Budget Report 27 (St. Louis, MO, and Washington, DC: Washington University's Weidenbaum Center and George Mason's Mercatus Center joint publication), 2005. Reprinted with permission.

combined budget for the sixty-eight federal regulatory agencies was approximately $41.4 billion in 2006, up from $39.5 billion in 2005 (see Figure 4.2). Another way to measure the direct cost of regulation is to look at the staffing levels of federal regulatory agencies. The expenditures and staffing of state and local regulatory agencies also generate direct costs to society. Approximately 242,376 individuals worked for an agency of the federal government in 2006, a 38 percent increase since 2000.[34]

Still another way to approach the measurement of the costs of regulation is to consider the burden that businesses incur in complying with regulations. Various federal regulations, for example, may require companies to change their manufacturing processes or facilities (e.g., smokestack "scrubbers" to clean air and wheelchair ramps to make facilities accessible to customers and employees with disabilities). Companies also must keep records to document their compliance and to obtain permits to implement plans that fall under the scope of specific regulatory agencies. Again, state regulatory agencies often add costs to this burden. Regulated firms may also spend large amounts of money and other resources to prevent additional legislation and to appear responsible. Philip Morris USA, for example, is spending more than $100 million a year to reduce underage smoking. The company operates a "parent resource center" on its main website, which includes a number of tools and insights for talking with kids, recognizing peer pressure, and providing others types of support to parents of teens and preteens.[35]

TABLE 4.5	Cost of Regulation
Type of Cost	**Description**
Administration & Enforcement	Expenditures by government to develop and administer regulatory requirements, including the salaries of government workers, hiring inspectors, purchasing office supplies, and other overhead expenses.
Compliance	Expenditures by organizations, both private and public, to meet regulatory requirements, such as hiring personnel, training employees, and monitoring compliance.

THE UNIVERSITY OF EDINBURGH

FIRE ACTION

On discovering a fire –
1. **Operate the nearest fire alarm point**
2. **Dial the emergency number**   **2222**
3. **Leave the building**

On hearing the fire alarm –

> The fire alarm signal is a
> **Continuous Electronic Sounder**

1. **Leave the building immediately by the nearest available exit, closing doors as you leave**
2. **Lifts MUST NOT be used**
3. **Proceed to the assembly point**

> The assembly point is
> **Middle Meadow Walk**

DO NOT RETURN TO THE BUILDING UNTIL AUTHORISED TO DO SO

All types of organizations are responsible for posting clear instructions on fire safety and related hazards, such as this sign at the University of Edinburgh.

Of course, businesses generally pass these regulatory costs on to their consumers in the form of higher prices, a cost that some label a "hidden tax" of government. Additionally, some businesses contend that the financial and time costs of complying with regulations stifle their ability to develop new products and make investments in facilities and equipment. Moreover, society must pay for the cost of staffing and operating regulatory agencies, and these costs may be reflected in federal income taxes. Table 4.5 describes the primary drivers to the cost of regulation, including those associated with administering, enforcing, and complying with the regulation.

Benefits of Regulation

Despite business complaints about the costs of regulation, it provides many benefits to business, consumers, and society as a whole. These benefits include greater equality in the workplace, safer workplaces, resources for disadvantaged members of society, safer products, more information about and greater choices among products, cleaner air and water, and the preservation of wildlife habitats to ensure that future generations can enjoy their beauty and diversity.

Antitrust laws and regulations strengthen competition by preventing monopolies. When markets are free and open to all, businesses must compete for consumers' dollars, and many try to differentiate their offerings by decreasing prices or raising their quality. Companies that fail to respond to consumer desires or that employ inefficient processes are often forced out of the marketplace by more efficient and effective firms. Truly competitive markets also spur companies to invest in researching and developing product innovations as well as new, more efficient methods of production. These innovations benefit consumers through lower prices and improved goods and services.[36] For example, companies such as Apple, IBM, and Dell Computer continue to engineer smaller, faster, and more powerful computers that help individuals and businesses be more productive.

REGULATORY REFORM Many businesses and individuals believe that the costs of regulation outweigh its benefits. They argue that removing regulation will allow Adam Smith's "invisible hand of competition" to more effectively and efficiently dictate business conduct. Some people desire complete **deregulation,** or removal of all regulatory authority. Proponents of deregulation believe that less government intervention allows business markets to work more effectively. For example, many businesses want their industries deregulated to decrease their costs of doing business. Many industries have been deregulated to a certain extent in recent years, including trucking, airlines, telecommunications (long-distance telephone and cable television), and more recently, electric utilities. For example, the Federal Communications Commission (FCC) is diminishing its role in monitoring telephone equipment.[37] In many cases, this deregulation has resulted in lower prices for consumers as well as in greater product choice, particularly in the long-distance telephone industry. In the airline industry, for example, one of every four tickets sold is on a discount airline.[38] However, critics of deregulation point to higher prices, poor service, and decreased product quality that have plagued some deregulated industries. The year 2000 was considered one of the worst ever for air travel because of the prevalence of flight delays, high prices, and other issues. The September 11, 2001, airline terrorist attacks also pointed to problems of security in a deregulated environment. The federal government soon created the Homeland Security Act and instituted a national security effort for airports. However, there is still considerable debate on the relative merits and costs of regulation.

deregulation
removal of all regulatory authority

SELF-REGULATION Many companies attempt to regulate themselves in an effort to demonstrate social responsibility and to preclude further regulation by federal or state government. In addition to complying with all relevant laws and regulations, many firms choose to join trade associations that have self-regulatory programs. Although such programs are not a direct outgrowth of laws, many were established to stop or delay the development of laws and regulations that would restrict the associations' business practices. Some trade associations establish codes of conduct by which their members must abide or risk discipline or expulsion from the association.[39]

Perhaps the best-known self-regulatory association is the Better Business Bureau (BBB), an organization supported by local member businesses. Founded in 1912, today there are more than 177 local bureaus extending over the United States and Canada. The bureaus help resolve problems for nearly 24 million consumers and businesses each year. When measured by each service request or encounter, the BBB has 90 million interactions per year, ranging from prepurchase requests for information to complaint handling programs.[40] Each bureau also works to champion good business practices within a community, although it usually does not have strong tools for enforcing its business conduct rules. When a company violates what the BBB believes to be good business practices, the bureau warns consumers through local newspapers or broadcast media.

| FIGURE 4.3 | The Credible Self-Regulatory Scheme |

- The scheme must be able to command public confidence.
- There must be strong external consultation and involvement with all relevant stakeholders in the design and operation of the scheme.
- As far as practicable, the operation and control of the scheme should be separate from the institutions of the industry.
- Consumer, public interest and other independent representatives must be fully represented (if possible, up to 75 per cent or more) on the governing bodies of self-regulatory schemes.
- The scheme must be based on clear and intelligible statements of principle and measurable standards—usually in a Code—which address real consumer concerns.
- The rules should identify the intended outcomes.
- There must be clear, accessible and well-publicised complaints procedures where breach of the code is alleged.
- There must be adequate, meaningful and commercially significant sanctions for non-observance.
- Compliance must be monitored (for example through complaints, research and compliance letters from chief executives).
- Performance indicators must be developed, implemented and published to measure the scheme's effectiveness.
- There must be a degree of public accountability, such as an Annual Report.
- The scheme must be well publicised, with maximum education and information directed at consumers and traders.
- The scheme must have adequate resources and be funded in such a way that the objectives are not compromised.
- Independence is vital in any redress scheme which includes the resolution of disputes between traders and consumers.
- The scheme must be regularly reviewed and updated in the light of changing circumstances and expectations.

Source: Copyright © 2006 by National Consumer Council. Reprinted with permission.

If the offending organization is a member of the BBB, it may be expelled from the local bureau. For example, the membership of Priceline.com was revoked by a Connecticut Better Business Bureau after the online retailer failed to address numerous complaints related to misrepresentation of products, failure to provide promised refunds, and failure to correct billing problems.[41] The BBB has also developed a website, BBBOnLine, to help consumers identify websites that collect personal information in an ethical manner. BBB members that use the site agree to binding arbitration with regard to online privacy issues.

Self-regulatory programs like the Better Business Bureau have a number of advantages over government regulation. Establishment and implementation of such programs are usually less costly, and their guidelines or codes of conduct are generally more practical and realistic. Furthermore, effective self-regulatory programs reduce the need to expand government bureaucracy. However, self-regulation also has several limitations. Nonmember firms are under no obligation to abide by a trade association's industry guidelines or codes. Moreover, most associations lack the tools or authority to enforce their guidelines. Finally, these guidelines are often less strict than the regulations established by government agencies. Figure 4.3 provides fifteen recommendations for building a credible and reputable self-regulatory program. The National Consumer Council, based in the United Kingdom, provides these recommendations but also recognizes five circumstances where self-regulation is not the best approach. These include (1) when fraud is an issue, (2) where there is a risk to life or health, (3) when unfair advantage is taken of vulnerable people, (4) when competition alone cannot deliver essential services to consumers who are not of commercial interest to suppliers, and (5) when regulation is needed to make competition work.[42]

BUSINESS'S INFLUENCE ON GOVERNMENT AND POLITICS

Although the government has a profound effect on business activities, especially through its regulatory actions, business has an equal influence on government, and that influence has grown in recent years. Managing this relationship with government officials while navigating the dynamic world of politics is a major challenge for firms, both large and small. In our pluralistic society, many participants are involved in the political process, and the economic stakes are high. Because government is a stakeholder of business (and vice versa), businesses and government can work together as both legitimately participate in the political process. For example, the Electronic Signatures in Global and National Commerce Act of 2000 was initiated by Internet businesses to improve efficiency and avoid the inconvenience and cost of written signatures. Contracts and documents electronically signed have the same legal status as those signed manually.[43] In promoting greater use of electronic signatures to authenticate transactions online, many businesses and consumers hope the bill will help reduce the incidence of fraud in e-commerce.

Obviously, many people believe that business should not be allowed to influence government because of its size, resources, and vested interests. Business participation can be either direct or indirect, positive or negative for society's interest depending not only on the outcome but also on the perspective of various stakeholders. For example, after China received the rights to host the 2008 Olympic Games, government leaders created a campaign to end five "boorish" behaviors commonly seen in Beijing and other cities. The illicit behaviors include spitting in public, littering, pushing and crowding on public transportation, jaywalking, and allowing pets to defecate on the street. The Olympics serve as a focal point for national pride, are watched and attended by millions of people around the world, and involve both private and public funding. As the Chinese government prepares for its debut on the global sports scene, it is sensitive to the prospects for business and industry that will result before, during, and after the Olympics. While business leaders may not have played an explicit role in the courtesy campaign decision, it is clear that the government understands the relationship between behavior on the streets and the economic attractiveness of China.[44]

Figure 4.4 describes four approaches to the relationship between social responsibility and political involvement by companies. Firms with a high level of social responsibility and political involvement are considered corporate activists because they take political actions that may be seen as positive or negative by stakeholder groups. For example, Shell was accused of being antiactivist after the company refused to intervene with the Nigerian government on the execution of the nine leaders of MOSOP, Movement for the Survival of the Ogoni People. Although Shell wrote to government officials asking for human treatment of the MOSOP leaders, the company maintained a policy against involvement in domestic politics. At the other end of the continuum, firms that are relatively weak in terms of social responsibility and political involvement may be called corporate tourists. This label implies that, much like tourists, these companies are relatively uninvolved on a social or political level and are able to exit with ease and a low level of consequence.

| FIGURE 4.4 | Social Responsibility and Political Involvement |

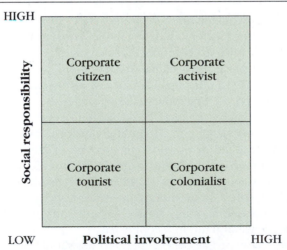

Source: Daniel Malan, "Corporate Citizens, Colonialists, Tourists or Activists? Ethical Challenges Facing South African Corporations in Africa," *Journal of Corporate Citizenship* 18 (Summer 2005): 49–60. Reprinted with permission.

Corporate citizens strive for strategic social responsibility but are not overly involved in the political climate of an area or country. In this regard, corporate citizens are focused on the four levels of social responsibility without resorting to aggressive activity in the political and governmental arena. This type of company would consider the needs of primary and secondary stakeholders without granting special privilege or resources to political stakeholders. Finally, firms with low levels of social responsibility but high levels of political interest are considered corporate colonialists. These companies are typically focused on obtaining competitive and economic power, even if it is detrimental to the local culture, environment, economy, or other social element. One example is the British South Africa Company, which was formed with the consent of the British government. The company had its own police force and flew a flag with the motto, "Justice, Commerce, Freedom." The company's founder, Cecil John Rhodes, stated that "Africa awaits us still, and it is our duty to seize every opportunity of acquiring more territory and we should keep this one idea steadily before our eyes. . . ."[45] Before we look at specific tactics businesses use to influence government policy, it is useful to briefly examine the current political environment to understand how business influence has grown.

The Contemporary Political Environment

Beginning in the 1960s, a significant "antiestablishment" public that was growing more hostile to business mounted protests to effect reform. Their increasingly vocal efforts spurred a fifteen-year wave of legislation and regulation to address a number of issues of the day, including product safety, employment discrimination, human rights, energy shortages, environmental degradation, and scandals related to bribery and payoffs. During the Republican-dominated 1980s, the pendulum swung back in favor of business. During the 1990s, economic prosperity driven by technological advances encouraged both the Republican and Democratic Parties to encourage the self-regulation of business while protecting competition and the natural environment. With the election of President George W. Bush in 2000, there is greater support of business. Environmental legislation passed under the previous Democratic leadership has been abandoned in recent years in favor of probusiness legislation. The balance between business interests and the environment may shift again. Critics have charged that Bush was too soft on business and environmental protection as governor of Texas and fear that this trend will continue, although after the terrorist attacks of September 11, 2001, national security emerged as the most important issue, and the emphasis on environmental regulation diminished. Then, the demise of Enron and WorldCom from corporate corruption created the need for the Bush administration to support major corporate reform legislation. Such changes in the political environment over the last forty years shaped the political environment in which businesses operate and created new avenues for businesses to participate in the political process. Among the most significant factors shaping the political environment were changes in Congress and the rise of special-interest groups.

CHANGES IN CONGRESS Among the calls for social reform in the 1960s were pressures for changes within the legislative process of the U.S. Congress itself. Bowing to this pressure, Congress enacted an amendment to the Legislative Reorganization Act in 1970, which effectively ushered in a new era of change for the political process. This legislation significantly revamped the procedures of congressional committees, most notably stripping committee chairpersons of much of their power, equalizing committee and chair assignments, and requiring committees to record and publish all roll-call votes taken in committee. By opening up the committee process to public scrutiny and reducing the power of senior members and committee leaders, the act reduced the level of secrecy surrounding the legislative process and effectively brought an end to an era of autonomous committee chairs and senior members.[46]

Another significant change occurred in 1974 when Congress amended the Federal Election Campaign Act to limit contributions from individuals, political parties, and special-interest groups organized to get specific candidates elected or policies enacted.[47] Around the same time, many states began to shift their electoral process from the traditional party caucus to primary elections, further eroding the influence of the party in the political process. These changes ultimately had the effect of reducing the importance of political parties by decreasing members' dependence on their parties. Many candidates for elected offices began to turn to special-interest groups to raise enough funds to mount serious campaigns and reelection bids.

RISE OF SPECIAL-INTEREST GROUPS The success of activists' efforts in the 1960s and 1970s spawned the rise of special-interest groups. The movements to promote African American and women's rights and to protest the Vietnam War and environmental degradation evolved into well-organized special-interest groups working to educate the public about significant social issues and to crusade for legislation and regulation of business conduct they deemed irresponsible. These progressive groups were soon joined on Capitol Hill by more conservative groups working to further their agendas on issues such as business deregulation, restriction of abortion and gun control, and promotion of prayer in schools. Businesses joined in by forming industry and trade associations. These increasingly powerful special-interest groups now focused on getting candidates elected who could further their own political agendas. Common Cause, for example, is a nonprofit, nonpartisan organization working to fight corrupt government and special interests backed by large sums of money. Since 1970, Common Cause, with more than 200,000 members, has campaigned for greater openness and accountability in government. Some of its self-proclaimed "victories" include reform of presidential campaign finances, tax systems, congressional ethics, open meeting standards, and disclosure requirements for lobbyists. Table 4.6 lists the dates and subject matter of Common Cause's major accomplishments over the past three decades.[48]

Corporate Approaches to Influencing Government

Although some businesses view regulatory and legal forces as beyond their control and simply react to conditions arising from those forces, other firms actively seek to influence the political process to achieve their goals. In some cases, companies publicly protest the actions of legislative bodies. More often, companies work for the election of political candidates who regard them positively. Lobbying, political action committees, and campaign contributions are some of the tools businesses employ to influence the political process.

| **TABLE 4.6** | Accomplishments of Common Cause |

1971: Helps pass the Twenty-Sixth Amendment, giving eighteen-year-olds the right to vote.

1974: Leads efforts to pass presidential public financing, contribution limits, and disclosure requirements.

1974–1975: Helps pass Freedom of Information Act (FOIA) and open meetings laws at federal, state, and local levels.

1978: Led effort to pass the historic Ethics in Government Act of 1978, requiring financial disclosure for government officials and restricting the "revolving door" between business and government.

1982: Works to pass extension of the Voting Rights Act.

1989: Successfully lobbies for passage of the Ethics in Government Act.

1990: Works to help pass the Americans with Disabilities Act, guaranteeing civil rights for the disabled.

1995: Lobbies for limits on gifts in the House and Senate and for passage of the Lobby Reform Act, providing disclosure of lobbyists' activity and spending.

2000: Successfully works for legislation to unmask and require disclosure of "527" political groups.

2001: Lobbies successfully with a coalition for the Help America Vote Act, which provided funding to states for improvement of the nation's system of voting.

2002: Leads successful multiyear campaign to enact the Bipartisan Campaign Reform Act, banning soft money in federal campaigns. In 2003, in a landmark decision, the U.S. Supreme Court upheld the law.

2004: Launches major voter mobilization and election monitoring programs for presidential election.

Source: Common Cause, "About Us," www.commoncause.org, accessed June 5, 2006. Copyright © 2006 by Common Cause. Reprinted with permission.

lobbying
the process of working to persuade public and/or government officials to favor a particular position in decision making

LOBBYING Among the most powerful tactics business can employ to participate in public policy decisions is direct representation through full-time staff that communicate with elected officials. **Lobbying** is the process of working to persuade public and/or government officials to favor a particular position in decision making. Organizations may lobby officials either directly or by combining their efforts with other organizations.

Many companies concerned about the threat of legislation or regulation that may negatively affect their operations employ lobbyists to communicate their concerns to officials on their behalf. Microsoft, for example, established a Washington office with a staff of fourteen lobbyists and spent $4.6 million to persuade federal officials that breaking up the company for antitrust violations would harm the computer industry and U.S. economy.[49] They were successful in preventing the breakup of the company.

Companies may attempt to influence the legislative or regulatory process more indirectly through trade associations and umbrella organizations that represent collective business interests of many firms. Virtually every industry has one or more trade associations that represent the interests of their members to federal officials and provide public education and other services for their members. Examples of such trade associations include the National Association of Home Builders, the Tobacco Institute, the American Booksellers Association, and the Pet Food Institute. The National Cable and Telecommunications Association (NCTA) responded to a lobbying campaign by Amazon.com, Apple Computers, Microsoft, eBay, and Yahoo!,

Competitive Intelligence in the Global Market

Collecting information about the competition is a standard practice in all industries. Gathering and interpreting data about rivals are crucial to staying competitive, developing new strategy, and keeping customers. It can be accomplished through profiling, studying competitor's websites, talking to customers, scanning the market, and other practices. But when does collecting information cross the line from competitive intelligence to industrial espionage?

Private investigators in Europe, acting on behalf of Proctor and Gamble (P&G), acquired sensitive documents of rival Unilever through "dumpster diving," where trash is rummaged through to discover invoices, memos, reports, and other information. The dumpster diving was clearly against Proctor and Gamble's own intelligence gathering guidelines, but the private investigators were very motivated to uncover Unilever's strategic plans. After learning how the competitive intelligence was retrieved, P&G decide to inform Unilever.

At the same time, the two multinational firms were involved in a competition for the purchase of the Clairol hair products line. P&G eventually won that deal, and Unilever followed with threats of legal action. The two settled out of court for $10 million. Even though P&G never admitted to improper actions, critics wonder if it is common for businesses to contract out competitive intelligence gathering and then claim to have no control over the third party. Other tactics include using surveillance to spy on competitors, reverse engineering, and posing as an employee or supplier of a competitor. Beyond these situations, some firms resort to illegal tactics, like burglarizing a competitor's place of business to gain competitive information. However, other organizations have adopted specific ethics guidelines for gathering information on competitors.

Another case involves employees at Ericsson, based in Sweden. The company known for producing cell phones is also involved with the Swedish government in developing radar and missile guidance systems for Swedish military aircraft. It was found that four employees and one former employee were giving out secret documents. The employees were caught quickly, so a major problem was avoided. The situation became more serious when two Russian diplomats were barred from Sweden, allegedly because they received the secret information. Neither the Swedish government nor

which asked the FCC to regulate high-speed Internet access to assure open availability to information products and services. The NCTA said that cable consumers had full access to Internet content, and regulation would have had unintended negative consequences.[50] Additionally, there are often state trade associations, such as the Hawaii Coffee Association and the Michigan Beer and Wine Wholesalers Association, that work on state- and regional-level issues. Umbrella organizations such as the National Federation of Independent Businesses and the U.S. Chamber of Commerce also help promote business interests to government officials. The U.S. Chamber of Commerce takes positions on many political, regulatory, and economic questions. With more than 200,000 member companies, its goal is to promote its members' views of the ideal free enterprise marketplace. There is growing interest and concern, however, about the relationship between corporations and the government. Lobbying by companies and their trade associations against social and environmental regulations or measures to help citizens in poorer countries has been identified as an emerging concern by Lifeworth.com in its recent Annual Review of Corporate Responsibility.[51]

Ericsson offered many details, but it is believed that the diplomats were passing the information on to the Russian government. If the actions had gone unnoticed any longer, there could have been serious implications.

These examples highlight the need for companies to create a clear and well-enforced competitive intelligence gathering and security plan. It is important to take action if one or more of the following is occurring:

1. The tactics used to gain competitive information exceed what is ethical, legal, or acceptable.

2. The information that is being sought about a competitor is private or confidential.

3. The information may cause harm to the public or another group.

Information that should not be available to outsiders for competitive reasons is considered private or confidential information. A primary concern in the global marketplace is that of intellectual property rights. Software, music, theories, inventions, and other intangible holdings of the company involve significant costs to create, and it is important to monitor their use and dis-semination. WestJet, a Canadian airline, recently settled a case of industrial espionage with Air Canada after WestJet employees gained unauthorized access to Air Canada's online flight information system.

Public safety issues can arise when a company uses practices to gain an unfair advantage of the competition and exploit the consumer. The public may also be in danger if confidential information of a defense contractor is released. The Ericsson example typifies this scenario. When a troubling or doubtful situation arises, examining these three criteria will enable the user to start the decision-making process. The answer will not be simple, especially for firms operating in several countries. Following these criteria will help the user obtain ethical decisions regarding competitive intelligence gathering, especially in today's competitive global market.

Sources: "WestJet Agrees to Pay $14 Million Settlement," *Wall Street Journal*, May 30, 2006, p. A11; Andrew Crane, "In the Company of Spies: When Competitive Intelligence Gathering Becomes Industrial Espionage," *Business Horizons* 48 (May–June 2005): 233–240; H. Keith Melton, "What? Me Worry?" *Harvard Business Review* 83 (November 2005): 11–36. ∎

POLITICAL ACTION COMMITTEES Companies can also influence the political process through political action committees. **Political action committees (PACs)** are organizations that solicit donations from individuals and then contribute these funds to candidates running for political office. Companies are barred by federal law from donating directly to candidates for federal offices or to political action committees, and individuals are limited to relatively small donations. However, companies can organize PACs to which their executives, employees, and stockholders can make significant donations as individuals. PACs operate independently of business and are usually incorporated. Labor unions and other special-interest groups, such as teachers and medical doctors, can also establish PACs to promote their goals.

political action committees (PACs)

organizations that solicit donations from individuals and then contribute these funds to candidates running for political office

The Federal Election Committee has established rules to restrict PAC donations to $5,000 per candidate for each election. However, many PACs exploit loopholes in these regulations by donating so-called soft money to political parties that do not support a specific candidate for federal office. Under current rules, these contributors can make unlimited donations to political parties for general activities. Microsoft, for example, contributed $1 million to help underwrite both the Republican and

TABLE 4.7	Political Contributions by Industry Sector	
Industry Sector	**To Democrats**	**To Republicans**
Finance, Insurance, & Real Estate	$18,553,697	$27,126,676
Lawyers & Lobbyists	$11,357,331	$5,716,720
Communication & Electronics	$5,926,199	$4,543,252
Health Care	$3,361,391	$9,149,947
Labor Unions	$3,027,871	$401,204
Construction	$1,629,462	$6,722,614

Source: Center for Responsive Politics, "2006 Sector Totals," http://www.opensecrets.org/parties/
sector.asp?Cmte=DPC&cycle=2006 and http://www.opensecrets.org/parties/sector.asp?Cmte=RPC&cycle=2006,
accessed June 18, 2006. Reprinted with permission from The Center for Responsive Politics/opensecrets.org

Democratic Party conventions in 2000. In addition, the company gave $522,150 in soft money to the Republican Party and $341,250 to the Democratic Party. The Bill and Melinda Gates Foundation contributed another $10 million to the U.S. Capitol Visitors Center. All of this largesse occurred while the Department of Justice was passing judgment on Microsoft for antitrust violations.[52] Some candidates form "leadership PACs" to avoid traditional PAC limitations since they are not specifically legislated by the FEC.[53]

CAMPAIGN CONTRIBUTIONS Although federal laws restrict direct corporate contributions to election campaigns, corporate money may be channeled into candidates' campaign coffers as corporate executives' or stockholders' personal contributions. Such donations can violate the spirit of corporate campaign laws. A sizable contribution to a candidate may carry with it an implied understanding that the elected official will perform some favor, such as voting in accordance with the contributor's desire on a particular law. Occasionally, some businesses find it so important to ensure favorable treatment that they make illegal corporate contributions to campaign funds. Former Louisiana Governor Edwin Edwards not only accepted campaign contributions; he extorted contributions from some businesspeople who applied for riverboat casino licenses during Edwards's tenure as governor.[54]

Although laws limit corporate contributions to specific candidates, it is acceptable for businesses and other organizations to make donations to political parties. Table 4.7 lists selected industry sectors and their contributions to political parties. Note that labor unions typically donate more to the Democratic Party, whereas the real estate, finance, and insurance industry contributes a significantly greater amount to the Republican Party. Most industry sectors choose to give to both major political parties.

THE GOVERNMENT'S APPROACH FOR LEGAL AND ETHICAL COMPLIANCE

Thus far, we have seen that although legal and regulatory forces have a strong influence on business operations, businesses can affect these forces through the political process. In addition, socially responsible firms strive to comply with society's wishes for responsible conduct through legal and ethical behavior. Indeed, the most effective way for businesses to manage the legal and regulatory environment is to establish values and policies that communicate and reward appropriate conduct. Most employees will try to comply with an organization's leadership and directions for responsible conduct. Therefore, top management must develop and implement a highly visible strategy for effective compliance. This means that top managers must take responsibility and be accountable for assessing legal risks and developing corporate programs that promote acceptable conduct.

Federal Sentencing Guidelines for Organizations

Federal Sentencing Guidelines for Organizations (FSGO)

established in 1991 to streamline the sentencing and punishment for organizational crimes and to hold companies, as well as their employees, responsible for misconduct

More and more companies are establishing organizational compliance programs to ensure that they operate legally and responsibly as well as generate a competitive advantage based on a reputation for responsible citizenship. There are also strong legal incentives to establish such programs. The U.S. Sentencing Commission established the **Federal Sentencing Guidelines for Organizations (FSGO)** in 1991 not only to streamline the sentencing and punishment for organizational crimes but also to hold companies, as well as their employees, responsible for misconduct. Previously, the law punished only those employees responsible for an offense, not the company. Under the FSGO, if a court determines that a company's organizational culture rewarded or otherwise created opportunities that encouraged wrongdoing, the firm may be subject to stiff penalties in the event that one of its employees breaks the law. The guidelines apply to all felonies and Class A misdemeanors committed by employees in association with their work. Table 4.8 shows the number of organizations receiving fines and/or ordered to make restitution for crimes sentenced in 2005.

The assumption underlying the FSGO is that good, socially responsible organizations maintain compliance systems and internal governance controls that deter

| TABLE 4.8 | Number of Organizations Fined or Ordered to Make Restitution Under FSGO in 2005 | | | |

Offense	No Fine or Restitution	Restitution Only	Fine Only	Both Fine and Restitution
Antitrust	0	0	8	3
Public corruption/bribery	1	0	4	0
Fraud	3	12	15	5
Import/export violation	0	0	8	0
Money laundering	4	1	4	1
Environmental—toxic pollutants	0	2	4	5
Environmental—water	0	0	19	7
Environmental—wildlife	0	1	1	1
Immigration	2	0	2	0

Source: *2005 Sourcebook of Federal Sentencing Statistics,* http://www.ussc.gov/ANNRPT/2005/Table51_post.pdf, accessed June 10, 2006.

TABLE 4.9	Seven Steps to Effective Compliance and Ethics Programs

1. Establish codes of conduct (identify key risk areas).
2. Appoint or hire high-level compliance manager (ethics officer).
3. Take care in delegating authority (background checks on employees).
4. Institute a training program and communication system (ethics training).
5. Monitor and audit for misconduct (reporting mechanisms).
6. Enforce and discipline (management implementation of policy).
7. Revise program as needed (feedback and action).

Source: U.S. Sentencing Commission, Federal Sentencing Guidelines for Organizations, 2005, http://www.ussc.gov/
2005guid/8b2_1.htm, accessed June 10, 2006.

misconduct by their employees. Thus, the guidelines focus on crime prevention and detection by mitigating penalties for firms that have implemented such compliance programs in the event that one of their employees commits a crime. To avoid or limit fines and other penalties as a result of wrongdoing by an employee, the employer must be able to demonstrate that it has implemented a reasonable program for deterring and preventing unlawful behavior.

The U.S. Sentencing Commission has delineated seven steps that companies must implement to demonstrate the existence of an effective compliance effort and thereby avoid penalties in the event of an employee's wrongdoing. These steps, which are listed in Table 4.9, are based on the commission's determination to emphasize compliance programs and to provide guidance for both organizations and courts regarding program effectiveness. The steps are not "a superficial checklist requiring little analysis or thought."[55] Rather, they help companies understand what is required of a compliance and ethics program that is capable of reducing employees' opportunities to engage in misconduct.

To cultivate an effective ethics and compliance program, an organization should first develop a code of conduct that communicates the standards it expects of its employees and identifies key risk areas for the firm. Next, oversight of the program should be assigned to high-ranking personnel in the organization (e.g., an ethics officer, a vice president of human resources, or a general counsel) who are recognized as individuals who abide by the legal and ethical standards of the industry. Authority should never be delegated to anyone with a known propensity to engage in misconduct. An effective compliance program also requires a meaningful communications system, often in the form of ethics training, to disseminate the company's standards and procedures. This system should provide for mechanisms, such as anonymous toll-free phone lines or company ombudsmen, through which employees can report wrongdoing without fear of retaliation. Monitoring and auditing systems designed to detect misconduct are also crucial ingredients for an effective compliance program. If a company does detect criminal behavior or other wrongdoing by an employee, it must take immediate, appropriate, and fair disciplinary action toward all individuals both directly and indirectly responsible for the offense. Finally, if a company discovers that a crime has occurred, it must take steps to prevent similar offenses in the future.

Members of eBay's Main Street Program receive updates on the legislative issues that affect businesses that operate via eBay, including sales taxes, privacy, licensing requirements, and fraud. These materials have been reproduced with the permission of eBay, Inc. © 2007 eBay, Inc. All rights reserved.

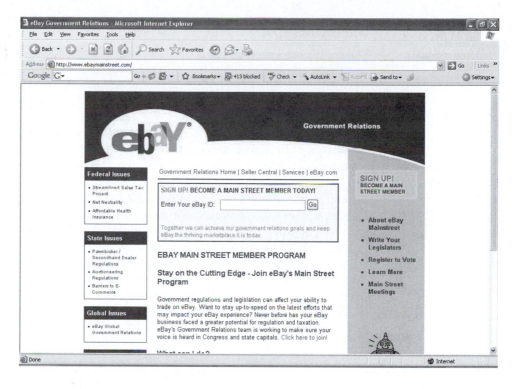

This usually involves modifications to the compliance program, additional employee training, and communications about specific types of conduct. The government expects continuous improvement and refinement of these seven steps for effective compliance and ethics programs. The guidelines were amended in 2004 to include the provision that a firm's governing authority (i.e., board of directors, executives) should be well informed about the content, implementation, and effectiveness of the compliance and ethics program. This clearly places the responsibility for ethics and compliance on top leadership.[56]

A strong program acts as a buffer to keep employees from committing crimes and to protect a company's reputation should wrongdoing occur despite its best efforts. If a firm can demonstrate that is has truly made an effort to communicate to its employees about their legal and ethical responsibilities, the public's response to any wrongdoing may be reduced along with any corporate punishment the courts mete out for the offense. It is important to point out, however, that executives who focus on strict legal compliance are missing part of the picture when it comes to social responsibility. By developing a work environment that supports and expects ethical decision making, management can avoid the perilous situation where employees ask, "Is this legal?" The buffer analogy is pivotal to this point: Strong corporate values and ethical standards, which are consistent with and more restrictive than legal standards, should minimize the missteps that are likely to occur in a compliance-driven firm. An effective program must feature ethics and values as the driving force, as we shall see in the next few chapters.

Sarbanes-Oxley Act

During probes into financial reporting fraud at Enron, WorldCom, and many other companies, investigators learned that hundreds of public corporations were not reporting their financial results accurately. Accounting firms, lawyers, top corporate officers, and boards of directors had developed a culture of deception to attempt to gain investor approval and competitive advantage. The downfall of many of these companies resulted in the loss to thousands of investors, and employees lost much of their savings. To restore stakeholder confidence and provide a new standard of ethical behavior for U.S. business, the **Sarbanes-Oxley Act** was enacted. The act had almost unanimous support by Congress, government regulatory agencies, and the general public. When President Bush signed the act, he emphasized the need for the standards it provides, especially for top management and boards of directors responsible for company oversight. Table 4.10 details the requirements of the act.

Sarbanes-Oxley Act (SOX)
legislation to protect investors by improving the accuracy and reliability of corporate disclosures

The section of SOX that has caused the most concern for companies has been compliance with section 404. Section 404 comprises three central issues: (1) it requires that management create reliable internal financial controls; (2) it requires that management attest to the reliability of those controls and the accuracy of financial statements that result from those controls; and (3) it requires an independent auditor to further attest to the statements made by management.

TABLE 4.10	Major Provisions of the Sarbanes-Oxley Act

1. Requires the establishment of an Independent Accounting Oversight Board in charge of regulations administered by the Securities and Exchange Commission.

2. Requires CEOs and CFOs to certify that their companies' financial statements are true and without misleading statements.

3. Requires that corporate board of directors' audit committees consist of independent members with no material interests in the company.

4. Prohibits corporations from making or offering loans to officers and board members.

5. Requires codes of ethics for senior financial officers; code must be registered with the SEC.

6. Prohibits accounting firms from providing both auditing and consulting services to the same client.

7. Requires company attorneys to report wrongdoing to top managers and, if necessary, to the board of directors; if managers and directors fail to respond to reports of wrongdoing, the attorney should stop representing the company.

8. Mandates "whistle-blower protection" for persons who disclose wrongdoing to authorities.

9. Requires financial securities analysts to certify that their recommendations are based on objective reports.

10. Requires mutual fund managers to disclose how they vote shareholder proxies, giving investors information about how their shares influence decisions.

11. Establishes a ten-year penalty for mail/wire fraud.

12. Prohibits the two senior auditors from working on a corporation's account for more than five years; other auditors are prohibited from working on an account for more than seven years; in other words, accounting firms must rotate individual auditors from one account to another from time to time.

Many company boards failed to provide the necessary oversight of the financial decisions of top officers and executives. At Adelphia Communications, for example, the Rigas family (Adelphia founders) collected more than $3 billion from the firm, using it as a kind of personal line of credit.[57] A former Kmart CEO, Charles Conaway, allegedly hired unqualified executives and consultants at fees that far exceeded the norm. There were also $24 million in board-approved loans to executives just one month before Kmart filed for Chapter 11 bankruptcy.[58]

To address fraudulent occurrences such as these, SOX required the creation of the Public Company Accounting Oversight Board, which provides oversight of the accounting firms that audit public companies and sets standards and rules for the auditors in these firms. The board has investigatory and disciplinary power over accounting firm auditors and securities analysts who issue reports about companies. Specific duties include (1) registration of public accounting firms; (2) establishment of auditing, quality control, ethics, independence, and other standards relating to preparation of audit reports; (3) inspection of accounting firms; (4) investigations, disciplinary proceedings, and imposition of sanctions; and (5) enforcement of compliance with accounting rules of the board, professionals standards, and securities laws relating to the preparation and issuance of audit reports and obligations and liabilities of accountants.

Conflicts of interest were eliminated because auditing firms are no longer able to act as both auditor and consultant without gaining special permission. Limitations on nonaudit services for clients have been imposed, as have limitations on the amount of time lead auditors may serve a particular client. The act also seeks to eliminate conflicts of interest among auditors, security analysts, brokers, dealers, and the public companies they serve to ensure enhanced financial disclosures of public companies' true condition. To accomplish auditor independence, section 201 of the act no longer allows registered public accounting firms to provide nonaudit service to a public company for which it provides audit services. Similar conflict of interest rules for security analysts, brokers, and dealers, who recommend equities in research reports, have already been adopted by national securities exchanges and registered securities associations. Wall Street is experiencing major changes. In early 2003, ten of the nation's largest securities firms agreed to pay a record $1.4 billion to settle government charges involving abuse of investors during the stock-market bubble of the late 1990s. Wall Street firms routinely issued overly optimistic stock research to investors to gain favor with corporate clients and win their lucrative investment-banking business.

SOX requires corporations to take more responsibility and to provide principles-based ethical leadership. Enhanced financial disclosures are required, including certification by top officers that audit reports are complete and that nothing material has been withheld from auditors. For example, registered public accounting firms are now required to identify all material correcting adjustments to reflect accurate financial statements. Also, all material off-balance-sheet transactions and other relationships with unconsolidated entities that affect current or future financial conditions of a public company must be disclosed in each annual and quarterly financial report. In addition, public companies must also report "on a rapid and current basis" material changes in the financial condition or operations.

CEOs and CFOs are now held personally accountable for the credibility and accuracy of their company's financial statements. A code of ethics for senior financial officers that addresses their specific areas of risk is now required.

Other provisions of the act include whistle-blower protection and changes in the attorney-client relationship so that attorneys are now required to report wrongdoing to top managers or to the board of directors. Employees of public companies and accounting firms, in general, are also accountable to report unethical behavior. SOX intends to motivate employees through "whistle-blower" protection that would prohibit the employer from taking certain actions against employees who lawfully disclose private employer information to, among others, parties in a judicial proceeding involving a fraud claim. Whistle-blowers are also granted a remedy of special damages and attorney's fees. Two years after Sarbanes-Oxley, the SEC received approximately 40,000 whistle-blowing reports per month, compared with 6,400 per month in 2001.[59] With only 11,000 publicly traded companies in the United States, it seems that even though 75 percent of the whistle-blowing reports have no validity, there are still more whistle-blowing reports every month than the number of companies listed.[60] Also, actions of retaliation that harm informants, including interference with the lawful employment or livelihood of any person, shall result in fines and/or imprisonment for ten years. Table 4.11 lists the benefits of the act.

There are some concerns with SOX, however. Although a law may help prevent misconduct, it will not stop executives who are determined to lie, steal, manipulate, or deceive for personal gain. The law requires that accountants and executives do the right thing, but a deep commitment by top company leadership is necessary to create an ethical corporate culture. In addition to these concerns, the implementation of SOX can take a great deal of organizational time and resources. Whereas very large corporations may be able to hire staff and make other arrangements for implementation, small and medium-sized organizations may have fewer resources at their disposal. Finally, publicly traded multinational companies with operations in the United States

TABLE 4.11	Benefits of Sarbanes-Oxley

1. Greater accountability by top management and board of directors to employees, communities, and society. The goals of the business will be to provide stakeholders with a return on their investment, rather than providing a vehicle for management to reap excessive compensation and other benefits.

2. Renewed investor confidence providing managers and brokers with the information they need to make solid investment decisions, which will ultimately lead to a more stable and solid growth rate for investors.

3. Clear explanations by CEOs of why their compensation package is in the best interest of the company. It will also eliminate certain traditional senior management perks, including company loans, and require disclosures about stock trades, thus making executives more like other investors.

4. Greater protection of employee retirement plans. Employees can develop greater trust that they will not lose savings tied to such plans.

5. Improved information from stock analysts and rating agencies.

6. Greater penalties and accountability of senior managers, auditors, and board members. The penalties now outweigh the rewards of purposeful manipulation and deception.

must implement SOX in addition to the regulatory requirements of other countries. Since there is no global standard on these responsibilities and accountability mechanisms, this implementation is costly and complicated for such firms.[61]

SUMMARY

In a pluralistic society, many diverse stakeholder groups attempt to influence the public officials who legislate, interpret laws, and regulate business. Companies that adopt a strategic approach to the legal and regulatory system develop proactive organizational values and compliance programs that identify areas of risks and include formal communication, training, and continuous improvement of responses to the legal and regulatory environment.

Economic reasons for regulation often relate to efforts to level the playing field on which businesses operate. These efforts include regulating trusts, which are generally established to gain control of a product market or industry by eliminating competition and eliminating monopolies, which occur when just one business provides a good or service in a given market. Another rationale for regulation is society's desire to restrict destructive or unfair competition. Social reasons for regulation address imperfections in the market that result in undesirable consequences and the protection of natural and social resources. Other regulations are created in response to social demands for safety and equality in the workplace, safer products, and privacy issues.

The Sherman Antitrust Act is the principal tool used to prevent businesses from restraining trade and monopolizing markets. The Clayton Antitrust Act limits mergers and acquisitions that could stifle competition and prohibits specific activities that could substantially lessen competition or tend to create a monopoly. The Federal Trade Commission Act prohibits unfair methods of competition and created the Federal Trade Commission (FTC). Legal and regulatory policy is also enforced through lawsuits by private citizens, competitors, and special-interest groups.

A company that engages in commerce beyond its own country must contend with the complex relationship among the laws of its own nation, international laws, and the laws of the nation in which it will be trading. There is considerable variation and focus among different nations' laws, but many countries' antitrust laws are quite similar to those of the United States.

Regulation creates numerous costs for businesses, consumers, and society at large. Some measures of these costs include administrative spending patterns, staffing levels of federal regulatory agencies, and costs businesses incur in complying with regulations. The cost of regulation is passed on to consumers in the form of higher prices and may stifle product innovation and investments in new facilities and equipment. Regulation also provides many benefits, including greater equality in the workplace, safer workplaces, resources for disadvantaged members of society, safer products, more information about and greater choices among products, cleaner air and water, and the preservation of wildlife habitats. Antitrust laws and regulations strengthen competition and spur companies to invest in research and development. Many businesses and individuals believe that the costs of regulation outweigh its benefits. Some people desire complete deregulation, or removal of regulatory authority.

Because government is a stakeholder of business (and vice versa), businesses and government can work together as both legitimately participate in the political process. Business participation can be a positive or negative force in society's interest, depending not only on the outcome but also on the perspective of various stakeholders.

Changes over the last forty years have shaped the political environment in which businesses operate. Among the most significant of these changes were amendments to the Legislative Reorganization Act and the Federal Election Campaign Act, which had the effect of reducing the importance of political parties. Many candidates for elected offices turned to increasingly powerful special-interest groups to raise funds to campaign for elected office.

Some organizations view regulatory and legal forces as beyond their control and simply react to conditions arising from those forces; other firms seek to influence the political process to achieve their goals. One way they can do so is through lobbying, the process of working to persuade public and/or government officials to favor a particular position in decision making. Companies can also influence the political process through political action committees, which are organizations that solicit donations from individuals and then contribute these funds to candidates running for political office. Corporate funds may also be channeled into candidates' campaign coffers as corporate executives' or stockholders' personal contributions, although such donations can violate the spirit of corporate campaign laws. Although laws limit corporate contributions to specific candidates, it is acceptable for businesses and other organizations to make donations to political parties.

More companies are establishing organizational compliance programs to ensure that they operate legally and responsibly as well as to generate a competitive advantage based on a reputation for good citizenship. Under the Federal Sentencing Guidelines for Organizations (FSGO), a company that wants to avoid or limit fines and other penalties as a result of an employee's crime must be able to demonstrate that it has implemented a reasonable program for deterring and preventing misconduct. To implement an effective compliance program, an organization should develop a code of conduct that communicates expected standards, assign oversight of the program to high-ranking personnel who abide by legal and ethical standards, communicate standards through training and other mechanisms, monitor and audit to detect wrongdoing, punish individuals responsible for misconduct, and take steps to continuously improve the program. A strong compliance program acts as a buffer to keep employees from committing crimes and to protect a company's reputation should wrongdoing occur despite its best efforts.

Enacted after many corporate financial fraud scandals, the Sarbanes-Oxley Act created the Public Company Accounting Oversight Board to provide oversight and set standards for the accounting firms that audit public companies. The board has investigatory and disciplinary power over accounting firm auditors and securities analysts. The act requires corporations to take responsibility to provide principles-based ethical leadership and holds CEOs and CFOs personally accountable for the credibility and accuracy of their company's financial statements. Ideally, the act will provide for a new standard of ethical behavior for U.S. business, especially for top management and boards of directors responsible for company oversight.

KEY TERMS

trust (p. 115)

monopoly (p. 115)

deregulation (p. 127)

lobbying (p. 133)

political action committees (PACs) (p. 135)

Federal Sentencing Guidelines for Organizations (FSGO) (p. 137)

Sarbanes-Oxley Act (SOX) (p. 140)

DISCUSSION QUESTIONS

1. Discuss the existence of both cooperation and conflict between government and businesses concerning the regulation of business.

2. What is the rationale for government to regulate the activities of businesses? How is our economic and social existence shaped by government regulations?

3. What was the historical background that encouraged the government to enact legislation such as the Sherman Antitrust Act and the Clayton Act? Do these same conditions exist today?

4. What is the role and function of the Federal Trade Commission in the regulation of business? How does the FTC engage in proactive activities to avoid government regulation?

5. How do global regulations influence U.S. businesses operating internationally? What are the major obstacles to global regulation?

6. Compare the costs and benefits of regulation. In your opinion, do the benefits outweigh the costs or do the costs outweigh the benefits? What are the advantages and disadvantages of deregulation?

7. Name three tools that businesses can employ to influence government and public policy. Evaluate the strengths and weaknesses of each of these approaches.

8. How do political action committees influence society, and what is their appropriate role in a democratic society?

9. Why should an organization implement the Federal Sentencing Guidelines for Organizations (FSGO) as a strategic approach for legal compliance?

10. What is the significance of Sarbanes-Oxley to business operations in the United States?

EXPERIENTIAL EXERCISE

Visit the website of the Federal Trade Commission (FTC) (http://www.ftc.gov/). What is the FTC's current mission? What are the primary areas for which the FTC is responsible? Review the last two months of press releases from the FTC. On the basis of these releases, what appear to be major issues of concern at this time?

WHAT WOULD YOU DO?

The election of a new governor brings many changes to any state capital, including the shuffling of a variety of appointed positions. In most cases, political appointees have contributed a great deal to the governor's election bid and have expertise in a specific area related to the appointed post. Joe Barritz was in that position when he became assistant agricultural commissioner in January 2003. He was instrumental in getting the governor elected, especially through his fundraising efforts. Joe's family owned thousands of acres in the state and had been farming and ranching since the 1930s. Joe earned a bachelor's degree in agricultural economics and policy and a law degree from one of the state's top institutions. He worked as an attorney in the state's capital city for over eighteen years and represented a range of clients, most of whom were involved in agriculture. Thus, he had many characteristics that made him a strong candidate for assistant commissioner. After about six months on the job, Joe had lunch with a couple of friends he had known for many years. During that June lunch, they had a casual conversation about the fact that Joe never did have a true "celebration" after being named assistant agricultural commissioner. His friends decided to talk with others about the possibility of holding that celebration in a few months. Before long, eight of Joe's friends were busy planning to hold a reception in his honor on October 5. Two of these friends were currently employed as lobbyists. One represented the beef industry association, and the other worked for the cotton industry council. They asked Joe if they could hold the celebration at his lake home in the capital city. Joe talked with the commission's ethics officer about the party and learned that these types of parties, between close friends, were common for newly appointed and elected officials. The ethics officer told Joe that the reception and location were fine, but only if his lobbyist friends paid for the reception with personal funds. The state's ethics rules did not allow a standing government official to take any type of gift, including corporate dollars, that might influence his or her decision making. Joe communicated this information to his friends.

During the next few months, Joe was involved in a number of issues that could potentially help or harm agriculture-based industries. Various reports and policy statements within the Agricultural Commission were being used to tailor state legislation and regulatory proposals. The beef and cotton councils were actively supporting a proposal that would provide tax breaks to farmers and ranchers. Staff on the Agricultural Commission were mixed on the proposal, but Joe was expected to deliver a report to a legislative committee on the commission's preferences. His presentation was scheduled for October 17.

On October 5, nearly sixty of Joe's friends gathered at the catered reception to reminisce and congratulate him on his achievements. Most were good friends and acquaintances, so the mood and conversation were relatively light that evening. A college football game between two big rivals drew most people to the big-screen TV. By midnight, the guests were gone. Back at the office the following week, Joe began working on his presentation for the legislative committee. Through a series of economic analyses, long meetings, and electronic discussions, he decided to support the tax benefits for farmers and ranchers. News reports carried information from his presentation.

It was not long before some reporters made a "connection" between the reception in Joe's honor and his stand on the tax breaks for agriculture industries. An investigation quickly ensued, including reports that the beef and cotton industry associations had not only been present but also financially supported the reception on October 5. The small company used to plan and cater the party indicated that checks from the cotton industry council and beef industry association were used to cover some of the expenses. A relationship between the "gift" of the reception and Joe's presentation to the legislative committee would be a breach of his oath of office and state ethics rules. If you were Joe, what would you do?

CHAPTER 5

Business Ethics and Ethical Decision Making

CHAPTER OBJECTIVES

- To define and describe the importance of business ethics
- To understand the diverse and complex nature of existing and emerging ethical issues
- To discuss the individual factors that influence ethical or unethical decisions
- To explore the effect of organizational relationships on ethical decision making
- To evaluate the role of opportunity in ethical or unethical decisions

CHAPTER OUTLINE

The Nature of Business Ethics

Foundations of Business Ethics

Ethical Issues in Business

Understanding the Ethical Decision-Making Process

Companies that provide services are becoming increasingly important in our society and our economy. Customers value high-quality service and organizational ethics that go above and beyond what is expected. The Allstate Corporation, the largest public personal insurance company in the United States, is one such service provider. The company offers thirteen lines of insurance, including auto, property, life, and business. It also offers retirement, investment, and banking services. Allstate serves about 17 million households and has offices in forty-nine U.S. states and in Canada. Allstate believes in bringing its customers value and prides itself on doing more than is expected of it in all areas—standing out in customer relationships, ethics, and social responsibility.

Allstate works hard to bring value to customers and all other stakeholders. The company has a strong commitment to high ethical standards. In today's climate of corporate scandal, this is a valuable asset for the company and in building long-term relationships with shareholders. Allstate maintains an effective organization ethics and compliance program. The company has also managed and invested its capital in an ethical manner, thereby providing shareholders with long-term financial stability. In addition, Allstate focuses on building long-term customers.

In 2004, more than 1 million customers switched their auto insurance coverage to Allstate, and now the company is working to keep them. One way the company has been working to retain happy customers is by offering excellent claim management services. Doing this both strengthens the connection between the company and its customers (customers know and trust that Allstate will be there for them in times of need) and keeps costs low (helping the company). Allstate also focuses on streamlining its relationships with all individuals working with the company—employees and independent agents alike—so that they can then better provide clear, effective help to customers. They believe strongly in being good corporate citizens.

In addition, the company is committed to giving back to individuals and communities. For example, contributions from its subsidiaries fund an independent charity—The Allstate Foundation, which donates millions of dollars each year to causes that focus on three specific areas: economic empowerment; tolerance, inclusion, and diversity; and safe and vital communities. In addition, each year the foundation donates $1 million to nonprofit organizations through Agency Hands in the Community grants. And in 2005, after an unusually large number of natural disasters, both The Allstate Corporation and The Allstate Foundation also came to the aid of those affected by hurricanes Katrina and Rita and the tsunami in South Asia, India, and Indonesia.

In the wake of these devastating disasters, The Allstate Foundation established a $1 million Allstate Foundation Hurricane Recovery Fund designed to help hurricane victims begin to rebuild. The Allstate Corporation also contributed $25,000 to the National Council of LaRaza Katrina Relief Fund and $50,000 to the Bush-Clinton Katrina Fund, and it agreed to match donations to the BlackAmericaWeb.com Relief Fund up to $250,000, as well as $1,000 to the American Red Cross Hurricane Katrina Relief Fund for each field goal completed by Allstate participating schools for the 2005 college football season. These contributions provided food, shelter, and schooling to those affected, as well as support to those who have offered to help hurricane victims. These significant donations came just months after the company raised $1.5 million for the Tsunami Disaster Recovery fund through employee and agency donations and company-matched contributions.

Allstate also invests in municipal bonds and low-interest loans to support and grow urban neighborhoods. In addition, it is committed to helping the environment. At the company headquarters, lighting has been replaced both in and outside the buildings to cut down on energy consumption. The company is part of the Climate Resolve initiative—aimed to reduce greenhouse gas intensity. Employees who make use of public transportation are rewarded with subsidized tickets and complimentary shuttles to train stations. Allstate also works primarily with suppliers using recycled materials.

The seventy-five-year-old Allstate comes to the aid of not only its customers but also the global community at large. Edward M. Liddy, chairman and chief executive officer, explains, "One of the most rewarding aspects of working at Allstate is to see the way our employees and agencies help others in a time of crisis. I know it is what we do as a business, but it's more than a business for Allstaters." This commitment rings true not only in times of disaster but in the day-to-day workings of the company managing ethical relationships with its customers and shareholders.[1] ■

As illustrated by the Allstate example, key business ethics concerns relate to questions about whether various stakeholders consider specific business practices acceptable. Wal-Mart, for example, has been accused of paying its female employees less than its male employees for the same jobs even after seniority, store location, and other factors have been considered. The retailer has also been accused of failing to advance women into higher level jobs at a rate comparable to that for men. It faces the largest private employer civil rights case in U.S. history, with possibly as many as 1.6 million former and current female Wal-Mart employees.[2] If the accusations prove to be true, Wal-Mart could face penalties in the hundreds of millions of dollars and could be forced to overhaul its entire pay and promotion system.[3] The Minnesota attorney general sued U.S. Bank for allegedly releasing customers' private information—including social security numbers, account numbers and balances, and credit-card numbers—to a telemarketing company.[4] Regardless of the legality of the actions of these companies, others have judged the conduct as unacceptable.

By its very nature, the field of business ethics is controversial, and no universally accepted approach has emerged for resolving its questions. Nonetheless, most businesses are establishing initiatives that include the development and implementation of ethics programs designed to deter conduct that some stakeholders might consider objectionable. Unisys, for example, provides ethics training for 34,000 employees working in 100 countries worldwide. It reaches about 90 percent of them annually through videos, an internal website, newsletters, and other ethics training.[5] This training helps Unisys communicate its values and policies to ensure that employees understand what the company expects of them, as well as what will happen if they violate the company's policies or the law.

The definition of social responsibility that appears in Chapter 1 incorporates society's expectations and includes four levels of concern: economic, legal, ethical, and philanthropic. Because ethics is becoming an increasingly important issue in business today, this chapter and Chapter 6 are devoted to exploring this dimension of social responsibility. First, we define business ethics, examine its importance from an organizational perspective, and review its foundations. Next, we define ethical issues in business to help understand areas of risk. We then look at the individual, organizational, and opportunity factors that influence ethical decision making in the workplace.

THE NATURE OF BUSINESS ETHICS

To support business decisions that are both acceptable and beneficial to society, it is necessary to examine business ethics from an organizational perspective. The term *ethics* relates to choices and judgments about acceptable standards of conduct that guide the behavior of individuals and groups. These standards require both organizations and individuals to accept responsibility for their actions and to comply with established value systems. Without a shared view of which values and conduct are appropriate and acceptable, companies may fail to balance their desires for profits against the wishes and needs of society. Maintaining this balance often demands compromises or trade-offs. For example, obesity in children is becoming an issue across groups and stakeholders. In the current Congress, there are fifty-five bills introduced that contain the word "obesity," which is approaching the number containing "gun."[6] According to a recent survey of readers in *The Wall Street Journal,* most people (60 percent) believed that consumers should bear the main burden of health-care costs. Only 28 percent believed the government should bear the burden, and a small 13 percent believed the employers should foot the bill for rising costs associated with obesity and other problems.[7] This example illustrates the legal and social pressures to act appropriately to protect children from the dangers of obesity. Society has developed rules—both legal and implied—to guide companies in their efforts to earn profits through means that do not bring harm to individuals or to society at large.

business ethics

the principles and standards that guide the behavior of individuals and groups in the world of business

Business ethics comprises the principles and standards that guide the behavior of individuals and groups in the world of business. Managers, employees, consumers, industry associations, government regulators, business partners, and special-interest groups all contribute to these conventions, and they may change over time. The most basic of these standards have been codified as laws and regulations to encourage companies to conform to society's expectations of business conduct. As we said in Chapter 4, public concerns about accounting fraud and conflicts of interest in the securities industry led to the passage of the Sarbanes-Oxley Act to restore the public's trust in the stock market. The chair of the Securities and Exchange Commission, who enforces many aspects of the act, issued the challenge for "American organizations to behave more ethically than the law requires to help restore investors' trust."[8]

It is vital to recognize that business ethics goes beyond legal issues. Ethical business decisions foster trust in business relationships, and as we discussed in Chapter 1, trust is a key factor in improving productivity and achieving success in most organizations. When companies deviate from the prevailing standards of industry and society, the result is customer dissatisfaction, lack of trust, and lawsuits. Table 5.1 reflects increasing distrust of business among Americans as reported by a leading polling organization, Yankelovich Partners, Inc. A global opinion poll for the World Economic Forum concluded that public trust in companies has eroded and dropped significantly over the last few years. Public trust in national governments and the United Nations has fallen significantly too.[9] Consumers in other countries also avoid businesses or products because of negative perceptions. According to a survey, two-thirds of consumers in their thirties and forties in the United Kingdom boycotted brands because of "unethical behavior" by the manufacturers. Ninety-five percent of the 1,000 consumers surveyed indicated they would never purchase the brands.[10]

TABLE 5.1	American Distrust of Business		
	80%	**70%**	**61%**
	American business is too concerned about profits, not concerned about responsibilities to workers, consumers, & the environment.	If the opportunity arises, most businesses will take advantage of the public if they feel they are not likely to be found out.	Even long established companies cannot be trusted to make safe, durable products without the government setting industry standards.

Source: J. Walker Smith, Ann Clurman, and Craig Wood of Yankelovich Partners, Inc., *Point,* February 2005, www.RacomBooks.com; results from Yankelovich MONITOR.

Largely in response to this crisis, business decisions and activities have come under greater scrutiny by many different constituents, including consumers, employees, investors, government regulators, and special-interest groups. Additionally, new legislation and regulations designed to encourage higher ethical standards in business have been put in place.

Some businesspeople choose to behave ethically because of enlightened self-interest or the expectation that "ethics pays." They want to act responsibly and assume that the public and customers will reward the company for its ethical actions. Avon, for example, is a company that achieves success, contributes to society, and has ethical management. CEO Andrea Jung works in the high-risk area of direct selling, without scandals or major ethical issues. In 2004, Jung was named one of *Fortune*'s 100 most powerful women.[11] According to *Business Week,* Jung's leadership has resulted in Avon's economic and social performance being recognized by many stakeholders. The company's contribution to breast cancer research, and awareness generation, has given it leadership in the area of strategic philanthropy. Avon has also won approval to conduct direct selling in China—the first approval for a U.S. company since China banned the practice in 1998.[12]

FOUNDATIONS OF BUSINESS ETHICS

Because all individuals and groups within a company may not have embraced the same set of values, there is always the possibility of ethical conflict. Most ethical issues in an organizational context are addressed openly whenever a policy, code, or rule is questioned. Even then, it may be hard to distinguish between the ethical issue and the legal means used to resolve it. Because it is difficult to draw a boundary between legal and ethical issues, all questionable issues need an organizational mechanism for resolution.

The legal ramifications of some issues and situations may be obvious, but questionable decisions and actions more often result in disputes that must be resolved through some type of negotiation or even litigation. A federal grand jury indicted Martha Stewart on charges of securities fraud, conspiracy, making false statements, and obstruction of justice but not insider trading. In 2004, the judge threw out the most serious charges against her—securities fraud. However, just one week later, a jury convicted her on four remaining charges of making false statements and conspiracy to obstruct justice, and she was sentenced to serve five months in jail and five months in home detention. She finished her jail time in 2005. After HealthSouth Corporation was investigated for allegedly inflating earnings by $2.5 billion, eleven former employees, including all of the firm's former chief financial officers, pleaded guilty to fraud charges.[13] In 2006, HealthSouth agreed to issue stocks and warrants valued at $215 million, and the company insurers agreed to pay $230 million cash.[14] Richard M. Scrushy, founder and former CEO, was acquitted of criminal charges. However, just a couple of months later, he was ordered to return nearly $50 million in bonuses paid to him during the massive accounting fraud at the health-care company.[15] Even though Scrushy triumphed over the Justice Department attempt to convict him of corporate fraud, in 2006 an Alabama jury convicted him of six charges of bribery, conspiracy, and mail fraud. He was convicted of funneling $500,000 to former Alabama Governor Don Siegelman in exchange for a seat on the state hospital regulatory board. He could face as many as thirty years in prison but will appeal the conviction.[16] Such highly publicized cases strengthen the perception that ethical standards in business need to be raised.

When ethical disputes wind up in court, the costs and distractions associated with litigation can be devastating to a business. In addition to the compensatory or nominal damages actually incurred, punitive damages may be imposed on a company that is judged to have acted improperly to punish the firm and to send an intimidating message to others. The legal system, therefore, provides a formal venue for businesspeople to resolve ethical as well as legal disputes; in fact, many of the examples we cite in this chapter had to be resolved through the courts. To avoid the costs of litigation, companies should develop systems to monitor complaints, suggestions, and other feedback from stakeholders. In many cases, issues can be negotiated or resolved without legal intervention. Strategic responsibility entails systems for listening to, understanding, and effectively managing stakeholder concerns.[17]

A high level of personal morality may not be sufficient to prevent an individual from violating the law in an organizational context in which even experienced attorneys debate the exact meaning of the law. Because it is impossible to train all the members of an organization as lawyers, the identification of ethical issues and the implementation of standards of conduct that incorporate both legal and ethical concerns are the best approach to preventing crime and avoiding civil litigation. Codifying ethical standards into meaningful policies that spell out what is and is not acceptable gives businesspeople an opportunity to reduce the probability of behavior that could create legal problems. Without proper ethical training and guidance, it is impossible for the average business manager to understand the exact boundaries for illegal behavior in the areas of price fixing, fraud, export–import violations, copyright violations, insider trading, and so on. Even top executives have been accused of violations such as insider trading. Sam Waksal, former CEO of ImClone, was arrested and charged with selling stock and sharing information with family members that ImClone's promising cancer drug Erbitux would not receive FDA approval. Waksal was sentenced to seven years and three months in prison, fined $3 million, and ordered to pay $1.26 million in restitution for insider trading that ensnared friends and family, including Martha Stewart.[18]

Although the values of honesty, respect, and trust are often assumed to be self-evident and universally accepted, business decisions involve complex and detailed discussions in which correctness may not be so clear-cut. Both employees and managers need experience within their specific industry to understand how to operate in gray areas or to handle close calls in evolving areas. The 2005 State of Corporate Citizenship in the U.S. report from the Center for Corporate Citizenship (CCC) at Boston College shows that although companies are active and are participating in a wide range of issues, their actions often lag behind their expressed attitudes. Corporate citizenship is viewed as a central part of good business practice, with 81 percent of respondents indicating that corporate citizenship needs to be a priority for companies and 69 percent saying the public has a right to expect good corporate citizenship. Despite their enthusiasm, however, 80 percent say good corporate citizenship should not be enforced through additional laws or regulations. In fact, 60 percent of those participating in the survey say they see businesses as societal stewards that integrate internal priorities with obligations to do right by society. Companies seem to be committed "more through words than deeds." According to a Roper poll, more than 72 percent of U.S. adults—up from 66 percent—say they believe wrongdoing is widespread and that executives are bent on "destroying the environment, cooking the books, and lining their own pockets."[19]

Many people who have limited business experience suddenly find themselves required to make decisions about product quality, advertising, pricing, sales techniques, hiring practices, privacy, and pollution control. For example, how do advertisers know when they are making misleading statements versus "puffery" in advertising? Bayer is "the world's best aspirin," Hush Puppies, "the earth's most comfortable shoes," and Firestone (before recalling 6.5 million tires) promised "quality you can trust."[20] The personal values learned through nonwork socialization from family, religion, and school may not provide specific guidelines for these complex business decisions. In other words, a person's experiences and decisions at home, in school, and in the community may be quite different from the experiences and the decisions he or she has to make at work. Moreover, the interests and values of individual employees may differ from those of the company in which they work, from industry standards, and from society in general. When personal values are inconsistent with the configuration of values held by the work group, ethical conflict may ensue. It is important that a shared vision of acceptable behavior develop from an organizational perspective to cultivate consistent and reliable relationships with all concerned stakeholders. A shared vision of ethics that is part of an organization's culture can be questioned, analyzed, and modified as new issues develop. However, business ethics should relate to work environment decisions and should not control or influence personal ethical issues.

ETHICAL ISSUES IN BUSINESS

Classification of Ethical Issues

ethical issue

a problem, situation, or opportunity requiring an individual, group, or organization to choose among several actions that must be evaluated as right or wrong, ethical or unethical

An **ethical issue** is a problem, situation, or opportunity requiring an individual, group, or organization to choose among several actions that must be evaluated as right or wrong, ethical or unethical. Surveys can render a useful overview of the many unsettled ethical issues in business. A constructive next step toward identifying and resolving ethical issues is to classify the issues relevant to most business organizations. In this section, we examine ethical issues related to abusive behavior, lying, conflict of interest, fraud, and discrimination. There are also issues related to business decisions that harm consumers, such as products that cause obesity, or that encourage socially unacceptable behavior in children, such as the consumption of alcohol. The Global Initiatives box in this chapter provides additional insights on ethical issues involved in marketing harmful products to children. Ethical issues related to information technology are addressed in Chapter 11.

Although not all-inclusive or mutually exclusive, these classifications provide an overview of some major ethical issues that business decision makers face. Just because an unsettled situation or activity is an ethical issue does not mean the behavior is necessarily unethical. An ethical issue is simply a situation, a problem, or even an opportunity that requires thought, discussion, or investigation to determine the moral impact of the decision. And because the business world is dynamic, new ethical issues are emerging all the time. Table 5.2 defines specific ethical issues identified by employees in the National Business Ethics Survey (NBES). Two types of misconduct have been considered the leading ethical issues since 2000. Abusive or intimidating behavior ranks as the most observed misconduct, and lying to various stakeholders is the second most observed misconduct. Conflicts of interest remain a strong number three ethical issue. Many of the issues discussed in this chapter are related to issues in Table 5.2.

Table 5.2 indicates the percentage of employees who observed specific types of misconduct. Employees could select more than one form of misconduct; therefore, each type of misconduct represents the percentage of employees who saw that

TABLE 5.2	Specific Types of Misconduct Observed	
	Abusive or intimidating behavior toward employees	21%
	Lying to employees, customers, vendors, or to the public	19%
	A situation that places employee interests over organizational interests	18%
	Violations of safety regulations	16%
	Misreporting of actual time worked	16%
	E-mail and Internet abuse	13%
	Discrimination on the basis of race, color, gender, age, or similar categories	12%
	Stealing or theft	11%
	Sexual harassment	9%
	Provision of goods or services that fail to meet specifications	8%
	Misuse of confidential information	7%
	Alteration of documents	6%
	Falsification or misrepresentation of financial records or reports	5%
	Improper use of competitors' inside information	4%
	Price fixing	3%
	Giving or accepting bribes, kickbacks, or inappropriate gifts	3%

Source: Copyright © 2005 Ethics Resource Center, *2005 National Business Ethics Survey: How Employees View Ethics in Their Organizations* (Washington, DC: 2005), p. 25. Reprinted with permission from The Ethics Resource Center.

Ethical Concerns About Kidsbeer in Japan

Kidsbeer is a drink developed and produced in Japan. It is a cola beverage that looks like beer; it has the same color, the same froth, and is packaged in a brown bottle. Kidsbeer is sold in a 330 milliliter (about 11.5 ounces) bottle and sells for roughly $3.30. The makers of Kidsbeer point out that children mimic adults, and Kidsbeer is a nonalcoholic drink that children can enjoy while their parents drink the more potent alternative. Kidsbeer's slogan is, "Even kids cannot stand life unless they have a drink."

The drink was originally called Guarana. It was sold at the Shitamachi-ya restaurant in Fukuoka, which is managed by Yuichi Asaba. After Asaba named the cola "Kidsbeer," it became a hit with children. The demand for the cola was so great that Asaba outsourced the production of Kidsbeer to a beverage maker called Tomomasu. Tomomasu made minor adjustments to the formula by increasing its frothiness and decreasing its sweetness. The manufacturer began sending out the first shipments late in 2003. The first shipment was only 200 bottles, but the beverage soon gained popularity. It is now offered in more than 150 restaurants and supermarkets throughout Japan. Monthly shipments increased to 75,000 by September 2005.

Many people feel that the beverage is dangerous and should not be consumed by children because it will entice children to participate in underage drinking. An advertisement for Kidsbeer shows a young boy crying after failing a math test and then shedding tears of joy after drinking a Kidsbeer. Another advertisement shows a man toasting his beer glass to a glass of his daughter's Kidsbeer. The president of Tomomasu, Satoshi Tomada, believes that Kidsbeer makes children feel more mature and a better part of special events and holidays.

Tomomasu has considered entering foreign markets such as Europe, New Zealand, and the United States. Officials in Britain want nothing to do with Kidsbeer. Tim Loughton, a British official said, "This product would be an alarming development for a nation which is already succumbing to a binge drinking culture. If manufacturers encourage children to have a dry run for drinking, it will only train children to experiment with real alcohol even earlier."

Alcohol Concern, an agency on alcohol abuse, has attacked Kidsbeer for glamorizing alcohol to children. Many advocates believe that Kidsbeer sends the wrong messages to young people. Despite the controversy, the British Soft Drinks Association believes there are no reasons Kidsbeer should not be offered in Britain if the firm develops better marketing sensitivity. Officials in New Zealand said they would fight the release but admitted that there is likely little that they could do to prevent Kidsbeer from entering New Zealand. They hope that pressure groups and the community deter market entry.

Anheuser-Busch caused an outrage in 1978 with the release of a beer-like drink called Chelsea. The beverage foamed like beer and had one-half of a percent alcohol content. Anheuser-Busch quickly removed the product from the market after critics called it "baby beer." Royal Crown was the last company to market a "children's beer." Its Royal Crown Draft Premium Cola got the attention of the White House drug policy advisor, Lee P. Brown, in 1995. The beverage looked similar to beer and was sold in a brown bottle. Royal Crown eventually changed its package to comply with officials' request. Most sugar-based drinks such as apple juice have a small percentage of alcohol, and it would be impossible to drink enough Chelsea to get drunk. However, some children consumed Chelsea and claimed to be drunk.

A similar ethical situation exists with candy cigarettes. World Candies and Necco still manufacture and sell candy cigarettes both in candy stores and on the Internet. Some cigarette companies actually once allowed candy cigarette manufacturers to replicate logos and package design. Research has shown that sixth graders who have used candy cigarettes are twice as likely to smoke tobacco cigarettes. Many countries have passed legislation banning the sale of candy cigarettes. Canada, Finland, Australia, Saudi Arabia, the United Kingdom, and Norway all have passed such laws. Legislation banning candy cigarettes in the United States has failed twice, once in 1970 and again in 1990.[21]

particular act. Although Table 5.2 documents many types of ethical issues that exist in organizations, due to the almost infinite number of ways that misconduct can occur, it is impossible in this chapter to list every conceivable ethical issue.

Abusive or Intimidating Behavior

Abusive or intimidating behavior is the most common ethical problem for employees, but what does it mean to be abusive or intimidating? The concepts can mean anything from physical threats, false accusations, annoying a coworker, profanity, insults, yelling, harshness, and ignoring someone, to being unreasonable, and the meaning of these words can differ by person. It is important to understand that each term falls along a continuum. For example, what one person may define as yelling might be another's definition of normal speech. Civility in our society has been a concern, and the workplace is no exception. The productivity level of many organizations has been damaged by the time spent unraveling abusive relationships.

Abusive behavior is difficult to assess and manage because of diversity in culture and lifestyles. What does it mean to speak profanely? Is profanity only related to specific words or other such terms that are common in today's business world? If you are using words that are normal in your language but others consider profanity, have you just insulted, abused, or disrespected them?

Within the concept of abusive behavior, intent should be a consideration. If the employee was trying to convey a compliment when the comment was considered abusive, then it was probably a mistake. The way (voice inflection) a word is said can be important. Add to this the fact that we now live in a multicultural environment doing business and working with many different cultural groups and the business-person soon realizes the depth of the ethical and legal issues that may arise. There are problems of word meanings by age and within cultures. For example, an expression such as, "Did you guys hook up last night?" can have various meanings, including some that could be considered offensive in a work environment.

These are only a few helpful points to remember in avoiding abusive or intimidating ethical issues in business today. Each company has formal and informal ways of interaction. Every company has different standards for this issue, and not all of them are ethical. It takes time within a firm to understand where the acceptable and unacceptable line is, and that the line can change at any time. Do not assume that communication used with close friends will fit into the work environment.

Bullying is associated with a hostile workplace when someone (or a group) considered a target is threatened, harassed, belittled, verbally abused, or overly criticized. Although bullying may create what some may call a hostile environment, this term is generally associated with sexual harassment. Although sexual harassment has legal recourse, bullying has little legal recourse at this time. Bullying can cause psychological damage that can result in health-endangering consequences to the target. As Table 5.3 indicates, bullying can use a mix of verbal, nonverbal, and manipulative threatening expressions to damage workplace productivity. One may wonder why workers tolerate such activities, but the problem is that 81 percent of workplace bullies are supervisors. A top officer at Boeing cited an employee survey indicating 26 percent had observed abusive or intimidating behavior by management.[22]

TABLE 5.3	Actions Associated with Bullies

1. Spreading rumors to damage others.

2. Blocking others' communication in the workplace.

3. Flaunting status or authority to take advantage of others.

4. Discrediting others' ideas and opinions.

5. Using e-mails to demean others.

6. Failing to communicate or return communication.

7. Insulting, yelling, and shouting.

8. Using terminology to discriminate by gender, race, or age.

9. Using eye or body language to hurt others or their reputation.

10. Taking credit for others' work or ideas.

Source: © O. C. Ferrell 2006.

Bullying can also occur between companies that are in intense competition. Even respected companies such as Intel have been accused of monopolistic bullying. A competitor, Advanced Micro Devices (AMD), claimed in a lawsuit that thirty-eight companies, including Dell and Sony, were strong-arming customers into buying Intel chips rather than those marketed by AMD. The AMD lawsuit seeks billions of dollars and will take years to litigate. In many cases, the alleged misconduct can not only have monetary and legal implications but can threaten reputation, investor confidence, and customer loyalty. A front cover *Forbes* headline stated "Intel to ADM: Drop Dead." An example of the intense competition and Intel's ability to use its large size won it the high-profile Apple account, displacing IBM and Freescale. ADM said it had no opportunity to bid because Intel offered to deploy 600 Indian engineers to help Apple software run more smoothly on Intel chips.[23]

Lying

To be honest is to tell the truth to the best of your ability; lying relates to distorting the truth. The three major types of lies include, first, joking without malice. A so-called white lie is not told to hurt someone's feelings. The second, lying by commission, is creating a perception or belief by words that intentionally deceives the receiver of the message. Examples include lying about being at work, on expense reports, or when carrying out work assignments. Commission also entails intentionally creating "noise" within the communication that knowingly confuses or deceives the receiver. Noise can be defined as technical explanations that the communicator knows the receiver does not understand. Using legal terms or terms relating to unfamiliar processes and systems to explain what was done in a work situation facilitates this type of lie. Lying by commission can involve complex forms, procedures, contracts, or words that are spelled the same but have different meanings or refuting the truth with a false statement.[24]

Third, lying by omission is intentionally not informing the receiver of material facts. A classic example for decades was the tobacco manufacturers that did not allow negative research results to appear on cigarettes and cigars. The drug Vioxx is being questioned because the manufacturer allegedly did not inform consumers as to the degree and occurrence of side effects, one of which is death. Finally, when lying damages others, it can be the focus of a lawsuit. For example, a fifty-state action against Ford for failing to disclose, once it became known, the safety risk associated with driving the Ford Explorer equipped with certain Firestone tires resulted in a $51.5 million nationwide settlement.[25]

You should be able to understand when a lie becomes unethical in business based on the context and intent to distort the truth. A lie becomes illegal if it is determined by the judgment of courts to damage others. Some businesspersons may believe that one must lie a little or that the occasional lie is sanctioned by the organization. The question you need to ask is whether lies are distorting openness, transparency, and other values that are associated with ethical behavior.[26]

Conflict of Interest

conflict of interest

the situation of an individual who must choose whether to advance his or her own interests, those of his or her organization, or those of some other group

A **conflict of interest** exists when an individual must choose whether to advance his or her own interests, those of his or her organization, or those of some other group. For example, a $1 million donation by Citigroup to the Ninety-second Street Y nursery school represents a possible conflict of interest. Jack Grubman, an analyst for Salomon Smith Barney, upgraded his rating for AT&T stock after Sanford Weill, the CEO of Citigroup (the parent company of Salomon Smith Barney), agreed to use his

A U.S. Customs Officer shows the results of a scan of a container off-loaded at the Port of Houston. Technology is an important component of the government's system to maintain security and the legality of imports.

influence to help Grubman's twins gain admission to the elite Manhattan nursery school. During the late 1990s, Grubman's boss, Citigroup Chairman Sandy Weill, an AT&T board member, had been upset that Citi wasn't getting any of AT&T's business. Grubman changed his AT&T rating to buy. A year later, he bragged in an e-mail that he had made the switch to placate Weill in exchange for Weill's help in getting Grubman's children into the exclusive Ninety-second Street Y nursery school. Grubman has denied elevating his rating for AT&T's stock to gain his children's admission to the school, but they were enrolled. Industry leaders still avoid him, publicly anyway, but on the fringes of the telecom industry, Grubman has had no trouble finding people who are willing to overlook his past or are simply unaware of it. According to a *Fortune* article, although Grubman was "banned from Wall Street, the former Telecom King wants to prove that he wasn't a huckster."[27] To avoid conflicts of interest, employees must be able to separate their private interests from their business dealings.

Organizations, too, must avoid potential conflicts of interest in providing goods or services. For example, Arthur Andersen LLP served as outside auditor for Waste Management, Inc., while providing consulting services to the firm—a situation that led the Securities and Exchange Commission to investigate charges that the consulting fees received by Arthur Andersen may have compromised the independence of its auditing of Waste Management's books. The accounting firm eventually agreed to pay $7 million to settle the case. Arthur Andersen later paid $100 million to settle a lawsuit brought against the firm by Waste Management shareholders. Within a year, Arthur Andersen found itself stuck in a pattern, paying out millions of dollars to settle similar federal charges and shareholder lawsuits surrounding accounting irregularities at Sunbeam and Qwest Communications, and investigations of its auditing of WorldCom, Enron, and Global Crossing resulted in Arthur Andersen closing its doors as an auditor.[28]

In many developed countries, it is generally recognized that employees should not accept bribes, personal payments, gifts, or special favors from people who hope to influence the outcome of a decision. However, as discussed later in this text, bribery is an accepted way of doing business in many countries. One source estimates that some $80 billion is paid out worldwide in the form of bribes or some other payoff every year.[29] According to a recent survey, four of ten companies say they have lost business in the last five years because a competitor paid a bribe. Companies in the United States were ranked fifth behind those in Canada, Germany, the Netherlands, and the United Kingdom in terms of complying with anticorruption laws.[30] Bribes also have been associated with the downfall of many managers, legislators, and government officials. When a government official accepts a bribe, it is usually from a business that seeks some favor, perhaps a chance to influence legislation that affects it. Giving bribes to legislators or public officials, then, is a business ethics issue.

Fraud

fraud
any false communication that deceives, manipulates, or conceals facts to create a false impression and damage others

When an individual engages in deceptive practices to advance his or her own interests over those of the organization or some other group, charges of illegal fraud may result. In general, **fraud** is any false communication that deceives, manipulates, or conceals facts to create a false impression when others are damaged or denied a benefit. It is

TABLE 5.4	Greatest Fraud Risks for Companies	
Conflicts of interest		63%
Fraudulent financial statements		57%
Billing schemes		31%
Expense and reimbursements schemes		29%
Bribery/economic extortion		25%

Source: 2005 Oversight Systems Report on Corporate Fraud questionnaire of 208 certified fraud examiners. In *USA Today,* Snapshots, February 2, 2006, p. B1.

considered a crime, and convictions may result in fines, imprisonment, or both. Fraud costs U.S. organizations more than $400 billion a year.[31] Insurance fraud alone costs the average American family between $200 and $300 annually.[32] Online fraud accounts for $2.6 billion stolen from online merchants by criminals per year.[33] Among the most common fraudulent activities employees report about their coworkers are stealing office supplies or shoplifting, claiming to have worked extra hours, and stealing money or products.[34] Table 5.4 indicates what fraud examiners view as the biggest risks to companies. In recent years, accounting fraud has become a major ethical issue, but as we will see, fraud can also relate to marketing and consumer issues as well.

ACCOUNTING FRAUD The field of accounting has changed dramatically over the last decade. The profession used to have a club-type mentality: Those who became certified public accountants (CPAs) were not concerned about competition. Now CPAs advertise their skills or short-term results in an environment in which competition has increased and overall billable hours have significantly decreased because of technological innovations. Pressures on accountants include time, reduced fees, client requests for altered opinions concerning financial conditions or for lower tax payments, and increased competition. Because of such pressures and the ethical predicaments they spawn, some accounting firms have had problems. Accounting firms have a responsibility to report a true and accurate picture of the financial condition of the companies for which they work. Failure to do so may result in charges and fines for both the accounting firm and the employing company. For example, Tyco International Ltd. agreed to pay $50 million to settle federal securities charges that it engaged in a $1 billion-plus accounting fraud and violated antibribery laws, putting an end to an ordeal that sent the company's former top executives to jail. As part of the settlement, in which Tyco did not admit or deny wrongdoing, the conglomerate agreed not to commit further accounting fraud and to pay a $50 million penalty. The agreement resolved Tyco's regulatory problems. However, the company, according to a spokeswoman, still faces "active litigation" from shareholders, including a class-action lawsuit alleging that Tyco investors lost billions from alleged Tyco wrongdoing stemming from its accounting from 1996 to 2002. The case lingered for nearly a year, in part because the SEC commissioners were sharply divided over when to penalize corporations involved in financial frauds and the SEC was working to finalize a list of factors to consider when fining a company.[35] Such scrutiny of financial reporting increased dramatically in the wake of the accounting scandals in the early 2000s. As a

TABLE 5.5	Major Firms Investigated for Accounting Fraud		
Enron	HealthSouth	Cendant
Credit Suisse First Boston	Computer Associates International	WorldCom
Imclone		Peregrine Systems
America On-Line	Royal Ahold	

Source: Federal Bureau of Investigation, http://www.fbi.gov/publications/financial/fcs_report052005/fcs_report052005.htm, accessed May 1, 2006. *The investigations in the table resulted in 120 indictments/informations and 79 convictions.*

result of the negative publicity surrounding the allegations of accounting fraud at a number of companies, many firms were forced to take a second look at their financial documents, and hundreds of companies chose to restate their earnings to avoid being drawn into accounting scandals.

Other issues that accountants face daily involve complex rules and regulations that must be followed, data overload, contingent fees, and commissions. An accountant's life is filled with rules and data that have to be interpreted correctly. As a result, accountants must abide by a strict code of ethics, which defines their responsibilities to their clients and the public interest. The code also discusses the concepts of integrity, objectivity, independence, and due care. Finally, the code delineates an accountant's scope and the nature of services that ethically should be provided. In this last portion of the code, contingent fees and commissions are indirectly addressed. Despite the standards provided by the code, the accounting industry has been the source of numerous fraud investigations in recent years. Table 5.5 shows major firms investigated for accounting fraud. At some companies, fraud is rewarded with stock options and bonuses for managing earnings.

Krispy Kreme, once a high-flying company, experienced a meltdown when two executives tried to manage earnings to meet Wall Street expectations. The company's stock, which had traded for $105/share in November 2000 before two stock splits, traded at $5/share in January 2006.[36] A poll by Harris Interactive found many scandal-plagued firms at the bottom of its annual survey of perceived corporate reputation, including Enron, Global Crossing, WorldCom, Andersen Worldwide, and Adelphia. The survey, which ranks companies according to how respondents rate them on twenty attributes, also found that public perceptions of trust had declined considerably as a result of the accounting scandals of the early twenty-first century. Joy Sever, a Harris vice president, reported, "The scandals cost many companies their emotional appeal, the strongest driver of reputation."[37] Former WorldCom CFO Scott Sullivan received a sentence of only five years for being chief architect of one of the biggest U.S. financial frauds because he cooperated with authorities. A U.S. district judge saluted his help in the prosecution of former WorldCom CEO Bernie Ebbers: "He provided information . . . without which Mr. Ebbers could not have been indicted." A jury convicted Ebbers of instigating an $11 billion fraud at WorldCom that cost thousands of employees their jobs and drove the company into bankruptcy protection.[38]

MARKETING FRAUD Communications that are false or misleading can destroy customers' trust in an organization. Lying, a major ethical issue within communications, may be a significant problem when there are material misrepresentations. It causes ethical predicaments in both external and internal communications because it destroys trust. False and deceptive advertising is a key issue in communications. Abuses in advertising can range from exaggerated claims and concealed facts to outright lying. Exaggerated claims are those that cannot be substantiated, as when a commercial states that a certain product is superior to any other on the market. Another form of advertising abuse involves making ambiguous statements with such imprecise words that the viewer, reader, or listener must infer the advertiser's intended message. These "weasel" words are inherently vague and enable the advertiser to deny any intent to deceive. The verb *help* is a good example (as in expressions such as "helps prevent," "helps fight," "helps make you feel").[39] Consumers may view such advertisements as unethical because they fail to communicate all the information needed to make a good purchasing decision or because they deceive the consumer outright.

The Federal Trade Commission and other agencies are monitoring more closely the advertisements for work-at-home business ventures. Consumers are losing millions of dollars each year responding to ads for phony business opportunities, such as those promising $50,000 a year for doing medical billing from a home computer.[40] Sometimes, differing interpretations of advertising messages create ethical issues that must be resolved in court. For example, the television ads for HMO Kaiser Permanente state that Kaiser is a place where "no one but you and your doctor decides what's right for you" and "there are no financial pressures to prevent your physician from giving you the medical care you need." According to a lawsuit filed by a California consumer group, however, Kaiser drastically reduced its medical budget as it added hundreds of thousands of new members. The consumer group also alleged that Kaiser set quotas for doctors to reduce the number of patients hospitalized, while tying a significant portion of physician pay to meeting the quotas.[41]

Labeling issues are even murkier. For example, Mott's, Inc., the nation's leading producer of applesauce and apple juice, agreed to revise the labels of some of its fruit products after New York's attorney general claimed they were misleading consumers. The products—often made by blending apple juice with enough grape juice or cherry juice to make the designated flavor—had labels with the phrase "100% Juice" and a picture of grapes or cherries and the fruits' names in large lettering underneath. The attorney general argued that placing the fruit's name under "100% Juice" could lead consumers to assume that the products were 100% grape juice or cherry juice. Mott's admitted no wrongdoing but agreed to pay $177,500 to cover the investigation costs and to institute a minor change to the labels in question.[42]

A jury awarded $7 million in compensatory damages to the widow and children of Leonel Garza, who died of a heart attack after taking Vioxx for less than a month. The jury also found that Merck had acted with "neglect" and awarded the Garza family $25 million in punitive damages. The decision struck a blow against Merck's assertion that it acted responsibly in developing and marketing Vioxx, which it took off the market in September 2004 after a study linked the drug to an increased risk of heart attacks and strokes in patients who took it for eighteen months or longer. Perhaps more damaging, it establishes a precedent of blaming Vioxx for even very short-term usage of the drug. Merck plans to appeal the verdict. Merck knew about Vioxx's risks years before it withdrew the drug from the market but put profit before patient safety. So far, Merck has won three of the six cases that have gone to trial. But the losses have been expensive.[43]

Advertising and direct sales communication can also mislead by concealing facts within a message. For instance, a salesperson anxious to sell a medical insurance policy might list a large number of illnesses covered by the policy but fail to mention that it does not include some commonly covered illnesses. The pharmaceutical industry has adopted new guidelines for direct-to-consumer advertising in the United States. The industry has been under heavy fire from doctors and politicians since the withdrawal of Vioxx. In response to its critics, who say the onslaught of advertising for Vioxx pushed patients who may not have needed the drug to take it, U.S. drug makers, in an unprecedented demonstration of cross-industry cooperation, have voluntarily agreed to take steps to limit the scope, timing, and content of their advertising.[44]

The fastest growth of fraudulent activity is in the area of direct marketing, which employs the telephone and nonpersonal media to communicate information to customers, who then purchase products via mail, telephone, or the Internet. In 2005, consumers reported losses of $680 million resulting from fraud to the Federal Trade Commission. Of these 685,000 complaints, 255,565 concerned identity theft and 431,118 were about other forms of fraud. Internet-related complaints accounted for 46 percent of fraud reports and $335 million of reported losses.[45]

Consumer Fraud

consumer fraud

consumers attempt to deceive businesses for their own gain

Consumer fraud occurs when consumers attempt to deceive businesses for their own gain. In 2005, the FTC estimated that 25 million consumers had engaged in consumer fraud.[46] Shoplifting, for example, accounts for nearly 32 percent of the losses of the 118 largest U.S. retail chains, although this figure is still far outweighed by the nearly 49 percent of losses perpetrated by store employees, according to the National Retail Security Survey. Together with vendor fraud and administrative error, these losses cost U.S. retailers more than $31 billion annually.[47]

Consumers engage in many other forms of fraud against businesses, including price-tag switching, item switching, lying to obtain age-related and other discounts, and taking advantage of generous return policies by returning used items, especially clothing that has been worn (with the price tags still attached). Such behavior by consumers affects retail stores as well as other consumers who, for example, may unwittingly purchase new clothing that has actually been worn.[48]

Consumer fraud involves intentional deception to derive an unfair economic advantage by an individual or group over an organization. Examples of fraudulent activities include shoplifting, collusion or duplicity, and guile. Collusion typically involves an employee who assists the consumer in fraud. For example, a cashier may not ring up all merchandise or may give an unwarranted discount. Duplicity may involve a consumer staging an accident in a grocery store and then seeking damages against the store for its lack of attention to safety. A consumer may purchase, wear, and then return an item of clothing for a full refund. In other situations, the consumer may ask for a refund by claiming a defect. Although some of these acts warrant legal prosecution, they can be very difficult to prove, and many companies are reluctant to accuse patrons of a crime when there is no way to verify it. Businesses that operate with the "customer is always right" philosophy have found that some consumers will take advantage of this promise and have therefore modified return policies to curb unfair use.

Discrimination

Another important ethics issue in business today is discrimination. Once dominated by white men, the U.S. workforce today includes significantly more women, African Americans, Hispanics, and other minorities, as well as workers with disabilities and older workers. Experts project that within the next fifty years, Hispanics will represent 24 percent of the population, while African Americans and Asians/Pacific Islanders will make up 15 percent and 9 percent, respectively.[49] These groups have traditionally faced discrimination and higher unemployment rates and have been denied opportunities to assume leadership roles in corporate America.[50]

Discrimination remains a significant ethical issue in business despite nearly forty years of legislation to outlaw it. The most significant piece of legislation is Title VII of the Civil Rights Act of 1964, which prohibits employment discrimination on the basis of race, national origin, color, religion, and gender. This law is fundamental to employees' rights to join and advance in an organization according to merit rather than one of the characteristics just mentioned. As a result of racial discrimination class-action settlements, some companies, such as Coca-Cola and ChevronTexaco, are being required to establish independent task forces to monitor and modify company practices to combat racial discrimination.

Additional laws passed in the 1970s, 1980s, and 1990s were designed to prohibit discrimination related to pregnancy, disabilities, age, and other factors. The Americans with Disabilities Act, for example, prohibits companies from discriminating on the basis of physical or mental disability in all employment practices and requires them

While there is much evidence of increasing equity in the workplace, men still tend to earn more than women who are in comparable positions.

'Three-fourths of a penny for your thoughts...'

to make facilities accessible to and usable by persons with disabilities.[51] The Age Discrimination in Employment Act specifically outlaws hiring practices that discriminate against people between the ages of forty-nine and sixty-nine, but it also bans policies that require employees to retire before the age of seventy. Despite this legislation, charges of age discrimination persist in the workplace.[52] The Supreme Court made it easier for any worker over forty to allege age discrimination, ruling that employers can be held liable even if they never intended any harm. The ruling means that workers age forty and older—about half the nation's workforce—now have less of a burden to raise their claim in court when suing under federal law. Currently, there are more than 70 million workers who are age forty or older, and the number is growing. The federal government predicts that by 2010, more than half of all workers will be forty or older. For example, Foot Locker Specialty paid $3.5 million to settle charges that it systematically laid off workers over forty to reduce costs, although the company denied any wrongdoing.[53] A survey by the American Association for Retired Persons (AARP), an advocacy organization for people fifty and older, highlighted how little most companies value older workers. When AARP mailed invitations to 10,000 companies for a chance to compete for a listing in *Modern Maturity* magazine as one of the "best employers for workers over 50," it received just fourteen applications. Given that nearly 20 percent of the nation's workers will be fifty-five years old or over by 2015, many companies need to change their approach toward older workers.[54]

affirmative action programs

programs that involve efforts to recruit, hire, train, and promote qualified individuals from groups that have traditionally been discriminated against on the basis of race, gender, or other characteristics

To help build workforces that reflect their customer base, many companies have initiated **affirmative action programs**, which involve efforts to recruit, hire, train, and promote qualified individuals from groups that have traditionally been discriminated against on the basis of race, gender, or other characteristics. Such initiatives may be imposed on an employer by federal law on federal government contractors and subcontractors, as part of a settlement agreement with a state or federal agency, or by a court order.[55] Many companies voluntarily implement affirmative action plans to build a more diverse workforce.[56] For example, a Chicago real estate developer launched the Female Employment Initiative, an outreach program designed to create opportunities for women in the construction industry through training programs, counseling and information services, and referral listings to help employers identify available women workers.[57]

Although many people believe that affirmative action requires the use of quotas to govern employment decisions, it is important to note that two decades of Supreme Court rulings have made it clear that affirmative action does *not* require or permit quotas, reverse discrimination, or favorable treatment of unqualified women or minorities. To ensure that affirmative action programs are fair, the Supreme Court has established a number of standards to guide their implementation: (1) there must be a strong reason for developing an affirmative action program, (2) affirmative action programs must apply only to qualified candidates, and (3) affirmative action programs must be limited and temporary and therefore cannot include "rigid and inflexible quotas."[58]

The Equal Employment Opportunity Commission (EEOC) monitors compliance with Title VII, with a mission to "promote equal opportunity in employment through administrative and judicial enforcement of the federal civil rights laws and through education and technical assistance."[59] A special type of discrimination, sexual harassment, is also prohibited through Title VII. As part of its settlement in

Internet Crime Complaint Center

iC3 INTERNET CRIME COMPLAINT CENTER

Data, Tools, and Resources for Enforcement Professionals

The Internet Crime Complaint Center (IC3) is an alliance between the National White Collar Crime Center (NW3C) and the Federal Bureau of Investigation (FBI). IC3's mission is to address crime committed over the Internet. For victims of Internet crime, IC3 provides a convenient and easy way to alert authorities of a suspected violation. For law enforcement and regulatory agencies, IC3 offers a central repository for complaints related to Internet crime, uses the information to quantify patterns, and provides timely statistical data of current trends.

Features

• Provides a central point for Internet crime victims to report and to alert an appropriate agency on-line at **www.ic3.gov**

• Collects, reviews, and refers Internet crime complaints to law enforcement agencies with jurisdiction to aid in preventive and investigative efforts

• Identifies current crime trends over the Internet

Benefits

• Provides an analytical repository for Internet crime complaints

• Analyzes and refers all fraudulent activity identified on the Internet to the appropriate local, state, or federal law enforcement authority

• Aids in the development of law enforcement training to address identified Internet crime problems

• Serves as the catalyst that allows law enforcement and regulatory agencies to network and share data

• Potentially reduces the amount of economic loss by Internet crime throughout the United States

To file an Internet crime complaint, visit the IC3 Web site at www.ic3.gov.

August 2005

NW3C NATIONAL WHITE COLLAR CRIME CENTER
Integrity Quality Service

The Internet Crime Complaint Center is a partnership between the government and nonprofit organizations in the fight against ethical and legal problems with technology.

a sexual discrimination lawsuit, Mitsubishi Motors of America promised to adopt a companywide, zero-tolerance program against harassment. The agreement also included a court-appointed panel to monitor company efforts.[60]

According to the EEOC, an employer may not fire, harass, or otherwise "retaliate" against an individual for filing a charge of discrimination, participating in a discrimination proceeding, or otherwise opposing discrimination. The Americans with Disabilities Act also protects individuals from coercion, intimidation, threat, harassment, or interference in their exercise of their own rights or their encouragement of someone else's exercise of rights granted by the act.[61] Legal specialists say employers can take steps to minimize retaliation complaints through beefed-up training, investigations, and follow-up efforts. Complaints to the Equal Employment Opportunity Commission that include retaliation allegations have more than doubled since 1992 and account for a record 30 percent of charges filed. Sometimes, employees win retaliation claims in court even when their bias allegations are dismissed. In a pending Supreme Court case, a jury ruled in favor of an employee's retaliation claims but struck down her sexual-harassment claims.[62]

Information Technology

The final category of ethical issues relates to technology and the numerous advances made in the Internet and other forms of electronic communications in the last few years. As the number of people who use the Internet increases, the areas of concern related to its use increase as well. Some issues that must be addressed by businesses include monitoring employee use of available technology, consumer privacy, site development and online marketing, and legal protection of intellectual properties, such as music, books, and movies. The recording companies have filed more than 10,000 lawsuits against song swappers, mostly against users of file-sharing programs such as Kazaa, Morpheus, and Grockster. Since the Recording Industry Association of America lawsuits began, file sharing has become more widespread. Millions of people log into peer-to-peer (P2P) networks at any one time.[63] This issue is discussed in detail in Chapter 11.

Recognizing an Ethical Issue

Although we have described a number of relationships and situations that may generate ethical issues, it can be difficult to recognize specific ethical issues in practice. Failure to acknowledge ethical issues is a great danger in any organization, particularly if business is treated as a game in which ordinary rules of fairness do not apply. Sometimes, people who take this view do things that are not only unethical but also illegal to maximize their own position or boost the profits or goals of the organization.

Figure 5.1 identifies the frequency of misconduct observed by employees in the most recent Ethics Resource Center Survey. Over half (52 percent) of the national sample of employees observed some type of misconduct. Figure 5.1 provides a view of how many different forms of misconduct were observed. These data provide evidence that misconduct is widespread and a significant issue in business.

An ethical issue reflects a concern, debate, or a decision that could be judged as either right or wrong. The whole process of ethical decision making means that thought, discussion, or even research is necessary to determine an appropriate action. The issues that often get the most publicity are not necessarily the issues that are most frequently dealt with in the workplace.

One way to determine whether a specific behavior or situation has an ethical component is to ask other individuals in the business how they feel about it and whether they approve. Another way is to determine whether the organization has adopted

| FIGURE 5.1 | Observed Frequency of Misconduct by Employees |

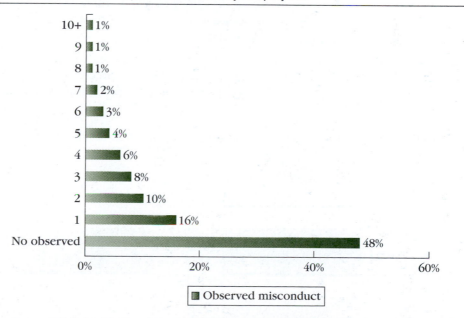

Source: *2005 National Business Ethics Survey: How Employees View Ethics at Work* (Washington, DC: Ethics Resource Center, 2005), p. 25. Reprinted with permission from The Ethics Resource Center.

specific policies on the activity. An activity approved of by most members of an organization, if it is also customary in the industry, is probably ethical. An issue, activity, or situation that can withstand open discussion between many stakeholders, both inside and outside the organization, and survive untarnished probably does not pose ethical problems. For instance, when engineers and designers at Ford Motor Co. discussed what type of gas-tank protection should be used in its Pinto automobile, they reached consensus within the organization, but they did not take into account the interests of various external stakeholders, such as the public's desire for maximum safety. Consequently, even though they might have believed the issue had no ethical dimension, Ford erred in not opening up the issue to public scrutiny. (As it turned out, the type of gas-tank protection used in the Pinto resulted in several fires and deaths when the cars were involved in rear-end collisions.)

UNDERSTANDING THE ETHICAL DECISION-MAKING PROCESS

To grasp the significance of ethics in business decision making, it is important to understand how ethical decisions are made within the context of an organization. Understanding the ethical decision-making process can help individuals and businesses design strategies to deter misconduct. Our descriptive approach to understanding ethical decision making does not prescribe what to do but, rather, provides a framework for managing ethical behavior in the workplace. Figure 5.2 depicts this framework, which shows how individual factors, organizational relationships, and opportunity interact to determine ethical decisions in business.

Individual Factors

Individuals make ethical choices on the basis of their own concepts of right or wrong, and they act accordingly in their daily lives. Studies suggest that individual ethics are reaching a new low. A survey of nearly 25,000 high school students revealed that

---

FIGURE 5.2   Factors That Influence the Ethical Decision-Making Process

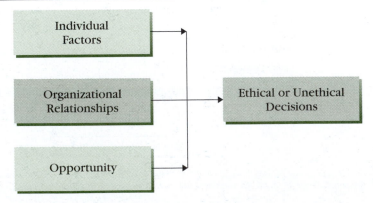

62 percent admitted to cheating on an exam at least once; 35 percent confessed to copying documents from the Internet; 27 percent admitted to shoplifting; and 23 percent owned up to cheating to win in sports.[64] If today's students are tomorrow's leaders, there is likely to be a correlation between acceptable behavior today and tomorrow, adding to the argument that the leaders of today must be prepared for the ethical risks associated with this downward trend. According to another poll by Deloitte and Touche of teenagers aged thirteen to eighteen years old, when asked if people who practice good business ethics are more successful than those who don't, 69 percent of teenagers agreed.[65] On the other hand, another survey indicated that many students do not define copying answers from another student's paper or downloading music or content for classroom work as cheating.[66] For example, a survey found that one of four Americans says it is acceptable to cheat on their taxes,[67] and according to *Golf Digest*, CEOs cheat at golf at four times the rate of average golfers.[68] Significant factors that affect the ethical decision-making process include an individual's personal moral philosophy, stage of moral development, motivation, and other personal factors such as gender, age, and experience.

MORAL PHILOSOPHY[69] Many people have justified difficult decisions by citing the golden rule ("Do unto others as you would have them do unto you") or some other principle. Such principles, or rules, which individuals apply in deciding what is right or wrong, are often referred to as **moral philosophies**. These philosophies are learned through socialization by family members, social groups, religion, and formal education. Most moral philosophies can be classified as consequentialism, ethical formalism, or justice.

Consequentialism is a class of moral philosophy that considers a decision right or acceptable if it accomplishes a desired result such as pleasure, knowledge, career growth, the realization of self-interest, or utility. For example, the nation's largest disability insurer, Unum Provident Insurance Co., has been accused by former employees of terminating legitimate policies and cheating people with disabilities out of money to which they were entitled in an effort to increase company profits. The employees allege that the company had an incentive structure that rewarded workers for cheating customers while saving money for the company.[70] Egoism and utilitarianism are two important consequentialist philosophies that often guide decision making in business.

Egoism is a philosophy that defines right or acceptable conduct in terms of the consequences for the individual. Egoists believe they should make decisions that maximize their own self-interest, which, depending on the individual, may be defined as physical well-being, power, pleasure, fame, a satisfying career, a good family life, wealth, and so forth. In a decision-making situation, the egoist will probably choose the alternative that most benefits his or her self-interest. Many people feel that egoists are inherently unethical, that they focus on the short term, and that they will take advantage of any opportunity to exploit consumers or employees. An example of egoism in the business world might be telemarketers who prey on elderly consumers who may be vulnerable because of loneliness or fear of losing their financial independence. Tens of thousands of senior citizens fall victim to telemarketing fraud every year. In Tucson, Arizona, for example, police uncovered a telemarketing scam in which elderly people received calls telling them they had won a lottery or sweepstakes contest.

moral philosophies

principles, or rules, that individuals apply in deciding what is right or wrong

consequentialism

a class of moral philosophy that considers a decision right or acceptable if it accomplishes a desired result such as pleasure, knowledge, career growth, the realization of self-interest, or utility

egoism

a philosophy that defines right or acceptable conduct in terms of the consequences for the individual

However, the victims were also told that they needed to pay a "tax" to receive the contest winnings. In one case, the tax was $10,000.[71] The Federal Trade Commission receives more than 10,000 complaints a year from consumers about gifts, sweepstakes, and prize promotions. Many people receive telephone calls or postcards telling them they have won a big prize—only to find out that to claim it, they have to buy something or pay as much as $10,000 in fees or other charges.[72]

utilitarianism

a consequentialist philosophy that is concerned with seeking the greatest good for the greatest number of people

Utilitarianism is another consequentialist philosophy but is concerned with seeking the greatest good for the greatest number of people. Using a cost-benefit analysis, a utilitarian decision maker calculates the utility of the consequences of all possible alternatives and then chooses the one that achieves the greatest utility. For example, the Occupational Safety and Health Administration (OSHA) recently proposed new standards for ensuring health and safety in the workplace. Thus, the federal agency has concluded that the greatest utility and benefits to society and employees will result from greater corporate efforts and leadership on safety and health issues on the job.[73]

ethical formalism

a class of moral philosophy that focuses on the rights of individuals and on the intentions associated with a particular behavior rather than on its consequences

In contrast with consequentialism, **ethical formalism** is a class of moral philosophy that focuses on the rights of individuals and on the intentions associated with a particular behavior rather than on its consequences. Ethical formalists regard certain behaviors as inherently right, and their determination of rightness focuses on the individual actor, not on society. Thus, these perspectives are sometimes referred to as nonconsequentialism and the ethics of respect for persons. A recent survey by the Institute of Ethics, an independent research arm of the American Medical Association, found that some doctors are manipulating insurance reimbursement rules to ensure treatment for their patients. For instance, a doctor might code a patient's illness as a sleep disorder, which is usually covered by insurance, rather than depression, which is not covered by most insurance plans, so that the insurance company would reimburse the patient for prescribed medications. According to the survey, 39 percent of the physicians reported sometimes or often exaggerating to insurance companies, and 10 percent admitted to outright lies.[74] These doctors may be applying ethical formalism in their decisions to flout the rules for their patients' benefit. But the application of formalism in this context could be illegal if it violated the doctor's requirement to report accurately to the insurance company.

Contemporary ethical formalism has been greatly influenced by German philosopher Immanuel Kant, who developed the so-called categorical imperative: "Act as if the maxim of thy action were to become by thy will a universal law of nature."[75] Unlike utilitarians, ethical formalists contend that there are some things that people should not do, even to maximize utility. For example, an ethical formalist would consider it unacceptable for a coal mine to continue to operate if some workers became ill and died of black lung disease. A utilitarian, however, might consider some disease or death an acceptable consequence of a decision that resulted in large-scale employment and economic prosperity.

justice theory

a class of moral philosophy that relates to evaluations of fairness, or the disposition to deal with perceived injustices of others

Justice theory is a class of moral philosophy that relates to evaluations of fairness, or the disposition to deal with perceived injustices of others. Justice demands fair treatment and due reward in accordance with ethical or legal standards. In business, this requires that the rules an individual uses to determine justice be based on the perceived rights of individuals and on the intentions associated with a business interaction. Justice, therefore, is more likely to be based on nonconsequentialist moral philosophies than on consequentialist philosophies. Justice primarily addresses the issue of what individuals feel they are due based on their rights and performance in the workplace. For example, the U.S. Equal Employment Opportunity Commission exists to help employees who suspect the injustice of discrimination in the workplace.

There are three types of justice that can be used to assess fairness in different situations. Distributive justice evaluates the outcomes or results of a business relationship. For example, if an employee feels that she is paid less than her coworkers for the same work, she has concerns about distributive justice. Procedural justice assesses the processes and activities employed to produce an outcome or results. Procedural justice concerns about compensation would relate to the perception that salary and benefit decisions were consistent and fair to all categories of employees. A recent study found that procedural justice is associated with group cohesiveness and helping behaviors.[76] Interactional justice evaluates the communication processes used in the business relationship. Being untruthful about the reasons for missing work is an example of an interactional justice issue.[77]

It is important to recognize that there is no one "correct" moral philosophy to apply in resolving ethical and legal issues in the workplace. It is also important to acknowledge that each philosophy presents an ideal perspective and that most people seem to adapt a number of moral philosophies as they interpret the context of different decision-making situations.[78] Moreover, research suggests that individuals may apply different moral philosophies in different decision situations.[79] Each philosophy could result in a different decision in a situation requiring an ethical judgment. And depending on the situation, people may even change their value structure or moral philosophy when making decisions.[80]

STAGE OF MORAL DEVELOPMENT[81] One reason that different people make different decisions when confronted with similar ethical situations may be that they are in different stages of moral development. Psychologist Lawrence Kohlberg proposed that people progress through stages in their development of moral reasoning or, as he called it, cognitive moral development.[82] He believes that people progress through the following six stages:

1. The stage of punishment and obedience. An individual in this stage of development defines right as literal obedience to rules and authority and responds to rules in terms of the physical power of those who determine such rules. Individuals in this stage do not associate right and wrong with any higher order or moral philosophy but instead with a person who has power. For example, a plant supervisor may choose to go along with a superior's order to release untreated wastewater into a nearby stream, even though she knows it would be illegal, because she fears the superior's power to fire her if she does not comply.

2. The stage of individual instrumental purpose and exchange. A person in this stage defines right as that which serves his or her own needs. In this stage, people evaluate behavior on the basis of its fairness to themselves rather than solely on the basis of specific rules or authority figures. For example, a corporate buyer may choose to accept an expensive gift from a salesperson, despite the presence of a company rule prohibiting the acceptance of gifts, because the gift is something he

needs or wants. This stage is sometimes labeled the stage of reciprocity because, from a practical standpoint, ethical decisions are based on "you-scratch-my-back-and-I'll-scratch-yours" agreements instead of on principles such as loyalty or justice.

3. The stage of mutual interpersonal expectation, relationships, and conformity. An individual in this stage emphasizes others over himself or herself. Although these individuals still derive motivation from obedience to rules, they also consider the well-being of others. For example, a production manager might choose to obey an order from upper management to speed up an assembly line because she believes this action will generate more profit for the company and thereby preserve her employees' jobs.

4. The stage of social justice and conscience maintenance. A person in this stage determines what is right by considering duty to society as well as to other specific people. Duty, respect for authority, and maintaining social order become fundamental goals in decision making. For example, Jeffrey Wigand, a former executive at Brown & Williamson Tobacco Corporation, believed that the company was hiding from the public the truth that cigarettes are addictive and dangerous. He chose to "blow the whistle" by testifying against his former employer after he was fired.[83] Wigand's story was later dramatized in the movie *The Insider.*

5. The stage of prior rights, social contract, or utility. In this stage, an individual is concerned with upholding the basic rights, values, and legal contracts of society. Such individuals feel a sense of obligation or "social contract" to other groups and recognize that legal and moral points of view may conflict in some instances. To minimize conflict, persons in this stage base decisions on a rational calculation of overall utilities. For example, a business owner may choose to establish an organizational compliance program because it will serve as a buffer to prevent legal problems and to protect the company's good name.

6. The stage of universal ethical principles. A person in this stage believes that right is determined by universal ethical principles that everyone should follow. Such individuals believe that there are inalienable rights that are universal in nature and consequence. Justice and equality are examples of such universal rights. Thus, a businessperson in this stage may be more concerned with social ethical issues and rely less on the company for direction in situations with an ethical component.[84] For example, a marketing manager may argue for the termination of a toy that has resulted in injury and death because she believes the product threatens the universal value of right to life.

Because there is some spillover effect among these stages, cognitive moral development can be viewed as a continuum. Kohlberg's theory suggests that people may change their moral beliefs and behavior as they gain education and experience in resolving conflicts, and this helps accelerate their progress along the moral development continuum. A survey by the Ethics Resource Center provides some confirmation that this occurs. Nearly half (49 percent) of 4,000 individuals surveyed believed that their business ethics had improved over the course of their careers. One-third (34 percent) thought their business ethics had improved because of their personal ethics. Surprisingly, nearly one in eight (12 percent) believed that their personal ethics had improved because of their business ethics.[85]

Kohlberg's model also suggests that there are universal values by which people in the highest level of moral development abide. These rights are considered valid not because of a particular society's laws or customs but because they rest on the premise of universality. Many organizations and researchers have attempted to identify a set of global or universal ethical standards that every individual should follow regardless of where they live or work.

MOTIVATION Another significant factor in the ethical decision-making process is an individual's motivation. Psychologist David McClelland identified three different social needs that may motivate an individual in an ethical decision-making situation: achievement, affiliation, and power.[86]

The need for achievement refers to an individual's preference for goals that are well defined and moderately challenging, include employee participation, and provide for feedback. People with a high need for achievement tend to be motivated, show great initiative, and work hard to accomplish common shared goals. McClelland's theory suggests that if employees are given role models that have high ethical standards, they will then emulate these values. At Home Depot, for example, community service is viewed as an important part of social responsibility. Arthur Blank, cofounder of Home Depot, the world's largest home improvement retailer, indicates principles and values are becoming more important in U.S. business. Blank says that success at Home Depot, which was founded in 1978, was due to sound business practices, such as hands-on management, putting employees and customers first, listening, giving back to the community, and recognizing that good ideas can come from anyone. The lessons learned at Home Depot helped Blank as the Atlanta Falcons' owner. For example, when he bought the team, Blank said players wanted one thing: to fill the Georgia Dome with fans on game day. By cutting ticket prices, resolving parking problems, and providing more entertainment during games, the Falcons increased ticket sales 100 percent during Blank's first year as owner and have sold out every home game since. Blank also said he asks his football players to visit schools and give back to the community. He said he talks to the players about winning "the Super Bowl of life."[87]

The need for affiliation relates to an individual's inclination to work with others in the organization rather than alone. Individuals with a high need for affiliation prefer to interact with others, guide others, and learn from coworkers. Therefore, they are more effective working in an environment with peers rather than working at home alone. Such employees will be easier to socialize into the core values of the organization compared to those who telecommute from home. Peers and coworkers have been found to have more influence on ethical decision making in an organizational context than any other factor.[88]

The need for power refers to an individual's desire to have influence and control over others. Business environments often limit or constrain what people are able to contribute. To exercise power successfully within an organization, an individual must be accepted, assertive, and capable. The greater the need for power, the greater is the probability that an individual or group may engage in questionable or unethical behavior. Although the need for power does not always lead to negative effects, it is important for employees to balance this need with organizational goals and standards. The emergence of team- and project-based organizational structures often means that power and control are decentralized. Such structures require a great deal of trust, communication, and relationship building, all key factors in both social responsibility and business performance.

Organizational Relationships

Although individuals can and do make ethical decisions, they do not operate in a vacuum.[89] Ethical choices in business are most often made jointly in committees and work groups or in conversations with coworkers. Moreover, people learn to settle ethical issues not only from their individual backgrounds but also from others with whom they associate in the business environment. The outcome of this learning process depends on the strength of each individual's personal values, opportunity for unethical behavior, and exposure to others who behave ethically or unethically. Consequently, the culture of the organization, as well as superiors, peers, and subordinates, can have a significant impact on the ethical decision-making process.

organizational, or corporate, culture

a set of values, beliefs, goals, norms, and rituals shared by members or employees of an organization

ORGANIZATIONAL CULTURE **Organizational, or corporate, culture** can be defined as a set of values, beliefs, goals, norms, and rituals shared by members or employees of an organization. It answers questions such as "What is important?" "How do we treat each other?" and "How do we do things around here?" Culture may be conveyed formally in employee handbooks, codes of conduct, memos, and ceremonies, but it is also expressed informally through dress codes, extracurricular activities, and anecdotes. A firm's culture gives its members meaning and offers direction as to how to behave and deal with problems within the organization. The

Floyd Landis took first place in the 2006 Tour de France, but later tested positive for substances banned by the international cycling community.

corporate culture at American Express, for example, includes numerous anecdotes about employees who have gone beyond the call of duty to help customers out of difficult situations. This strong tradition of customer service might encourage an American Express employee to take extra steps to help a customer who encounters a problem while traveling overseas.

On the other hand, an organization's culture can also encourage employees to make decisions that others may judge as unethical, or it can encourage actions that may be viewed as socially responsible. Most misconduct comes from employees trying to attain the performance objectives of the firm. Consider oil traders at Royal Dutch Shell who created fictitious sales that eliminated price competition and market risk for their companies. Trades by Houston-based Shell Trading U.S. Co. and London-based Shell International Trading & Shipping Co. violated futures trading rules on the New York Mercantile Exchange and resulted in a combined $300,000 in fines.[90] However, Texas Instruments, which has always been a company very concerned about ethics and ranked fiftieth on *Business Ethics* magazine's 100 Best Corporate Citizens in 2005, proposed a challenge to its design team. If the team could find a way to build the new factory for $180 million less than the last Dallas factory built in the late 1990s, then Texas Instruments would locate in Dallas. The team managed to design the new building with two floors instead of three and a completely new design that is expected to cut utility costs by 20 percent and water usage by 35 percent.[91]

ethical climate
part of a corporate culture that relates to an organization's expectations about appropriate conduct that focuses specifically on issues of right and wrong

Whereas a firm's overall culture establishes ideals that guide a wide range of behaviors for members of the organization, its **ethical climate** focuses specifically on issues of right and wrong. We think of ethical climate as the part of a corporate culture that relates to an organization's expectations about appropriate conduct. To some extent, ethical climate is the character component of an organization. Corporate policies and codes, the conduct of top managers, the values and moral philosophies of coworkers, and opportunity for misconduct all contribute to a firm's ethical climate. When top managers strive to establish an ethical climate based on responsibility and citizenship, they set the tone for ethical decisions.

Such is the case at the White Dog Café in Philadelphia. Owner Judy Wicks pays a living wage to all restaurant employees, including dishwashers, with a minimum of $9 an hour after three months' employment; however, most employees at the White Dog Café make well above this amount. The restaurant is run using 100 percent wind-powered electricity, and 10 to 20 percent of the profits are donated to their nonprofit, White Dog Café Foundation, which works to build a more socially just and environmentally sustainable local economy in the greater Philadelphia region, and other nonprofits. They also give food, employee services, and gift certificates for local fundraisers and events. Wicks purchases only organic produce and humanely raised meats. She says, "Business is about relationships more than money." White Dog Enterprises employs more than 100 people and grosses more than $5 million annually, demonstrating the concept of "doing well by doing good."[92] Thus, the White Dog Café management has established an ethical climate that promotes responsible conduct. Ethical climate also determines whether an individual perceives an issue as having an ethical component. Recognizing ethical issues and generating alternatives to address them are manifestations of ethical climate.

significant others

superiors, peers, and sub-ordinates in the organization who influence the ethical decision-making process

SIGNIFICANT OTHERS **Significant others** include superiors, peers, and subordinates in the organization who influence the ethical decision-making process. Although people outside the firm, such as family members and friends, also influence decision makers, organizational structure and culture operate through significant others to influence ethical decisions. The Ethics Resource Center's National Business Ethics Survey (NBES) found that observed misconduct is higher in large organizations—those with more than 500 employees—than in smaller organizations and that there are also differences in observed misconduct across employee levels. Reporting misconduct is most likely to come from upper levels of management compared to lower level supervisors and nonmanagement employees. Employees in lower level positions have a greater tendency not to understand misconduct or to be complacent about the misconduct they observe. Figure 5.3 is based on the percentage of employees who indicated that they did observe misconduct during the past year. Each bar represents the percentage of employees who reported misconduct. Among senior managers, 77 percent of employees report observing misconduct, but among nonmanagement, only 48 percent of employees report observing misconduct.[93]

Most experts agree that the chief executive officer establishes the ethical tone for the entire firm. Lower level managers obtain their cues from top managers, and they in turn impose some of their personal values on the company. This interaction between corporate culture and executive leadership helps determine the ethical value system of the firm. However, obedience to authority can also explain why many people resolve workplace issues by following the directives of a superior. An employee may feel obligated to carry out the orders of a superior even if those orders conflict with the employee's values of right and wrong. If that decision is later judged to have

Diversity in the workplace is usually characterized by differences in age, gender, ethnicity, background, and other personal qualities.

| **FIGURE 5.3** | Employee Reporting of Misconduct by Employee Level |

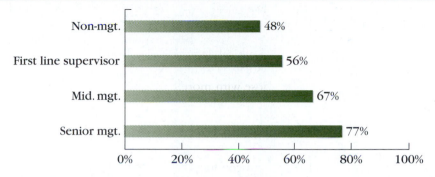

Source: *2005 National Business Ethics Survey: How Employees Perceive Ethics at Work* (Washington, DC: Ethics Resource Center, 2005), p. 30. Reprinted with permission from The Ethics Resource Center.

been wrong, the employee may justify it by saying, "I was only carrying out orders" or "My boss told me to do it this way."

Coworkers' influence on ethical decision making depends on the person's exposure to unethical behavior in making ethical decisions. The more a person is exposed to unethical activity by others in the organization, the more likely it is that he or she will behave unethically, especially in ethically "gray" areas. Thus, a decision maker who associates with others who act unethically is more likely to behave unethically as well. Within work groups, employees may be subject to the phenomenon of "groupthink," going along with group decisions even when those decisions run counter to their own values. They may rationalize the decision with "safety in numbers" when everyone else appears to back a particular decision. Most businesspeople take their cues or learn from coworkers how to solve problems—including ethical dilemmas.[94] "We evaluate other people based upon their behavior; we evaluate ourselves based upon our intentions."[95] Close friends at work exert the most influence on ethical decisions that relate to roles associated with a particular job.

Superiors and coworkers can create organizational pressure, which plays a key role in creating ethical issues. For example, Mitsubishi employees kept silent for eight years about potential defects in large-screen televisions the firm manufactured between 1987 and 1990. Despite ten major cases of TV sets overheating, six of which caused extensive home fires, employees chose not to disclose the liability until recently, when the firm announced a major recall.[96] Concealing evidence of defects that could result in a recall is not uncommon in Japanese culture, which views product recalls as a source of great humiliation. In such a culture, pressure from superiors and coworkers to remain silent may be enormous.

Nearly all businesspeople face difficult issues where solutions are not obvious or where organizational objectives and personal ethical values may conflict. For example, a salesperson for a Web-based retailer may be asked by a superior to lie to a customer over the telephone about a late product shipment. In one survey, 47 percent of human resources managers said they had felt pressured by other employees or managers to compromise their firm's standards of business conduct to attain business

FIGURE 5.4 | Sources of Pressure to Compromise Ethics Standards

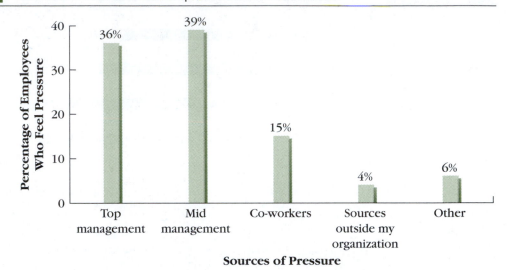

Source: *2005 National Business Ethics Survey: How Employees Perceive Ethics at Work* (Washington, DC: Ethics Resource Center, 2005), p. 43. Reprinted by permission from The Ethics Resource Center.

objectives.[97] A study by the Ethics Resource Center found that 44 percent of those surveyed said they had experienced pressure from superiors or coworkers to compromise ethics standards to achieve business objectives.[98] Figure 5.4 shows the sources of pressure reported by employees.

Opportunity

opportunity
a set of conditions that limits barriers or provides rewards

Together, organizational culture and the influence of coworkers may foster conditions that either hinder or permit misconduct. **Opportunity** is a set of conditions that limits barriers or provides rewards. When these conditions provide rewards—be it financial gain, recognition, promotion, or simply the good feeling from a job well done—the opportunity for unethical conduct may be encouraged or discouraged. For example, a company policy that fails to specify the punishment for employees who violate the rules provides an opportunity for unethical behavior because it allows individuals to engage in such behavior without fear of consequences. Thus, company policies, processes, and other factors may create opportunities to act unethically. Advancing technology associated with the Internet is challenging companies working to limit opportunities to engage in unethical and illegal behavior. In a survey of online retailers, 83 percent reported that fraud is a problem in online transactions, and 61 percent indicated that they were taking precautions to limit the opportunity to engage in fraud.[99] Individual factors as well as organizational relationships may influence whether an individual becomes opportunistic and takes advantage of situations in an unethical or even illegal manner.

Opportunity usually relates to employees' immediate job context—where they work, with whom they work, and the nature of the work. This context includes the

| FIGURE 5.5 | Items Employees Pilfer in the Workplace |

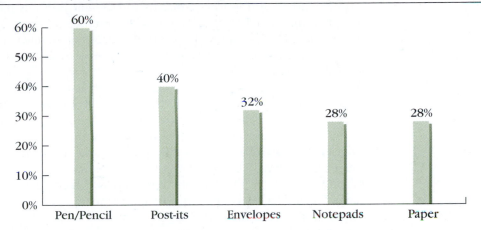

Source: "Top Items Employees Pilfer." Most popular items employees take from office supply rooms for matters unrelated to the job. Vault's office survey of 1,152 respondents. In *USA Today,* Snapshots, March 29, 2006, p. B1.

motivational "carrots and sticks," or rewards and punishments, that superiors can use to influence employee behavior. Rewards, or positive reinforcers, include pay raises, bonuses, and public recognition, whereas reprimands, pay penalties, demotions, and even firings act as negative reinforcers. For example, a manager who decides to sell customers' personal data may be confident that such behavior is an easy way to boost revenue because other companies sell customer account information. Even if this activity violates the employee's personal value system, it may be viewed as acceptable within the organization's culture. This manager may be motivated by opportunities to increase company revenue and his or her performance standing within the organization. A survey by Vault.com indicates that 67 percent of employees take office supplies for personal use. As Figure 5.5 shows, many employees pilfer office supply rooms for matters unrelated to the job. It is possible that the opportunity is provided, and in some cases, there are no concerns if employees take pens, Post-its, envelopes, notepads, and paper. Respondents to the Vault survey indicate that 25 percent feel that no one cares if they take office supplies, 34 percent indicate they never got caught, and 1 percent say they got caught.[100] One concern, if there is no policy against this practice, is that employees will not learn where to draw the line and will get into the habit of taking even more expensive items for personal use.

Often, opportunity can arise from someone whose job is to create opportunity for others. Barbara Toffler, an ethics consultant and professor, learned firsthand how difficult it can be to follow one's own moral compass when she worked as a consultant at Arthur Andersen creating ethics programs for Andersen clients (the firm itself had no internal ethics program). After charging a client $1 million for developing an ethics program that should have cost $500,000, the praise Toffler earned from Andersen "was the only day in four years that I felt truly valued by Arthur Andersen." Despite her expertise, she learned that "unethical or illegal behavior happens when decent people are put under the unbearable pressure to do their jobs and meet ambitious goals without the resources to get the job done right."[101] A natural gas trader for Dynegy Inc. was indicted for allegedly manipulating gas price indexes during the California energy crisis to increase prices. The trader pleaded not guilty when arrested on federal criminal fraud charges. Although it is alleged that the trader sent fictitious trade information, the deception may have had rewards if it increased profits. If convicted, the trader faces a fine of up to $2.75 million and a prison sentence of up to thirty-five years.[102]

If an employee takes advantage of an opportunity to act unethically and is rewarded or suffers no penalty, he or she may repeat such acts as other opportunities arise. Securities regulators asked an administrative law judge to bar a unit of Raymond James Financial Inc. from hiring any new brokers or opening any new branch offices until it hires an independent consultant to oversee compliance at the securities firm. Raymond James Financial Services' attitude toward compliance "is too lax and not sufficiently proactive to offer any assurances that the investing public will be protected against future fraud" by the firm's registered representatives. An employee allegedly bilked investors out of $16.5 million. The SEC filed an administrative complaint against Raymond James and two former executives, saying they failed to supervise a former broker who promised investors returns of more than 100 percent. The employee in question used the Raymond James letterhead to solicit investors, who deposited $44.5 million in a Raymond James account. The employee began siphoning off the money and transferred $16.5 million to a Raymond James account controlled by his wife.[103] When company managers get away with unethical conduct, their behavior is reinforced and a culture of manipulation and misconduct can develop. Indeed, opportunity to engage in unethical conduct is often a better predictor of unethical activities than personal values.[104]

In addition to rewards and the absence of punishment, other elements in the business environment tend to create opportunities. Professional codes of conduct and ethics-related corporate policies also influence opportunity by prescribing what behaviors are acceptable. Compliance programs are necessary to provide internal controls to prevent situations such as the Raymond James issue just discussed. The larger the rewards and the milder the punishment for unethical behavior, the greater is the probability that unethical behavior will be practiced.

SUMMARY

Business ethics comprises principles and standards that guide individual and work group behavior in the world of business. Stakeholders determine these conventions, and they may change over time. The most basic of these standards have been codified as laws and regulations. Business ethics goes beyond legal issues.

Because individuals and groups within a company may not have embraced the same set of values, ethical conflict may occur. Questionable decisions and actions may result in disputes that must be resolved through some type of negotiation or even litigation. Codifying ethical standards into meaningful policies that spell out what is and is not acceptable gives businesspeople an opportunity to reduce the possibility of behavior that could create legal problems. Business decisions involve complex and detailed discussions in which correctness may not be clear-cut. It is important that a shared vision of acceptable behavior develop from an organizational perspective to create consistent and reliable relationships with all concerned stakeholders.

Understanding the ethical decision-making process can help individuals and businesses design strategies to prevent misconduct. Three of the important components of ethical decision making are individual factors, organizational relationships, and opportunity.

Significant individual factors that affect the ethical decision-making process include personal moral philosophy, stage of moral development, motivation, and other personal factors such as gender, age, and experience. Moral philosophies are the principles or rules that individuals apply in deciding what is right or wrong. Most moral philosophies can be classified as consequentialism, ethical formalism, or justice. Consequentialist philosophies consider a decision to be right or acceptable if it accomplishes a desired result such as pleasure, knowledge, career growth, the realization of self-interest, or utility. Consequentialism may be further classified as egoism and utilitarianism. Ethical formalism focuses on the rights of individuals and on the intentions associated with a particular behavior rather than on its consequences. Justice theory relates to evaluations of fairness, or the disposition to deal with perceived injustices of others. Kohlberg proposed that people progress through six stages in their cognitive moral development. McClelland identified three different social needs that may motivate an individual in an ethical decision-making situation: achievement, affiliation, and power.

The culture of the organization, as well as superiors, peers, and subordinates, can have a significant impact on the ethical decision-making process. Organizational, or corporate, culture can be defined as a set of values, beliefs, goals, norms, and rituals shared by members or employees of an organization. Whereas a firm's overall culture establishes ideals that guide a wide range of behaviors for members of the organization, its ethical climate focuses specifically on issues of right and wrong. Significant others include superiors, peers, and subordinates in the organization who influence the ethical decision-making process. Interaction between corporate culture and executive leadership helps determine the ethical value system of the firm, but obedience to authority can also explain why many people resolve workplace issues by following the directives of a superior. The more a person is exposed to unethical activity by others in the organization, the more likely it is that he or she will behave unethically. Superiors and coworkers can create organizational pressure, which plays a key role in creating ethical issues.

Opportunity is a set of conditions that limit barriers or provide rewards. If an individual takes advantage of an opportunity to act unethically and escapes punishment or gains a reward, that person may repeat such acts when circumstances favor them.

KEY TERMS

business ethics (p. 150)
ethical issue (p. 153)
conflict of interest (p. 158)
fraud (p. 159)
consumer fraud (p. 163)
affirmative action programs (p. 165)
moral philosophies (p. 169)

consequentialism (p. 169)
egoism (p. 169)
utilitarianism (p. 170)
ethical formalism (p. 170)
justice theory (p. 170)
organizational, or corporate, culture (p. 174)
ethical climate (p. 175)
significant others (p. 176)
opportunity (p. 178)

DISCUSSION QUESTIONS

1. Why is business ethics a strategic consideration in organizational decisions?
2. How do individual, organizational, and opportunity factors interact to influence ethical or unethical decisions?
3. How do moral philosophies influence the individual factor in organizational ethical decision making?
4. How can ethical formalism be used in organizational ethics programs and still respect diversity and the right for individual values?
5. What are the potential benefits of an emphasis on procedural justice?
6. How can knowledge of Kohlberg's stages of moral development be useful in developing an organizational ethics program?
7. How do organizations create an ethical climate?
8. Why are we seeing more evidence of widespread ethical dilemmas within organizations?

EXPERIENTIAL EXERCISE

Visit www.bbb.org, the home page for the Better Business Bureau. Locate the International Marketplace Ethics award criteria. Find recent winners of the award and summarize what they did to achieve this recognition. Describe the role of the BBB in supporting self-regulatory activities and business ethics.

WHAT WOULD YOU DO?

On Sunday, Armando went to work to pick up a report he needed to review before an early Monday meeting. While at work, he noticed a colleague's light on and went over to her cubicle for a short visit. Monica was one of the newest systems designers on the department's staff. She was hired six weeks ago to assist with a series of human resources (HR) projects for the company. Before joining the firm, she worked as an independent consultant to organizations trying to upgrade their human resources systems that track payroll, benefits, compliance, and other issues. Monica was very well qualified,

detail oriented, and hard working. She was the only female on the systems staff.

In his brief conversation with Monica, Armando felt that he was not getting the full story of her reason for being at work on a Sunday. After all, the systems team completed the first HR systems proposal on Thursday and was prepared to present its report and recommendations on Monday. Monica said she was "working on a few parts" of the project but did not get more specific. Her face turned red when Armando joked, "With the beautiful sunshine outside, only someone hoping to earn a little extra money would be at work today."

Armando and another coworker, David, presented the systems team's report to the HR staff on Monday. HR was generally pleased with the recommendations but wanted a number of specifications changes. This was normal and the systems designers were prepared for the changes. Everyone on the team met that afternoon and Tuesday morning to develop a plan for revamping the HR system. By Tuesday afternoon, each member was working on his or her part of the project again.

On Friday afternoon, David went up and down the hall, encouraging everyone to go to happy hour at the pub down the street. About ten people, including Monica and Armando, went to the pub. The conversation was mainly about work and the new HR project. On several occasions, Monica offered ideas about other systems and companies with which she was familiar. Most of the systems designers listened, but a few were quick to question her suggestions. Armando assumed her suggestions were the result of work with previous clients. Over the weekend, however, Armando began to wonder whether Monica was talking about current clients. He remembered their conversation on Sunday and decided to look into the matter.

On Monday, Armando asked Monica directly whether she still had clients. Monica said yes and that she was finishing up on projects with two of them. She went on to say that she worked late hours and on the weekends and was not skimping on her company responsibilities. Armando agreed that she was a good colleague but was not comfortable with her use of company resources on personal, moneymaking projects. He was also concerned that the team's intellectual capital was being used. What would you do?

CHAPTER 6

Strategic Approaches to Improving Ethical Behavior

CHAPTER OBJECTIVES

- To provide an overview of the need for an organizational ethics program

- To consider crucial keys to development of an effective ethics program

- To examine effective implementation of an ethics program

CHAPTER OUTLINE

Honda Engineering North America, Inc. has 400 associates and sales of between $100 and $200 million per year. It provides engineering services such as designing, building, and installing production tooling for Honda's plants in North America. There are many reasons small companies should have an ethics program, especially to reduce the risk of compliance problems, because small companies usually have fewer internal controls and therefore have higher risks of compliance problems. It also gives small companies a competitive advantage, as their customers increasingly have a program and want their suppliers to have one too; it can also improve hiring and reduce turnover, as more and more employees become concerned about a corporation's ethical reputation when accepting a job offer. However, there are also problems that may not occur in a larger company; for example, there may be a limited or nonexistent budget, a leaner staff, cultural differences, and difficulty getting management buy-in.

Honda Engineering was asked by its largest customer to establish an ethics program. The main issues about implementing the program included concerns about workforce and budget. Honda Engineering overcame these problems by using Honda of America (HAM) as a resource. They used the code of conduct from HAM as a base and made minor changes to it using the same consultant as HAM. For code revisions, costs were kept low by not using a consultant, and using only two colors. It has also been made available online, which reduces costs, as well as in a brochure format, which is only four pages. To address the workforce problem, Honda Engineering provided a toll-free number with a message; they provided short, live training classes for all associates, which consisted of two hours for management and two hours for associates. All of the training was designed in house with HAM support.

Honda Engineering runs an effective program by relying on the basic principles of building and maintaining trust. It does this through live training with frank discussions, asking the employees what they need, and maintaining independence and confidentiality. They use databases, surveys, and interviews with management to target the training and always follow up. Through effective communication, Honda Engineering ensures that employees are kept updated on changes to the code of conduct and any issues that arise. They send out an e-mail Ethics@Work quarterly newsletter that is based on real situations and real concerns; Honda Engineering also addresses issues in the company newsletter. In this way, the company communicates the code to its employees while at the same time ensuring that the employees know that it is everyone's responsibility to comply with the code at all times.[1]

http://world.honda.com/profile/governance/, "Corporate Governance: To Be a Company that our Shareholders, Customers and Society Want," accessed May 15, 2006.
http://world.honda.com/conductguideline/ "Conduct Guideline: The Basis of Honda's Group Companies," May 15, 2006 ■

A strategic approach to ethical decisions will contribute to both business and society. This chapter provides a framework that is consistent with research, best practices, and regulatory requirements. Business ethics programs have not been implemented effectively by many companies, but they are good systems to manage organizational misconduct. Our framework for developing effective ethics programs is consistent with the ethical decision-making process described in Chapter 5. In addition, the strategic approach to an ethics program presented here is consistent with the Federal Sentencing Guidelines for Organizations and the Sarbanes-Oxley Act described in Chapter 3. These legislative reforms require managers to assume responsibility and ensure that ethical standards are implemented properly on a daily basis. Ethics programs include not only the need for leadership from top executives but also responsibility by boards of directors for corporate governance.

Unethical and illegal business conduct occurs even in organizations that have ethics programs. For example, although Enron had a code of ethics and was a member of the Better Business Bureau, the company was devastated by unethical activities and corporate scandal. Many business leaders believe that personal moral development and character are all that is needed for corporate responsibility. There are those who feel that ethics initiatives should arise inherently from a company's culture and that hiring good employees will limit unethical behavior within the organization. Many executives and board members do not understand how organizational ethical decisions are made and how to develop an ethical corporate culture. Customized ethics programs may help many organizations provide guidance for employees from diverse backgrounds to gain an understanding of acceptable behavior within the organization. Many ethical issues in business are complex and include considerations that require organizational agreement regarding appropriate action. Top executives and boards of directors must provide the leadership, a system to resolve these issues, and support for an ethical corporate culture.

In this chapter, we provide an overview of why businesses need to develop an organizational ethics program. Next, we consider the factors that are crucial for the development of such a program: a code of conduct, an ethics officer and appropriate delegation of authority, effective ethics training, a system to monitor and support ethical compliance, and continual efforts to improve the ethics program. Finally, we discuss implementation of an organizational ethics program, including the roles of leadership and corporate culture.

THE NEED FOR ORGANIZATIONAL ETHICS PROGRAMS

Usually, an organization is held accountable for the conduct of its employees. Companies must assess their ethical risks and develop values and compliance systems to avoid legal and ethical mistakes that could damage the organization. The Federal Sentencing Guidelines for Organizations holds corporations responsible for conduct they engage in as an entity. Some corporate outcomes cannot be tied to one individual or even a group, and misconduct can result from a collective pattern of decisions supported by a corporate culture. Therefore, corporations can be held accountable, fined, and even receive the death penalty when they are operating in a manner inconsistent with major legal requirements. Organizations are sensitive to avoid infringing on employees' personal freedoms and ethical beliefs. In cases where an individual's personal beliefs and activities are inconsistent with company policies on ethics, conflict may develop. If the individual feels that ethical systems in the organization are deficient or directed in an inappropriate manner, some type of open conflict resolution may be needed to deal with the differences.

Former Wal-Mart Stores Inc. vice president Tom Coughlin pleaded guilty to fraud and filing a false tax return in 2006. The former executive stole gift cards, money, and merchandise from Wal-Mart.

Understanding the factors that influence how individuals make decisions to resolve ethical issues, as discussed in Chapter 5, can help companies encourage ethical behavior and discourage undesirable conduct. Fostering ethical decisions within an organization requires eliminating unethical behavior and improving the firm's ethical standards. Some people are "bad apples" who will always do things in their own self-interest regardless of organizational goals or accepted standards of conduct. For example, major league baseball players know the use of steroids is prohibited. Random drug tests are conducted to determine such abuses. Baltimore Orioles first baseman Rafael Palmeiro tested positive for steroid use and was suspended from the team in 2005. Palmeiro admitted to steroid use that season, even though he had testified before Congress denying such activity. Such abuses have ruined careers and the reputation of the sport.[2] Eliminating such bad apples through screening techniques and enforcement of the firm's ethical standards can help improve the firm's overall ethical conduct.

Organizations can create unethical corporate cultures not because individuals within them are bad but because the pressures to succeed create opportunities that reward unethical decisions. In the case of an unethical corporate culture, the organization must redesign its ethical standards to conform to industry and stakeholder standards of acceptable behavior. Most businesses attempt to improve ethical decision making by establishing and implementing a strategic approach to improving organizational ethics. Companies such as Texas Instruments, Starbucks, Levi's, and Johnson & Johnson take a strategic approach to organizational ethics but monitor their programs on a continuous basis and make improvements when problems occur.

To be socially responsible and promote legal and ethical conduct, an organization should develop an organizational ethics program by establishing, communicating, and monitoring ethical values and legal requirements that characterize its history, culture, industry, and operating environment. Without such programs and uniform standards and policies of conduct, it is difficult for employees to determine what behaviors are acceptable within a company. As discussed in Chapter 5, in the absence of such programs and standards, employees generally will make decisions based on their observations of how their coworkers and managers behave. A strong ethics program includes a written code of conduct, an ethics officer to oversee the program, care in the delegation of authority, formal ethics training, auditing, monitoring, enforcement, and revision of program standards. Without a strong customized program, problems are much more likely to arise. Figure 6.1 outlines the causes of organizational misconduct.

The corporate ethics crises in the United States have destroyed trust in top management and significantly lowered the public's trust of business. According to a survey by Golin/Harris International, there are five top recommendations to CEOs for rebuilding trust and confidence in American firms. These are making customers the top priority, assuming personal responsibility and accountability, communicating openly and frequently with customers, handling crises more honestly, and finally, sticking to the code of business ethics no matter what.[3] This is a recurring theme among primary stakeholders. Consumers are looking for clear, creative, and constructive leadership from CEOs that demonstrates trust is a priority. Survey respondents were asked to make recommendations they considered essential or important to establishing and maintaining trust.

FIGURE 6.1   Root Causes of Misconduct

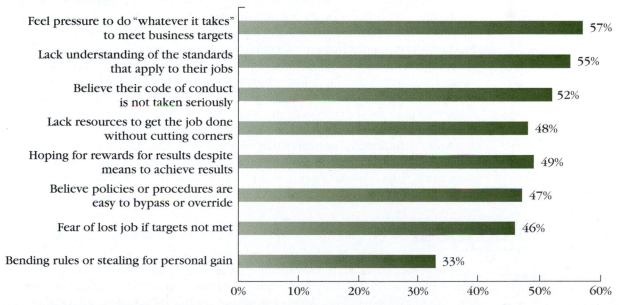

Source: KPMG Forensic Integrity Survey 2005–2006, http://www.kpmginsiders.com/display_analysis.asp?cs_id=148597, accessed March 9, 2006.

There are no universal standards that can be applied to organizational ethics programs, but most companies develop codes, values, or policies for guidance about business behavior. The majority of companies that have been in ethical or legal trouble usually have stated ethics codes and programs. Often, the problem is that top management, as well as the overall corporate culture, has not integrated these codes, values, and standards into daily decision making. Tyco CEO Dennis Kozlowski allegedly used millions of dollars of company funds for personal use and was indicted for criminal tax avoidance schemes.[4] If a company's leadership fails to provide the vision and support needed for ethical conduct, then an ethics program will not be effective. Ethics is not something to be delegated to lower level employees while top managers break the rules.

No matter what their goals, ethics programs are developed as organizational control systems, the aim of which is to create predictability in employee behavior. Two types of control systems can be created. A compliance orientation creates order by requiring that employees identify with and commit to specific required conduct. It uses legal terms, statutes, and contracts that teach employees the rules and penalties for noncompliance. The other type of system is a values orientation, which strives to develop shared values. Although penalties are attached, the focus is more on an abstract core of ideals such as respect and responsibility. Instead of relying on coercion, the company's values are seen as something to which people willingly aspire.[5]

Research into compliance- and values-based approaches reveals that both types of programs can interact or work toward the same end, but a values orientation can better help explain and influence employees. Values-based programs increase employees' awareness of ethics at work, their integrity, their willingness to deliver bad news to supervisors, and the perception that better decisions are made. Compliance-based programs are linked to employees' awareness of ethical issues at work and their perception that decision making is better because of the expectations of its employees.

To meet the public's escalating demands for ethical decision making, companies need to develop plans and structures for addressing ethical considerations. Some directions for the improvement of ethics have been mandated through regulations, but companies must be willing to have in place a values and ethics implementation system that exceeds the minimum regulatory requirements. According to a study by the Open Compliance and Ethics Group (OCEG), among companies with an ethics program in place for ten years or more, none have experienced "reputational damage" in the last five years—"a testament to the important impact these programs can have over time." In addition, companies that have experienced reputational damage in the past are much further along compared to their peers in establishing ethics and compliance programs. Companies in the study spent an average of $5.8 million in total compliance or ethics efforts for every $1 billion in revenues.[6]

CODES OF CONDUCT

codes of conduct
formal statements that describe what an organization expects of its employees

Because people come from diverse family, educational, and business backgrounds, it cannot be assumed that they know how to behave appropriately when they enter a new organization or job. Most companies begin the process of establishing organizational ethics programs by developing **codes of conduct** (also called codes of ethics), which are formal statements that describe what an organization expects of its

FIGURE 6.2	Presence of Written Standards of Conduct

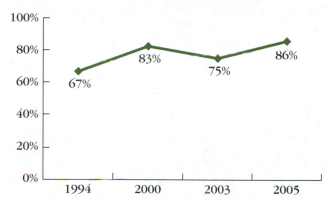

A year to year comparison of the percentage of employees who are aware that their organizations have a written set of ethics standards.

Source: National Business Ethics Survey, *How Employees View Ethics in Their Organizations 1994–2005,* Ethics Resource Center, p. 12.

employees. Figure 6.2 indicates increases in codes of conduct over time, with 86 percent of employees aware of their organization's code of conduct. These codes may address a variety of situations from internal operations to sales presentations and financial disclosure practices.

A code of ethics has to reflect the board of directors' and senior management's desire for organizational compliance with the values, mission, rules, and policies that support an ethical climate. Development of a code of ethics should involve the board of directors, president, and senior managers who will be implementing the code. Legal staff should be called on to ensure that the code has correctly assessed key areas of risk and that potential legal problems are buffered by standards in the code. A code of ethics that does not address specific high-risk activities within the scope of daily operations is inadequate for maintaining standards that can prevent misconduct. Table 6.1 shows considerations in developing and implementing a code of ethics.

A large multinational firm, Texas Instruments manufactures computers, calculators, and other high-technology products. Its code of ethics resembles that of many other organizations. The code addresses issues relating to policies and procedures; government laws and regulations; relationships with customers, suppliers, and competitors; acceptance of gifts, travel, and entertainment; political contributions; expense reporting; business payments; conflicts of interest; investment in TI stock; handling of proprietary information and trade secrets; use of TI employees and assets to perform personal work; relationships with government officials and agencies; and enforcement of the code. TI's code emphasizes that ethical behavior is critical to maintaining long-term success and that each individual is responsible for upholding the integrity of the company.

Our reputation at TI depends upon all of the decisions we make and all the actions we take personally each day. Our values define how we will evaluate our decisions and actions . . . and how we will conduct our business. We are working in a difficult and

TABLE 6.1	Developing and Implementing a Code of Ethics

1. Consider areas of risk and state values as well as conduct necessary to comply with laws and regulations. Values are an important buffer in preventing serious misconduct.

2. Identify values that specifically address current ethical issues.

3. Consider values that link the organization to a stakeholder orientation. Attempt to find overlaps in organizational and stakeholder values.

4. Make the code understandable by providing examples that reflect values.

5. Communicate the code frequently and in language that employees can understand.

6. Revise the code every year with input from organizational members and stakeholders.

demanding, ever-changing business environment. Together we are building a work environment on the foundation of Integrity, Innovation, and Commitment. Together we are moving our company into a new century . . . one good decision at a time. Our high standards have rewarded us with an enviable reputation in today's marketplace . . . a reputation of integrity, honesty, and trustworthiness. That strong ethical reputation is a vital asset . . . and each of us shares a personal responsibility to protect, to preserve, and to enhance it. Our reputation is a strong but silent partner in all business relationships. By understanding and applying the values presented on the following pages, each of us can say to ourselves and to others, "TI is a good company, and one reason is that I am part of it." Know what's right. Value what's right. Do what's right.[7]

To ensure that its employees understand the nature of business ethics and the ethical standards they are expected to follow, TI also provides the "ethics quick test" to help employees when they have doubts about the ethics of specific situations and behaviors:

Is the action legal?

Does it comply with our values?

If you do it, will you feel bad?

How will it look in the newspaper?

If you know it's wrong, don't do it!

If you're not sure, ask.

Keep asking until you get an answer.[8]

Texas Instruments explicitly states what it expects of its employees and what behaviors are unacceptable. By enforcing the codes wholeheartedly, TI has taken logical steps to safeguard its excellent reputation for ethical and responsible behavior. When such standards of behavior are not made explicit, employees sometimes base ethical decisions on their observations of the behavior of peers and management. The use of rewards and punishments to enforce codes and policies controls the opportunity to behave unethically and increases employees' acceptance of ethical standards.

As we stated, codes of conduct may address a variety of situations, from internal operations to sales presentations and financial disclosure practices. As seen in Figure 6.3, associations such as the Public Relations Society of America provide general code for organizations operating within the industry. Research has found that corporate codes

FIGURE 6.3   Public Relations Society of America Member Code of Ethics

Our Primary Obligation

The primary obligation of membership in the Public Relations Society of America is the ethical practice of Public Relations.

The PRSA Member Code of Ethics is the way each member of our Society can daily reaffirm a commitment to ethical professional activities and decisions.

- The Code sets forth the principles and standards that guide our decisions and actions.
- The Code solidly connects our values and our ideals to the work each of us does every day.
- The Code is about what we should do, and why we should do it.

The Code is also meant to be a living, growing body of knowledge, precedent, and experience. It should stimulate our thinking and encourage us to seek guidance and clarification when we have questions about principles, practices, and standards of conduct.

Every member's involvement in preserving and enhancing ethical standards is essential to building and maintaining the respect and credibility of our profession. Using our values, principles, standards of conduct, and commitment as a foundation, and continuing to work together on ethical issues, we ensure that the Public Relations Society of America fulfills its obligation to build and maintain the framework for public dialogue that deserves the public's trust and support.

This statement presents the core values of PRSA members and, more broadly, of the public relations profession. These values provide the foundation for the Member Code of Ethics and set the industry standard for the professional practice of public relations. These values are the fundamental beliefs that guide our behaviors and decision-making process. We believe our professional values are vital to the integrity of the profession as a whole.

ADVOCACY

We serve the public interest by acting as responsible advocates for those we represent. We provide a voice in the marketplace of ideas, facts, and viewpoints to aid informed public debate.

HONESTY

We adhere to the highest standards of accuracy and truth in advancing the interests of those we represent and in communicating with the public.

EXPERTISE

We acquire and responsibly use specialized knowledge and experience. We advance the profession through continued professional development, research, and education. We build mutual understanding, credibility, and relationships among a wide array of institutions and audiences.

INDEPENDENCE

We provide objective counsel to those we represent. We are accountable for our actions.

LOYALTY

We are faithful to those we represent, while honoring our obligation to serve the public interest.

FAIRNESS

We deal fairly with clients, employers, competitors, peers, vendors, the media, and the general public. We respect all opinions and support the right of free expression.

Source: Public Relations Society of America, http://www.prsa.org/_About/ethics/values.asp?ident=eth4, accessed April 26, 2006. Reprinted with permission.

of ethics often have five to seven core values or principles in addition to more detailed descriptions and examples of appropriate conduct.[9] The six values that have been suggested as desirable elements in a code of ethics include (1) trustworthiness, (2) respect, (3) responsibility, (4) fairness, (5) caring, and (6) citizenship.[10] These values will not be effective without distribution of the code, training, and the support of top management in making the values a part of the corporate culture. Employees need specific examples of how the values can be implemented.

Codes of conduct will not resolve every ethical issue encountered in daily operations, but they help employees and managers deal with ethical dilemmas by prescribing or limiting specific actions. Many companies have a code of ethics, but is it communicated effectively? According to an Ethics Resource Center survey, 86 percent of employees surveyed reported that their firm has written standards of ethical business conduct such as codes of ethics or conduct, policy statements on ethics, or guidelines on proper business conduct.[11] A code that is placed on a website or in a training manual is useless if it is not reinforced on a daily basis. By communicating to employees both what is expected of them and what punishments they face if they violate the rules, codes of conduct curtail opportunities for unethical behavior and thereby improve ethical decision making. Fidelity's code, for example, specifies that sanctions for violating it range from cautions and warnings to dismissal and criminal prosecution.[12] Codes of conduct do not have to be so detailed that they take into account every situation, but they should provide guidelines and principles that are capable of helping employees achieve organizational ethical objectives and address risks in an accepted manner.

ETHICS OFFICERS

ethics officer

usually a high-ranking person known to respect legal and ethical standards who is responsible for assessing the needs and risks addressed in an organizational ethics program, developing and distributing a code of conduct or ethics, conducting training programs for employees, establishing and maintaining a confidential service to answer questions about ethical issues, making sure that the company is in compliance with government regulation, monitoring and auditing ethical conduct, taking action on possible violations of the company's code, and reviewing and updating the code

Organizational ethics programs also must have oversight by a high-ranking person known to respect and understand legal and ethical standards. This person is often referred to as an **ethics officer**. According to the Ethics Resource Center survey, 65 percent of respondents reported that their firm has a designated office, person, or telephone line where they can get advice about ethical issues.[13] Corporate wrongdoings and scandal-grabbing headlines have a profound negative impact on public trust. To ensure compliance with state and federal regulations, many corporations are now appointing chief compliance officers and ethics and business conduct professionals to develop and oversee corporate compliance programs.[14]

Consistent enforcement and necessary disciplinary action are essential to a functional ethical compliance program. The ethics or compliance officer is usually responsible for companywide disciplinary systems, implementing all disciplinary actions the company takes for violations of its ethical standards. Many companies are including ethical compliance in employee performance appraisals. During performance appraisals, employees may be asked to sign an acknowledgment that they have read the company's current guidelines on its ethical policies. The company must also promptly investigate any known or suspected misconduct. The appropriate company official, often the ethics officer, needs to make a recommendation to senior management on how to deal with a particular ethical infraction.

Ethics officers meet with company employees on a regular basis to provide training and updates on the company's code of conduct and ethics policies.

The Ethics and Compliance Officer Association (ECOA) has over 1,200 members, who are at the front lines of managing ethics programs.[15] They have members representing nearly every industry, they have members from more than 62 percent of the Fortune 100 companies, and they conduct business in more than 160 countries. In addition to U.S.–based organizations, members are based in Belgium, Canada, Germany, Great Britain, Greece, Hong Kong, India, Japan, the Netherlands, and Switzerland.[16] Ethics and compliance officers now have the attention of top managers and boards of directors.[17] The ethics officer position has existed for over two decades, but its role increased tremendously when the Federal Sentencing Guidelines for Organizations (FSGO) were passed in 1991. The guidelines gave companies that faced federal charges for misconduct the incentive of fine reductions up to 95 percent if they had an effective comprehensive ethics program in place. The financial reporting requirements of the Sarbanes-Oxley Act put more pressure on ethics officers to monitor financial reporting, as well as reporting of sales and inventory movements, to prevent fraud in reporting revenue and profits.[18] In most firms, ethics officers do not report directly to the board of directors, but this is changing rapidly.

Building an ethics program and hiring an ethics officer to avoid fines will not be effective alone. Only with the involvement of top management and the board can an ethics officer earn the trust and cooperation of all key decision makers. Ethics officers are responsible for knowing the contents of thousands of pages of regulations as well as for communicating and reinforcing values that build an ethical corporate culture.

ETHICS TRAINING AND COMMUNICATION

Instituting a training program and a system to communicate and educate about the firm's ethical standards is a major step in developing an effective ethics program. Such training can educate employees about the firm's policies and expectations, relevant laws and regulations, and general social standards. Training programs can make employees aware of available resources, support systems, and designated personnel who can assist them with ethical and legal advice. Training also can help empower employees to ask tough questions and make ethical decisions. Figure 6.4 indicates that by 2005, 69 percent of employees knew that their organization provided ethics training.

Ethics officers provide the oversight and management of most ethics training. Although training and communication should reinforce values and provide learning opportunities about rules, it is only one part of an effective ethics program. The employee's capacity to exercise judgments that result in ethical decisions must be reinforced and developed. Ethics training that is done only because it is required or because ethics involvement is considered something that other companies do will not be effective. Ethics training must be customized to the specific nature of the employees in the organization and the risk areas they face.

The majority of ethics officers surveyed by the Conference Board said that even ethics training would not have prevented the collapse of Enron. Even if Enron's senior management had extensive ethics training, it would have made little or no difference in preventing misconduct.[19] This is because Enron knew that it had the support of Arthur Andersen, its auditing and accounting consulting partner, as well as that of law firms, investment analysts, and in some cases, government regulators. Enron's top management thought they would not be caught in their fraud and manipulation.

FIGURE 6.4   Presence of Ethics Training

The response of employees when asked if their organization provides ethics training.

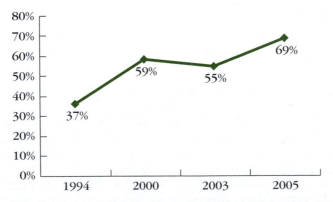

Source: National Business Ethics Survey, *How Employees View Ethics in Their Organizations 1994–2005*, Ethics Resource Center, p. 13. Copyright, Reprinted with permission from The Ethics Resource Center, Washington, DC.

TABLE 6.2	Factors Crucial to Ethics Training

1. Identify the key ethical risk areas.

2. Relate ethical decisions to the organization's values and culture.

3. Communicate company codes, policies, and procedures regarding ethical business conduct.

4. Provide leadership training to model desired behavior.

5. Provide directions for internal questions and reporting mechanisms.

6. Engage in regular training events using a variety of educational tools.

7. Establish manuals, websites, and other communication to reinforce ethics training.

8. Evaluate and use feedback to improve training.

Source: © O. C Ferrell 2006.

If ethical performance is not a part of regular performance appraisals, the message is that ethics is not an important component of decision making. For ethics training to make a difference, employees must understand why it is conducted, how it fits into the organization, and their own role in its implementation.

Top corporate executives must communicate with managers at the operations level (e.g., in production, sales, and finance) and enforce overall ethical standards within the organization. Table 6.2 lists the factors crucial to successful ethics training. It is most important to help employees identify ethical issues and give them the means to address and resolve such issues in ambiguous situations. In addition, employees must be offered direction on seeking assistance from managers or other designated personnel in resolving ethical problems. An effective ethics program can reduce criminal, civil, and administrative consequences, including fines, penalties, judgments, debarment from government contracts, and court control of the organization. An ineffective ethics program that results in many unethical acts may cause negative publicity and a decrease in organizational financial performance. An ethical disaster can do as much damage (or more) to a company than a natural disaster.

Companies can implement ethical principles in their organizations through training programs. Discussions conducted in ethical training programs sometimes break down into personal opinions about what should or should not be done in particular situations. To be successful, business ethics programs need to educate employees about formal ethical frameworks and models for analyzing business ethics issues. Then, employees are able to base ethical decisions on their knowledge of choices rather than on emotions.

Training and communication initiatives should reflect the unique characteristics of an organization: its size, culture, values, management style, and employee base. It is important for the ethics program to differentiate between personal and organizational ethics. If ethics training is to be effective, it must start with a foundation, a code of ethics, an ethical concerns procedure, line and staff involvements, and executive priorities on ethics that are communicated to employees. Managers from every department must be involved in the development of an ethics training program.

Most experts on training agree that one of the most effective methods of ethics training is involvement in resolving ethical dilemmas that relate to actual situations

While research has shown that "good ethics is good business," some business-people still assume that ethical behavior is ultimately costly to the bottom line.

"A 34% cut in our corporate ethics should return us to profitability."

that employees experience in carrying out their responsibilities. For example, Lockheed Martin developed a training game called *Gray Matters*. This training device is available on your textbook website and includes dilemmas that can be resolved by teams. Each member of the team can offer his or her perspective and understand the ramifications of the decision for coworkers and the organization. Figure 6.5 gives an example of the type of issues covered in the game.

A relatively new training device is the behavioral simulation or role-play exercise in which participants are given a short hypothetical ethical issue situation to review. The participants are assigned roles within the hypothetical organization and are provided with varying levels of information about the issue. They then must interact to provide recommended courses of action representing short-term, midrange, and long-term considerations. The simulation re-creates the complexities of organizational relationships and of having to address a situation without complete information. Learning objectives of the simulation exercise include (1) increased awareness by participants of the ethical, legal, and social dimensions of business decision making; (2) development of analytical skills for resolving ethical issues; and (3) exposure to the complexity of ethical decision making in organizations. According to recent research, "the simulation not only instructs on the importance of ethics but on the processes for managing ethical concerns and conflict."[20]

A growing number of small businesses deliver "learning-management" systems software and content to train and certify employees on everything from how to write legally sound e-mails to keeping up with the mandates of the Patriot Act. In addition to streamlined training, the systems provide real-time records of instruction that

FIGURE 6.5	Gray Matters

MINI-CASE

For several months now, one of your colleagues has been slacking off, and you are getting stuck doing the work. You think this is unfair. What do you do?

POTENTIAL ANSWERS

A. Recognize this as an opportunity for you to demonstrate how capable you are.

B. Go to your supervisor and complain about this unfair workload.

C. Discuss the problem with your colleague in an attempt to solve the problem without involving others.

D. Discuss the problem with the human resources department.

MINI-CASE

Your coworker is copying company-purchased software and taking it home. You know a certain program costs $400, and you have been saving for a while to buy it. What do you do?

POTENTIAL ANSWERS

A. You figure you can copy it too since nothing had ever happened to your coworker.

B. You tell your coworker he can't legally do this.

C. You report the matter to the ethics office.

D. You mention this to your boss.

MINI-CASE

You are aware that a fellow employee uses drugs on the job. Another friend encourages you to confront the person instead of informing the supervisor. What do you do?

POTENTIAL ANSWERS

A. You speak to the alleged user and encourage him to get help.

B. You elect to tell your supervisor that you suspect an employee is using drugs on the job.

C. You confront the alleged user and tell him to quit using drugs or you'll "turn him in."

D. You report the matter to employee assistance.

Source: George Sammet, Jr., *Gray Matters: The Ethics Game*. Mr. Sammet published the game while serving as Vice President of Ethics for Martin Marietta. © 1992. Reprinted with permission.

increasingly are the first line of defense for companies facing litigation or questions about whether they're accountable for an employee's actions. The e-learning market is expected to grow to roughly $13.48 billion by 2008. Helping fuel the growth in the post-Enron culture is a renewed zeal among companies to show they've made a good-faith effort to promote an ethically sound culture. Well-documented training records that are easily accessible by computer facilitate a company's effort to protect itself from an employee's errors. For multinational companies, the computerized training element of such systems also helps coordinate getting employees in far-flung locations all trained by the same standards. LRN, for one, now translates its courses into multiple languages, among them Flemish, Russian, Japanese, and Spanish.[21]

Some of the goals of an ethics training program might be to improve employee understanding of ethical issues and the ability to identify them, to inform employees of related procedures and rules, and to identify the contact person who could help in resolving ethical problems. In keeping with these goals, the purpose of the Boeing Corporation's "Boeing Ethics and Business Conduct" program is as follows:

- Communicate Boeing's values and standards of ethical business conduct to employees.
- Inform employees of company policies and procedures regarding ethical business conduct.
- Establish processes to help employees obtain guidance and resolve questions regarding compliance with the company's standards of conduct and values.
- Establish criteria for ethics education and awareness programs and for coordinating compliance oversight activities.[22]

Boeing also asks employees to take ethics refresher training each year. On the company's "Ethics Challenge" webpage, employees (as well as the general public) can select from a variety of ethical dilemma scenarios, discuss them with their peers, and select from several potential answers. After clicking the answer they think is most ethically correct, employees get feedback: the company's own opinion of the correct response and its rationale for it.

Ethical decision making is influenced by organizational culture, by coworkers and supervisors, and by the opportunity to engage in unethical behavior.[23] All three types of influence can be affected by ethics training. Full awareness of the philosophy of management, rules, and procedures can strengthen both the organizational culture and the ethical stance of peers and supervisors. Such awareness also arms employees against opportunities for unethical behavior and reduces the likelihood of misconduct. Thus, the existence and enforcement of company rules and procedures limit unethical practices in the organization. If adequately and thoughtfully designed, ethics training can ensure that everyone in the organization (1) recognizes situations that might involve ethical decision making, (2) understands the values and culture of the organization, and (3) is able to evaluate the impact of ethical decisions on the company in the light of its value structure.[24]

ESTABLISHING SYSTEMS TO MONITOR AND ENFORCE ETHICAL STANDARDS

Ethical compliance involves comparing employee ethical performance with the organization's ethical standards. Ethical compliance can be measured through employee observation, internal audits, surveys, reporting systems, and investigations. An effective ethical program uses a variety of resources to effectively monitor ethical conduct. Sometimes, external auditing and review of company activities are helpful in developing benchmarks of compliance.

The existence of an internal system for employees to report misconduct is especially useful in monitoring and evaluating ethical performance. A number of firms have set up ethics assistance lines, often called help lines, or help desks to offer support and give employees an opportunity to register ethical concerns. Although there is always some worry that people may misreport a situation or misuse a help line to retaliate against another employee, help lines have become widespread, and employees do utilize them. The ethics line at Boeing is available not only to all Boeing employees, including those in subsidiaries, but also to concerned individuals outside the company.[25]

Systems to Monitor and Enforce Ethical Standards

A survey of Fortune 500 companies indicates that 90 percent offer toll-free help lines to report and request assistance when there are ethical concerns. It is interesting that Kenneth Lay, who was often a featured ethics speaker at conferences, did not offer employees at Enron a help line when he was Enron's CEO. His supportive auditor, Arthur Andersen, did not have a help line either.[26] About half of the issues raised on help lines relate to human resources and complaints such as coworker abuse, failure of management to intervene in such abuse, and inappropriate language. Ethical issues have ranged from an employee who used the corporation to advance a personal business to human-resource-related issues such as sexual harassment.[27]

Organizations need a help or assistance line or place where employees and managers can report suspected cases of unethical conduct. Critical comments, dilemmas, and advice can be handled at a central contact point where the most appropriate person can deal with a specific case.[28] A help line or desk is characterized by ease of accessibility and simple procedures, and it serves as a safety net that facilitates monitoring and reporting. Outside companies, such as Ethics Power, can provide help line services that enable employees and consumers to voice concerns twenty-four hours a day, seven days a week. This reporting approach increases the chance of detecting unethical conduct and enables responsible management to take adequate and timely measures to maintain compliance with standards.[29]

Observation and Feedback

To determine whether a person is performing his or her job adequately and ethically, observation might focus on how the person handles an ethically charged situation. For example, many businesses use role-playing in the training of salespeople and managers. Ethical issues can be introduced into the discussion, and the results can be videotaped so that both the participant and the superior can evaluate the results of the ethical dilemma.

Questionnaires that survey employees' ethical perceptions of their company, their superiors, their coworkers, and themselves, as well as ratings of ethical or unethical practices within the firm and industry, can serve as benchmarks in an ongoing assessment of ethical performance. Then, if unethical behavior is perceived to increase, management will have a better understanding of what types of unethical practices may be occurring and why. A change in the ethics training within the company may be necessary.

Appropriate action involves rewarding employees who comply with company policies and standards and punishing those who do not. When employees comply

FIGURE 6.6 Percentage of Employees Nationally Who Report Misconduct

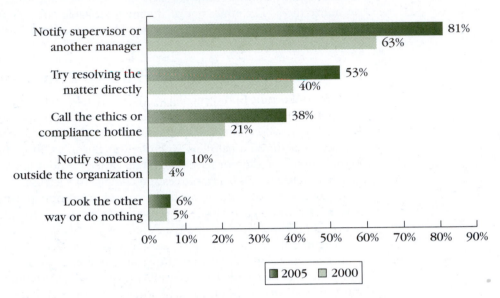

There were gains between 2000 and 2005 in the propensity of employees to report misconduct, as evidenced below.

Notify supervisor or another manager — 81% / 63%

Try resolving the matter directly — 53% / 40%

Call the ethics or compliance hotline — 38% / 21%

Notify someone outside the organization — 10% / 4%

Look the other way or do nothing — 6% / 5%

■ 2005 □ 2000

Source: KPMG Forensic Integrity Survey 2005–2006, http://www.kpmginsiders.com/display_analysis.asp?cs_id=148597, accessed March 9, 2006.

with organizational standards, their efforts may be acknowledged and rewarded through public recognition, bonuses, raises, or some other means. Conversely, when employees deviate from organizational standards, they may be reprimanded, transferred, docked, suspended, or even fired.

Figure 6.6 provides an overview of changes in employee propensity to report misconduct. Employees prefer to deal with ethical issues through their supervisor or manager or try to resolve the matter directly before using an anonymous reporting system such as a hotline. Companies are increasingly using firms that provide professional case management services and software. Software is becoming popular as it provides reports of employee concerns, complaints, or observations of misconduct that can then be tracked and managed. It allows the company to track investigations, analysis, resolutions, and documentation of reported misconduct. This helps prevent lawsuits, and the shared management and prevention can help a company analyze and learn about ethical lapses. However, it is important for companies to choose the right software. They need to assess their current position and determine what they need going forward. Although only 10 to 15 percent of companies currently use some type of compliance management tool, many are moving toward the automated process that technology and software provide.

GLOBAL INITIATIVES

Use of an Ombudsman to Resolve Ethical Conflict

The history of the ombudsman goes back more than 2,000 years. The Chinese and the Romans were the first to use the ombudsman, a position originally designed to safeguard ordinary citizens against crime and corruption by public officials. After the fall of the Han Dynasty and the Roman Empire, ombudsmen were not used for several centuries. In the 1700s, the Scandinavian countries brought back the ombudsman and finely tuned its function. The word *ombudsman* is Scandinavian in origin. The first Scandinavian ombudsman was appointed by Swedish King Charles XII in 1713 to watch over various government functions. The king had been out of the country for several years, and subsequently, the country and government had fallen into disarray. The purpose of the ombudsman was to ensure that public officials acted lawfully.

Today, an ombudsman may be employed by any organization, including companies, governments, universities, and nonprofit firms. Essentially, the ombudsman acts as a third party to help resolve disputes between two parties by receiving complaints from individuals, investigating the complaints, and taking corrective action when needed. Much like its origins suggest, an ombudsman deals with two primary issues:

1. a decision, process, recommendation, or act that is contrary to law, rules, regulations, is a departure from established practice or procedure, or is perverse, arbitrary or unreasonable, unjust, biased, oppressive, or discriminatory

2. neglect, inattention, delay, incompetence, inefficiency, and ineptitude in the discharge of duties and responsibilities

Since 1713, many countries have implemented the use of the ombudsman, including New Zealand, the United Kingdom, and several Australian provinces. Since its revival in Scandinavia, the ombudsman has spread to over 100 countries and many private industries. Ombudsmen have also found their way into colleges and universities. Eastern Montana College at Billings was the first to appoint a campus ombudsman in 1966. Most universities today employ the ombudsman or similar system for resolving internal disputes, such as decisions made on personnel matters.

Ethics ombudsmen are also very common in today's business workplace and often serve an important role in developing an effective ethical compliance program. Employees will call upon the ombudsman when they have questions or concerns that, for some reason, cannot be resolved by their supervisor or department. Thus, an ombudsman offers an alternative for conflict resolution and essentially serves as a third party, so the individual occupying this position must be highly respected and trusted. However, the ombudsman is not considered "management," and employees must believe that he or she is neutral and reliable. Company ombudsmen also track new issues within the organization or its environment, make policy recommendations, and take on other projects that ensure employee and stakeholder interests are fully respected. There are several professional associations that provide training and guidance for ombudsmen, including the American Bar Association.

The Ayr Farmers Mutual Insurance Company asks its policyholders to send their complaints to the company ombudsman. Their policy is to treat policyholders in a fair, courteous, and timely manner, and complainants who have unresolved complaints will be advised how to contact the Office of the Insurance Ombudsman. In this way, ethical conflicts can be resolved in a fair and unbiased manner to prevent escalation into crisis events.

Sources: Kevin Jasser, "The Ombud's Perspective: A Critical Analysis of the ABA 2004 Ombuds Standards," *Dispute Resolution Journal*, 60 (August–October 2005): 56–61; Russell G. Smith, ed., *Crime in the Professions* (Burlington, VT: Ashgate, 2002); "Ombudsman," in Wikipedia, http://en.wikipedia.org/wiki/Ombudsman, accessed January 27, 2006; http://www.ayrmutual.com/ombudsman_service.htm, accessed May 10, 2006. ■

Whistle-Blowing

Interpersonal conflict ensues when employees think they know the right course of action in a situation, yet their work group or company promotes or requires a different, unethical decision. In such cases, employees may choose to follow their own values and refuse to participate in the unethical or illegal conduct. If they conclude that they cannot discuss what they are doing or what should be done with their coworkers or immediate supervisors, these employees may go outside the organization to publicize and correct the unethical situation. **Whistle-blowing** means exposing an employer's wrongdoing to outsiders, such as media or government regulatory agencies.

Whistle-blowers have provided pivotal evidence documenting corporate malfeasance at a number of companies. The importance of their role was highlighted when *Time* magazine named three whistle-blowers as its 2002 "Persons of the Year": Sherron Watkins of Enron, Cynthia Cooper of WorldCom, and Coleen Rowley of the

whistle-blowing
exposing an employer's wrongdoing to outsiders, such as media or government regulatory agencies

By posting these instructions for making anonymous reports, the University of California encourages employees and others to report improper activities.

UNIVERSITY OF CALIFORNIA HASTINGS COLLEGE OF THE LAW
HOW TO BLOW THE WHISTLE ON SUSPECTED IMPROPER ACTIVITIES
The UC Hastings College of the Law wants you to report improper activities, and will protect you from retaliation for whistleblowing

What You Can Report
Any activity by Hastings or a Hastings employee that violates any state or federal law or regulation (e.g., corruption, malfeasance, bribery, theft or misuse of government property, fraud, coercion, or conversion); or wastes money, or involves gross misconduct, gross incompetence, or gross inefficiency

Where To Report
- Your supervisor (or other appropriate administrator within your unit), who will report it to the Executive Director of Human Resources.
- Directly to the Executive Director of Human Resources. (Direct Line: 415-581-8868)

How To Report
- In writing or orally
- With as much specific factual information possible (report what you know, but don't investigate—leave that to the experts!)
- Anonymously, if preferred
Confidentiality will be maintained, to the extent possible

Protection from Retaliation
If you believe you have been retaliated against for whistleblowing, you may file a complaint with the Executive Director of Human Resources or your supervisor

For More Information
The Whistleblower and Whistleblower Protection policies can be found online at: www.uchastings.edu.

In addition to the above procedures, you have the option of reporting improper activities directly to the State Auditor whistleblower hotline at 1 (800) 952-5665 or to the California Attorney General hotline at 1 (800) 952-5225.

A Message from the State Auditor:
CALL THE STATE AUDITOR'S WHISTLEBLOWER HOTLINE TO REPORT THE IMPROPER ACTS OF STATE AGENCIES OR EMPLOYEES
Blow The Whistle on State Government Fraud and Waste

WHAT WE INVESTIGATE:
- Illegal acts like theft, fraud, or conflicts of interest by state employees.
- Misuse or abuse of state property or time by state employees.
- Gross misconduct, incompetence, or inefficiency by state employees.

WE FOLLOW THROUGH WHEN OUR INVESTIGATION SUBSTANTIATES YOUR ALLEGATION
Although we have no enforcement power, we keep the ball rolling by reporting the results of investigations that substantiate improprieties to:
- The head of the employing agency
- The attorney general or other enforcement agencies, legislative committees, and any other authority with jurisdiction
- The general public, keeping identities confidential

STATE LAW GOES TO BAT FOR YOU
- It requires the Bureau of State Audits to shield your identity (except from law enforcement).
- It helps guard against intimidation, threats, or coercion by state employees that could interfere with your right to disclose improper government activities.
- It helps keep you safe from reprisal, retaliation, threats, or coercion for reporting such information.

IF YOU EXPERIENCE RETALIATION, SPEAK UP!
If you're a state employee, contact the State Personnel Board in writing at 801 Capitol Mall, MS53, Sacramento, CA 95814. For additional information, call (916) 653-1403.
- University of California (UC) has its own system. If you work for UC, check our web site, www.bsa.ca.gov/bsa/hotline/filecomp.html, for a link to information on its current policy.
- California State University (CSU) has its own system. If you work for CSU, check our web site, www.bsa.ca.gov/bsa/hotline/filecomp.html for a link to information on its current policy.

REPORT WHAT YOU KNOW—Call 1(800) 952-5665 or
Mail the information to: Investigations, Bureau of State Audits, 555 Capitol Mall, Suite 300, Sacramento, CA 95814.

We cannot accept complaints via our web site or email. However, visit our web site at www.bsa.ca.gov/bsa/hotline/filecomp.html for more information on filing complaints.

Remember! The Bureau of State Audits can only investigate state government improprieties. We do not investigate misconduct by federal or local governments or by private businesses or organizations.

Rev. 6/29/06

FBI. Watkins, an Enron vice president, warned Kenneth Lay, the firm's CEO, that the company was using improper accounting procedures. "I am incredibly nervous that we will implode in a wave of accounting scandals," she told him, and the energy firm did exactly that within a few short months. Soon after, Watkins testified before Congress that Enron had concealed billions of dollars in debt through a complex scheme of off-balance-sheet partnerships.[30]

Historically, the fortunes of whistle-blowers have not been as positive: Most were labeled traitors, and many lost their jobs. A study of 300 whistle-blowers by researchers at the University of Pennsylvania found that 69 percent lost their jobs or were forced to retire after exposing their companies' misdeeds.[31] Ted Beatty, for example, worked for Houston-based Dynegy. After he was passed over for promotion, he began collecting information on Dynegy's complex energy trades. When Beatty gave the information to the Securities and Exchange Commission, an investment fund, and the media, it led to the resignation of the firm's top officers. Beatty did not benefit financially from blowing the whistle on Dynegy. In fact, he has been unable to find another job, had his home broken into, and received numerous threats.[32] Although most whistle-blowers do not receive positive recognition for pointing out corporate misconduct, some have turned to the courts and obtained substantial settlements. For example, the whistle-blowers who exposed Medicare fraud at SmithKline Beecham were awarded $42 million. In subsequent appeals, however, they learned that they might not be entitled to the full amount because it was unclear whether they were solely responsible for uncovering the abuses.[33] The third U.S Circuit Court of Appeals later overturned the awards and ordered the judge to take a look at whether one of the three whistle-blowers was the original source. The judge later ruled that only one of the three should get any money, saying that two of the three were "original sources" but that only one had the right to a reward since his lawsuit was the first filed. Robert Merena, the first to file the suit, was awarded more than $24 million while the others received nothing due to the strict "first to file" rule in the False Claims Act.[34] Table 6.3 provides a checklist of questions an employee should ask before blowing the whistle.

Figure 6.7 shows that nearly one in four employees experienced retaliation after reporting misconduct. Nearly half of all employees who reported misconduct received positive feedback for having done so.

TABLE 6.3 Questions to Ask Before Engaging in External Whistle-Blowing

1. Have I exhausted internal anonymous reporting opportunities within the organization?

2. Have I examined company polices and codes that outline acceptable behavior and violations of standards?

3. Is this a personal issue that should be resolved through other means?

4. Can I manage the stress that may evolve from exposing potential wrongdoing in the organization?

5. Can I deal with the consequences of resolving an ethical or legal conflict within the organization?

Source: © O. C. Ferrell 2006.

| FIGURE 6.7 | Outcome for Internal Whistle-Blowers Reporting Misconduct |

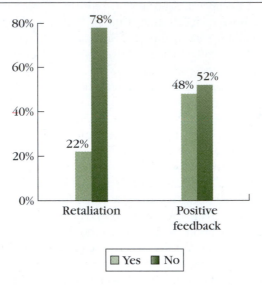

Source: National Business Ethics Survey, *How Employees View Ethics in Their Organizations 1994–2005*, Ethics Resource Center, p. 32. Copyright, Reprinted with permission from The Ethics Resource Center, Washington, DC.

CONTINUOUS IMPROVEMENT OF THE ETHICS PROGRAM

Improving the system that encourages employees to make more ethical decisions is not very different from implementing other types of business strategies. Implementation means putting strategies into action. Implementation in ethical compliance means the design of activities to achieve organizational objectives using available resources and given existing constraints. Implementation translates a plan for action into operational terms and establishes a means by which organizational ethical performance will be monitored, controlled, and improved.

A firm's ability to plan and implement ethical business standards depends in part on the organization's structuring resources and activities to achieve its ethical objectives in an effective and efficient manner. Some U.S. companies are setting up computer systems that encourage whistle-blowing. With more than 5,500 employees, Marvin Windows (one of the world's largest custom manufacturers of wood windows and doors) is concerned about employees feeling comfortable reporting violations of safety conditions, bad management, fraud, or theft. The system is anonymous and allows for reporting in native country languages. This system is used to alert management to potential problems in the organization and facilitate an investigation.[35] Systems such as these help alleviate employee concerns when reporting observed misconduct. As reported by the National Business Ethics Survey, employees' feelings that there will be no corrective action or there will be retaliation are leading factors influencing their decisions not to report observed misconduct. Other factors that play a role

TABLE 6.4	Mutual of Omaha's "Values for Success"

Openness and Trust—We encourage an open sharing of ideas and information, displaying a fundamental respect for each other as well as our cultural diversity.

Teamwork (Win/Win)—We work together to find solutions that carry positive results for others as well as ourselves, creating an environment that brings out the best in everyone.

Accountability/Ownership—We take ownership and accept accountability for achieving end results, and empower team members to do the same.

Sense of Urgency—We set priorities and handle all tasks and assignments in a timely manner.

Honesty and Integrity—We are honest and ethical with others, maintaining the highest standards of personal and professional conduct.

Customer-Focus—We never lose sight of our customers, and constantly challenge ourselves to meet their requirements even better.

Innovation and Risk—We question "the old way of doing things" and take prudent risks that can lead to innovative performance and process improvements.

Caring/Attentive (Be Here Now)—We take time to clear our minds to focus on the present moment, listening to our teammates and customers, and caring enough to hear their concerns.

Leadership—We provide direction, purpose, support, encouragement, and recognition to achieve our vision, meet our objectives and our values.

Personal and Professional Growth—We challenge ourselves and look for ways to be even more effective as a team and as individuals.

Source: "Transforming Our Culture: The Values for Success," Mutual of Omaha, www.careerlink.org/emp/mut/corp.htm, accessed March 30, 2006. Reprinted with permission.

when employees neglect to report wrongdoing include lack of anonymity, deciding someone else will report the action, and uncertainty about who should receive a report.[36]

A firm's values statement (see Table 6.4) is its foundation. It guides the company in all of its actions. People's attitudes and behavior must be guided by a shared commitment to the business instead of by obedience to traditional managerial authority. Encouraging diversity of perspectives, disagreement, and the empowerment of people within the organization helps to align the company's leadership with its employees.

If a company determines that its performance has not been satisfactory in ethical terms, that company's management may want to reorganize the way certain kinds of ethical decisions are made. For example, a decentralized organization may need to centralize key decisions, if only for a time, so that top-level managers can ensure that the decisions are ethical. Centralization may reduce the opportunity for lower level managers and employees to make unethical decisions. Top management can then focus on improving the corporate culture and infusing more ethical values throughout the organization by providing rewards for positive behavior and sanctions for negative behavior. General Motors and Dell Computer are examples of centralized organizations, possibly because of their focus on manufacturing processes. In other companies, decentralization of important decisions may be a better way to attack ethical problems so that lower level managers, familiar with the forces of the local business environment and local culture and values, can make more decisions. Coca-Cola is a more decentralized company due to its use of independent distributors and unique localized cultures. Whether the ethics function is centralized or decentralized, the key need is to delegate authority in such a way that the organization can achieve ethical performance.

IMPLEMENTING ORGANIZATIONAL ETHICS PROGRAMS

There is increasing support for the belief that it is good business for an organization to be ethical and that ethical cultures emerge from strong leadership. Many agree that the character and success of the most admired companies emanate from their leader. John Kotter noted that there are four things that a leader must do. First, leaders should create a common goal or vision for the company. Leaders are also good at getting "buy-in" or support from significant partners. Great leaders are also great motivators and know how to use the resources available to them. The last characteristic is the spirit of great leaders who enjoy their jobs and approach them with an almost contagious tenacity, passion, and commitment.[37]

If a company is to maintain ethical behavior, its policies and standards must be modeled by top management. Maintaining an ethical culture can be difficult if top management does not support such behavior. In an effort to keep earnings high and boost stock prices, many firms have engaged in falsifying revenue reports. Top executives in these firms encouraged the behavior because they held stock options—and could receive bonus packages—tied to the company's performance. Thus, higher reported revenues meant larger executive payoffs.

Along with strong ethical leadership, a strong corporate culture in support of ethical behavior can also play a key role in guiding employee behavior. Note in Figure 6.8 that the majority of firms have at least some of the critical elements installed in their ethics programs.

FIGURE 6.8   Prevalence of Formal Program Elements

One in four organizations across the United States has implemented all the elements of a formal ethics program, as defined in NBES.

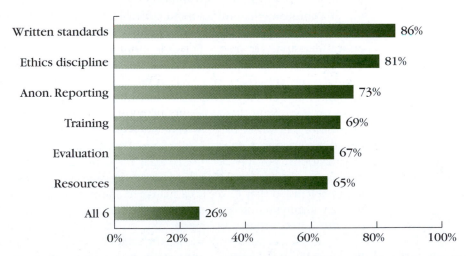

Source: National Business Ethics Survey, *How Employees View Ethics in Their Organizations 1994–2005,* Ethics Resource Center, p. 56. Copyright, Reprinted with permission from The Ethics Resource Center, Washington, DC.

FIGURE 6.9 Perceived Tone and Culture, Tone at the Top, Perceptions of the CEO and Other Senior Executives

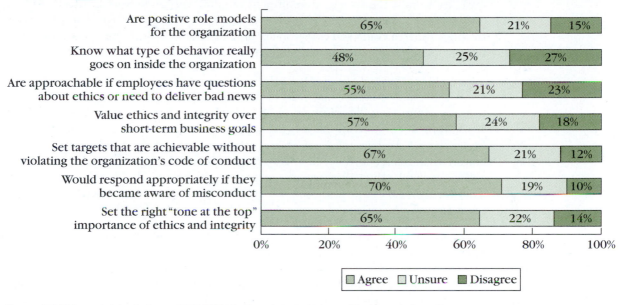

Source: KPMG Forensic Integrity Survey 2005–2006 http://www.kpmginsiders.com/display_analysis.asp?
cs_id=148597, accessed March 9, 2006.

In the following sections, we discuss the roles of leadership and culture in shaping organizational ethics. The "tone at the top" is often cited as a determining factor in creating a high-integrity organization.

A KPMG Forensic Integrity Survey (Figure 6.9) asked employees whether their chief executive officer (CEO) and other senior executives exhibited characteristics attributable to personal integrity and ethical leadership. Nearly two-thirds of employees believed that their leaders served as positive role models for their organizations. However, roughly half suggested a lack of confidence (based on "unsure" and "disagree" responses) that their CEOs knew about behaviors further down in the organization. Nearly half suggested a lack of confidence that their leaders would be approachable if employees had ethics concerns. Seventy percent agreed that their CEOs would respond appropriately to matters brought to their attention. Overall, nearly two-thirds of employees agreed their leaders set the right tone at the top, leaving one-third unsure or in disagreement.

The Role of Leadership

Leadership influences many aspects of organizational behavior, including employees' acceptance of and adherence to organizational norms and values. Leadership that focuses on building strong organizational values among employees creates agreement on norms of conduct. Leaders in highly visible positions in the organization play a key role in transmitting values and diffusing values, norms, and codes of ethics.[38] Two dominant styles are transactional and transformational leadership. Transactional leadership attempts to create employee satisfaction through negotiating for levels of performance or "bartering" for desired behaviors. Transformational leaders, in contrast, try to raise the level of commitment of employees and create greater trust and motivation.[39] Transformational leaders attempt to promote activities and behavior through a shared vision and common learning experiences. Both transformational and transactional leaders can positively influence the organizational climate.

TRANSFORMATIONAL LEADERSHIP Transformational leaders communicate a sense of mission, stimulate new ways of thinking, and enhance as well as generate new learning experiences. Transformational leadership considers the employees' needs and aspirations in conjunction with organizational needs. Therefore, transformational leaders have a stronger influence on coworker support and the building of an ethical culture than transactional leaders. Transformational leaders also build a commitment and respect for values that provide agreement on how to deal with ethical issues. Transformational ethical leadership is best suited for higher levels of ethical commitment among employees and strong stakeholder support for an ethical climate.

TRANSACTIONAL LEADERSHIP Transactional leadership focuses on making certain that the required conduct and procedures are implemented. The "barter" aspects of negotiation to achieve the desired outcomes result in a dynamic relationship between leaders and employees where reactions, conflicts, and crises influence the relationship more than ethical concerns. Transactional leaders produce employees who achieve a negotiated level of required ethical performance or compliance. As long as employees and leaders find the exchange mutually rewarding, the compliance relationship is likely to be successful. However, transactional leadership is best suited to quickly changing ethical climates or reacting to ethical problems or issues. Michael Capellas used transactional leadership to change WorldCom's—now called MCI—culture and ethical conduct when he took over as CEO and chair after an accounting scandal forced the company into bankruptcy proceedings. Capellas sought to restore WorldCom's credibility in the marketplace by bringing in a new board of directors, creating a corporate ethics office, enhancing the code of ethics, and launching new employee financial reporting and ethics training initiatives.[40]

LEADERS INFLUENCE CORPORATE CULTURE

Organizational leaders use their power and influence to shape corporate culture. Power refers to the influence that leaders and managers have over the behavior and decisions of subordinates. An individual has power over others when his or her presence causes them to behave differently. Exerting power is one way to influence the ethical decision-making framework we described in Chapter 5. Significant others and opportunity provide the cultural context for gaining conformity.

The status and power of leaders are directly related to the amount of pressure they can exert on employees to conform to their expectations. A superior in an authority position can put strong pressure on employees to comply, even when their personal ethical values conflict with the superior's wishes. For example, a manager might say to a subordinate, "I want the confidential data about our competitor's sales on my desk by Monday morning, and I don't care how you get it." A subordinate who values his or her job or who does not realize the ethical questions involved may feel pressure to do something unethical to obtain the data.

There are five power bases from which one person may influence another: (1) reward power, (2) coercive power, (3) legitimate power, (4) expert power, and (5) referent power.[41] These five bases of power can be used to motivate individuals either ethically or unethically.

REWARD POWER Reward power refers to a person's ability to influence the behavior of others by offering them something desirable. Typical rewards might be money, status, or promotion. Consider, for example, a retail salesperson who has two watches (a Timex and a Casio) for sale. Let us assume that the Timex is of higher quality than the Casio but is priced about the same. In the absence of any form of reward power, the salesperson would logically attempt to sell the Timex watch. However, if Casio gave him an extra 10 percent commission, he would probably focus his efforts on selling the Casio watch. Such "carrot dangling" and incentives have been shown to be very effective in getting people to change their behavior in the long run. In the short run, however, it is not as effective as coercive power.

COERCIVE POWER Coercive power is essentially the opposite of reward power. Instead of rewarding a person for doing something, coercive power penalizes actions or behavior. As an example, suppose a valuable client asks an industrial salesperson for a bribe and insinuates that he will take his business elsewhere if his demands are not met. Although the salesperson believes bribery is unethical, she has been told by her boss that she must keep the client happy or lose her chance at promotion. The boss is imposing a negative sanction if certain actions are not performed. Every year, 20 percent of Enron's workforce was asked to leave because they were ranked as "needs improvement" or other issues were noted. Employees not wanting to fall into the bottom 20 percent engaged in corruption or exhibited complacency toward corruption.[42]

Coercive power relies on fear to change behavior. For this reason, it has been found to be more effective in changing behavior in the short run than in the long run. Coercion is often employed in situations where there is an extreme imbalance in power. However, people who are continually subjected to coercion may seek a counterbalance by aligning themselves with other more powerful persons or simply by leaving the organization. In firms that use coercive power, relationships usually break down in the long run. Power is an ethical issue not only for individuals but also for work groups that establish policy for large corporations.

LEGITIMATE POWER Legitimate power stems from the belief that a certain person has the right to exert influence and that certain others have an obligation to accept it. The titles and positions of authority that organizations bestow on individuals appeal to this traditional view of power. Many people readily acquiesce to those who wield legitimate power, sometimes committing acts that are contrary to their beliefs and values. Betty Vincent, an accountant at WorldCom, objected to her supervisor's requests to produce improper accounting entries in an effort to conceal WorldCom's deteriorating financial condition. She finally gave in to their requests, being told this was the only way to save the company. She and other WorldCom accountants eventually pleaded guilty to conspiracy and fraud charges. She was sentenced to five months in prison and five months of house arrest.[43]

Such staunch loyalty to authority figures can also be seen in corporations that have strong charismatic leaders and centralized structures. In business, if a superior tells an employee to increase sales "no matter what it takes" and that employee has a strong affiliation to legitimate power, the employee may try anything to fulfill that order.

EXPERT POWER Expert power is derived from a person's knowledge (or the perception that the person possesses knowledge). Expert power usually stems from a superior's credibility with subordinates. Credibility, and thus expert power, is positively related to the number of years a person has worked in a firm or industry, the person's education, or the honors he or she has received for performance. Expert power can also be conferred on a person by others who perceive him or her as an expert on a specific topic. A relatively low-level secretary may have expert power because he or she knows specific details about how the business operates and can even make suggestions on how to inflate revenue through expense reimbursements.

Expert power may cause ethical problems when it is used to manipulate others or to gain an unfair advantage. Physicians, lawyers, or consultants can take unfair advantage of unknowing clients, for example. Accounting firms may gain extra income by ignoring concerns about the accuracy of financial data they are provided in an audit.

REFERENT POWER Referent power may exist when one person perceives that his or her goals or objectives are similar to another's. The second person may attempt to influence the first to take actions that will lead both to achieve their objectives. Because they share the same objectives, the person influenced by the other will perceive the other's use of referent power as beneficial. For this power relationship to be effective, however, some sort of empathy must exist between the individuals. Identification with others helps to boost the decision maker's confidence when making a decision, thus increasing his or her referent power.

Consider the following situation: Lisa Jones, a manager in the accounting department of a manufacturing firm, has asked Michael Wong, a salesperson, to speed up the delivery of sales contracts, which usually take about one month to process after a deal is reached. Michael protests that he is not to blame for the slow process. Rather than threaten to slow delivery of Michael's commission checks (coercive power), Lisa makes use of referent power. She invites Michael to lunch, and they discuss some of their work concerns, including the problem of slow-moving documentation. They agree that if document processing cannot be speeded up, both will be hurt. Lisa then suggests that Michael start faxing contracts instead of mailing them. He agrees to give it a try, and within several weeks, the contracts are moving faster. Lisa's job is made easier, and Michael gets his commission checks a little sooner.

The five bases of power are not mutually exclusive. People typically use several power bases to effect change in others. Although power in itself is neither ethical nor unethical, its use can raise ethical issues. Sometimes, a leader uses power to manipulate a situation or a person's values in a way that creates a conflict with the person's value structure. For example, a manager who forces an employee to choose between staying home with his sick child and keeping his job is using coercive power, which creates a direct conflict with the employee's values.

The Role of an Ethical Corporate Culture

Top management provides a plan for the corporate culture. If executives and CEOs do not explicitly address these issues, a culture may emerge where unethical behavior is sanctioned and rewarded. To be most successful, ethical standards and expected behaviors should be integrated throughout every organizational process from hiring, training, compensating, and rewarding to firing. Many employees who view unethical conduct do not report it because they fear inaction, they are afraid they will not remain anonymous, or they believe their organization is not concerned about the activity. Frank Navran, a consultant to the Ethics Resource Center, has identified seven steps to changing the ethical culture of an organization (see Table 6.5).

Organizational ethical culture is important to employees. A fair, open, and trusting organizational climate supports an ethical culture and can contribute to lower turnover and higher employee satisfaction. Starbucks offers excellent health benefits to its employees as well as a stock ownership plan called Bean Stock. These benefits are available to the entire employee workforce, which is mostly part time. Turnover at Starbucks has historically been one-seventh of the industry standard, while its sales and profits continue to soar. Starbucks was noted as one of the 100 Best Companies to Work For in *Fortune*'s annual survey in every year since 1998 except 2001. Howard Schultz, founder and CEO, was voted one of the "Top 25 Managers" by *Business Week*.[44] In 2003, 2004, and 2005, Starbucks was named in the top ten of America's most admired companies.[45]

Some leaders assume that hiring or promoting good, ethical managers will automatically produce an ethical organizational climate. This ignores the fact that an individual may have limited opportunity to enforce his or her own personal ethics on management systems and informal decision making that occurs in the organization. The greatest influence on employee behavior is that of peers and coworkers.[46] Many times, workers do not know what constitutes specific ethical violations such as price fixing, deceptive advertising, consumer fraud, and copyright violations. The more ethical the culture of the organization is perceived to be, the less likely it is that unethical decision making will occur. Over time, an organization's failure to monitor or manage its culture may foster questionable behavior. FedEx maintains a strong ethical culture and has woven its values and expectations throughout the company.

TABLE 6.5	Steps for Changing the Ethical Culture of an Organization

1. State your position, philosophy, or belief.
2. Create formal organizational systems.
3. Communicate expectations through informal (leadership) systems.
4. Reinforce the policy through measurements and rewards.
5. Implement communications and education strategies.
6. Use responses to critical events to underscore commitment.
7. Avoid the perception of hidden agendas.

Source: Ethics Resource Center, www.ethics.org/resources/article_detail.cfm?id=785, accessed April 26, 2006. Copyright, Reprinted with permission from The Ethics Resource Center, Washington, DC.

Employees who work in an open environment may be more likely to communicate freely and share information, including perspectives on ethical issues.

FedEx's open-door policy specifies that employees may bring up any work issue or problem with any manager in the organization.[47]

Variation in Employee Conduct

Although the corporation is required to take responsibility for conducting its business ethically, a substantial amount of research indicates that there are significant differences in the values and philosophies that influence how the individuals that comprise corporations make ethical decisions.[48] In other words, because people are culturally diverse and have different values, they interpret situations differently and will vary in the ethical decisions they make on the same ethical issue.

Table 6.6 shows that approximately 10 percent of employees take advantage of situations to further their own personal interests. These individuals are more likely to manipulate, cheat, or be self-serving when the benefits gained from doing so are greater than the penalties for the misconduct. Such employees may choose to take office supplies from work for personal use if the only penalty they may suffer if caught is having to pay for the supplies. The lower the risk of being caught, the higher the chance that the 10 percent most likely to take advantage will be involved in unethical activities.

Another 40 percent of workers go along with the work group on most matters. These employees are most concerned about the social implications of their actions and want to fit into the organization. Although they have their own personal opinions, they are easily influenced by what people around them are doing. These individuals may know that using office supplies for personal use is improper, yet they view it as acceptable because their coworkers do so. These employees rationalize their action by

TABLE 6.6	Variation in Employee Conduct		
10 Percent	**40 Percent**	**40 Percent**	**10 Percent**
Follow their own values and beliefs; believe that their values are superior to those of others in the company	Always try to follow company policies	Go along with the work group	Take advantage of situations if the penalty is less than the benefit—the risk of being caught is low

These percentages are based on a number of studies in the popular press and data gathered by the authors. The percentages are not exact and represent a general typology that may vary by organization. The 10 percent that will take advantage is adapted from John Fraedrich and O. C. Ferrell, "Cognitive Consistency of Marketing Managers in Ethical Situations," *Journal of the Academy of Marketing Science* 20 (Summer 1992): 243–252.

saying that the use of office supplies is one of the benefits of working at their particular business, and it must be acceptable because the company does not enforce a policy precluding the behavior. Coupled with this philosophy is the belief that no one will get into trouble for doing what everybody else is doing, for there is safety in numbers.

About 40 percent of a company's employees, as shown in Table 6.6, always try to follow company policies and rules. These workers not only have a strong grasp of their corporate culture's definition of acceptable behavior, but they also attempt to comply with codes of ethics, ethics training, and other communications about appropriate conduct. If the company has a policy that prohibits taking office supplies from work, these employees probably would observe it. However, they likely would not speak out about the 40 percent who choose to go along with the work group, for these employees prefer to focus on their jobs and steer clear of any organizational misconduct. If the company fails to communicate standards of appropriate behavior, members of this group will devise their own.

The final 10 percent of employees try to maintain formal ethical standards that focus on rights, duties, and rules. They embrace values that assert certain inalienable rights and actions, which they perceive to be always ethically correct. In general, members of this group believe that their values are right and superior to the values of others in the company, or even to the company's value system, when an ethical conflict arises. These individuals have a tendency to report the misconduct of others or to speak out when they view activities within the company as unethical. Consequently, members of this group would probably report colleagues who take office supplies.

The significance of this variation in the way individuals behave ethically is simply this: Employees use different approaches when making ethical decisions. Because of the probability that a large percentage of any work group will either take advantage of a situation or at least go along with the work group, it is vital that companies provide communication and control mechanisms to maintain an ethical culture. Companies that fail to monitor activities and enforce ethics policies provide a low-risk environment for employees who are inclined to take advantage of situations to accomplish their personal, and sometimes unethical, objectives.

Good business practice and concern for the law require organizations to recognize this variation in employees' desire to be ethical. The percentages in Table 6.6 are only estimates, and the actual percentages of each type of employee may vary widely across organizations based on individuals and corporate culture. The specific percentages are less important than the fact that our research has identified these variations as existing within most organizations. Organizations should focus particular attention on managers who oversee the day-to-day operations of employees within the company. They should also provide training and communication to ensure that the business operates ethically; that it does not become the victim of fraud or theft; and that employees, customers, and other stakeholders are not abused through the misconduct of people who have a pattern of unethical behavior.

As we have seen throughout this book, many examples can be cited of employees and managers who have no concern for ethical conduct but are nonetheless hired and placed in positions of trust. Some corporations continue to support executives who ignore environmental concerns, poor working conditions, or defective products or who engage in accounting fraud. Executives who can get results, regardless of the consequences, are often admired and lauded, especially in the business press. When their unethical or even illegal actions become public knowledge, however, they risk more than the loss of their positions. Table 6.7 summarizes the penalties that corporate executives have experienced over the past several years.

TABLE 6.7   Penalties for Convictions of Organizational Wrongdoing

Executive/Company	Trial Outcome
Franklin Brown former general counsel Rite Aid	Convicted. Sentenced to 10 years in prison.
Bernard Ebbers former chairman, CEO WorldCom	Convicted. Sentenced to 25 years to life. Lost his appeal in 2006 and is now in prison.
Dennis Kozlowski former CEO, Tyco	Mistrial in first trial; in second, convicted and sentenced to 8 1/3 years to 25 years.
Jamie Olis former VP of finance Dynegy	Convicted. Sentenced to 24 years in prison without the chance of parole. Sentence overturned on appeal and is under review.
Frank Quattrone former investment banker, CSFB	Convicted in second trial, but conviction overturned due to error in jury instructions.
John Rigas Adelphia founder	Convicted. Sentenced to 15 years in prison.
Richard Scrushy HealthSouth founder	Acquitted on all counts of corporate fraud but convicted on six counts of bribery, conspiracy, and mail fraud.
Theodore Sihpol Bank of America broker	Acquitted on 29 of 33 criminal counts. No retrial on remaining counts.
Martha Stewart Martha Stewart Living Omnimedia founder	Convicted. Sentenced to five months in prison, five months of home confinement and is settling civil charges filed by the SEC.

Source: "White-Collar Defendants: Take the Stand, or Not?" April 2, 2006, WSJ.com Research, http://online.wsj.com/article/SB114382340584213619.html?mod=article-outset-box, accessed April 6, 2006.

Reducing unethical behavior is a business goal no different from increasing profits. If progress is not being made toward creating and maintaining an ethical culture, the company needs to determine why and take corrective action, either by enforcing current standards more strictly or by setting higher standards. If the code of ethics is aggressively enforced and becomes part of the corporate culture, it can be effective in improving ethical behavior within the organization. If a code is merely window-dressing and not genuinely part of the corporate culture, it will accomplish very little.

SUMMARY

A strategic approach to ethical decisions will contribute to both business and society. To be socially responsible and promote legal and ethical conduct, an organization should develop an organizational ethics program by establishing, communicating, and monitoring ethical values and legal requirements that characterize its history, culture, industry, and operating environment. Most companies begin the process of establishing an organizational ethics program by developing a code of conduct, a formal statement that describes what the organization expects of its employees. A code should reflect senior management's desire for organizational compliance with values, rules, and policies that support an ethical climate. Codes of conduct help employees and managers address ethical dilemmas by prescribing or limiting specific activities.

Organizational ethics programs must have oversight by high-ranking persons known to respect legal and ethical standards. Often referred to as ethics officers, these persons are responsible for assessing the needs and risks to be addressed in an organization-wide ethics program, developing and distributing a code of conduct, conducting training programs for employees, establishing and maintaining a confidential service to answer questions about ethical issues, making sure the company is in compliance with government regulations, monitoring and auditing ethical conduct, taking action on possible violations of the organization's code, and reviewing and updating the code. Instituting a training program and a system to communicate and educate employees about the firm's ethical standards is a major step in developing an effective ethics program.

Ethical compliance involves comparing employee ethical performance with the organization's ethical standards. Ethical compliance can be measured through employee observation, internal audits, reporting systems, and investigations. An internal system for reporting misconduct is especially useful. Employees who conclude that they cannot discuss current or potential unethical activities with coworkers or superiors and go outside the organization for help are known as whistle-blowers.

Consistent enforcement and necessary disciplinary action are essential to a functional ethical compliance program. Continuous improvement of the ethics program is necessary. Ethical leadership and a strong corporate culture in support of ethical behavior are necessary to implement an effective organizational ethics program.

KEY TERMS

codes of conduct (p. 188)
ethics officer (p. 192)
whistle-blowing (p. 202)

DISCUSSION QUESTIONS

1. How can an organization be socially responsible and promote legal and ethical conduct?
2. What are the elements that should be included in a strong ethics program?
3. What is a code of conduct and how can a code be communicated effectively to employees?
4. How and why are a training program and a communications system important in developing an effective ethics program?
5. What does ethical compliance involve and how can it be measured?
6. What role does leadership play in influencing organizational behavior?
7. Compare transformational leadership and transactional leadership.

EXPERIENTIAL EXERCISE

Visit the website of the Ethics and Compliance Officer Association (http://www.theecoa.org). What is the association's current mission and membership composition? Review the website to determine the issues and concerns that comprise the ECOA's most recent programs, publications, and research. What trends do you find? What topics seem most important to ethics officers today?

WHAT WOULD YOU DO?

Robert Rubine flipped through his messages and wondered which call he should return first. It was only 3:30 P.M., but he felt as though he had been through a week's worth of decisions and worries. Mondays were normally busy, but this one was anything but normal. Robert's employer, Medic-All, is in the business of selling a wide array of medical supplies and equipment. The company's products range from relatively inexpensive items, like bandages, gloves, and syringes, to more costly items, such as microscopes, incubators, and examination tables. Although the product line is broad, it represents the "basics" required in most health-care settings. Medic-All utilizes an inside sales force to market its products to private hospitals, elder care facilities, government health-care institutions, and other similar organizations. The company employs 275 people and is considered a small business under government rules.

The inside sales force has the authority to negotiate on price, which works well in the highly competitive market of medical supplies and equipment. The salespeople are compensated primarily on a commission basis. The sales force and other employees receive legal training annually. All employees are required to sign Medic-All's code of ethics each year and attend an ethics training session. Despite the importance of the inside sales force, Medic-All has experienced a good deal of turnover in its sales management team. A new lead manager was hired about four months ago. Robert oversees the sales division in his role as vice president of marketing and operations.

Late Friday afternoon last week, Robert received word that two employees in the company's headquarters were selling products to the government at a higher price than they were selling them to other organizations. Both employees have been on the job for over two years and seem to be good performers. A few of their sales colleagues have complained to the lead sales manager about the high quarterly commissions that the two employees recently received. They insinuated that these commissions were earned unfairly by charging government-run hospitals high prices. A cursory review of their accounts showed that, in many instances, the government is paying more than other organizations. Under procurement rules, the government is supposed to pay a fair price, one that other cost-conscious customers would pay. When asked about the situation, the two employees said that the price offered was based on volume, so the pricing always varied from customer to customer.

Robert took the information to his boss, the company president. The president and Robert discussed how these employees received legal and ethics training, signed the company code of ethics, and should have been knowledgeable about rules related to government procurement. The president said that these two salespeople sounded liked "rogue employees," who committed acts without management approval to increase their commissions. Robert and the president discussed many issues and scenarios, such as how to deal with the two salespeople, whether to continue the investigation and inform the government, strategies for preventing the problem in the future, how to protect the firm's good name, whether the company could face suspension from lucrative government business, and others. What would you do?

Employee Relations

CHAPTER 7

CHAPTER OBJECTIVES

- To discuss employees as stakeholders

- To examine the economic, legal, ethical, and philanthropic responsibilities related to employees

- To describe an employer of choice and the employer of choice's relationship to social responsibility

CHAPTER OUTLINE

Although large oil and energy companies are often the target of criticism, Royal Dutch Shell has invested many resources into its social responsibility initiatives. Environmental issues remain at the forefront of the company's agenda, but Shell collaborates and innovates with stakeholders on a variety of other issues. This global firm, which has ventures in nearly 150 countries, operates on the basis of eight business principles. These principles were first established in 1976 and have been revised several times, with the latest revision in 2005. Some of the principles include (1) communication and engagement, (2) compliance, (3) business integrity, and (4) local communities. Even in the midst of shutting down industrial operations in one Norwegian city, Shell recently proved its solid commitment to communities.

When Shell decided to close an oil refinery in Sola, Norway, the company engaged various groups in the decision-making process. Shell provided job assistance and worked with area employers and organizations to find new positions for employees. Shell also created a dialog with the local government and other constituencies, who had a voice in how the plant closing was implemented. Based on these conversations, the community was able to benefit from the refinery closing. Laboratory equipment was donated to local schools. The refinery's boiling system was installed in a retirement community. To date, over 98 percent of the refinery plant and materials have been recycled or used for another purpose. So that the city does not have an abandoned and dilapidated area, new businesses occupy the land where the refinery once stood. Shell recognizes that, far beyond the economic impact, business affects communities and local infrastructure in many other ways. Health, safety, local culture, natural resources, security, and secondary economic effects are also part of Shell's stakeholder assessment for strategic social responsibility. Even when faced with the difficult task of workforce reduction, the company is committed to engaging stakeholders so that various interests and needs are considered from a long-term perspective.[1] ■

This vignette illustrates the extent to which some firms consider the needs, wants, and characteristics of employees and other stakeholders in designing various business processes and practices. Although it is widely understood that employees are of great importance, beliefs about the extent and types of responsibilities that organizations should assume toward employees are likely to vary. For example, some managers are primarily concerned with economic and legal responsibilities, whereas proponents of the stakeholder interaction model would advocate for a broader perspective. As this chapter will show, a delicate balance of power, responsibility, and accountability resides in the relationships a company develops with its employees.

Because employee stakeholders are so important to the success of any company, this chapter is devoted to the employer-employee relationship. We explore the many issues related to the social responsibilities employers have to their employees, including the employee-employer contract, workforce reduction, wages and benefits, labor unions, health and safety, equal opportunity, sexual harassment, whistle-blowing, diversity, and work/life balance. Along the way, we discuss a number of significant laws that affect companies' human resources programs. Finally, we look at the concept of employer of choice and what it takes to earn that reputation and distinction.

EMPLOYEE STAKEHOLDERS

Think for a minute about the first job or volunteer position you held. What information were you given about the organization's strategic direction? How were you managed and treated by supervisors? Did you feel empowered to make decisions? How much training did you receive? The answers to these questions may reveal the types of responsibilities that employers have toward employees. If you worked in a restaurant, for example, training should have covered safety, cleanliness, and other health issues mandated by law. If you volunteered at a hospital, you may have learned about the ethical and economic considerations in providing health care for the uninsured or poor and the philanthropic efforts used to support the hospital financially. Although such issues may have seemed subtle or even unimportant at the time, they are related to the responsibilities that employees, government, and other stakeholders expect of employing organizations.

RESPONSIBILITIES TO EMPLOYEES

In her book *The Working Life: The Promise and Betrayal of Modern Work*, business professor Joanne B. Ciulla writes about the different types of work, the history of work, the value of work to a person's self-concept, the relationship between work and freedom, and as the title implies, the rewards and pitfalls that exist in the employee-employer relationship. Ciulla contends that two common phrases—"Get a job!" and "Get a life!"—are antithetical in today's society, meaning they seem diametrically opposed goals or values.[2] For the ancient Greeks, work was seen as the gods' way of punishing humans. Centuries later, Benedictine monks, who built farms, church abbeys, and villages, were considered the lowest order of monks because they labored. By the eighteenth century, the Protestant work ethic had emerged to imply that work was a method for discovering and creating a person.[3] Today, psychologists, families, and friends lament how work has become the primary source of many individuals' fulfillment, status, and happiness. Just as in the complicated history of work, the responsibilities, obligations, and expectations between employees and employers are also fraught with challenges and debates. In this section, we review the four levels of corporate social responsibilities as they relate to employees. Although we focus primarily on the responsibilities of employers to employees, we also acknowledge the role that employees have in achieving strategic social responsibility.

Economic Issues

Perhaps no story in recent memory underscores the economic realm of employment more vividly than the saga of Malden Mills Industries. In 1995, 750,000 square feet of factory and office space at Malden Mills burned to the ground. It was just a few weeks before the winter holidays, and in addition, workers were injured. In an unusual move, CEO Aaron Feuerstein paid end-of-year bonuses and employees' full wages and benefits while the buildings were reconstructed. Human resource managers set up a temporary job-training center, collected Christmas gifts for employees' children, and worked with community agencies to support employees and their families.[4] Even after injured employees filed a workers' compensation claim against Malden Mills, Feuerstein said, "The welfare of our employees has always been and continues to be a priority of Malden Mills."[5] When economic factors forced Malden Mills through several employee layoffs in the late 1990s, employees were offered jobs at another plant and received career transition assistance. Essentially, Feuerstein believes in an unwritten contract that considers the economic prospects of both employer and employees. Several years later, Malden Mills filed for bankruptcy protection, part of which was blamed on losses from the fire. Lenders provided funding for the company to continue operations and develop a reorganization strategy to emerge from bankruptcy. The company emerged from bankruptcy, but the plan took the CEO's responsibility from Feuerstein and placed it with lenders and creditors. Today, Malden Mills is thriving and well known for its Polartec fabric and textiles. The U.S. government recently authorized $15 million in armed services contracts with the company.[6]

EMPLOYEE-EMPLOYER CONTRACT As we discussed in Chapter 1, the recent history of social responsibility has brought many changes to bear on stakeholder relationships. One of the more dramatic shifts has been in the "contract" and mutual understanding that exist between employee and employer. At the beginning of the twenty-first century, many companies had to learn and accept new rules for recruiting, retaining, and compensating employees. For example, although employers held the position of power for many years, the new century brought record employment rates and the tightest job market in years. Huge salaries, signing bonuses, multiple offers, and flexible, not seniority-based, compensation plans became commonplace throughout the late 1990s. The economic downturn, September 11, 2001, attacks, and a series of business scandals in the early 2000s brought a decline in lucrative employment opportunities and forced many firms to implement layoffs and other cost-cutting measures. Pay raises, health-care benefits, mental health coverage, retirement funding, paid maternity leave, and other benefits were reduced or costs were shifted to employees.[7]

psychological contract

the beliefs, perceptions, expectations, and obligations that make up the agreement between individuals and the organizations that employ them

Regardless of salary, perks, and specific position, a **psychological contract** exists between an employee and employer. This contract is largely unwritten and includes the beliefs, perceptions, expectations, and obligations that make up the agreement between individuals and the organizations that employ them.[8] Details of the contract develop through communications, via interactions with managers and coworkers, and through perceptions of the corporate culture.[9] This contract, though informal, has a significant influence on the way employees act. When promises and expectations are not met, a psychological contract breach occurs, and employees may become less loyal, less trusting, inattentive to work, or otherwise dissatisfied with their employment situation.[10] On the other hand, when employers present information in a credible, competent, and trustworthy manner, employees are more likely to be supportive of and committed to the organization. This commitment is revealed through employee interactions with important stakeholders and ultimately has a positive influence on shareholder value, as we discussed in Chapter 1.[11] Just as in other stakeholder relationships, expectations in the employment psychological contract are subject to a

TABLE 7.1	Changes in Employees' Psychological Contract with Employers	
Characteristic	**Old**	**New**
Attachment to employer	Long term	Near term
Readiness to change jobs	Not interested	Not looking, but will listen
Priorities on the job	Company and its goals	Personal life and career
Devotion to employer goals	Follows orders	Usually buys in
Effort on the job	100 percent	110 percent
Motto	Semper fidelis ("Always faithful")	Carpe diem ("Seize the day")

Source: Neil Conway and Rob B. Briner, *Understanding Psychological Contracts at Work* (London: Oxford University Press, 2006).

variety of influences. This section discusses how the contract has evolved over the last 100 years. Table 7.1 profiles six characteristics that have changed over time in employees' psychological contract with employers.

Until the early 1900s, the relationship between employer and employee was best characterized as a master-servant relationship.[12] In this view, there was a natural imbalance in power that meant employment was viewed as a privilege that included few rights and many obligations. Employees were expected to work for the best interests of the organization, even at the expense of personal and family welfare. At this time, most psychologists and management scholars believed that good leadership required aggressive and domineering behavior.[13] Images from Upton Sinclair's novel *The Jungle,* which we discuss briefly in the next chapter, characterized the extreme negative effects of this employment contract.[14]

In the 1920s and 1930s, employees assumed a relationship with an employer that was more balanced in terms of power, responsibilities, and obligations. This shift meant that employees and employers were coequals, and in legal terms, employees had many more rights than under the master-servant model.[15] Much of the employment law in the United States was enacted in the 1930s, when legislators passed laws related to child labor, wages, working hours, and labor unions.[16] Throughout the twentieth century, the employee-employer contract evolved along the coequals model, although social critics began to question the influence large companies had on employees.

In the 1950s, political commentator and sociologist C. Wright Mills criticized white-collar work as draining on employees' time, energy, and even personalities. He also believed that individuals with business power were apt to keep employees happy in an attempt to ward off the development of stronger labor unions and unfavorable government regulations.[17] A few years later, the classic book *The Organization Man* by William H. Whyte was published. This book examined the social nature of work, including the inherent conflict between belonging and contributing to a group on the job while maintaining a sense of independence and identity.[18] Organizational researchers and managers in the 1960s began to question authoritarian behavior and consider participatory management styles that assumed employees were motivated and eager to assume responsibility for work. A study by the U.S. Department of

Health, Education, and Welfare in the early 1970s confirmed that employees wanted interesting work and a chance to demonstrate their skills. The report also recommended job redesign and managerial approaches that increased participation, freedom, and democracy at work.[19] By the 1980s, a family analogy was being used to describe the workplace. This implied strong attention to employee welfare and prompted the focus on business ethics that we explored in Chapters 5 and 6. At the same time, corporate mission statements touted the importance of customers and employees, and *In Search of Excellence,* a best-selling book by distinguished professor Thomas J. Peters and business consultant Robert H. Waterman Jr. profiled companies with strong corporate cultures that inspired employees toward better work, products, and customer satisfaction.[20] The total quality management (TQM) movement increased empowerment and teamwork on the job throughout the 1990s and led the charge toward workplaces simultaneously devoted to employee achievement at work and home.[21]

Although there were many positive initiatives for employees in the 1990s, the confluence of economic progress with demands for global competitiveness convinced many executives of the need for cost cutting. For individuals accustomed to messages about the importance of employees to organizational success, workforce reduction was both unexpected and traumatic. These experiences effectively ended the loyalty- and commitment-based contract that employees had developed with employers. A study of young employees showed that their greatest psychological need in the workplace is security but that they viewed many employers as "terminators."[22]

WORKFORCE REDUCTION[23] At different points in a company's history, there are likely to be factors that beg the question, "How can we decrease our overall costs?" In a highly competitive business environment, where new companies, customers, and products emerge and disappear every day, there is a continuous push for greater organizational efficiency and effectiveness. This pressure often leads to difficult decisions, including ones that require careful balance and consideration for the short-run survival and long-term vision of the company. This situation can create the need for **workforce reduction**, the process of eliminating employment positions. This process places considerable pressure on top management, causes speculation and tension among employees, and raises public ire about the role of business in society.[24]

There are several strategies that companies use to reduce overall costs and expenditures. For example, organizations may choose to reduce the number of employees, simplify products and processes, decrease quality and promises in service delivery, or develop some other mechanism for eliminating resources or nonperforming assets. Managers may find it difficult to communicate about cost reductions, as this message carries both emotional and social risk. Employees may wonder, "What value do I bring to the company?" and "Does anyone really care about my years of service?" Customers may inquire, "Can we expect the same level of service and product quality?" Governments and the community may ask, "Is this really necessary? How will it affect our economy?" For all of these questions, company leadership must have a clear answer. This response should be based on a thorough analysis of costs within the organizational system and how any changes are likely to affect business processes and outcomes. In 2005, IBM announced it would cut its American and European

workforce reduction
the process of eliminating employment positions

When stores and malls close, especially in small towns, there can be a strong impact on employment rates in the area.

workforces by 13,000. This would appear to be a reduction, but the company is actually adding 14,000 workers in India. Many companies have already outsourced certain positions to places outside the United States and Europe, where labor is much cheaper and cost savings can be realized.

In the last two decades, many firms chose to adopt the strategy that also creates the most anxiety and criticism—the reduction of the workforce. Throughout the 1990s, the numbers were staggering, as Sears eliminated 50,000 jobs, Kodak terminated nearly 17,000 people, and scandals in the early 2000s also created a wave of layoffs. These actions effectively signaled the "end of the old contract" that employees had with employers.[25] This strategy, sometimes called *downsizing* or *rightsizing,* usually entails employee layoffs and terminations. In other cases, a company freezes new hiring, hopes for natural workforce attrition, offers incentives for early retirement, or encourages job sharing among existing employees. Table 7.2 provides information on the different tactics that may be used to effect downsizing in the workplace. The reality is that some employees will lose their current positions one way or another. Thus, although workforce reduction may be the strategy chosen to control and reduce costs, it may have profound implications for the welfare of employees, their families, and the economic prospects of a geographical region and other constituents as well as for the corporation itself.

As with other aspects of business, it is difficult to separate financial considerations for costs from other obligations and expectations that develop between a company and its stakeholders. Depending on a firm's resource base and current financial situation, the psychological contract that exists between an employer and employee is likely to be broken through layoffs, and the social contract between employers,

TABLE 7.2　Three Downsizing Tactics

Tactic	Characteristics	Examples
Workforce reduction	Aimed at headcount reduction Short-term implementation Fosters transition and 　transformation	Attrition Transfer and outplacement Retirement incentives Buyout packages Layoffs
Organization redesign	Aimed at organization change Moderate-term implementation Fosters transition and 　transformation	Eliminates functions Merges units Eliminates layers Eliminates products 　and services Redesigns tasks
Systemic redesign	Aimed at culture change Long-term implementation Fosters transformation	Change responsibility Involves all constituents Fosters continuous 　improvement and innovation Simplification Downsizing: a way of life

Source: Thomas G. Cummings and Christopher G. Worley, *Organization Development and Change* (Cincinnati, OH: South-Western, 2005).

communities, and other groups may also be threatened. Downsizing makes the private relationship between employee and employer a public issue that affects many stakeholders and subsequently draws heavy criticism.[26]

The impact of the workforce reduction process depends on a host of factors, including corporate culture, long-term plans, and creative calculations on both quantitative and qualitative aspects of the workplace. Because few human resource directors and other managers have extensive experience in restructuring the workforce, there are several issues to consider before embarking on the process.[27] First, a comprehensive plan must be developed that takes into account the financial implications and qualitative and emotional toll of the reduction strategy. This plan may include a systematic analysis of workflow so that management understands how tasks are currently completed and how they will be completed after restructuring. Second, the organization should commit to assisting employees who must make a career transition as a result of the reduction process. To make the transition productive for employees, this assistance should begin as soon as management is aware of possible reductions. Through the Worker Adjustment and Retraining Notification Act (WARN), U.S. employers are required to give at least sixty days' advance notice if a layoff will affect 500 or more employees or more than one-third of the workforce.[28] Offering career assistance is beneficial over the long term, as it demonstrates a firm's commitment to social responsibility.

External factors also play a role in how quickly employees find new work and affect perceptions of a firm's decision to downsize. When the Opryland Hotel in Nashville, Tennessee, laid off 160 employees, other hotels in the area quickly hired them. With the unemployment rate in Nashville below 2.7 percent at the time, the other hotels appreciated the service training and competence of the former Opryland employees.[29] Thus, the Opryland Hotel probably did not suffer the types of reputation problems that other firms may have experienced in less favorable labor markets. Individuals who are reemployed quickly, whether through company efforts or market circumstances, experience fewer negative economic and emotional repercussions. In addition, employees who are kept well informed of the downsizing decision process are more likely to retain positive attitudes toward the company, even if they experienced job loss.[30]

Companies must be willing to accept the consequences of terminating employees. Although workforce reduction can improve a firm's financial performance, especially in the short run, there are costs to consider, including the loss of intellectual capital.[31] The years of knowledge, skills, relationships, and commitment that employees develop cannot be easily replaced or substituted, and the loss of one employee can cost a firm between $50,000 and $100,000.[32] Skandia Assurance and Financial Services, based in Stockholm, Sweden, is one of a few firms to measure and report its intellectual capital to investors, a move that illuminates an intangible asset for better decision making. Skandia has been recognized by *Fortune* magazine as one of ten great companies in Europe.[33] Although workforce reduction lowers costs, it often results in lost intellectual capital, strained customer relationships, negative media attention, and other issues that drain company resources. Employees who retain their jobs may suffer guilt, depression, or stress as a result of the reduction in workforce. Thus, a long-term understanding of the qualitative and quantitative costs and benefits should guide downsizing decisions.[34]

Although workforce reduction is a corporate decision, it is also important to recognize the potential role of employees in these decisions. Whereas hiring and job growth reached a frantic pace by the late 1990s, a wave of downsizings in the early 1990s and 2000s meant that some individuals had embraced the reality of having little job security. Instead of becoming cynical or angry, employees may have reversed roles and began asking, "What is this company doing for me?" and "Am I getting what I need from my employer?" Employees of all types began taking more responsibility for career growth, demanding balance in work and personal responsibilities, and seeking opportunities in upstart firms and emerging industries. Thus, although workforce reduction has negative effects, it has also shifted the psychological contract and power between employee and employer. The following suggestions examine how individuals can potentially mitigate the onset and effects of downsizing.

First, all employees should understand how their skills and competencies affect business performance. Not recognizing and improving this relationship makes it more difficult to prove their worth to managers faced with workforce reduction decisions. Second, employees should strive for cost-cutting and conservation strategies regardless of the employer's current financial condition. This is a workforce's first line of defense against layoffs—assisting the organization in reducing its costs before drastic measures are necessary. Third, today's work environment requires that most employees fulfill diverse and varying roles. For example, manufacturing managers must understand the whole product development and introduction process, ranging from engineering to marketing and distribution activities. Thus, another way of ensuring worth to the company, and to potential employers, is through an employee's ability to navigate different customer environments and organizational systems. It is now necessary to "cross-train," show flexibility, and learn the entire business, even if a company does not offer a formal program for gaining this type of experience and exposure. Although this advice may not prevent workforce reduction, it does empower employees against some of its harmful effects. Through laws and regulations, the government has also created a system for ensuring that employees are treated properly on the job. The next section covers the myriad of laws that all employers and employees should consider in daily and strategic decisions.

Legal Issues

Employment law is a very complex and evolving area. Most large companies and organizations employ human resource managers and legal specialists who are trained in the detail and implementation of specific statutes related to employee hiring, compensation, benefits, safety, and other areas. Smaller organizations often send human resource managers to workshops and conferences to keep abreast of legal imperatives in the workplace. Table 7.3 lists the major federal laws that cover employer

TABLE 7.3	Major Employment Laws	
Act (Date Enacted)	**Purpose**
National Labor Relations Act (1935)	Established the rights of employees to engage in collective bargaining and to strike.
Fair Labor Standards Act (1938)	Established minimum wage and overtime pay standards, recordkeeping, and child labor standards for most private and public employers.
Equal Pay Act (1963)	Protects women and men who perform substantially equal work in the same establishment from gender-based wage discrimination.
Civil Rights Act, Title VII (1964)	Prohibits employment discrimination on the basis of race, national origin, color, religion, and gender.
Age Discrimination in Employment Act (1967)	Protects individuals age forty or older from age-based discrimination.
Occupational Safety and Health Act (1970)	Ensures safe and healthy working conditions for all employees by providing specific standards that employers must meet.
Employee Retirement Income Security Act (1974)	Sets uniform minimum standards to assure that employee benefit plans are established and maintained in a fair and financially sound manner.
Americans with Disabilities Act (1990)	Prohibits discrimination on the basis of physical or mental disability in all employment practices and requires employers to make reasonable accommodation to make facilities accessible to and usable by persons with disabilities.
Family and Medical Leave Act (1993)	Requires certain employers to provide up to twelve weeks of unpaid, job-protected leave to eligible employees for certain family and medical reasons.

Sources: "Federal Laws Prohibiting Job Discrimination Questions and Answers," Equal Employment Opportunity Commission, http://www.eeoc.gov/facts/qanda.html, accessed April 24, 2006; Gillian Flynn, "Looking Back on 100 Years of Employment Law," *Workforce* 78 (November 1999): 74–77; Roger LeRoy Miller and Gaylord A. Jentz, *Business Law Today* (Cincinnati, OH: West Legal Studies in Business, 2000); U.S. Department of Labor, Employment Law Guide, http://www.dol.gov/compliance/guide/index.htm, accessed April 24, 2006.

GLOBAL CHALLENGES

Employing Illegal Workers

In April 2006, United States Immigration and Customers Enforcement agents raided the offices and manufacturing sites of IFCO Systems in nearly ten states. After the raid, seven executives were arrested and over 1,000 employees were detained for further questioning. Many employees were handed deportation orders. The executives were charged with conspiracy to transport, harbor, and encourage illegal aliens to reside in the United States for commercial advantage and private financial gain. The federal government alleges that IFCO was able to produce record profits because it heavily utilized an illegal workforce. The company claims that many of these workers produced fraudulent or altered documentation when they were hired. IFCO Systems, a pallet services company, operates sixty facilities in the United States. The arrests were made after a year-long criminal investigation. Although IFCO may have noticed irregularities in worker documentation, the company apparently did not take effective action to investigate the problem. The government insists that illegal aliens were a fundamental part of IFCO's business plan and that working conditions were unsafe. A tip from a former employee, who witnessed illegal workers tearing up their W-2 tax forms, led to the investigation, raids, and arrests. With the IFCO incident, top government officials declared a heightened enforcement strategy against companies and executives who violate immigration law.

IFCO is not alone. Wal-Mart stores agreed to pay $11 million to settle allegations that the company knowingly contracted with cleaning services that employed illegal immigrants. The allegations also pointed to the mistreatment of the workers, including long working hours and few breaks. There were no criminal charges filed against Wal-Mart executives, and the company agreed to implement assurance standards to prevent it from hiring or contracting with undocumented workers. The case came to light when these employees filed a civil suit against Wal-Mart, demanding to be paid for overtime they allegedly worked.

Two temporary employment agencies that place employees in New Jersey, Ohio, and Pennsylvania were charged in a $5.3 million scheme for employing and harboring illegal aliens. Three restaurant operators in Baltimore, Maryland, pleaded guilty to immigration charges. Forty illegal workers were arrested while working for a construction subcontractor on a New Mexico military base. Because of these cases and others like them, a national debate was forged on the topic of immigration and employment. Business owners often claim that undocumented workers will take jobs that regular U.S. citizens refuse to consider and, therefore, are adding positively to business and the economy. Employee rights advocates question whether these workers are taking jobs away from U.S. citizens or whether they are paid fairly and treated well by the employers. Relatives of illegal aliens do not understand the reasoning behind the law, as they are often supported by lucrative wages sent to them from the United States.

Sources: Nicole Gaouette, "What Was Behind the Big Raid," *Los Angeles Times*, April 22, 2006, p. A1; Abigil Goldman, "Wal-Mart Looks to Polish Image, but Detractors Gear Up, Too," *Los Angeles Times*, April 19, 2006, p. C1; Armando Villafranca, "Raided Company Says Hirers Duped by Fake ID Papers," *Houston Chronicle*, April 22, 2006, p. 1. ■

---

employment at will

a common-law doctrine that allows either the employer or the employee to terminate the relationship at any time as long as it does not violate an employment contract

responsibilities with respect to wages, labor unions, benefits, health and safety, equal opportunity, and other areas. Until the early 1900s, employment was primarily governed by the concept of **employment at will**, a common-law doctrine that allows either the employer or the employee to terminate the relationship at any time as long as it does not violate an employment contract. Today, many states still use the employment-at-will philosophy, but laws and statutes may limit total discretion in this regard.[35] The following discussion highlights employment laws and their fundamental contribution to social responsibility.[36]

WAGES AND BENEFITS After the Great Depression, the U.S. Congress enacted a number of laws to protect employee rights and extend employer responsibilities. The Fair Labor Standards Act (FLSA) of 1938 prescribed minimum wage and overtime pay, recordkeeping, and child labor standards for most private and public employers. The minimum wage is set by the federal government and is periodically revised, although states have the option to adopt a higher standard. For example, the federal minimum wage was raised from $4.45 per hour to $5.15 per hour in September 1997. The majority of states abide by the federal standard, although Alaska, California, Oregon, Vermont, Washington, and several others have adopted a higher minimum wage. Most employees who work more than forty hours per week are entitled to overtime pay in the amount of one and a half times their regular pay. There are exemptions to the overtime pay provisions for four classes of employees: executives, outside salespeople, administrators, and professionals.[37]

The FLSA also affected child labor, including the provision that individuals under the age of fourteen are allowed to do only certain types of work, such as delivering newspapers and working in their parents' businesses. Children under age sixteen are often required to get a work permit, and their work hours are restricted so that they can attend school. Persons between the ages of sixteen and eighteen are not restricted in terms of number of work hours, but they cannot be employed in hazardous or dangerous positions. Although passage of the FLSA was necessary to eliminate abusive child labor practices, its restrictions became somewhat problematic during the booming economy of the late 1990s, when unemployment rates were extremely low in the United States. Some business owners may have even considered lobbying for relaxed standards in very restrictive states so that they could hire more teens. In addition, general FLSA restrictions have created problems in implementing job-sharing and flextime arrangements with employees who are paid on an hourly basis.[38]

Two other pieces of legislation relate to employer responsibilities for benefits and job security. The Employee Retirement Income Security Act (ERISA) of 1974 set uniform minimum standards to assure that employee benefit plans are established and maintained in a fair and financially sound manner. ERISA does not require companies to establish retirement pension plans; instead, it developed standards for the administration of plans that management chooses to offer employees. A key provision relates to **vesting**, the legal right to pension plan benefits. In general, contributions an employee makes to the plan are vested immediately, whereas company contributions are vested after five years of employment. ERISA is a very complicated aspect of employer responsibilities because it involves tax law, financial investments, and plan participants and beneficiaries.[39]

The Family and Medical Leave Act (FMLA) of 1993 requires certain employers to provide up to twelve weeks of unpaid, job-protected leave to eligible employees for certain family and medical reasons. However, if the employee is paid in the top 10 percent of the entire workforce, the employer does not have to reinstate him or her in the same or comparable position.[40] Typical reasons for this type of leave include the birth or adoption of a child, personal illness, or the serious health condition of a close relative. The FMLA applies to employers with fifty or more employees, which means that its provisions do not cover a large number of U.S. employees. In addition, employees must have worked at least one year for the firm and at least twenty-five hours per week during the past year before the FMLA is required.

vesting
the legal right to pension plan benefits

LABOR UNIONS In one of the earliest pieces of employment legislation, the National Labor Relations Act (NLRA) of 1935 legitimized the rights of employees to engage in collective bargaining and to strike. This law was originally passed to protect employee rights, but subsequent legislation gave more rights to employers and restricted the power of unions. Before the NLRA, many companies attempted to prohibit their employees from creating or joining labor organizations. Employees who were members of unions were often discriminated against in terms of hiring and retention decisions. This act sought to eliminate the perceived imbalance of power between employers and employees. Through unions, employees gained a collective bargaining mechanism that enabled greater power on several fronts, including wages and safety.[41] For example, after a weeks-long strike against Verizon Communications, members of the Communications Workers of America (CWA) and International Brotherhood of Electrical Workers (IBEW) negotiated a deal that gave workers of the telecommunications firm a 12 percent pay raise (over three years), a cap on overtime hours, and other provisions, including the elimination of the threat of layoffs for the period of the labor contract. Verizon also upgraded its website for delivering information and services to its employees.[42]

HEALTH AND SAFETY In 1970, the Occupational Safety and Health Act (OSHA) sought to ensure safe and healthy working conditions for all employees by providing specific standards that employers must meet. This act led to the development of the Occupational Safety and Health Administration, also known as OSHA, the agency that oversees the regulations intended to make U.S. workplaces the safest in the world. In

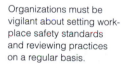

Organizations must be vigilant about setting workplace safety standards and reviewing practices on a regular basis.

its more than thirty-five years of existence, OSHA has made great strides to improve and maintain the health and safety of employees. For example, since the 1970s, the workplace death rate in the United States has been reduced by 50 percent, and the agency's initiatives in cotton dust and lead standards have reduced disease in several industries. The agency continues to innovate and uses feedback systems for improving its services and standards. For example, OSHA recently translated a variety of its documents into Spanish and posted them to a prominent place on its website. OSHA officials were concerned about Spanish-speaking workers' understanding of the agency and their rights in the workplace.[43] OSHA has the authority to enter and make inspections of most employers. Because of its far-reaching power and unwarranted inspections made in the 1970s, the agency's relationship with business has not always been positive. For example, OSHA recently proposed rules to increase employer responsibility for **ergonomics**, the design, arrangement, and use of equipment to maximize productivity and minimize fatigue and physical discomfort. Without proper attention to ergonomics, employees may suffer injuries and long-term health issues as a result of work motion and tasks. Many business and industry associations have opposed the proposal, citing enormous costs and unsubstantiated claims. A federal ergonomics rule was established under the Clinton presidency but was repealed by President George W. Bush. However, the issue continues to be raised on the regulatory agenda. OSHA is currently focusing its ergonomics efforts on one industry at a time, while individual states, such as Alaska, Washington, and California, are forging ahead with their own ergonomics rules.[44] Despite differences between this federal agency and some states and companies on a number of regulations, most employers are required to display the poster shown in Figure 7.1 or one required by their state safety and health agency. The John Deere Company has become a leader in workplace ergonomics. At its Waterloo Works facility in Iowa, employees are helping create safer and more ergonomic workplaces. Workstations are tested in three dimensions before actually being built.[45]

An emerging issue in the area of health and safety is the increasing rate of violence in the workplace. According to OSHA, 1.5 million workers are assaulted and nearly 1,000 are murdered in the workplace every year.[46] A recent survey of *Fortune* 1000 companies indicates that workplace violence is one of the most important security issues they face, costs $36 billion annually, and results in three deaths daily and thousands of injuries each year. The third leading cause of all occupational fatalities is homicide.[47] Surveys in the insurance industry show that nearly 25 percent of insurance employees have been threatened, harassed, or attacked in job-related circumstances.[48]

The state of California's Occupational Safety and Health Agency has identified three types of workplace violence: (1) crimes committed by strangers and intruders in the workplace; (2) acts committed by nonemployees, such as customers, patients, students, and clients, who have expected or normal contact with employees; and (3) violence committed by coworkers.[49] Taxi drivers and clerks working late-night shifts at convenience stores are often subject to the first type of violence. Airline attendants are increasingly experiencing the second category of workplace violence when passengers become unruly, drunk, or otherwise violent while in flight. Airline employees across the United States, Australia, and Switzerland staged a campaign to combat "air rage," the uncivil and dangerous acts of passengers that are not only punishable by large fines but can also threaten the safety of everyone aboard the aircraft. The groups asked

ergonomics

the design, arrangement, and use of equipment to maximize productivity and minimize fatigue and physical discomfort

FIGURE 7.1   Job Safety and Health Protection Poster

You Have a Right to a Safe and Healthful Workplace.

IT'S THE LAW!

- You have the right to notify your employer or OSHA about workplace hazards. You may ask OSHA to keep your name confidential.

- You have the right to request an OSHA inspection if you believe that there are unsafe and unhealthful conditions in your workplace. You or your representative may participate in the inspection.

- You can file a complaint with OSHA within 30 days of discrimination by your employer for making safety and health complaints or for exercising your rights under the *OSH Act*.

- You have a right to see OSHA citations issued to your employer. Your employer must post the citations at or near the place of the alleged violation.

- Your employer must correct workplace hazards by the date indicated on the citation and must certify that these hazards have been reduced or eliminated.

- You have the right to copies of your medical records or records of your exposure to toxic and harmful substances or conditions.

- Your employer must post this notice in your workplace.

The *Occupational Safety and Health Act of 1970 (OSH Act)*, P.L. 91-596, assures safe and healthful working conditions for working men and women throughout the Nation. The Occupational Safety and Health Administration, in the U.S. Department of Labor, has the primary responsibility for administering the *OSH Act*. The rights listed here may vary depending on the particular circumstances. To file a complaint, report an emergency, or seek OSHA advice, assistance, or products, call 1-800-321-OSHA or your nearest OSHA office: • Atlanta (404) 562-2300 • Boston (617) 565-9860 • Chicago (312) 353-2220 • Dallas (214) 767-4731 • Denver (303) 844-1600 • Kansas City (816) 426-5861 • New York (212) 337-2378 • Philadelphia (215) 861-4900 • San Francisco (415) 975-4310 • Seattle (206) 553-5930. Teletypewriter (TTY) number is 1-877-889-5627. To file a complaint online or obtain more information on OSHA federal and state programs, visit OSHA's website at **www.osha.gov**. If your workplace is in a state operating under an OSHA-approved plan, your employer must post the required state equivalent of this poster.

1-800-321-OSHA
www.osha.gov

U.S. Department of Labor • Occupational Safety and Health Administration • OSHA 3165

☆ U.S. GOVERNMENT PRINTING OFFICE: 2000-467-940

Source: "New OSHA Workplace Poster," Occupational Safety and Health Administration, http://www.osha.gov/Publications/poster.html, accessed April 21, 2006.

government officials to toughen penalties and control of air rage perpetrators. The terrorist attacks on the World Trade Center and the Pentagon further highlighted workplace risks and violence, including the steps that many organizations are taking to protect employees and other stakeholders. Some organizations with employees who travel frequently are hiring training firms to educate employees on aircraft evacuation, air rage, how to respond to hijackers, and other safety measures.[50]

Finally, disagreements and stress in the workplace may escalate into employee-on-employee violence. For example, a Xerox Corporation warehouse employee opened fire during a team meeting at a facility in Honolulu, killing seven coworkers. The employee, Bryan Uyesugi, was eventually convicted of murder and sentenced to life in prison without parole for the shooting, which Xerox officials described as the "worst tragedy" in the company's history. The Hawaii Occupational Safety and Health Division later cited Xerox for failing to enforce workplace-violence policies that might have prevented the deaths.[51] In many of these cases, the perpetrator had been recently reprimanded, dismissed, or received other negative feedback that prompted the violent attack. Although crimes reflect general problems in society, employers have a responsibility to assess risks and provide security, training, and safeguards to protect employees and other stakeholders from such acts. Experts estimate that 50 percent of all companies have no workplace-violence prevention program, whereas 40 percent have a program "in name only."[52] Companies often purchase insurance policies to cover the costs of workplace violence, including business interruption, psychological counseling, informant rewards, and medical claims related to injuries. One expert suggests that all organizations publish and communicate an antiviolence policy and make employees and managers aware of antecedents to workplace violence.[53]

EQUAL OPPORTUNITY Title VII of the Civil Rights Act of 1964 prohibits employment discrimination on the basis of race, national origin, color, religion, and gender. This law is fundamental to employees' rights to join and advance in an organization according to merit rather than one of the characteristics just mentioned. For example, employers are not permitted to categorize jobs as only for men or women unless there is a reason gender is fundamental to the tasks and responsibilities. Additional laws passed in the 1970s, 1980s, and 1990s were also designed to prohibit discrimination related to pregnancy, disabilities, age, and other factors. For example, the Americans with Disabilities Act prohibits companies from discriminating on the basis of physical or mental disability in all employment practices and requires them to make facilities accessible to and usable by persons with disabilities. The Pregnancy Discrimination Act was created to help protect the rights of mothers and mothers-to-be in the workplace. The act has been modified many times since its inception. The increasing number of women in the workforce has led to a 39 percent increase in pregnancy-related complaints in the past decade.[54] Figure 7.2 depicts the number of complaints and resolutions on pregnancy discrimination cases over a ten-year period.

These legal imperatives require that companies formalize employment practices to ensure that no discrimination is occurring. Thus, managers must be fully aware of the types of practices that constitute discrimination and work to ensure that hiring, promotion, annual evaluation, and other procedures are fair and based on merit. The spread of HIV and AIDS has prompted multinational firms with operations in Africa

FIGURE 7.2	Growth in Filings and Resolutions of Pregnancy Discrimination Act Complaints to the EEOC

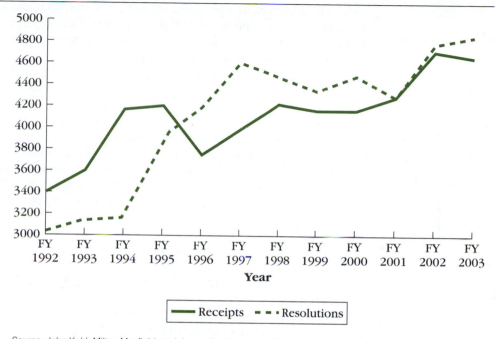

Source: John Kohl, Milton Mayfield, and Jacqueline Mayfield, "Recent Trends in Pregnancy Discrimination Law," *Business Horizons* (September–October 2005): 48–52.

to distribute educational literature and launch prevention programs. Some companies work with internal and external stakeholders and even fund medical facilities that help prevent the disease and treat HIV/AIDS patients. Another component to their initiatives involves education on fair treatment of employees with the disease. Recently, multinational companies in Mexico produced a written commitment to eliminate the stigma and discrimination often surrounding HIV/AIDS in the workplace.[55]

To ensure that they build balanced workforces, many companies have initiated affirmative action programs, which involve efforts to recruit, hire, train, and promote qualified individuals from groups that have traditionally been discriminated against on the basis of race, sex, or other characteristics. Safeway, a chain of supermarkets, established a program to expand opportunities for women in middle and upper level management after settling a sex-discrimination lawsuit.[56] However, many companies voluntarily implement affirmative action plans to build a more diverse workforce.[57] A key goal of these programs is to reduce any bias that may exist in hiring, evaluating, and promoting employees. A special type of discrimination, sexual harassment, is also prohibited through Title VII.

SEXUAL HARASSMENT The flood of women into the workplace during the last half of the twentieth century brought new challenges and opportunities for organizations. Although harassment has probably always existed in the workplace, the presence of both genders in roughly equal numbers changed norms of behavior. When men dominated the workplace, photos of partially nude women or sexually suggestive materials may have been posted on walls or in lockers. Today, such materials could be viewed as illegal if they contribute to a work environment that is intimidating, offensive, or otherwise interferes with an employee's work performance. The U.S. government indicates the nature of this illegal activity:

Unwelcome sexual advances, requests for sexual favors, and other verbal or physical conduct of a sexual nature constitutes **sexual harassment** when submission to or rejection of this conduct explicitly or implicitly affects an individual's employment, unreasonably interferes with an individual's work performance, or creates an intimidating, hostile, or offensive work environment.[58]

Prior to 1986, sexual harassment was not a specific violation of federal law in the United States. In *Meritor Savings Bank v. Vinson*, the U.S. Supreme Court ruled that sexual harassment creates a "hostile environment" that violates Title VII of the Civil Rights Act, even in the absence of economic harm or demand for sexual favors in exchange for promotions, raises, or related work incentives.[59] In other countries, sexual harassment in the workplace is considered an illegal act, although the specific conditions may vary by legal and social culture. In Mexico, the law protects employees only if their jobs are jeopardized on the basis of the exchange of sexual favors or relations. Employees of Mexican public entities, such as government offices, will be fired if found guilty of the offending behavior.[60] In the European Union (EU), sexual harassment legislation focuses on the liability that employers carry when they fail to promote a workplace culture free of harassment and other forms of discrimination. The EU recently strengthened its rules on sexual harassment, including definitions of direct and indirect harassment, the removal of an upper limit on victim compensation, and the requirement that businesses develop and make "equality reports" available to employees.[61]

There are two general categories of sexual harassment: quid pro quo and hostile work environment.[62] **Quid pro quo sexual harassment** is a type of sexual extortion, where there is a proposed or explicit exchange of job benefits for sexual favors. For example, telling an employee, "You will be fired if you do not have sex with me," is a direct form of sexual harassment. Usually, the person making such a statement is in a position of authority over the harassed employee, and thus, the threat of job loss is real. One incident of quid pro quo harassment may create a justifiable legal claim. **Hostile work environment sexual harassment** is less direct than quid pro quo harassment and can involve epithets, slurs, negative stereotyping, intimidating acts, graphic materials that show hostility toward an individual or group, and other types of conduct that affect the employment situation. For example, an e-mail message containing sexually explicit jokes that is broadcast to employees could be viewed as contributing to a hostile work environment. Some hostile work environment harassment is nonsexual, meaning the harassing conduct is based on gender without explicit reference to sexual acts. For example, in *Campbell v. Kansas State University* (1991), the courts found repeated remarks about women "being intellectually inferior to men" to be part of a hostile environment. Unlike quid pro quo cases, one incident may not justify a legal claim. Instead, the courts will examine a range of acts and circumstances to determine if the work environment was intolerable and the victim's job performance was impaired.[63] From a social responsibility perspective, a key issue in both types of

sexual harassment

unwelcome sexual advances, requests for sexual favors, and other verbal or physical conduct of a sexual nature when submission to or rejection of this conduct explicitly or implicitly affects an individual's employment, unreasonably interferes with an individual's work performance, or creates an intimidating, hostile, or offensive work environment

quid pro quo sexual harassment

a type of sexual extortion, where there is a proposed or explicit exchange of job benefits for sexual favor

hostile work environment sexual harassment

conduct that shows hostility toward an individual or group in a work environment. It can involve epithets, slurs, negative stereotyping, intimidating acts, and graphic materials; less direct than quid pro quo harassment.

sexual harassment is the employing organization's knowledge and tolerance for these types of behaviors. A number of court cases have shed more light on the issues that constitute sexual harassment and organizations' responsibility in this regard.

In *Harris v. Forklift Systems* (1993), Teresa Harris claimed that her boss at Forklift Systems made suggestive sexual remarks, asked her to retrieve coins from his pants pocket, and joked that they should go to a motel to "negotiate her raise." Courts at the state level threw out her case because she did not suffer major psychological injury. The U.S. Supreme Court overturned these decisions and ruled that employers can be forced to pay damages even if the worker suffered no proven psychological harm. This case brought about the "reasonable person" standard in evaluating what conduct constitutes sexual harassment. From this case, juries now evaluate the alleged conduct with respect to commonly held beliefs and expectations.[64]

Several global firms have been embroiled in sexual harassment suits. For example, Ford Motor Company settled a class-action lawsuit for $7.75 million in the late 1990s, the fourth-largest sexual harassment settlement in the Equal Employment Opportunity Commission's history, after more than 500 female employees claimed they were groped and sexually harassed at two different Ford plants. The settlement also required that the company spend an additional $10 million on sensitivity training programs.[65] Mitsubishi Motors agreed in 1998 to pay $34 million in a settlement with 350 women who made serious allegations of harassment and brought lawsuits against the company. Their allegations of sexual harassment included the distribution of lewd videos and photos, inappropriate conversations and jokes, and general tolerance by management for these actions and overtones. As part of the settlement, the company also agreed to periodic monitoring by a three-member panel and implemention of an effective sexual harassment policy.[66]

Recent U.S. Supreme Court decisions on sexual harassment cases indicate that (1) employers are liable for the acts of supervisors; (2) employers are liable for sexual harassment by supervisors that culminates in a tangible employment action (loss of job, demotion, etc.); (3) employers are liable for a hostile environment created by a supervisor but may escape liability if they demonstrate that they exercised reasonable care to prevent and promptly correct any sexually harassing behavior and that the plaintiff employee unreasonably failed to take advantage of any preventive or corrective measures offered by the employer; and (4) claims of hostile environment sexual harassment must be severe and pervasive to be viewed as actionable by the courts.[67]

Much like the underlying philosophy of the Federal Sentencing Guidelines for Organizations that we discussed in earlier chapters, these decisions require top managers in organizations to take the detection and prevention of sexual harassment seriously. To this end, many firms have implemented programs on sexual harassment. To satisfy current legal standards and set a higher standard for social responsibility, employees, supervisors, and other close business partners should be educated on the company's zero-tolerance policy against harassment. Employees must be educated on the policy prohibiting harassment, including the types of behaviors that constitute harassment, how offenders will be punished, and what employees should do if they experience harassment. Just as with an organizational compliance program, employees must be assured of confidentiality and no retaliation for reporting harassment. Training on sexual harassment should be balanced in terms of legal definitions and practical tips

TABLE 7.4	Sexual Harassment in the Workplace

Facts

Sexual harassment is a form of sex discrimination that violates Title VII of the Civil Rights Act of 1964.

Unwelcome sexual advances, requests for sexual favors, and other verbal or physical conduct of a sexual nature constitute sexual harassment when submission to or rejection of this conduct explicitly or implicitly affects an individual's employment, unreasonably interferes with an individual's work performance, or creates an intimidating, hostile, or offensive work environment.

Sexual harassment can occur in a variety of circumstances including but not limited to the following:

- The victim as well as the harasser may be a woman or a man. The victim does not have to be of the opposite sex.
- The harasser can be the victim's supervisor, an agent of the employer, a supervisor in another area, a coworker, or a nonemployee.
- The victim does not have to be the person harassed but could be anyone affected by the offensive conduct.
- Unlawful sexual harassment may occur without economic injury to or discharge of the victim.
- The harasser's conduct must be unwelcome.

It is helpful for the victim to inform the harasser directly that the conduct is unwelcome and must stop. The victim should use any employer complaint mechanism or grievance system available.

When investigating allegations of sexual harassment, the Equal Employment Opportunity Commission looks at the whole record: the circumstances, such as the nature of the sexual advances, and the context in which the alleged incidents occurred. A determination of the allegations is made from the facts on a case-by-case basis.

Source: "Facts About Sexual Harassment," U.S. Equal Employment Opportunity Commission, www.eeoc.gov/facts/fs-sex.html, accessed April 21, 2006.

and tools. Although employees need to be aware of the legal issues and ramifications, they also may need assistance in learning to recognize and avoid behaviors that may constitute quid pro quo harassment, create a hostile environment, or appear to be retaliatory in nature. In fact, retaliation claims have more than doubled since the early 1990s, prompting many companies to incorporate this element into sexual harassment training. Finally, employees should be aware that same-sex conduct may also constitute sexual harassment.[68] Table 7.4 lists facts about sexual harassment that should be used in company communication and training on this workplace issue.

WHISTLE-BLOWING[69] An employee who reports individual or company wrongdoing to either internal or external sources is considered a whistle-blower.[70] Whistle-blowers usually focus on issues or behaviors that need corrective action, although managers and other employees may not appreciate reports that expose company weaknesses, raise embarrassing questions, or otherwise detract from organizational tasks. Although not all whistle-blowing activity leads to an extreme reaction, whistle-blowers have been retaliated against, demoted, fired, and even worse as a result of their actions. For example, Jacob F. Horton, senior vice president at Gulf Power, was on his way to talk with company officials about alleged thefts, payoffs, and cover-ups at the utility when he died in a plane crash in 1989. Allegations that his death was related to whistle-blowing still linger.[71]

The U.S. Office of Special Counsel investigates confidential allegations about federal agencies, including violations of law, mismanagement, abuse of power, and waste of funds.

Whistleblowing

A "whistleblower" discloses information he or she reasonably believes evidences:

- A violation of any law, rule or regulation

- Gross mismanagement

- A gross waste of funds

- An abuse of authority

- A substantial and specific danger to public health

- A substantial and specific danger to public safety

The Office of Special Counsel (OSC) provides a secure channel through which current and former federal employees and applicants for federal employment may make confidential disclosures. OSC evaluates the diclosures to determine whether there is a substantial likelihood that one of the categories listed above has been disclosed. If such a determination is made, OSC has the authority to require the head of the agency to investigate the matter.

To make a disclosure contact:

U.S. OFFICE OF SPECIAL COUNSEL
1730 M STREET, N.W., SUITE 218
WASHINGTON, DC 20036-4505

PHONE: (202) 254-3640*   **TOLL FREE: 1-800-572-2249***
*Hearing and Speech Disabled: Federal Relay Service 1-800-877-8339

WWW.OSC.GOV

Rev. 12/05

Partly as a result of business and industry scandals in the 1980s, most large corporations have formal organizational ethics and compliance programs, including toll-free phone lines and other anonymous means for employees to ask questions, gain clarification, or report suspicious behavior. These programs are designed to facilitate internal whistle-blowing, as they engender a more ethical organizational culture and provide mechanisms for monitoring and supporting appropriate behavior. Thus, an effective ethics and legal compliance program should provide employees and other stakeholders with opportunities to make possible transgressions known (e.g., ethics hot line, open-door policy, and strong ethical climate).

The federal government and most state governments in the United States have enacted measures to protect whistle-blowers from retaliation. For example, the Whistleblower Protection Act of 1986 shields federal employees from retaliatory behavior. The Sarbanes-Oxley Act provides solid protection to whistle-blowers and strong penalties for those who retaliate against them. Other legislation actually rewards whistle-blowers for revealing illegal behavior. Under the False Claims Act of 1986, an individual who reports fraud perpetrated against the federal government may receive between 15 and 25 percent of the proceeds if a suit is brought against the perpetrator.

Ethical Issues

Laws are imperative for social responsibility. The ethical climate of the workplace, however, is more subjective and dependent on top management leadership and corporate culture. In this section, we examine several trends in employment practices that have not fully reached the legal realm. Company initiatives in these areas indicate a corporate philosophy or culture that respects and promotes certain ethical values.

TRAINING AND DEVELOPMENT As discussed in the business ethics chapters, organizational culture and the associated values, beliefs, and norms operate on many levels and affect a number of workplace practices. Some organizations value employees as individuals, not just "cogs in a wheel." Firms with this ethical stance fund initiatives to develop employees' skills, knowledge, and other personal characteristics. Although this development is linked to business strategy and aids the employer, it also demonstrates a commitment to the future of the employee and his or her interests. The Cracker Barrel restaurant chain offers Spanish-speaking employees a program to help them learn English. The interactive kit utilizes a laptop and microphone. Employees complete the six-level program at home.[72]

Store managers with Domino's Pizza participated in a four-day boot camp designed to promote leadership in the workplace.

Professionals also appreciate and respect a training and development focus from their employers. For example, the Los Angeles–based law firm of Latham & Watkins launched a series of initiatives, including "Latham & Watkins University," for first- and fourth-year associates. This training program covers legal updates, professional skill development, and information on career management and planning. Other law firms have upgraded their development opportunities, including mentoring programs, sabbaticals, and feedback sessions for commenting on firm policies and procedures.[73] These firms are finding many benefits of employee training and development, including stronger employee recruitment and retention strategies. Indeed, there is a link between investments in employees and the amount of commitment, job satisfaction, and productivity demonstrated by them. Happier employees tend to stay with their employer and to better serve coworkers, customers, and other constituents, which has a direct bearing on the quality of relationships and financial prospects of a firm. Leadership training is also critical, as the main reason employees leave a company is because of poor or unskilled leadership, not salary, benefits, or related factors. In exit interviews, departing employees often mention their desire for more meaningful feedback and steady communication with managers.[74]

Employees recognize when a company is diligently investing in programs that not only improve operations but also increase empowerment and provide new opportunities to improve knowledge and grow professionally. Through formal training and development classes, workers get a better sense of where they fit and how they contribute to the overall organization. This understanding empowers them to become more responsive, accurate, and confident in workplace decisions. Training also increases conflict resolution skills, accountability, and responsibility, a situation most employees prefer to micromanaging or "hand-holding." All these effects contribute to the financial and cultural health of an organization.[75] Thus, a commitment to training enables a firm to enhance its organizational capacity to fulfill stakeholder expectations.

Training and development activities require resources and the commitment of all managers to be successful. For example, a departmental manager must be supportive of an employee using part of the workday to attend a training session on a new software package. At the same time, the organization must pay for the training, regardless of whether it uses inside or outside trainers and develops in-house materials or purchases them from educational providers. A study by the American Society for Training and Development indicates that, on average, employers in developed countries spend about $630 per employee on training every year. Survey respondents in Latin America reported spending the least per employee ($311), whereas their Middle Eastern counterparts reported the highest rate per employee ($783). Companies in all regions indicated they were training more employees than ever before, with an average of 76.7 percent of employees being trained in a given year. Australia and New Zealand had the highest figures, with over 90 percent of all employees receiving training in those companies surveyed. Despite the differences in training expenditures, the types of training programs and workplace practices in effect in these regions are remarkably similar. Managerial skills, supervisory strategies, information technology skills, occupational safety and compliance, and customer relations are the topics of training programs in all countries.[76] Another area that has received much attention in the United States but less focus in other countries involves the diverse nature of today's workforce.

workplace diversity

initiatives focused on
recruiting and retaining
a diverse workforce as a
business imperative

DIVERSITY Whereas Title VII of the Civil Rights Act grants legal protection to different types of employees, initiatives in **workplace diversity** focus on recruiting and retaining a diverse workforce as a business imperative.[77] With diversity programs, companies assume an ethical obligation to employ and empower individuals regardless of age, gender, ethnicity, physical or mental ability, or other characteristics. These firms go beyond compliance with government guidelines to develop cultures that respect and embrace the unique skills, backgrounds, and contributions of all types of people. Thus, legal statutes focus on removing discrimination, whereas diversity represents a leadership approach for cultivating and appreciating employee talent.[78] Firms with an effective diversity effort link their diversity mission statement with the corporate strategic plan, implement plans to recruit and retain a diverse talent pool, support community programs of diverse groups, hold management accountable for various types of diversity performance, and have tangible outcomes of the diversity strategy. Each firm must tailor its diversity initiative to meet unique employee, market, and industry conditions.[79]

Many firms embrace employee diversity to deal with supplier and customer diversity. Their assumption is that to effectively design, market, and support products for different target groups, a company must employ individuals who reflect its customers' characteristics.[80] Organizations and industries with a population-wide customer base may use national demographics for assessing their diversity effort. For example, the Newspaper Association of America implemented a minority recruitment and diversity strategy in the early 1990s to help the industry better align staff demographics to community demographics. A study in the newspaper industry found that although racial and ethnic minorities make up nearly 30 percent of the U.S. population, fewer than 12 percent of all news reporters fall into that category. This finding prompted the National Association of Black Journalists to call for greater attention to diversity in the newsroom. Several years later, the Scripps Howard Foundation, associated with the Cincinnati media conglomerate, funded a media school at Hampton University, a historically African American school in Virginia.[81] After the 2000 U.S. census data were released, some companies began to reconsider marketing strategy, including the link between employee and customer characteristics. For example, census data revealed sharp growth in the Hispanic population and, for some firms, prompted hiring of Hispanic employees and consultants. Frito-Lay introduced Guacamole Chips after its diverse product team tapped into the ideas and perspectives of the company's Latino/Hispanic Advisory Board and Hispanic Employee Network.[82]

As we discussed in Chapter 1, there are opportunities to link social responsibility objectives with business performance, and many firms are learning the benefits of employing individuals with different backgrounds and perspectives. For example, at New York Life, diversity is treated like all other business goals. The company employs a chief diversity officer to create accountability and inclusion strategies with employees, suppliers, community members, and other stakeholders.[83] Even small businesses are discovering these advantages. Global Products, Inc. makes a point of hiring mentally challenged workers, especially those who have suffered head injuries. The company established a flexible workplace that designs jobs around workers' abilities instead of trying to fit the person into a job description. By partnering with the Center for Head Injury Services, Global Products has been richly rewarded with loyal, creative, hardworking employees who stay for years and enhance the company's culture of social responsibility.[84] Verizon,

TABLE 7.5   Profiles of Generations at Work

Generation Name	Birth Years	Key Characteristics
Veterans	1922–1943	Hardworking, detail-oriented, uncomfortable with conflict
Baby boomers	1943–1960	Service-oriented, good team players, sensitive to feedback
Generation X	1960–1980	Adaptable, independent, impatient
Millennials (Generation Y)	After 1980	Optimistic, technologically and financially savvy, need supervision, multitaskers

Source: Ron Zemke, Claire Raines, and Bob Filipczak, *Generations at Work: Managing the Clash of Veterans, Boomers, Xers, and Nexters in Your Workplace* (New York: AMACOM, 2000).

a global provider of wireless communication services, is also committed to including people with disabilities into the workplace. The company was recently named Private-Sector Employer of the Year by *CAREERS and the disABLED* magazine, a publication that provides career advice for people with disabilities.[85]

Conflicting views and voices of different generations abound in the workplace, and this is the first time in history that the workforce has been composed of so many generations at one time. Generations have worked together in the past, but these groups were usually divided by organizational stratification. Many workplaces now include members of multiple generations sitting side by side and working shoulder to shoulder. The result may be greater dissension among the age groups than when they were stratified by the organizational hierarchy. Because employees serve an important role in the social responsibility framework, managers need to be aware of generational differences and their potential effects on teamwork, conflict, and other workplace behaviors. Table 7.5 lists the four generations in today's workplace as well as their key characteristics.

Veterans tend to bring stability and loyalty to the workplace. Although veterans are very hardworking and detail oriented, they are often uncomfortable with conflict and ambiguity and reluctant to buck the system. The baby boomers are service oriented, good team players, and want to please. However, they are also known for being self-centered, overly sensitive to feedback, and not budget minded. People in Generation X are adaptable, technologically literate, independent, and not intimidated by authority. However, their liabilities include impatience, cynicism, and inexperience. The latest generation to enter the workforce, the Nexters or the Millennials, is technologically savvy. They also bring the assets of collective action, optimism, multitasking ability, and tenacity to the workplace. However, they bring the liabilities of inexperience, especially with difficult people issues, and a need for supervision and structure.

Although generational issues existed in the workforce in the 1920s and the 1960s, there are some new twists today. The older generations no longer have all the money and power. Times of anxiety and uncertainty can aggravate differences and generational conflict, and these conflicts need to be handled correctly when they occur. Understanding the different generations and how they see things is a crucial part of handling this conflict. The authors of *Generations at Work: Managing the Clash of Veterans, Boomers, Xers, and Nexters in Your Workplace* developed the ACORN acronym to describe five principles that managers can use to deal with generational issues.

*A*ccommodating employee differences entails treating employees as customers and giving them the best service that the company can give. *C*reating workplace choices as to what and how employees work can allow for change and satisfaction. *O*perating from a sophisticated management style requires that management be direct but tactful. *R*especting competence and initiative assumes the best from the different generations and responds accordingly. *N*ourishing retention means keeping the best employees. When combined with effective communication efforts, the ACORN principles can help managers mend generational conflicts for the benefit of everyone in the company.[86]

Although workplace diversity reaps benefits for both employees and employers, it also brings challenges that must be addressed. For example, diverse employees may have more difficulty communicating and working with each other. Although differences can breed innovation and creativity, they can also create an atmosphere of distrust, dissatisfaction, or lack of cooperation.[87] Many companies found a way to turn fear and confusion over the September 11, 2001, terrorist strikes into an opportunity for discussing diversity and creating stronger bonds among employees of different ethnicities, religions, beliefs, and experiences. Other firms engage employees in community service projects and similar initiatives that promote teamwork and cohesion and help to minimize any negative effects of diversity.

Finally, the diversity message will not be taken seriously unless top management and organizational systems fully support a diverse workforce. After Home Depot settled a gender-discrimination lawsuit, it developed an automated hiring and promotion computer program. Although the Job Preference Program (JPP) was originally intended as insurance against discrimination, the system opens all jobs and applicants to the companywide network, eliminates unqualified applications, and enables managers to learn employee aspirations and skills in a more effective manner. JPP has also brought positive change to the number of female and minority managers within Home Depot.[88] In contrast to this success story, some employees of companies with diversity training programs have viewed such training as intended to blame or change white men only. Other training has focused on the reasons diversity should be important, not the actual changes in attitudes, work styles, expectations, and business processes that are needed for diversity to work.[89]

WORK/LIFE BALANCE A recent in-depth study focused on two women and their career and family progression over sixteen years. Both women had great work achievements in their twenties and later decided to marry, have children, and devote more time to family than career. From this study and many others, the authors note the inherent trade-offs between work and family life. They conclude that most working women are typically forced to make tough trade-offs among career goals, child rearing, household management, and economic realities. These are not easy decisions for everyone, thus giving rise to potential stress and conflict at home and work.[90] Just as increasing numbers of women in the workplace have changed the norms of behavior at work and prompted attention to sexual harassment, they have also brought challenges in work/life balance. This balance is not just an issue for women, as men also have multiple roles that can create the same types of stress and conflict.[91]

Because employees have roles within and outside the organization, there is increasing corporate focus on the types of support that employees have in balancing these obligations. Deloitte & Touche (now Deloitte Touche Tohmatsu), an international professional services firm, recently came to grips with issues of work/life balance when it discovered the alarming rate at which women were leaving the firm. In the early 1990s, only four of the fifty employees being considered for partner status were women, despite the company's heavy recruitment of women from business schools. A closer examination of the company's turnover rate also illuminated the gender issue, although many executives assumed the women had left to have and raise children. The company convened the Initiative for the Retention and Advancement of Women task force and soon uncovered cultural beliefs and practices that needed modification. The task force found that younger employees—both male and female—wanted a balanced life, were willing to forgo some pay for more time with family and less stress, and had similar career goals. Thus, Deloitte & Touche set out to change its culture and operating practices so that all employees were given similar opportunities and to ensure that concerns and issues were open for discussion. A major initiative included reduced travel schedules and flexible work arrangements to benefit both men and women employees of the firm. According to a recent survey, issues related to telecommuting, flexible scheduling, and assistance with child care and elder care are almost equally important to male and female employees. Whereas men rarely utilized these benefits in the past, this is no longer the case. Many midlevel executives, both male and female, are part of dual-earner couples "sandwiched" between raising children and caring for aging parents.[92]

work/life programs

programs to assist employees in balancing work responsibilities with personal and family responsibilities

Such **work/life programs** assist employees in balancing work responsibilities with personal and family responsibilities. A central feature of these programs is flexibility so that employees of all types are able to achieve their own definition of balance. For example, a single parent may want child care and consistent work hours, whereas another employee may need assistance in finding elder care for a parent with Alzheimer's disease. A working mother may need access to "just-in-time" care when a child is sick or school is out of session. Employees of all types appreciate flextime arrangements, which allow them to work forty hours per week on a schedule they develop within a range of hours specified by the company. Other employees work some hours at home or in a location more conducive to their personal obligations. DuPont, for example, has been recognized by *Working Mother* magazine for its exceptional flexibility to support work/life balance. At nearly all of its eighty-five locations, DuPont's employees enjoy compressed scheduling, telecommuting, job sharing, and other arrangements. More than half of DuPont's 28,000 employees use a flextime arrangement. The company has installed data lines to support employee telecommuting, which benefits nearly one-third of its workforce.[93] Work/life balance not only enhances employee productivity, but it is also an imperative to attracting and maintaining a healthy workforce.

More than 65 million Americans suffer from symptoms of stress at work, including headaches, sleeplessness, and other physical ailments. To remedy these concerns, Americans spend more than $370 million per year on stress-reducing products, services, and strategies. Compared to Japanese workers, however, the U.S. figures are moderate. A study by the Japanese government found that nearly 60 percent of Japanese employees feel fairly fatigued from work, whereas less than 30 percent of U.S. workers feel the same way. Nearly 10,000 Japanese men die every year as a result of job-related stressors, physical problems, and associated psychological ramifications. The Japanese Ministry of Health, Labour and Welfare recently proposed legislation that would require companies to encourage employees to take breaks for holidays and vacations.[94]

Managers must become sensitive to cues that employees need to create a stronger work/life balance. Frustration, anger, moodiness, a myopic focus, and physiological symptoms are often present when an employee needs to take vacation, work fewer hours, utilize flexible scheduling, or simply reduce his or her workload. One manager of a telecommunications firm in California returned to the workplace around 11:30 P.M. every night to send people home. Otherwise, she knew many of them would sleep on the floor in the office. Not only do some employees work too many hours, but they may largely ignore nutrition and fitness, friendships, community involvement, and other aspects of work/life balance.[95]

There is no generic work/life program. Instead, companies need to consider their employee base and the types of support their employees are likely to need and appreciate. For the employees of SAS Institute, the world's largest private software company, the workplace resembles a modern-day utopia. Although the North Carolina company competes with Silicon Valley firms, its workplace bears little resemblance to the demanding atmosphere that often characterizes high-tech companies. James Goodnight, SAS's founder, believes that dinnertime should be spent with family and friends, not in the office. Most employees leave by 5:00 P.M., and others participate in flextime or job-sharing arrangements. Other perks, such as on-site day care and a health center staffed with dentists and physicians, also contribute to the company's high ranking on *Fortune* magazine's annual list of the 100 Best Companies to Work For. The company has also been named to *Working Mother* magazine's 100 Best Companies for Working Mothers.[96]

Successful work/life programs, like that developed by the SAS Institute, are an extension of the diversity philosophy in that employees are respected as individuals in the process of contributing to company goals. Thus, connecting employees' personal needs, lives, and goals to strategic business issues can be fruitful for both parties. This perspective is in contrast to the "employee goals versus business goals" trade-off mentality that has been pervasive. IBM implemented a work/life strategy over two decades ago and periodically conducts employee surveys to see if changes or additions are needed.[97]

A study by jobtrack.com found that nearly 50 percent of all applicants consider work/life balance the most important consideration in identifying potential employers and considering job offers.[98] For this reason, companies have become quite innovative in their approach to work/life balance. DaimlerChrysler, for example, developed the work/family account, where employees allocate $4,000 for child care, adoption costs, elder care, education costs, or retirement. The allocation was gradually increased to $8,000.[99] Texas Instruments holds summer camps for employees' children at its Dallas headquarters and two other locations. For a reasonable fee, each child is involved in supervised and educational field trips, arts and crafts, sports, community projects, and other fun activities, which ease parents' worries about dependable child care and aids in children's personal development.[100] Such efforts demonstrate the company's willingness to accommodate employee needs and concerns beyond the workplace.

Philanthropic Issues

In Chapter 9, we examine the philanthropic efforts of companies and the important role that employees play in the process of selecting and implementing projects that contribute time, resources, and human activity to worthy causes. In social responsibility, philanthropic responsibilities are primarily directed outside the organization, so they are not directly focused on employees. However, employees benefit from participating in volunteerism and other philanthropic projects. A recent study by the Points of Light Foundation asked corporate executives about the effect of employee volunteerism on organizational competitiveness and success. The surveyed executives reported that this aspect of philanthropy increases employee productivity and builds teamwork skills. In a tight job market, employees may even view philanthropic activity, such as volunteer opportunities, as an important criterion in evaluating potential employers.[101]

Many employers help organize employees to participate in walkathons, marathons, bikeathons, and similar events. The executive vice president of FedEx Kinkos, Ken May, says, "The esprit de corps it builds is incredible." While employees exercise and feel a part of the "team," charitable organizations also benefit financially, as these types of events raise over $1 billion annually.[102] Thus, the benefits of corporate philanthropy in the community reflect back positively on the organization. There are many strategies for demonstrating community involvement and care. McDonald's launched a series of websites intended to serve both employment needs and community relations goals. On a state-by-state basis, the venerable fast-food chain set up sites, such as www.McWisconsin.com and www.McMinnesota.com, to aid both corporate and local franchisees' ability to hire new employees, educate consumers, deliver promotional materials, and reach other business goals. McDonald's released its first corporate responsibility report in the United States recently, which included a section on the ways in which the company and its franchises positively affect local communities.[103]

STRATEGIC IMPLEMENTATION OF RESPONSIBILITIES TO EMPLOYEES

As this chapter has demonstrated, responsibilities toward employees are varied and complex. Legal issues alone require full-time attention from lawyers and human resource specialists. These issues are also emotional because corporate decisions have ramifications for families and communities as well as employees. In light of this complexity, many companies have chosen to embrace these obligations to benefit both employee and organizational goals. This philosophy stands in stark contrast to the master-servant model popular more than 100 years ago. Today, companies are using distinctive programs and initiatives to set themselves apart and to become known as desirable employers. Low unemployment levels in the late 1990s, along with diversity, work/life balance, outsourcing, and generational differences, prompted companies to use marketing strategy and business insight normally applied to customer development in the employee recruitment and retention realm. Even in a time of economic downturn, employers will need to be mindful of keeping top talent and maintaining employee satisfaction. For example, Small Dog Electronics, a small Vermont retailer, offers a rather unusual perk to satisfy and retain its fourteen employees: dog insurance. The firm allows employees to bring their dogs to work and picks up 80 percent of veterinarians' bills, minus a deductible. T3, an integrated marketing agency, also has a pet-friendly workplace and other types of progressive policies. "T3 and Under" is the name of the agency's family-friendly work program. At this Austin, Texas-based firm, employees bring their babies to work, which relieves the stress of finding trustworthy and reliable day care for infants. In both cases, the companies' policies differentiate its work environment.[104]

employer of choice

an organization of any size in any industry that is able to attract, optimize, and retain the best employee talent over the long term

An **employer of choice** is an organization of any size in any industry that is able to attract, optimize, and retain the best employee talent over the long term. ENSR, a European environmental consulting firm, created a cross-functional and geographically diverse committee to provide guidance for maintaining and strengthening the company's positive culture. The committee focuses on ways in which ENSR's top management can better operationalize integrity, respect, balance, and other core values.[105] Advertising, websites, and other company communications often use the term to describe and market the organization to current and potential employees. These messages center on the various practices that companies have implemented to create employee satisfaction. Firms with this distinction value the human component of business, not just financial considerations, ensure that employees are engaged in meaningful work, and stimulate the intellectual curiosity of employees. These businesses have strong training practices, delegate authority, and recognize the link between employee morale, customer satisfaction, and other performance measures.[106] Thus, becoming an employer of choice is an important manifestation of strategic social responsibility.

From employees' perspectives, one traditional way to strengthen trust is through employee stock ownership plans (ESOPs), which provide the opportunity both to contribute to and gain from organizational success. Such programs confer not only ownership but also opportunities for employees to participate in management planning, which foster an environment that many organizations believe increases profits. Several studies of companies with ESOPs cast a positive light on these plans. ESOPs appear to increase sales by about 2.3 to 2.4 percent over what would have been expected without an ESOP. ESOP companies were also found to pay better benefits, higher wages, and provide nearly twice the retirement income for employees than their non-ESOP counterparts. Under these plans, employees must take on an ownership perspective, work as a team in an environment that forges trust, and provide excellent interactions and service to customers. ESOPs are also thought to improve employee loyalty and lower employee turnover rates. Some of the 10,000 "employee-owned" firms include Lowe's, Acadian Ambulance, Publix Supermarkets, Procter & Gamble, Hallmark Cards, and Ferrellgas.[107] Despite the advantages of ESOPs, experts also warn that some plans are potentially risky for employees, as in the case of Enron.[108] Becoming an employer of choice has many benefits, including an enhanced ability to hire and retain the best people. The expectations of such businesses are very high because employee stakeholders have specific criteria in mind when assessing the attractiveness of a particular employer. Although top managers must decide how the firm will achieve strategic social responsibility with employees, Table 7.6 provides general guidance on some of the best practices that are implemented by employers of choice.

TABLE 7.6	Best Practices of Employers of Choice

Practice	Explanation
Foster openness	Give all employees full access to company information.
Foster community	Instill in employees a concern for coworkers and society at large.
Foster creativity	Allow workers to create their own work environments.
Foster loyalty	Train workers extensively and pay them generously for greater productivity.
Foster responsibility	Put new workers in charge and move them quickly through the ranks.
Foster individuality	Allow workers to do their own thing, no matter how wacky their thing is.
Foster teamwork	Throw out the old management hierarchy and encourage group over individual success.

Sources: "Main Page," Employer of Choice.net, http://www.employerofchoice.net/, accessed April 23, 2006; Roger E. Herman and Joyce L. Gioia, *How to Become an Employer of Choice* (Winchester, VA: Oakhill Press, 2000).

Finally, the global dimensions of today's workplace shape an organization's ability to effectively work with employee stakeholders and to become an employer of choice. Firms with offices and sites around the world must deal with a complex array of norms and expectations, all of which can affect its reputation at home. For example, when Nike was first accused of dealing with suppliers that used child labor in the mid-1990s, the company claimed that it was not in the business of manufacturing shoes and that therefore it could not be blamed for the practices of Asian manufacturers. Following media criticism, Nike publicized a report claiming that the employees of its Indonesian and Vietnamese suppliers were living quite well. The veracity of this report was tarnished by contradictory evidence produced by activists. Next, Nike started introducing workers' rights and environmental guidelines for its suppliers. Yet some company representatives explained that any additional social responsibility initiative would damage the competitive position of the firm. In the late 1990s, Nike designed a suppliers' auditing process that invited student representatives along with other activists to visit manufacturing plants and provide recommendations for better practices. Before the company's shift, many media reports discussed Nike's manufacturing practices, and it is likely that some consumers and potential employees turned their attention away from Nike. Nike actually settled the legal case that rose all the way to the Supreme Court. Nike agreed to pay $1.5 million to the Fair Labor Association to help fund worker development programs. In this case, Nike's relationships with its manufacturing suppliers and their employees affected the company's ability to achieve strategic social responsibility.[109]

SUMMARY

Throughout history, people's perceptions of work and employment have evolved from a necessary evil to a source of fulfillment. The relationship between employer and employee involves responsibilities, obligations, and expectations as well as challenges.

On an economic level, many believe there is an unwritten, informal psychological contract that includes the beliefs, perceptions, expectations, and obligations that make up the agreement between individuals and their employers. This contract has evolved from a primarily master-servant relationship, in which employers held the power, to one in which employees assume a more balanced relationship with employers. Workforce reduction, the process of eliminating employment positions, breaches the psychological contract that exists between an employer and employee and threatens the social contract among employers, communities, and other groups. Although workforce reduction lowers costs, it often results in lost intellectual capital, strained customer relationships, negative media attention, and other issues that drain company resources.

Employment law is a complex and evolving area. In the past, employment was primarily governed by employment at will, a common-law doctrine that allows either the employer or employee to terminate the relationship at any time as long as it does not violate an employment contract. Many laws have been enacted to regulate business conduct with regard to wages and benefits, labor unions, health and safety, equal employment opportunity, sexual harassment, and whistle-blowing. Title VII of the Civil Rights Act, which prohibits employment discrimination on the basis of race, national origin, color, religion, and gender, is fundamental to employees' rights to join and advance in an organization according to merit. Sexual harassment is defined as unwelcome sexual advances, requests for sexual favors, and other verbal or physical conduct of a sexual nature when submission to or rejection of this conduct explicitly or implicitly affects an individual's employment, unreasonably interferes with an individual's work performance, or creates an intimidating, hostile, or offensive work environment. Sexual harassment may take the form of either quid pro quo harassment or hostile work environment harassment. An employee who reports individual or corporate wrongdoing to either internal or external sources is considered a whistle-blower.

Although legal compliance is imperative for social responsibility, the ethical climate of the workplace is more subjective and dependent on top management support and corporate culture. Companies with a strong ethical stance fund initiatives to develop employees' skills, knowledge, and other personal characteristics. With diversity programs, companies assume an ethical obligation to employ and empower individuals regardless of age, gender, physical and mental ability, and other characteristics. Work/life programs assist employees in balancing work responsibilities with personal and family responsibilities.

Employees may play an important role in a firm's philanthropic efforts. Employees benefit from such initiatives through participation in volunteerism and other projects.

In light of the complexity of and emotions involved with responsibilities toward employees, many companies have chosen to embrace these obligations to benefit both employee and organizational goals. An employer of choice is an organization of any size in any industry that is able to attract, optimize, and retain the best employee talent over the long term. One traditional way to strengthen trust is through ESOPs, which provide the opportunity both to contribute to and gain from organizational success. Finally, the global dimensions of today's workplace shape an organization's ability to effectively work with employee stakeholders and to become an employer of choice.

KEY TERMS

psychological contract (p. 220)
workforce reduction (p. 222)
employment at will (p. 227)
vesting (p. 228)
ergonomics (p. 230)
sexual harassment (p. 234)
quid pro quo sexual harassment (p. 235)
hostile work environment sexual
    harassment (p. 235)
workplace diversity (p. 240)
work/life programs (p. 243)
employer of choice (p. 246)

DISCUSSION QUESTIONS

1. Review Table 7.1, Changes in Employees' Psychological Contract with Employers. Create additional columns to indicate the positive and negative effects associated with the "old" and "new" contract characteristics. For example, what is positive and negative about the belief that employees should follow orders? What is positive and negative about giving 110 percent effort on the job?

2. What is workforce reduction? How does it affect employees, consumers, and the local community? What steps should a company take to address these effects?

3. What responsibilities do companies have with respect to workplace violence? Using the three categories of violence presented in the chapter, describe the responsibilities and actions that you believe are necessary for an organization to demonstrate social responsibility in this area.

4. Describe the differences between workplace diversity and equal employment opportunity. How do these differences affect managerial responsibilities and the development of social responsibility programs?

5. Why is it important to understand the profiles of different generations at work? How can managers use the ACORN principles to develop a strong sense of community and solidarity among all employee groups?

6. Why are organizations developing work/life programs? What trends have contributed to these programs?

7. What is an employer of choice? Describe how a firm could use traditional marketing concepts and strategies to appeal to current and potential employees.

8. Review the best practices in Table 7.6 for becoming an employer of choice. What are some potential drawbacks to each practice? Rank the seven practices in terms of their importance to you.

EXPERIENTIAL EXERCISE

Develop a list of five criteria that describe your employer of choice. Then, visit the websites of three companies in which you have some employment interest. Peruse each firm's website to find evidence on how it fulfills your criteria. On the basis of this evidence, develop a chart to show how well each firm meets your description and criteria of your employer of choice. Finally, provide three recommendations on how these companies can better communicate their commitment to employees and the employer of choice criteria.

WHAT WOULD YOU DO?

Dawn Burke, director of employee relations, glanced at her online calendar and remembered her appointment at 3:00 P.M. today. She quickly found the file labeled "McCullen and Aranda" and started preparing for the meeting. She recalled that this was essentially an employee-supervisor case, where the employee had been unwilling or unable to meet the supervisor's requests. The employee claimed that the supervisor was too demanding and impatient. Their conflict had escalated to the point that both were unhappy and uncomfortable in the work environment. Other employees had noticed, and overheard, some of the conflict.

In her role, Dawn was responsible for many programs, including a new mediation initiative to resolve workplace conflict. The program was designed to help employees develop stronger communication and conflict resolution skills. In this case, the program was also providing an intermediary step between informal and formal discipline. Today, she was meeting with both parties to discuss mediation guidelines, a time line, their goal, and their general points of conflict.

John McCullen, fifty-one, a buyer in the facilities department, and Terry Aranda, the director of facilities procurement, arrived separately. John had been with the company for thirty-two years and had started his career with the company right out of high school. Terry, thirty-one, was hired from another firm to oversee the procurement area a year ago and recently graduated from a prestigious M.B.A. program. Dawn started the meeting by reviewing the mediation guidelines and time line. She reminded John and Terry that their goal was to develop a workable and agreeable solution to the current situation. Dawn then asked for each party to explain his or her position on the conflict.

John began, "Ms. Aranda is a very smart lady. She seems to know the buying and procurement area, but she knows less about the company and its history. I am not sure she has taken the time to learn our ways and values. Ms. Aranda is impatient with our use of the new software and computer system. Some of us don't have college degrees, and we haven't been using computers since we were young. I started working at this company about the time she was born, and I am not sure that her management style is good for our department. Everything was going pretty well until we starting changing our systems."

Terry commented, "John is a valuable member of the department, as he knows everyone at this company. I appreciate his knowledge and loyalty. On the other hand, he has not completed several tasks in a timely manner, nor has he asked for an extension. I feel that I must check up on his schedule and proof all of his work. John has attended several training classes, and I asked that he use an electronic calendar so that projects are completed on time. He continues to ignore my advice and deadlines. We've had several conversations, but John's work has not substantially improved. We have many goals to achieve in the department, and I need everyone's best work in order to make that happen."

Dawn thanked them for their candor and told them she would meet with them next week to start the mediation process. As she contemplated what each had said, she remembered an article that discussed how people born in different generations often have contrasting perceptions about work. Dawn started to jot a few notes about the next steps in resolving their conflict. What would you do?

CHAPTER 8

Consumer Relations

CHAPTER OBJECTIVES

- To describe customers as stakeholders
- To investigate consumer protection laws
- To examine six consumer rights
- To discuss the implementation of responsibilities to consumers

CHAPTER OUTLINE

Consumer Stakeholders

Responsibilities to Consumers

Strategic Implementation of Responsibilities to Consumers

Banco Azteca, Mexico's first bank aimed at the country's middle and working class, opened its doors in late 2002. For a security guard and father of four like Humberto Vidal, Banco Azteca is a welcome sight. He received a personal loan of $350 and commented, "Now I have a place where I can go if I need support." Before the bank opened, most Mexican consumers had little access to credit unless they chose to pay exorbitant interest rates. Banco Azteca is targeting the 73 million people in Mexico who live in households with combined incomes of $250 to $1,300 a month. This mass market has been neglected by Mexico's traditional banking system. Not only is the bank going after a new market, but it is bucking the trend of bank closures or mergers with foreign banks. Company executives also speak of a greater mission: improving the personal financial situation of millions of Mexican citizens.

Most of the bank's 800 branches are located inside the retail stores of Elektra, Salinas & Rocha, and Bodega de Ramates, all owned by Grupo Elektra S.A. de C.V., Latin America's leading specialty retailer and consumer finance company. The retail stores have offered consumer credit options for some time and claim several million active accounts but will eventually close down consumer financing operations to drive business to Banco Azteca. Unlike the retail financing operation, the bank has access to interbank borrowing rates, which average around 8 percent annually. This status opens new doors for consumer credit in Mexico.

In its first few months of operation, Banco Azteca opened nearly 250,000 savings accounts. One customer, Stephanie Diaz, started a savings account with only $5 but plans to have her employer deposit her paycheck with Banco Azteca, some of which will go into the savings account. Consumers who work in the informal business sector, such as taxi drivers, street merchants, and electricians, will now have access to loans. In the past, these workers could not receive loans because they could not meet lending requirements, including proof of income. Small business owners and would-be entrepreneurs will also benefit from Banco Azteca.

In addition to savings accounts and personal loans, Banco Azteca offers car loans, mortgage loans, installment plans, debit cards, and other services. Elektra is taking its understanding of these underserved consumers from the retail store into the banking operations. The company is fervent in its belief that low and middle income is not necessarily synonymous with loan defaults and high risk, as long as the right control mechanisms are in place. The bank's business model and focus on the ordinary consumer are consistent with its vision: *Our vision is to develop plain financial products and services to improve the lives of our clients.*"[1] ∎

This vignette illustrates that organizations with profit objectives, operations expertise, customer insights, and related competencies can also be focused on implementing social responsibility and satisfying stakeholder groups. From a social responsibility perspective, the key challenge is how an organization assesses its stakeholders' needs, integrates them with company strategy, reconciles differences between stakeholders' needs, strives for better relationships with stakeholders, achieves mutual understandings with them, and finds solutions for problems. In this chapter, we explore relationships with consumers and the expectations of the economic, legal, ethical, and philanthropic responsibilities that must be addressed by business.

CONSUMER STAKEHOLDERS

Throughout the 1980s and much of the 1990s, "green marketing," the promotion of more environmentally friendly products, became a much-discussed strategy in the package goods industry. Both Energizer and Rayovac, for example, marketed environmentally friendly batteries. Today, those products have disappeared from most store shelves, replaced by the alkaline batteries needed to run electronic devices that have become so common for both children and adults. Around the same time, Procter & Gamble (P&G), the venerable manufacturer of soap, paper goods, and other household products, feared that increasing environmental consciousness among consumers would lead to a resurgence in the use of cloth diapers, which would have had a negative effect on its disposable diaper business. P&G launched a marketing campaign touting the benefits of disposables, including the fact that their use does not require hot water for laundering or fuel for diaper service trucks. P&G also initiated a pilot project for composting disposable diapers. Today, the debate over cloth versus disposables has largely faded, and the P&G marketing campaign has disappeared.

The dawn of the twenty-first century brought many new products, including disposable tableware, food containers that can be used repeatedly or thrown away, hybrid automobiles, and electrostatic mops with cloths that are disposed of after one use. Although these product introductions suggest a decline in environmental consciousness among consumers, other initiatives counter this assumption. Whole Foods Markets, a grocery chain that specializes in organic and environmentally friendly items, reports $689 sales per square foot versus the $400 sales per square foot earned by most supermarkets. With nearly 200 stores, the company is the world's largest retailer of natural and organic goods and underwrote a thirteen-part PBS special, "Chefs A'Field," to expose consumers to sustainable practices, from the field to the table. About one-third of its stores compost their waste, and the chief executive has promised to implement humane animal treatment standards.[2] Indeed, environmental and related social initiatives have become a global phenomenon. One goal of the annual International Buy Nothing Day, sponsored by consumer associations around the world, is to encourage consumers to consider the environmental consequences of their buying habits. The event's organizers remind consumers that the richest 20 percent of people consume 80 percent of the world's resources.[3]

Although the future of different marketing strategies can be debated, the real test of effectiveness lies in the expectations, attitudes, and ultimate buying patterns of consumers. The preceding examples illustrate that there is no true consensus around issues such as environmental responsibility, and companies therefore face complex decisions about how to respond to them. This is true for all types of expectations, including the ones we explore in this chapter. In the sections that follow, we examine the economic, legal, ethical, and philanthropic responsibilities that businesses have to **consumers**, those individuals who purchase, use, and dispose of products for themselves and their homes.

consumers
individuals who purchase, use, and dispose of products for themselves and their homes

RESPONSIBILITIES TO CONSUMERS

Consumers International, a London-based nonprofit federation of more than 230 consumer organizations and government agencies in 113 countries, is dedicated to protecting and promoting consumers' interests and rights and implementing campaigns and research programs to aid governments, businesses, and nonprofit groups in decision making.[4] The federation sponsors an annual World Consumer Rights Day every March 15 to further solidarity among the global consumer movement by promoting consumer rights, demanding the protection of these rights, and protesting abuses and injustices. Each observance has a particular theme—a pressing issue that is likely to affect a majority of consumers around the world. Issues over the last few years have included access to electricity, genetically modified foods, the safety and affordability of water, the natural environment, and consumer representation in government decision making. Another recent project evaluated the credibility and integrity of information found on the Internet. Consumers International worked with researchers in thirteen consumer organizations around the world and concluded that most consumers have difficulty evaluating the credibility of information sources on the Web.[5] The association's many efforts have led to the development of the Consumer Charter for Global Business, which offers guidance on a variety of business practices, including product standards, marketing, service guarantees, information and labeling, consumer complaint procedures, and competitive tactics. At a minimum, the charter asks companies to consider their economic relationship with consumers through all stages of the production, distribution, and marketing process; to obey all relevant laws; and to establish clear ethical standards for business practice.[6] Figure 8.1 provides the preamble to the charter, which covers three of the four responsibilities we have discussed throughout this book.

Economic Issues

As we saw in Chapter 2, consumers are primary stakeholders because their awareness, purchase, use, and repurchase of products are vital to a company's existence. Fundamentally, therefore, consumers and businesses are connected by an economic relationship. This relationship begins with an exchange, usually of a good or service for money, which often leads to deeper attachments or affiliation. An advertising campaign slogan, "You are what you drive," typifies the close relationship that some consumers develop with the products they purchase. Other consumers may choose to shun particular brands or opt for the environmentally sensitive products described earlier. In all of these cases, however, consumers expect the products they purchase to perform as guaranteed by their sellers. Thus, a firm's economic responsibilities include following through on promises made in the exchange process. Although this responsibility seems basic today, business practices have not always been directed in this way. In the early part of the 1900s, the caveat "Let the buyer beware" typified the power that business—not consumers—wielded in most exchange relationships.[7] In less developed parts of the world, this phrase still accurately describes the consumer marketplace. For example, despite recent government regulation, investors in Bangladesh are wary of company prospectuses and other financial documents used to make sound

| **FIGURE 8.1** | Consumer Charter for Global Business |

Intent of This Charter

This Charter was prepared by Consumers International, the international federation of consumer organisations. It is based on the eight consumer rights: the right to basic needs, safety, information, choice, a fair hearing, redress, consumer education and a healthy environment. The Charter sets out best business practice in areas of interest to consumers such as ethical standards, competition, product standards, marketing, labelling, disclosure of information and consumer redress. It draws on the experience of consumer organisations and is modelled on existing international codes of practice. The aim of the Charter is to develop corporate practice in light of consumer concerns. The accompanying Charter Assessment Form translates the Charter's principles into practical goals for business. The Form helps assess the company's progress in attaining the standards set by the Charter. The Charter's provisions can also be the basis for national and international regulation of business practices. They provide a focus for consumer education campaigns and highlight how different corporate activities can affect consumer rights.

Source: Consumers International, www.consumersinternational.org, accessed May 29, 2006. Copyright © 2006 by Consumers International. Reprinted with permission.

investment decisions. Experts believe that this lack of investor confidence is the primary reason Bangladesh securities markets have not flourished.[8]

consumer fraud
intentional deception to derive an unfair economic advantage over an organization

Fulfillment of economic responsibilities depends on interactions with the consumer. However, there are situations in which the consumer does not act as a fair participant in the exchange.[9] **Consumer fraud** involves intentional deception to derive an unfair economic advantage over an organization. Examples of fraudulent activities include shoplifting, collusion or duplicity, and guile. Collusion typically involves an employee who assists the consumer in fraud. For example, a cashier may not scan all merchandise or may give an unwarranted discount. Duplicity may involve a consumer staging an accident in a grocery store and then seeking damages against the store for its lack of attention to safety. A consumer may purchase, wear, and then return an item of clothing for a full refund. In other situations, the consumer may ask for a refund by claiming a defect that either is nonexistent or was caused by consumer misuse.[10] Although some of these acts warrant legal prosecution, they can be very difficult to prove, and many companies are reluctant to accuse patrons of a crime when there is no way of verifying it. Businesses that operate with the "customer is always right" philosophy have found that some consumers will take advantage of this promise and have therefore modified return policies to curb unfair use. However, some people persist in illegitimate complaining. Table 8.1 describes six motivations that consumers may have when committing this type of behavior.

Because of the vague nature of some types of consumer fraud, its full financial toll has been difficult to tally. However, rough estimates indicate that inventory shrinkage

TABLE 8.1   Motivations for Illegitimate Consumer Complaints

Motivation	Description
Freeloaders	Consumer attempts to obtain free goods or services by making a fraudulent complaint
Fraudulent Return	Consumer buys product and knows that he or she will attempt to return it for a refund
Fault Transferors	Consumer avoids fault by making fraudulent claims and trying to shift responsibility to company
Solitary Ego Gains	While alone, consumer voices illegitimate complaints to enhance his or her feelings of self-worth and ego
Peer-Induced Esteem Seekers	If there is an audience, consumer perceives there to be benefits of voicing fraudulent complaints
Disruptive Gains	Consumer expresses insincere complaints solely to cause disruption (e.g., get employee into trouble)

Source: Kate L. Reynolds and Lloyd C. Harris, "When Service Failure Is Not Service Failure: An Exploration of the Forms and Motives of 'Illegitimate' Customer Complaining," *Journal of Services Marketing* 19 (August 2005): 321–335.

costs U.S. businesses more than $40 billion per year, with half of the shrinkage perpetrated by employees. While shrinkage is most often considered in the context of brick-and-mortar establishments, companies in many industries have problems with fraud and related issues that raise costs and lower profitability. Figure 8.2 provides the results of a study of online merchants who were asked about their fraud detection and prevention strategies. Online merchants have developed a number of strategies, including customer follow-up, credit-card verification, address verification, and other techniques to stay ahead of sophisticated criminals. The survey was sponsored by the Merchant Risk Council, a trade association representing 7,500 businesses, law enforcement agencies, financial institutions, and other organizations committed to establishing best practices in cyberfraud prevention.[11]

FIGURE 8.2   Company Use of Online Fraud Prevention Tools

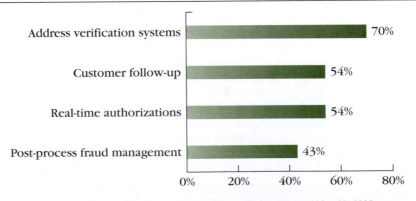

Source: Merchant Risk Council, www.merchantriskcouncil.org, accessed May 29, 2006.

Many consumers, of course, do not engage in such activities. However, there are cases when buyers and sellers disagree on whether or how well companies have satisfied their economic responsibilities. Thus, a consumer may believe that a product is not worth the price paid, perhaps because he or she believes the product's benefits have been exaggerated by the seller. For example, although some marketers claim that their creams, pills, special massages, and other techniques can reduce or even eliminate cellulite, most medical experts and dermatologists believe that only exercise and weight loss can reduce the appearance of this undesirable condition. Products for reducing cellulite remain on the market, but many consumers have returned these products and complained about the lack of results. In the United Kingdom, a number of cosmetic companies have been reprimanded by the Advertising Standards Authority for making misleading claims in advertising and packaging.[12] If a consumer believes that a firm has not fulfilled its basic economic responsibilities, he or she may ask for a refund, tell others about the bad experiences, discontinue patronage, contact a consumer agency, and even seek legal redress. Many consumer and government agencies keep track of consumer complaints. For example, district attorneys in California recently reported the top five consumer scams being investigated by their offices. Problems related to identity theft, Internet fraud, unreasonable interest rates, bogus charities, and unlicensed professionals topped the list.[13] To protect consumers and provide businesses with guidance, a number of laws and regulations have been enacted to ensure that economic responsibility is met in accordance with institutionalized standards.

Legal Issues

As we discussed in Chapter 4, legal issues with respect to consumers in the United States primarily fall under the domain of the Federal Trade Commission (FTC), which enforces federal antitrust and consumer protection laws. Within this agency, the Bureau of Consumer Protection works to protect consumers against unfair, deceptive, and fraudulent practices. The bureau is further organized into eight divisions, including those focused on marketing practices, privacy and identity protection, advertising practices, and international consumer protection.[14] For example, consumer complaints about problems with credit counseling agencies prompted the FTC to investigate. Under a recent settlement, Lighthouse Credit Foundation Inc. and its codefendants will pay more than $2.4 million in consumer redress. They are prohibited from making deceptive claims about credit counseling or debt management services. Consumers did not receive individualized credit counseling or the significantly lower interest rates promised by Lighthouse and several other firms.[15] In this case, the companies' inability to honor the economic exchange agreement resulted in legal action and continuing oversight on behalf of consumers. To aid consumers who are facing economic distress, the FTC publishes a guide entitled "Fiscal Fitness: Choosing a Credit Counselor."

In addition to the FTC, several other federal agencies regulate specific goods, services, or business practices to protect consumers. The Food and Drug Administration, for example, enforces laws and regulations enacted to prevent distribution of adulterated or misbranded foods, drugs, medical devices, cosmetics, veterinary products, and potentially hazardous consumer products. The Consumer Product Safety Commission enforces laws and regulations designed to protect the public from unreasonable risk of injury from consumer products. Many states also have regulatory agencies that enforce laws and regulations regarding business practices within their states. Most federal agencies and states have consumer affairs or information offices to help consumers. The Federal Communications Commission's Consumer Affairs and Outreach Division educates consumers on issues related to cable and satellite service, telecommunications, wireless technology, and other areas under the FCC's domain.[16] In Iowa, the attorney general's Consumer Protection Division publishes brochures to assist consumers in complaining effectively, buying a new or used car, recognizing scams, and avoiding identity theft.[17]

In this section, we focus on U.S. laws related to exchanges and relationships with consumers. Table 8.2 summarizes some of the laws that are likely to affect a wide

TABLE 8.2	Major Consumer Laws
Act (Date Enacted)	**Purpose**
Pure Food and Drug Act (1906)	Established the Food and Drug Administration; outlaws the adulteration or mislabeling of food and drug products sold in interstate commerce.
Cigarette Labeling and Advertising Act (1965)	Requires manufacturers to add to package labels warnings about the possible health hazards associated with smoking cigarettes.
Fair Packaging and Labeling Act (1966)	Outlaws unfair or deceptive packaging or labeling of consumer products.
Truth in Lending Act (1968)	Requires creditors to disclose in writing all finance charges and related aspects of credit transactions.
Child Protection and Toy Safety Act (1969)	Requires childproof devices and special labeling.
Fair Credit Reporting Act (1970)	Promotes accuracy, fairness, and privacy of credit information; gives consumers the right to see their personal credit reports and to dispute any inaccurate information therein.
Consumer Product Safety Act (1972)	Established the Consumer Product Safety Commission to regulate potentially hazardous consumer products.
Odometer Act (1972)	Provides protections for consumers against odometer fraud in used-car sales.
Equal Credit Opportunity Act (1974)	Outlaws denial of credit on the basis of race, color, religion, national origin, sex, marital status, age, or receipt of public assistance and requires creditors to provide applicants, on request, with the reasons for credit denial.
Magnuson-Moss Warranty (FTC) Act (1975)	Establishes rules for consumer product warranties, including minimum content and disclosure standards; allows the FTC to prescribe interpretive rules in policy statements regarding unfair or deceptive practices.
Consumer Goods Pricing Act (1975)	Prohibits the use of price maintenance agreements among manufacturers and resellers in interstate commerce.
Fair Debt Collection Practices Act (1977)	Prohibits third-party debt collectors from engaging in deceptive or abusive conduct when collecting consumer debts incurred for personal, family, or household purposes.
Toy Safety Act (1984)	Authorizes the Consumer Product Safety Commission to recall products intended for use by children when they present substantial risk of injury.
Nutrition Labeling and Education Act (1990)	Prohibits exaggerated health claims and requires all processed foods to contain standardized labels with nutritional information.
Telephone Consumer Protection Act (1991)	Establishes procedures to avoid unwanted telephone solicitations; prohibits marketers from using automated telephone dialing systems or an artificial or prerecorded voice to certain telephone lines.
Home Ownership and Equity Protection Act (1994)	Requires home equity lenders to disclose to borrowers in writing the payment amounts, the consequences of default, and the borrowers' right to cancel the loan within a certain time period.

TABLE 8.2	Major Consumer Laws (*continued*)
Act (Date Enacted)	**Purpose**
Telemarketing and Consumer Fraud and Abuse Prevention Act (1994)	Authorizes the FTC to establish regulations for telemarketing, including prohibiting deceptive, coercive, or privacy-invading telemarketing practices; restricting the time during which unsolicited telephone calls may be made to consumers; and requiring telemarketers to disclose the nature of the call at the beginning of an unsolicited sales call.
Identity Theft Assumption and Deterrence Act (1998)	Makes the FTC a central clearinghouse for identity theft complaints and requires the FTC to log and acknowledge such complaints, provide victims with relevant information, and refer their complaints to appropriate entities (e.g., the major national consumer reporting agencies and other law enforcement agencies).
Children's Online Privacy Protection Act (1998)	Protects children's privacy by giving parents the tools to control what information is collected from their children online.
Do-Not-Call Registry Act (2003)	Allows the FTC to implement and enforce a do-not-call registry.
Fair and Accurate Credit Transactions Act (2003)	Amends the Fair Credit Reporting Act (FCRA), gives consumers the right to one free credit report a year from the credit reporting agencies, adds provisions designed to prevent and mitigate identity theft, and grants consumers additional rights with respect to how information is used.

Sources: "Statutes Relating to Consumer Protection Mission," Federal Trade Commission, www.ftc.gov/ogc/stat3.htm, accessed May 10, 2006; O. C. Ferrell, John Fraedrich, and Linda Ferrell, *Business Ethics: Ethical Decision Making and Cases,* 6th ed. (Boston: Houghton Mifflin, 2007); Roger L. Miller and Gaylord A. Jentz, *Business Law Today* (Cincinnati, OH: Thomson South-Western, 2004).

range of companies and consumers. State and local laws can be more stringent than federal statutes, so it is important that businesses fully investigate the laws applicable to all markets in which they operate. In Texas, for example, the Deceptive Trade Practices Act prohibits a business from selling anything to a consumer that he or she does not need or cannot afford.[18]

HEALTH AND SAFETY One of the first consumer protection laws in the United States came about in response to public outrage over a novel. In *The Jungle,* Upton Sinclair exposed atrocities, including unsanitary conditions and inhumane labor practices, by the meat-packing industry in Chicago at the turn of the twentieth century. Appalled by the unwholesome practices described in the book, the public demanded reform. Congress responded by passing the Pure Food and Drug Act in 1906, just six months after *The Jungle* was published.[19] In addition to prohibiting the adulteration and mislabeling of food and drug products, the new law also established one of the nation's first federal regulatory agencies, the Food and Drug Administration.

Since the passage of the Pure Food and Drug Act, public health and safety have been major targets of federal and state regulation. For example, the Consumer Product Safety Act established the Consumer Product Safety Commission (CPSC), and the Flammable Fabrics Act set standards for the flammability of clothing, children's sleepwear, carpets and rugs, and mattresses. The Standard Mattress Co. paid $460,000 to settle charges that it violated the Flammable Fabrics Act by manufacturing and selling futons that failed to meet flammability standards. Despite its agreement with the CPSC, the company denied that it violated any consumer product

The Consumer Affairs department of Victoria, Australia, provides retirees with information on choosing the best retirement villages to fit their needs, income, and expectations.

safety laws.[20] Other laws attempt to protect children from harm, including the Child Protection and Toy Safety Act and the Children's Online Privacy Protection Act.

CREDIT AND OWNERSHIP Abuses and inequities associated with loans and credit have resulted in the passage of laws designed to protect consumers' rights and public interests. The most significant of these laws prohibits discrimination in the extension of credit, requires creditors to disclose all finance charges and related aspects of credit transactions, gives consumers the right to dispute and correct inaccurate information on their credit reports, and regulates the activities of debt collectors. For example, the Home Ownership and Equity Protection Act requires home equity lenders to disclose, in writing, the borrower's rights, payment amounts, and the consequences of defaulting on the loan. Together, the U.S. Department of Justice and Department of

Housing and Urban Development (HUD) enforce laws that ensure equal access to sale and rental housing. Every April, the government sponsors Fair Housing Month to educate property owners, agents, and consumers on rights with respect to housing. After Hurricane Katrina wreaked havoc on Louisiana, Alabama, and Mississippi, HUD located temporary and permanent housing for many displaced citizens. HUD also developed a campaign to encourage fairness and equity in housing during this difficult time.[21]

While home ownership is often considered part of the American Dream, specific business practices in the banking and finance industry have been questioned. So-called predatory mortgage loans usually have one of the following four characteristics. First, the bank charges more in fees and interest than is needed to cover the additional risk associated with poor credit. Second, the bank traps individuals into loans and, possibly, increased debt. Third, the bank does not consider the individual's ability to pay the loan back. Fourth, the bank violates the law by targeting minorities and the poor. Financial institutions in other countries have also been accused of similar practices. For example, one Irish bank allegedly required African immigrants to take HIV/AIDS tests to qualify for home loan packages. However, Irish nationals were not asked to take the medical tests. Whereas many financial institutions are now providing credit for traditionally underserved markets, equitable access to affordable credit is not always clearly available.[22]

MARKETING, ADVERTISING, AND PACKAGING Legal issues in marketing often relate to sales and advertising communications and information about product content and safety. Abuses in promotion can range from exaggerated claims, concealed facts, and deception to outright lying. Such misleading information creates ethical issues because the communicated messages do not include all the information consumers need to make sound purchasing decisions. Publishers Clearing House recently settled charges brought by twenty-six states and the District of Columbia that it used deceptive sweepstakes promotions to get consumers to buy magazines. The settlement required the company to pay $34 million to the states to give refunds to customers, especially the elderly, who bought magazines under the belief that such purchases would boost their chances of winning the oft-touted million-dollar sweepstakes. Although Publishers Clearing House did not admit to any wrongdoing, it agreed to stop using the phrase "You are a winner," unless adequately balanced with statements specifying the conditions necessary to win, and to clearly indicate the odds of winning in sweepstakes promotions. In the same year, United States Sales Corporation and Time Inc. agreed to similar settlements over allegations of deceptive sweepstakes promotions with forty-eight states and the District of Columbia. An academic review of sweepstakes letters and promotions concluded that, rather than being merely "junk mail," these efforts were actually quite skillful and elegant. Researchers concluded that the language used in letters and other materials did an excellent job of establishing rapport, building excitement, and persuading readers to take action.[23]

Although a certain amount of exaggeration and hyperbole is tolerated, deceptive claims or claims that cannot be substantiated are likely to invite legal action from the FTC. For example, the FTC levied a $3 million fine against the marketers of Blue

FIGURE 8.3   Red Flags: Bogus Weight Loss Claims

- Cause weight loss of two pounds or more a week for a month or more without dieting or exercise
- Cause substantial weight loss no matter what or how much the consumer eats
- Cause permanent weight loss (even when the consumer stops using product)
- Block the absorption of fat or calories to enable consumers to lose substantial weight
- Safely enable consumers to lose more than three pounds per week for more than four weeks
- Cause substantial weight loss for all users
- Cause substantial weight loss by wearing on the body or rubbing into the skin

Source: Federal Trade Commission, "Bogus Weight Loss Claims," http://www.ftc.gov/bcp/conline/edcams/redflag/falseclaims.html, accessed May 29, 2006.

Stuff pain relievers for marketing campaigns that used unsupported claims. The FTC also sued Body Solutions over ads that declared consumers could eat pizza, tacos, and other fatty foods and burn away the fat while sleeping. Cases such as these prompted the FTC to develop a list of phrases that should alert both consumers and marketers to unsubstantiated or false claims about weight loss products (see Figure 8.3).[24]

Since the Federal Trade Commission Act of 1914 outlawed all deceptive and unfair trade practices, additional legislation has further delineated which activities are permissible and which are illegal. For example, the Telemarketing and Consumer Fraud and Abuse Prevention Act requires telemarketers to disclose the nature of the call at the beginning of an unsolicited sales call and restricts the times during which such calls may be made to consumers. Another legal issue in marketing has to do with the promotion of products that involve health or safety. Numerous laws regulate the promotion of alcohol and tobacco products, including the Public Health Cigarette Smoking Act (1970) and the Cigarette Labeling and Advertising Act (1965). The Eighteenth Amendment to the U.S. Constitution prohibited the manufacture and sale of alcoholic beverages in 1919; the prohibition was repealed in 1933 by the Twenty-first Amendment. However, this amendment gave states the power to regulate the transportation of alcoholic beverages across state lines. Today, each state has unique regulations, some of which require the use of wholesalers and retailers to limit direct sales of alcoholic beverages to final consumers in other states. In this case, a law aimed at protecting consumers by promoting temperance in alcohol consumption now affects wine sellers' ability to implement e-commerce and subsequent interstate sales. Currently, roughly nineteen states prohibit the interstate sale of wine, nineteen states allow interstate sales on a limited basis, and twelve states provide for reciprocal transactions only (e.g., between the states of Colorado and New Mexico).[25]

GLOBAL INITIATIVES

Stokke's Sustainable Furniture

Stokke was established in 1932 in Oslo, Norway, with a focus on creating functional furniture that improves the quality of life for customers. The company has two separate divisions, including a children's division that creates furniture that grows with the child through adolescence. Thus, the furniture is sustainable throughout many years of a child's growth and development.

Stokke has become an international company that employs people in fourteen European countries, the United States, and Japan. All Stokke products either meet or exceed governmental product and safety standards. Stokke has received several awards internationally for ergonomics, functionality, quality, and design. Recently, the company received the award for Best Product at the International Furniture Fair in Japan and the Most Innovative Product of the Year from the British Association of Nursery and Pram Retailers.

The KinderZeat is one of Stokke's most popular children's products. The chair is so adjustable, it allows children as young as eighteen months old and children into their teens to sit comfortably. The seat and footrest can also support up to 300 pounds. Other booster seats and highchairs do not compare to the KinderZeat. An ordinary highchair sets the child apart from the rest of the family at the table, leaving the child feeling isolated and alone. The KinderZeat allows children to sit at the same table and feel closer to the rest of the family. Traditional booster seats leave the child's legs hanging and restrict circulation. Children tend to move around and squirm when in such a position. The KinderZeat has an adjustable footrest to fit each child perfectly, thus eliminating the squirming.

Other Stokke products like the sleigh-style Kathryn crib convert from a crib to a youth bed to a double bed. Another product converts from a diaper changing table to a play table, a desk, or a bookshelf. Stokke products are fully convertible and functional for years.

The newest Stokke product to hit the market is the Xplory, a stroller. The firm realizes that parents can get by with a $100 stroller but believe the innovative design and functionality of the Xplory will lead to future success. The company initially distributed 1,000 units of Xplory to its best twenty-three retailers, while insisting that the sales staff should receive complete training on the innovative stroller. Stokke hit its six-month sales mark in the first nine weeks. It soon expanded the product offering to several other stores throughout the country.

The unique design of the Xplory is what makes it stand out from its competitors. The central pole allows the child to sit at eye level with the parent. Sitting up higher gets the child away from passing animals and car exhaust fumes. The stroller allows for navigation on stairs and escalators with the baby safely strapped inside. The stroller can also be converted from front facing to rear facing. The Xplory and KinderZeat are just two of the many products produced by the Stokke furniture company. The wide assortment of convertible products makes Stokke a one-of-a-kind furniture company, which takes a long-term view of its consumers' needs, life stages, and pocketbooks.

Sources: Stokke USA, http://www.stokkeusa.com/; Ryan Underwood, "Hot Wheels," *Fast Company*, May 2005, pp. 64–65. ∎

SALES AND WARRANTIES Another area of law that affects business relationships with consumers has to do with warranties. Many consumers consider the warranty behind a product when making a purchase decision, especially for expensive durable goods such as automobiles and appliances. One of the most significant laws affecting warranties is the Magnuson-Moss Warranty (FTC) Act of 1975, which established rules for consumer product warranties, including minimum content and standards for disclosure. All fifty states have enacted "lemon laws" to ensure that automobile sales are accompanied by appropriate warranties and remedies for defects that impair the safety, use, or value of the vehicle. Courts have recently ruled that consumers who lease instead of purchase automobiles are also entitled to warranty protection under Magnuson-Moss.[26]

product liability
a business's legal responsibility for the performance of its products

PRODUCT LIABILITY One area of law that has a profound effect on business and its relations with consumers is **product liability**, which refers to a business's legal responsibility for the performance of its products. This responsibility, which has evolved through both legislation and court interpretation (common law), may include a legal obligation to provide financial compensation to a consumer who has been harmed by a defective product. To receive compensation, a consumer who files suit in the United States must prove that the product was defective, that the defect caused an injury, and that the defect made the product unreasonably dangerous. Under the concept of *strict liability,* an injured consumer can apply this legal responsibility to any firm in the supply chain of a defective product, including contractors, suppliers of component parts, wholesalers, and retailers. Companies with operations in other countries must understand the various forms of product liability law that exist. For example, South Korea recently passed a new law making it easier for consumers to win product liability cases. In response to the law, many South Korean firms developed product liability teams for assessing risk and safety issues, reviewing insurance coverage, and educating employees on the importance of product safety. Product recalls jumped 50 percent in the first year after the law was enacted. In addition, the market for business insurance has grown substantially.[27]

Because the law typically holds businesses liable for their products' performance, many companies choose to recall potentially harmful products; such recalls may be required by legal or regulatory authorities as well. Warner-Lambert, for example, was asked by the Food and Drug Administration to recall Rezulin, a diabetes drug, after thirty-five cases of liver damage occurred in patients using the drug during its first year on the market. Roche Diagnostics recalled certain models of its ACCU-CHECK diabetes monitors after the company discovered the potential for electronic malfunction and improper readings.[28]

Product liability lawsuits have increased dramatically in recent years, and many suits have resulted in huge damage awards to injured consumers or their families. In a much-publicized case, a jury awarded a McDonald's customer $2.9 million after she was scalded when she spilled hot McDonald's coffee on her lap. Although that award was eventually reduced on appeal, McDonald's and other fast-food restaurants now display warning signs that their coffee is hot to eliminate both further injury and liability. Because of multimillion-dollar judgments like that against McDonald's, companies sometimes pass on the costs of damage awards to their customers in the form of higher prices. Most companies have taken steps to minimize their liability, and some firms—such as pharmaceutical firms making serum for the DPT (diphtheria-pertussis-tetanus) vaccine and manufacturers of small planes—have stopped making products or withdrawn completely from problematic markets because of the high risk of expensive liability lawsuits. Although some states have limited damage awards and legislative reform is often on the agenda, the issue of product liability remains politically sensitive. Recently, several product liability lawsuits against TASER International have been dismissed. The firm manufactures and markets the TASER technology, which is used by law enforcement officials as an alternative to other types of physical force. Plaintiffs have claimed that the electroshock devices cause injury or death.[29]

A police officer demonstrates the Air Taser stun gun, which can deliver a paralyzing electric shock to its target from 15 feet away.

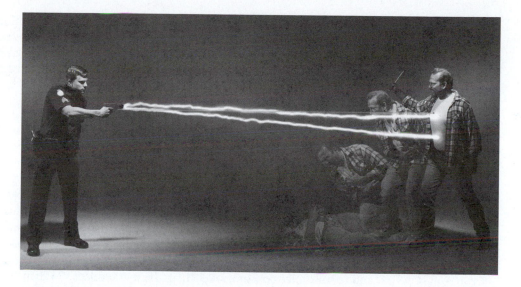

INTERNATIONAL ISSUES Concerns about protecting consumers' legal rights are not limited to the United States. Most developed nations have laws and offices devoted to this goal. For example, the Chinese government recently enacted tougher safety standards for automobiles, bringing Chinese expectations in line with safety standards in the United States and Europe.[30] In the European Union (EU), the health and consumer protection directorate general oversees efforts to increase consumer confidence in the unified market. Its initiatives center on health, safety, economic, and public-health interests. One recently passed EU directive establishes minimum levels of consumer protection in member states. For example, EU consumers now have a legal guarantee of two years on all consumer goods. If they find a defective product, they may choose repair or replacement or, in special circumstances, ask for a price reduction or rescind the contract altogether.[31]

In Japan, unlike in the United States, product liability lawsuits are much less common. In the early 1990s, Chikara Minami filed one of the first such lawsuits against Japanese automaker Mitsubishi. Minami's suit alleged a defect in the Mitsubishi Pajero. Although the court sided with the automaker in that case, ten years later Mitsubishi was accused of deliberately covering up consumer complaints. Despite this revelation and an enhanced product liability law in 1995, consumer rights are often subverted to preserve the power and structure of big business in Japan.[32] Much like that in Japan, China's consumer rights movement is also relatively new and resulted from economic policy changes away from isolationism and central economic planning. The China Consumers' Association was established in 1984 and has helped create consumer expectations and company responses that are starting to resemble those found in Western economies.[33]

As we have discussed in this section, there are many laws that influence business practices with respect to consumers all over the world. Every year, new laws are enacted, and existing rules are modified in response to the changing business environment. For example, the EU recently implemented new accountability standards for the chemical industry. Under the new guidelines, approximately 30,000 chemicals will be registered, evaluated, and approved for use by an EU agency. A key focus of the agency will be the effects of chemicals on human and environmental health.[34] Although companies must monitor and obey all laws and regulations, they also need to keep abreast of the ethical obligations and standards that exist in the marketplace.

Ethical Issues

In 1962, President John F. Kennedy proclaimed a Consumer Bill of Rights that includes the rights to choose, to safety, to be informed, and to be heard. Kennedy also established the Consumer Advisory Council to integrate consumer concerns into government regulations and processes. These four rights established a philosophical basis on which state and local consumer protection rules were later developed.[35] Around the same time, Ralph Nader's investigations of auto safety and his publication of *Unsafe at Any Speed* in 1965 alerted citizens to the dangers of a common consumer product. Nader's activism and Kennedy's speech provided support for **consumerism**, the movement to protect consumers from an imbalance of power on the side of business and to maximize consumer welfare in the marketplace.[36] When Nader ran for the U.S. presidency in 2000, his platform included many of the same concerns about consumers and business that were being discussed thirty-five years earlier.[37] As we have pointed out, the consumer movement is a global phenomenon, including the World Consumer Rights Day celebrated every year.

consumerism
movement to protect consumers from an imbalance of power on the side of business and to maximize consumer welfare in the marketplace

Over the last four decades, consumerism has affected public policy through a variety of mechanisms. Early efforts were aimed primarily at advocating for legislation and regulation, whereas more recent efforts have shifted to education and protection programs directed at consumers.[38] Consumers Union (CU), for example, works with regional and federal legislators and international groups to protect consumer interests, sponsors conferences and research projects, tests consumer products, and publishes the results in its *Consumer Reports*® magazine. A recent posting on www.ConsumersUnion.org detailed business practices that the CU deems unfair to consumers, including predatory lending, the poor value of some life insurance products, and advertisements aimed at vulnerable people, like children.[39] The Internet and electronic communication have also created new vehicles for consumer advocacy, education, and protection. Visitors to the National Consumers League website at http://www.nclnet.org/ or www.consumerworld.org find publications on many consumer issues, research and campaign reports, product reviews, retailer rankings, updates on legal matters, ways to track used-car histories, and many other types of services. Thus, consumer groups and information services have shifted the balance of power between consumer and business because consumers are able to compare prices, read independent rankings, communicate with other buyers, and in general, have greater knowledge about products, companies, and competitors.[40]

Despite the opportunities to exert more power, some researchers question whether most consumers take the time and energy to do so. For example, although the Internet provides a great deal of information and choices, access to the Internet partly depends on educational level and income. In addition, the volume of information available online may actually make it more difficult to analyze and assimilate. Even with these issues, Consumers Union has developed a legion of e-activists, who e-mail legislators and regulators through CU-sponsored websites. In its first eighteen

| FIGURE 8.4 | Consumers Union's Guidelines for Letters |

General Guidelines for Letters

Thank you for your interest in writing a letter! The letter you write can influence actions taken by government and corporations.

The sample letter included in each CU action alert is designed so that it can be changed. We encourage you to personalize the message you send. Adding your own personal experience makes letters more effective.

Below are some suggested guidelines to make sure your letter is as effective as possible.

Style and Format

- Be brief.
- Be specific.
- Ask for a response.
- Thank the recipient for his/her attention and cooperation.

Substance

- Identify yourself (and your organization, if applicable).
- If you're writing to a legislator, member of Congress, or Senator, let them know if you're from their home district/state.
- If you're writing to a company, let them know if you are a customer.
- Be polite and show respect, and give reasons for the requested action.
- Try to put the issue in terms of your own personal experience.
- Avoid technical jargon. Put the argument in layman's terms.
- Do not make threats. He/she is far more likely to do what you want if you build a responsible and credible relationship.
- Do not use profanity or language that slanders or disrespects others. You will only hurt your case.

months of existence, nearly 1 million messages were sent through these websites, which are organized by state and legislative agenda. Because of this consumer action, cell phone companies in California, Georgia, and Washington state must get permission before listing subscribers' cell phone numbers in a directory. Several states, including Missouri and Virginia, are now required to provide public information on infection rates at hospitals. CU provides a number of consumer advocacy tools on its website, including recommendations for writing letters to government agencies and corporations (see Figure 8.4).[41]

All U.S. presidents since Kennedy have confirmed the four basic consumer rights and added new ones in response to changing business conditions. President William J. Clinton, for example, appointed a commission to study the changing health-care environment and its implications for consumer rights. The result was the proposal of a Patient's Bill of Rights and Responsibilities to ensure rights to confidentiality of patient information, to participate in health-care decisions, to access emergency services, and

| **TABLE 8.3** | Basic Consumer Rights |

Right	General Issues
To choose	Access to a variety of products at competitive and reasonable prices
To safety	Protection of health, safety, and financial well-being in the marketplace
To be informed	Opportunity to have accurate and adequate information on which to base decisions and protection from misleading or deceptive information
To be heard	Consideration given to consumer interests in government processes
To redress	Opportunity to express dissatisfaction and to have the complaint resolved effectively
To privacy	Protection of consumer information and its use

Source: Adapted from E. Thomas Garman, *Consumer Economic Issues in America* (Stamford, CT: Thomson Learning, 2005).

other needs.[42] During the same period, a Financial Consumer's Bill of Rights Act was proposed in the U.S. House of Representatives to curb high bank fees, automated teller machine surcharges, and other practices that have angered consumers.[43]

Although consumer rights were first formalized through a presidential speech and subsequent affirmations, they have not yet reached the legal domain of social responsibility. Some specific elements of these rights have been mandated through law, but the relatively broad nature of the rights means they must be interpreted and implemented on a company-by-company basis. Table 8.3 lists six consumer rights that have become part of the ethical expectations of business. Although these rights are not necessarily provided by all organizations, our social responsibility philosophy requires their attention and implementation.

RIGHT TO CHOOSE The right to choose implies that, to the extent possible, consumers have the opportunity to select from a variety of products at competitive prices. This right is based on the philosophy of the competitive nature of markets, which should lead to high-quality products at reasonable prices. Antitrust activities that reduce competition may jeopardize this right. This right has been called into question with respect to safety in some parts of the United States. Domino's Pizza, for example, was accused of discriminating against African American customers through a delivery policy that seemed to be based on a neighborhood's racial composition rather than on a legitimate threat of danger to drivers delivering in those neighborhoods. In effect, consumers in these neighborhoods were denied access to pizza delivery service. Although no lawsuit was filed, Domino's worked with the U.S. Department of Justice to revise the delivery policy to narrowly define delivery limitations on the basis of real safety threats and to reevaluate the status of excluded areas on a yearly basis.[44]

RIGHT TO SAFETY The right to safety means that businesses have an obligation not to knowingly market a product that could harm consumers. Some consumer advocates believe that this right means that the manufacture and sale of firearms should be outlawed in the United States. Although organizations like the National Rifle Association have vehemently opposed this view, questions about gun safety, especially

In this busy area of Manchester, England, tourists and residents are warned about thieves.

around children, have prompted a number of state laws to regulate the manufacture and sale of guns. For example, Massachusetts recently required that all guns sold in that state meet stringent standards and carry internal identification numbers. Maryland requires that all guns be equipped with trigger locks.[45]

The right to safety also implies that all products should be safe for their intended use, include instructions for proper and safe use, and have been sufficiently tested to ensure reliability. Companies must take great care in designing warning messages about products with potentially dangerous or unsafe effects. These messages should take into account consumers' ability to understand and respond to the information. Warnings should be relevant and meaningful to every potential user of the product. Some warnings use symbols or pictures to communicate. Companies that fail to honor the right to safety risk expensive product liability lawsuits. In 1998, the five largest tobacco manufacturers in the United States reached a landmark $246 billion settlement with the attorneys general of forty-six states. The master settlement agreement (MSA) required the companies to give billions of dollars to the state governments every year to help relieve the burden that smoking-related illnesses put on state health-care systems and to fund campaigns designed to discourage smoking, especially among children. Under the settlement, the companies agreed to stop using cartoon characters, like R. J. Reynolds's Joe Camel. The MSA barred companies from a number of traditional marketing strategies, such as using billboards or direct-mail advertising or passing out samples at shopping malls to tout their products. To help pay for the costs of the settlement, the companies raised prices. Thus, the settlement was designed to force the tobacco firms to bear more of the costs of illnesses caused by their product and to make them act more responsibly. Although corporate executives point to declining teen smoking rates as evidence of their responsibility, many anti-smoking activists believe that the responsible thing to do is to stop selling a product that causes illness and death.[46]

RIGHT TO BE INFORMED Consumers also have the right to be informed. Any information, whether communicated in written or verbal format, should be accurate, adequate, and free of deception so that consumers can make a sound decision. This general assertion has also led to specific legislation, such as the Nutrition Labeling and Education Act of 1990, which requires certain nutrition facts on food labels and limits the use of terms such as *low fat*. This right can be associated with safety issues if consumers do not have sufficient information to purchase or use a product effectively. For example, a woman in New York leveled a $50 million lawsuit against Robert's American Gourmet Food, Inc., for mislabeling its snack products and causing her "weight gain . . . mental anguish, outrage and indignation." The snacks, branded Pirate's Booty, Veggie Booty, and Fruity Booty, were sold in packages that claimed to have 120 calories and 2.5 grams of fat. When independently tested, however, the Good Housekeeping Institute published numbers that came as a shock to many dieters; the snack actually contained 147 calories and 8.5 grams of fat. Bags that claimed to have 1 ounce of product actually had 1.25 ounces of the product. Robert's recalled the snacks prior to the *Good Housekeeping* magazine report and blamed new manufacturing equipment on the mislabeling and fat content problem. The snack, once so popular that it made the pages of *Vanity Fair*, reminded consumers that "if something tastes too good to be true, it probably is too good to be true."[47]

In an age of rapid technological advances and globalization, the degree of complexity in product marketing is another concern related to consumers' right to information. This complexity can impact the ways in which product features and benefits are discussed in advertising, how effective salespeople are in answering consumer questions, the expertise needed to operate or use the product, and the ease of returning or exchanging the product. To help consumers make decisions based on adequate and timely information, some organizations sponsor consumer education programs. For example, pharmaceutical companies and health maintenance organizations sponsor free seminars, health screenings, websites, and other programs to educate consumers about their health and treatment options. The proliferation of websites devoted to consumer health information prompted the American Accreditation Healthcare Commission to develop a Health Web Site Accreditation program. The program's "seal of approval" should let consumers know that the website's content is trustworthy and reliable.[48] In Russia, consumer advocacy organizations have established a telephone hot line to educate consumers about their rights and to advise them when they encounter poor-quality products marketed as leading consumer brands. According to the hot line director, Yelena Poluektova, "Although there has been a law on consumer rights since 1992 it turns out very many people have no knowledge of their rights."[49]

RIGHT TO BE HEARD The right to be heard relates to opportunities for consumers to communicate or voice their concerns in the public policy process. This also implies that governments have the responsibility to listen and take consumer issues into account. One mechanism for fulfilling this responsibility is through the FTC and state consumer affairs offices. Another vehicle includes congressional hearings held to educate elected officials about specific issues of concern to consumers. At the same time, consumers are expected to be full participants in the process, meaning they must be informed and willing to take action against wrongs in the marketplace.

RIGHT TO SEEK REDRESS In addition to the rights described by Kennedy, consumers also have the right to express dissatisfaction and seek restitution from a business when a good or service does not meet their expectations. However, consumers need to be educated in the process for seeking redress and to recognize that the first course of action in such cases should be with the seller. At the same time, companies need to have explicit and formal processes for dealing with customer dissatisfaction. Although some product problems lead to third-party intervention or legal recourse, the majority of issues should be resolvable between the consumer and the business. One third party that consumers may consult in such cases is the Better Business Bureau (BBB), which promotes self-regulation of business. To gain and maintain membership, a firm must agree to abide by the ethical standards established by the BBB. This organization collects complaints on businesses and makes this information, along with other reports, available for consumer decision making. The BBB also operates the dispute resolution division to assist in out-of-court settlements between consumers and businesses. For example, this division has a program, BBB Auto Line, to handle disputes between consumers and twenty-five automobile manufacturers.[50] This self-regulatory approach not only provides differentiation in the market but can also stave off new laws and regulations.

RIGHT TO PRIVACY The advent of new information technology and the Internet has prompted increasing concerns about consumer privacy. This right relates to consumers' awareness of how personal data are collected and used, and it places a burden on firms to protect this information. How information is used can create concerns for consumers. Although some e-commerce firms have joined together to develop privacy standards for the Internet, many websites do not meet the FTC's criteria for fair information practices, including notice, choice, access, and security.[51] We will take a closer look at the debate surrounding privacy rights in Chapter 11.

A firm's ability to address these consumer rights can serve as a competitive advantage. CMC Properties, a recent recipient of the National Torch Award for Marketplace Ethics given by the Better Business Bureau, is highly regarded for the ethical approach to consumers of its real estate and property management services. Instead of viewing its business as "bricks and mortar," the company is focused on "bodies and souls." As the company's mission states, CMC strives to simplify the lives of its customers.[52] Another example is in the highly competitive market for air travel. Many airlines have developed a strong focus on customer service and satisfaction. Together with the air transport association, several airlines launched the airline customer service commitment to demonstrate an industry focus on alleviating passenger frustrations and complaints. Southwest Airlines established a lengthy Customer Service Commitment that details the airline's practices before, during, and after a customer flight (see Figure 8.5).[53]

| FIGURE 8.5 | Southwest Airlines' Customer Service Commitment |

Source: Southwest Airlines, "Customer Service Commitment," http://www.southwest.com/about_swa/ customer_service_commitment/customer_service_commitment.html, accessed May 15, 2006. Copyright © 2006 by Southwest Airlines. Reprinted with permission.

When consumers believe a firm is operating outside ethical or legal standards, they may be motivated to take some type of action. As we discussed earlier, there are a number of strategies consumers can employ to communicate their dissatisfaction, such as complaining or discontinuing the exchange relationship. For example, some people believe Wal-Mart's presence has contributed to the demise of locally owned pharmacies and variety stores in many small towns. The chain's buying power ensures lower prices and wider product variety for consumers but also makes it difficult for smaller retailers to compete. Other consumers and community leaders worry about the traffic congestion and urban sprawl that accompany new retail sites. Some Wal-Mart critics have taken their discontent with the retailer to the Internet. Disgruntled customers and others share complaints about the retail chain, provide updates about legal action, and promote campaigns against the retailer on http://www.wakeupwalmart.com/. Another website, http://www.walmartsurvivor.com, details court rulings against Wal-Mart and lists attorneys who have been successful in opposing the retail giant.[54]

Stakeholders may use the three types of power—symbolic, utilitarian, and coercive—discussed in Chapter 2 to create organizational awareness on an important issue. For example, some Chinese consumers feel that Japanese people believe they are

Wal-Mart has been the subject of criticism from anti-corporate activists, including *Wal-Mart: The High Cost of Low Price,* a recent movie that examined the company's business and employment practices.

racially superior to the Chinese. This sentiment stems from Japan's occupation of China in the 1940s. More recently, Toshiba has been accused of racism for not compensating Chinese users of potentially faulty Toshiba laptop computers. This perceived slight, along with feelings of nationalism, have prompted Chinese consumers to dismiss Toshiba and other Japanese manufacturers. Chinese retailers have pulled Japanese products off their shelves as well.[55] These consumers are engaging in another form of consumer action, a **boycott**, by abstaining from using, purchasing, or dealing with an organization. The World Jewish Congress encouraged its members to boycott the insurance company Transamerica after its parent company, Aegon NV, refused to join the international commission on Holocaust-era insurance claims. The commission was established to resolve insurance claims that resulted from the Holocaust and World War II.[56]

> **boycott**
> consumer action of abstaining from using, purchasing, or dealing with an organization

Other boycotts, while of corporate interest, may not be based on traditional social responsibility issues. For example, fans of the James Bond movies boycotted a new production that starred a young and inexperienced Bond. The movie's director explained, "He's just got his 007 stripes when he gets into the story so he's got some rough edges on him to begin with and hopefully, by the end of it, he'll become the 007 we all know and love." Fans created a website, where the prequel was denounced and derided for several reasons, including the replacement of Pierce Brosnan with a much younger and relatively unknown actor named Daniel Craig. Craig was said to be less attractive, less experienced, and less suited to the role. The website urged fans to write Sony Pictures, get friends involved, and take other actions to ensure a successful boycott of the film.[57]

Philanthropic Issues

Although relationships with consumers are fundamentally grounded in economic exchanges, the previous sections demonstrate that additional levels of expectations exist. A national survey by Cone/Roper reported that 70 percent of consumers would be likely to switch to brands associated with a good cause, as long as price and quality were equal. These results suggest that today's consumers take for granted that they can obtain high-quality products at reasonable prices, so businesses need to do something to differentiate themselves from the competition.[58] More firms are therefore investigating ways to link their philanthropic efforts with consumer interests. Eastman Kodak, for example, has funded environmental literacy programs of the World Wildlife Fund. These programs not only forge a link between the company's possible effects and its interest in the natural environment but also provide a service to its customers and other stakeholders.[59]

From a strategic perspective, a firm's ability to link consumer interests to philanthropy should lead to stronger economic relationships. As we shall see in Chapter 9, philanthropic responsibilities to consumers usually entail broader benefits, including those that affect the community. For example, large pharmaceutical and health insurance firms provided financial support to the Foundation for Accountability (FACCT), a nonprofit organization that assists health-care consumers in making better decisions. FACCT initiated an online system for patients to evaluate their physician on several quality indicators. Although FACCT ceased its operations in 2004, the Markle

Foundation continues to host the nonprofit's legacy documents and white papers. The foundation partners with other organizations to improve the role of technology in addressing critical public health needs.[60]

Companies will have more successful philanthropic efforts when the cause is a good fit with the firm's product category, industry, customer concerns, and/or location. This alignment is an important contributor to the long-term relationships that often develop between specific companies and cause-related organizations. Many firms involved in technology and electronics will contribute to causes that advance educational attainment, fund math and science initiatives, democratize the access to the Internet, or otherwise enable people better access to technology. Many technology firms, including Advanced Micro Devices and National Semiconductor, have established corporate foundations with large endowments, which means that annual contributions are relatively unaffected by corporate profitability and the economic cycle. Nonprofits prefer consistent donations rather than wide variance from year to year.[61]

STRATEGIC IMPLEMENTATION OF RESPONSIBILITIES TO CONSUMERS

As this chapter has demonstrated, social responsibility entails relationships with many stakeholders—including consumers—and many firms are finding creative ways to meet these responsibilities. Just as in other aspects of social responsibility, these relationships must be managed, nurtured, and continuously assessed. Resources devoted to this effort may include programs for educating and listening to consumers, surveys to discover strengths and weaknesses in stakeholder relationships, hiring consumer affairs professionals, the development of a community relations office, and other initiatives. Understanding stakeholder issues can be especially complex in the global environment. For example, a group of 150 Nigerian women led a peaceful protest that shut down most of ChevronTexaco's Nigerian oil operations for a week. These women, who live in the Niger Delta, are among the poorest in Nigeria, although they live on oil-rich land. The women demanded that ChevronTexaco hire their sons and provide electricity in their villages. The company viewed the women's complaints as unjustified and pointed to its local employment rates and contributions to development projects in the area. Because the government has failed to develop good roads, schools, and utility systems in the area, these activists turned to a multinational corporation for some resolution.[62]

The utility industry represents an interesting case study in its resource investments and relationships with both consumers and the community. There is much public interest in issues related to utility prices, environmental impact, plant closures, plant location, and more. In the late 1980s and early 1990s, larger utilities held "town hall" meetings and other sessions to obtain stakeholder views and feedback. This approach, along with sophisticated and directed programs, is making a comeback. Kansas City Power & Light (KCPL), for example, held an open house that attracted more than 1,000 people. Employees of KCPL served as babysitters while parents learned more about electric and magnetic fields and other emerging topics. The open house not only addressed the information needs of customers but also provided for their family needs by utilizing employee time and talent.[63] KCPL understands the importance of integrating all stakeholders in its social responsibility effort, including employees, as we explored in Chapter 7.

SUMMARY

Companies face complex decisions about how to respond to the expectations, attitudes, and buying patterns of consumers, those individuals who purchase, use, and dispose of products for personal and household use. Consumers are primary stakeholders because their awareness, purchase, use, and repurchase of products are vital to a company's existence.

Consumers and businesses are fundamentally connected by an economic relationship. Economic responsibilities include following through on promises made in the exchange process. Consumer fraud involves intentional deception to derive an unfair economic advantage over an organization. If consumers believe that a firm has not fulfilled its economic responsibility, they may ask for a refund, tell others about the bad experience, discontinue their patronage, contact a consumer agency, or seek legal redress.

In the United States, legal issues with respect to consumers fall under the jurisdiction of the Federal Trade Commission (FTC), which enforces federal antitrust and consumer protection laws. Other federal and state agencies regulate specific goods, services, or business practices. Among the issues that may have been addressed through specific state or federal laws and regulations are consumer health and safety, credit and ownership, marketing and advertising, sales and warranties, and product liability. Product liability refers to a business's legal responsibility for the performance of its products. Concerns about protecting consumers' legal rights are not limited to the United States.

Ethical issues related to consumers include the Consumer Bill of Rights enumerated by President Kennedy. Consumerism refers to the movement to protect consumers from an imbalance of power with business and to maximize consumer welfare in the marketplace. Some specific elements of consumer rights have been mandated by law, but the relatively broad nature of the rights means they must be interpreted and implemented on a company-by-company basis. Consumer rights have evolved to include the right to choose, the right to safety, the right to be informed, the right to be heard, the right to seek redress, and the right to privacy. When consumers believe a firm is operating outside ethical or legal standards, they may be motivated to take action, including boycotting—abstaining from using, purchasing, or dealing with an organization.

More firms are investigating ways to link their philanthropic efforts with consumer interests. From a strategic perspective, a firm's ability to link consumer interests to philanthropy should lead to stronger economic relationships.

Many companies are finding creative ways to satisfy their responsibilities to consumers. Much like employee relationships, these responsibilities must be managed, nurtured, and continuously assessed. Resources devoted to this effort may include programs for educating and listening to consumers, surveys to discover strengths and weaknesses in stakeholder relationships, hiring consumer affairs professionals, working with industry groups, and the development of other initiatives that engage consumers.

KEY TERMS

consumers (p. 253)
consumer fraud (p. 255)
product liability (p. 264)
consumerism (p. 266)
boycott (p. 273)

DISCUSSION QUESTIONS

1. List and describe the consumer rights that have become social expectations of business. Why have some of these rights been formalized through legislation? Should these rights be considered ethical standards?
2. Review Southwest Airlines' plan for customer service in Figure 8.5. Create a chart to link each of the twelve points to a specific economic, legal, ethical, or philanthropic responsibility that the airline has to its customers.
3. What is the purpose of a boycott? Describe the characteristics of companies and consumers that are likely to be involved in a boycott situation. What circumstances would cause you to consider participating in a boycott?
4. How can companies strive for successful relationships with consumers, including meeting their economic, legal, ethical, and philanthropic expectations?
5. How will consumer rights and activism change over the next decade? Will the movement strengthen or decline? Why?

EXPERIENTIAL EXERCISE

Visit the website of IdealsWork (http://www.idealswork.com/). What is the purpose of this website? Select any category at the site's "Compare brands now" feature to examine companies in a particular industry for ratings on various social responsibility issues. Using the basic form, choose five issues on which to evaluate the companies. Print out at least one page of the ratings results and then examine the detail for a few company ratings. How useful is this information to you? What information could a business derive from this site to improve its reputation for social responsibility?

WHAT WOULD YOU DO?

Justin Thompson was excited. He really enjoyed his job at the Kingston's department store downtown. This location housed Kingston's first store and still had many of its original features. As he rode the subway into the city center, Justin thought about the money he would earn this summer and the great car he hoped to buy before school started. He was lucky to have secured this type of job, since many of his friends were working early or late hours at fast-food chains or out in the summer heat. The management team at Kingston's had initiated a program with his high school counselors, hoping to attract top high school seniors into retail management throughout their college career and beyond. Justin was a strong student from a single-parent background, and his counselor was highly complimentary of his work ethic and prospects for professional employment.

Justin's first week was consumed with various training sessions. There were eight students in the special high school program. They watched a company video that discussed Kingston's history, ethics policy, current operations, and customer service philosophy. They met with staff from Human Resources to fill out paperwork. They learned how to scan merchandise and operate the computer software and cash register. They toured the store's three levels and visited with each department manager. Justin was especially excited about working in the electronics department, but he was assigned to men's clothing.

Justin worked alongside several employees during the first few weeks on the store floor. He watched the experienced employees approach customers, help them, and ring up the sale. He noticed that some employees took personal telephone calls and that others did not clean up the dressing rooms or restock items very quickly.

On slower days, he eventually worked alone in the department. Several times when he came to work in the afternoon, he had to clean up the mess left behind by the morning shift. When he spoke to various colleagues about it in the break room, they told him it was best to keep quiet. After all, he was a high school student earning money for a car, not a "real employee" with kids to feed and bills to pay. Justin assumed that retail work was much like team projects in school—not everyone pulled their weight but it was hard to be the tattletale.

One Saturday morning was extremely busy, as Kingston's was running a big sale. People were swarming to the sales racks, and Justin was amazed at how fast the time was passing. In the late afternoon, several friends of one of his coworkers dropped by the men's section. Before long, their hands were filled with merchandise. The crowd was starting to wane, so Justin took a few minutes to clean up the dressing room. When he came out of the dressing room, his coworker was ringing up the friends' merchandise. Justin saw two ties go into the bag, but only one was scanned into the system. He saw an extra discount provided on an expensive shirt. Justin was shocked to see that not every item was scanned or that improper discounts were applied, and his mind was racing. Should he stop his coworker? Should he "take a break" and get security? Was there another alternative? What would you do?

CHAPTER 9

Community Relations and Strategic Philanthropy

CHAPTER OBJECTIVES

- To describe the community as a stakeholder
- To discuss the community relations function
- To distinguish between strategic philanthropy and cause-related marketing
- To identify the benefits of strategic philanthropy
- To explain the key factors in implementing strategic philanthropy

CHAPTER OUTLINE

The Kansas City Chiefs were founded in 1960 by owner Lamar Hunt. The Chiefs are known as a one-of-a-kind professional sports franchise. Administrative employees, players, coaches, and other staff give back to the community that provides so much support and enthusiasm for the team.

The Chiefs' organization is what it is today because of Hunt and Carl Peterson. Peterson was hired in 1988 as president, general manager, and CEO. He has helped turn the team around both on and off the field. Hunt is more concerned about creating an ambience at Arrowhead Stadium than about draft picks and the roster for the next game. For example, Hunt and his family have planted many trees around the stadium to create an environmentally friendly atmosphere at Arrowhead. In 2002, they planted forty redwoods to mark the fortieth anniversary of the Chiefs in Kansas City.

The Chiefs were the first professional sports franchise to contractually obligate players to attend charitable events. Today, many sports team have similar agreements with players. Since the early days of the Chiefs, Hunt has taken players to school functions, fundraising events, parades, and Rotary Club meetings. Many players have started nonprofits through the Greater Kansas City Community Foundation. Since 1998, more than $8 million has been raised for charitable organizations through the Chiefs.

An example of the fundraising efforts occurred after September 11, 2001, when the Chiefs faced off against the New York Giants. Hunt announced that the team would match the total donations collected from fans at the game. At the end of the game, a total of $225,000 had been raised by fans. The Chiefs kept the promise, and $450,000 was donated to charities of the NYPD, FDNY, and the Port Authority.

Through these efforts, and a deep commitment to social responsibility, the Chiefs have become winners both on and off the field. New franchises and other owners come to Kansas City to observe the Chiefs' operations. The organization is a role model for community and philanthropic success in the world of professional sports.[1] ∎

The Kansas City Chiefs, like most organizations with operational expertise and other core competencies, can also focus on implementing social responsibility and satisfying stakeholder groups. From a social responsibility perspective, the key challenge is how an organization assesses its stakeholders' needs, integrates them with company strategy, reconciles differences among stakeholders' needs, strives for better relationships with stakeholders, achieves mutual understandings with them, and finds solutions for problems. In this chapter, we explore community stakeholders and how organizations deal with stakeholder needs through philanthropic initiatives. We explore the relationship with communities and the economic, legal, ethical, and philanthropic responsibilities that must be addressed by business. We define strategic philanthropy and integrate this concept with other elements of social responsibility. Next, we trace the evolution of corporate philanthropy and distinguish the concept from cause-related marketing. We also provide examples of best practices of addressing stakeholders' interests that meet our definition of strategic philanthropy. From there, we consider the benefits of investing in strategic philanthropy to satisfy both stakeholders and corporate objectives. Finally, we examine the process of implementing strategic philanthropy in business. Our approach in this chapter is to demonstrate how companies can link strategic philanthropy with economic, legal, and ethical concerns for the benefit of all stakeholders.

COMMUNITY STAKEHOLDERS

The concept of *community* has many varying characteristics that make it a challenge to define. The community does not always receive the same level of acceptance as other stakeholders. Some people even wonder how a company determines who is in the community. Is a community determined by city or county boundaries? What if the firm operates in multiple locations? Or is a community prescribed by the interactions a firm has with various constituents who do not fit neatly into other stakeholder categories? For a small restaurant in a large city, the owner may define the community as the immediate neighborhood where most patrons live. The restaurant may demonstrate social responsibility by hiring people from the neighborhood, participating in the neighborhood crime watch program, donating food to the elementary school's annual parent-teacher meetings, or sponsoring a neighborhood Little League team. For example, Merlino's Steak House in North Conway, New Hampshire, sponsors an annual golf tournament that benefits the Center for Hope, an organization that provides transportation for local individuals with disabilities. Merlino's has raised roughly $1 million for local charities with tournament proceeds.[2] For a corporation with facilities in North and South America, Europe, and Africa, the community may be viewed as virtually the entire world. To focus its social responsibility efforts, the multinational corporation might employ a community relations officer in each facility who reports to and coordinates with the company's head office.

community
those members of society who are aware of, concerned with, or in some way affected by the operations and output of an organization

Under our social responsibility philosophy, the term *community* should be viewed from a global perspective, beyond the immediate town, city, or state where a business is located. Thus, we define **community** as those members of society who are aware of, concerned with, or in some way affected by the operations and output of an organization. With information technology, high-speed travel, and the emergence of global business interests, the community as a constituency can be quite geographically, culturally, and attitudinally diverse. Issues that could become important include pollution of the environment, land use, economic advantages to the region, and discrimination within the community, as well as exploitation of workers or consumers.

neighbor of choice
an organization that builds and sustains trust with the community

From a positive perspective, an organization can significantly improve the quality of life through employment opportunities, economic development, and financial contributions for educational, health, artistic, and recreational activities. Through such efforts, a firm may become a **neighbor of choice**, an organization that builds and sustains trust with the community.[3] To become a neighbor of choice, a company should strive for positive and sustainable relationships with key individuals, groups, and organizations; demonstrate sensitivity to community concerns and issues; and design and implement programs that improve the quality of community life while promoting the company's long-term business strategies and goals.[4] Home Depot's

Neighbor of Choice program involves the following considerations: partnering with cities and towns, reflecting the community in hiring associates, creating jobs and opportunities for other businesses, purchasing locally to keep dollars in the community, valuing volunteerism, generating local tax revenue, and offering home solutions in your neighborhood.[5] As a part of its Neighbor of Choice program, FedEx, headquartered in Memphis, Tennessee, serves as a major corporate sponsor of the National Civil Rights Museum in Memphis. This museum exists to help the public understand the lessons of the Civil Rights Movement and its impact and influence on the human rights movement worldwide. The museum is a key component in the company's diversity training, and FedEx has helped fund the Exploring the Legacy project, which expanded the museum's exhibit space by almost 13,000 square feet.[6]

Similar to other areas of life, the relationship between a business and the community should be symbiotic. A business may support educational opportunities in the community because the owners feel it is the right thing to do, but it also helps develop the human resources and consumer skills necessary to operate the business. Customers and employees are also community members who benefit from contributions supporting recreational activities, environmental initiatives, safety, and education. Many firms rely on universities and community colleges to provide support for ongoing education of their employees. Sykes Enterprises, for example, often locates its customer call and support centers in towns where the local community college is willing to

Fans and athletes enjoyed an exhibition soccer game in Italy that raised funds for refugee children from Kosovo. Many sports teams are involved in charitable activities in their communities.

develop courses that educate employees in the skills and aptitude needed to effectively operate a call center.

To build and support these initiatives, companies may invest in **community relations**, the organizational function dedicated to building and maintaining relationships and trust with the community. In the past, most businesses have not viewed community relations as strategically important or associated them with the firm's ultimate performance. Although the community relations department interacted with the community and often doled out large sums of money to charities, it essentially served as a buffer between the organization and its immediate community. Today, community relations activities have achieved greater prominence and responsibility within most companies, especially due to the rise of stakeholder power and global business interests. The function has gained strategic importance through linking to overall business goals, professionalizing its staff and their knowledge of business and community issues, assessing its performance in quantitative and qualitative terms, and recognizing the breadth of stakeholders to which the organization is accountable.[7] Community relations also assist in short-term and crisis situations, such as disaster relief. Cisco was honored with an Excellence Award on corporate Philanthropy Day by the Committee to Encourage Corporate Philanthropy for employees donating over 200,000 hours of community service in seven months. Cisco offers an innovative program to encourage employees to volunteer their time, including post–Hurricane Katrina rebuilding and a global Leadership Fellows Program, which allows employees to work full time for nonprofits for up to one year (at no cost to the nonprofit).[8]

Corporate support for philanthropy is growing. According to the Foundation Center, an authority in philanthropy, corporate giving rose to $3.6 billion in recent years. Corporate giving is also becoming more effective and strategic. Companies are working to align their stakeholder interests and develop partnerships that are more closely aligned to business goals, community interests, and sustainable activities.[9]

In a diverse society, however, there is no general agreement as to what constitutes the ideal model of responsibility to the community. Businesses are likely to experience conflicts among stakeholders as to what constitutes a real commitment to the community. Therefore, the community relations function should cooperate with various internal and external constituents to develop community mission statements and assess opportunities and develop priorities for the types of contributions it will make to the community. Table 9.1 provides several examples of company missions and programs with respect to community involvement. As you can see, these missions are specific to the needs of the people and areas in which the companies operate and are usually aligned with the competencies of the organizations involved and their employees.

Community mission statements are likely to change as needs are met and new issues emerge. For example, when Delphi Automotive opened a manufacturing site in Mexico, it worked with the Mexican government to build subsidized housing for Delphi employees. The project helped more than 2,000 employees find better housing and was recently extended to serve nonemployees through a partnership with Habitat for Humanity.[10] This effort addressed a basic need in life, and now

| **TABLE 9.1** | Community Mission Statements |

Organization	Community Mission
Aetna, Inc (Hartford, CT)	Aetna Employees Reaching Out (AERO), Aetna's employee volunteering and giving program, integrates community involvement and business. When employees get involved in communities to teach underprivileged children dental hygiene, serve on hospital governance boards, and conduct other caring acts, they help Aetna to "build trusting, value-added relationships" with constituents, "anticipate the future" in health care, and invigorate other values expressed in The Aetna Way—Aetna's business approach.
Cisco Systems, Inc. (San Jose, CA)	Cisco's corporate giving and citizenship programs build stakeholder trust and loyalty which have a powerful impact on the global community. Cisco's community investment programs are designed to help build stronger and more productive communities by providing resources to nonprofit organizations that address critical needs in the community. Cisco employees volunteer their time and technical expertise to develop strategies that help nonprofits maximize their reach and effectiveness.
Federated Department Stores, Inc. (Cincinnati, OH, and New York, NY)	Federated Department Stores' community commitment is put into action with Partners in Time—an employee volunteer program founded in 1989. Since that year, employees have given 1.1 million hours of volunteer time to serve 230 cities nationwide. About 50,000 volunteers in 500 Macy's and Bloomingdale's stores and Federated support divisions participate in 2,500 community service projects annually.
Georgia Natural Gas (Atlanta, GA)	The 60 employees at Georgia Natural Gas have made a tremendous difference in the lives of children and senior citizens in the community near the company's Atlanta headquarters. Employees have counseled low-income job seekers, tutored children in a community school, introduced a reading program for preschoolers, and served as counselors for a child abuse prevention program.
The Home Depot (Atlanta, GA)	The Home Depot's associate volunteer program, Team Depot, was formalized in 1992 as a way to support the communities where its associates live and work. Through The Home Depot Foundation, Team Depot, and ongoing partnerships with nonprofit groups, The Home Depot donates millions of hours, tools, and supplies each year to community service projects.
The Washington Trust Company (Westerly, RI)	Washington Trust's service to the community, through both its employee volunteerism and charitable contributions, unites its employees, customers, and community by spreading a sense of social responsibility and goodwill among them. This creates a positive response that reflects the importance of Washington Trust's employee-selected core values—quality, integrity, and community.

Source: "Awards for Excellence in Workplace Volunteer Programs," Points of Light Foundation, http://www.pointsoflight.org/about/mediacenter/releases/2005/08-05a.cfm, accessed May 10, 2006.

that it has largely been met, Delphi may consider investments in other community areas, such as education or health care. Thus, as stakeholder needs and concerns change, the organization will need to adapt its community relations efforts. To determine key areas that require support and to refine the mission statement, a company should periodically conduct a community needs assessment like the one presented in Table 9.2.[11]

TABLE 9.2	Community Needs Assessment

For each of the questions in the survey, circle the number that corresponds to your assessment:

Community Issues	Exceptional	Adequate	Inadequate	Don't know
Parks	3	2	1	0
Culinary water system	3	2	1	0
Street maintenance	3	2	1	0
Garbage collection	3	2	1	0
Snow removal	3	2	1	0
Fire protection	3	2	1	0
Police protection	3	2	1	0
Ambulance service	3	2	1	0
Building inspection	3	2	1	0
Animal control	3	2	1	0
Other code enforcement (weeds, junk cars, etc.)	3	2	1	0
Arts	3	2	1	0
Street lighting	3	2	1	0

Other issues that can be evaluated: grocery stores, pharmacies, clothing stores, fast-food restaurants, entertainment, hardware/lumber stores, auto services, banking/financial services, affordable housing, business offices, warehouses, convenience stores, community colleges, higher education satellite campuses.

Source: "Utah State University Extension, Community Needs Assessment Survey Guide" http://extension.usu.edu/files/survey/draper.htm, accessed April 22, 2006. Courtesy Utah State University Extension Community Development.

RESPONSIBILITIES TO THE COMMUNITY

It is important for a company to view community stakeholders in a trusting manner, recognizing the potential mutual benefit to each party. In a networked world, much about a company can be learned with a few clicks of a mouse. Activists and disgruntled individuals have used websites to publicize the questionable activities of some companies. McDonald's Corporation, like Wal-Mart, has been the target of numerous "hate" websites that broadcast concerns about the company's products, pricing strategies, and marketing to children. Because of the visibility of business activities and the desire for strategic social responsibility, successful companies strive to build long-term mutually beneficial relationships with relevant communities. Achieving these relationships may involve some trial and error. Table 9.3 illustrates some of the common mistakes organizations make in planning for and implementing community responsibilities. In contrast, Eli Lilly Pharmaceuticals, headquartered in Indianapolis, Indiana, is a strong supporter of the Indianapolis Symphony Orchestra. In return, the orchestra stages private concerts for Eli Lilly employees. Dell Computer has a similar relationship with the Round Rock Express, a minor league (Texas League) baseball team.

TABLE 9.3	Ten Common Myths and Mistakes About Community Relations

We Won't Need Consent or Support From Our Local Government Officials or Local Community.

Many organizations have learned the importance of community relations the hard way when they have tried to clean up sites; get permits; and site, expand, and operate facilities. It is difficult to put a dollar value on community relations until negative relations threaten or jeopardize a company's goals or operations. Organizations often do not allocate sufficient resources to community relations until it is too late. Unresolved conflicts which result from inadequate communication or poor relations can have ugly and expensive ramifications for companies, including injunctions from localities, permit denials, delays in projects, negative press, cease-and-desist orders, lawsuits, new legislation, etc. Community relations are much more rewarding and well received than crisis management.

We Will be Stirring Up Trouble If We Talk to the Community.

Many project managers are afraid to talk with the community because they are afraid that they will make things worse by stirring up issues that might not already exist. It generally works the opposite. In fact, they are usually flattered and disarmed (and maybe a tad suspicious) when organizations care enough to talk with them. If you have never initiated dialog before, you can expect the first few times to be contentious, as negative comments, complaints, and fears are expressed. But if you are committed to establishing and maintaining good relations, you have the opportunity to turn those negative comments into positive ones, or at least neutral and balanced ones, as long as your organization's plans are solid. Proactive community relations efforts are very rewarding and can actually make your job much easier in the future. You can even establish yourself as a leader in the community.

We Can Improve Relations With One-Way Communications Efforts (Without Interaction With Interested Parties).

If your company or facility is experiencing negative press or strained relations with the community, controlled one-way communication is not the answer. Human nature causes us to want to play it close to the chest. Productive (and perhaps facilitated) interaction is necessary to allow both parties to work through and resolve the issues. Many conflicts are caused by a lack of information, misinformation, different interpretations, stereotypes, repetitive negative behavior, and a perception of different interests. Many of these conflicts can only be resolved through improved, effective communication and joint problem solving, which can only occur through interaction and dialog.

The Community Cannot Add Anything Meaningful to This Process Because It Is Too Technically Complex.

I am consistently amazed at the level of contribution communities have made to a number of very complex projects that we have been involved with. When given the opportunity and sufficient time to review technical information, it is amazing how much local residents can grasp and contribute to projects. Local involvement and buy-in on engineering projects may even reduce the liability of technical decisions in the future.

Community Leaders Will Request the Most Unreasonable or Costly Solutions.

We usually approach issues based on the way we define them. As a community relations firm, we often find that the way our clients define community relations issues and the way the community defines them are quite different. We can't truly know how people will react until we talk with them. We often find that community leaders are sympathetic to companies and facilities in terms of the cost associated with regulatory compliances and environmental cleanup and are much more practical (e.g., when it comes to cleanup levels etc.) than one might imagine.

We Shouldn't Talk to the Community Until We Have All the Answers.

Actually, you gain more credibility by being open enough to allow the community to be involved throughout the process. There is a comfort in knowing all the layers, steps, models, assumptions, and coordination that organizations are undertaking to develop and implement cleanup and other engineering projects. The more the community knows about this effort, the more credible the information will be.

Consulting With Elected Officials Is Enough Community Relations.

The old-fashioned public affairs approach focused on covering your bases with the media and with elected officials. The truth is that elected officials and the media usually tend to their constituents when issues stir up. Your efforts are better spent on improving relations with the local community. This is not to suggest that you shouldn't have relations with the local media and elected officials, but be careful of relying too heavily (or exclusively) on them when an issue escalates.

(continued)

| **TABLE 9.3** | Ten Common Myths and Mistakes About Community Relations (*continued*) |

If Our Relations Are Currently Strained, We Will Make Relations Worse by Communicating With the Community Now.

The first step is to find out why relations are strained (which may require an independent reliable source to uncover). If your intentions are sound and mutually beneficial in some way, how can communication make relations worse? How can relationships get better if you don't communicate?

It Will be Easier to Implement Our Project Without Community Relations.

Reactive communication efforts resulting from unexpected community concern or media interest always seem to cause more upheaval, require more time and money, and are more disruptive to my clients than planned communication efforts.

We Need to Do a Better Job Communicating the Technical Issues.

Don't underestimate the value of the trust and credibility factors that are less technically based: caring and empathy, commitment, openness, and honesty. Messages that communicate these are much more powerful in relations building than technical knowledge.

Source: "10 Common Myths About Community Relations," Chaloux Environmental Communications, Inc., www.ce-com.com/10commonmyths.htm, accessed May 10, 2006. © 2006 Chaloux Environmental Communications, Inc. All rights reserved.

A community focus can be integrated with concerns for employees and consumers. Chapter 1 provided evidence that satisfied customers and employees are correlated with improved organizational performance.

Economic Issues

From an economic perspective, business is absolutely vital to a community. Companies play a major role in community economic development by bringing jobs to the community and allowing employees to support themselves and their families. These companies also buy supplies, raw materials, utilities, advertising services, and other goods and services from area firms; this in turn produces more economic effects. In communities with few employers, an organization that expands in or moves to the area can reduce some of the burden on community services and other subsidized support. Even in large cities with many employers, some companies choose to address social problems that tax the community. In countries with developing economies, a business or industry can also provide many benefits. A new company brings not only jobs but also new technology, related businesses, improvements to infrastructure, and other positive factors. Conversely, the "McDonaldization" of developing countries is a common criticism regarding the effects of U.S. businesses on other parts of the world. For example, although Coca-Cola has been criticized for selling sugared water and exploiting consumers in developing countries, the firm's market expansion strategy often involves creating a network of distributors that improves both employment and entrepreneurship opportunities in a given area.[12]

Interactions with suppliers and other vendors also stimulate the economy. Some companies are even dedicated to finding local or regional business partners in an effort to enhance their economic responsibility. For example, BP feels its most valuable contribution to local economies is to encourage enterprise through job creation, the use of local suppliers, sharing business skills, and the promotion of investment in the economy.[13] Furthermore, there is often a contagion effect when one business moves into an area: By virtue of its prestige or business relationships, such a move can signal to other firms that the area is a viable and attractive place for others to locate. There are parts of the United States that are highly concentrated with automotive manufacturing, financial services, or technology. Local chambers of commerce and economic development organizations often entice new firms to a region because of the positive reputation and economic contagion it brings. Finally, business contributions to local health, education, and recreation projects not only benefit local residents and employees but also may bring additional revenue into the community from tourism and other businesses that appreciate the region's quality of life. FedEx, for example, hosts the FedEx St. Jude Classic PGA golf tournament. The tournament has raised more than $15.5 million for St. Jude's Children's Hospital and has generated significant tourism for the city of Memphis.[14]

Just as a business brings positive economic effects by expanding in or relocating to an area, it can also cause financial repercussions when it exits a particular market or geographical location. Thus, workforce reduction, or downsizing—a topic discussed in Chapter 7—is a key issue with respect to economic responsibility. The impact of layoffs due to plant closings and corporate restructuring often extends well beyond the financial well-being of affected employees. Laid-off employees typically limit their spending to basic necessities while they look for new employment, and many may ultimately leave the area altogether. Even employees who retain their jobs in such a downsizing may suffer from poor morale, distrust, guilt, and continued anxiety over their own job security, further stifling spending in a community.

Because companies have such a profound impact on the economic viability of the communities in which they operate, firms that value social responsibility consider both the short- and long-term effects on the community of changes in their workforce. Today, many companies that must reduce their workforce—regardless of the reasons—strive to give both employees and the community advance notice and offer placement services to help the community absorb employees who lose their jobs. For example, when Ford Motor Company announced layoffs in St. Paul, Minnesota, they noted that laid-off employees would receive unemployment benefits and additional benefits that would bring them close to their normal wages. The laid-off workers will ultimately be placed on Ford's "GEN pool," which continues to pay out most of their pay and benefits. GEN stands for Guaranteed Employment Number and is part of the UAW contract. Minnesota Governor Tim Pawlenty is working on strategies with Ford that might keep the plant open, knowing the potential economic impact of losing 1,770 workers.[15] Other companies may choose to offer extra compensation commensurate with an employee's length of employment which gives laid-off employees a financial cushion while they find new work.

Legal Issues

To conduct business, a company must be granted a "license to operate." For many firms, a series of legal and regulatory matters must be resolved before the first employee is hired or the first customer is served. If you open a restaurant, for example, most states require a business license and sales tax number. These documents require basic information, such as business type, ownership structure, owner information, number of expected employees, and other data.

On a fundamental level, society has the ability to dictate what types of organizations are allowed to operate. In exchange for the license to operate, organizations are expected to uphold all legal obligations and standards. We have discussed many of these laws throughout this book, although individual cities, counties, and municipalities will have additional laws and regulations that firms must obey. For example, five fishing companies were charged with dumping squid parts and wastewater that contaminated a suburban Los Angeles harbor, killing sharks, sting rays, and other sea life. These fishing companies violated city ordinances and state water and fish and game regulations.[16]

Other communities have concerns about whether and how businesses fit into existing communities, especially those threatened by urban sprawl and small towns working to preserve a traditional way of life. Some states, cities, and counties have enacted legislation that limits the square footage of stores in an effort to deter "big-box stores," such as Wal-Mart and Home Depot, unless local voters specifically approve their being allowed to build. In most cases, these communities have called for such legislation to combat the noise and traffic congestion that may be associated with such stores, to protect neighborhoods, and to preserve the viability of local small businesses.[17] Thus, although living wages and store location may be ethical issues for business, some local governments have chosen to move them into the legal realm.

Ethical Issues

As more companies view themselves as responsible to the community, they will contemplate their role and the impact of their decisions on communities from an ethical perspective. Consider Clyde Oatis, who is renovating an abandoned rice mill in Houston's Fifth Ward to house a business that he hopes will address both environmental and economic issues in the low-income neighborhood. Oatis's U.S. Custom Feed will process food waste once destined for landfills into nutritious food pellets customized for the needs of different species of animals. The company will also employ and pay a living wage to workers in an area that desperately needs the jobs. Says Oatis, "You've got to have some social responsibility. . . . I think I should do my part."[18]

Business leaders are increasingly recognizing the significance of the role their firms play in the community and the need for their leadership in tackling community problems. Bill Daniels was an extremely successful entrepreneur having founded Cablevision. The Daniels Fund is having a significant impact on business ethics education and other social concerns in the states of Wyoming, Colorado, New Mexico, and Utah. The Daniels Fund donated over $3.5 million to the University of Wyoming to support a statewide business ethics initiative impacting students at the University of Wyoming and throughout the community college system.[19]

These examples demonstrate that the ethical dimension of community responsibility can be multifaceted. This dimension and related programs are not legally mandated but emanate from the particular philosophy of a company and its top managers. For example, since many cities have not mandated a living wage, Clyde Oatis's actions in Houston are based on an ethical obligation that he feels to employees and the community. There are many ways that a company can demonstrate its ethical commitment to the community. As Bill Daniels's commitment to business ethics illustrates, a common extension of "doing the right thing" ethically is for companies and individuals to begin to allocate funds to assist communities and others in need.

Philanthropic Issues

The community relations function has always been associated with philanthropy, as one of the main historical roles of community relations was to provide gifts, grants, and other resources to worthy causes. Today, that thinking has shifted. Although businesses have the potential to help solve social issues, the success of a business can be enhanced from the publicity generated by and through stakeholder acceptance of community activities. For example, Colorado-based New Belgium Brewing Company donates $1 for every barrel of beer brewed the prior year to charities within the markets it serves. The brewery tries to divide the funds among states in proportion to interests and needs, considering environmental, social, drug and alcohol awareness, and cultural issues. Donation decisions are made by the firm's philanthropy committee, which is a volunteer group of diverse employees and one or two of the owners; employees are encouraged to bring philanthropy suggestions to the committee.[20] However, New Belgium belongs to an industry that some members of society believe contributes to social problems. Thus, regardless of the positive contributions such a firm makes to the community, some members will always have a negative view of the business.

volunteerism
when employees spend company-supported time in support of social causes

One of the most significant ways that organizations are exercising their philanthropic responsibilities is through volunteer programs. **Volunteerism** in the workplace, when employees spend company-supported time in support of social causes, has been increasing among companies of all sizes. Roughly 44 percent of U.S. adults volunteer, and 71 percent of those asked to volunteer do so.[21] Benefits of volunteering accrue to both the individual, in terms of greater motivation, enjoyment, and satisfaction, and to the organization through employee retention and productivity increases.[22] Communities benefit from the application of new skills and initiatives toward problems, better relations with business, a greater supply of volunteers, assistance to stretch limited resources, and social and economic regeneration.[23] Philanthropic issues are just another dimension of voluntary social responsibility and relate to business's contributions to stakeholders.

Americans spend millions of hours supporting formal volunteer activities. At Toyota, for example, the Volunteers in Place (VIP) program offers incentives to encourage employees to volunteer at least thirty hours per year. The top volunteers win recognition and additional cash contributions to the charity of their choice. A spokesperson for Toyota Motor Manufacturing states, "Employee morale, productivity, and turnover have all improved since the VIP program was implemented four years ago."[24] IBM contributes $1,500 to the charity of any employee who donates more than 100 hours of volunteer time to a community school each year.[25] Vanderbilt University's Owen Graduate School of Management is targeting 100 percent volunteerism among its business students, faculty, and staff. The 100 percent Owen Club has raised money for disaster relief and supported Habitat for Humanity, Boys and Girls Clubs of Middle Tennessee, and numerous other causes.[26]

There are several considerations in deciding how to structure a volunteer program. Attention must be paid to employee values and beliefs; therefore, political

After a massive tsunami hit Sri Lanka and other areas, volunteers from the Sri Lanka Oil Corporation helped to clean up the debris and destruction.

or religious organizations should be supported on the basis of individual employee initiative and interest. Warner Brothers, the motion picture company, allows its employees to select from a menu outlining volunteer opportunities. One very successful program for Time Warner Communications is Time to Read, which pairs tutors with children throughout the company's 300 sites.[27] Another issue is what to do when some employees do not wish to volunteer. If the company is not paying for the employees' time to volunteer and volunteering is not a condition of employment or an aspect of the job description, it may be difficult to convince a certain percentage of the workforce to participate. If the organization is paying for one day a month, for example, to allow the employee exposure to volunteerism, then individual compliance is usually expected.

PHILANTHROPIC CONTRIBUTIONS

philanthropy
involves any acts of benevolence and goodwill, such as making gifts to charities, volunteering for community projects, and taking action to benefit others

Philanthropy provides four major benefits to society. First, it improves the quality of life and helps make communities places where people want to do business, raise families, and enjoy life. Thus, improving the quality of life in a community makes it easier to attract and retain employees and customers. Second, philanthropy reduces government involvement by providing assistance to stakeholders. Third, philanthropy develops employee leadership skills. Many firms, for example, use campaigns by the United Way and other community service organizations as leadership- and skill-building exercises for their employees. Philanthropy helps create an ethical culture and the values that can act as a buffer to organizational misconduct.[28] In the United States, charitable giving has remained fairly consistent at 1.9 percent of gross domestic product annually. Natural disasters such as hurricanes, floods, and earthquakes can divert giving from traditional causes, with 80 percent of nonprofits surveyed indicating their contributions were flat or down from 2005.[29] Corporate donations in 2005 decreased among the largest U.S. companies. The $8.56 billion donated represented a decline of 0.9 percent from the previous year.[30] The decline in organizational giving has caused charities to pursue individual donors more aggressively.

The most common way that businesses demonstrate philanthropy is through donations to local and national charitable organizations. Corporations gave more than $12 billion to environmental and social causes in 2004.[31] Wells Fargo & Co., for example, contributed $93 million to 15,000 different organizations. It helped finance the construction of single-family homes on or near Native American reservations in seven states, bringing private mortgage capital to those historically denied access.[32] Indeed, many companies have become concerned about the quality of education in the United States after realizing that the current pool of prospective employees lacks many basic work skills. Recognizing that today's students are tomorrow's employees and customers, firms such as Kroger, Campbell Soup Co., Eastman Kodak, American Express, Apple Computer, Xerox, and Coca-Cola have donated money, equipment, and employee time to help improve schools in their communities and throughout the nation. Corporations are increasingly giving merchandise, and not cash, as charitable contributions. In 2004, 54.2 percent of corporate contributions were merchandise versus 35 percent in 2002. The pharmaceutical industry with medical donations has been a key contributor.[33]

Wal-Mart donated more than $200 million in 2005 to help charities and organizations throughout the United States. More than 90 percent of the contributions were directed at the local level. Wal-Mart was recognized by *The Chronicle of Philanthropy* as the largest corporate cash contributor in America. They helped more than 100,000 charitable organizations around the country and gave back $547,945 each day. The money supported a variety of causes such as child development, education, the environment, and disaster relief. Wal-Mart feels that they can make the greatest impact on communities by supporting issues and causes that are important to their customers and associates in their own neighborhoods. Wal-Mart relies on their own associates to know which organizations are the most important to their hometowns, and they empower them to determine how money will be spent in their communities. Wal-Mart supports charities such as the American Cancer Society and The Salvation Army as well as helping soldiers wounded in Iraq and donating more than $2.5 million to tsunami relief efforts. After Hurricane Katrina, Wal-Mart donated more than $17 million in cash to help the victims of the hurricane and contributed much-needed supplies right after the disaster. By supporting communities at the local level, it encourages customer loyalty and goodwill.[34]

Figure 9.1 displays the major recipients of the more than $240 billion in philanthropic donations made in 2002. Religious organizations received 35 percent of all contributions, with educational causes collecting 13 percent of the funds. Individuals made 75 percent of these donations, with corporations contributing 5 percent, or just over $12 billion.[35]

In a general sense, philanthropy involves any acts of benevolence and goodwill, such as making gifts to charities, volunteering for community projects, and taking action to benefit others. For example, your parents may have spent time on nonwork projects that directly benefited the community or a special population. Perhaps you have participated in similar activities through work, school groups, or associations. Have you ever served Thanksgiving dinner at a homeless shelter? Have you ever raised money for a neighborhood school? Have you ever joined a social club that volunteered member services to local charities?

Most religious organizations, educational institutions, and arts programs rely heavily on philanthropic donations from both individuals and organizations. Philanthropy is a major driver of the nonprofit sector of the economy, as these organizations rely on the time, money, and talents of both individuals and organizations to operate and fund their programs. Consider the Sakharov Museum in Moscow. The museum, named for the Nobel Peace Prize winner and human rights activist Andrei

---

FIGURE 9.1   Sources and Recipients of Charitable Giving

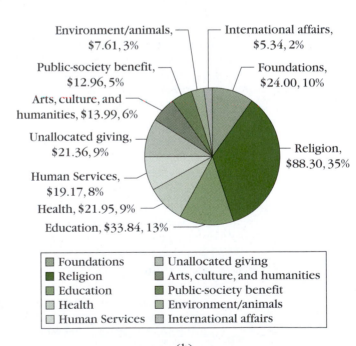

**Source of Charitable Contributions
($ millions)**

Corporations, $12.00, 5%
Foundations, $28.80, 12%
Bequests, $19.80, 8%
Individuals, $187.92, 75%

- Corporations
- Foundations
- Bequests
- Individuals

(a)

**Recipients of Charitable Giving
($ millions)**

Environment/animals, $7.61, 3%
International affairs, $5.34, 2%
Public-society benefit, $12.96, 5%
Foundations, $24.00, 10%
Arts, culture, and humanities, $13.99, 6%
Unallocated giving, $21.36, 9%
Religion, $88.30, 35%
Human Services, $19.17, 8%
Health, $21.95, 9%
Education, $33.84, 13%

- Foundations
- Religion
- Education
- Health
- Human Services
- Unallocated giving
- Arts, culture, and humanities
- Public-society benefit
- Environment/animals
- International affairs

(b)

(c)

Number	Donors	Background	2001–2005 Given or Pledged ($ millions)	Causes
1	Gordon and Betty Moore	Intel cofounder	$7,046	Environment, science
2	Bill and Melinda Gates	Microsoft cofounder	5,458	Health, education, libraries
3	Warren Buffett	Berkshire Hathaway CEO	2,622	Reproductive choice, reducing nukes
4	George Soros	Investor	2,367	Open and democratic societies
5	Eli and Edythe Broad	SunAmerica, KB Home founder	1,475	Public education, arts, science
6	James and Virginia Stowers	American Century founder	1,205	Biomedical research
7	Walton Family	Family of Wal-Mart founder	1,100	Education
8	Michael and Susan Dell	Dell founder	933	Children's health and education
9	Alfred Mann	Medical devices	993	Biomedical education and research
10	George Kaiser	Oil and gas, banking, real estate	617	Antipoverty in Oklahoma
11	John Templeton	Investor	562	Spirituality and science
12	Ruth Lilly	Eli Lilly heiress	560	Poetry, libraries, culture, scholarships
13	Michael Bloomberg	Bloomberg founder, NYC mayor	528	Education, health care, arts and culture
14	Veronica Atkins	Widow of Dr. Robert Atkins	500	Eradication of obesity and diabetes
15	Jeff Skoll	Founding president of eBay	489	Social entrepreneurs
16	Ted Turner	CNN founder	457	Environment, global security
17	Kirk Kerkorian	Investor	453	Humanitarian and Armenian causes
18	Donald Bren	Real estate	447	Education, environment
19	Pierre and Pam Omidyar	eBay chairman, founder	433	Individual self-empowerment
20	Patrick and Lore Harp McGovern	IDG founder	370	Brain research

Sources: (a) "Contributions: $248.52 Billion by Source of Contributions," American Association of Fundraising Council, Giving USA Foundation™, http://www.aafrc.org/index.htm (accessed May 11, 2006). (b) "Contributions: $248.52 Billion by Type of Recipient Organization," American Association of Fundraising Council, Giving USA Foundation™, http://www.aafrc.org/index.htm, (accessed May 11, 2006). (c) Susan Wooley, "The 50 Most Generous Philanthropists" *BusinessWeek,* November 28, 2005, p. 61.

Sakharov, recently faced a severe financial crisis because Russia lacks a culture of corporate philanthropy and the associated funding of nongovernment museums. The museum's political bent, along with Russian laws prohibiting tax benefits from charitable donations, caused museum managers to look outside their country for funding. As a result, the Moscow office of the U.S.-based Ford Foundation has partnered with the museum.[36]

STRATEGIC PHILANTHROPY DEFINED

strategic philanthropy

the synergistic use of an organization's core competencies and resources to address key stakeholders' interests and to achieve both organizational and social benefits

Our concept of corporate philanthropy extends beyond financial contributions and explicitly links company missions, organizational competencies, and various stakeholders. Thus, we define **strategic philanthropy** as the synergistic use of an organization's core competencies and resources to address key stakeholders' interests and to achieve both organizational and social benefits. Strategic philanthropy goes well beyond the traditional benevolent philanthropy of donating a percentage of sales to social causes by involving employees (utilizing their core skills), organizational resources and expertise (equipment, knowledge, and money), and the ability to link employees, customers, suppliers, and social needs with these key assets. Strategic philanthropy involves both financial and nonfinancial contributions to stakeholders (employee time, goods and services, and company technology and equipment as well as facilities), but it also benefits the company.

John Damonti, president of the Bristol-Myers Squibb Foundation, reflected, "When you align your contributions with your business focus, you then can draw on the greater wealth of the corporation's people, information, and resources."[37] Organizations are best suited to deal with social or stakeholder issues in areas with which they have some experience, knowledge, or expertise. From a business perspective, companies want to refine their intellectual capital, reinforce their core competencies, and develop synergies between business and philanthropic activities. The process of addressing stakeholder concerns through philanthropy should be strategic to a company's ongoing development and improvement. For example, American Express, a global financial and travel company, contributed funds and know-how to initiate the development of the Academy of Travel and Tourism in Hungary. This project benefited the Hungarian economy, tested the entrepreneurial spirit and skills of American Express employees, and reinforced the company's understanding of the Hungarian market.[38] Some critics would argue that this was not true philanthropy because American Express received business benefits. Because social responsibility takes place on many levels, effective philanthropy depends on the synergy between stakeholder needs and business competencies and goals. Thus, the fact that each partner to the Academy of Travel and Tourism had different goals and earned unique benefits does not diminish the overall good that resulted from the project. As global competition escalates, companies are increasingly responsible to stakeholders in justifying their philanthropic endeavors. This ultimately requires greater planning and alignment of philanthropic efforts with overall strategic goals. Table 9.4 provides additional examples of philanthropic activities.

| **TABLE 9.4** | Examples of Corporate Philanthropy |

- After British Petroleum (now BP Amoco) was criticized by Greenpeace for its environmental practices, the company created a $1 billion business and many new jobs in solar power, a renewable and nonpolluting source of energy.

- Dayton-Hudson Corporation regularly donates 5 percent of its pretax income to charities, whereas employees both select and volunteer in many of these community-based organizations.

- Altria spent over $1 billion in the past decade to combat domestic abuse, feed the ill and elderly, and respond to natural disasters.

- Customers of Hanna Andersson, a manufacturer of high-quality children's clothes, can return worn clothing for credit toward their next purchase, with the used clothing donated to needy children.

- Boeing Company donated $15 million to the National Air and Space Museum. Since the museum opened in 1976, Boeing has been deeply involved in the aircraft collection and restoration of artifacts.

- Businesspeople from the toy industry in Brazil created the Abrinq Foundation for Children's Rights, which is dedicated to promoting the rights of children and youth at risk in Brazil.

- Seafirst Bank's partnership with Indian Nations in the state of Washington resulted in education programs for Native Americans in financial management and tribal economic development and helped Seafirst employees better understand cultural issues related to business relationships and development.

- More than 6,000 companies sponsor matching-gift programs, where an employee's personal donation to an educational institution is matched by the employer.

Sources: Peggy Dulany and David Winder, "The Status of and Trends in Private Philanthropy in the Southern Hemisphere," Synergos Institute, http://www.synergos.org/globalphilanthropy/02/philanthropyinsouthernhemisphere.htm, accessed January 28, 2003; Reynold Levy, *Give and Take: A Candid Account of Corporate Philanthropy* (Boston: Harvard Business School Press, 1999); "Better to Give and to Receive," *Hemispheres* (January 1997); Luba Krekhovetsky, "Charity Begins with Homes," *Canadian Business,* December 30, 2002, pp. 91–93; Glen Peters, *Waltzing with the Raptors: A Practical Roadmap to Protecting Your Company's Reputation* (New York: John Wiley, 1999); Ann Svendsen, *The Stakeholder Strategy* (San Francisco: Berrett-Koehler, 1998); Nanette Byrnes, "Smarter Corporate Giving," *Business Week Online,* November 28, 2005, http://www.businessweek.com/print/magazine/content/05_48/b39616707.htm, accessed May 11, 2006; Jacqueline Trescott, "Boeing Donates $15 Million to Expand Smithsonian Aviation Annex at Dulles," *Washington Post,* April 11, 2006, p. C01.

The American Library Association organized a philanthropic effort to rebuild libraries in Alabama, Louisiana, and Mississippi destroyed by Hurricane Katrina.

STRATEGIC PHILANTHROPY AND SOCIAL RESPONSIBILITY

It is important to place strategic philanthropy in the context of organizational responsibilities at the economic, legal, ethical, and philanthropic levels. Most companies understand the need to be economically successful for the benefit of all stakeholders and to comply with the laws required within our society and others in which they do business. Additionally, through the establishment of core values and ethical cultures, most firms are recognizing the many benefits of good ethics. As we saw in Chapter 1, evidence is accumulating that there is a positive relationship between social responsibility and performance, especially with regard to customer satisfaction, investor loyalty, and employee commitment. Strategic social responsibility can reduce the cost of business transactions, establish trust among stakeholders, improve teamwork, and preserve the social capital necessary for an infrastructure for doing business. In sum, these efforts improve the context and environment for corporate operations and performance.[39]

When Noah's Bagels began expanding beyond its original Berkeley, California, location in the late 1980s, the company focused not only on opening new retail stores but also on helping surrounding neighborhoods. Noah's sought to be a positive, dynamic force in its local communities because it "recognizes the importance of giving the community more than just exhilarated taste buds." Thus, the company began to link its philanthropic efforts directly with the core operations and skills required to run the business. For example, Noah's donates bagels and other foods to fight community hunger. The company also gives employees paid time off to work on service projects that benefit surrounding neighborhoods. Store managers can choose a local charity and apply for matching funds from corporate headquarters. Customers are encouraged to comment on the company's bagels, coffee, and community affairs. All of these efforts directly link Noah's philanthropy to issues that positively affect, and reflect, its operations and marketing. Because the company carefully chooses projects and charities that are aligned with its core competencies, Noah's Bagels is taking a strategic approach to its philanthropy.[40]

Many companies consider philanthropy only after they have met their financial, legal, and ethical obligations. As companies strive for social responsibility, their ability to meet each obligation lays the foundation for success with other responsibilities. In addition, there is synergy in corporate efforts directed at the four levels of responsibility. As one of the most voluntary dimensions of social responsibility, philanthropy has not always been linked to profits or business ethics. In fact, the traditional approach to philanthropy disconnects giving from business performance and its impact on stakeholders. Before the evolution of strategic philanthropy, most corporate gift programs separated the company from the organizations, causes, and individuals that its donations most benefited.[41]

Research has begun to highlight organizations' formalization of philanthropic activities and their efforts to integrate philanthropic goals with other business strategies and implementation. U.S. companies are adopting a more businesslike approach to philanthropy and experiencing a better image, increased employee loyalty, and improved customer ties.[42] Philanthropy involves using organizational resources, and specific methods are used to measure its impact on key stakeholders. In this case, philanthropy is an investment from which a company can gain some type of value.

The traditional approach to corporate philanthropy is characterized by donations and related activities that are not purposefully aligned with the strategic goals and resources of the firm. For instance, employees may be encouraged to volunteer in the community but receive little direction on where or how to spend their time. Employees of Fuji Bank of Japan, for example, may apply for leaves of absence to take part in volunteer opportunities.[43] After the September 11, 2001, terrorist attacks, companies and employees became quite creative in their philanthropic efforts. One result was "leave-based donation programs," which allow employees to donate the value of accumulated vacation and sick- and personal-leave days to a nonprofit cause. The U.S. Treasury Department approved the idea and clarified regulations to benefit employees, companies, and nonprofits.[44] Indeed, there are numerous examples of companies supporting community involvement. Although these actions are noble, they are not always considered in tandem with organizational goals and strengths.

In some cases, corporate contributions may be made to nonprofit organizations in which top managers have a personal interest. When Unilever acquired Ben and Jerry's Homemade, they agreed to support the following causes and initiatives that are extremely important to founders Ben Cohen and Jerry Greenfield. Unilever agreed to maintain the Vermont employment and manufacture base, pay workers a livable wage with complete benefits, by milk from Vermont dairy farmers who do not use bovine growth hormones, contribute over $1.1 million annually to the Ben and Jerry's Foundation, open more Partner Shops owned by nonprofit organizations providing employment opportunities for disadvantaged persons, and maintain relationships with alternate suppliers.[45] Finally, many companies will match employees' personal gifts to educational institutions. Although gift-matching programs instill employee pride and assist education, they are rarely linked to company operations and competencies.[46] In the traditional approach to corporate philanthropy, then, companies have good intentions, but there is no solid integration with organizational resources and objectives.

In the social responsibility model that we propose, philanthropy is only one focal point for a corporate vision that includes both the welfare of the firm and benefits to stakeholders. This requires support from top management as well as a strategic planning structure that incorporates stakeholder concerns and benefits. Corporate giving, volunteer efforts, and other contributions should be considered and aligned not only with corporate strategy but also with financial, legal, and ethical obligations. The shift from traditional benevolent philanthropy to strategic philanthropy has come about as companies struggled in the 1980s, 1990s, and early 2000s to redefine their missions, alliances, and scope, while becoming increasingly accountable to stakeholders and society.

Strategic Philanthropy Versus Cause-Related Marketing

The first attempts by organizations to coordinate organizational goals with philanthropic giving emerged with cause-related marketing in the early 1980s. Whereas strategic philanthropy links corporate resources and knowledge to address broader

TABLE 9.5   Strategic Philanthropy Contrasted with Cause-Related Marketing

	Strategic Philanthropy	**Cause-Related Marketing**
Focus	Organizational	Product or product line
Goals	Improvement of organizational competence or tying organizational competence to social need or charitable cause; builds brand equity	Increase of product sales
Time frame	Ongoing	Traditionally of limited duration
Organizational members involved	Potentially all organizational employees	Marketing department and related personnel
Cost	Moderate—alignment with organizational strategies and mission	Minimal—alliance development and promotion expenditures

cause-related marketing

business strategy that ties an organization's product(s) directly to a social concern through a marketing program

social, customer, employee, and supplier problems and needs, **cause-related marketing** ties an organization's product(s) directly to a social concern. Table 9.5 compares cause-related marketing and strategic philanthropy.

With cause-related marketing, a percentage of a product's sales is usually donated to a cause appealing to the relevant target market. The Avon Breast Cancer Crusade, for example, generates proceeds for the breast cancer cause through several fundraising efforts, including the sale of special "pink ribbon" products by Avon independent sales representatives nationwide (see Figure 9.2). Gifts are awarded by the Avon Products Foundation, Inc., a nonprofit 501(c)(3) accredited public charity, to support six vital areas of the breast cancer cause with a focus on medically underserved women, biomedical research, clinical care, financial assistance and support services, educational seminars and advocacy training, and early detection and awareness programs nationwide. Both the cause and Avon Crusade "pink ribbon" products appeal to Avon's primary target market, women. Between 1992 and 2005, the Avon Breast Cancer Crusade generated more than $400 million net in total funds raised worldwide to fund access to care and finding a cure for breast cancer.[47]

American Express was the first company to use cause-related marketing widely, when it began advertising in 1983 that it would give a percentage of credit-card charges to the Statue of Liberty and Ellis Island Restoration Fund.[48] As is the case with Avon, American Express companies generally prefer to support causes that are of interest to their target markets. In a single year, organizations paid more than $500 million for the rights to support various social programs, ultimately raising roughly $2.5 billion for these causes.[49] Thus, a key feature of cause-related marketing is the promise of donations to a particular social cause based on customer sales or involvement. Whereas strategic philanthropy is tied to the entire organization, cause-related marketing is linked to a specific product and marketing program. The program may involve in-store promotions, messages on packages and labels, and other marketing communications.[50]

FIGURE 9.2	The Avon Breast Cancer Crusade

Source: "Avon Breast Cancer Crusade," http://www.avoncompany.com/women/avoncrusade/, accessed January 28, 2003. Courtesy of Avon Products, Inc.

Although cause-related marketing has its roots in the United States, the marketing tool is gaining widespread usage in other parts of the world. A study by Saatchi & Saatchi found that about 40 percent of European senior marketers were aligning their cause-related marketing budgets with brand communication programs. For example, the New Covent Garden Soup Co. recently partnered with a homeless charity in Great Britain. During the Christmas season, portions of sales of New Covent Garden's pea and ham soup were donated to help renovate the charity's kitchens. Tesco, a large European grocery chain, also joined the cause by donating funds based on every soup carton sold in the six-week holiday season.[51] Business in the Community, a nonprofit group in the United Kingdom, sponsors annual awards for British firms that demonstrate excellence in cause-related marketing. Walkers, a manufacturer of cookies and biscuits, is a recent winner due to its distribution of more than 2.3 million books to schools in the United Kingdom. Bettys and Taylors of Harrogate Yorkshire Tea also received an award for its cause-related marketing program to plant trees and slow forest degradation in regions where it sources its teas and commodities.[52]

Cause-related marketing activities have the potential to affect buying patterns. For cause-related marketing to be successful, consumers must have awareness and affinity for the cause, the brand and cause must be associated and perceived as a good fit, and consumers should be able to transfer feelings toward the cause to their brand perceptions and purchase intentions. Studies have found that a majority of consumers said that, given equal price and product quality, they would be more likely to buy the product associated with a charitable cause. Eighty percent of customers say they have more positive perceptions of firms that support causes about which they personally care. These surveys have also noted that most marketing directors felt that cause-related marketing would increase in importance over the coming years.[53] Through cause-related marketing, companies first become aware that supporting social causes, such as environmental awareness, health and human services, education, and the arts, can support business goals and help bolster a firm's reputation, especially those with an ethically neutral image. However, firms that are perceived as unethical may be suspected of ulterior motives in developing cause-related campaigns.[54] One of the main weaknesses with cause-related marketing is that some consumers cannot link specific philanthropic efforts with companies.[55] Consumers may have difficulty recalling exact philanthropic relationships because many cause-related marketing campaigns have tended to be of short duration and have not always had a direct correlation to the sponsoring firm's core business. Because strategic philanthropy is more pervasive and relates to company attributes and skills, such alliances should have greater stakeholder recognition, appreciation, and long-term value.

STAKEHOLDERS IN STRATEGIC PHILANTHROPY

Although more businesses are moving toward adopting a strategic philanthropy model, others are still focusing only on the needs of individual stakeholders. Although these efforts are important and commendable, companies may not be realizing the full benefits for themselves and their stakeholders. For example, the implementation of cause-related marketing efforts may not reinforce employee skills and competencies. Instead, such campaigns usually focus on generating product sales and donations to a specific cause. Volunteer programs may benefit the community and employee morale, but the value of this service could be greatly enhanced through synergies between current and future job-related aptitude and nonprofit needs.

In this section, we offer examples of organizations that have effectively collaborated with various stakeholders in the pursuit of mutual benefits. Their efforts serve as examples of best practices in implementing and managing strategic philanthropy by engaging, not just managing, stakeholder relationships.[56] The following strategic philanthropic efforts demonstrate a dual concern for meeting stakeholder needs while strengthening organizational competencies.

By providing a free networking curriculum to schools, Cisco contributes to education and also ensures an ongoing supply of skilled maintenance people who can service Cisco equipment. In addition, in consideration of varied stakeholder interests, Cisco believes such involvement boosts brand equity with customers, investors, and the community in general.[57] Sony's philanthropic efforts reflect the diverse interests of their key businesses and focus on several distinct areas and stakeholder interests: arts education; arts and culture; health and human services; civic and community outreach; education; and volunteerism. Each operating company has its own philanthropic priorities and unique resources, from product donations to recordings and screenings that benefit a multitude of causes. Sony Corporation of America is a strong supporter of arts and culture, and education and volunteerism are key components of Sony Electronics' philanthropic efforts.[58]

Employees

A key to organizational success is the ability of organizations to attract, socialize, and retain competent and qualified employees. Through strategic philanthropy initiatives, companies have the opportunity to increase employee commitment, motivation, and skill refinement. For example, United Airlines Foundation supports and encourages volunteerism among its 63,000 employees. Every holiday season for years, United employees in communities around the world have hosted Fantasy Flights—magical flights that take disadvantaged or seriously ill children on a trip to Santa's workshop at the North Pole. Clowns, magicians, and elves entertain the children in specially decorated gate areas. The children also receive goodies and presents to take home for the holidays. Many local companies and charitable organizations join in these festivities. United Airlines' strengths include the ability to allow employees to link the company's competencies to social causes of interest.[59]

BE&K, an international construction and engineering firm headquartered in Birmingham, Alabama, has mobilized its retirees for supporting special community service projects. Because these retirees have years of experience in the construction business, they are particularly suited for philanthropic efforts that involve renovation, design, and related skills. For example, one retired employee heads a YWCA effort to renovate housing for disabled and low-income women.[60] BE&K has also extended its employee safety and drug abuse programs into the philanthropic realm. These programs were originally designed to assist employees, reduce accidents, and help the business perform more effectively. After taking this experience and program to others in the industry and beyond, the company received the FBI Director's Community Leadership Award for outstanding contributions to the community in the prevention of drug abuse.[61]

Customers

As industries become increasingly competitive, companies are seeking ways to differentiate themselves in customers' minds. Home Depot, for example, has been progressive in the way it approaches philanthropy. The company has aligned its expertise and resources to address community needs. Its relationship with Habitat for Humanity gives employees a chance to improve their skills and bring direct knowledge back into the workplace to benefit customers. It also enhances Home Depot's image of expertise as the do-it-yourself center. Home Depot is also investing $57 million to support rebuilding efforts throughout the Gulf region as a result of numerous natural disasters. Combining capital construction with philanthropic support, this investment will create jobs, drive economic activity, and support local community efforts to rebuild homes.[62]

Bankers Trust Private Bank, part of German-headquartered Deutsche Bank AG, introduced its Wealth with Responsibility program to assist wealthy families in planning for philanthropy. In addition to financial experts, the bank employs consultants and advisors who help families set goals, invest for future wealth, and provide funds to charities and other groups. Thus, the bank is providing services that not only benefit wealthy clients but also direct assets into philanthropic directions to benefit society. The program targets clients around the world, with a focus on Europeans who are just beginning to become interested in philanthropy.[63]

The Verizon Reads program is multifaceted to affect the largest number of stakeholders. With an estimated 40 million U.S. citizens classified as illiterate, Verizon feels it can influence customers' quality of life with such broad-based initiatives, most of which are chronicled on www.verizonreads.net. Employees are encouraged to volunteer in education-related programs and to take part in initiatives that will strengthen their own literacy and technology use.[64] Target is another firm that contributes significant resources to education, including direct donations of $170 million to schools as well as fundraising and scholarship programs to assist teachers and students. Through the retailer's Take Charge of Education program, customers using a Target Guest Card can designate a specific school to which Target donates 1 percent of that customer's total purchases. This program is designed to make customers feel that their purchases are benefiting their community while increasing the use of Target Guest Cards.[65]

Business Partners

More companies are using philanthropic goals and social concerns as a measure of those with whom they would like to do business. Companies are increasingly requiring social audits and the adoption of industry codes of ethics on the part of their business partners. The Freeplay Group, based in South Africa, is an example of a company founded on the principle of "making money and making a difference." The company manufactures and markets wind-up radios that were originally intended for use in poor nations where electricity and batteries are scarce. For example, these radios have been used to transmit elementary school lessons in South Africa and election results in Ghana. The radios now sell in many countries at retailers such as Sharper Image, Radio Shack, and Harrod's. Rotary International and other community organizations are using the radios to implement programs that benefit society and communities. Freeplay's investors include the General Electric Pension Trust and Liberty Life, a South African insurance firm. These investors and customers have chosen Freeplay for its solid business plan founded on broader social goals.[66]

BJC Health System is working with other area health-care systems to make health insurance available to St. Louis, Missouri, residents who cannot afford it. BJC manages Care Partners and ConnectCare. Care Partners offers twenty-four-hour emergency care and primary-care facilities to anyone in need, whether they are insured or not. ConnectCare was launched by city officials and community leaders with the same goal of providing health services to all citizens. BJC has won praise for its ability to work with insurers, other systems, and the public in supporting health insurance initiatives with the collective goal of improving people's lives. These collaborative ventures allocate the costs of caring for indigent and uninsured patients across the community, a strategy that benefits all hospitals and care providers representing suppliers and business partners' best interests.[67]

Community and Society

Society expects businesses to be socially responsible and to contribute to the well-being of the communities in which they operate. The Coca-Cola Company takes a strategic view of its role in society by linking its company resources and operating practices to stakeholder issues. Although it acknowledges the profusion of problems in today's world, Coca-Cola has chosen to focus its energies and resources on environmental issues where the company has an impact and relevant expertise. Water quality, water conservation, and waste reduction are therefore key considerations in its packaging and operational decisions.[68] Coca-Cola has also contributed funds and expertise around the world to support collaborations that respond to these environmental concerns. These projects involve bottlers, employees, suppliers, regulators, customers, and other corporations interested in building strategies for environmental excellence.

Merck developed a drug to combat river blindness, a disease afflicting more than 18 million people worldwide. Merck's expertise as a pharmaceutical laboratory allowed it to develop Mectizan to treat river blindness, and its humanitarian orientation led it to donate the drug to nearly 25 million people at risk in ten African countries. Jimmy Carter, former U.S. president and cofounder of the Carter Center, notes, "I think Merck has set a standard of the highest possible quality. [The Mectizan Donation Program has] been one of the most remarkable and exciting and inspiring partnerships that I have ever witnessed."[69] The decision to develop and donate the drug to heavily afflicted areas demonstrates Merck's understanding of strategic philanthropy and the positive effects on society, as well as on employees, investors, and even customers.

LensCrafters has pledged to give 3 million pairs of glasses to the needy. Not wanting the firm's motives questioned, the CEO directed employees not to seek publicity. He states, "I do not want anyone thinking the company is doing this for any reason other than it's the right thing to do." Employees can engage in other philanthropy,

Trabajo Voluntario is a social entrepreneurship venture in Peru that links citizens with volunteer activities, such as this event for children. Copyright © 2006 by Trabajo Voluntario. Reprinted with permission.

Global Social Entrepreneurs

Many companies worldwide have become increasingly concerned with the society and communities in which they operate. This new breed of business is concerned about bettering the lives of the surrounding community while providing a profitable good or service at the same time. This new type of business is called *social entrepreneurship*. Leaders in organizations from the United States to Egypt are becoming social entrepreneurs.

Social entrepreneurs typically follow a four-stage process. In the first stage of envisioning, a clear need, gap, and opportunity are identified. The second stage is engaging in the opportunity and doing something about it. Enabling something to happen is the third stage. The final stage is enacting and leading the project to completion.

The Institute of OneWorld Health, based in San Francisco, has been a leader in social entrepreneurship. OneWorld's focus is on creating medicines to cure diseases that affect Third World countries. The nonprofit organization is currently working on creating a cure for VL. VL is known as the black fever and is carried by sand flies. Over 1.5 million people are infected with the black fever worldwide. It is estimated that 200,000 people die of VL annually, and about 500,000 new

cases are discovered each year. The black fever has a devastating effect in Third World countries.

The efforts of OneWorld have not gone unnoticed. The institute has received a $10 million grant from the Bill and Melinda Gates Foundation to help continue its fight against diseases. The Institute of OneWorld also received the 2005 Skoll Award for Social Entrepreneurship. The award comes with a $615,000 donation over the next few years. The Skoll Foundation awards funds to several organizations yearly that are leaders in social entrepreneurship.

The nonprofit status offers many advantages to OneWorld. Most of its funding comes from the government or philanthropic organizations. Biotech companies have gained a channel for intellectual property that might normally have gone unused because of lack of profit potential. Many members of the scientific community donated time and effort to help fight disease in Third World countries.

Social entrepreneurs are present all over the world. Take, for example, Sekem, located just north of Cairo, Egypt. Sekem was founded in 1977 by Dr. Ibrahim Abouleish. Since 1977, the organization has grown from one person to several business firms. Sekem produces several organic products on its

but this effort makes more sense because it leverages LensCrafters' eye-care provision skills and competencies.[70]

Finally, groups of companies and industry associations are also working to extend the philanthropic efforts of their member companies. For example, the American Apparel and Footwear Association assists manufacturers in donating surplus apparel to the needy, homeless, and disaster victims.[71] By working with their trade association, apparel manufacturers have been able to benefit from strategic philanthropy.

NATURAL ENVIRONMENT As we will see in Chapter 10, environmental causes have become increasingly important to stakeholders in recent years. Environmental abuses have damaged company and industry reputations and resulted in lost sales. 3M is one company that has been very aggressive in implementing environmentally friendly processes and procedures throughout its operations. This commitment extends to employees, as the company provides van transportation to work for employees within a fifteen-mile radius of the corporate office. If a van has only a few riders, farms. The company focuses on these long-term objectives.

- We endeavor to build our economic, social and cultural activities so that they invigorate each other.

- We wish to build a long-term, trusting and fair relationship with our partners.

- We nurture the development of all co-workers by facilitating the possibility to learn through their work, to commit themselves to their task and to practice agriculture.

- We intend to restore the earth through implementing and developing biodynamic agriculture.

- We want to provide various products and services of the highest standards to meet the needs of the consumer.

- We educate and train children and youth according to contemporary human sciences.

- We provide Primary Health Care and therapy using holistic medicine.

- We strive through our research to meet the questions of all aspects of life for the present age.

Sekem developed an alternative method for using pesticides to protect cotton crops. This new system led to a ban on crop dusting in Egypt. In 2003, Sekem received the Right Livelihood Award. The award is given by the Swedish Parliament for advancing social and cultural developments. This award is known as the "Alternative Nobel Prize." The award recipient also receives $230,000 to help further social responsibility.

Sekem has also opened a school for holistic education. The profits earned by Sekem helped fund medical centers and education for both children and adults. They are committed to helping the community break away from the poverty that has taken control of their lives. Sekem is continually expanding operations to help the community achieve a higher quality of life.

Sources: Anonymous, "Two Awards for the Institute of OneWorld Health," *Appropriate Technology,* June 2005, p. 26; Christian Seelos and Johanna Mair, "Social Entrepreneurship," *Business Horizons* 48, no. 3 (May–June 2005): 241–246; http://www.sekem.com/objectives.html; http://www.skollfoundation.org/aboutsocialentrepreneurship/index.asp; John L. Thompson, "The World of the Social Entrepreneur," *The International Journal of Public Sector Management* 15 (2002): 412–432. ∎

each rider pays a minimal monthly fee to help offset some of the costs of the program. If the number of employees using the program increases to a specified level, 3M drops the monthly fee. The van-pooling initiative has minimized pollution levels.[72] 3M is able to coordinate its commitment to various stakeholders, including employees, customers, the natural environment, and the community. For this reason, 3M recently ranked second among the top fifty chemical manufacturers and users in the world for environmental performance.[73] The company also scores very highly on *Fortune* magazine's annual Most Admired Companies list.

BENEFITS OF STRATEGIC PHILANTHROPY

To pursue strategic philanthropy successfully, organizations must weigh both the costs and benefits associated with planning and implementing it as a corporate priority. Companies that assume a strategic approach to philanthropy are using an investment model with respect to their charitable acts and donations. In other words, these

Guests enjoy dinner and entertainment at the charity gala benefiting Sidaction, a nonprofit organization based in France that raises money and awareness for AIDS projects around the world.

firms are not just writing checks; they are investing in solutions to stakeholder problems and corporate needs. Such an investment requires the commitment of company time, money, and human talent to succeed. Companies often need to hire staff to manage projects, communicate goals and opportunities throughout the firm, develop long-term priorities and programs, handle requests for funds, and represent the firm on other aspects of philanthropy. In addition, philanthropy consumes the time and energy of all types of employees within the organization. Thus, strategic philanthropy involves real corporate costs that must be justified and managed.

Most scholars and practitioners agree that the benefits of strategic philanthropy ultimately outweigh its costs. The positive return on strategic philanthropy is closely aligned with benefits obtained from strong social responsibility. First, in the United States, businesses can declare up to 10 percent of pretax profits as tax-deductible contributions. Most firms do not take full advantage of this benefit, as 10 percent is viewed as a very generous contribution level. In fact, corporate giving has averaged just over 1 percent of pretax profits in the last several decades. Second, companies with a strategic approach to philanthropy experience rewards in the workplace. Employees involved in volunteer projects and related ventures not only have the opportunity to refine their professional skills, but they also develop a stronger sense of loyalty and commitment to their employer. A national survey of employees demonstrated that corporate philanthropy is an important driver in employee relations. Those who perceive their employer as strong in philanthropy were four times more likely to be very loyal than those who believed their employer was less philanthropic. Employees in firms with favorable ratings on philanthropy are also more likely to recommend the company and its products to others and have intentions to stay with the employer. Positive impressions of the executives' role in corporate philanthropy also influenced employees' affirmative attitudes toward their employer.[74] Results such as these lead to improved productivity, enhanced employee recruitment results, and reduced employee turnover, each contributing to the overall effectiveness and efficiency of the company.

As a third benefit, companies should experience enhanced customer loyalty as a result of their strategic philanthropy. By choosing projects and causes with links to its core business, a firm can create synergies with its core competencies and customers. For example, Rosie O'Donnell used her celebrity status and television talk show to establish the For All Kids Foundation to support the social and cultural development of disadvantaged children. The foundation has been funded by a number of creative projects, including *Kids Are Punny,* a compilation of riddles, puns, and drawings sent by kids to the *Rosie O'Donnell Show.* Warner Books, the publisher, agreed to contribute its net profits to the foundation. Warner-Lambert, the manufacturer of Listerine Antiseptic mouthwash, donated $500,000 for kisses ($1,000 a kiss) Rosie received from guests on her show. In addition to grants from corporations, the foundation is also funded through celebrity charity auctions on eBay.[75] To the benefit of Warner Brothers studio and production, these creative projects not only support hundreds of children's causes and charities but also earned the show critical praise and customer loyalty. Because a majority of Rosie O'Donnell's viewers are women with children, her For All Kids Foundation was a natural and strategic vehicle.

Finally, strategic philanthropy should improve a company's overall reputation in the community and ease government and community relations. Research indicates a strong negative relationship between illegal activity and reputation, whereas firms that contribute to charitable causes enjoy enhanced reputations. Moreover, companies that contribute to social causes, especially to solve problems that arise as a result of their actions, may be able to improve their reputations after committing a crime.[76] A business engaged in a strategic approach to contributions, volunteerism, and related activities, demonstrates a clear intention to enhance and benefit the community. By properly implementing and communicating these achievements, the company will "do well by doing good." Essentially, community members and others use cues from a strategic philanthropy initiative, along with other social responsibility programs, to form a lasting impression—or reputation—of the firm. These benefits, together with others discussed in this section, are consistent with research conducted on European firms. Table 9.6 highlights the perceived benefits of corporate philanthropy to companies located in France, Germany, and the United Kingdom. The table suggests that companies in these countries believe that their charitable activities generally have a positive effect on goodwill, public relations, community relations, employee motivation, and customer loyalty.[77]

TABLE 9.6	Benefits of Socially Responsible Corporate Philanthropy

- advancing financial performance
- boosting employee motivation
- increasing customer loyalty
- enhancing corporate image and reputation
- reducing investor/executive conflicts
- improving stakeholder relationship overall

Source: *Insight Business* published by USC's Center for Management Communication, www.marshallinsight.com
© copyright 2006 by USC Marshall School of Business. All Rights Reserved.

IMPLEMENTATION OF STRATEGIC PHILANTHROPY

To be fully effective in attaining the benefits of strategic philanthropy, a company must integrate corporate competencies, business stakeholders, and social responsibility objectives. However, fruitfully implementing a strategic philanthropy approach is not simple and requires organizational resources and strategic attention. In this section, we examine some of the key factors associated with implementing strategic philanthropy.

Although some organizations and leaders see beyond economic concerns, other firms are far less progressive and collaborative in nature. To the extent that corporate leaders and others advocate for strategic philanthropy, planning and evaluation practices must be developed just as with any other business process. Almost all effective actions taken by a company come from well-thought-out business plans. However, although most large organizations have solid plans for philanthropy and other community involvement, these activities typically do not receive the same attention that other business endeavors garner. A study by the American Productivity and Quality Center found that many organizations are not yet taking a systematic or comprehensive approach in evaluating the impact of philanthropy on the business and other stakeholders.[78]

Top Management Support

The implementation of strategic philanthropy is impossible without the endorsement and support of the chief executive officer and other members of top management. Although most executives care about their communities and social issues, there may be debate or confusion over how their firms should meet stakeholder concerns and social responsibility. When Al Dunlap became CEO of Sunbeam, for example, he eliminated the company's annual giving program of $1 million. He was very clear that he felt Sunbeam's primary responsibility was to shareholders, noting that the company was giving to society by making money for shareholders.[79] Bernie Ebbers, former CEO of WorldCom, engaged in a much more minor cost-cutting tactic by eliminating free coffee for his employees. In contrast, Robert Allen, chair of the board for AT&T, observed that although some corporations are solely motivated by financial returns, he is confident that "the men and women who guide AT&T firmly believe that our business has the responsibility to contribute to the long-term well-being of the society."[80]

Top managers often have unique concerns with respect to strategic philanthropy. For example, chief executive officers may worry about having to defend the company's commitment to charity. Some investors may see these contributions as damaging to their portfolios. A related concern involves the resources required to manage a philanthropy effort. Top managers must be well versed in the performance benefits of social responsibility that we discussed in Chapter 1. Additionally, some executives may believe that less philanthropic-minded competitors have a profit advantage. If these competitors have any advantage at all, it is probably just a short-term situation. The tax benefits and other gains that philanthropy provides should prevail over the long run.[81] In today's environment, there are many positive incentives and reasons that strategic philanthropy and social responsibility make good business sense.

Planning and Evaluating Strategic Philanthropy

As with any initiative, strategic philanthropy must prove its relevance and importance. For philanthropy and other stakeholder collaborations to be fully diffused and accepted within the business community, a performance benefit must be evident. In addition, philanthropy should be treated as a corporate program that deserves the same professionalism and resources as other strategic initiatives. Thus, the process for planning and evaluating strategic philanthropy is integral to its success.

To make the best decisions when dealing with stakeholder concerns and issues, there should be a defensible, workable strategy to ensure that every donation is wisely spent. Author Curt Weeden, CEO of the Contributions Academy, has developed a multistep process for ensuring effective planning and implementation of strategic philanthropy.

1. **Research** If a company has too little or inaccurate information, it will suffer when making philanthropic decisions. Research should cover the internal organization and programs, organizations, sponsorship options, and events that might intersect with the interests and competencies of the corporation.

2. **Organize and Design** The information collected by research should be classified into relevant categories. For example, funding opportunities can be categorized according to the level of need and alignment with organizational competencies. The process of organizing and designing is probably the most crucial step in which management should be thoroughly involved.

3. **Engage** This step consists of engaging management early on so as to ease the approval process in the future. Top managers need to be co-owners of the corporate philanthropy plan. They will have interest in seeing the plan receive authorization, and they will enrich the program by sharing their ideas and thoughts.

Eddy Bayardelle, first vice president for global philanthropy at Merrill Lynch, stands in the "Merrill Lynch Field of Dreams." The company donated $500,000 to build the much-needed athletic facility.

4. **Spend** Deciding what resources and dollars should be spent where is a very important task. A skilled manager who has spent some time with the philanthropy program should preferably handle this. If the previous steps were handled appropriately, this step should go rather smoothly.[82]

Evaluating corporate philanthropy should begin with a clear understanding of how these efforts are linked to the company's vision, mission, and resources. As our definition suggests, philanthropy can only be strategic if it is fully aligned with the values, core competencies, and long-term plans of an organization. Thus, the development of philanthropic programs should be part of the strategic planning process.

Assuming that key stakeholders have been identified, organizations need to conduct research to understand stakeholder expectations and their willingness to collaborate for mutual benefit. Although many companies have invested time and resources to understand the needs of employees, customers, and investors, fewer have examined other stakeholders or the potential for aligning stakeholders and company resources for philanthropic reasons. Philanthropic efforts should be evaluated for their effects on and benefits to various constituents.[83] Although philanthropists have always been concerned with results, the aftermath of September 11 brought not only widespread contributions but also a heightened sensitivity to accountability. For example, the American Red Cross suffered intense scrutiny after its leaders initially decided to set aside a portion of donations received in response to the terrorist strikes. The rationale for setting aside $200 million was that a long-term program on terrorism response needed to be developed and funded. Other funds were earmarked for expansion, maintenance, and other purposes not directly related to September 11. Many donors rejected this plan, and the Red Cross reversed its decision. There were outright scams after the attacks, including people who, to collect money, claimed loved ones were killed in the World Trade Center entrepreneurs who sold patriotic items supposedly for charitable reasons, and fake charities for police and fire personnel. A survey in late 2002 indicated that 42 percent of Americans have less confidence in charities than they did before the September 11 attacks. Major philanthropists are also stepping up their expectations for accountability, widespread impact, strategic thinking, global implications, and results.[84] Figure 9.3 lists ten guidelines that potential donors should use in evaluating and choosing organizations with which to partner or provide funding.

Methods to evaluate strategic philanthropy should include an assessment of how these initiatives are communicated to stakeholders. Vancouver City Savings and Credit Union of Canada (VanCity) initiated the process of increasing its social accountability to its various stakeholders when its executives and board of directors recognized that VanCity's level of disclosure, not necessarily its social responsibility, was below that of many other financial institutions in Canada. By increasing its disclosure and reporting, VanCity improved awareness of its commitment to social responsibility and ultimately refined its corporate strategy to meet other stakeholder concerns.[85] Such reporting mechanisms not only improve stakeholder knowledge but also lead to improvements and refinements. Although critics may deride organizations for communicating their philanthropic efforts, the strategic philanthropy model is dependent on feedback and learning to create greater value for the organization and its stakeholders, as we shall see in the next chapter.

FIGURE 9.3	A Donor Bill of Rights

Philanthropy is based on voluntary action for the common good. It is a tradition of giving and sharing that is primary to the quality of life. To assure that philanthropy merits the respect and trust of the general public and that donors and prospective donors can have full confidence in the not-for-profit organizations and causes they are asked to support, we declare that all donors have these rights:

1. To be informed of the organization's mission, of the way the organization intends to use donated resources, and of its capacity to use donations effectively for their intended purposes

2. To be informed of the identity of those serving on the organization's governing board and to expect the board to exercise prudent judgment in its stewardship responsibilities

3. To have access to the organization's most recent financial statements

4. To be assured their gifts will be used for the purposes for which they were given

5. To receive appropriate acknowledgment and recognition

6. To be assured that information about their donations is handled with respect and with confidentiality to the extent provided by law

7. To expect that all relationships with individuals representing organizations of interest to the donor will be professional in nature

8. To be informed whether those seeking donations are volunteers, employees of the organization, or hired solicitors

9. To have the opportunity for their names to be deleted from mailing lists that an organization may intend to share

10. To feel free to ask questions when making a donation and to receive prompt, truthful, and forthright answers

The text of this statement in its entirety was developed by the American Association of Fundraising Counsel (AAFRC), Association for Healthcare Philanthropy (AHP), Council for Advancement and Support of Education (CASE), and the Association of Fundraising Professionals (AFP).

Source: American Association of Fundraising Counsel, "A Donor Bill of Rights," http://www.aafrc.org/choose_counsel/donor.html, accessed May 15, 2006. The Donor Bill of Rights is reprinted with permission of the Giving Institute: Leading Consultants to Non-Profits (formerly AAFRC), the Association for Healthcare Philanthropy (AHP), the Council for Advancement and Support of Education (CASE), and the Association of Fundraising Professionals (AFP), and endorsed by Independent Sector, National Catholic Development Conference (NCDC), National Committee on Planned Giving (NCPG), National Council for Resource Development (NCRD), and United Way of America.

SUMMARY

More firms are investigating ways to link their philanthropic efforts with consumer interests. From a strategic perspective, a firm's ability to link consumer interests to philanthropy should lead to stronger economic relationships. Community relations are the organizational functions dedicated to building and maintaining relationships and trust with the community. To determine the key areas that require support and to refine the mission statement, a company should periodically conduct a community needs assessment.

Companies play a major role in community economic development by bringing jobs to the community, interacting with other businesses, and making contributions to local health, education, and recreation projects that benefit residents and employees. When a company leaves an area, financial repercussions may be devastating.

Because they have such a profound impact on the economic viability of their communities, firms that value social responsibility consider both the short- and long-term effects of changes in their workforce on the community.

For many firms, a series of legal and regulatory matters must be resolved before launching a business. On a basic level, society has the ability to dictate what types of organizations are allowed to operate. As more companies view themselves as responsible to the community, they consider their role and the impact of their decisions on communities from an ethical perspective.

The success of a business can be enhanced by the publicity generated from and through stakeholder acceptance of community activities. One way that organizations are exercising their philanthropic responsibilities is through volunteerism, the donation of employee time by companies in support of social causes. In structuring volunteer programs, attention must be paid to employee values and beliefs.

Many companies are finding creative ways to satisfy their responsibilities to consumers and the community. These relationships must be managed, nurtured, and continuously assessed. Resources devoted to this effort may include programs for educating and listening to consumers, surveys to discover strengths and weaknesses in stakeholder relationships, hiring consumer affairs professionals, the development of a community relations office, and other initiatives.

Generally, philanthropy involves any acts of benevolence and goodwill. Strategic philanthropy is defined as the synergistic use of organizational core competencies and resources to address key stakeholders' interests and to achieve organizational and social benefits. Strategic philanthropy involves both financial and nonfinancial contributions to stakeholders, but it also benefits the company. As such, strategic philanthropy is part of a broader philosophy that recognizes how social responsibility can help an organization improve its overall performance. Research suggests that companies that adopt a more businesslike approach to philanthropy will experience a better image, increased employee loyalty, and improved customer ties.

Corporate giving, volunteer efforts, and other philanthropic activities should be considered and aligned with corporate strategy and financial, legal, and ethical obligations. The concept of strategic philanthropy has evolved since the middle of the twentieth century, when contributions were prohibited by law, to emerge as a management practice to support social responsibility in the 1990s. Whereas strategic philanthropy links corporate resources and knowledge to address broader social, customer, employee, and supplier problems and needs, cause-related marketing ties an organization's product(s) directly to a social concern. By linking products with charities and social causes, organizations acknowledge the opportunity to align philanthropy to economic goals and to recognize stakeholder interests in organizational benevolence.

Many organizations have skillfully used their resources and core competencies to address the needs of employees, customers, business partners, the community and society, and the natural environment. To pursue strategic philanthropy successfully, organizations must weigh the costs and benefits associated with planning and implementing it as a corporate priority. The benefits of strategic philanthropy are closely aligned with benefits obtained from social responsibility. Businesses that engage in strategic philanthropy often gain a tax advantage. Research suggests that they may also enjoy improved productivity, stronger employee commitment and morale, reduced turnover, and greater customer loyalty and satisfaction. In the future, many companies will devote more resources to understand how strategic philanthropy can be developed and integrated to support their core competencies.

The implementation of strategic philanthropy is impossible without the support of top management. To integrate strategic philanthropy into the organization successfully, the efforts must fit with the company's mission, values, and resources. Organizations must also understand stakeholder expectations and the propensity to support such activities for mutual benefit. This process relies on the feedback of stakeholders in improving and learning how to better integrate the strategic philanthropy objectives with other organizational goals. Finally, companies will need to evaluate philanthropic efforts and assess how these results should be communicated to stakeholders.

KEY TERMS

community (p. 280)
neighbor of choice (p. 280)
community relations (p. 282)
volunteerism (p. 289)
philanthropy (p. 290)
strategic philanthropy (p. 294)
cause-related marketing (p. 298)

DISCUSSION QUESTIONS

1. What are some of the issues you might include in a defense of strategic philanthropy to company stockholders?
2. Describe your personal experiences with philanthropy. In what types of activities have you participated? Which companies that you do business with have a philanthropic focus? How did this focus influence your decision to buy from those companies?
3. How have changes in the business environment contributed to the growing trend of strategic philanthropy?
4. Compare and contrast cause-related marketing with strategic philanthropy. What are the unique benefits of each approach?
5. What role does top management play in developing and implementing a strategic philanthropy approach?
6. Describe the four-stage process for planning and implementing strategic philanthropy.

EXPERIENTIAL EXERCISE

Choose one major corporation and investigate how closely its philanthropic efforts are strategically aligned with its core competencies. Visit the company's website, read its annual reports, and use other sources to justify your conclusions. Develop a chart or table to depict how the company's core competencies are linked to various philanthropic projects and stakeholder groups. Finally, provide an analysis of how these efforts have affected the company's performance.

WHAT WOULD YOU DO?

As a new vice president of corporate philanthropy, Jack Birke was looking forward to the great initiatives and partnerships the company could create through his office. During his eighteen-year career, Jack worked for several large nonprofit organizations and earned an excellent reputation for his ability to raise funds, develop advisory boards, and in general, work well with the business community.

About a year ago, Jack decided to investigate other opportunities within the fundraising industry and started looking at companies that were formalizing their philanthropy efforts. He was hired as vice president less than a month ago and was in the process of developing an office structure, getting to know the organization, and creating a strategic plan. His charge over the next year was to develop a stronger reputation for philanthropy and social responsibility with the company's stakeholders, including employees, customers, and the community. An executive assistant, director of volunteerism, and director of community relations were already on board, and Jack was looking for additional staff.

The position and office were new to the company, and Jack had already heard dissent from other employees, who openly questioned how important philanthropy was to the business. After all, the economy was slowing, and it seemed that customers were more concerned about price and value than any "touchy feely" program. About half of the company's employees worked on the manufacturing line, and the other half was employed in administrative or professional positions. Both groups seemed to be equally suspicious of Jack and his office. The company developed an employee volunteer program two years ago, but it was never very successful. A program to gather food, gifts, and money to support needy families at Christmas, however, drew strong support. The firm had fairly good relationships in the community, but these were primarily the top executives' connections through the chamber of commerce, industry associations, nonprofit boards, and so forth. In sum, while Jack had the support of top management, many employees were unsure about philanthropy and its importance to the company. Jack was starting to think about short-term policies and long-term strategy for "marketing" his office and goals to the rest of the organization. What would you do?

CHAPTER 10

Environmental Issues

CHAPTER OBJECTIVES

- To define the nature of the natural environment as it relates to social responsibility

- To explore a variety of environmental issues faced by business and society

- To examine the impact of environmental policy and regulations

- To discuss a strategic approach to respond to environmental issues

CHAPTER OUTLINE

Global Environmental Issues

Environmental Policy and Regulation

Business Response to Environmental Issues

Strategic Implementation of Environmental Responsibility

Many companies today face a dilemma: Should they invest resources in creating, supporting, and maintaining organizational initiatives that protect the natural environment? By striving to be one of the most environmentally conscious companies, Interface has answered that question with a resounding yes.

In the mid-1990s, Interface introduced a new fabric made from 100 percent waste and reclaimed wool. It's now the leading brand in the company's fabric division. During the same time frame, this leading manufacturer of carpet and textile products cut its greenhouse gas emissions by 52 percent. The company estimates that it has saved over $260 million from waste-reduction strategies, including its work with suppliers, customers, and others in Interface's supply chain. The company's chief purchasing executive is clear on the role of sustainability in evaluating and choosing suppliers: "At every meeting, we look at their performance on the environment. We motivate the suppliers and identify the mutual benefits of being 'green.'" Interface is now making use of the biobased polymer PLA (polylactic acid) in its manufacturing processes to become even more environmentally sustainable. The Atlanta, Georgia-based firm is also looking into composting its woven products at the end of their lives. Interface developed a program called ReSKU that recovers fabric waste. Its ReEntry program takes back postconsumer carpet, regardless of manufacturer, for recycling. As part of its initiatives to "close the loop completely," Interface is partnering with Herman Miller, Inc., an environmentally conscious furniture maker, to keep manufacturing scraps out of the landfill. The two companies are developing a method for composting fabric scraps, sawdust, and other leftovers from the carpet and furniture manufacturing processes.

Interface has been recognized for its environmental efforts and was recently awarded the Environmental Protection Agency's Green Power Leadership Award. In announcing the award, government officials noted: "Interface strives to reduce greenhouse gas emissions in its North American facilities to 15 percent below 2001 levels, per unit of production, by 2010. By 2020, the company wants to be powered 10 percent by renewable sources. Interface has also won EPA's Climate Protection and Environmental Merit Awards in 2004 and the Lone Star Award for Green Energy in 2003. Interface is a true leader in advancing corporate markets for renewable energy." Its Atlanta showroom was awarded with the first Platinum Award from the U.S. Green Building Council's Leadership in Energy & Environmental Design for Commercial Interiors. The showroom meets or exceeds criteria for site selection, water and energy efficiency, atmosphere, construction waste diversion from landfills, reuse of furniture and fixtures, and indoor environmental quality.

Not surprisingly, Interface's founder and Chairman of the Board Ray Anderson is an advocate for environmental responsibility both inside and outside the company. He wasn't always so focused, however. In 1994, an employee sent him a copy of Paul Hawken's classic book, *The Ecology of Commerce*. While reading the book, Anderson says, "A new definition of success burst into my consciousness, and the latent sense of legacy asserted itself. I got it. I was a plunderer of Earth, and *that* is not the legacy one wants to leave behind." Today, both Interface and Anderson are widely recognized for cutting-edge approaches to minimizing environmental impact while maximizing positive returns for a variety of stakeholders.[1] ■

As Interface's efforts illustrate, public and business support for environmental causes has increased since the first Earth Day was held in 1970. Four of five respondents in a Gallup poll reported that they agree with the goals of the environmental movement, and another 80 percent indicated that they have participated in environmentally conscious activities such as recycling, avoiding products that harm the environment, trying to use less water, and reducing household consumption of energy.[2] Another survey found that 83.5 percent of *Fortune* 500 respondents have a written environmental policy, 74.7 percent recycle, and 69.7 percent have made investments in waste-reduction efforts.[3]

In this chapter, we explore the concept of the natural environment in the context of social responsibility in today's complex business environment. First, we define the natural environment and explore some of the significant environmental issues that businesses and society face. Next, we consider the impact of government environmental policy and regulation on business and examine how some companies are going beyond the scope of these laws to address environmental issues and act in an environmentally responsible manner. Finally, we highlight a strategic approach to environmental issues, including risk management and strategic audits.

GLOBAL ENVIRONMENTAL ISSUES

Most people probably associate the term *environment* with nature, including wildlife, trees, oceans, rivers, mountains, and prairies. Until the twentieth century, people generally thought of the environment solely in terms of how these resources could be harnessed to satisfy their needs for food, shelter, transportation, and recreation. As Earth's population swelled throughout the twentieth century, however, humans began to use more and more of these resources and, with technological advancements, to do so with ever greater efficiency. Although these conditions have resulted in a much-improved standard of living, they come with a cost. Plant and animal species, along with wildlife habitats, are disappearing at an accelerated rate; water use has become a critical issue in some parts of the globe; and pollution has rendered the atmosphere of some cities a gloomy haze. How to deal with these issues has become a major concern for business and society in the twenty-first century.

Although the scope of the natural environment is quite broad—including plants, animals, human beings, oceans and other waterways, land, and the atmosphere—in this book, we discuss the term from a strategic business perspective. Thus, we define the **natural environment** as the physical world, including all biological entities, as well as the interaction among nature and individuals, organizations, and business strategies. In recent years, business has played a significant role in adapting, using, and maintaining the quality of the natural environment.

natural environment
the physical world, including all biological entities, as well as the interaction among nature and individuals, organizations, and business strategies

The protection of air, water, land, biodiversity, and renewable natural resources emerged as a major issue in the twentieth century in the face of increasing evidence that pollution, uncontrolled use of natural resources, and population growth were putting increasing pressure on the long-term sustainability of these resources. As the environmental movement sounded the alarm over these issues, governments around the globe responded with environmental protection laws during the 1970s. In recent years, companies have been increasingly incorporating these issues into their overall business strategies. Most of these issues have been the focus of concerned citizens as well as government and corporate efforts. Some nonprofit organizations have stepped forward to provide leadership in gaining the cooperation of diverse groups in responsible environmental activities. For example, the Coalition for Environmentally Responsible

CERES, the Coalition for Environmentally Responsible Economies, has established goals and processes for businesses to achieve global environment standards. Copyright © 2006 Ceres. Reprinted with permission.

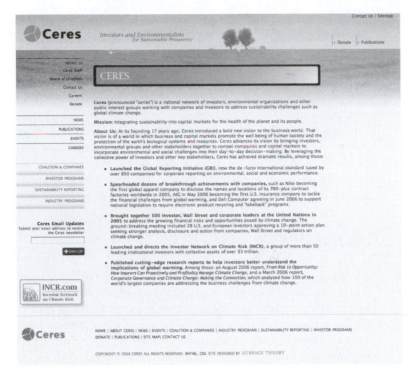

Economies (CERES), a union of businesses, consumer groups, environmentalists, and other stakeholders, has established a set of goals for environmental performance.

In this section, we examine some of the most significant environmental issues facing business and society today, including air pollution, acid rain, global warming, water pollution and water quantity, land pollution, waste management, deforestation, urban sprawl, biodiversity, and genetically modified foods.

Atmospheric Issues

Among the most far-reaching and controversial environmental issues are those that relate to the air we breathe. These include air pollution, acid rain, and global warming.

AIR POLLUTION Air pollution typically arises from three different sources: stationary sources such as factories and power plants; mobile sources such as cars, trucks, planes, and trains; and natural sources such as windblown dust and volcanic eruptions.[4] These sources discharge gases, as well as particulates, that can be carried long distances by surface winds or linger on the surface for days if lack of winds or geographical conditions permit. Mexico City, for example, is surrounded by mountains, which trap the emissions from automobiles and industry and leave that city with the poorest air quality in the world. Such conditions can cause respiratory problems (e.g., asthma, bronchitis, and allergies) in humans and animals, especially in the elderly and the very young. Some of the chemicals associated with air pollution may contribute to birth defects, cancer, and brain, nerve, and respiratory system damage. Air pollution can also harm plants, animals, and water bodies. Haze caused by air pollution can reduce visibility, interfering with aviation, driving, and recreation.[5]

ACID RAIN In addition to the health risks posed by air pollution, when nitrous oxides and sulfur dioxides emitted from manufacturing facilities react with air and rain, the result is acid rain. This phenomenon has contributed to the deaths of many valuable forests and lakes in North America as well as in Europe. Acid rain can also corrode paint and deteriorate stone, leaving automobiles, buildings, and cultural resources such as architecture and outside art vulnerable unless they are protected from its effects.[6]

GLOBAL WARMING When carbon dioxide and other gases collect in Earth's atmosphere, they trap the sun's heat like a greenhouse and prevent Earth's surface from cooling. Without this process, the planet would become too cold to sustain life. However, during the twentieth century, the burning of fossil fuels—gasoline, natural gas, oil, and coal—accelerated dramatically, increasing the concentration of "greenhouse" gases like carbon dioxide and methane in Earth's atmosphere. Chlorofluorocarbons—from refrigerants, coolants, and aerosol cans—also harm Earth's ozone layer, which filters out the sun's harmful ultraviolet light. The United States produces over 20 percent of all the greenhouse gases emitted (see Figure 10.1).[7] The United States plans to reduce greenhouse gases through incentives to businesses over the next ten years.

| **FIGURE 10.1** | Leading Emitters of Greenhouse Gases (by 1,000 million tons) |

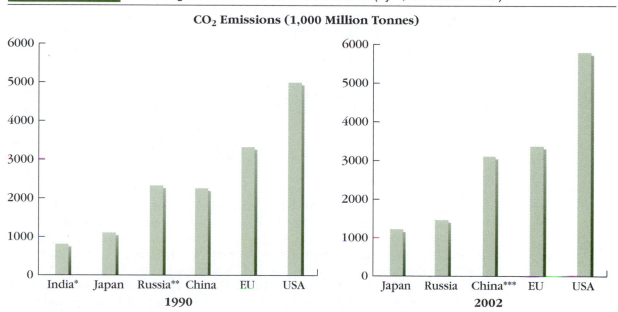

CO_2 Emissions (1,000 Million Tonnes)

*1994, **1999, ***2001

Note: Both China figures include Hong Kong

Source data from: BBC News, "Climate Change: The Big Emitters," http://news.bbc.co.uk/1/hi/sci/tech/3143798.stm, accessed June 10, 2006.

Within the plan, the government hopes to set mandatory targets to reduce power plant emissions by 70 percent by the year 2018.[8]

Many scientists believe that increasing concentrations of greenhouse gases like methane and carbon dioxide in the atmosphere are warming the planet. In fact, accumulations of greenhouse gases have increased dramatically since preindustrial times.[9] However, a new study conducted and funded by NASA says the growth of so-called greenhouse gas emissions in the atmosphere continues, but the growth rate peaked in 1980 and has slowed ever since.[10] The year 1995—with many cities breaking records for the longest period without rain since the Dust Bowl of the 1930s and for the highest number of days over 100°F—was the hottest year on record. The second hottest year on record was 2005, and 2003 was recorded as the third hottest around the world. In 2003, however, Europe was hotter than it had been in 500 years. The accumulation of gases does appear to have increased average temperatures by an estimated 1°F over the last century. Although 1° doesn't sound like much of a change, it is sufficient to increase the rate of polar ice sheet melting, which has already started to occur. Additionally, larger than normal icebergs are breaking away from the Antarctic ice shelf and drifting into shipping lanes. If this global warming continues, scientists warn that the planet's polar icecaps will begin to melt, potentially raising the sea level and perhaps flooding some of the world's most populated areas. With less snow and ice cover to reflect the sun's rays, Earth absorbs even more of the sun's heat, accelerating the warming process. Some scientists also think that global warming may alter long-term weather patterns, causing drought in some parts of the world while bringing floods to others. The 2005 hurricane season was especially devastating in the United States, which some researchers linked to the effects of global warming.[11]

The theory of global warming has been rather controversial, and some scientists continue to dispute its existence. Critics of global warming argue that apparent temperature increases are part of a natural cycle of temperature variation that the planet has experienced over millions of years. Many companies and organizations have also maligned the theory. Indeed, one of the most aggressive critics has been the Global Climate Coalition, an alliance of electric utilities, coal and oil companies, petrochemical manufacturers, automakers, and related trade associations. The coalition has sponsored scientific research, public speaking tours, and advertising campaigns in an effort to thwart the **Kyoto Protocol,** a treaty among industrialized nations to slow global warming. In the face of mounting evidence in support of global warming, however, many corporations have failed to support the initiative in recent years, including BP Amoco, Royal Dutch/Shell, Dow Chemical, Ford, DaimlerChrysler, and Texaco.[12] The Kyoto Protocol continues to be a controversial and contentious issue in global politics. The United States balked at signing the treaty, which would require slashing its level of greenhouse gas emissions to 6 percent that of 1990 by 2012, because leaders fear that compliance would jeopardize U.S. businesses and the economy.[13] After the European Union, Argentina, Mexico, Russia, Israel, and many other countries ratified the agreement, however, there was enough international support to put the treaty into effect on February 16, 2005. By 2006, the number of signatories topped 150, but both the governments of the United States and Australia had no intention of ratifying the agreement. In 2002, Canada ratified the agreement, but by 2006, it was clear that

Kyoto Protocol
a treaty among industrialized nations to slow global warming

TABLE 10.1	Elements of the U.S. Global Climate Change Initiative

- Enhancement of the 1605(b) Voluntary Reporting of Greenhouse Gases Program

- Significantly expanded funding for basic scientific research and advanced technology development

- Tax incentives, such as credits for renewable energy, cogeneration, and new technology

- Challenges for business to undertake voluntary initiatives and commit to greenhouse gas intensity goals, such as through recent agreements with the semiconductor and aluminum industries

- Transportation programs, including technology research and development and fuel economy standards

- Carbon sequestration programs, which include increased funding for U.S. Department of Agriculture conservation programs under the Farm Bill

- Investments in climate observation systems in developing countries

- Funding for "debt-for-nature" forest conservation programs

- Use of economic incentives to encourage developing countries to participate in climate change initiatives

- Expanding technology transfer and capacity building in the developing world

- Joint research with Japan, Italy, and Central America

Source: Energy Information Administration, U.S. Department of Energy, "Voluntary Reporting of Greenhouse Gases 2004—Summary," http://www.eia.doe.gov/oiaf/1605/vrrpt/summary/special_topic.html, accessed June 20, 2006.

the Canadian government was withdrawing from the protocol. For this reason and others, experts suggest that global leaders are moving away from the Kyoto Protocol toward environmental solutions based on scientific evidence and market factors.[14]

Although President George W. Bush did not sign the treaty, many U.S. businesses are committing to self-regulatory standards with respect to global warming and related areas. Table 10.1 describes many facets of the self-regulatory and voluntary program that the U.S. created instead of signing the Kyoto Protocol. These standards have been successful, so far, in suppressing the escalation of greenhouse gas emissions. For example, the U.S. Environmental Protection Agency (EPA) reports that in the United States, greenhouse gas emissions have increased only 1.3 percent since 2000, which is much lower than rates experienced in Canada and Greece. Other countries are also creating self-regulatory programs. Japan, China, India, and South Korea formed the Asia-Pacific Partnership on Clean Development and Climate, which includes voluntary standards and a focus on creating technologies that reduce emissions without harming the economy.[15] PricewaterhouseCoopers, a global consulting firm, recommends that companies incorporate legal, environmental, and financial expertise in decision making about environmental strategy. There is an emphasis on stakeholder management and communication. Figure 10.2 depicts the process of embedding a climate change strategy into a utility company, although many aspects of the process would be similar in other industries.[16]

Water Issues

WATER POLLUTION Water pollution results from the dumping of raw sewage and toxic chemicals into rivers and oceans, from oil and gasoline spills, and from the burial of industrial wastes in the ground where they may filter into underground water supplies. Fertilizers and pesticides used in farming and grounds maintenance also drain into water supplies with each rainfall. When these chemicals reach the oceans,

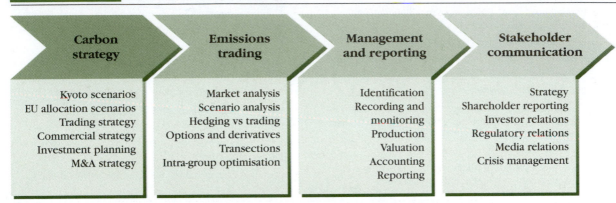

they encourage the growth of algae that use up all the nearby oxygen, thus killing the sea life. According to the Environmental Protection Agency (EPA), more than a third of the nation's rivers, lakes, and coastal waters are not safe for swimming or fishing as a result of contaminated runoff. Lake Champlain and the Great Lakes, for example, have been polluted by mercury-contaminated rain caused by air pollution from coal-burning power plants, making the waters' fish unsafe to eat.[17] Water pollution problems are especially notable in heavily industrialized areas.

Water pollution can affect drinking water quality, whether a community obtains its water from surface reservoirs (rivers and lakes) or underground aquifers. In central Texas, for example, local citizens concerned about gasoline leaks contaminating drinking water supplies have vehemently protested a project to refit a fifty-year-old pipeline to carry gasoline across the state directly over one major aquifer. One of five drinking water systems in the United States is in violation of federal safety standards, and nearly 1 million Americans get sick every year because of contaminated water, according to a report by the EPA.[18] There are 218 million Americans living within ten miles of a polluted lake, river, stream, or coastal area, and over one-third of the nation's assessed waters are still unsafe for fishing, swimming, or supporting aquatic life.[19] One source of water contamination may be somewhat surprising. Researchers have found traces of antibiotics and other pharmaceuticals in streams, rivers, and municipal water supplies in the United States and Europe. Scientists worry that the presence of antibiotics in water supplies may encourage the development of "superbugs," infection-causing bacteria that are immune to currently available antibiotics.[20] The EPA stated that millions of pounds of antibiotics and steroids used by U.S. agriculture are seeping into waterways, their effects still unknown. Animal-feeding operations are a significant part of the water pollution caused by U.S. agriculture, the leading source of pollution of the nation's lakes and rivers. Across the Great Plains, many communities are fighting increasingly vast animal-feeding operations. Some worry about the health effects from breathing the dust and gases produced by animal waste and from being exposed to chemicals that might get into the water or air.[21]

A dog drinks polluted water from a dried canal connected to the river Buriganga in Bangladesh.

Mark Van Putten, president of the National Wildlife Federation, believes that many states are ignoring federal legislation and regulations that would improve water quality. Many states have not aggressively enforced federal requirements, and many sources of pollution—agribusiness, logging, and power plants—often have strong political power to resist efforts to regulate their operations in ways that would reduce discharges that contaminate water supplies.[22] Special interests make it even more difficult to regulate water pollution in other parts of the world. Tougher regulations are needed globally to address pollution from activities such as dumping wastes into the ocean, large animal-feeding operations, logging sites, public roads, parking lots, and industrial waste created by production operations. The Sierra Club noted that 2002 marked the twenty-fifth anniversary of the Clean Water Act, one of the most successful environmental laws in our nation's history. Since the act was passed, nearly two-thirds of our lakes and rivers have become safe for swimming compared to just 36 percent in 1970. However, members of the Sierra Club believe that the United States has not yet achieved the act's goal to make all waters safe for fishing and swimming; nor have we eliminated the discharge of all pollutants into the nation's lakes, rivers, and coastal waters.[23]

WATER QUANTITY In addition to concerns about the quality of water, some parts of the globe are increasingly worried about its quantity. There has been a sixfold increase in water use worldwide since 1990, and as a result, one-fifth of the world's population now has no access to safe drinking water. Since 1960, irrigation has jumped by 60 percent, with serious consequences for the global water supply. After several years of scorching summer months and below-average precipitation across most of the nation, as much as 49 percent of the United States is in the grips of a drought, according to the National Climatic Data Center. By summer 2003, long-term moisture deficits persisted, especially in western states and parts of the Great Lakes to northeast regions. These conditions put added pressure on facility managers to conserve water. The world's supply of accessible fresh water is decreasing drastically, in no small part because of U.S. consumption. The average American uses 86.2 gallons of fresh water per day—40 percent of which is flushed down toilets. New low-consumption toilets have proved they can assist in reducing water use.[24]

In other areas, poor weather conditions in conjunction with growing demand for water by booming populations have outpaced nature's ability to replenish surface and underground water sources, especially during periods of prolonged drought. A severe drought hit Colorado, Texas, New Mexico, and Mexico, but increased snow and rain the following year provided some replenishment of the water supply. Nearly 500 emergency drilling permits were issued for farms and residences where groundwater wells, some 150 years old, went dry.[25] Concerns about water quantity have led to intense political and legal wrangling in a number of states. Indeed, Mark Twain (Samuel Clemens) once said, "Whiskey is for drinking, water is for fighting over."

Land Issues

LAND POLLUTION Land pollution results from the dumping of residential and industrial wastes, strip mining, and poor forest conservation. Such pollution jeopardizes wildlife habitats, causes erosion, alters watercourses (leading to flooding), poisons groundwater supplies, and can contribute to illnesses in humans and animals. For example, the dumping of toxic industrial wastes into Love Canal, near Niagara Falls, New York, caused residents who moved to the area years later to experience high rates of birth defects and cancer.

WASTE MANAGEMENT Another aspect of the land pollution problem is the issue of how to dispose of waste in an environmentally responsible manner. Consumers contribute an average of 1,500 pounds of garbage per person each year to landfills, and landfill space is declining. Within a few years, 70 percent of the nation's landfills will be full. Also compounding the waste-disposal problem is the fact that more than 50 percent of all garbage is made out of plastic, most of which does not decompose. Some communities have passed laws that prohibit the use of plastics such as Styrofoam for this reason.

DEFORESTATION With a global population that exceeds 6.45 billion, human beings are squeezing other life from the planet. In Brazil and other South American countries, rain forests are being destroyed—at a rate of one acre per minute—to make way for farms and ranches, at a cost of the extinction of the many plants and animals (including some endangered species) that call the rain forest home. Nearly 60 percent of the world's rain forests have been lost to agricultural or timber interests.[26] Many of Africa's tropical forests and jungles are threatened by deforestation and development by humans. Large-scale deforestation also depletes the oxygen supply available to humans and other animals. Deforestation may also contribute to flooding when it destroys erosion-controlling plants. The causes of deforestation are very complex. A competitive global

FIGURE 10.3   Deforestation of the United States

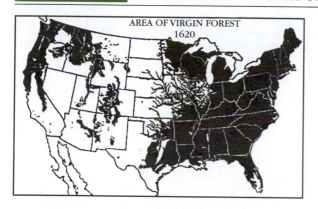

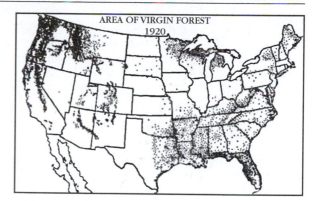

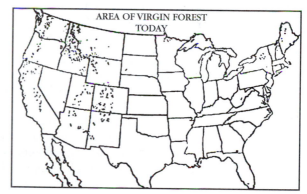

Source: Deforestation, http://en.wikipedia.org/wiki/Deforestation, accessed June 21, 2006. Compiled by George Draffan from roadless area map in *The Big Outside: A Descriptive Inventory of the Big Wilderness Areas of the United States,* by Dave Foreman and Howie Wolke (Harmony Books, 1992).

economy drives the need for money in economically challenged tropical countries. At the national level, governments sell logging concessions to raise money for projects, to pay international debt, or to develop industry. For example, Brazil has billions of dollars in international debt on which it must make payments each year. The logging companies seek to harvest the forest and profit from the sales of pulp and valuable hardwoods such as mahogany. Figure 10.3 includes forestation maps of the United States in 1620, 1850, 1920, and present. The shaded areas represent forest, so it is easy to see that most of the virgin forest in the United States has disappeared over the last four centuries.[27]

URBAN SPRAWL One cause of deforestation in the United States is urban sprawl. Author James Howard Kunstler has defined urban sprawl as "a degenerate urban form that is too congested to be efficient, too chaotic to be beautiful, and too dispersed to possess the diversity and vitality of a great city."[28] Urban sprawl began with the post–World War II building boom that transformed the nation from primarily low-density communities designed to accommodate one-car households, bicyclists, and pedestrians to large-scale suburban developments at the edges of established towns and

TABLE 10.2	U.S. Cities Threatened by Urban and Suburban Sprawl

Large Cities (Population One Million or More)	Medium Cities (Population 500,000 to One Million)	Small Cities (Population 200,000–500,000)
1. Atlanta, GA	1. Orlando, FL	1. McAllen, TX
2. St. Louis, MO	2. Austin, TX	2. Raleigh, NC
3. Washington, DC	3. Las Vegas, NV	3. Pensacola, FL
4. Cincinnati, OH	4. West Palm Beach, FL	4. Daytona Beach, FL
5. Kansas City, MO	5. Akron, OH	5. Little Rock, AR
6. Denver, CO		
7. Seattle, WA		
8. Minneapolis-St. Paul, MN		
9. Ft. Lauderdale, FL		
10. Chicago, IL		

Source: "Thirty Most Sprawl-Threatened Cities," *The Dark Side of the American Dream: The Costs and Consequences of Suburban Sprawl,* Sierra Club, www.sierraclub.org/sprawl/report98/map.html, accessed June 10, 2006. Reprinted by permission from Sierra Club.

cities. Downtowns and inner cities deteriorated as strip and shopping malls, office parks, corporate campuses, and residential developments sprang up on what was once forest, prairie, or farm and ranch land. As the places where people live, work, and shop grew farther apart, people began spending more time in automobiles, driving ever-greater distances.[29] According to the Surface Transportation Policy Project (STPP), almost 70 percent of the increase in driving between 1983 and 1990 was due to the effects of such sprawl.[30] Urban sprawl has not only consumed wildlife habitat, wetlands, and farmland, but it has also contributed to land, water, and especially air pollution. Table 10.2 lists the U.S. cities most threatened by sprawl. This sprawl is not just a problem in big cities, as many smaller cities and towns are also experiencing the effects of a burgeoning population, traffic density, economic growth, and inefficient land use.

Because of the problems associated with urban sprawl, some communities have taken drastic steps to limit it. Oregon, for example, has established an Urban Growth Boundary around the city of Portland to restrict growth and preserve open space and farm and ranch land around the city. In Texas, the city of Austin implemented a Smart Growth initiative that directs development away from environmentally sensitive areas. A number of Colorado cities, including Boulder and Fort Collins, require as much as 80 percent of new residential housing developments to be devoted to agriculture, wetlands, or open spaces for wildlife.

Biodiversity

Deforestation, pollution, development, and urban sprawl have put increasing pressure on wildlife, plants, and their habitats. Many plants and animals have become extinct, and thousands more are threatened. In the Florida Everglades, for example, channeling, damming, and diverting water for urban and agricultural uses have dramatically altered the sensitive ecosystem. As a result, 68 percent of the Everglades' native resident species, including the manatee and the panther, are now endangered.[31]

The world's tropical forests, which cover just 7 percent of Earth's land surface, account for more than half of the planet's biological species.[32] The importance of these ecosystems is highlighted by the fact that 25 percent of the world's prescription drugs are extracted from plants primarily growing in tropical rain forests. Seventy percent of the 3,000 plants identified as sources of cancer-fighting drugs come from tropical forests, and scientists suspect that many more tropical plants may have pharmaceutical benefits. However, these forests are being depleted at alarming rates because of commercial logging, mining, and drilling and to make way for roads, farms, and ranches. More than half of the world's tropical forests have disappeared in the last century and, with them, many plant and animal species.[33] The most recent extinction is the Miss Waldron's red colobus monkey, a primate that once frequented the tropical forests of West Africa. With experts predicting that West Africa will lose 70 percent of its remaining forests, scientists fear that many more primates will become extinct during the twenty-first century.[34]

Many ecologists believe that the loss of such species threatens the success of entire ecosystems, which require a diversity of organisms to function properly. Recent global research indicates that declining numbers of available plant species result in lower ecosystem productivity, whereas increasing the number of species raises productivity.[35] Because each biological species plays a unique role in its ecosystem, the loss of any one of them may threaten the entire ecosystem. Pollinators, for example, play a significant role in any ecosystem. However, increasing development and widespread use of pesticides have reduced the populations of bees, insects, and bats that help plants reproduce. Among honeybees, the primary pollinators of food-producing plants, populations of domestic honeybees have declined by one-third, whereas many wild honeybees have become virtually extinct in many places around the world. Declines in pollinating species not only threaten the success of their relevant ecosystems but also may harm long-term global food production because one-third of all food products require pollinators to reproduce.[36]

Despite evidence of the importance of biodiversity in ecosystems, many people argue that human beings are more important than any single plant or animal species. This argument lies at the heart of environmental battles over endangered species' habitats throughout the United States and around the globe. In the Pacific Northwest, for example, old-growth forests are prime habitat for the endangered northern spotted owl, but their valuable timber provides jobs for hundreds of families as well as lumber to house a multiplying society. Although statistical evidence suggests that timber-related job losses in the Pacific Northwest are due as much to decades of overcutting of timberlands as to conservation measures to protect the owl, the battle of people's needs versus endangered species' needs continues there and elsewhere around the globe.[37] For example, Figure 10.4 depicts human population growth in the Brazilian Amazon forest over the past fifty years. Urban populations have experienced the most dramatic growth, and subsequently, there is more pressure for deforestation, heightened demand for water and natural resources, an increase in mining activities, and other effects of economic development.

FIGURE 10.4   Human Population Growth in the Brazilian Amazon

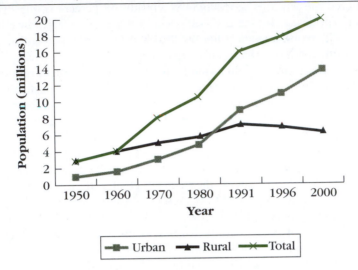

Source: World Resources Institute, "Human Pressure on the Brazilian Amazon Forest," http://pdf.wri.org/amazon_glossy_overview.pdf, accessed June 19, 2006.

Genetically Modified Foods

New technologies are also creating environmental issues, especially with regard to manipulating genes in plants and animals. Genetic engineering involves transferring one or more genes from one organism to another to create a new life form that has unique traits. Many of these genetically modified organisms have been developed to provide natural immunity against insects and viruses. Companies like Monsanto and DuPont marketed the idea that genetically modified (GM) corn, soybeans, potatoes, canola oil seeds, and cotton plants are more pest resistant, require fewer chemicals to produce, and have higher yields.[38] Indeed, one of the primary goals of using these GM plants is the reduction in the use of pesticides and other farming practices that harm the environment. Moreover, the resulting increase in crop yields can reduce costs, thereby making potentially more food available for world consumption.

On the other hand, the long-term impact of this genetic tinkering is not known. A study sponsored by the National Academy of Sciences reported that the GM varieties developed so far do not pose allergy problems. However, the report called for further research to determine how to prevent GM crops from killing beneficial and harmless insects, such as the monarch butterfly, and to deter herbicide-resistant genes from spreading into weeds.[39] Health, safety, and environmental concerns have prompted consumers around the world, particularly in Europe and Japan, to boycott products made from GM crops.

Even while a backlash against GM products builds, biotech companies are extending genetic engineering by experimenting with inserting artificial chromosomes into the cells of animals. For example, genetically engineered animal milk can be used as a culture for producing a vast range of drugs. However, many consumers are finding this technology as unpalatable as GM plants. Regulators in Germany and France have already banned its use, and the U.S. Food and Drug Administration has not approved the testing of artificial chromosomes in people as therapies for genetic diseases. As with GM plants, the problem with genetic engineering of animal cells is that the long-run effects cannot currently be predicted. Large numbers of genetically altered animals could upset the balance in relationships among various species with undetermined effects, such as the ability to reproduce or fight diseases and pests.[40] Until further research addresses public concerns about the safety and long-term environmental effects of these technologies, their success in the marketplace is uncertain.

ENVIRONMENTAL POLICY AND REGULATION

The United States, like most other nations, has passed numerous laws and established regulatory agencies to address environmental issues. Most of these efforts have focused on the activities of businesses, government agencies, and other organizations that use natural resources in providing goods and services.

Environmental Protection Agency

The most influential regulatory agency that deals with environmental issues and enforces environmental legislation in the United States is the Environmental Protection Agency (EPA). The EPA's founding in 1970 was the culmination of a decade of growing protests over the deterioration of the natural environment. This movement reached a significant climax with the publication of Rachel Carson's *Silent Spring,* an attack on the indiscriminate use of pesticides, which rallied scientists, activists, and citizens from around the country to crusade to protect the environment from abuses of the time. Twenty million Americans joined together on April 22, 1970, for Earth Day, a nationwide demonstration for environmental reforms. President Richard Nixon responded to these events by establishing the EPA as an independent agency to establish and enforce environmental protection standards, conduct environmental research, provide assistance in fighting pollution, and assist in developing and recommending new policies for environmental protection.[41] The agency is also charged with ensuring that

- All Americans are protected from significant risks to their health and to the environment in which they live and work.

- National efforts to manage environmental risk are based on the best scientific information available.

- Federal laws protecting human health and the environment are enforced fairly and effectively.

- Environmental protection is an integral consideration in U.S. policies concerning natural resources, human health, economic growth, energy, transportation, agriculture, industry, and international trade, and these factors are considered in establishing environmental policy.

- All parts of society have access to accurate information sufficient to participate effectively in managing human health and environmental risks.

- Environmental protection contributes to diverse, sustainable, and economically productive communities and ecosystems.
- The United States plays a leadership role in working with other nations to protect the environment.[42]

With these charges, the EPA has become one of the most powerful regulatory forces in the United States. For example, the agency recently reached an agreement with Syngenta, the leading manufacturer of diazinon, to phase out home and garden use of the commonly used pesticide and permit only limited commercial use of the product, which belongs to a class of pesticides linked to neurological disorders and other health problems in children. Although diazinon is considered less risky than other organophosphates, Syngenta executives said the company could not justify paying for the research needed to prove the pesticide's safety for consumer use and therefore agreed to the phaseout.[43]

To fulfill its primary mission to protect human health and the natural environment into the twenty-second century, the EPA recently established ten long-term strategic goals to define its planning, budgeting, analysis, and accountability processes (see Table 10.3). To determine these goals, the agency solicited and evaluated significant stakeholder input on priority areas related to human health and environmental protection activities. Thus, these goals reflect public priorities as voiced by Congress in the form of statutes and regulations designed to achieve clean air and water, proper waste management, and other important concerns.[44]

To achieve these goals and carry out its public mission, the EPA may also file civil charges against companies that violate the law. For example, the EPA, along with the U.S. Department of Justice and the state of Texas, settled two lawsuits against Koch Industries over more than 300 oil spills from the Kansas-based firm's pipelines and facilities in six states. The settlement imposed $30 million in civil penalties—the

TABLE 10.3	Goals of the Environmental Protection Agency

Goal	Long-Term Outcome
1.	Clean air
2.	Clean and safe water
3.	Safe food
4.	Preventing pollution and reducing risk in communities, homes, workplaces, and ecosystems
5.	Better waste management, restoration of contaminated waste sites, and emergency response
6.	Reduction of global and cross-border environmental risks
7.	Quality environmental information
8.	Sound science, improved understanding of environmental risk, and greater innovation to address environmental problems
9.	A credible deterrent to pollution and greater compliance with the law
10.	Effective management

Source: "Strategic Plan," Office of the Chief Financial Officer, Environmental Protection Agency, www.epa.gov/ocfo/plan/plan.htm, accessed June 20, 2006.

largest ever in the history of federal environmental law—against Koch and required the firm to hire an independent auditor to oversee repairs on 2,500 miles of pipeline, to improve its maintenance and training programs, and to spend $5 million on environmental projects in Kansas, Oklahoma, and Texas.[45] In comparison, Exxon's settlement with state and federal governments amounted to nearly $6 billion in compensatory and punitive damages after its tanker, the *Exxon Valdez,* ran aground and leaked 11 million gallons of oil into Alaska's Prince William Sound. The company also paid more than $2 billion to clean up damage from the ecological disaster and to reimburse government agencies for their expenses in response to the spill. Although the Exxon oil spill occurred more than a decade ago, the legal, political, and social implications of this event are still evolving.[46]

Environmental Legislation

A significant number of laws have been passed to address both general and specific environmental issues, including public health, threatened species, toxic substances, clean air and water, and natural resources. Table 10.4 summarizes some of the most significant laws related to environmental protection.

CLEAN AIR ACT The Clean Air Act, passed in 1970, is a comprehensive federal law that regulates atmospheric emissions from a variety of sources.[47] Among its most significant provisions is the requirement that the Environmental Protection Agency establish national air quality standards as well as standards for significant new pollution sources and for all facilities emitting hazardous substances. These maximum pollutant standards, called National Ambient Air Quality Standards (NAAQS), were mandated for every state to protect public health and the environment. The states were further directed to develop state implementation plans (SIPs) pertinent to the industries in each state. The law also established deadlines for reducing automobile emission levels—90 percent reductions in hydrocarbon and carbon monoxide levels by 1975 and a 90 percent reduction in nitrogen oxides by 1976. Because many areas of the country failed to meet these deadlines, the Clean Air Act was amended in 1977 to set new dates for attainment of the NAAQS.[48] The Clean Air Act was revised again as the Clean Air Act Amendments of 1990 to address lingering problems or issues that were not acknowledged in the original law, such as acid rain, ground-level ozone, stratospheric ozone depletion, and air toxins. The amended act also increased the number of regulated pollutants from fewer than 20 to more than 380.[49]

FEDERAL INSECTICIDE, FUNGICIDE, AND RODENTICIDE ACT The primary focus of the Federal Insecticide, Fungicide, and Rodenticide Act of 1972 was to place the distribution, sale, and use of pesticides under federal control. The law granted the EPA the authority to study the consequences of pesticide use and to require all users to register when purchasing pesticides. All pesticides used in the United States must be registered (licensed) with the EPA to assure that they will be properly labeled and that, if used according to specifications, they will not cause unreasonable harm to the environment. Later amendments to the law also require users to take exams to be certified as applicators of pesticides.[50]

| TABLE 10.4 | Major Environmental Laws |

Act (Date Enacted)	Purpose
National Environmental Policy Act (1969)	Established national environmental policy, set goals, and provided a means for implementing the policy; promotes efforts to prevent damage to the biosphere and to stimulate human health and welfare; established a Council on Environmental Quality.
Occupational Safety and Health Act (1970)	Ensures worker and workplace safety by requiring employers to provide a place of employment free from health and safety hazards.
Clean Air Act (1970)	Regulates emissions from natural, stationary, and mobile sources; authorized the EPA to establish National Ambient Air Quality Standards (NAAQS) to protect public health and the environment.
Federal Insecticide, Fungicide, and Rodenticide Act (1972)	Provides for federal control of pesticide distribution, sale, and use; requires users to register when purchasing pesticides.
Endangered Species Act (1973)	Established a conservation program for threatened and endangered plants and animals and their habitats; prohibits the import, export, interstate, and foreign commerce or any action that results in a "taking" of a listed species or that adversely affects habitat.
Safe Drinking Water Act (1974)	Protects the quality of drinking water in the United States; authorized the EPA to establish water purity standards and required public water systems to comply with health-related standards.
Toxic Substances Control Act (1976)	Empowered the EPA to track industrial chemicals currently produced or imported into the United States; authorized the EPA to require reporting or testing of chemicals and to ban the manufacture and import of chemicals that pose an unreasonable risk.
Resource Conservation Recovery Act (1976)	Empowered the EPA to control the generation, transportation, treatment, storage, and disposal of hazardous waste.
Clean Water Act (1977)	Authorized the EPA to set effluent standards on an industrywide basis and to continue to set water quality standards for all contaminants in surface waters; made it unlawful for any person to discharge any pollutant from a point source into navigable waters without a permit.
Comprehensive Environmental Response, Compensation, and Liability Act (1980)	Established prohibitions and requirements concerning closed and abandoned hazardous waste sites; authorized a tax on the chemical and petroleum industries to establish a "superfund" to provide for cleanup when no responsible party could be identified.
Superfund Amendments Reauthorization Act (1986)	Amended the Comprehensive Environmental and Response, Compensation, and Liability Act to increase the size of the superfund; required superfund actions to consider the standards and requirements found in other state and federal environmental laws and regulations; provided new enforcement authorities and tools.
Emergency Planning and Community Right-to-Know Act (1986)	Enacted to help local communities protect public health and safety and the environment from chemical hazards; requires each state to appoint a State Emergency Response Commission (SERC) and to establish Emergency Planning Districts.
Oil Pollution Act (1990)	Requires oil storage facilities and vessels to submit plans detailing how they will respond to large spills; requires the development of area contingency plans to prepare and plan for responses to oil spills on a regional scale.
Pollution Prevention Act (1990)	Promotes pollution reduction through cost-effective changes in production, operation, and use of raw materials and practices that increase efficiency and conserve natural resources, such as recycling, source reduction, and sustainable agriculture.
Food Quality Protection Act (1996)	Amended the Federal Insecticide, Fungicide, and Rodenticide Act and the Federal Food, Drug, and Cosmetic Act to change the way the EPA regulates pesticides; applies a new safety standard—reasonable certainty of no harm—to all pesticides used on foods.

Source: "Major Environmental Laws," Environmental Protection Agency, http://www.epa.gov/epahome/laws.htm, accessed June 20, 2006.

The World Wildlife Federation campaigns to protect certain animals and reduce trade in endangered species, including the hawksbill turtle.

ENDANGERED SPECIES ACT The Endangered Species Act of 1973 established a program to protect threatened and endangered species as well as the habitats in which they live.[51] An endangered species is one that is in danger of extinction, whereas a threatened species is one that may become endangered without protection. The U.S. Fish and Wildlife Service of the Department of the Interior maintains the list of endangered and threatened species, which currently includes 632 endangered species (326 are plants) and 190 threatened species (78 are plants). The Endangered Species Act prohibits any action that results in the harm to or death of a listed species or that adversely affects endangered species habitat. It also makes the import, export, and interstate and foreign commerce of listed species illegal. Protected species may include birds, insects, fish, reptiles, mammals, crustaceans, flowers, grasses, cacti, and trees.[52]

The Endangered Species Act has become one of the most controversial environmental laws passed in the United States. Some environmentalists fear the law may backfire if landowners who find endangered or threatened species on their property fail to notify authorities to avoid the expense and hassle of complying with the law; in some cases, threatened or endangered species have been harmed by landowners seeking to avoid the law. Concerns about the restrictions and costs associated with the law are not entirely unfounded. Consider the case of Brandt Child, who purchased 500 acres in Utah with the intention of building a campground and golf course. However, the U.S. Fish and Wildlife Service ordered Child not to use the land because 200,000 federally protected Kanab ambersnails inhabited three lakes on the premises. The federal government not only refused to compensate Child for his loss of the use of the property, but it also threatened to fine him $50,000 per snail if geese that wandered onto the property had eaten any of the snails (the geese were later found to be snail free).[53] Such anecdotes have angered many property rights activists who believe that the Endangered Species Act goes too far in protecting threatened species at the expense of human rights.

TOXIC SUBSTANCES CONTROL ACT Congress passed the Toxic Substances Control Act in 1976 to empower the Environmental Protection Agency with the ability to track the 75,000 industrial chemicals currently produced or imported into the United States. The agency repeatedly screens these chemicals and can require reporting or testing of those that may pose an environmental or human health hazard. It can also ban the manufacture and import of chemicals that pose an unreasonable risk. The EPA has the ability to track the thousands of new chemicals developed by industry each year with either unknown or dangerous characteristics. It then can control these chemicals as necessary to protect human health and the environment.[54]

CLEAN WATER ACT In 1977, Congress amended the Federal Water Pollution Control Act of 1972 as the Clean Water Act. This law granted the EPA the authority to establish effluent standards on an industry basis and continued the earlier law's requirements to set water quality limits for all contaminants in surface waters. The Clean Water Act makes it illegal for anyone to discharge any pollutant from a point source into navigable waters without a permit.[55] A five-year investigation found that ships owned by Royal Caribbean Cruises Ltd. used secret bypass pipes to dump oil and hazardous materials overboard, often at night. Government officials accused the company of dumping to save the expense of properly disposing of the waste. At the time, the company was also promoting itself as environmentally friendly. Royal Caribbean eventually paid $27 million in fines and spent up to $90,000 per ship to install new water treatment systems. The company also placed environmental officers on board each vessel.[56]

EMERGENCY PLANNING AND COMMUNITY RIGHT-TO-KNOW ACT The Emergency Planning and Community Right-to-Know Act was enacted in 1986 to help local communities identify and protect public health, safety, and the environment from chemical hazards. To achieve this goal, the law requires that businesses report the locations and quantities of stored chemicals to state and local governments to help them respond to chemical spills and similar emergencies. Additionally, the law mandates that most manufacturers file a **Toxics Release Inventory (TRI)** of all releases of specified chemicals into the air, water, or land, as well as transfers of chemicals for treatment or disposal. TRIs must also be filed with the U.S. EPA, which compiles the reports in a publicly accessible online database. As such, the TRI program serves as a "public report card" of chemical pollution from U.S. manufacturing facilities. It also creates a powerful incentive for manufacturers to reduce their emissions and wastes. Table 10.5 lists the top ten facilities in the United States based on TRI reports filed with the EPA.[57]

Toxics Release Inventory (TRI)

"public report card" filed with the U.S. EPA that contains all releases of specified chemicals into the air, water, or land, as well as transfers by manufacturers of chemicals for treatment or disposal

POLLUTION PREVENTION ACT The Pollution Prevention Act of 1990 focused industry, government, and public attention on reducing pollution through cost-effective changes in production, operation, and raw materials use. Practices include recycling, source reduction, sustainable agriculture, and other practices that increase

TABLE 10.5	Top Ten Facilities Based on Chemical Releases to the Environment		
	Company	**Facility Location**	**Pounds Released**
	1. Red Dog Operations	Kotzebue, Alaska	481,578,816
	2. Newmont Mining Corp.	Golconda, Nevada	291,128,400
	3. BHP Copper	San Manuel, Arizona	248,695,440
	4. Kennecott Utah Copper Mine Concentrators & Power Plant	Copperton, Utah	113,640,793
	5. Barrick Goldstrike Mines	Elko, Nevada	79,410,838
	6. Newmont Mining Corp.	Valmy, Nevada	58,686,703
	7. Newmont Mining Corp.	Carlin, Nevada	43,143,578
	8. Kennecott Greens Creek Mining Co.	Juneau, Alaska	37,103,243
	9. Asarco Inc. Ray Complex Hayden Smelter & Concentrator	Hayden, Arizona	34,941,191
	10. US Ecology Idaho Inc.	Grand View, Idaho	28,895,378

Source: Scorecard: The Pollution Information Site, "Facilities Releasing TRI Chemicals to the Environment," http://www.scorecard.org/env-releases/us-map.tcl, accessed June 20, 2006.

efficiency in the use of energy, water, or other natural resources and protect resources through conservation.[58]

FOOD QUALITY PROTECTION ACT In 1996, the Food Quality Protection Act amended the Federal Insecticide, Fungicide, and Rodenticide Act and the Federal Food, Drug, and Cosmetic Act to fundamentally change the way the EPA regulates pesticides. The law included a new safety standard—reasonable certainty of no harm—that must be applied to all pesticides used on foods.[59] The legislation establishes a more consistent, science-based regulatory environment and mandates a single health-based standard for all pesticides in all foods. The law also provides special protections for infants and children, expedites approval of safer pesticides, provides incentives for the development and maintenance of effective crop protection tools for farmers, and requires periodic reevaluation of pesticide registrations and tolerances to ensure that they are up-to-date and based on good science.[60]

BUSINESS RESPONSE TO ENVIRONMENTAL ISSUES

Partly in response to federal legislation such as the National Environmental Policy Act of 1969 and partly due to stakeholder concerns, businesses are applying creativity, technology, and business resources to respond to environmental issues. In many cases, these firms not only have improved their reputations with interested stakeholders but also have seen dramatic cost savings by making their operations more efficient. Moreover, many companies, including Staples, Walt Disney, Chevron, U.S. Steel, and Scott Paper, have created a new executive position, vice president of environmental affairs. This position is designed to help these companies achieve their business goals in an environmentally responsible manner. In an effort to protect our resources, AT&T supports and helps publish the *Green Business Letter,* a hands-on journal for environmentally conscious companies. Corporate efforts to respond to environmental issues focus on green marketing, recycling, emissions reductions, and socially responsible buying.

For example, disposable cameras are increasingly popular because of their size and convenience. They account for 40 percent of worldwide film sales, which equates to about $2 billion annually. Fujifilm (Fuji), the world's number two film maker, holds the key patent for disposable cameras. No matter how convenient these disposable cameras are, they tend to be thrown away and added to the ever-growing amount of waste. As landfills continue to bulge with waste, companies are responding to the challenge of protecting and preserving our environment in a socially responsible manner. To accomplish this, Fuji decided to conduct a recycling program for the Quick-Snap camera in 1990. They added it as an essential attribute to their corporate philosophy, in part because of their sensitivity and commitment to worldwide environmental concerns. Part of their challenge with this new initiative was to get people to stop thinking "disposable" and start thinking recyclable.[61]

Green Marketing

green marketing
the specific development, pricing, promotion, and distribution of products that do less harm to the environment

Green marketing refers to the specific development, pricing, promotion, and distribution of products that do less harm to the environment. General Motors, for example, is developing new "hybrid" pickup trucks and buses that employ electric motors to augment their internal-combustion engines, improving the vehicles' fuel economy without a loss in power. The full-size trucks, for example, will get nearly 15 percent better gas mileage than a conventional pickup.[62]

One truly "green" firm is the Parks Company, which donates 5 percent of the gross profit from its catalog sales to U.S. national parks to help bridge their $9 billion budget shortfall. Since the company was founded in 1995, the mailing list for its catalog of parks-related gift items has grown to 60,000, and the firm donated $20,000 in its first twenty-eight months of business. The company also succeeded in its grass-roots campaign, One for the Parks, a crusade for assigning 1 percent of the federal budget surplus to meet the parks' budget needs.[63]

Even some real estate developers are attempting to integrate environmental concerns into new communities to protect the land. One example is Meadow Ranch in Colorado. The developer of Meadow Ranch deliberately designed a community that spares wildlife habitat to ensure that new homeowners do not evict the hawks and red foxes that have long roamed the land. Homes in Meadow Ranch are on land once zoned light industrial, which, had it been developed as such, would have destroyed thirty of the forty wetland acres preserved on the site today. The developers also consulted the Colorado National Plant Society, the Army Corps of Engineers, and the Soil Conservation District to ensure that new landscaping harmonized with the native plants. The firm also prints its brochures on recycled paper.[64]

Many products are certified as "green" by environmental organizations such as Green Seal and carry a special logo identifying them as such. In Europe, companies can voluntarily apply for an Eco-label (see Figure 10.5) to indicate that their product is less

| FIGURE 10.5 | The European Eco-label (German) |

Source: "European Union Eco-label Logo," *Europa*, European Union, http://ec.europa.eu/environment/ecolabel/index_en.htm/, accessed June 19, 2006.

harmful to the environment than competing products, based on scientifically determined criteria. The European Union supports the Eco-label program, which has been utilized in product categories as diverse as refrigerators, mattresses, vacuum cleaners, footwear, and televisions. Certification does not include food and medicine.[65] Lumber products at Home Depot and the U.K.-based B&Q may carry a seal from the Forest Stewardship Council to indicate that they were harvested from sustainable forests using environmentally friendly methods.[66] Likewise, Chiquita bananas are certified through the Better Banana Project as having been grown with more environmentally conscious and labor-friendly practices. The company also works with the Rainforest Alliance to implement a market-based conservation system, which ensures that the banana operations meet 200 criteria to verify that they are operating in a sustainable manner.[67]

However, a recent study by Consumers International suggests that consumers are being confused and even misled by green marketing claims. Researchers compared claims on products sold in ten countries, including the United States, to labeling guidelines established by the International Organization for Standardization (ISO), which prohibit vague and misleading claims as well as unverifiable ones such as "environmentally friendly" and "nonpolluting." The study found that many products' claims are too vague or misleading to meet ISO standards. For example, one brand of flour claimed to be "nonpolluting," and a German compost was described as "earthworm friendly." Among the products with the highest number of misleading or unverifiable claims were laundry detergents, household cleaners, and paints. Anna Fielder, the director of Consumers International, contends the study shows that although there are many useful claims made about the environmental responsibility of products, there is still a long way to go to ensure that shoppers are adequately informed about the environmental impact of the products they buy.[68]

Although the demand for legal and practical solutions to environmental issues is widespread, the environmental movement includes many diverse groups, whose values and goals often conflict. There is growing agreement among environmentalists and businesses, however, that companies should work to protect and preserve the natural environment by implementing a number of goals. First, companies should strive to eliminate the concept of waste. Because pollution and waste usually stem from inefficiency, the issue should not be what to do with waste but, rather, how to make things more efficiently so that no waste is produced. Second, companies should rethink the concept of a product. Products can be classified as consumables, which are eaten or biodegradable; durable goods, such as cars, televisions, computers, and refrigerators; and unsalables, including such undesirable by-products as radioactive materials, heavy metals, and toxins. The design of durable goods should utilize a closed loop system of manufacture and use, and a return to the manufacturing process that allows products and resources to be disassembled and recycled and minimizes the disposal of unsalables. Third, the price of products should reflect their true costs, including the costs of replenishing natural resources that are utilized or damaged during the production process. Finally, businesses should seek ways to make their commitment to the environment profitable.[69] For example, Sharon de Cloet founded Caeran, a manufacturer of environmentally responsible cleaning and personal care products, in 1989. At the time, she was a frustrated consumer, who was unable to learn the ingredients in common laundry detergent that were causing her young son's allergic reaction. Today, Caeran manufactures thirty products and utilizes a 150-person sales team to market in Canada. Each product label details the ingredients, which are fully explained in the company catalog. Customers receive only two mailings a year, including a newsletter that focuses on environmental issues and new products. De Cloet is a mentor to other entrepreneurs and uses her business success to better the community and support environmental causes.[70]

Recycling Initiatives

recycling
the reprocessing of materials, especially steel, aluminum, paper, glass, rubber, and some plastics, for reuse

Many organizations engage in **recycling,** the reprocessing of materials, especially steel, aluminum, paper, glass, rubber, and some plastics, for reuse (see Figure 10.6). Procter & Gamble, for example, uses recycled materials in some of its packaging and markets refills for some products, which reduce packaging waste. Sonoma County (California) Stable and Livestock markets rubber mats recycled from used tires for use in horse stalls.[71] More than 50 percent of all products sold in stores are packed in 100 percent recycled paperboard. Other markets using 100 percent recycled paperboard include book covers, jigsaw puzzles, board games, greeting cards, and video and CD covers.[72] Starbucks makes coffee grounds available free to those who wish to use them for compost to add nutrition to their gardens. Ben Pachard, Starbucks' environmental affairs manager, says, "Recycling the grounds back into the garden is a better alternative then throwing them away into the trash."[73]

A number of beverage companies have formed an alliance called WasteWise to represent and share industry goals and best practices with respect to recycling and waste management. Anheuser-Busch Companies, for example, reduced its total solid waste by 15 percent, or 19 million pounds, in one year through waste prevention and recycling. Coca-Cola purchases more than $2 billion in recycled content materials in the United States alone. Pepsi-Cola switched to reusable plastic shipping cases and saved $44 million. Coors, by using a lighter weight bottle, saved more than 1 million pounds of glass.[74] Table 10.6 shows some of the goals and techniques the beverage industry maintains in managing waste.

FIGURE 10.6   Recycling Steel Cans

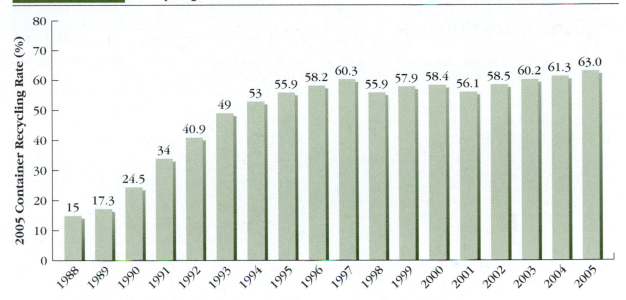

Source: "Steel Recycling Rates at a Glance," Steel Recycling Institute, http://www.recycle-steel.org/PDFs/ 2005Graphs.pdf, accessed June 20, 2006. Reprinted by permission from the Steel Recycling Institute.

TABLE 10.6   A Sampling of Beverage Industry Waste Management Initiatives

Initiative	Companies Supporting the Beverage Industry Wastewise Initiatives
Utilize lightweight plastic and glass bottles.	7Up/RC Bottling
Switch from corrugated shippers to reusable plastic cases.	Coors Brewing Companies
Institute a glove-reuse program in manufacturing facilities.	Coca-Cola Company
Develop a waste tracking system for syrup production facilities that measures and tracks the amount of waste generated on a per-unit basis.	Veryfine Products
	Anheuser-Busch Companies
Refurbish, rather than replace, vending equipment.	Pepsi-Cola Company
Implement a six-pack ring-recycling program.	Poland Spring Natural Spring Water
Collect and bale corrugated shipping containers from the public.	Fetzer Vineyards
Establish a facility to buy back used beverage containers from the public.	
Increase recycled content in glass bottles.	
Increase recycled content in corrugated shipping containers.	

Source: "Doing What It Takes to Be Wastewise," Environmental Protection Agency, http://www.epa.gov/ wastewise/pubs/bevfact.pdf, accessed June 19, 2006.

Precautionary Principle

The precautionary principle was developed internationally in 1992 at the United Nations Conference on Environment and Development. Developed over a decade ago, the precautionary principle is gaining more acceptance today. The Rio Declaration that was developed at that time stated:

> In order to protect the environment, the precautionary principle shall be widely applied by States according to their capabilities. Where there are threats of serious or irreversible damage, lack of full scientific certainty shall not be used as a reason for postponing cost effective measures to prevent environmental degradation.

The precautionary principle has its roots in Germany with the Vorsorge principle. This principle was based on using foresight to avoid possible environmental damage that could be caused by harmful human activity. Key issues with the principles include risk prevention, cost effectiveness, ethical responsibilities toward maintaining the integrity of natural systems, and the fallibility of human understanding. The application of the precautionary principle is much more advanced in Germany and other European countries than in the United States. This has led to a strong environmental consciousness in European nations.

In the United States, there is no explicit mention of the precautionary principle, but it is the underlying force behind many environmental laws. The National Environmental Policy mandates an environmental impact study on all projects receiving federal funds that could pose harm to the environment. The Clean Water Act sets forth strict standards to renew and maintain U.S. waters. The Occupational Safety and Health Act was created to help maintain the safest possible work environment for American workers. Despite these and many other related laws, the U.S. government has done little to address the precautionary principle.

The *Precautionary Principle in Action Handbook* suggests answering the following three questions when addressing the issues involving the precautionary principle:

1. How much contamination can be avoided?

2. What are the alternatives to this product or activity and are they safer?

3. Is this activity even necessary?

Answering these questions can help a leader make a choice concerning the precautionary principle. It can also slow down the development of technology by requiring that all potential consequences are taken into consideration. The handbook goes into further detail

Future Solutions, Inc., distributes recycled products ranging from automated teller machine (ATM) supplies and toilet bowl brushes to recycled mouse pads and vacuum cleaners from more than 300 manufacturers. Among the firm's clients are the U.S. Department of Energy and the states of Colorado, California, and Arizona. Plans for Future Solutions include constructing a new office headquarters out of 100 percent recycled material that utilizes both energy-efficient and water-conserving products.[75]

Companies are finding ways to recycle water to avoid discharging chemicals into rivers and streams and to preserve diminishing water supplies. DaimlerChrysler, for example, has three manufacturing plants that operate wastewater-recycling facilities. The company's facility in Toluca, Mexico, which manufactures the PT Cruiser, operates a comprehensive recycling system that treats more than 610,000 gallons of wastewater—enough to fill up ten medium-sized baseball stadiums—each day from both manufacturing operations and sanitary operations (like restrooms, showers, and cafeterias). Because the plant totally recycles all the water used, it draws less from the by listing the exact components of the precautionary principle. They are as follows:

- Taking precautionary action before scientific certainty of cause and effect.

- Setting goals

- Seeking out and evaluating alternatives

- Shifting burdens of proof
  - Financial responsibility
  - The duty to monitor, understand, investigate, inform, and act

- Developing more democratic and thorough decision-making criteria and methods

Governments have several ways to show precaution in a situation. One of the strongest precautionary actions is the ban or phase out. An example is Sweden's ban on toxic chemicals like mercury and cadmium. Many other countries have similar bans on toxic chemicals that could have an adverse effect on humankind or the environment.

Another example of precaution is the use of clean production and pollution prevention. A change of production operations is likely needed to help clean up production and reduce pollution. Creating a sustainable

product would be a great way to accomplish clean production. Producing organic agriculture is another example of using the precautionary principle. The practice of organic agriculture actively uses the precautionary principle by staying away from potentially harmful practices. Alternatively, conventional agriculture waits for proof of harm before discontinuing any practices.

Other examples of the precautionary principle are alternative assessment, health-based occupational exposure limits, reverse onus chemical listings, ecosystem management, and premarket or preactivity testing requirements. All of these practices will help guide an organization to better follow the precautionary principle. The precautionary principle stresses identifying the possible effects that decisions will have. Specifically, the decision maker should ascertain if there is a possibility that serious, irreversible damage could be done.

Sources: Joel Tickner, Carolyn Raffensperger, and Nancy Myers, *Precautionary Principle in Action Handbook*, http://www.mindfully.org/Precaution/Precaution-In-Action-Handbook.htm, accessed May 10, 2006; "Precautionary Principle," http://en.wikipedia.org/wiki/Precautionary_principle, accessed May 9, 2006; Gary E. Marchant and Kenneth L. Mossman, *Arbitrary and Capricious: The Precautionary Principle in the European Union Courts* (London: International Policy Press, 2005). ■

---

area's receding aquifer and minimizes the potential for polluted water to reach a nearby river system. Moreover, the system allows DaimlerChrysler's water quality standards to be stricter than those set by Mexico or the United States.[76]

Emissions Reduction Initiatives

To combat air pollution and the threat of global warming, many companies have begun to take steps to reduce the emissions of greenhouse gases from their facilities. Many firms, such as Herman Miller, Inc., which designs and manages production facilities to function as efficiently as possible, are finding new ways to light and heat their buildings and factories to improve efficiency, thereby reducing waste and energy use. Making improvements in energy efficiency can save a company approximately $1 per square foot of office or factory space per year.[77] There is even a new term, **green power,** defined as energy sources that are commonly accepted as having relatively low impact on human, animal, and ecosystem health. Renewable energy

green power
energy sources that are commonly accepted as having relatively low impact on human, animal, and ecosystem health

sources including solar, wind, biomass, landfill gas, and geothermal qualify as green power. Companies such as General Motors, IBM, and Johnson & Johnson are helping pave the way for the creation of cost-competitive clean power options. A few of the benefits of using this type of energy are that it provides on-site electricity generation, helps stabilize corporate energy costs, and provides a hedge against the uncertainty of future environmental regulations.[78]

Many companies are going beyond the emission reductions called for by the Kyoto Protocol, which set a goal of reducing greenhouse emissions by signing countries by 7 percent from their 2000 levels. DuPont, for example, is slashing its greenhouse gas emissions to 58 million tons, or 40 percent of their 1991 levels. Royal Dutch/Shell is working to reduce greenhouse gas emissions from its plants to 100 million tons, or 25 percent below 1990 levels. To achieve an equivalent reduction, every car in New England would have to be taken off the road for five years.[79] Companies that achieve reductions in excess of that called for by the Kyoto Protocol earn credits that may then be "traded" to other firms that have not yet achieved their targets. Nations may also trade credits earned from reducing emissions to other nations that have yet to do so. Russia, for example, plans to use the revenue from the sale of these credits to fund clean-energy projects.[80]

Socially Responsible Buying

Socially responsible buying initiatives are another way that companies are finding to incorporate environmental responsibility into their business strategies. Minette

Hudson's Bay's code of vendor conduct details the company's commitment to socially responsible buying and ethical sourcing. Copyright Hudson's Bay Company, used with their permission.

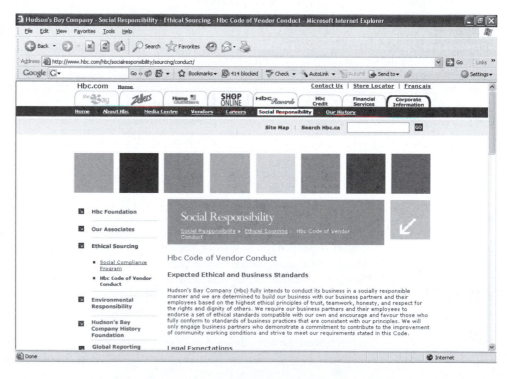

Drumwright has defined socially responsible buying (SRB) as "that which attempts to take into account the public consequences of organizational buying or bring about positive social change through organizational buying behavior."[81] For example, Tesco, Alda, and Sainsbury, all European grocers, are committed to socially responsible buying. The grocery chains work with suppliers and packaging firms to ensure that recycled and reclaimable materials are used in food packaging solutions. These companies, along with manufacturers and other vendors, formed the Retail Packaging Work Group in the United Kingdom to develop industrywide effort for ensuring socially responsible buying in the grocery industry.[82]

A company that takes a proactive approach to socially responsible buying is likely to (1) be actively involved in the development of SRB principles and practices both inside and outside its own operations, (2) routinely and objectively evaluate its suppliers' achievements with respect to the social responsibilities involved, and (3) communicate its achievements and failures to its primary stakeholders. How companies implement SRB strategies ranges from terminating relations with suppliers who will not abide by the firm's environmental goals to seeking out partners who can supply environmentally friendly parts and supplies to forming industrywide agreements. In the United Kingdom, for example, Co-operative Bank, after discovering that one of its furniture suppliers was unknowingly using endangered tropical hardwoods, introduced the manufacturer to a firm that could supply it with more sustainable resources.[83]

STRATEGIC IMPLEMENTATION OF ENVIRONMENTAL RESPONSIBILITY

Businesses have responded to the opportunities and threats created by environmental issues with varying levels of commitment. The World Resources Institute states that the "principle of environmental governance is decision-making that is 'accessible'"— that is, decisions that are transparent and open to public input and oversight.[84] As Figure 10.7 indicates, a low-commitment business attempts to avoid dealing with environmental issues and hopes that nothing bad will happen or that no one will ever find out about an environmental accident or abuse. Such firms may try to protect themselves against lawsuits. Hooker Chemical, for example, disposed of its chemical wastes in and around Love Canal near Niagara Falls, New York, because the area was sparsely populated. When the area was developed years later, new residents were surprised when toxic fumes were detected in some basements. Many families were ultimately forced to abandon their homes. Many people felt that Hooker had failed by not being actively involved in preventing this tragedy. On the other hand, some companies take a high-commitment approach toward natural environment issues. Such firms develop strategic management programs, which view the environment as an opportunity for advancing organizational interests. These companies respond to stakeholder interests, assess risks, and develop a comprehensive environmental strategy. Home Depot, for example, has established a set of environmental principles that includes selling responsibly marketed products, eliminating unnecessary packaging, recycling and encouraging the use of products with recycled content, and conserving

FIGURE 10.7   Strategic Approaches to Environmental Issues

Low Commitment	Medium Commitment	High Commitment
Deals only with existing problems	Attempts to comply with environmental laws	Has strategic programs to address environmental issues
Makes only limited plans for anticipated problems	Deals with issues that could cause public relations problems	Views environment as an opportunity to advance the business strategy
Fails to consider stakeholder environmental issues	Views environmental issues from a tactical, not a strategic, perspective	Consults with stakeholders about their environmental concerns
Operates without concern for long-term environmental impact	Views environment as more of a threat than an opportunity	Conducts an environmental audit to assess performance and adopts international standards

natural resources by using them wisely. The company also makes contributions to many environmental organizations, including Keep America Beautiful, the Tampa Audubon Society, and the World Wildlife Fund.[85]

Stakeholder Assessment

Stakeholder analysis, as discussed in Chapter 2, is an important part of a high-commitment approach to environmental issues. This process requires acknowledging and actively monitoring the environmental concerns of all legitimate stakeholders. Thus, a company must have a process in place for identifying and prioritizing the many claims and stakes on its business and for dealing with trade-offs related to the impact on different stakeholders. Although no company can satisfy every claim, all risk-related claims should be evaluated before a firm decides to take action on or ignore a particular issue. To make accurate assumptions about stakeholder interests, managers need to conduct research, assess risks, and communicate with stakeholders about their respective concerns.

Based on an understanding of its stakeholders, Herman Miller, the ergonomic furniture maker, has implemented a comprehensive strategy to protect the environment. The firm's environmental responsibility initiatives encompass every element of its product supply chain, from the acquisition of raw materials through production and design, to the end user who ultimately purchases its furniture. Herman Miller is committed to designing and manufacturing environmentally friendly furniture that has minimal impact on the environment. The strategy begins with an analysis of the "life cycle" of raw materials and finished goods to identify opportunities to reduce, reuse, and recycle. Miller's environmental initiatives not only have supported its founder's and managers' own personal beliefs of environmental stewardship and self-actualization but also have proven effective in reducing costs, building shareholder value, and earning stakeholder respect. The company also received a WasteWise award from the EPA in 2005.[86]

However, not all stakeholders are equal. There are specific regulations and legal requirements that govern some aspects of stakeholder relationships, such as air and water quality. Additionally, some special-interest groups take extreme positions that, if adopted, would undermine the economic base of many other stakeholders (e.g., fishing rights, logging, and hunting). Regardless of the final decision a company makes with regard to particular environmental issues, information should be communicated consistently across all stakeholders. This is especially important when a company faces a crisis or negative publicity about a decision. Another aspect of strong relationships is the willingness to acknowledge and openly address potential conflicts. Some degree of negotiation and conciliation will be necessary to align a company's decisions and strategies with stakeholder interests.

Risk Analysis

The next step in a high-commitment response to environmental concerns is assessing risk. Through industry and government research, an organization can usually identify environmental issues that relate to manufacturing, marketing, and consumption and use patterns associated with its products. Through risk analysis, it is possible to assess the environmental risks associated with business decisions. The real difficulty is measuring the costs and benefits of environmental decisions, especially in the eyes of interested stakeholders. Research studies often conflict, which only adds to the confusion and controversy over the natural environment. For example, a well-respected researcher reported in a leading journal that a certain type of genetically modified corn kills significant numbers of monarch butterflies. However, twenty other studies and the EPA have found that genetically modified corn does not pose a significant risk to the monarch butterfly. In fact, in the year before the study was reported, Monarch Watch found a 30 percent increase in the monarch butterfly population when 40 percent more genetically modified corn was planted.[87]

Debate surrounding environmental issues will force corporate decision makers to weigh the evidence and take some risks in final decisions. The important point for high-commitment organizations is to continue to evaluate the latest information and to maintain communication with all stakeholders. For example, if the 68 million sport utility vehicles (SUVs) on U.S. roads today were replaced with fuel-efficient electric-powered cars and trucks, there would be a tremendous reduction of greenhouse gas emissions.[88] However, the cooperation and commitment needed to gain the support of government, manufacturers, consumers, and other stakeholders to accomplish this would be almost impossible to achieve. Although SUVs may harm the environment, many of their owners believe they provide greater protection in an accident.

The issue of environmental responsibility versus safety in SUVs illustrates that many environmental decisions involve trade-offs for various stakeholders' risks. Through risk management, it is possible to quantify these trade-offs in determining whether to accept or reject environmentally related activities and programs. Usually, the key decision is between the amount of investment required to reduce the risk of damage and the amount of risk acceptable in stakeholder relationships. A company should assess these relationships on an ongoing basis. Both formal and informal methods are needed to get feedback from stakeholders. For example, the employees of a firm can use formal methods such as exit interviews, an open-door policy, and toll-free telephone hot lines. Conversations between employees could provide informal feedback. But it is ultimately the responsibility of the business to make the best decision possible after processing all available research and information. Then, if it is later discovered that a mistake has been made, change is still possible through open disclosure and thoughtful reasoning. Finally, a high-commitment organization will incorporate new information and insights into the strategic planning process.

The Strategic Environmental Audit

ISO 14000
a comprehensive set of environmental standards that encourage a cleaner, safer, and healthier world

Organizations that are highly committed to environmental responsibility may conduct an audit of their efforts and report the results to all interested stakeholders. Table 10.7 provides a starting point for examining environmental sensitivity. Such organizations may also wish to use globally accepted standards, such as ISO 14000, as benchmarks in a strategic environmental audit. The International Organization for Standardization developed **ISO 14000** as a comprehensive set of environmental standards that encourage a cleaner, safer, and healthier world. There is currently considerable variation among the environmental laws and regulations of nations and regions, making it difficult for high-commitment organizations to find acceptable solutions on a global scale. The goal of the ISO 14000 standards is to promote a common approach to

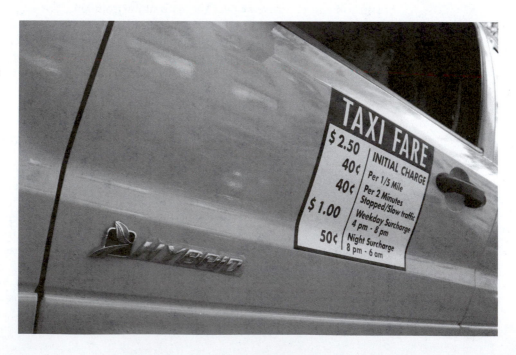

Ford Motor Company unveiled a fleet of Ford Escape Hybrid taxi cabs in New York City. The hybrid vehicles get about 36 miles-per-gallon in the city.

TABLE 10.7	Strategic Natural Environment Audit

Yes	No	Checklist
O	O	Does the organization show a high commitment to a strategic environmental policy?
O	O	Do employees know the environmental compliance policies of the organization?
O	O	Do suppliers and customers recognize the organization's stand on environmental issues?
O	O	Are managers familiar with the environmental strategies of other organizations in the industry?
O	O	Has the organization compared its environmental initiatives with those of other firms?
O	O	Is the company aware of the best practices in environmental management regardless of industry?
O	O	Has the organization developed measurable performance standards for environmental compliance?
O	O	Does the firm reconcile the need for consistent responsible values with the needs of various stakeholders?
O	O	Do the organization's philanthropic efforts consider environmental issues?
O	O	Does the organization comply with all laws and regulations that relate to environmental impact?

environmental management and to help companies attain and measure improvements in environmental performance.[89] Companies that choose to abide by the ISO standards receive a certificate to indicate their compliance. Ford was the first automaker to require all suppliers and manufacturing facilities to be ISO 14000 certified. The initiative was designed to reduce Ford's environmental impact and save millions in business expenses.[90] Other performance benchmarks available for use in environmental audits come from nonprofit organizations such as CERES, which has also developed standards for reporting information about environmental performance to interested stakeholders.

As this chapter has demonstrated, social responsibility entails responding to stakeholder concerns about the environment, and many firms are finding creative ways to address environmental challenges. Although many of the companies mentioned in this chapter have chosen to implement strategic environmental initiatives to capitalize on opportunities and achieve greater efficiency and cost savings, most also believe that responding to stakeholders' concerns about environmental issues will both improve relationships with stakeholders and make the world a better place.

SUMMARY

Although the scope of the natural environment is quite broad, we define the term as the physical world, including all biological entities, as well as the interaction among nature and individuals, organizations, and business strategies. In recent years, companies have been increasingly incorporating environmental issues into their business strategies.

Air pollution arises from stationary sources such as factories and power plants; mobile sources such as cars, trucks, planes, and trains; and natural sources such as windblown dust and volcanic eruptions. Acid rain results when nitrous oxides and sulfur dioxides emitted from manufacturing facilities react with air and rain. Scientists believe that increasing concentrations of greenhouse gases in the atmosphere are warming the planet, although this theory is still controversial. The Kyoto Protocol is a treaty proposed among industrialized nations to slow global warming.

Water pollution results from the dumping of raw sewage and toxic chemicals into rivers and oceans, from oil and gasoline spills, from the burial of industrial waste in the ground where it may filter into underground water supplies, and from the runoff of fertilizers and pesticides used in farming and grounds maintenance. The amount of water available is also a concern and the topic of political disputes.

Land pollution results from the dumping of residential and industrial waste, strip mining, and poor forest conservation. How to dispose of waste in an environmentally responsible manner is another issue. Deforestation to make way for agriculture and development threatens animal and plant species. Urban sprawl, the result of changing human development patterns, consumes wildlife habitat, wetlands, and farmland.

Deforestation, pollution, and urban sprawl threaten wildlife, plants, and their habitats and have caused many species to become extinct or endangered. Genetic engineering involves transferring one or more genes from one organism to another to create a new life form that has unique traits. However, the long-term impact of this technology is not known, and many people fear its use.

The U.S. Environmental Protection Agency (EPA) is an independent regulatory agency that establishes and enforces environmental protection standards, conducts environmental research, provides assistance in fighting pollution, and assists in developing and recommending new policies for environmental protection. The Clean Air Act regulates atmospheric emissions from a variety of sources, whereas the Federal Insecticide, Fungicide, and Rodenticide Act regulates the distribution, sale, and use of pesticides. The Endangered Species Act protects threatened and endangered species as well as the habitats in which they live. The Toxic Substances Control Act empowered the EPA to track, test, and ban industrial chemicals. The Clean Water Act authorized the EPA to establish effluent standards and to set water quality limits for all contaminants in surface waters. The Emergency Planning and Community Right-to-Know Act required most manufacturers to file Toxics Release Inventories detailing their releases of chemicals into the air, water, and land. The Pollution Prevention Act focused industry, government, and public attention on pollution reduction efforts. The Food Quality Protection Act changed the way the EPA regulates pesticides by applying the same standard to all pesticides used in food products.

Businesses are applying creativity, technology, and business resources to respond to environmental issues. Some firms have created a new executive position, vice president of environmental affairs, to help them achieve their business goals in an environmentally responsible manner. Green marketing refers to the specific development, pricing, promotion, and distribution of products that do less harm to the environment. There is growing agreement among environmentalists and businesses, however, that companies should work to protect and preserve the natural environment by implementing a number of goals: (1) eliminate the concept of waste, (2) rethink the concept of a product, (3) make the price of products reflect their true costs, and (4) seek ways to make business's commitment to the environment profitable. Many organizations engage in recycling, the reprocessing of materials—especially steel, aluminum, paper, glass, rubber, and some plastics—for reuse. To combat air pollution and the threat of global warming, many companies are striving for greater efficiency, waste reduction, and the reduction of greenhouse-gas emissions. Socially responsible buying initiatives are another way that companies incorporate environmental responsibility into their business strategies.

Businesses have responded to the opportunities and threats created by environmental issues with varying levels of commitment. A high-commitment business develops strategic management programs, which view the environment as an opportunity for advancing organizational interests. Stakeholder analysis requires a process for identifying and prioritizing the many claims and stakes on its business and for dealing with trade-offs related to the impact on different stakeholders. Risk analysis tries to assess the environmental risks and trade-offs associated with business decisions. Organizations that are highly committed to environmental responsibility may conduct an audit of their efforts and report the results to all interested stakeholders. Such organizations may use globally accepted standards, such as ISO 14000, as benchmarks in a strategic environmental audit.

KEY TERMS

natural environment (p. 317)
Kyoto Protocol (p. 320)
Toxics Release Inventory (TRI) (p 334)
green marketing (p. 336)
recycling (p. 338)
green power (p. 341)
ISO 14000 (p. 346)

DISCUSSION QUESTIONS

1. Define the natural environment in the context of social responsibility. How does this definition differ from your definition of the environment?
2. Identify how some of the environmental issues discussed in this chapter are affecting your community. What steps have local businesses taken to address these issues?
3. How serious is the issue of global warming? Discuss the need for global cooperation in addressing this issue.
4. Discuss some of the potential problems associated with attempts to manage biodiversity and endangered species.

5. What is the role of the EPA in U.S. environmental policy? What impact does this agency have on businesses?
6. What federal laws seem to have the greatest impact on business efforts to be environmentally responsible?
7. What role do stakeholders play in a strategic approach to environmental issues? How can businesses satisfy the interests of diverse stakeholders?
8. What is environmental risk analysis? Why is it important for an environmentally conscious company?
9. What is ISO 14000? What is its potential impact on key stakeholders, community, businesses, and global organizations concerned about environmental issues?
10. How can businesses plan for and manage environmental responsibility?

EXPERIENTIAL EXERCISE

Visit the website of the U.S. EPA (http://www.epa.gov/). What topics and issues fall under the authority of the EPA? Peruse the agency's most recent news releases. What are the themes, issues, regulations, and other areas that EPA is most concerned with today? How can this site be useful to consumers and businesses?

WHAT WOULD YOU DO?

The Sustainability Committee's first meeting was scheduled for Thursday afternoon. Although it was only Tuesday, several people had already dropped by committee members' offices to express their opinions and concerns about the company's new focus on sustainability. Some colleagues had trouble with the broad definition of sustainability—"to balance the economic, environmental, and social needs of today's world while planning for future generations." Others worried the sustainability project was just another passing fad. A small group of colleagues believed the company should be most concerned with performance and should forget about trying to become a leader in the social responsibility movement. In general, however, most employees were either supportive or neutral on the initiative.

As the committee's meeting started, the committee chair reminded the group that the company's CEO was very committed to sustainability for several reasons. First, the company was engaged in product development and manufacturing processes that had environmental effects. Second, most companies in the industry were starting initiatives on sustainable development. Third, recent scandals had negatively affected public opinion about business in general. Finally, the company was exploring markets in Europe where environmental activism and rules were often more stringent. With these reasons in mind, the committee set out to develop plans for the next year.

For an hour, the committee discussed the general scope of sustainability in the company. They agreed that sustainability was concerned with increasing positive results while reducing negative effects on a variety of stakeholders. They also agreed that sustainability focused on the "triple bottom line" of financial, social, and environmental performance. For example, a company dedicated to sustainability could design and build a new facility that used alternative energy sources, minimized impact on environmentally sensitive surrounding areas, and encouraged recycling and composting. Another firm might implement its sustainability objectives by requiring suppliers to meet certain standards for environmental impact, business ethics, economic efficiency, community involvement, and others.

After this discussion, the committee made a list of current and potential projects that were likely to be affected by the company's new sustainability focus. These projects included

Energy consumption	Philanthropy
Manufacturing emissions and waste	Product development
Employee diversity	Technology
Community relations	Supplier selection
Corporate governance	Employee health and safety
Regulations and compliance	Volunteerism

After much discussion, the committee agreed that each member would take one of these twelve projects and prepare a brief report on its link to the environmental component of sustainability. This report should review the ways environmental issues can be discussed, changed, improved, or implemented within that area to demonstrate a commitment to sustainability. What would you do?

Technology Issues

CHAPTER 11

CHAPTER OBJECTIVES

- To examine the nature and characteristics of technology

- To explore the economic impact of technology

- To examine technology's influence on society

- To provide a framework for the strategic management of technology issues

CHAPTER OUTLINE

The Nature of Technology

Technology's Influence on the Economy

Technology's Influence on Society

Strategic Implementation of Responsibility for Technology

Increases in cybercrime, widespread worm and virus outbreaks, and regulatory requirements have boosted the profile of computer security. It has become a regular agenda item at board meetings, employee training sessions, consumer shows, and other events. Every day, it seems the media report on new viruses or attacks by hackers. Although many of these crimes are relatively harmless, others do billions of dollars in damage, defraud innocent people, and frighten potential online shoppers away. CEOs must justify spending that has been allocated to security initiatives. Shareholders need to see that this expense is delivering value by ensuring that the company isn't vandalized by hackers or shut down by damaging viruses.

The term *hacker* has evolved over the years to mean a person who breaks into a computer system or network to explore, steal, or wreak havoc. The more secure the system, the more desirable a target it becomes. Hackers often use specialized software that can enter millions of possible passwords until one is accepted by the system. Once inside a system, they may use other specialized programs to search for sensitive information. Although many hackers simply explore the contents of a computer network and later brag about their exploits to other hackers, some have much more malicious intents. Some hackers deface websites to express political or personal opinions or to damage the site's reputation. Hackers may sell the information they find, such as customers' credit-card numbers, telephone calling-card numbers, or plans for new products or marketing strategies. A credit-card transaction processing company confirmed that 8 million credit-card numbers were stolen when someone hacked into its computers. Computer-savvy hackers use text messages on wireless telephones to crash cell phones.

Other hackers may damage systems by altering or deleting files or unleashing "denial-of-service attacks," mail bombs, or computer viruses. Denial-of-service attacks inundate a computer system with fake requests for access to webpages to slow its performance. Mail bombs are similar but involve attacks to mail servers. No matter what form hackers choose, companies need to be on the lookout.

These occurrences have forced companies to spend extra for "network risk insurance," which costs about $5,000 to $30,000 a year for $1 million in coverage. Insurers are delivering an ultimatum: Invest in stand-alone hacker policies or go unprotected. Losses from computer crime are expected to soar 25 percent to $2.8 billion in the United States. Successful website attacks nearly doubled to 600 a day. Many companies are purchasing "hacker insurance," to protect them in the case of data theft and consequences with intellectual property, customer trust, and related areas. That may result in higher costs for consumers as the cost of doing business goes up. Some predict that hacker insurance will be ubiquitous in a few years. Companies cannot budget for the next computer worm, but insurance is a fixed cost that reduces risk.

The threat of computer worms underscores corporate America's growing dependence on the Internet and the vulnerability of its computer networks. The Code Red worm in 2001 caused an estimated $2 billion in damages and cleanup costs. Such security breaches prompted the government to urge companies to insure against losses and for insurance companies to offer more cyberrisk policies as part of its National Strategy to Secure Cyberspace plan. However, security experts warn that hacker insurance is not entirely foolproof.

Hackers may also unleash viruses, which are self-replicating programs. A virus may attach itself to a file, such as an e-mail message or a word-processing macro. Some viruses are relatively harmless, leaving behind nothing more than simple "hello" messages. Others may crash the affected computer by using up all its resources, attacking and corrupting critical files, or erasing the hard drive. History has shown that during a time of increased international tension, illegal cyberactivity often escalates. Attacks may have several motivations. Two of the most common are political activism by self-described "patriot" hackers and criminal activity to further personal goals.

Regardless of the motivation, such activity is illegal and punishable as a felony. During times of potentially increased cyberdisruption, owners and operators of computers and networked systems should review their defensive postures and procedures and stress the importance of increased vigilance in system monitoring. Computer users and system administrators can limit potential problems through the use of "security best practices." Some of the most basic and effective measures that can be taken are:

- Increase user awareness.
- Update antivirus software.
- Stop potentially hostile/suspicious attachments at the e-mail server.
- Utilize filtering to maximize security.

- Establish policies and procedures for responding and recovery.

To combat cybercrime, companies are spending millions of dollars to hire security consultants and purchase specialized software to deter or detect unauthorized entry. Even so, cybercrime is detected only about 40 percent of the time. The problem is further compounded by the fact that companies are reluctant to report such crimes, often because it makes both customers and shareholders uncomfortable and damages the companies' reputations. As the Internet grows ever more popular, the threat of losses from cybercrime will only grow.[1] ■

*I*n this chapter, we explore the nature of technology and its positive and negative effects on society. Technology's influence on the economy is very powerful, especially with regard to growth, employment, and working environments. This influence on society includes issues related to the Internet, privacy, intellectual property, health, and the general quality of life. The strategic direction for technology depends on government as well as on business's ability to plan, implement, and audit the influence of technology on society.

THE NATURE OF TECHNOLOGY

technology
the application of knowledge, including the processes and applications to solve problems, perform tasks, and create new methods to obtain desired outcomes

Technology relates to the application of knowledge, including the processes and applications to solve problems, perform tasks, and create new methods to obtain desired outcomes. It includes intellectual knowledge as well as the physical systems devised to achieve business and personal objectives. The evolution of civilization is tied to developments in technology. Through technological advances, humans have moved from a hunter-gatherer existence to a stable agricultural economy to the Industrial Revolution. Today, our economy is based more on information technology and services than on manufacturing. This technology is changing the way we take vacations, have dinner, do homework, track criminals, know where we are, and maintain friendships. Technology has made it possible to go to work or attend meetings without leaving the house. Our new economy is based on these dynamic technological changes in our society.

Characteristics of Technology

Some of the characteristics of technology include the dynamics, reach, and self-sustaining nature of technological progress. The dynamics of technology relate to the constant change that often challenges the structure of social institutions. The automobile, airplane, and personal computer all created major changes and influenced government, the family, social relationships, education, the military, and leisure. These changes can happen so fast that they require significant adjustments in the political, religious, and economic structures of society. Some societies have difficulty adjusting to this rate of change to the point that they even attempt to legislate against new technologies to isolate themselves. In the past, China tried to isolate its citizens from innovations such as the Internet and social trends that result from the application of new technology to music, movies, and other carriers of culture. But even China responded to the new Internet technology by issuing online advertising licenses in a country where advertising has not been widely accepted, allowing the Internet to be used for market research purposes and permitting the establishment of over 100,000 cybercafés. Since then, Internet use in China has grown, with the number of people logging on regularly totaling 75 million users. Today, China ranks number two in the world, with only the United States having more Internet users. However, the government utilizes a number of strategies for overseeing Chinese citizens and monitoring their behavior when they are surfing on the Internet, including the use of "cybercops" who are able to have real-time, online discussions with Internet users.[2]

The future dynamics of technology are challenging many traditional products, including books. E Ink and Xerox, for example, are developing thin paper and plastic films that can function as screens with digital ink. Users of the technology would still be able to turn the pages as with a traditional book or newspaper, but the pages could be reloaded with a new article or bestseller through wireless transmission. The flat sheet of enhanced paper could even be used to receive a movie. E Ink has joined Lucent Technologies to get the rights to use plastic transistors developed by Lucent needed to show color.[3] The challenges to traditional ways of receiving information are accelerating change in every aspect of life. In many cases, a new technology may become obsolete very shortly after its introduction. Thus, the dynamic characteristic of technology keeps challenging society to adjust.

Reach relates to the broad nature of technology as it moves through society. For instance, every community in both developed and developing countries has been influenced by cellular and wireless telephones. The ability to make a call from almost any location has many positive effects, but negative side effects include increases in traffic accidents and noise pollution as well as fears about potential health risks. Through telecommunications, businesses, families, and governments have been linked from far distances. Satellites allow instant visual and voice electronic connections almost anywhere in the world. These technologies have reduced the need for in-person meetings via business travel, as shown in Figure 11.1. Web conferencing and video conferencing are becoming more popular alternatives, although it may be difficult for technology to replace the nature of face-to-face encounters.

The self-sustaining nature of technology relates to the fact that technology acts as a catalyst to spur even faster development. As innovations are introduced, they stimulate the need for more technology to facilitate further development. For example, the Internet has created the need for broadband transmission of electric signals through phone lines (DSL), satellites, and cable. Broadband allows connections to

| **FIGURE 11.1** | Technology and Business Travel: Percentage of Business Meetings Held in Various Formats |

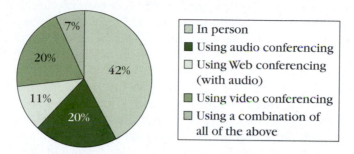

Percentage of business meetings held in various formats

- ☐ In person
- ■ Using audio conferencing
- ☐ Using Web conferencing (with audio)
- ■ Using video conferencing
- ☐ Using a combination of all of the above

Source: Wainhouse Research, "Usage Trends of Collaboration Technology by Business Travelers," http://www.wainhouse.com/surveys/WR-survey-travhab0404.pdf, accessed June 10, 2006. Reprinted with permission of Beattie, Marc, Wainhouse Research, LLC.

the Internet to be fifty times faster than through a traditional telephone modem, allows users to download large files, and creates the opportunity for a rich multimedia experience. As broadband becomes available to more businesses and households, other technologies will have to advance to keep up with the ability to access so much data quickly.[4] In the future, it could be possible to have broadband transmission to computers through electric lines. This means that users could have a broadband connection anywhere that a computer can be plugged in. The invention of the personal computer resulted in changes in personal financial management related to banking, insurance, taxes, and stock trading. Technology starts a change process that creates new opportunities for new technologies in every industry segment or personal life experience that it touches. At some point, there is even a multiplier effect that causes an even greater demand for more change to improve performance. In the marketing sense, technology is not really fulfilling a new need; it is simply filling an old need more efficiently and effectively.

Effects of Technology

Civilizations must harness and adapt to changes in technology to maintain a desired quality of life. The cell phone, for example, has dramatically altered communication patterns, particularly in developing countries where there are few telephone lines. Innovations can also change entire industries. Companies like IBM are creating supercomputers that will be 2 million times more powerful than today's PCs. The computers are revolutionizing financial markets, as stock exchanges are now able to handle very large orders electronically, perform complex trading strategies, and manage many more transactions each day.[5] Such examples illustrate how technology can provide new methods to accomplish tasks that were once thought impossible. These advancements create new processes, new products, and economic progress and ultimately have profound effects on society.

Over the last decade, the global economy experienced the greatest acceleration of technological advancement that has ever occurred, propelling increased productivity, output, corporate profits, and stock prices.[6] Among the positive contributions of these advances were reductions in the number of worker hours required to generate the nation's output. At the same time, the economic conditions that accompanied this period of technical innovation resulted in increased job opportunities. But in the early 2000s, with the fall of the dot-coms and the integrity meltdown of major U.S. corporations, the economy had taken a downturn, along with the falling stock market. Many information technology firms expanded too rapidly and misreported revenue and earnings to maintain high stock prices, to please executives and investors. The result was incidences of massive accounting fraud that damaged confidence and the economy. Chapters 3 and 4 discussed many of these cases and their effect on social responsibility expectations. The traditional work environment has also changed because new forms of telecommunications (e.g., e-mail and video conferencing) reduce the need for face-to-face interaction. Through online shopping, the Internet can also reduce the need for trips to a shopping center and has increased the amount of business done by UPS and FedEx. In addition, the ease and number of business-to-business transactions have expanded.

However, there are concerns that dramatic shifts in the acceleration and innovations derived from technology may be spurring imbalances not only in the economy but also in our social existence. The flow of technology into developing countries can serve as a method to jump-start economic development. On the other hand, a failure to share technology or provide methods to disseminate technology could cause a major divide in the quality of life. It is in the best interest of the United States to be supportive of technology development throughout the world. Limited resources in underdeveloped countries and the lack of a technology infrastructure will lead to many social, political, and economic problems in the future. In addition, trade with the United States would be affected by these problems.

In the United States, the federal government is stepping in with plans to spend $50 million to subsidize computers and Internet access for 300,000 low-income households across the nation. Although this initiative is somewhat controversial, proponents believe it has the potential to raise the standard of living for low-income families much as the Rural Electrification Administration (REA) did in the 1930s, after President Franklin Delano Roosevelt established it to extend electrical power and telephone services to remote communities and rural areas.[7] Some companies are also trying to help bridge the technology gap that is developing between those who can afford technology and those who are on the other side of the so-called digital divide. Gateway, Inc., in partnership with the Hispanic Association of College and Universities (HACU), provides discounted pricing and rebate programs to colleges and universities affiliated with HACU. Gateway also works with these universities to provide paid internship and other career opportunities to encourage Hispanic employment in the technology sector.[8] Gateway is an example of a corporate attempt to keep the positive effects of the reach of technology available to all segments of society.

There are concerns about the way information technology can improve the quality of life for society. In addition, there are concerns about the negative consequences

Access to technology is a social responsibility issue. The pictured book, as well as many other programs, ensure that people with disabilities have the opportunity to reap the benefits of technology.

of the reduction of privacy and the emergence of cybercrime. At some point, abrupt adjustment could occur from changes in our economy, and members of society could become unhappy about changes in their lifestyles or the role of business and government in their lives. Public advocacy organizations are helping by participating in charting the future of computer networks to integrate these technological innovations into the way we live.[9] Timothy Berners-Lee, the crafter of the Internet, has a new futuristic scenario. The Semantic Web, a sequel to the World Wide Web, offers controlled access to U.S. health-care data, plus databases charting the location and status of rivers, underground water, and forests and local vegetation, along with economic data on local industries and what they produce—all marked up in special vocabularies. These allow scientists to run global queries across the Web, fishing randomly for correlations that might exist between where sick people live, worked, and played, such as a polluted stream or industrial dump. He is trying to create a tool that might replace our aging Web browsers, letting us display data by color codes, by geographical maps, or by types of sources searched.[10]

TECHNOLOGY'S INFLUENCE ON THE ECONOMY

Technological advancements have had a profound impact on economic growth and employment, but they raise concerns as well.

Economic Growth and Employment

Over the past fifty years, technology has been a major factor in the economic growth of the United States. Investments in educational technologies, increased support for basic government research, and continued commitment to the mission of research and development (R&D) in both the public and private sectors have become major drivers of economic growth. Through deficit reduction, lower interest rates, tax credits, and liberalization of export controls, the government established the economic infrastructure for using technology to drive economic development. The expansion of industry-led technology partnerships among corporations, governments, and nonprofit organizations has also been a key component of growth. Table 11.1 shows the industries that have received the highest federal support for research and development.

Investments in research and development are among the highest-return investments a nation can make. A report by the Council of Economic Advisors notes that over the past fifty years, technological innovation has been responsible for half or more of the nation's growth in productivity.[11] For example, the ability to access information in real time through the electronic data interface among retailers, wholesalers, and manufacturers has reduced delivery lead times as well as the hours required to produce and deliver products. Likewise, product design times and costs have declined because computer modeling has minimized the need for architectural drafters

TABLE 11.1	Industries with the Highest Federal Support for Research and Development
Industry	**Payoff**
Computers and communications	Defense-related research and development to provide for communications in the event of war led to what has become the Internet.
Semiconductors	The U.S. semiconductor industry developed as a direct result of federal R&D investments and procurement activities.
Biotechnology	Federally funded discoveries in biology, food science, agriculture, genetics, and drugs enabled the private sector to build and expand a world-class industry.
Aerospace	The federal government traditionally has funded the lion's share of aerospace R&D, and this support has made U.S. aerospace companies the world's most advanced.
Environmental technologies	The federal government provides nearly $2 billion a year in support of R&D related to environmental technologies.
Energy efficiency	Many of the products sold and installed by this industry are the product of partnerships between the federal government and private industry.
Lasers	Refined through government, industry, and university research, lasers are now one of the most powerful, versatile, and pervasive technologies in our lives.
Magnetic resonance imaging	Nuclear physicists and chemists worked out the fundamental technique of using radio beams and magnetic fields to analyze the chemical structure of biomedical and other materials.

Source: "Technology and Economic Growth: Producing Real Results for the American People," The White House, November 8, 1995.

and some engineers required for building projects. Medical diagnoses have become faster, more thorough, and more accurate thanks to access to information and records over the Internet, hastening treatment and eliminating unnecessary procedures.[12]

The relationship between businesses and consumers already is being changed by the expanding opportunities for e-commerce, the sharing of business information, maintaining business relationships, and conducting business transactions by means of telecommunications networks. Business-to-business (B2B) e-commerce involving companies buying from and selling to each other online is the fastest growing segment of e-commerce. It has facilitated supply chain management as more companies outsource purchasing over the Internet.[13]

More and more people are turning to the Internet to purchase computers and related peripherals, software, books, music, and even furniture; consumers are increasingly using the Internet to book travel reservations, transact banking business, and trade securities. The forces unleashed by the Internet are particularly important in business-to-business relationships, where the improved quantity, reliability, and timeliness of information have reduced uncertainties. This is the case in companies such as General Motors, IBM, and Procter & Gamble, which are learning to consolidate and rationalize their supply chains using the Internet.[14] Consider the Covisint alliance among Ford, General Motors, DaimlerChrysler, Renault, Nissan, Oracle, and Commerce One, which makes parts from suppliers available through a competitive online auction, reducing months of negotiations to a single day. The goal of the alliance is to reduce the time it takes to bring a new vehicle to market from fifty-four months to eighteen.[15] In many cases, companies are moving toward making most of their purchases online.[16] The downturn in the economy hasn't stopped the momentum of the Contract Division of office supplies retailer Staples Inc., the company's main business-to-business arm. The unit had annual sales of $1 billion and managed double-digit quarterly growth for more than three years.[17]

Economic growth means more jobs and improved living standards. Americans hold millions of jobs in industries that have grown as a result of public and private investment in R&D. These include biotechnology, computers, communications, software, aerospace, and semiconductors; even retailing, wholesaling, and other commercial institutions have been transformed by technology. Average pay for workers in these high-technology industries is about 60 percent higher than the average wage for all U.S. workers.

Science and technology are powerful drivers of economic growth and improvements in the quality of life in the United States. Advances in technology have created not only millions of new jobs but also better health and longer lives, new opportunities, and enrichment of our lives in ways we could not have imagined half a century ago. For example, electric plugs and outlets are becoming a thing of the past. Because of improved battery technologies and better utilization of radio frequencies (RFs), we are becoming a wireless society. Wireless devices in use today include almost everything—PDAs, laptop Internet connections, radios, cell phones, TVs, pagers, and car keys. In the future, most long-distance communication will likely be through fiber optics, and short-distance communication will be wireless. The *Wireless News Factor* has a special report that says free wireless broadband may be coming in the future. But the article says that while some people enjoy free wireless broadband now, the day when it is free to all is still a ways off for a variety of reasons, including "shifting business models and a lack of public commitment."[18] There is also concern about "wacking," or tapping onto other people's wireless connection.

Demand for wireless technology is accelerating, with 50 percent of *Fortune* 1000 companies expected to commit 15 percent of all network spending to wireless voice and data technology. *Computerworld*'s Mark Hall stated that by 2012, every new digital device in the enterprise will be wirelessly connected.[19] In the future, refrigerators, medicine cabinets, and even product packaging may contain wireless microdevices that broadcast product characteristics, features, expiration dates, and other information. Wireless LANs are being installed on Navy warships to free up personnel, reduce crew sizes, and improve monitoring of a range of mechanical and electrical systems.[20]

Economic Concerns About the Use of Technology

Despite the staggering economic growth fostered by technological advancements, there are economic downsides to technology. Small businesses in particular may have difficulty taking advantage of the opportunities surrounding the Internet. Consider the case of Joseph Serna, who thought the Internet could be a powerful tool to attract more customers to his seven-employee print shop in Denver. However, like millions of other small businesspeople and thousands of communities, Serna now fears the new medium will crush his small business instead. Serna's customers want to send art, photos, and layouts to him via e-mail, but his conventional computer modem requires a laborious twenty minutes to send or receive a simple eight-page brochure. A new high-speed Internet connection could slash that time to seconds if it was available in his area. Telephone companies are now offering high-speed service in other, often more upscale, Denver areas, but they have no immediate plans to bring service to Serna's neighborhood. His choice: Pay more than $1,000 a month for a dedicated T-1 telephone line or stand by and watch while competitors with greater resources steal his customers. High-speed connections, also known as broadband, are becoming a must-have for businesses of any size.[21] Over 40 percent (42 percent) of U.S. Internet users have broadband access at home.[22]

The study "Broadband Revolution 2: The Media World of Speedies" found that 64 percent of Internet users who have broadband access (identified as "speedies" in the report) are connected through their workplace, and 37 percent have access at home. In addition, the study found little overlap between those with broadband at work and at home. Of consumers with access to broadband at home and/or work, 58 percent have access only at work; 27 percent have access only at home. Only 15 percent have access at both locations. More important for those with a stake in widespread broadband access, the study found that college students with broadband access are likely to get residential broadband service in the future. More than one-third (38 percent) of college "speedies" say they would be either very likely or somewhat likely to get broadband at home if they were no longer in school. Nearly one-quarter (22 percent) use broadband as a source of entertainment. On average, broadband households pay nearly twice what dial-up households pay each month for their Web connection ($35.40 versus $18.05).[23] Without greater access to the latest technology, especially high-speed Internet services, economic development could suffer in underserved communities, especially poor suburban neighborhoods, inner cities, and rural areas. The ability to purchase other types of technology may affect the nature of competition and the success of various types of businesses.

There are several ways to address these problems that are the inevitable consequences of accelerating change in the technology drivers of the new economy. One way is to examine the outcomes associated with the attempts to use technology. For example, the small town of Glasgow, Kentucky, thanks to the foresight of local leaders, was hard-wired for high-speed Internet access years before the technology was available in many larger urban areas. Community leaders thought the technology would not only benefit citizens but also lead to a high-tech boom for the town of 14,000. The city exploits the high-speed wiring to control traffic lights, share computerized maps to coordinate utility repairs, and monitor electric meters, and a number of businesses have incorporated Internet access into their business strategies. However, only two-thirds of the community's businesses and one-quarter of its residences have signed up for the service, and the high-tech boom has yet to begin. Nonetheless, many other small communities are installing similar high-speed links in preparation for the future.[24] Another way to address the negative consequences of accelerating new technology is to assess problems related to its impact on competition. Restraining competition, domestic or international, to suppress competitive turmoil is a major concern of governments. Allowing anticompetitive practices, price fixing, or other unfair methods of competition would be counterproductive to rising standards of living.[25] Online shoppers may get a tax break, as members of Congress move to ban taxes on Internet access, taxes on Internet transactions involving several jurisdictions, and discriminatory taxes that treat Internet purchases differently from other types of commerce.[26]

TECHNOLOGY'S INFLUENCE ON SOCIETY

Information and telecommunications technology minimizes the borders between countries, businesses, and people and allows people to overcome the physical limitations of time and space. Technological advances also enable people to acquire customized goods and services that cost less and are of higher quality than ever imagined.[27] For example, parents can give their children robotic pets and dolls, which often cost less than $50, that can be programmed to respond to their child's voice.[28] Airline passengers can purchase tickets online and print out boarding passes on their home or office printers so that they can go straight to their plane on arrival at the airport after clearing security.[29] Cartographers and geologists can create custom maps—even in three dimensions—that may help experts manage water supplies, find oil, and pinpoint future earthquakes.[30] In this section, we explore four broad issues related to technology and its impact on society, including the Internet, privacy, intellectual property, and health and biotechnology. Although there are many other pressing issues related to technology, these seem to be the most widely debated at this time. As technology advances, there will probably be more issues by the time you read this book.

The Internet

The Internet, the global information system that links many computer networks together, has profoundly altered the way people communicate, learn, do business, and find entertainment. Although many people believe the Internet began in the early

While technology has made a positive impact on society, it may also be used for illegal activity, such as the printing of counterfeit currency. This counterfeit currency was found by the U.S. Secret Service before it made it into circulation.

TABLE 11.2	History of the Internet

Year	Event	Significance
1836	Telegraph	The telegraph revolutionized human (tele)communications with Morse Code, a series of dots and dashes used to communicate between humans.
1858–1866	Transatlantic cable	Transatlantic cable allowed direct instantaneous communication across the Atlantic Ocean.
1876	Telephone	The telephone created voice communication, and telephone exchanges provide the backbone of Internet connections today.
1957	USSR launched *Sputnik*.	*Sputnik* was the first artificial Earth satellite and the start of global communications.
1962–1968	Packet switching	The Internet relies on packet-switching networks that split data into tiny packets that may take different routes to a destination.
1971	Beginning of the Internet	People communicate over the Internet with a program to send messages across a distributed network.
1973	Global networking becomes a reality.	Ethernet outlined—this is how local networks are basically connected today, and gateways define how large networks (maybe of different architecture) can be connected together.
1991	World Wide Web with text-based, menu-driven interface to access Internet resources	User-friendly interface to World Wide Web is established.
1992	Multimedia changes the face of the Internet.	The term *surfing the Internet* is coined.
1993	World Wide Web revolution begins.	Mosaic, a user-friendly Graphical Front End to the World Wide Web, makes the Web more accessible and evolves into Netscape.
1995	Internet service providers advance.	Online dial-up systems (CompuServe, America Online, and Prodigy) begin to provide Internet access.
2000	Broadband emerges.	Provides fast access to multimedia and large text files.
2002	Wireless expands.	Devices for wireless linkage to the Internet grow rapidly.

Source: Adapted from "History of the Internet," NetValley, www.internetvalley.com/archives/mirrors/davemarsh-timeline-1.htm, accessed June 19, 2006.

1990s, its origins can be traced to the late 1950s (see Table 11.2). Over five decades, the network evolved from a system for government and university researchers into an information and entertainment tool used by millions around the globe. With the development of the World Wide Web, which organizes the information on the Internet into interconnected "pages" of text, graphics, audio, and video, use of the Internet exploded in the 1990s.

Today, nearly half a billion people around the world utilize the Internet. In the United States alone, about 145 million Americans access the Internet at home, with some citizens accessing the Internet only at work. Internet use by consumers in other countries, especially Japan (42 million users), the United Kingdom (24 million), Germany (33 million), and Spain (12 million), is escalating rapidly. Table 11.3 shows the recent pattern of active Internet usage in households.[31] To keep up with the growing demand for new e-mail and website addresses, the Internet Corporation for Assigned

TABLE 11.3	Active Home Use of the Internet

Active Home Internet Users by Country, April and May 2006

Country	April 2006	May 2006	Change (%)	One-Month Difference
Australia	10,222,090	10,585,433	3.55	363,343
Brazil	13,431,424	13,246,186	−1.38	−185,238
France	17,907,014	18,414,460	2.83	507,446
Germany	32,112,698	33,373,792	3.93	1,261,093
Italy	17,280,253	16,946,925	−1.93	−333,329
Japan	41,139,368	42,405,468	3.08	1,266,100
Spain	11,715,596	12,484,324	6.56	768,728
Switzerland	3,824,662	3,769,940	−1.43	−54,722
U.K.	24,200,841	24,235,940	0.15	35,098
U.S.	143,596,769	143,229,214	−0.26	−367,554
Total	**315,430,716**	**318,691,682**	**1.03**	**3,260,966**

Source: Nielsen/NetRatings, 2006. Copyright © 2006 NetRatings. Reprinted with permission.

Names and Numbers has added seven new domain name suffixes to allow for the creation of millions of new addresses. Now, in addition to .com (for companies), .edu (schools and universities), .gov (government agencies and offices), .mil (military use), .net (networks), and hundreds of country codes, computer users will see addresses followed by .zero (air-transport industry), .biz (businesses), .coop (nonprofit cooperatives), .info (unrestricted), .museum (museums), .name (personal names), and .pro (professionals such as doctors and accountants).[32]

The interactive nature of the Internet has created tremendous opportunities for businesses to forge relationships with consumers and business customers, target markets more precisely, and even reach previously inaccessible markets. The Internet also facilitates supply chain management, allowing companies to network with manufacturers, wholesalers, retailers, suppliers, and outsource firms to serve customers more efficiently.[33] Despite the growing importance and popularity of the Internet, fraud has become a major issue for businesses and consumers. Because shopping via the Internet does not require a signature to verify transactions, credit-card fraud online is more than three and a half times greater than credit-card fraud through mail-order catalogs and almost nine times greater than for traditional storefront retailers.[34] More than $700 million in online sales were lost to fraud in 2001, representing 1.14 percent of total annual online sales of $61.8 billion. Some are attempting to fight fraud by embracing two new credit-card protection systems: Visa's Verified by Visa and MasterCard's Universal Cardholder Authentication Field (UCAF) standard and Secure Payment Application (SPA).[35]

Consumers are also increasingly worried about becoming victims of fraud online. For example, complaints about fraud in online auctions have risen dramatically over the last decade.[36] A survey conducted by Harris Interactive found that 31 percent of Americans who go online, or approximately 35 million people, participate in online auctions. However, the survey found that online auctions made up 78 percent of Internet fraud complaints, with an average loss of $326 per victim. Still, a majority of respondents who have participated as bidders said they are somewhat or very confident that as the winning bidder in an online auction, they will get what they pay for from a seller.[37] The online auction site eBay has more than 16 million regular customers exchanging $14 million every day. The company received 10,700 fraud complaints in one year. Among the complaints are accusations of "shill bidding," which involves sellers bidding on their own items to heighten interest, and competitive bidding. Another problem is sellers not delivering promised items after receiving the buyers' funds. The formula for fraud is enhanced by anonymity, quick access, low overhead, satellite access, and little regulation.[38] Corporations are buying industrial-strength IT gear via online auctions. Todd Lutwak, director of San Jose–based eBay Inc.'s Technology Marketplace, says that in fiscal 2001, $1.8 billion worth of equipment was sold in that division (which includes consumer electronics and computers in addition to enterprise IT equipment). eBay has auction offerings in used business equipment that are complemented by both financial and inspection services. Customers interested in purchasing used farm tractors, printing presses, forklifts, trailers, and other capital equipment are assured of fair pricing and quality through eBay's Business Equipment Purchase Protection program.[39] Despite such programs in the business-to-business market, complaints about online auctions have made them one of the Federal Trade Commission's top ten "dot cons" (see Figure 11.2). With online auctions generating an estimated $6.1 billion, consumers and merchants alike are exploring options, including regulation, to protect the security of online transactions.[40]

Privacy

The extraordinary growth of the Internet has generated issues related to privacy. Businesses have long tracked consumers' shopping habits with little controversy. However, observing the contents of a consumer's shopping cart or the process a consumer goes through when choosing a box of cereal generally involves the collection of aggregate data rather than specific personally identifying data. And although some consumers' use of credit cards, shopping cards, and coupons involves giving up a certain degree of anonymity in the shopping process, consumers could still choose to remain anonymous by paying cash. Shopping on the Internet, however, allows businesses to track consumers on a far more personal level, from their online purchases to the websites they favor.[41] More than 71 percent of respondents surveyed in a UCLA study indicated they will probably make more purchases online in the future, up from 66 percent in 2001 and 54 percent in 2000. Privacy concerns, while still high, have declined slightly, and the most experienced users show lower levels of concern about credit-card security than do new users.[42] Indeed, current technology has made it possible to amass vast quantities of personal information, often without consumers' knowledge. The Internet allows for the collection, sharing, and selling of this information to interested third parties. The website peoplesearch.com, for example, permits anyone to do asset verification checks and criminal background checks on any individual for a fee of $39 to $125. Another website, UsSearch.com, supplies

FIGURE 11.2	The Top Ten "Dot Cons"

1. Internet Auctions

The Bait: Shop in a "virtual marketplace" that offers a huge selection of products at great deals.

The Catch: After sending their money, consumers say they've received an item that is less valuable than promised or, worse yet, nothing at all.

The Safety Net: When bidding through an Internet auction, particularly for a valuable item, check out the seller and insist on paying with a credit card or using an escrow service.

2. Internet Access Services

The Bait: Free money, simply for cashing a check.

The Catch: Consumers say they've been "trapped" into long-term contracts for Internet access or another Web service, with big penalties for cancellation or early termination.

The Safety Net: If a check arrives at your home or business, read both sides carefully and look inside the envelope to find the conditions you're agreeing to if you cash the check. Read your telephone bill carefully for unexpected or unauthorized charges.

3. Credit-Card Fraud

The Bait: Surf the Internet and view adult images online for free, just for sharing your credit-card number to prove you're over eighteen.

The Catch: Consumers say that fraudulent promoters have used their credit-card numbers to run up charges on their cards.

The Safety Net: Share credit-card information only when buying from a company you trust. Dispute unauthorized charges on your credit-card bill by complaining to the bank that issued the card. Federal law limits your liability to $50 in charges if your card is misused.

4. International Modem Dialing

The Bait: Get free access to adult material and pornography by downloading a "viewer" or "dialer" computer program.

The Catch: Consumers complain about exorbitant long-distance charges on their telephone bill. Through the program, their modem is disconnected, then reconnected to the Internet through an international long-distance number.

The Safety Net: Don't download any program to access a so-called free service without reading all the disclosures carefully for cost information. Just as important, read your telephone bill carefully and challenge any charges you didn't authorize or don't understand.

5. Web Cramming

The Bait: Get a free custom-designed website for a thirty-day trial period, with no obligation to continue.

The Catch: Consumers say they've been charged on their telephone bills or received a separate invoice, even if they never accepted the offer or agreed to continue the service after the trial period.

The Safety Net: Review your telephone bills and challenge any charges you don't recognize.

6. Multilevel Marketing Plans/Pyramids

The Bait: Make money through the products and services you sell as well as those sold by the people you recruit into the program.

The Catch: Consumers say that they've bought into plans and programs, but their customers are other distributors, not the general public. Some multilevel marketing programs are actually illegal pyramid schemes. When products or services are sold only to distributors like yourself, there's no way to make money.

The Safety Net: Avoid plans that require you to recruit distributors, buy expensive inventory, or commit to a minimum sales volume.

7. Travel and Vacation

The Bait: Get a luxurious trip with lots of "extras" at a bargain-basement price.

The Catch: Consumers say some companies deliver lower quality accommodations and services than they've advertised or no trip at all. Others have been hit with hidden charges or additional requirements after they've paid.

(*continued*)

| FIGURE 11.2 | The Top Ten "Dot Cons" (*continued*) |

The Safety Net: Get references on any travel company you're planning to do business with. Then, get details of the trip in writing, including the cancellation policy, before signing on.

8. Business Opportunities

The Bait: Be your own boss and earn big bucks.

The Catch: Taken in by promises about potential earnings, many consumers have invested in a "biz op" that turned out to be a "biz flop." There was no evidence to back up the earnings claims.

The Safety Net: Talk to other people who started businesses through the same company, get all the promises in writing, and study the proposed contract carefully before signing. Get an attorney or an accountant to take a look at it, too.

9. Investments

The Bait: Make an initial investment in a day trading system or service and you'll quickly realize huge returns.

The Catch: Big profits always mean big risk. Consumers have lost money to programs that claim to be able to predict the market with 100 percent accuracy.

The Safety Net: Check out the promoter with state and federal securities and commodities regulators, and talk to other people who invested through the program to find out what level of risk you're assuming.

10. Health-Care Products/Services

The Bait: Items not sold through traditional suppliers are "proven" to cure serious and even fatal health problems.

The Catch: Claims for "miracle" products and treatments convince consumers that their health problems can be cured. But people with serious illnesses who put their hopes in these offers might delay getting the health care they need.

The Safety Net: Consult a health-care professional before buying any "cure-all" that claims to treat a wide range of ailments or offers quick cures and easy solutions to serious illnesses.

Source: "Top 10 Dot Cons," Federal Trade Commission, http://www.ftc.gov/opa/2000/10/topten.htm, accessed June 10, 2006.

background information, including property ownership, civil judgments, driver's license, physical description, and summary of assets, on any individual in its database for $39.95 and up.[43] In all, 88.8 percent of respondents in the UCLA survey—users and nonusers alike—expressed some concern about the privacy of their personal information when or if they buy on the Internet, down from 94.6 percent in 2001.[44]

On the positive side, today's technology makes it easier for law enforcement agents to catch criminals, for banks to detect fraud, and for consumers to learn about goods and services and to communicate directly with businesses about their needs. Because of the ease of access to personal information, however, unauthorized use of this information may occur.[45] Spam has reached an epidemic level, affecting hundreds of millions of e-mail users worldwide, impairing productivity, and sapping network resources. Estimates now claim about 50 percent of e-mail consists of spam. A real need has emerged for spam-blocking software to revitalize productivity and to stop unwanted e-mails.[46]

Information can be collected on the Internet with or without a person's knowledge. Many websites follow users' tracks through their site by storing a "cookie," or identifying string of text, on their computers. These cookies permit website operators to track how often a user visits the site, what he or she looks at while there, and in what sequence. Cookies also allow website visitors to customize services, such as

GLOBAL CHALLENGES

Technology Issues Around the World

As Beijing prepares for the 2008 Olympics, questions about the Chinese government's stance on piracy and trademark violations are being asked. It is common to find phony Adidas, Mickey Mouse, Diesel, and Nike merchandise across China, but there are additional precautions being taken on official Olympic merchandise. Although shop owners in the counterfeit center of Xu Chao are accustomed to selling Western knock-offs, they are also aware that the penalties for selling fake Olympic items can be quite steep.

Much like the Chinese government protects high-end brands such as Burberry, Chanel, and Prada, it has also taken steps to protect the Olympic brand. In 2002, the government passed a national law to defend the intellectual property rights associated with Olympic symbols. An executive of the Beijing Olympiad Committee noted, "We have no fixed assets. So the Olympic logo is the most valuable thing we own."

Official manufacturers are under very strict orders to keep the Olympic merchandise in the formal supply chain. Unlike other supply chains, the route of products from manufacturer to retailers is highly controlled for the Olympic merchandise. The channel is kept necessarily tight, so the products do not become diffused and distributed into unapproved retail stores. In addition, manufacturing output is carefully monitored so that no black market merchandise appears. The Olympic merchandise carries innovative and sophisticated tags, including ones with holograms, watermarks, bar codes, and serial numbers. There are only twenty-four official retail stores that will carry Beijing commemorative items.

China is not the first country to guard its Olympic brand; Australia passed a similar law in anticipation of the 2000 Sydney games. By the time the Olympics started there, however, the city was flooded with counterfeit items. Beijing officials are hoping that the nationalistic pride of Chinese citizens will make them less inclined to manufacture, buy, or sell fake Olympic merchandise because the honor of the 2008 games belongs to the whole country.

Sources: "Handbags at Dawn" *Economist.com*, April 21, 2006, p. 1; "Silk Market Victory Could Open New Anti-Fake Front," *Managing Intellectual Property* (February 2006): 1; Geoffrey A. Fowler, "China's Logo Crackdown," *Wall Street Journal*, November 4, 2005, p. B1. ∎

virtual shopping carts, as well as the particular content they see when they log on to a webpage. However, if a website operator can exploit cookies to link a visitor's interests to a name and address, that information could be sold to advertisers and other parties without the visitor's consent or even knowledge. The potential for misuse has left many consumers rather uncomfortable with this technology.[47] Identity theft is one of the fastest growing crimes in the nation, hitting nearly 1.1 million people a year for an average of $6,767 each. In 2002, federal authorities broke up one of the biggest identity-theft cases in U.S. history and charged three men with stealing credit information via the Internet from more than 30,000 people, draining bank accounts, and ruining credit ratings.[48]

Cookies aren't the only way that businesses can track consumers online. Companies such as DoubleClick, Digital Envoy, and Quova are developing technology that can match Internet addresses with geographical locations. This technology involves bouncing homing bits to a browser's computer from multiple locations and then analyzing the data to triangulate the computer's actual location. Quova says that it can provide its customers with a website visitor's city in a fiftieth of a second with 90 percent accuracy. These companies claim that they are not collecting specific customer names and addresses, only their city of origin so that website operators can tailor their content—and advertisements—to different users. The technology also gets around the problem of savvier users who block webpages from storing cookies on their computers.[49]

A growing number of Internet websites require visitors to register and provide information about themselves to access some or all of their content. How this information will be used is also generating concern. For example, 75 percent of users of health-related websites worry that the information they supply when they register for access to the site or respond to surveys may be sold to third parties without their permission.[50] Some people are concerned that personal information about their health may be sold to insurance companies that may deny them coverage on the basis of that information. Although many health-oriented and other websites post privacy policies that specify whether and how they will use any personal information they gather, some consumers still worry that such policies are just "lip service." Amazon.com received complaints through the Federal Trade Commission (FTC) after it modified its privacy policy, which allows it to disclose personal information to third parties and to sell customer information in the event it goes out of business or sells assets.[51] According to the FTC, about two-thirds of commercial websites post information on their privacy policies. However, about 93 percent of these sites collect at least one type of personally identifying information from visitors, and 57 percent gather some type of demographic information.[52] Moreover, only 20 percent of sites have voluntarily implemented adequate privacy-protection standards.[53] Even the Federal Trade Commission's own website fails to meet its privacy standards.[54]

Privacy issues related to children are generating even more debate, as well as laws to protect children's interests. Concerns about protecting children's privacy were highlighted in a recent study by the Annenberg Public Policy Center, which reported that two-thirds of children ages ten to seventeen would divulge their favorite online stores to receive a free gift, whereas more than half would reveal their parents' favorite stores, and another quarter would disclose details about their parents' activities on the weekend. The study also found that many children would share information about the family car and the amount of their allowance. It should be noted that this survey was conducted before the U.S. Children's Online Privacy Protection Act (COPPA) went into effect in 2000. That law prohibits websites and Internet providers from seeking personal information from children under age thirteen without parental consent.[55] Recent Census Bureau statistics bear out the increasing use of computers and the Internet among children. That's provoking a lot of worries and assorted attempts to tame the Internet. The government has waded in with the Children's Internet Protection Act, which requires schools and libraries that receive federal funds to block access to inappropriate content. The measure as it applies to libraries was struck down on First Amendment grounds and is on appeal to the U.S. Supreme Court.[56] Table 11.4 provides recommendations for improving child safety on the Internet, courtesy of Microsoft.

Another area of growing concern is "identity theft," which occurs when criminals obtain personal information that allows them to impersonate someone else and use their credit to obtain financial accounts and make purchases. Because of the Internet's

TABLE 11.4   Ten Ideas to Improve Child Safety on the Internet

1. Encourage your kids to share their Internet experiences with you.

2. Teach your kids to trust their instincts.

3. If your kids visit chat rooms, use instant messaging (IM) programs, online video games, or other activities on the Internet that require a login name to identify themselves, help them choose that name and make sure it doesn't reveal any personal information about them.

4. Insist that your kids never give out your address, phone number, or other personal information, including where they go to school or where they like to play.

5. Teach your kids that the difference between right and wrong is the same on the Internet as it is in real life.

6. Show your kids how to respect others online. Make sure they know that rules for good behavior don't change just because they're on a computer.

7. Insist that your kids respect the property of others online. Explain that making illegal copies of other people's work—music, video games, and other programs—is just like stealing it from a store.

8. Tell your kids that they should never meet online friends in person. Explain that online friends may not be who they say they are.

9. Teach your kids that not everything they read or see online is true.

10. Control your children's online activity with advanced Internet software. Parental controls can help you filter out harmful content, monitor the sites your child visits, and find out what they do there.

Source: Microsoft Corporation, "10 Things You Can Teach Kids to Improve Their Web Safety," http://www.microsoft.com/athome/security/children/kidsonlinetips.mspx, accessed June 19, 2006. © 2006 Microsoft Corporation. All rights reserved.

relative anonymity and speed, it fosters legal and illegal access to databases containing social security numbers, driver's license numbers, dates of birth, mothers' maiden names, and other information that can be used to establish a credit-card or bank account in another person's name to make transactions. According to the National Fraud Center, arrests for identity theft fraud have increased to nearly 10,000 a year, with losses from such fraud reaching $745 million. The Federal Trade Commission said complaints about identity theft represent 37 percent of all consumer fraud complaints, with victims reporting hijacked credit cards, drained bank accounts, and tarnished reputations.[57] To deter identity theft, the National Fraud Center wants financial institutions to implement new technologies, such as digital certificates, digital signatures, and biometrics—the use of fingerprinting or retina scanning.[58] Legislation was introduced to protect people from identity theft, with a focus on cases involving the Internet. The bill would require social security numbers to be removed from public records published on the Web; it would also prohibit the sale of social security numbers to the general public and remove such numbers from government checks and driver's licenses. The measure would permit legitimate business and government use of the numbers. Identity theft topped the Federal Trade Commission's annual report on consumer complaints in 2002, accounting for 43 percent of the complaints lodged with the FTC and losses for consumers of about $343 million.[59]

Some measure of protection for personal privacy is already provided by the U.S. Constitution as well as Supreme Court rulings and federal laws (see Table 11.5).

TABLE 11.5	Privacy Laws

Act (Date Enacted)	Purpose
Privacy Act (1974)	Requires federal agencies to adopt minimum standards for collecting and processing personal information; limits the disclosure of such records to other public or private parties; requires agencies to make records on individuals available to them on request, subject to certain conditions.
Right to Financial Privacy Act (1978)	Protects the rights of financial institution customers to keep their financial records private and free from unjust government investigation.
Computer Security Act (1987)	Brought greater confidentiality and integrity to the regulation of information in the public realm by assigning responsibility for the standardization of communication protocols, data structures, and interfaces in telecommunications and computer systems to the National Institute of Standards and Technology (NIST), which also announced security and privacy guidelines for federal computer systems.
Computer Matching and Privacy Protection Act (1988)	Amended the Privacy Act by adding provisions regulating the use of computer matching, the computerized comparison of individual information for purposes of determining eligibility for federal benefits programs.
Video Privacy Protection Act (1988)	Specifies the circumstances under which a business that rents or sells videos can disclose personally identifiable information about a consumer or reveal an individual's video rental or sales records.
Telephone Consumer Protection Act (1991)	Regulates the activities of telemarketers by limiting the hours during which they can solicit residential subscribers, outlawing the use of artificial or prerecorded voice messages to residences without prior consent, prohibiting unsolicited advertisements by telephone facsimile machines, and requiring telemarketers to maintain a "do not call list" of any consumers who request not to receive further solicitation.
Driver Privacy Protection Act (1993)	Restricts the circumstances under which state departments of motor vehicles may disclose personal information about any individual obtained by the department in connection with a motor vehicle record.
Fair Credit Reporting Act (amended in 1997)	Promotes accuracy, fairness, and privacy of information in the files of consumer reporting agencies (e.g., credit bureaus); grants consumers the right to see their personal credit reports, to find out who has requested access to their reports, to dispute any inaccurate information with the consumer reporting agency, and to have inaccurate information corrected or deleted.
Children's Online Privacy Protection Act (2000)	Regulates the online collection of personally identifiable information (name, address, e-mail address, hobbies, interests, or information collected through cookies) from children under age thirteen by specifying what a website operator must include in a privacy policy, when and how to seek consent from a parent, and what responsibilities an operator has to protect children's privacy and safety online.

Sources: "Privacy Act of 1974," U.S. Bureau of Reclamation, http://www.usbr.gov/foia/privacy.html, accessed August 15, 2006; Federal Deposit Insurance Corporation, "Financial Institutions Regulatory and Interest Rates Control Act of 1978," http://www.fdic.gov/regulations/laws/rules/6500-2550.html, accessed August 23, 2006; E. Maria Grace, "Privacy vs. Convenience: The Benefits and Drawbacks of Tax System Modernization," *Federal Communications Law Journal* 47 (December 1994), www.law.indiana.edu/fclj/pubs/v47/no2/grace.html; "Sec. 2710. Wrongful Disclosure of Video Tape Rental or Sale Records," Legal Information Institute, www4.law.cornell.edu/uscode/18/2710.text.html, accessed December 27, 2000; "Comments Sought in Important FCC Proceeding Impacting Non-Profit Organizations and Other Entities That Make Unsolicited Telephone Calls," Arent Fox, PLLC, http://www.arentfox.com/legal_updates/content660.htm, accessed August 25, 2006; "Sec. 2721. Prohibition on Release and Use of Certain Personal Information from State Motor Vehicle Records," Legal Information Institute, www4.law.cornell.edu/uscode/18/2721.text.html, accessed August 15, 2006; "A Summary of Your Rights Under the Fair Credit Reporting Act," Federal Trade Commission, http://www.ftc.gov/bcp/conline/pubs/credit/fcrasummary.pdf, accessed August 25, 2006; "How to Comply with the Children's Online Privacy Protection Rule According to the Federal Trade Commission," COPPA, http://www.coppa.org/comply.htm, accessed August 25, 2006.

The U.S. Federal Trade Commission (FTC) also regulates and enforces privacy standards and monitors websites to ensure compliance. A recent study commissioned by the FTC reported that 98 percent of the 100 top websites collect at least one type of personal information, and 93 percent have posted at least one type of disclosure (privacy policy notice or the site practices).[60] The 2002 Online Customer Respect Study of *Fortune* 100 Companies rated Verizon as sixth best overall, third in online privacy, and first in how well it explains online policies to customers, called "transparency" in the survey.[61] As the FTC Chair Robert Pitofsky told a Senate panel, "Companies say self-regulation will work, but it's becoming clear that companies on the Net are not protecting the privacy of consumers."[62] For example, the FTC accused GeoCities, a popular entertainment website, of misrepresenting the purposes for which it was harvesting personal information from both children and adults. GeoCities did not disclose the information collected, the purpose for which it was collected, or to whom it would be disclosed. The company settled the charges, agreeing to post an explicit privacy policy detailing what information it collects, for what purpose, to whom it will be disclosed, and how consumers can access and remove the information.[63]

INTERNATIONAL INITIATIVES ON PRIVACY Privacy concerns are not limited to the United States. The European Union (EU) has made great strides in protecting the privacy of its citizens. The 1998 European Union Directive on Data Protection specifically requires companies that want to collect personal information to explain how the information will be used and to obtain the individual's permission. Companies must make customer data files available on request, just as U.S. credit-reporting firms must grant customers access to their personal credit histories. The law also bars website operators from selling e-mail addresses and using cookies to track visitors' movements and preferences without first obtaining permission. Because of this legislation, no company may deliver personal information about EU citizens to countries whose privacy laws do not meet EU standards.[64] Some European countries have taken further steps to protect their citizens. Italy, for example, established an Italian Data Protection Commission to enforce its stringent privacy laws. Such agencies highlight the differences in how Europeans and Americans approach the online privacy issue.[65]

In Canada, private industry has taken the lead in creating and developing privacy policies through the Direct Marketing Association of Canada (DMAC). The DMAC's policies resulted in the proposal of legislation to protect personal privacy. The Personal Information Protection and Electronic Documents Act, which went into effect on January 1, 2001, established a right of personal privacy for information collected by Canadian businesses and organizations. The new law instituted rules governing the collection, use, and disclosure of personal information in the private sector. The law also works in conjunction with other legislation that protects personal information collected by federal and/or provincial governments. The Canadian Standards Association (CSA) was also instrumental in bringing about privacy protection guidelines in Canada. The CSA Model Code for the Protection of Personal Information requires organizations to protect personal information and to allow individuals access to their own personal information, allowing for correction if necessary.[66]

In Japan, the Ministry of International Trade and Industry established the Electronic Network Consortium (ENC) to resolve issues associated with the Internet. The ENC (which comprises ninety-two corporate members, fifty-one local community organizations, and fifteen special members) has prepared guidelines for protecting personal data gathered by Japanese online service providers. These guidelines require websites to obtain an individual's consent before collecting personal data or using or transferring such data to a third party. The guidelines also call for organizations to appoint managers who understand the ENC guidelines to oversee the collection and use of personal data and to utilize privacy information management systems such as the Platform for Privacy Protection (P3P).[67] P3P is a set of standards under development by the World Wide Web Consortium that would permit websites to translate their privacy statements and standards into a uniform format that Web-browsing software could access to supply users with relevant information about a particular firm's policies. Website visitors could then decide what information, if any, they are willing to share with websites.[68]

Protection of citizens' privacy on the Internet is not a major public concern in Russia. Few Russian websites have privacy policy or disclosure statements explaining how collected information will be used. International companies conducting business in Russia or managing Russian subsidiaries often maintain online privacy information for their U.S. and European customers but not for Russian customers.[69] The country is not currently looking to tighten its information privacy laws. Corporate databases as well as comprehensive files on customers of retail product and service providers are readily available across Russia. It is a common practice in Russia to sell databases.[70] Until recently, Russian law gave authorities the right to monitor private e-mail. However, Nail Murzakhanov, the founder of a small Internet service provider in Volgograd, challenged this right when he refused to purchase the equipment that would have permitted Russian security agencies to eavesdrop on his customers' e-mail. Murzakhanov stood firm in his belief that complying with the law would jeopardize his guarantee of privacy to his customers, even after the Ministry of Communications threatened to revoke his license to operate. Eventually, the Ministry of Communications dropped all charges against Murzakhanov's company, setting a precedent for other Internet service providers who wish to protect their customers' privacy.[71] Russian antitrust regulators are also examining the last space where Russian vodka makers can still advertise: the Internet. An official of the antitrust service said that advertising for alcohol was allowed neither on television nor in the street, and therefore, it was not allowed on the Internet either. More than many other countries, the future prospects of the Internet in Russia are largely controlled by the government.[72]

PRIVACY OFFICERS AND CERTIFICATION Businesses are beginning to recognize that the only way to circumvent further government regulation with respect to privacy is to develop systems and policies to protect consumers' interests. In addition to creating and posting policies regarding the gathering and use of personal information, more companies—including American Express, AT&T, Citigroup, and Prudential Insurance—are beginning to hire chief privacy officers (CPOs). New laws requiring companies to protect consumer privacy will create 30,000 jobs. Most health-care-related businesses must appoint a privacy official to safeguard patient data. About 20 percent of

FIGURE 11.3   Fair Information Practices

The Fair Information Practices

- **Notice.** Web sites should provide full disclosure of what personal information is collected and how it is used.
- **Choice.** Consumers at a Web site should be given choice about how their personal information is used.
- **Access.** Once consumers have disclosed personal information, they should have access to it.
- **Security.** Personal information disclosed to Web sites should be secured to ensure the information stays private.
- **Redress.** Consumers should have a way to resolve problems that may arise regarding sites, use and disclosure of their personal information.

Source: Federal Trade Commission, "Fair Information Practice Principles," http://www.ftc.gov/reports/privacy3/fairinfo.htm, accessed June 19, 2006.

the new jobs will be for executives, such as at Ford, where privacy officers typically earn between $100,000 and $350,000 a year and report either to a company's general counsel or its chief operating officer.[73] These high-level executives are typically given broad powers to establish policies to protect consumer privacy and, in so doing, to protect their companies from negative publicity and legal scrutiny. Figure 11.3 lists the major provisions of the FTC's Fair Information Practices, which can be used as a starting point in developing a corporate privacy policy.

Several nonprofit organizations have also stepped in to help companies develop privacy policies. Among the best known are TRUSTe and the BBBOnLine. TRUSTe is a nonprofit organization devoted to promoting global trust in Internet technology by providing a standardized, third-party oversight program that addresses the privacy concerns of consumers, website operators, and government regulators. Companies that agree to abide by TRUSTe's privacy standards may display a "trustmark" on their websites. These firms must disclose their personal information collection and privacy policies in a straightforward privacy statement. TRUSTe is supported by a network of corporate, industry, and nonprofit sponsors, including the Electronic Frontier Foundation, CommerceNet, America Online, Compaq, Ernst & Young, Excite, IBM, MatchLogic, Microsoft, Netcom, and Netscape.[74] For example, eBay's website is TRUSTe certified, which means that its online privacy practices fulfill TRUSTe's requirements. The online auction company's privacy policy promises that eBay will not share any personal information gathered from customers with any third parties and specifies how it will use the information it obtains. TRUSTe maintains the largest privacy seal program with more than 1,500 websites certified throughout the world. The organization is very active in educating

reviewed by

TRUST·e
site privacy statement

There are a number of organizations dedicated to improving and protecting privacy on the Internet and with technology. TRUSTe is a nonprofit, independent group dedicated to protecting privacy on the Internet, building users' confidence and trust in the Internet, and helping to accelerate Web-based economic growth.

and encouraging companies to improve privacy, security, and related aspects of business. Table 11.6 describes a real-life case scenario, along with an explanation of how TRUSTe's version 2.0 security guidelines could be applied to improve the situation.[75]

The mission of BBBOnLine is to promote trust and confidence in the Internet by encouraging ethical business practices. The BBBOnLine program provides verification, monitoring and review, consumer dispute resolution, a compliance seal, enforcement mechanisms, and an educational component. It is managed by the Council of Better Business Bureaus, an organization with considerable experience in conducting self-regulation and dispute-resolution programs, and it employs guidelines and requirements outlined by the Federal Trade Commission and the U.S. Department of Commerce.[76] More than 12,000 websites have qualified to display the BBBOnLine trustmarks, which include separate programs for security, privacy, and safe shopping. Together with PlanetFeedback.com, whose 400,000 registered users make it one of the largest online consumer feedback services, BBBOnLine has created consumer feedback solutions for several top companies, including Procter & Gamble,

TABLE 11.6	Applying TRUSTe Guidelines to a Case Study
Case Study 1	**How the TRUSTe Guidelines Would Help**
Company ABC maintains a database containing customers' names, addresses, and account numbers. The database is unencrypted, but is only accessible by employees using the proper usernames and passwords. Some employees have access to laptops for their jobs. ABC has a security policy requiring all laptops to be locked in employee cabinets while not in use. However, ABC does not enforce this aspect of the policy.	The Security Guidelines (v. 2.0) suggest that all companies establish an employee awareness and training program. If all employees undergo basic initial and refresher security training, they are more likely to remember company policies and abide by them.
One night, Employee 1 left a laptop on his desk. Even though the building was locked, somehow a thief broke in and stole the laptop. A disgruntled former Employee 2 was contacted by the thief and was convinced to sell her old username and password.	If ABC had implemented an incident investigation and notification procedure, it is more likely that security personnel could have changed the passwords as soon as the theft was discovered and the thief would not have been able to access the database on that laptop.
The former Employee 2's username and password worked for both the laptop and the database. The thief was able to use the laptop to get access to the network and the database. Thousands of customers were impacted.	Assigning access privileges based on a need to know might have prevented this breach. Additionally, forcing password expiration would have prevented access to the network and the database. If the company had terminated inactive accounts or the accounts of terminated employees, access would have likewise been prevented.
Because it had never considered what it should do in the event of a breach, ABC had a significant delay before it could assemble a list of affected customers and notify them of the incident. Major media picked up the story and portrayed the company as unprepared and sloppy in their response.	If the company had abided by the guidelines, the information would have been encrypted and the impact of the breach would have been less severe.
	Motion detectors, micro-switches, or pressure pads, used to indicate when doors are opened and rooms entered, may have been useful to alert security personnel and prevent the theft in the first place. Another option would be closed-circuit cameras.
	Having an incident response and breach notification plan would have helped the company respond more quickly and avoid bad publicity.

Source: TRUSTe, "Security Guidelines Examples," http://www.truste.org/docs/Security_Guidelines_Examples.doc, accessed June 11, 2006. Copyright © 2006 by TRUSTe. Reprinted with permission.

Nokia, and others. This venture will help companies meet whistle-blower provisions of the recent corporate reform legislation.[77]

Intellectual Property

In addition to protecting personal privacy, Internet users and others are concerned about protecting their rights to property they create, including songs, movies, books, and software. Such **intellectual property** consists of the ideas and creative materials developed to solve problems, carry out applications, educate, and entertain others. It is the result, or end product, of the creative process. Intellectual property is generally protected by patents and copyrights. However, technological advancements are increasingly challenging the ownership of such property. For example, the FTC sued to block Internet retailer Toysmart.com from selling the names, addresses, billing information, family profiles, and buying habits of customers who have visited its website. The company, which filed for bankruptcy, had posted a privacy policy specifying that it would not share such information with third parties and had once been certified by TRUSTe. The FTC's suit opens the door for litigation against other failing Internet companies that attempt to sell their only significant assets—their databases, which often contain both customer contact information and intellectual insights on buying behavior gleaned through sophisticated technologies.[78]

Intellectual property losses in the United States total more than $11 billion a year in lost revenue from the illegal copying of computer programs, movies, compact discs, and books. This issue has become a global concern because of disparities in enforcement of laws throughout the world. For example, according to the trade association International Intellectual Property Alliance, more than half of the business software used in Israel is pirated, costing U.S. companies roughly $170 million in one year.[79] The Business Software Alliance says business software producers, including alliance members, such as Microsoft Corp., Adobe Systems Inc., and Apple Computer Inc., are losing $34 billion a year to piracy worldwide. The price of software lost to piracy ranges from $40 for desktop utilities to $13,000 for computer-aided design programs. According to trade group officials, roughly 35 percent of all commercial software is pirated. Illegal use of software downloaded from the Internet is a growing concern for the trade group. Another major concern is software piracy rates, which are finally starting to decline slightly.[80] Russia and China are the two worst countries in terms of piracy violations. It is predicted that the trade-related aspects of intellectual property rights disputes will make countries more accountable for adhering to copyright standards.[81] Cisco Systems Inc. announced that it has filed a lawsuit against Chinese network equipment maker Huawei Technologies and its subsidiaries, claiming unlawful copying of its intellectual property. Cisco claims that Huawei copied extensively from Cisco's copyrighted technical documentation and portions of the Cisco IOS source code and included the technology in its operating system.[82]

Microsoft has been particularly aggressive in battling software piracy. The company has initiated legal action against 7,500 Internet listings in thirty-three countries for products it says are pirated. The company's efforts to stamp out piracy have been facilitated by software that searches the Internet for offers to sell counterfeit or illegally copied software.[83] If Microsoft is successful in its attempts, by showing

TABLE 11.7	Electronic Document Theft
Employee theft	Employees with legitimate access to confidential documents pass information to competitors, journalists or government agencies.
Accidental distribution	E-mail allows documents to be transmitted anywhere in the world within seconds. A careless employee can send documents to the wrong parties with virtually no paper trail to follow.
Hackers	Companies make a significant investment in firewalls and other security software and systems. Even so, determined hackers can still cause security breaches.
No perceived value	An employee may pass on information that he considers valueless, not realizing the continued sensitivity of the information.
Change in trust	An employee who is planning to leave the firm may take sensitive documents to a new job with a competitor.
Lost devices	There are countless stories of notebook PCs and storage devices (floppy disks, flash drives and zip disks) that were stolen or mislaid in hotels or airports.

Source: Copyright © 2004 From Edward H. Freeman, "Document Theft: Appropriate Responses," *EDPACS*. Reproduced by permission of Taylor & Francis Group, LLC., http://www.taylorandfrancis.com

courage, foresight, and leadership on this issue, it could transform the economics of the software business, allowing cheaper, more innovative software to be available for legitimate, paying customers.[84] Microsoft has even opened up a howtotell.com website for people to consult when loading software onto their computers. The website helps educate customers on how to tell if their software is genuine. Microsoft is also employing a new Office Registration Wizard that authorizes purchasers of its software to load the programs onto only one desktop and one portable computer. If a purchaser attempts to register the software on more than two computers, the program will abort.[85] Can you think of another industry that would tolerate 40 percent of its products being stolen? Table 11.7 provides a list of ways in which electronic documents may be stolen. Known also as digital leakage, electronic document theft is the undesired distribution of confidential information stored in electronic form. The distribution may be unintentional or malicious.

U.S. copyright laws protect original works in text form, pictures, movies, computer software, musical multimedia, and audiovisual work. Owners of copyrights have the right to reproduce, derive from, distribute, and publicly display and perform the copyrighted works. Copyright infringement is the unauthorized execution of the rights reserved by a copyright holder. Congress passed the Digital Millennium Copyright Act (DMCA) in 1998 to protect copyrighted materials on the Internet and to limit the liability of online service providers (OSPs). The DMCA provides a "safe harbor" provision that limits judgments that can be levied against OSPs for copyright infringement by their customers. To limit their liability, service providers must pay a nominal fee and comply with the act's reporting requirements.[86] In a lawsuit brought by Ticketmaster against Tickets.com under the DMCA, a judge ruled that Tickets.com could legally place a hypertext link to Ticketmaster on its website. Although Ticketmaster claimed that the link infringed its copyrights, Tickets.com

TABLE 11.8	Facts About Copyrights

- A copyright notice is not necessary to protect private and original work created after April 1, 1989.

- Granting work to the public domain relinquishes all of the copyright holder's rights.

- The "fair use" exemption to copyright law allows for commentary, parody, news reporting, as well as research and education without seeking the copyright holder's permission, but giving acknowledgment is appropriate.

- Legal defense of a copyright is not necessary for maintaining the copyright—unlike trademarks, which may be damaged if not defended.

- Derivative works, based on another copyrighted work, come under the control of the original copyright holder. A notable exception is parody—making fun of an original work.

- Most copyright litigation is civil rather than criminal in nature, but criminal litigation is possible with more than ten copies of an original work and a valuation of over $2,500 (representing a commercial copyright violation).

Source: Brad Templeton, "10 Big Myths About Copyrights Explained," Brad Templeton's homepage, www.templetons.com/brad/copymyths.html, accessed June 10, 2006.

contended that it placed the Ticketmaster and other similar hot links on its website so that its customers could access those sites to obtain tickets not available through Tickets.com. Because the link automatically directed potential customers to Ticketmaster's actual website, the court ruled no copyright violation occurred.[87] Table 11.8 provides additional facts about copyrights.

The Internet has created other copyright issues for some organizations that have found that the Web addresses (URLs) of other online firms either match or are very similar to their own trademarks. In some cases, "cybersquatters" have deliberately registered Web addresses that match or relate to other firms' trademarks and then have attempted to sell the registration to the trademark owners. A number of companies, including Taco Bell, MTC, and KFC, have paid thousands of dollars to gain control of names that match or parallel company trademarks.[88] Registering a domain name is currently done on the honor system; a registrant simply fills out an online form, to automatically reserve a domain name. Thus, the process is ideal for cybersquatters or other scammers looking to defraud businesses and consumers. On November 11, 2002, a scammer who set up a spoof eBay website that has since been taken down was allowed to register the domain name Ebaylogin.com with VeriSign using 555–555–5555 as his fax number.[89] The Federal Trademark Dilution Act of 1995 was enacted to help companies resolve this conflict. The law gives trademark owners the right to protect their trademarks, prevents the use of trademark-protected entities by others, and requires cybersquatters to relinquish trademarked names.[90]

The Internet Corporation for Assigned Names and Numbers (ICANN), a nonprofit organization charged with overseeing basic technical matters related to addressing on the Internet, has had success, including the introduction of a competitive domain registrar and registration market, the Uniform Dispute Resolution Policy (UDRP), and the creation of seven new top-level domains.[91] Many trademark holders immediately turn to the Internet Corporation for Assigned Names and Numbers' Uniform Dispute Resolution Policy as a vehicle for combating cybersquatters. However, remedies available in federal court under the Anti-Cybersquatting Consumer

Production Act may better protect the rights of trademark holders. All ICANN-authorized registrars of domain names in the .com, .net, and .org top-level domains must agree to abide by the UDRP. Under the terms of the UDRP, a domain name will be transferred between parties only by agreement between them or by order of a court of competent jurisdiction or a UDRP-authorized dispute resolution provider.[92]

Since ICANN is overseen by the U.S. Department of Commerce, leaders in other countries have begun to question whether the United States has too much control of the Internet. Under the philosophy that the Internet is above the domain of any one government, these leaders pose several concerns. First, ICANN controls the master root file that provides users with access to the Internet. Some countries have threatened to develop a competing master root file, which would create parallel Internets. China has already developed a competing file and is encouraging other countries to join its effort. Second, ICANN has the power to affect selective parts of the Internet. For example, ICANN recently delayed adoption of a new .xxx top-level domain (TLD) for adult content because of pressure from U.S. government agencies. Third, because ICANN is a private corporation performing a significant public service, critics point to a lack of transparency and effectiveness in its operations and decisions. Finally, some leaders worry that ICANN will serve as a social and cultural gatekeeper, since all new TLD names and other requests must be approved by ICANN. The debate over governance of the Internet is related to a number of significant issues, including intellectual property, privacy, security, and other top-level concerns of the public and government.[93]

Health and Biotechnology

bioethics
the study of ethical issues in the fields of medical treatment and research, including medicine, nursing, law, philosophy, and theology, though today medical ethics is also recognized as a separate discipline

The advance of life-supporting technologies has raised a number of medical and health issues related to technology. **Bioethics** refers to the study of ethical issues in the fields of medical treatment and research, including medicine, nursing, law, philosophy, and theology, though today medical ethics is also recognized as a separate discipline.[94] All of these fields have been influenced by rapid changes in technology that require new approaches to solving issues. New genetic technologies promise to give medical ethics an even greater role in social decision making. For example, the Human Genome Project, a fifteen-year, $3 billion federally funded program to decode the entire human genetic map, identified a number of genes that may contribute to particular diseases or traits.

Because so many of our resources are spent on health care, the role of the private sector in determining the quality of health care is an important consideration to society. The pharmaceutical industry, for example, has been sharply criticized by politicians, health-care organizations, and consumers because of escalating drug costs. Investigators from federal and state agencies have threatened legal action over allegations that Medicare and Medicaid overpaid for drugs by $1 billion or more a year.[95] Pfizer Inc. agreed to pay $49 million to settle a whistle-blower case that lawyers predict will be followed by others. The case involved claims that Pfizer had bilked the federal government out of millions when selling Lipitor, an anticholesterol drug. This case, in essence, signifies a new niche of cases against the drug industry that fall under the federal False Claims Act. Under federal law, it is illegal for a drug company to pay

FIGURE 11.4   Research and Development Expenditures in Health

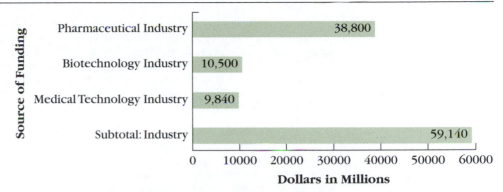

Source: Research America, "2004 Investment in U.S. Health Research," http://www.researchamerica.org/publications/appropriations/healthdollar2004.pdf, accessed June 19, 2006.

a doctor or an organization, such as an HMO, as an inducement for that company to give a drug preferred status.[96] On the other hand, pharmaceutical companies claim that the development of new lifesaving drugs and tests requires huge expenditures in research and development. Figure 11.4 provides evidence that large amounts of money are spent in this process and others in the health-care field. The pharmaceutical industry is among the most profitable U.S. industries and spends nearly $14 billion a year in marketing, including drug samples provided to doctors, advertising in medical journals, and other strategies. The visibility of pharmaceutical advertising and promotion prompted Pharmaceutical Research & Manufacturers of America, an industry association, to develop its Guiding Principles on Direct-to-Consumer (DTC) Advertising. The voluntary guidelines are designed to ensure that DTC advertising is accurate, accessible, and useful. Figure 11.5 shows the preamble that accompanies the association's booklet on the fifteen guiding principles.[97]

BIOTECHNOLOGY Driven by human genome projects in the late 1990s, the value of biotech firms increased by three and a half times in less than two years.[98] According to a recent world study by KPMG, for the third consecutive year, Canada is the fastest growing country in biomedical research and development. A Statistics Canada report states that the Canadian biotechnology sector, which is second only to the United States', saw revenues increase by 53 percent in the early 2000s.[99] The remarkable feat of mapping the human genome has spurred a rush to cash in on the booming business of genetic research. In fact, genetic research is one of the fastest growing areas of high technology. Patent applications from biotechnology companies are flooding into the U.S. Patent Office at a rate of 400 a week, and there are some 20,000 applications pending for gene-related discoveries. There are 1,283 biotechnology companies with 153,000 employees and a stock worth of almost $100 billion.[100] More than 500,000 patents have been applied for on genes or gene sequences worldwide according to the activist group GeneWatch UK. The U.S. Patent and Trademark Office alone has

FIGURE 11.5 Preamble to PhRMA Guiding Principles for Direct-to-Consumer Advertisements

Given the progress that continues to be made in society's battle against disease, patients are seeking more information about medical problems and potential treatments so they can better understand their health care options and communicate effectively with their physicians. An important benefit of direct-to-consumer (DTC) advertising is that it fosters an informed conversation about health, disease and treatments between patients and their health care practitioners.

A strong empirical record demonstrates that DTC communications about prescription medicines serve the public health by:

- Increasing awareness about diseases;
- Educating patients about treatment options;
- Motivating patients to contact their physicians and engage in a dialogue about health concerns;
- Increasing the likelihood that patients will receive appropriate care for conditions that are frequently under-diagnosed and under-treated; and
- Encouraging compliance with prescription drug treatment regimens.

Source: Pharmaceutical Research & Manufacturers of America, "PhRMA Guiding Principles: Direct-to-Consumer Advertisements About Prescription Medicines," http://www.phrma.org/files/DTCGuidingprinciples.pdf, accessed June 10, 2006. Copyright © 2006 by PhRMA. Reprinted with permission.

issued approximately 20,000 patents on genes or gene-related molecules, and 25,000 more applications are pending.[101]

The government and the private sector often partner with academic researchers and nonprofit institutes to develop new technologies in health and biotechnology. Research ranges from mapping the human genetic code to finding drugs that cure cancer to genetically modifying food products. Many of these collaborative efforts to improve health involve scientists, funded globally by a variety of sources. For example, the Avon Foundation granted nearly $30 million through the Avon Kiss Goodbye to Breast Cancer Crusade, which supports virtually every facet of the cause by funding five critical areas: breast cancer biomedical research, clinical care, support services, education, and early detection programs.[102] National Institutes of Health scientists created great excitement when they reported that embryonic stem cells had been coaxed to form pancreatic cells that make insulin, a potential treatment for diabetes. But a new study suggests that the cells didn't really make insulin and instead just absorbed it from the culture medium they were grown in and later released it.[103] Using cell-engineering techniques, scientists may have found a way to generate unlimited supplies of brain cells for transplanting into patients with Parkinson's disease. These examples illustrate technology advances that could result in commercially viable products that save and/or prolong life.

Cloning, the replication of organisms that are genetically identical to their parent, has become a highly controversial topic in biotechnology and bioethics. Human cloning has raised unanswered questions about the future of human reproduction.

Since Scottish scientists first cloned Dolly the sheep, scientists have also successfully cloned mice, cows, pigs, goats, and cats but with mixed reports about the health of the cloned progeny. While cloning humans would appear to be the final step of scientific reproduction, indisputable proof of the first human clone will actually serve as a starting point for many years of research. Like in vitro fertilization, human clones will need to grow up before scientists know the effects that this process will have on a person's physical, mental, and emotional states.[104] Cloning has the potential to revolutionize the treatment of diseases and conditions such as Parkinson's disease and cancer. Cloning technology might also allow doctors to create replacement organs, thereby lengthening human lives. Some scientists believe that cloning could be used to re-create extinct or endangered species in a last-ditch conservation effort. The ability to create and modify life processes is often generated through business and government collaborative research; the results of such research may contribute to life-altering products of tomorrow.

Despite the potential of this technology, many people have negative views about cloning. Some contend that it is unethical to "meddle with nature," whereas others believe that cloning is wrong because every time it is used to treat a patient, a cloned human embryo is destroyed, one that might otherwise have been capable of life.[105] The cloning of a miniature pig, named Goldie, lacking both copies of a gene involved in immediate immune rejection has brought the prospect of transplanting pig organs into people a little closer. The small pig's organs are similar in size to those of humans, and the missing genes make the organs less likely to be rejected. But although Goldie's creation may have solved the problem of immediate transplant rejection, there is a slower rejection in which the transplant is attacked by the recipient's white blood cells.[106] Some people argue that cloning of human beings should be banned, and several bills have been introduced in Congress and various state legislatures to do just that. Additionally, nineteen European nations have signed an agreement prohibiting the genetic replication of humans. Harvesting stem cells from surplus in vitro fertilization (IVF) embryos was given the go-ahead by the Australian Senate by a vote of nearly two to one in favor of a bill legalizing the procedure. The new Australian law lies between those in the United Kingdom and the United States. In the United Kingdom, the law already allows researchers to harvest stem cells from surplus IVF embryos and to conduct therapeutic cloning. But in the United States, federally funded researchers cannot pursue therapeutic cloning or harvest stem cells from discarded embryos, although private companies can.[107]

Genetic research holds the promise to revolutionize how many diseases are diagnosed and treated. However, consumer advocates have urged the World Trade Organization (WTO) to place limits on gene patents, which they claim are tantamount to "ownership of life." Patents dealing with human DNA have increased dramatically in the last decade as researchers have identified more genes that play a role in a number of diseases. The WTO rules governing patents on intellectual property currently permit patents to be owned for twenty years and allow patent holders to prevent other firms from profiting from a particular technology during that period. But some consumer groups, including Ralph Nader's Public Citizen, fear that these patents have the potential to permit a company to "corner the market" on the diagnosis and treatment of specific diseases for years. These groups worry that such long-term protection

In Ireland, consumer groups against the use of genetically modified foods are vocal and visible, including the GM-Free Ireland organization.

could prohibit other companies from developing alternative tests and treatments that might result in improved care at lower prices.[108] The fact that genes are both material molecules and informational systems helps explain the difficulty that the patent system is going to continue to have.[109]

A final concern with genetics is the increasing availability of direct-to-consumer testing kits. With these kits, consumers can proactively manage their health, including gaining access to knowledge about predispositions to cancer, diseases, and illnesses. Most specialists agree that the results of such tests are best delivered in a professional medical setting, not via the Internet or mail. For example, through a mail-order kit, a consumer could receive a positive finding on a DNA-based prostate cancer screening test. The consumer may have cancerous growths that can be removed, cancer that has spread, or neither because the test is a false positive. Medical advice is warranted at this point because the consumer has no way of determining the appropriate course of action.[110]

GENETICALLY MODIFIED FOODS As many as 800 million people around the world don't have enough to eat. Increasing food production to satisfy the growing demand for food without increasing land use will require farmers to achieve significant increases in productivity. Genetically modified (GM) foods offer a way to quickly improve crop characteristics such as yield, pest resistance, or herbicide tolerance, often to a degree not possible with traditional methods. Further, GM crops can be manipulated to produce completely artificial substances, from the precursors of plastics to consumable vaccines.[111] As we discussed in Chapter 10, genetically modified, or transgenic, crops are created when scientists introduce a gene from one organism to another. Scientists believe that genetically engineered crops could raise overall crop production in developing countries by as much as 25 percent.[112] According to a report by seven independent academies from both developed and developing countries, to combat world hunger, developed countries must boost funding for research into genetically modified crops, and poor farmers must be protected from corporate control of the technology.[113] The European public calls GM products "Frankenfood" for fear it could pose a health threat or create an environmental disaster where genes jump from GM crops to wild plants and reduce biodiversity or create superweeds. For four years, Europe has held up new approvals of U.S. exports of Frankenfood. The European Parliament voted to require extensive labeling and traceability of food containing genetically modified organisms, even if no remnants of genetic modification are detectable. With European public confidence in food safety badly shaken by foot-and-mouth and mad-cow disease, no new GM products have been authorized for use in Europe since 1998. European Union officials admit this is likely illegal under WTO rules and hurts largely U.S. farm exporters. In an effort to restart the approval process by addressing public concerns over consumer choice and environmental protection, the EU proposed burdensome new rules for biotech food and animal feed labeling and for "farm-to-fork" traceability measures on products.[114] Table 11.9 lists some examples of genetically modified foods. Genetic modification has raised numerous health, ethical, and environmental questions. We looked at some of the environmental issues in Chapter 10.

TABLE 11.9	Genetically Modified Foods	
Product	**Genetic Modification**	**Purpose**
Tomatoes, peas, peppers, tropical fruit, broccoli, raspberries, melons	Controlled ripening	Allows shipping of vine-ripened tomatoes; improves shelf life, quality
Tomatoes, potatoes, corn, lettuce, coffee, cabbage family, apples	Insect resistance	Reduces insecticide use
Peppers, tomatoes, cucumbers	Fungal resistance	Reduces fungicide use
Potatoes, tomatoes, cantaloupe, squash, cucumbers, corn, oilseed rape (canola), soybeans, grapes	Viral resistance	Reduces diseases caused by plant viruses and, because insects carry viruses, reduces use of insecticides
Soybeans, tomatoes, corn, oilseed rape (canola), wheat	Herbicide tolerance	Improves weed control
Corn, sunflowers, soybeans, and other plants	Improved nutrition	Increases amount of essential amino acids, vitamins, or other nutrients in the host plants
Oilseed rape (canola), peanuts	Heat stability	Improves the processing quality, permits new food uses for healthier oils

Source: Food Marketing Institute, "Bioengineered Food and You," http://www.fmi.org/consumer/biotech/biotechnology.pdf, accessed June 19, 2006. Courtesy of Food Marketing Institute.

Many people do not realize that some of the foods they eat were made from genetically engineered crops. Consumer groups are increasingly concerned that these foods could be unhealthy and/or harmful to the environment. Concerns about the safety of genetically altered crops have led to a backlash in Europe and, more recently, in the United States and Japan. For example, Campbell Soup, the first firm to license a genetically modified food—the FlavSavr tomato, which was engineered for a longer shelf life—has been the target of a massive letter-writing campaign by consumers worried about the lack of safety testing and labels on foods containing gene-altered crops.[115] The power of genetic modification techniques raises the possibility of human health, environmental, and economic problems, including unanticipated allergic responses to novel substances in foods, the spread of pest resistance or herbicide tolerance to wild plants, inadvertent toxicity to benign wildlife, and increasing control of agriculture by biotechnology corporations.[116] Many consumers are boycotting products made from genetically modified materials. Several countries have opposed trade in GM foods through the World Trade Organization, and Japan has asked U.S. corn producers not to include genetically modified corn in animal feed exported to Japan. The European Parliament has called for all GM foods to be labeled.[117] Insects and birds transport seeds from one field to the next, allowing cross-pollination geneticists never intended. Unlike chemical or nuclear contamination, gene pollution can never be cleaned up. Table 11.10 demonstrates the millions of hectares that are being used to cultivate GM crops in various countries. There has been solid growth of GM crops since 1998.[118]

TABLE 11.10	Commercial Cultivation of Genetically Modified Crops (in millions of hectares)

Country	1998	1999	2000	2001	2002	2003	2004	2005
USA	20.5	28.7	30.3	35.7	39.0	42.8	47.6	49.8
Argentina	4.3	6.7	10.0	11.8	13.5	13.9	16.2	17.1
Canada	2.8	4.0	3.0	3.2	3.5	4.4	5.4	5.8
Brazil	0.0	0.0	0.0	0.0	0.0	3.0	5.0	9.4
China	<0.1	0.3	0.5	1.5	2.1	2.8	3.7	3.3
Paraguay	0.0	0.0	0.0	0.0	0.0	0.0	0.0	1.8
India	0.0	0.0	0.0	0.0	<0.1	0.1	0.5	1.3
South Africa	<0.1	0.1	0.2	0.3	0.3	0.4	0.5	0.5
Australia	0.1	0.1	0.2	0.2	0.1	0.1	0.2	0.3
Uruguay	0.0	0.0	<0.1	<0.1	<0.1	<0.05	0.3	0.3
Mexico	<0.1	<0.1	<0.1	<0.1	<0.1	<0.05	0.1	0.1

Source: GeneWatch UK, "Briefing 34: Genetic Technologies: A Review of Developments in 2005," www.genewatch.org, accessed June 19, 2006. © ISAAA, Clive James. Reprinted with permission.

A number of companies have responded to public concerns about genetically modified food products by limiting or avoiding their use altogether. Major European supermarkets are considering banning GM foods, and Nestlé UK and Unilever have stopped using them in their food products. Archer Daniels Midland, the largest buyer of genetically modified crops in the United States, has asked farmers and grain merchants to segregate GM crops from traditionally grown plants. The company may discard a load of grain when tests detect even a tiny amount of altered genes. In fact, large agribusiness purchasers of farm crops are paying less per bushel for genetically altered products.[119] Genetically engineered food crops, virtually unknown ten years ago, now occupy over 100 million acres of U.S. farmland. This is an astonishing 167,000 square miles, an area larger than the entire state of California. McDonald's and Frito-Lay have asked their suppliers to stop using GM potatoes developed by Monsanto.[120] Gerber and Heinz both announced that they will not permit genetically engineered corn or soybeans in their baby-food products. Corn growers in the United States say they are losing $300 million annually because their GM crops are largely barred—along with many other modified products—from the European market.[121]

Ethical questions about the use of some types of genetically modified products have also been raised. For example, Monsanto and other companies are developing so-called terminator technology to create plants that are genetically engineered to produce sterile seeds. Dr. Jane Rissler, a scientist with the Union of Concerned Scientists, says, "The fact that terminator technology will work to the disadvantage of the subsistence farmer who depends on harvesting seeds for the next year's crops illustrates the intent of the companies, which is to get the maximum return on their investment." Other plants in development will require spraying with chemicals supplied by the seed companies to produce desired traits, such as resistance to certain pests or disease. Farmers say the issue isn't the technology itself but, rather, who controls the technology—in most cases, the multinational seed companies. In response to global concerns about this issue, Monsanto announced that it would halt commercial development of the terminator technology, although it plans to continue researching it.[122]

Defenders of biotechnology say consumer fears about genetically modified foods have not been substantiated by research.[123] India froze food-aid shipments of corn and soy from the United States, and Zambia turned away 18,000 tons of U.S. corn, even though 3 million of its citizens teeter on the brink of starvation. So far, genetic technologies haven't led to drastically lowered prices, but as supplies increase, some experts think 30 percent drops are likely. As the U.S. agriculture industry is eager to point out, the technology has been a big success: It has reduced the amount of pesticides farmers have had to spray on their cornfields, with happy consequences for the environment and human health. U.S. health regulators have not been able to find anything wrong with eating Bt (*Bacillus thuringiensis*) corn. It is now found in roughly two-thirds of all corn products on U.S. store shelves.[124]

STRATEGIC IMPLEMENTATION OF RESPONSIBILITY FOR TECHNOLOGY

To accrue the maximum benefits from the technologies driving the new economy, many parties within society have important roles to play. While the media and public continue to debate the issues associated with technology, the government must take steps to provide support for continued technological advancements and establish regulations, as needed, to ensure that the benefits of technology apply to as many people as possible while minimizing any potential for harm, especially to competition, the environment, and human welfare. Various stakeholders, including employees, customers, and special-interest groups, as well as the general public, can influence the use and control of technology through the public policy process. Businesses also have a significant role to play in supporting technology. New technologies are developed, refined, and introduced to the market through the research and development and marketing activities of business. Businesses that aspire to be socially responsible must monitor the impact of technology and harness it for the good of all.

The Role of Government

With an economy that is increasingly driven by technology, the government must maintain the basic infrastructure and support for technology in our society. The Department of Defense, for example, explores ways that technology can improve the quality of life. The government also serves as a watchdog to ensure that technology benefits society, not criminals. However, as the pace of technology continues to escalate, law enforcement agencies ranging from the FBI to local police forces are struggling to recruit and retain officers and prosecutors who are knowledgeable about the latest technology and the ways criminals can exploit it. The nation currently has only a few hundred high-caliber forensic computer experts, but many of these officers are being lured to technology firms and private security outfits by salaries more than twice their government paychecks. Only a handful of police and sheriffs' departments across the country have enough money to support squads of high-tech investigators, and many top detectives leap to the corporate realm anyway.[125] Computer crimes currently share sentencing guidelines with larceny, embezzlement, and theft, where the most significant sentencing factor is the amount of financial loss inflicted, and additional points are awarded for using false ID or ripping off more than ten victims. But in a congressional session that heard much talk about "cyberterrorism," lawmakers became convinced that computer outlaws had more in common with al-Qaeda than with common thieves. The U.S. Supreme Court's Federal Sentencing Guidelines set the range of sentences a court can choose from in a given case on the basis of a point system that sets a starting value for a particular crime and then adds or subtracts points for specific aggravating or mitigating circumstances.[126]

In addition to cybercriminals, many commercial users of the Internet are implementing new technologies in ways that our existing legal system could not have conceived of when our laws were framed. Hollywood film studios, for example, are concerned that new technology will allow computer users to copy and trade entire videos on the Internet, much like they traded music recordings via Napster and other peer-to-peer file-sharing services. The recording and movie industry saw the threat of this technology when Shawn Fanning, the creator of the peer-to-peer file-swapping service, was a child.

Indeed, the road to the controversial Digital Millennium Copyright Act (DMCA) probably began in 1975, when Sony Corp. introduced the Betamax VCR. That was the start of a long series of court battles and legislative fights over electronic duplication of copyrighted material. But it wasn't until PCs were in wide use that Congress acted in a broad way to extend copyright protections to the digital domain. President Clinton signed the DMCA in October 1998. Five years later, copyright holders, such as the Recording Industry Association of America (RIAA), are using the DMCA to successfully fight Napster-like services and protect their anticopying technology. But the law has many critics and challengers, who say it impinges on the right of consumers to copy content and creates a predicament for scientists conducting certain kinds of security research.[127]

Both the Napster and RIAA lawsuits illustrate a significant difference in opinion in the interpretation of existing laws when exploiting the evolving multimedia potential of the Internet. Although the government's strategy thus far has been not to interfere with the commercial use of technology, disputes and differing interpretations of current laws increasingly bring technology into the domain of the legal system. New laws related to breakthrough technologies that change the nature of competition are constantly being considered. Usually, the issues of privacy, ownership of intellectual property, health and safety, environmental impact, competition, or consumer welfare are the legislative platforms for changing the legal and regulatory system.

The Role of Business

Business, like government, is involved in both reactive and proactive attempts to market and make effective use of technology. Reactive concerns relate to issues that have legal and/or ethical implications as well as issues of productivity, customer welfare, or other stakeholder concerns. One example of a reactive response to the consequences of new technologies relates to employee access to and use of the World Wide Web.

Websense is the worldwide leader of employee Internet management (EIM) solutions. Websense Enterprise software enables businesses to manage how their employees use the Internet, improving productivity, conserving network bandwidth and storage costs, and mitigating legal liability. Founded in 1994, Websense serves more than 18,100 worldwide customers, ranging in size from 100-person firms to global corporations. Clients include Blue Bell Creameries, Harvey Nichols department store, Carnival Cruise Lines, and the City of Cincinnati.[128] At any given time, about 20 percent of employee PCs are surfing nonbusiness-related sites, such as ESPN.com or sexually oriented websites. This includes both staff and executives, such as the CIO, chief technology officer, and even the CEO.[129] Many large firms have suffered public embarrassment, legal bills, compensation claims, and clean-up costs when employees seek inappropriate material online, send e-mail to people they shouldn't, accidentally circulate confidential information outside a business, or spread a computer virus. The Department of Trade and Industry security survey conducted in the United Kingdom revealed that 62 percent of businesses have suffered a security breach of some type, a figure that has climbed in every survey.[130]

Some companies are purchasing software that assists employees in managing the Internet time they spend on personal activities. Kozy Shack Enterprises, the manufacturer of ready-to-eat pudding, allows employees one hour per day to shop, browse, chat, and complete other personal tasks. Harvey Nichols, a high-end retailer in London, uses similar software to ensure that employees do not have access to pornography, gambling, and other inappropriate sites. A majority of large U.S. companies are monitoring employee communications, including telephone calls, e-mail, and Internet connections.[131] The courts have ruled that because communications occurring on company-provided equipment are not private under current law, such monitoring is legal.[132] However, established high-tech companies like Microsoft and Oracle, and many technology startups, often choose not to monitor or limit employees' Web usage or e-mail. Managers at these companies believe they cannot be innovators with technology while strictly monitoring employee use and time on the Web.[133]

Concerns about undesirable employee use of telecommunications equipment represent reactions to changes in information technology that affect the workplace. Even though companies may be legally within their right to monitor and control the use of certain websites by employees, such control raises strategic issues related to trust and the type of long-run relationships that firms want to have with their employees.

On the other hand, a strategic, proactive approach to technology will consider its impact on social responsibility. Proactive management of technology requires developing a plan for utilizing resources to take advantage of competitive opportunities. For example, there is great demand for high-speed Internet connections, including cable modems, DSL, and other broadband connections, because computing speed and power have moved beyond current bandwidth capacity. Many telecommunications firms are racing to install and market the infrastructure for broadband connections to satisfy this demand. In a few years, however, new technologies, probably wireless connections, will more than likely provide even greater connection speeds, and the opportunity for new companies to provide broadband service will vanish.

With competition increasing, companies are spending more time and resources to establish technology-based competitive advantages. The strategic approach to technology requires an overall mission, strategy, and coordination of all functional activities, including a concern for social responsibility, to have an effective program. To promote the responsible use of technology, a firm's policies, rules, and standards must be integrated into its corporate culture. Reducing undesirable behavior in this area is a goal that is no different from reducing costs, increasing profits, or improving quality that is aggressively enforced and integrated into the corporate culture to be effective in improving appropriate behavior within the organization.

Top managers must consider the social consequences of technology in the strategic planning process. When all stakeholders are involved in the process, everyone can better understand the need for and requirements of responsible development and use of technology. There will always be conflicts in making the right choices, but through participation in decision making, the best solutions can be found. Individual participants in this process should not abdicate their personal responsibility as concerned members of society. Organizations that are concerned about the consequences of their decisions create an environment for different opinions on important issues. As Richard Purcell, Microsoft's chief privacy officer, says, "No matter what legislation is enacted, it is the responsibility of the leaders in the online industry to provide and implement technologies that help consumers feel safer and more comfortable online."[134]

Strategic Technology Assessment

technology assessment

a procedure that companies can use to foresee the effects new products and processes will have on their operation, on other business organizations, and on society in general

To calculate the effects of new technologies, companies can employ a procedure known as **technology assessment** to foresee the effects new products and processes will have on their firm's operation, on other business organizations, and on society in general. This assessment is a tool that managers can use to evaluate their firm's performance and to chart strategic courses of action to respond to new technologies. With information obtained through a technology assessment or audit, managers can estimate whether the benefits of adopting a specific technology outweigh costs to the firm and to society at large. The assessment process can also help companies ensure compliance with government regulations related to technology. Remember that one of the four components of social responsibility is legal compliance. Because technology is evolving so rapidly, even lawyers are struggling to keep up with the legal implications of these advances. Social institutions, including religion, education, the law, and business, have to respond to changing technology by adapting or developing new approaches to address the evolving issues. A strategic technology assessment or audit can help organizations understand these issues and develop appropriate and responsible responses to them (see Table 11.11).[135]

If the assessment process indicates that the company has not been effective at utilizing technologies or is using them in a way that raises questions, changes may be necessary. Companies may need to consider setting higher standards, improving reporting processes, and improving communication of standards and training programs, as well as participating in aboveboard discussions with other organizations. If performance has not been satisfactory, management may want to reorganize the way certain kinds of decisions are made. Table 11.11 contains some issues to assess for proactive and reactive technology responsibility issues. Some social concerns might relate to a technology's impact on the environment, employee health and working conditions, consumer safety, and community values.

TABLE 11.11	Strategic Technology Assessment Issues

Yes	No	Checklist
O	O	Are top managers in your organization aware of the federal, state, and local laws related to technology decisions?
O	O	Does your organization have an effective system for monitoring changes in the federal, state, and local laws related to technology?
O	O	Is there an individual, committee, or department in your organization responsible for overseeing government technology issues?
O	O	Does your organization do checks on technology brought into the organization by employees?
O	O	Are there communications and training programs in your organization to create an effective culture to protect employees and organizational interests related to technology?
O	O	Does your organization have monitoring and auditing systems to determine the impact of technology on key stakeholders?
O	O	Does your organization have a method for reporting concerns about the use or impact of technology?
O	O	Is there a system to determine ethical risks and appropriate ethical conduct to deal with technology issues?
O	O	Do top managers in your organization understand the ramifications of using technology to communicate with employees and customers?
O	O	Is there an individual or department in your organization responsible for maintaining compliance standards to protect the organization in the areas of privacy and intellectual property?

Finally, the organization should focus on the positive aspects of technology to determine how it can be used to improve the work environment, its products, and the general welfare of society. Technology can be used to reduce pollution, encourage recycling, and save energy. Also, information can be made available to customers to help them maximize the benefits of products. Technology has been and will continue to be a major force that can improve society.

SUMMARY

Technology relates to the application of knowledge, including the processes and applications to solve problems, perform tasks, and create new methods to obtain desired outcomes. The dynamics of technology relate to the constant change that requires significant adjustments in the political, religious, and economic structures of society. Reach relates to the far-reaching nature of technology as it moves through society. The self-sustaining nature of technology relates to the fact that technology acts as a catalyst to spur even faster development. Civilizations must harness and adapt to changes in technology to maintain a desired quality of life. Although technological advances have improved our quality of life, they have also raised ethical, legal, and social concerns.

Advances in technology have created millions of new jobs, better health and longer lives, new opportunities, and the enrichment of lives. Without greater access to the latest technology, however, economic development could suffer in underserved areas. The ability to purchase technology may affect the nature of competition and business success. Information and telecommunications technology minimizes borders, allows people to overcome the physical limitations of time and space, and enables people to acquire customized goods and services that cost less and are of higher quality.

The Internet, a global information system that links many computer networks together, has altered the way people communicate, learn, do business, and find entertainment. The growth of the Internet has generated issues never before encountered, issues that social institutions, including the legal system, have been slow to address.

Because current technology has made it possible to collect, share, and sell vast quantities of personal information, often without consumers' knowledge, privacy has become a major concern associated with technology. Many websites follow users' tracks through their site by storing a cookie, or identifying string of text, on the users' computers. What companies do with the consumer information they collect through cookies and other technologies is generating concern. Privacy issues related to children are generating even more debate and laws to protect children's interests. Identity theft occurs when criminals obtain personal information that allows them to impersonate someone else to use that individual's credit to obtain financial accounts and to make purchases. Some measure of protection of personal privacy is provided by the U.S. Constitution, as well as by Supreme Court rulings and federal laws. Europe and other regions of the world are also addressing privacy concerns. In addition to creating and posting policies regarding the gathering and use of personal information, more companies are beginning to hire chief privacy officers.

Intellectual property consists of the ideas and creative materials developed to solve problems, carry out applications, educate, and entertain others. Copyright infringement is the unauthorized execution of the rights reserved by a copyright holder. Technological advancements are challenging the ownership of intellectual property. Other issues relate to "cybersquatters" who deliberately register Web addresses that match or relate to other firms' trademarks and then attempt to sell the registration to the trademark owners.

Bioethics refers to the study of ethical issues in the fields of medical treatment and research, including medicine, nursing, law, philosophy, and theology. Genetic research, including cloning, may revolutionize how diseases are diagnosed and treated. Genetically modified crops are created when scientists introduce a gene from one organism to another. However, these technologies are controversial because some people believe they are immoral, unsafe, or harmful to the environment.

To accrue the maximum benefits from the technology driving the new economy, many parties within society have important roles to play. With an economy that is increasingly driven by technology, the government must maintain the basic infrastructure and support for technology in our society. The government also serves as a watchdog to ensure that technology benefits society, not criminals.

Business is involved in both reactive and proactive attempts to make effective use of technology. Reactive concerns relate to issues that have legal or ethical implications as well as to productivity, customer welfare, or other stakeholder issues. Proactive management of technology requires developing a plan for utilizing resources to take advantage of competitive opportunities. The strategic approach to technology requires an overall mission, strategy, and coordination of all functional activities, including a concern for social responsibility, to produce an effective program. To calculate the effects of new technologies, companies can employ a procedure known as technology assessment to foresee the effects of new products and processes on their firm's operation, on other business organizations, and on society in general.

KEY TERMS

technology (p. 353)
intellectual property (p. 375)
bioethics (p. 378)
technology assessment (p. 388)

DISCUSSION QUESTIONS

1. Define technology and describe three characteristics that can be used to assess it.
2. What effect has technology had on the U.S. and global economies? Have these effects been positive or negative?
3. Many people believe that the government should regulate business with respect to privacy online, but companies say self-regulation is more appropriate. Which approach would benefit consumers most? Business?
4. What is intellectual property? How can owners of intellectual property protect their rights?
5. What is bioethics? What are some of the consequences of biomedical research?
6. Should genetically modified foods be labeled as "genetically modified"? Why or why not?
7. How can a strategic technology assessment help a company?

EXPERIENTIAL EXERCISE

Visit three websites that are primarily designed for children or that focus on products of interest to children under age thirteen. For example, visit the websites for new movies, games, action figures, candy, cereal, or beverages. While visiting these sites, put yourself in the role and mind-set of a child. What type of language and persuasion is used? Is there a privacy statement on the site that can be understood by children? Are there any parts of the site that might be offensive or worrisome to parents? Provide a brief evaluation of how well these sites attend to the provisions of the Children's Online Privacy Protection Act.

WHAT WOULD YOU DO?

James Kitling thought about his conversation with Ira Romero earlier that day. He was not really surprised that the human resources (HR) department was concerned about the time employees were spending on personal issues during the workday. Several departments were known for their rather loose management approach. Internet access for personal tasks, like shopping, using Instant Messaging services, and answering nonwork e-mails, had been a concern for several months. Recent news reports indicated that over 50 percent of large companies now filter or monitor e-mail. Companies are also monitoring Web browsing, file downloads, chat room use, and group postings. A survey published in the media reported that workers spend an average of eight hours a week looking at nonwork Internet sites.

As the director of information technology, James was very dedicated to the effective use of technology to enhance business productivity. Although he was knowledgeable about technology, James was equally attuned to the ways in which technology can be abused in a work setting. He knew that some employees were probably using too much Internet time on personal tasks.

On the other hand, his company mainly employed professionals, administrative staff, and customer service personnel. All 310 employees were expected to use the computer a great deal throughout the day. At present, the company had a skeleton code of ethics and policy on the use of company resources, including the Internet.

A couple of managers and now HR had spoken with James about the prospects of monitoring employee computer and Internet use. Ira's inquiry about the software, however, was a bit more serious. An employee had recently been formally reprimanded for downloading and printing nonwork documents from the Internet. These documents were designed to help the employee's spouse in a new business venture. Although the employee did most of the searching and downloading during lunch, the supervisor felt this was an improper use of company resources. Other employees had been informally spoken with about their use of the Internet for personal matters. Ira believed this was a growing problem that definitely affected productivity. He had read the news reports and believed that monitoring software was becoming a necessary tool in today's workplace.

So far, James had been hesitant to purchase and implement one of these systems. The employee Internet management software was somewhat expensive, running approximately $25 per computer. He felt that the software could cause employee trust to sharply decline, resulting in even greater problems than currently existed. After all, employees engage in some personal tasks during work hours, including making telephone calls home, getting coffee, chatting with coworkers, going to the doctor, and so forth. James wondered if the Internet was that much different from these other personal activities. He recalled a discussion in a management class in his MBA program, where they learned that employees in the early 1900s were only allowed to use the telephone to call the police. Thus, the telephone was once thought of as a great distracter, much like the Internet today.

Ira and a few other managers were pretty firm in their beliefs about the Internet monitoring system. James was still not convinced that it was the best route to curbing the problem. In his role, however, he was expected to provide leadership in developing a solution. What would you do?

The Social Audit

CHAPTER 12

CHAPTER OBJECTIVES

- To define social auditing
- To identify the benefits of social auditing
- To discuss the potential limitations of social auditing
- To compare the process of social auditing with that of financial auditing
- To explore the stages of the social auditing process
- To explore the strategic role of social auditing

CHAPTER OUTLINE

The Nature of Social Auditing

The Challenges of Measuring Nonfinancial Performance

The Social Auditing Process

The Strategic Importance of Social Auditing

Deere & Company is the world's leading manufacturer of agricultural equipment and has a significant global presence in lawn and garden, construction, heavy engines, forestry, and related markets. Most people recognize the company's products from the green and yellow John Deere logo, which features a deer leaping into the future. Deere & Company has become highly respected for the integrity, innovation, quality, and commitment the company and its employees demonstrate in many ways. The company has received numerous awards in the last few years. These accolades include being named one of America's 100 Best Corporate Citizens by *Business Ethics* magazine and Most Trusted Illinois Company by *Crain's Chicago Business* publication.

Deere has flourished under Chairman and CEO Robert Lane, who joined the company in 1982 and was named to the top position in 2000. Today, Deere is a multinational company offering products in 160 countries. The company has 46,000 employees and generates about $20 billion in annual sales. The social responsibility approach the firm developed in the United States also affects international operations. For example, John Deere Brazil was honored with the Excellence in Social Management prize by *Editoria Expressao* magazine.

A recent book entitled the *John Deere Way* reveals some of the key components to the longevity and success of the company founded in 1837, including:

- If we don't improve our products, others will make them in our place.
- Always maintain integrity.
- I will not put my name on a product that does not have in it the best that is in me.
- Concentrate on areas where you have a clear competitive advantage.
- It is more important in business to listen than to lead.
- It is more valuable to lean than laden.
- In a rigorously competitive market, virtue is necessary for sustained value creation.

- It is important to build a business as great as your products.

In keeping with this approach, Deere publishes an annual review of its environmental, health, and safety performance. The review, which is managed and published by the company, includes media reports, manufacturing innovations, awards, milestones, and metrics for measuring its progress. A key focus over the last few years has been on improving ergonomics for employees.

Ergonomics examines the body in relation to work demands. If the work demands are too strenuous for the body, injury will likely occur. Deere engineers are developing new programs to make sure that production processes consider ergonomics. At the John Deere Waterloo Works facility in Iowa, employees are creating safer workplaces using advanced three-dimensional and virtual reality technology. Employees are allowed to test new production facilities before they are actually built. Engineers may set up the demonstration for the entire production process or for a single workstation and then examine the potential strain that will be put on the body in each stage. The facility is one of only four in the world dedicated to ergonomics in the manufacturing environment.

Deere & Company has proven its commitment to many stakeholders, especially employees. This firm not only publicizes its specific efforts and invests in innovative systems but provides a widely available self-evaluation on an annual basis. Although this company often has positive news to report, its annual review also discloses areas for improvement. Employee ergonomics is one example of an area where Deere has recently invested much time and many resources. As CEO Lane noted in the opening letter of a recent annual review, "We strive to manage our resources in ways that are environmentally responsible. Not only does this create a safer and healthier workplace for our employees, it also creates safer and healthier communities. We also believe it gives our employees another reason to be proud of John Deere, as a company that endeavors to do the right thing."[1] ■

*J*ust as Deere & Company did, more companies around the globe are beginning to assess their social performance and report the results of those assessments as a means of demonstrating their commitment to social responsibility. These audits can help companies identify risks, noncompliance with laws and company policies, and areas that need improvement. An audit should provide a systematic and objective survey of the firm's ethical culture and values. Audits can also spotlight social responsibility activities and accomplishments related to environmental impact, sustainable development, consumer welfare, fair trade, and treatment of employees. More organizations are reporting about their impact on and relationships with a variety of stakeholders as well as their performance on social issues ranging far beyond the environment or sustainable development. These reports are often called "social audits," "social responsibility reports," or "corporate citizenship audits." For example, Nestlé publishes social responsibility reports for regions of the world such as Africa and Latin America.

Regardless of what name they go by, the reports of such auditing efforts are important for demonstrating a firm's commitment to and ensuring the continuous improvement of its social responsibility efforts. Without reliable measurements of the achievement of social objectives, a company has no concrete way to verify their importance, link them to organizational performance, justify expenditures to stockholders and investors, or address any stakeholder concerns.[2] Because the well-conducted social audit has the ability to do all these things, we devote this chapter to this leading-edge social responsibility tool. We begin by defining the social audit and explore the reasons for conducting the audit and its benefits and limitations. The challenges of measuring nonfinancial ethical performance are examined and evolving standards are reviewed from AA1000, the Integrity Institute, and the Open Compliance Ethics Group. Next, we compare the social audit to financial audits to derive standards that may be applied to social auditing and reporting. We also describe an auditing procedure that can be used to measure and improve the social responsibility effort. Finally, we look at the strategic importance of social auditing and provide a framework for smaller companies.

THE NATURE OF SOCIAL AUDITING

social auditing

the process of assessing and reporting a business's performance on fulfilling the economic, legal, ethical, and philanthropic social responsibilities expected of it by its stakeholders

Social auditing is the process of assessing and reporting a business's performance on fulfilling the economic, legal, ethical, and philanthropic social responsibilities expected of it by its stakeholders. Social audits are tools that companies can employ to identify and measure their progress and challenges to stakeholders—including employees, customers, investors, suppliers, community members, activists, the media, and regulators—who are increasingly demanding that companies be transparent and accountable for their commitments and performance.[3] The auditing process is important to business because it can improve financial performance, increase attractiveness to investors, improve relationships with stakeholders, identify potential liabilities, improve organizational effectiveness, and decrease the risk of misconduct and adverse publicity.[4] A firm's reputation depends on transparency and openness in reporting and improving its activities.

The social audit provides an objective approach for an organization to demonstrate its commitment to improving strategic planning, including showing social accountability and commitment to monitoring and evaluating social issues. Thus, it is critical that top managers understand and embrace the strategic importance of the social audit. Key stakeholders of the company should also be involved in the audit to ensure the integration of their perspectives into the firm's economic, legal, ethical, and philanthropic responsibilities.[5] Companies are working to incorporate accountability into actions ranging from long-term planning to everyday decision making, including corporate governance, financial reporting, and diversity. The strategic responsibility goals and outcomes measured in the social audit need to be communicated throughout the organization and to all of its stakeholders so that everyone is aware of what the company would like to achieve and what progress has been made in achieving its goals. The social audit should provide regular, comprehensive, and comparative verification of the views of stakeholders. Disclosure is a key part of auditing to encourage constructive feedback. Directions for finding best practices and continuous improvement on legal, social, ethical, philanthropic, and other issues can come from all stakeholders.

Reasons for Social Audits

Throughout this book, we have examined the various forces affecting social responsibility. There are many reasons companies choose to understand, report on, and improve their social performance. The increased visibility of corporate social responsibility has encouraged companies to better account for their actions in a wide range of areas, including human resources, environmental policies, ethics programs, and community involvement. At one extreme, a company may want to achieve the best social performance possible, whereas at the other extreme, a firm may desire to project a good image to hide misconduct. Still other companies may see the auditing process as a key component of organizational improvement. Thus, the reasons companies exceed their legally prescribed duties lie along a vast spectrum, as the social responsibility continuum in Chapter 1 indicated.[6] For example, it is common for firms to conduct audits of business practices with legal ramifications, such as harassment, employee safety, and environmental impact. Although these concerns are important to a firm's social responsibility, they are also legally prescribed and indicative of minimal social responsibility.

Stakeholders are demanding increased transparency and are taking a more active role through external organizations representing the interests of these groups. Government regulators are calling on companies to increase the quantity and quality of information disclosed aimed at increasing the companies' accountability to society. For example, the Sarbanes-Oxley Act requires top financial officers to file their company's code of ethics with the Securities and Exchange Commission. A number of financial and auditing decisions must also be reported on a regular basis.

In general, social auditing is not usually associated with regulatory requirements, whereas financial audits are required of public companies that issue securities. Because social audits are more voluntary, there are fewer standards that a company can apply with regard to reporting frequency, disclosure requirements, and remedial actions that it should take in response to results. This may change as more companies build ethics

and social responsibility programs in the current environment—where regulatory agencies support giving boards of directors oversight of corporate responsibility. For boards to track the effectiveness of oversight of social responsibility programs, audits will be required. In addition, nonfinancial auditing standards are developing with data available for benchmarking and comparing a firm's nonfinancial social performance.

Benefits of Social Auditing

Social auditing provides benefits for both organizations and their stakeholders. For example, regular audits permit stockholders and investors to judge whether a firm is achieving the goals it has established and whether it abides by the values it has specified as important. Moreover, they permit stakeholders to influence the organization's behavior.[7] Increasingly, a broad range of stakeholder groups are seeking specific, often quantifiable, information from companies. These stakeholders expect companies to take a deeper look at the nature of their operations and to publicly disclose both their progress and problems in addressing these issues. Some investors, for example, are using their rights as stockholders to encourage companies to modify their plans and policies to address specific social issues. Tyco International Ltd. shareholders voted to eliminate some benefits to top executives on the basis of the reported scandal that occurred in the past. Greater transparency related to social auditing assists stakeholders in making decisions related to corporate governance.[8] Every year, managers of Shell companies worldwide are required to write and sign three different letters covering performance in business integrity, health, safety, and environment and executing the Statement of General Business Principles. Writing the letters is a mandatory part of a senior manager's duties, and the task is taken seriously because managers are held personally responsible for the accuracy of the contents. Those who give false information or fail to reveal the truth can be dismissed. Shell has also opened communications to stakeholders through an annual series of Shell reports.[9]

For organizations, one of the greatest benefits of the auditing process is improved relationships with stakeholders. Many stakeholders have become wary of corporate public relations campaigns. Verbal assurances by corporate management are no longer sufficient to gain the trust of stakeholders. Consider that former Enron leaders often spoke to stakeholders about the importance of appropriate conduct, yet Enron demonstrated little concern for shareholders and employees when it concealed millions of dollars in debt in off-balance-sheet partnerships. When companies and their employees, suppliers, and investors trust each other, the costs of monitoring and managing these relationships are lower. Companies experience less conflict with these stakeholders, which results in a heightened capacity for innovation and relationship building.

As a result, shareholders and investors have welcomed the increased disclosure that comes with corporate responsibility. Figure 12.1 illustrates issues that are expected to have the most impact on shareholder value over the next five years. These issues can be considered major risk areas to audit. Therefore, they represent subject matter areas that could be important in a social audit. A growing number of investors are considering nonfinancial measures—such as the existence of ethics programs, legal compliance, board diversity and independence, and other corporate governance issues such as CEO compensation—when they analyze the quality of current and potential investments. Research suggests that investors may be willing to pay higher prices for the stock of companies they deem to be accountable.[10]

Consider that the "most admired companies" in the United States—General Electric, FedEx, Southwest Airlines, Procter & Gamble, Starbucks—have generally avoided major ethical problems.[11] However, some companies have experienced some legal issues or had their ethics questioned. Wal-Mart, who ranked number twelve in 2006, for example, has been accused of treating its men and women employees differently. It faces the largest private civil rights class-action discrimination suit from as many as 1.6 million female employees who say the giant retailer paid them lower wages and salaries than it did men in comparable positions. Pretrial proceedings uncovered discrepancies not only between the pay of men and women but also in the

| FIGURE 12.1 | Risk and Opportunity |

Which three issues are likely to have the most impact, positive of negative, on shareholder value for companies in your industry over the next five years? For each of the three issues selected, what mix of risks and opportunities does each issue pose to shareholder value?

	Only Opportunity or Mostly Opportunity and Limited Risk	Equal Balance Between Risk and Opportunity	Only Risk or Mostly Risk and Limited Opportunity
Pension and retirement benefits	7%	21%	70%
Health-care benefits and other employee benefits	10%	26%	63%
Political influence and/or political involvement of companies	11%	32%	56%
Opposition to foreign investment and freer trade	15%	23%	61%
Pay inequality between senior executives and other employees	16%	19%	63%
Privacy and data security	16%	29%	54%
Environmental issues, including climate change	18%	39%	41%
Affordability of products for poorer countries	29%	38%	30%
Ethical standards for advertising and marketing	30%	38%	30%
Demand for more investment in poor developing countries	30%	48%	22%
Workplace conditions and safety	31%	35%	33%
Job loss and offshoring	32%	41%	26%
Human-rights standards	33%	31%	30%
Demand for healthier or safer products	38%	45%	15%
Demand for more ethically produced products	40%	39%	20%

All data weighted by GDP of constituent countries to adjust for differences in response rates from various regions. Figures do not sum to 100%, because respondents answering "don't know" are not shown.

Source data from: "McKinsey Global Survey of Business Executives: Business & Society," January 2006. The McKinsey Quarterly conducted the survey in December 2005 and received responses from 4,238 executives— more than a quarter of them CEOs or other C-level executives—in 116 countries.

fact that men dominate higher paying store manager positions while women occupy more than 90 percent of cashier jobs, most of which pay about $14,000 a year. Wal-Mart faces fines and penalties in the millions of dollars if found guilty of sexual discrimination.[12] Such problems could have been uncovered and addressed with a regular audit related to gender discrimination. Even with its problems, Wal-Mart is the tenth most admired firm in the world, and Microsoft, with a significant antitrust issue, ranked sixth as the world's most admired company.[13]

Independent verification of social and environmental reports is one way companies are addressing this lack of trust. Verification can provide stakeholders with a measure of assurance that the company has reported honestly and fairly, together with an assessment of the quality of its social reporting systems. Accessibility and distribution of the report, as well as its direct relevance to stakeholders, help to facilitate a more beneficial, ongoing relationship between a company and its stakeholders.[14] When firms and their suppliers trust each other, the costs of monitoring and managing contracts are lower. Companies experience less conflict with their suppliers, resulting in fewer lawsuits, and there is a heightened capacity for innovation. In addition, social auditing and reporting can identify the effectiveness of programs and policies, often improving operating efficiencies and reducing costs. Information from audits and reports can also help identify priorities among corporate social responsibility activities to ensure the company is achieving the greatest possible impact with available resources.

The process of social auditing can also help an organization identify potential risks and liabilities and improve its compliance with the law. Accountable companies may be better prepared to address the concerns of customers or other stakeholders who might otherwise take negative action on social issues. For example, by engaging in a dialog with stakeholders about their interests and concerns and addressing those concerns in business implementation processes, companies may be able to head off or minimize the impacts of boycotts organized by consumer groups. Similarly, companies that proactively address the concerns of shareholders can reduce the risk of adverse publicity stemming from high-profile shareholder disputes.[15] Furthermore, the audit report may help to document the firm's compliance with legal requirements as well as demonstrate its progress in areas of previous noncompliance, including the systems implemented to reduce the likelihood of recurrence.[16] Firms may want to comply with the Federal Sentencing Guidelines for Organizations requirements that the board of directors oversee the discovery of ethical risk, design and implement an ethics program, and evaluate performance. Still other companies may see the auditing process as a key component of improving the financial performance of the organization. Shareholders and investors welcome the increased disclosure that comes with corporate accountability. A growing number of investors are including new nonfinancial metrics in their analysis of the quality of their investments. New metrics include legal compliance, the board of directors' independence, corporate governance, employee assistance through help lines, and a wide variety of other social responsibility concerns.

There seems to be a correlation between companies that are judged to treat their stakeholders well and those same companies being rated by their peers as having superior management. Stakeholders, including government regulators, may look more favorably on a company that identifies such problems through an audit, especially when the firm publicly reports the problems, demonstrates that it is attempting to resolve them, and implements systems that will reduce the likelihood of their recurrence.[17] Documentation of improvement through auditing is important proof of a corporate culture that is responsible. Thus, the social audit is a form of due diligence that provides evidence of a strategic attempt to benchmark and comply with standards.

Social auditing may also help a company coordinate its social responsibility initiatives throughout the firm, resulting in more effective and efficient use of company resources to address community and social concerns. Information from audits and reports can help identify priorities among corporate social responsibility activities to ensure the company is achieving the greatest possible impact with available resources. Because a well-designed audit can document the effectiveness and efficiency of social and accountability initiatives, the audit process may uncover areas where operations can be made more efficient (e.g., through recycling) and thereby reduce costs and increase profits.[18] Indeed, many companies are finding that the audit reduces operating costs while at the same time creating social benefits. One study by Smith O'Brien, a leader in the social audit industry, found dramatic savings for some companies conducting social audits. Examples of these savings ranged from nearly $200,000 from lower production costs in a small manufacturing plant to $1.7 million from a 10 percent decline in paper use in a company switching to electronic communication.[19] The auditing process helps organizations establish priorities for social responsibility, thereby allowing them to focus on those that will generate the greatest economic and social impact.[20]

Reporting on social responsibilities also allows a company to quantify the nonfinancial aspects of its community involvement. To illustrate, consider the fact that many organizations commit significant resources to activities such as providing volunteers for community activities. Sometimes, volunteers engage in activities during regular work hours. The time and effort an organization's staff spends on projects such as providing dinners at a homeless shelter or painting a youth center do not appear on a company's balance sheet. In addition, many companies donate products to help their communities. Bottled water companies, for example, often donate their products after disasters such as hurricanes.[21] Microsoft, IBM, and Hewlett-Packard have a reputation for donating their products to educational institutions.

Investors view companies that engage in social reporting more favorably. According to the Dow-Jones Sustainability Indexes (DJSI), the average sustainability performance of companies has improved significantly. Reasons for this include the integration of economic, environmental, and social issues moving up on the business agenda in all sectors and reaching a high level of sophistication in particularly exposed industries. The DJSI also recognized an increase in the number of sustainability-driven investors. People are realizing that sustainability trends have an impact on their investment decisions. Recent corporate scandals have emphasized the need for greater transparency and accountability on all social issues. As a result, investors are turning to the concept of sustainability to identify well-managed and future-oriented companies.[22]

Managing the Risks of Auditing and Risks of Not Auditing

Although social audits provide many benefits for individual organizations and their stakeholders, they do have potential risks, which could create as many problems as the audits solve. A firm may uncover a serious problem that it would prefer not to disclose until it can remedy the situation. An audit could discover an environmental problem or an employee who is creating an antitrust violation. For example, special-interest groups may be concerned about the amount of fat in fast-food meals. The audit may find that one or more of the firm's stakeholders' criticisms cannot be dismissed or easily addressed. Executive pay may be out of control, or serious misconduct may be discovered. Occasionally, the process of conducting a social audit may foster stakeholder dissatisfaction instead of eliminating it. Asking employees about discrimination or other unethical conduct in the workplace can stimulate employee complaints and

The Body Shop is recognized as a pioneer in the field of social auditing.

THE BODY SHOP®

COMPANY PROFILE
THE BODY SHOP A COMPANY WITH A DIFFERENCE

WHO WE ARE
The Body Shop International plc has over 2,000 stores in 54 countries, trading across 25 different languages and 12 time zones. We have a range of over 1,200 products – from our world-famous Body Butters, our much-loved fragrances including the best-selling White Musk®, inspiring accessories and gifts, and fabulous make-up.

We were the first international cosmetics brand to be awarded the Humane Cosmetics Standard for our Against Animal Testing policy. And over 15 years ago The Body Shop created its own fair trade programme called Community Trade. By satisfying our demand for ingredients, gifts and accessories in a fair way we help create sustainable trading relationships with marginalised communities around the world.

We believe business has the power to make the right kind of difference to the world, and the best way to convince others is to lead by example. All our products are made with a love of life, the world we live in, individuality, community spirit and a commitment to trading fairly.

WHERE WE ARE FROM
The Body Shop was founded by entrepreneur Dame Anita Roddick, when in 1976 she started selling around 25 hand-mixed naturally inspired products with minimal packaging from one small shop in Brighton, England.

Dame Anita was appointed a Dame of the British Empire in 2003 for services to retailing, the environment and to charity in recognition of her success in these key areas.

Over the years The Body Shop has run campaigns against human rights abuses, protecting animals and the environment and shown commitment to boosting self-esteem, winning the support of a generation of consumers.

Dame Anita Roddick is a non-executive director on the Board of The Body Shop, delivering essential expertise on product, marketing and values.

Since 2002 The Body Shop has been led by Peter Saunders, CEO of the Group and Director of the Board, while the Non-Executive Chairman is Adrian Bellamy.

WHAT WE BELIEVE IN
The Body Shop has been a leader in the trend towards greater corporate transparency, and has been a force for positive social and environmental change through its lobbying and campaigning programmes around five core principles: Support Community Trade, Defend Human Rights, Against Animal Testing, Activate Self-Esteem, and Protect Our Planet.

We set ourselves and our business partners clear standards of business practice, engage stakeholders with our aims, and report on our performance and our intent to improve within the overall context of our business.

We have also published details of our social, economic and environmental performance globally via web-based dissatisfaction. Moreover, the auditing process imposes burdens (especially with regard to recordkeeping) and costs for firms that undertake it. Finally, the process of auditing and reporting a firm's social efforts is no guarantee that the firm will not face challenges to its social responsibility.[23] In addition, because this type of auditing is relatively new, there are fewer common standards to judge disclosure and effectiveness or to make comparisons, but this issue is changing rapidly as new standards emerge.[24] In environmental auditing, it has been noted that some assurance providers engage in what is called selective disclosure; that is, they deliberately fail to give an opinion or judgment on so-called gray areas or activities that could be negative to the client's interests. The need for organizations to be seen by the public as being audited can be the motivating factor for conducting the audit and, in this case, of signaling that nothing is wrong.[25]

Despite the high costs of misconduct, a PricewaterhouseCoopers survey indicates that U.S. companies are failing to identify and manage ethical, social, economic, and environmental risks. Although most companies recognize that these issues have the potential to harm their reputations and threaten their relationships with customers, suppliers, and other stakeholders, few are taking steps to identify, evaluate, and respond to them.[26] Figure 12.2 indicates that where employees are exposed to situations posing risk, there is a high likelihood that they will also observe a violation taking place. For example, of those who felt they were poorly prepared or felt pressure to deal with risk, 94 percent observed misconduct. Of those who encountered situations that they believed could result in misconduct, 74 percent observed at least one form of misconduct, and even 64 percent of those in transitional organizations observed misconduct. Therefore, if employees feel pressured or aware of a risk factor in their work situation, they tend to observe misconduct. These findings mean that social audits could help more companies identify potential risks and liabilities so they can implement plans to discover and eliminate or reduce risks before they reach crisis dimensions.

| **FIGURE 12.2** | Employee Observed Misconduct by Risk Factors |

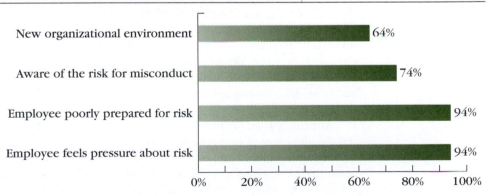

Where employees are exposed to situations posing risk, there is high likelihood that they will also observe a violation taking place.

Source: National Business Ethics Survey, *How Employees View Ethics in Their Organizations 1994–2005*, Ethics Resource Center, p. 36. Copyright, Reprinted with permission from The Ethics Resource Center, Washington, DC.

Crisis and Conflict from Anticorporate Interest Groups

Although there is very little academic literature on the subject, anticorporatism has been gaining the attention of the public, companies, governments, and nonprofit agencies. Using the Internet, anticorporate groups have been able not only to increase their power and impact but also share their views with the rest of the world. These groups are using technological advances to achieve different goals for all kinds of causes. Recently, the terms *anticorporatism* and *antiglobalism* have been used interchangeably. Opponents of corporatism and globalism both resist the expanding nature of corporations and businesses worldwide. They are fighting to limit the control and impact of corporations. They oppose the cultural shifts, new products, and other changes often brought to foreign countries by large multinational firms.

A British sociology professor uses an "iceberg" analogy to describe the current anticorporatism movement. The four levels are high-level protest events, less visible protests and related activities, social movement organizations and networks, and the interested and sympathetic.

The first level, which is the tip of the iceberg, is the high-level protest events. The protest in Seattle in 1999 at the World Trade Organization meeting, the protest in Prague at the IMF and World Bank meetings, the protest against the European Summit in Nice, and the protest in Montreal against the North American Free Trade Agreement are all examples of the tip of the iceberg. The World Bank called off its 2001 meeting in Barcelona because of anticipated protest and elected to have a virtual meeting instead. These events are the most visible level of the anticorporatism movement.

The people who participate in these protests come from all walks of life. They are college students, church members, environmentalists, union members, farmers, and others. The protestors want more democratic control as opposed to more corporate control of organizations such as the IMF, WTO, and the World Bank. In Europe, some of the groups wish to slow the advancement of the European Union.

The next three levels are not as visible as the first. The second level, less visible protests, includes webpages, magazine articles, debates, and other less visible

Misconduct can be caused by organizational members who engage in questionable or even illegal conduct. These rogue employees can threaten the overall integrity of the organization. Top leaders in particular can magnify ethical misconduct to disastrous dimensions. Organizational disasters resulting from individuals' misconduct include Rigas family members at Adelphia Communications, Andrew Fastow at Enron, Dennis Kozlowski at Tyco, and Bernie Ebbers at WorldCom.[27] A social audit can discover rogue employees who are violating the firm's ethical standards and policies or laws and regulations.

Although social responsibility is defined and perceived differently by various stakeholders, a core of minimum standards for corporate social performance is evolving. These standards represent a fundamental step in the development of a socially responsible company. The minimum standards are specific and measurable, and they are achievable and meaningful in terms of business impact on communities, employees, consumers, the environment, and economic systems. These standards help companies set measurable and achievable targets for improvement and form an objective foundation for reporting the firm's efforts to all stakeholders. There may still be disagreements on key issues and standards, but through these standards, progress should be made.[28]

outlets. The third level of the iceberg is the social movement organizations, or SMOs. These groups organize and fund the first- and second-level movements. An example of an SMO is the Adbusters group of Canada. The mission of Adbusters is to "halt the erosion of our physical and cultural environments by commercial forces, and forge a major shift in the way we live in the 21st century." They are currently suing several Canadian TV networks because they won't allow Adbusters to air its advertisements. The networks feel that the ads are too controversial and don't fit their business model.

The fourth level is an integral part of the third level. The fourth level is the interested and sympathetic. These individuals visit websites of the SMOs and often contribute financially and nonfinancially. An individual may contribute through a cash donation, volunteer time, or simply spreading the word about the movement and educating others on the movement's purpose. This final level supports the rest of the levels by financially funding efforts of the SMOs and furthering the movement through word of mouth.

Crisis management brought on by anticorporatism can be a difficult task. A crisis can be managed if, through the practice of reputation management, the issue has been identified by the organization before the pressure groups and media have a chance to exploit it. The recent increase in the power of anticorporate pressure groups poses new threats to the success of crisis management; hence, the organization's power to maintain control of a crisis brought about by these groups must be reassessed. Different groups have different goals, some specific and some broad. The more specific the aim of the group, the easier it is to pinpoint actions that may come under attack, thus making it easier to manage a crisis should one occur. Groups with a broader perspective create situations where it is difficult to identify potential crises, which in turn makes it harder to create an effective crisis management plan. The effects of anticorporatism can be softened by maintaining a strong reputation, incorporating stakeholder assessments and dialog, and realizing the impact that globalization potentially has on other countries and areas.[29] ■

Social Auditing Versus Financial Auditing

The social audit is much like the internal audit companies have used for years to verify the accuracy of their financial reports. In many cases, the standards used in financial auditing can be adapted to provide an objective foundation for social reporting. Thus, it is constructive to compare the financial audit and the social audit to better understand the reasons for and benefits of the social auditing process. With major scandals in accounting, such as HealthSouth and U.S. Foodservice, the reforms to prevent fraud in financial reporting provide some guidance in conducting a social audit.

Whereas a financial audit is concerned primarily with a company's claims about its financial performance, a social audit is interested in a company's nonfinancial social responsibility performance. Financial auditing focuses on all systems related to money flows and financial assessments of value for tax purposes and managerial accountability. Social auditing deals with nonfinancial aspects of operations from both their internal and external impacts. Issues such as abusive behavior, diversity, privacy, human resource decisions, and environmental impact are included in a social audit.

Another significant difference is that social auditing is a voluntary process today, whereas financial auditing is required of public companies that issue securities. Because social audits are voluntary, there are few standards that a company can apply with regard to reporting frequency, disclosure requirements, and remedial actions that a company should take in response to results. A variety of organizations and initiatives are attempting to standardize social and environmental reporting procedures to let stakeholders more easily compare companies across facilities, sectors, and borders. For example, the Global Reporting Initiative, an alliance of international organizations headed by the U.S.-based organization CERES, was established in 1998 to streamline the numerous initiatives on corporate environmental reporting that have developed independently around the world and to shape them into a set of consistent global standards. Also, the Institute of Social and Ethical Accountability introduced standards that aim to help companies understand and improve their social and ethical performance, describing how to identify key issues and report on them in a way that outsiders can rely on and suggesting how those reports should be audited. The AA1000 standard, discussed in more detail later in this chapter, sets out principles for ensuring that social reports are comprehensive, meaningful, and reliable. Even without such initiatives, many companies have been steadily improving the quality and quantity of information featured in their annual reports, voluntarily including greater amounts of data related to their environmental and social performance. A wide variety of standards are emerging that apply to corporate accountability. These include industry benchmarking tools and frameworks, legislation, and voluntary codes developed by nongovernmental organizations and private-sector consultancies.

The International Organization for Standardization (ISO) has tried to establish a corporate responsibility standard, the ISO 26000, and although the ISO 26000 has been demoted to a "guideline" rather than a standard, the discussion and debate surrounding the process are valuable. Although corporate responsibility needs quantitative credibility, significant aspects are more qualitative in nature: employee satisfaction, customer motivation, company values, and ethical decision-making processes, for instance. All to some extent can be broken down into quantitative data, but the essence of them cannot.[30] ISO has created six stakeholder categories in which experts are grouped for the social responsibility process: industry, labor, consumers, nongovernmental organization, government, and "other." ISO standards are the most widely respected and used nongovernmental standards. There are more than a half million sites certified to ISO 9000 worldwide, and a further 66,000 certified to ISO 14001. But those are just certifications, and estimates suggest that up to ten times as many sites are using these standards as guidance documents. ISO 26000 will not be for certification, but literally hundreds of thousands of organizations will hear about it and trust it.[31]

Social auditing is similar to financial auditing in that both employ the same procedures and processes to create a system of integrity with objective reporting. An independent expert must verify both types of audits. The financial auditor will employ external sources to certify the assertions in financial statements, such as comparing the company's accounts receivable with its accounts payable. To vouch for a company's claims about its social performance, a social auditor will contact customers and other stakeholders and compare their perceptions of the firm's social performance with the company's assessments. Like financial audits, social audits are often performed by certified public accountants. Table 12.1 illustrates the social responsibility auditing standards established by one of these accounting and consulting firms.

TABLE 12.1	Social Auditing Standards

Competence

The engagement shall be performed by a practitioner having adequate technical training and proficiency.

The engagement shall be performed by a practitioner having adequate knowledge in the subject matter.

The practitioner shall perform an engagement only if he or she has reason to believe that the following two conditions exist:

- The assertion is capable of evaluation against reasonable criteria that have been established by a recognizable body or are stated in the presentation of the assertion in a sufficiently clear and comprehensive manner for a knowledgeable reader to be able to understand them.
- The assertion is capable of reasonably consistent estimation or measurement using such criteria.

Independence

An independence in mental attitude shall be maintained by the practitioner who shall not have participated in the assertion.

Due Care

Due professional care shall be exercised in the performance of the engagement.

Planning

The work shall be adequately planned and assistants, if any, shall be properly supervised.

Control Structure

A sufficient understanding of the communications and control structures is to be obtained to plan the audit and to determine the nature, timing, and extent of tests to be performed.

Evidence

Sufficient evidence shall be obtained to provide a reasonable basis for the conclusion that is expressed in the report.

Standards of Reporting

The report shall identify the assertion being reported on and state the character of the engagement.

The report shall state the practitioner's conclusion about whether the assertion is presented in conformity with the established or stated criteria against which it was measured.

The report shall state all of the practitioner's significant reservations about the engagement and the presentation of the assertion.

The report on an engagement to evaluate an assertion that has been prepared in conformity with agreed-upon criteria or on an engagement to apply agreed-upon procedures should contain a statement limiting its use to the parties who have agreed upon such criteria or procedures.

Source: "Social Responsibility Auditing Standards," Vasin, Heyn & Company, www.vhcoaudit.com/SRAarticles/SRAStandards.htm, accessed April 27, 2006. Reprinted by permission of Vasin, Heyn & Company.

Both financial and social audits begin with planning. In each audit, planning involves collecting information to understand the company's industry, determining the scope of the audit, and documenting the details of the audit program. This information must be of high quality, consistent, complete, material, segregated, and collected in a controlled environment. The auditor cannot start the program assuming management is in compliance with legal and ethical standards. Nor can the auditor assume management is not in compliance with standards. It is a practice that is based on judgment with the use of professional skepticism. The failure to use professional skepticism in financial audits created the accounting audit fraud scandals associated with WorldCom and Enron.

The quality of information gathered affects management's capacity to direct the company's social responsibility activities and therefore influences the social auditor's ability to conduct the audit. The auditor is primarily concerned with how the company records, processes, summarizes, and reports on its social responsibilities and how the company communicates these responsibilities to involved stakeholders. Accuracy in measurement and due diligence and professionalism in reporting are required to ensure quality.

Consistency is also essential in both financial and social audits. For example, an auditor of financial statements will use analytical procedures, such as comparing current-year account balances to those of prior years, to test specific claims. The methods of reporting must be consistent to be meaningful. Thus, a company is not permitted to change its method of reporting without adequate disclosure. A common example of this would be an announcement of a change in the method of valuing inventory accounts from "last in, first out" (LIFO) to "first in, first out" (FIFO). For the same reasons, a company should not alter its method of reporting about social responsibility results for a particular stakeholder group from one year to the next without disclosing that fact. For example, if the sample size of community groups surveyed in a subsequent social audit is significantly reduced, the auditor should question whether this reduction provides consistency with the results of the prior year's audit. Perhaps more favorable results were obtained in a prior year because the company surveyed more community groups that responded positively than negatively in the prior audit. Although this type of practice undermines the purpose and continuous improvements that a company can gain from a social responsibility effort, its possibility should not be overlooked. For these reasons, a social balance sheet has been created. It is defined as a representation of a given enterprise's social and socioeconomic development. Modern versions attempt to cover not only the point of view of owners and shareholders but also that of other stakeholders. The social balance sheet and the provision of socioeconomic information in general have come into being as a result of the change in the traditional notion of the enterprise, which is no longer identified solely with the interest of its owners (maximizing profit) and is seen as a coalition of interests of various stakeholders. This means that greater attention has to be paid to the interests and concerns of all stakeholders.[32]

Both social and financial auditors are particularly concerned about the completeness of the records used to document a company's assertions. In a financial audit, the auditor will trace from the source documents to the financial statements to ensure that accounts are complete. Likewise, a social audit must include all aspects of the company's "social footprint," including all the places, people, and stakeholders that are affected by the firm and all the company's activities, standards, and perceived organizational culture as related to social performance. Did the company record all of its responsibilities and performance related to social responsibility?

The concept of materiality is related to the audit's completeness. In a financial audit, something is deemed material if it is probable that the judgment of a reasonable person relying on the information would have been changed or influenced by its omission or misstatement. Materiality applies to social audits as well because users of a social audit could be misled if the audit fails to include material measures of stakeholders' perspectives, such as those of the company's customers. It is important for materiality that research methods and measurement procedures provide an accurate and timely audit. For example, Enron concealed off-balance-sheet partnerships that materially influenced the value of the corporation.

To avoid misstatements in the social report, it is important for social auditors to clearly segregate certain functions. For example, the individual responsible for gathering stakeholder perspectives should not be the same individual who records the results. Obviously, if the duty of gathering evidence as well as recording the findings is conducted by the same person, there is no way to independently verify the accuracy of the recorded perspectives. The segregation of audit activities is facilitated by assigning accountants or consultants responsibility for certain audit functions. Even financial audits need to be conducted by an independent auditor that does not have conflicts of interest related to consulting income.

Perhaps the most significant component of the auditing process is the control environment, which relates to the values or philosophy and operating style of management. The corporate culture is captured in social audits to address this key leadership and control environment. The control environment facilitates establishing standards and reducing differences between desired and actual performance. The control environment represents the collective effect of both formal and informal methods to achieve desired results. Does management strongly emphasize the need for compliance with standards to ensure that the firm's social responsibility claims are managed and implemented? Are ethical values part of the corporate culture? In a financial audit, it is standard procedure for an audit firm to determine the integrity of management before accepting an auditing engagement. Auditors lend credibility to a company's assertions, and this credibility can never be compromised. It is better for an outside audit consultant to decline an engagement than be associated with a company that lacks integrity. Arthur Andersen made the mistake of being the auditor of clients such as Enron, WorldCom, Qwest, Sunbeam, Waste Management, and others that wanted to manipulate expenses and revenues to inflate earnings. If there is limited commitment to the auditing process, then the company may plan to use the audit for public relations rather than for improvement.

Skewed financial results appear in financial statements primarily because management's compensation is often tied to the financial results, and management feels pressure to meet analyst expectations. As the demand for social responsibility grows in importance, the temptation for management to conceal and perpetuate social irregularities will also grow. The unavoidable result will be for social audits to emphasize internal control variables in a manner similar to financial audits. When internal control is overemphasized, there is a movement away from proactive value-driven activities that are harder to measure to emphasizing required, objective, legalistic audits. Firms that take a legalistic approach to social auditing are avoiding the spirit of existing legislation and are missing the opportunity to develop an innovative corporate culture that values and embraces social responsibility.

THE CHALLENGES OF MEASURING NONFINANCIAL PERFORMANCE

Much of the regulatory focus of social responsibility and compliance is driven by financial measures, but the integrity of an organization must also focus on nonfinancial areas of performance. The word *integrity* implies a balanced organization that not only makes responsible financial decisions but also is ethical in the more subjective aspects of its corporate culture. For example, the Sarbanes-Oxley Act has focused on questionable accounting and the metrics that destroy shareholder value. On the other hand, there are models that have been developed such as Six Sigma, the Balanced Scorecard, and the Triple Bottom Line to capture structural and behavioral organizational ethical performance. Six Sigma is a methodology to manage process variations that cause defects, defined as unacceptable deviation from the mean or target; and to systematically work toward managing variation to eliminate those defects. The objective of Six Sigma is to deliver world-class performance, reliability, and value to the end customer.[33] The Balanced Scorecard is a method for measuring a company's activities in terms of its vision and strategies. It gives managers a comprehensive view of the performance of a business. It is a strategic management system that forces managers to focus on the important performance metrics that drive success. It balances a financial perspective with customer, internal process, and learning and growth perspectives.[34] The Triple Bottom Line captures an expanded spectrum of values and criteria for measuring organizational (and societal) success—economic, environmental, and social. For some, a commitment to corporate social responsibility brings with it a need to institute triple bottom line reporting.[35]

The purpose of nonfinancial measures is to determine the wholeness and soundness of the many aspects of a business that enhance responsibility and profits without increasing risk. Companies that capitalize on ethical culture, communications, and other nonfinancial issues realize a financial "return on integrity."[36]

AccountAbility is an international membership organization committed to enhancing the performance of organizations and to developing the competencies of individuals in social and ethical accountability and sustainable development. Figure 12.3 illustrates the AccountAbility AA1000 framework for ethics and social responsibility. The AA1000 process standards link the definition and embedding of an organization's values to the development of performance targets and to the assessment and communication of organizational performance. By this process, focused around the organization's engagement with stakeholders, AA1000 ties social and ethical issues into the organization's strategic management and operations. AA1000 recognizes these different traditions. It combines the terms *social and ethical* to refer to the systems and to individual behavior within an organization and to the *direct and indirect* impact of an

FIGURE 12.3   AA1000 Framework for Ethics and Social Accountability

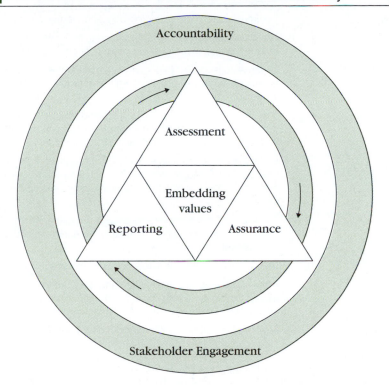

Source: Adapted from AccountAbility AA1000 Series, http://www.accountability.org.uk/aa1000/default.asp, accessed April 4, 2006.

organization's activities on stakeholders. *Social and ethical issues* (relating to systems, behavior, and impacts) are defined by an organization's values and aims, through the influence of the interests and expectations of its stakeholders, and by societal norms and expectations. Assessment is measuring organizational responsiveness or the extent to which an organization takes action on the basis of stakeholder engagement. This is followed by assurance, including control mechanisms, and then reporting to document the process. Embedding of an organization's values to assure performance is a continuous process.

The Integrity Institute has developed ten validated models that create a diagnostic tool to help organizations recognize the structural weaknesses early on to avoid or address problems appropriately rather than to respond to and recover from a crisis, which often proves too late. Rather than focusing on single-issue assessments, a comprehensive model provides nonfinancial information that discovers and assesses the soundness, wholeness, and incorruptibility of a corporation and makes it possible to pinpoint more accurately where weaknesses may exist that influence the health and welfare of a company and its sustainability. By measuring these components, it is possible to assess an organization's ability to withstand market forces (e.g., ethical misconduct disasters) that may influence the company and destroy shareholder value.[37]

TABLE 12.2	The Integrity Institute Integrated Model to Standardize the Measure of Integrity
Communication Integrity	Communicated information, messages, meta-messages, and processes
Compensation Integrity	Excessive compensation, tactics used to motivate employees to take certain actions that can jeopardize the integrity of an organization.
Compliance and Ethical Integrity	Organizations that fail to comply with minimum legal requirements on a variety of fronts or have ethical disasters are being regularly dropped from investment and insurance portfolios.
Corporate Citizenship Integrity (Environmental and Social Responsibility)	Integrity of the environmental policies and social responsibility practices of an organization. It measures the structure—not the morality—of corporate citizenship and identifies pressure being placed on companies to do the right thing.
Cultural Integrity	Collective consciousness and values define the culture of the organization and whether it has integrity. Whether the culture is sound, whole, and incorruptible and what predictive "markers" exist that may weaken the organization's ability to stand strong.
Earnings Integrity	The extent to which corporate earnings are managed vs. manipulated has long been of interest to analysts, regulators, researchers, and other investment professionals.
Leadership Integrity	Behavioral complexity in leadership and the strategy of ethical leadership.
Risk Integrity	Risks associated with intelligence and the sharing of data and related privacy issues. Risk integrity begins and ends with information and the transfer of that information.
Stakeholders' Perceptions of Organizational Integrity	After analyzing the nine nonfinancial performance indicators outlined above, measure them against the stakeholders' perceptions.

Source: Lynn Brewer, "Capitalizing on the Value of Integrity: An Integrated Model to Standardize the Measure of Non-Financial Performance as an Assessment of Corporate Integrity," Appendix B in Lynn Brewer, Robert Chandler, and O. C. Ferrell, *Managing Risks for Corporate Integrity: How to Survive an Ethical Misconduct Disaster* 1st edition (Mason, OH: Texere/Thomson, 2006). Reprinted with permission of South-Western, a division of Thomson Learning: www.thomsonrights.com. Fax 800 730-2215.

The Integrity Institute's integrated model to standardize the measure of integrity is illustrated in Table 12.2. The model integrates ten drivers or markers that have the potential to weaken the overall structural soundness of the organization. These components include (1) communication, (2) compensation, (3) compliance and ethics, (4) corporate citizenship, (5) culture, (6) earnings, (7) governance, (8) leadership, (9) risk, and (10) stakeholder perceptions. While investors may already use many of these variables, the Integrity Institute Integria™ model establishes a standard that can predict the sustainability and success of the organization. This measurement to an established standard is used as a basis of certification of integrity by the Integrity Institute.

Figure 12.4 shows the Open Compliance Ethics Group Framework Overview. The Open Compliance Ethics Group (OCEG), www.oceg.org, has worked with over 100 companies to create a universal framework for compliance and ethics management. The OCEG focuses on nonfinancial compliance and the more qualitative elements of internal controls. The OCEG framework deals with complex issues of compliance and actual solutions to address the development of organizational ethics. The framework integrates some of the best thinking in several disciplines to address compliance and ethics management. Using expertise from these disciplines, guidelines were developed. By establishing guidelines rather than standards, OCEG provides a tool for each company to use as it sees fit, given its size, scope, structure, industry, and other factors

| **FIGURE 12.4** | Open Compliance Ethics Group Framework |

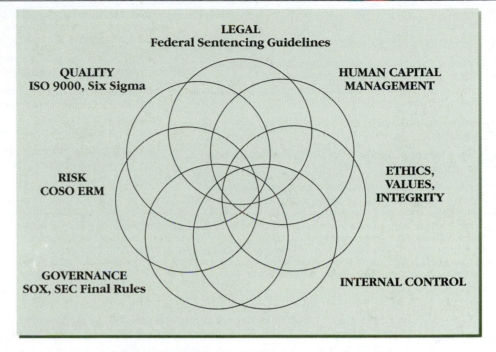

Source: Adapted from Open Compliance Ethics Group, www.oceg.org, accessed October 4, 2004.

that create individualized needs. The OCEG guidelines and benchmarking studies can be very valuable to a firm conducting an ethics audit. Most significant is the opportunity to benchmark an organization's current activities to those of other organizations.

THE SOCIAL AUDITING PROCESS

There are relatively few standards available for companies to follow in conducting a social audit, such as what standards of performance should be used, how often to conduct an audit, whether and how to report an audit's results to stakeholders, and what actions should be taken in response to audit results. A survey conducted by one of the big four accounting firms found that only a few social reports contained any form of external verification. Such a general lack of third-party assurance has probably contributed to the general critique that social reporting is simply about corporate spin and public relations. However, the number of outside-verified reports is growing. Thus, corporate approaches to social auditing are as varied as their approaches to social responsibility.[38]

It is our belief that a social audit should be unique to each company based on its size, industry, and corporate culture, as well as the regulatory environment in which it operates and the commitment of its top management to social responsibility. For this reason, we have mapped out a framework that is somewhat generic and can therefore be expanded by all companies that want to conduct a social audit. The

TABLE 12.3	Framework for a Social Audit

- Secure commitment of top management and/or board of directors.

- Establish an audit committee.

- Define the scope of the audit process, including subject matter areas important to the social audit (e.g., environment, discrimination, employee rights, privacy, philanthropy, legal compliance, etc.).

- Review organizational mission, policies, goals, and objectives.

- Define the organization's social priorities as they relate to stakeholders.

- Identify the tools or methods the organization can employ to measure its achievement of objectives.

- Collect relevant information in each designated subject matter area, including internal data and data from concerned stakeholders.

- Summarize and analyze the data collected and compare the internal information to stakeholder expectations.

- Have the results verified by an independent agent (i.e., a social audit consultant, accounting firm that offers social auditing services, or nonprofit special-interest organization with social auditing experience).

- Report the findings to the audit committee and, if approved, to managers and stakeholders.

Sources: These steps are compatible with the social auditing methods prescribed by Warren Dow and Roy Crowe, *What Social Auditing Can Do for Voluntary Organizations* (Vancouver, WA: Volunteer Vancouver, 1999); Business for Social Responsibility, "CSR Reporting," http://www.bsr.org/CSRResources/IssueBriefDetail.cfm?DocumentID= 50962, accessed April 27, 2006; Sandra Waddock and Neil Smith, "Corporate Responsibility Audits: Doing Well by Doing Good," *Sloan Management Review* 41 (Winter 2000): 79.

steps of this framework are presented in Table 12.3. As with any new initiative, companies may choose to begin their effort with a smaller, less formal audit and then work up to a more comprehensive social audit. For example, a firm may choose to focus on primary stakeholders in its initial audit year and then expand to secondary groups in subsequent audits.

When creating a framework, companies should be aware of the development of standards such as the Integrity Institute, AA1000 Series, and the Open Compliance Ethics Group discussed in the last section. Although no regulation exists, AA1000 lays out guidelines that can be used to judge the quality of the audit. The guidelines build on the core principle of inclusiveness and are based on three propositions: (1) stakeholder engagement remains at the core of the accountability processes of accounting, embedding values, assurance, and reporting; (2) accountability is about organizational responsiveness, or the extent to which an organization takes action on the basis of stakeholder engagement; and (3) responsiveness requires the organizational capacities to learn and innovate effectively on the basis of stakeholder engagement. The Integrity Institute provides ten markers of structural integrity, and the Open Compliance Ethics Group provides benchmarking for a firm to compare its performance against industry performance.

Our framework encompasses a wide range of business responsibilities and relationships. The audit entails an individualized process and outcomes for a particular firm, as it requires the careful consideration of the unique issues that face a particular organization. For example, the auditing process at Kellogg Company includes the following:

The Social Responsibility Committee of the Board of Directors shall identify, evaluate and monitor the social, political, environmental, occupational safety and health trends, issues, and concerns, domestic and foreign, which affect or could affect the Company's business or performance.

The Committee shall make recommendations to assist in the formulation and adoption of policies, programs and practices concerning the matters set forth above including, but not limited to, environmental protection, employee and community health and safety, ethical business conduct, consumer affairs, alcohol and drug abuse, equal opportunity matters, and government relations, and shall monitor the Company's charitable contributions.[39]

Figure 12.5 depicts The Body Shop's framework for its social auditing and disclosure process. Although this chapter presents a structure and recommendations for a social audit, there is no generic approach to satisfy every firm's circumstances.

FIGURE 12.5   Framework for Social Auditing and Disclosure at The Body Shop International

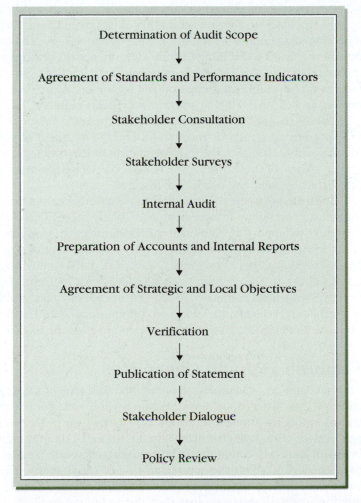

Determination of Audit Scope

↓

Agreement of Standards and Performance Indicators

↓

Stakeholder Consultation

↓

Stakeholder Surveys

↓

Internal Audit

↓

Preparation of Accounts and Internal Reports

↓

Agreement of Strategic and Local Objectives

↓

Verification

↓

Publication of Statement

↓

Stakeholder Dialogue

↓

Policy Review

Source: Maria Sillanpaa and David Wheeler, "Integrated Ethical Auditing: The Body Shop International, UK," in *Building Corporate Accountability: The Emerging Practices in Social and Ethical Accounting, Auditing and Reporting,* ed. Simon Zadek, Peter Pruzan, and Richard Evans (London: Earthscan Publications Ltd., 1997), p. 116.

However, the benefits and limitations that companies derive from social auditing are relatively consistent.

Secure Commitment of Top Management and/or Board of Directors

The first step in conducting a social audit is securing the commitment of the firm's top management and/or its board of directors. In some cases, the push for a social audit may come directly from the board of directors in response to stakeholder concerns. Changes in corporate governance associated with the Sarbanes-Oxley Act would suggest that the board of directors should be providing oversight for all auditing activities. In addition, pressure for a social audit may come from top managers looking for ways to create a competitive advantage for their firm by publicizing its social efforts. Some companies now have a senior officer in charge of social responsibility, and this individual may campaign for a social audit as a means of demonstrating the effectiveness of the firm's social initiatives. In addition, court decisions and the 2004 amendments related to the Federal Sentencing Guidelines for Organizations hold board members responsible for the ethical and legal compliance programs of the firms they oversee as well as developing an ethical corporate culture.

The Sarbanes-Oxley Act requires the board's financial audit committee to examine ethical standards throughout the organization as they relate to financial matters and to deal with the implementation of the code of ethics from top financial officers. Many of these issues relate to such corporate governance issues as compensation, stock options, and conflicts of interest.

Regardless of where the impetus for an assessment comes from, its success hinges on the full support of top management, particularly the CEO and the board of directors. Without this support, an assessment will not be effective in improving the ethics program and corporate culture. For example, after a negative publicity documentary, "Wal-Mart: The High Cost of Low Prices," was released, the company asked economists to assess its effect on the economy. A conference, "An In-Depth Look at Wal-Mart and Society," was part of a campaign to address criticism of wages, health-care benefits, workplace policies, and economic impact on communities. Wal-Mart attempted to develop an objective and balanced assessment to respond to a very one-sided documentary.[40]

Establish an Audit Committee

The next step in our framework is the establishment of a committee to oversee the audit process. This committee works best when it establishes the scope of the audit and monitors its progress to ensure that it stays on track. On the basis of the best practices of corporate governance, audits should be monitored by an independent board of directors committee. The committee should include some members who have knowledge about the nature and role of social audits. The internal or external auditors should report directly to the board audit committee. The company being audited must get all services, other than the audit, approved by the audit committee if they are to be performed by the external auditors. It is important that external consultants do not have conflicts of interest or relationships with top management that may affect their independence. Companies may consider inputs from stakeholder members such as customers, employees, and shareholders in determining the scope of the audit. It is important to document the scope of the social audit in the beginning stages, even if modifications of the preliminary scope are made later.

Define the Scope of the Audit Process

The next step after establishing an audit committee is to define the scope of the audit process, including subject matter areas that are important to the social audit. The scope of an audit depends on the type of business, the risks faced by the business, and the available opportunities to manage social responsibility. The scope will determine the key subject matter areas of the company's social responsibilities (e.g., environment, governance, discrimination, employee rights, privacy, philanthropy, and legal compliance) that the audit should cover and on what basis they should be assessed. Assessments can be made on the basis of direct consultation, observation, surveys, or focus groups.[41] For example, the Chris Hani Baragwanath Hospital (CHBH) in Johannesburg, South Africa, conducted an audit that included focus groups with hospital management, doctors, nurses, related health professionals, support staff, and patients. On the basis of the trends uncovered in these focus groups, CHBH then developed a questionnaire for a survey, which it administered to a larger group of individual stakeholders.[42] The greater the number of stakeholders included in this stage, the more time and resources will be required to carry out the audit; however, a larger sample of stakeholders may yield a more useful variety of opinions about the company. Table 12.4 lists some sample subject matter areas and audit items for each of those areas.

Review Organizational Mission, Policies, Goals, and Objectives

Because social audits generally involve a comparison of organizational performance to the firm's policies and objectives, the audit process should include a review of the current mission statement and strategic objectives. The company's overall mission may incorporate social responsibility objectives, but these may also be found in separate documents focused on social responsibility. For instance, the Furniture Resource Centre states:

> Founded in 1988 by Nic Frances, we have grown from having a small community based response to poverty in inner city Liverpool to being today one of Britain's best known social businesses turning over millions of pounds. We are about personal and social change. We have a passion about all we do, aspire to be professional in all areas, and believe that our ambitious goals require relentless creativity and bravery.[43]

For example, the firm's ethics statement or statement of values may offer guidance for management on the transactions and human relationships that support the firm's reputation, thereby fostering confidence from stakeholders outside the firm.[44] This step should examine the formal documents that make explicit commitments to environmental or social responsibility, as well as less formal documents, including marketing materials, workplace policies, and ethics policies and standards for suppliers or vendors. Such a review may reveal a need to create additional statements or a new

TABLE 12.4	Sample Subject Matter and Stakeholder Audit Items

Please check the response (yes or no) that best answers the following questions:

Yes	No	**Human Resource Issues**
O	O	Does the company have a formal training program that focuses on social responsibility issues?
O	O	If training sessions exist, are they designed to cover legal, ethical, and subject matter social concerns that relate to daily operations?
O	O	Has someone been appointed to provide oversight for training and compliance of ethical, legal, and social issues?
O	O	Do employees have an independent mechanism, such as an 800 number or e-mail address, to report social responsibility concerns?
O	O	Does the company have programs for helping employees manage work-related stress and conflict?

Yes	No	**Customer Relations Issues**
O	O	Does the company have a feedback mechanism to obtain customer concerns/complaints?
O	O	Has the company established policies and a shared value system of fairness and honesty toward customers?
O	O	Is there a long-term focus on all aspects of customer welfare at the expense of short-run profits?
O	O	Are product quality, pricing, and service designed to deliver customers' expectations of value?
O	O	Are all the laws and legal rights related to customers communicated to employees?

Yes	No	**Community Issues**
O	O	Does the company achieve its goals without compromising community ethical norms?
O	O	Are there environmental impact considerations for operations and organizational activities?
O	O	Does the company contribute resources to the community?
O	O	Are there programs to empower or reward employees who contribute to recognized community activities?
O	O	Does top management express organizational commitment to improving the quality of life and the general welfare of society?

Yes	No	**Diversity Issues**
O	O	Are all laws protecting specific classes of employees and customers properly communicated?
O	O	Are systems in place to ensure compliance with all discrimination laws?
O	O	Does the company value and proactively embrace diversity in the workplace?
O	O	Is all communication designed to incorporate a philosophy of culture and diversity?
O	O	Has the company developed special educational or employment opportunities to contribute to diversity objectives?

comprehensive mission statement or ethics policy to address deficiencies uncovered during this step.[45]

It is also important to examine all of the firm's policies and practices for the specific areas covered by the audit. For example, in an audit that includes environmental issues in its scope, this step would consider the company's goals and objectives on environmental matters, the company's environmental policies, the means for communicating these policies, and the effectiveness of this communication. This assessment should also look at whether and how managers are rewarded for meeting their goals and the systems available for employees to give and receive feedback. An effective social audit should review all these systems and assess their strengths and weaknesses.[46]

Define the Organization's Social Priorities

The next step in the auditing process is defining the organization's social priorities. Determining a company's social priorities is a balancing act, as it can be difficult to identify the needs and assess the priorities of each stakeholder. Because there are no legal requirements for social priorities, it is up to the board of directors' and management's strategic planning processes to determine appropriate duties and required action to deal with social issues. It is very important in this stage to articulate these priorities and values as a set of parameters or performance indicators that can be objectively and quantitatively assessed. Because the social audit is a structured report that offers quantitative and descriptive assessments, actions should be measurable by quantitative indicators. However, it is sometimes not possible to go beyond description.[47]

At some point, the firm must demonstrate action-oriented responsiveness to those social issues given top priority. Wells Fargo, for example, believes that education, jobs, and housing are fundamental community issues, and therefore, these are

A market researcher in Las Vegas waits for passers-by at the MGM Grand hotel and casino. Las Vegas is increasingly the city of choice for researchers, some of whom seek consumer opinion on the social responsibility activities and reputations of various companies.

the focus of the firm's philanthropy programs. In line with these priorities, the bank has donated $300 million to nonprofit organizations and made $45 billion in loans for community reinvestment projects, including affordable housing development, commercial economic development, and small-business loans, especially to firms owned by women and minorities.[48] Likewise, Home Depot has identified affordable housing, at-risk youth, and the natural environment as social priorities. To address its environmental priority—and satisfy stakeholders' concerns about deforestation—the world's largest home-improvement retailer recently pledged to stop selling lumber and other products made from wood from endangered forests and to focus instead on wood products that have been certified as having come from responsibly managed forests. Also, the company has a social responsibility report on its website to account for how it strives to be the best neighbor by contributing to local communities.[49]

Identify Tools or Methods for Accurate Measurement of Social Objectives

The sixth step in our framework is identifying the tools or methods that can be employed to measure the firm's achievement of social responsibility objectives. In this age of globalization and intense competitive pressures, such measurement tools are important to ensure that corporate social responsibilities are not compromised for higher profitability. Performance indicators can be used to quantitatively and qualitatively measure an organization's social as well as its financial performance. Some organizations, for example, have found that quantifying their community involvement can lead to more efficient and effective use of company resources to address community needs. The London Benchmarking Group has developed a template for companies to monitor and measure community involvement activities. This template helps companies to assess their community efforts and make continual improvement.[50]

Some social areas of concern, such as fair trade, present challenges in measurement. Trying to ensure fair wages, safe working conditions, and sustainable production associated with fair trade is receiving greater awareness for products such as coffee and fruit grown in developing countries. On the other hand, there is considerable lack of agreement about what fair trade means and how to measure or certify it, especially the types of workers or commodities that relate to fair trade.[51]

Smith O'Brien, a leading social audit firm, has identified some useful measurement techniques for social audits. The social balance sheet assigns dollar values to social impact as well as financial performance. The social performance index uses a numerical ranking system relating to corporate social performance. Stakeholder surveys incorporate the perceptions of the company from the stakeholders' point of view. The Body Shop has conducted such surveys based on interviews with its key stakeholders. Reading The Body Shop's latest values report, it is easy to believe that the company means what it says and that the company's strongly held values really go to the core of the organization and permeate through all of its practices. Integrating values into an organization is surely much easier when a company holds them from its inception, rather than when it tries to tack them on as an afterthought to mitigate risks posed by changing social trends. The Body Shop is not without its critics, and although the organization has a distinguished history as a pioneer of corporate responsibility, it is the first to admit it has neglected meaningful social and environmental reporting for a number of years. But now it has made a concerted effort to get back to the cutting edge, and it is even rumored to have recently been recruiting for a director of values. The Body Shop's return to serious social reporting started with reports tailored for specific stakeholders; however, the publication of tailored reports was short lived and the company has returned to the all-in-one format again. McSpotlight claims that The Body Shop's products are far from natural and are almost wholly synthetic. The company participates in many stakeholder initiatives, including the Ethical Trading Initiative, the Forest Stewardship Council, the Roundtable for Sustainable Palm Oil, and the Business Leaders' Initiative for Human Rights. But overall, the report is surprisingly scant when it comes to hard data about its impacts. It is obvious to many in the corporate social responsibility world that the company has slipped backward since the late 1990s. On the evidence of this report, despite many good points, it is clear that The Body Shop is still trying to find its feet as it tries to reestablish itself as a leader in the corporate responsibility debate. The attempt to hire a star corporate responsibility director suggests The Body Shop knows this.[52] Disclosure audits are similar to those provided in a company's financial statements but relate to a firm's social responsibilities. Ben & Jerry's (owned by Unilever) has employed disclosure accounts in its social audit.

Collect Relevant Information

The next step in the auditing process is to collect relevant information for each designated subject matter area. To understand employee issues, for example, the auditing committee will work with the firm's human resources department in gathering employee survey information and other statistics and feedback. A thorough audit will include a review of all relevant reports, including external documents sent to government agencies and others. The information collected in this step will help determine baseline levels of compliance as well as the internal and external expectations of the company. This step will also identify where the company has, or has not, met its commitments, including those dictated by its mission statement and other policy documents. The documents reviewed in this process will vary from company to company, depending on the firm's size, nature of its business, and the scope of the audit process.[53]

Some techniques of evidence collection might involve examination of both internal and external documents, observation of the data-collection process (e.g., stakeholder consultation), and confirmation of information in the organization's accounting records. Ratio analysis of relevant indicators may also be used to identify any inconsistencies or unexpected patterns. The importance of objective measurement is the key consideration of the social auditor.[54] As with the financial audit, reliability depends on the source of all information collected. A document or acknowledgment that has been generated and circulated externally provides the most objective evidence. For example, New Belgium Brewing Company received the Better Business Bureau Marketplace Ethics Award and the Annual Business Ethics Award granted by *Business Ethics* magazine. In response to this, an NBC *Today Show* segment about New Belgium's environmental stewardship provided evidence of how these actions can be favorable for a company. Another example of such a document might be the minutes of a focus group taken by an external stakeholder group that is sent directly to the social auditor. Documents that are internally generated and circulated are more subjective because they can more easily be altered. Sometimes, internal documents are used for publicity or to motivate employees. In the context of a social audit, an example of the least objective document would be an internally generated and circulated report on the staff hours spent in community volunteering. This document might count hours that are questionable.[55]

Because stakeholder integration is so crucial to the social audit, a company's stakeholders need to be defined and interviewed during the data-collection stage. For most companies, stakeholders include employees, customers, investors, suppliers, community groups, regulators, nongovernmental organizations, and the media. Social audits typically include interviews and focus groups with these stakeholders to gain an understanding of their perceptions of the company. In multinational corporations, a decision must also be made on whether to include only the main office or headquarters region or to use all facilities around the globe in the audit.[56] Coca-Cola must be concerned about the hundreds of independent bottlers and distributors around the world. All of these relationships are a part of Coca-Cola's social performance. Recently, Coca-Cola bottlers who serve as the firm's wholesalers sued Coca-Cola, claiming that the plan to send the Powerade product directly to retailers such as Wal-Mart was a breach of contract.[57] Although Coca-Cola disputes or denies these allegations, the net result means that shares of Coca-Cola trade today at the same level they did nearly ten years ago, while Pepsi continues to gain market share in the beverage market.

Because employees carry out a business's operations, including its social initiatives, understanding employee issues is vital. Indicators that are useful for assessing employee issues include staff turnover and employee satisfaction. High turnover rates could indicate poor working conditions, an unethical climate, inadequate compensation, or general employee dissatisfaction. Companies can analyze these factors to determine key areas for improvement.[58] For example, Wild Planet Toys, as part of its annual social assessment, surveys employees on a range of issues, including company mission, product quality, diversity, the workplace, the environment, and community outreach. The results of this process, which are provided to employees, have led to clearer priorities and better internal coordination, as well as to a revised mission statement and the addition of long-term disability insurance to the benefits package.[59] Most companies recognize that employees will behave in ways that result in recognition and rewards and avoid behavior that results in punishment. Thus, companies can design and implement human resources policies and procedures for recruiting, hiring, promoting, compensating, and rewarding employees to encourage behaviors that further social responsibility efforts.[60]

Figure 12.6 indicates the communication channels that employees feel comfortable with when providing feedback during data collection. Employees were asked to whom they would "feel comfortable" reporting misconduct if they suspected or became aware of it. Supervisors and local managers received the most favorable response, suggesting the need for organizations to ensure that front-line managers are equipped to respond appropriately to allegations. It is worth noting that those functions that are primarily charged with taking action in response to

| FIGURE 12.6 | Channels Employees "Feel Comfortable" Using to Report Misconduct |

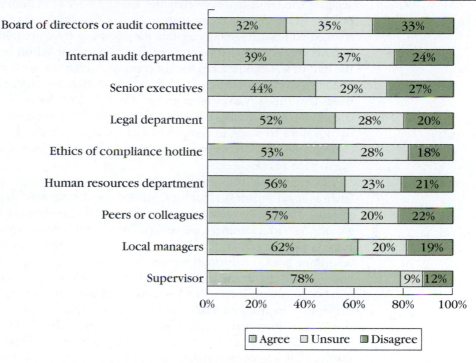

Source: KPMG Forensic Integrity Survey 2005–2006, http://www.kpmginsiders.com/display_analysis.asp?cs_id=148597, accessed March 9, 2006.

alleged misconduct (legal, internal audit, and board or audit committee functions) were cited among the least likely channels employees would feel comfortable using to report allegations.

Customers are another primary stakeholder group because their patronage determines financial success. Providing meaningful feedback through a number of mechanisms is critical to creating and maintaining customer satisfaction. Through surveys and customer-initiated communication systems such as response cards, e-mail, and toll-free telephone systems, an organization can monitor and respond to customer issues and social performance. Sears, for example, surveyed more than 2 million customers to investigate attitudes toward products, advertising, and the social performance of the company.

A growing number of investors are seeking companies that conduct social audits to include in their investment portfolios. They are becoming more aware of the financial benefits desired from socially responsible management systems—as well as the negative consequences of a lack of responsibility. Investors are also increasingly taking legal action for financial losses resulting from ethical misconduct. For example, after the Securities and Exchange Commission filed civil fraud charges against HealthSouth Corporation for overstating its earnings by $1.4 billion over a three-and-a-half-year period, the company's stock price plummeted 44 percent. The suit, which also accused the company of overstating assets by $800 million and its chief executive officer, Richard Scrushy, of instructing staff to inflate earnings to meet estimates, sparked additional lawsuits against the company by shareholders (although Scrushy himself was acquitted for fraud but later was convicted on bribery charges).[61] Even the hint of wrongdoing can harm a company's relations with shareholders if the value of their portfolio declines. It is, therefore, critical for companies to understand the issues that this very important group of stakeholders have and what they expect from corporations financially, ethically, and socially.[62] Additionally, many investors simply do not want to invest in companies that engage in certain business practices, such as cigarette production, or in companies that fail to provide adequate working conditions, such as sweatshops.

The community is another significant stakeholder group. Community groups such as local business chambers, schools, and hospitals, as well as environmental groups, can be asked to comment on the social responsibility initiatives of an organization. As with customers, surveys can be used to obtain community feedback. Such surveys may be administered on a random basis (e.g., every tenth listing in the local telephone book) or through regular contact with various groups. Websites and e-mail also provide opportunities for interaction with community stakeholder groups.

Social responsibility should be assessed from the vantage point of each of the previously mentioned stakeholders. Their respective assessments can be broken down into four main components: economic, legal, ethical, and philanthropic. Table 12.5 provides sample questions that ensure a company is assessing its social responsibility from each stakeholder perspective and should be modified to meet the unique attributes of each company.

Feedback from these stakeholders may be obtained through standardized surveys, interviews, and focus groups. Companies can also encourage stakeholder exchanges by inviting specific groups together for discussions. Such meetings also may include an office or facility tour or a field trip by company representatives to sites in the community. Regardless of how information about stakeholder views is collected, the primary objective is to generate a variety of opinions about how the company is perceived and whether it is fulfilling stakeholders' expectations.[63]

Analyze the Data

The next step in the auditing process is to compare the company's internal perceptions to those discovered during the stakeholder assessment stage and then to summarize these findings. During this phase, the audit committee should draw some conclusions about the information obtained in the previous stages. These conclusions may involve descriptive assessments of the findings, including the costs and benefits of social responsibility, strengths and weaknesses in the firm's policies and practices, and feedback from stakeholders, as well as issues that should be addressed in future audits. In some cases, it may be appropriate to weigh the findings against standards identified earlier, both quantitatively and qualitatively.[64]

Data analysis should also include an examination of how other organizations in the industry are performing in the designated subject matter areas. The audit

TABLE 12.5 Sample Stakeholder Social Responsibility Concerns

| Stakeholders | Social Responsibilities | | | |
	Economic	Legal	Ethical	Philanthropic
Employees	Are salary, benefits, and promotions perceived to be fair and equitable to all employees?	Does the organization train employees on effective legal compliance?	Have the company's ethical standards been communicated to employees?	Does the organization encourage and enable employees to contribute to the community?
Customers	Does the company adhere to fair pricing and maintain acceptable product quality?	Does the company participate in deceptive or unfair marketing activities?	Are customers' rights and concerns about products considered in all decisions?	Does the company seek to share in philanthropic activities important to customers?
Investors	Has the organization increased its profitability through socially responsible business practices?	Are there any potential illegal activities that could damage investors?	Is there an effective values program to enhance organizational performance?	Is the company using its resources to strategically improve its philanthropic efforts?
Community Groups	Does the community benefit from the economic impact of the company?	Are the legal rights of all community stakeholders considered?	Are the ethical standards of the company consistent with those of the community?	Does the company invest in the community through grants, fund raising, and community service?

The questions in the table are mere examples of potential questions that can be asked of the stakeholders. Stakeholder perceptions related to each component of social responsibility should be obtained through additional questions.

committee can investigate the successes of some other firm that is considered the best in a particular area and compare the auditing company's performance to the benchmark established by that firm. Some common examples of benchmark information available from most corporate social audits include employee or customer satisfaction, the perception of the company by community groups, and the impact of the company's philanthropy. For example, the Ethics and Compliance Officer Association (ECOA) conducts research on legal and ethical issues in the workplace. The studies allow members of the ECOA to compare their responses to the aggregate results obtained through the study.[65] The Open Compliance and Ethics Group Benchmarking study evaluates key elements of compliance, and ethics programs could help assess best practices across industries. Such comparisons can help the audit committee identify best practices for a particular industry or establish a baseline of minimum requirements for ethical compliance programs. It is important to note that a wide variety of standards are emerging that apply to social corporate accountability. The aim of these standards is to create a tool for benchmarking and a framework for businesses to follow.[66]

Verify the Results

The next step is to have the results of the data analysis verified by an independent party, such as a social audit consultant, a financial accounting firm that offers social auditing services (e.g., KPMG), or a nonprofit special-interest group with auditing experience (e.g., the New Economics Foundation). The international consulting firm Arup is committed to social responsibility and discusses with clients and governments the promotion of more sustainable performance. From this, the company identified the need for a robust and accepted high-quality social responsibility reporting system for organizations. They created a program called Corporate SpeAR, which is an independent, auditable, transparent reporting tool. It measures and records an organization's sustainable performance and guides the development of strategic policy. The tool is groundbreaking in the way it will provide the financial community with a transparent and verifiable means of analyzing a company's performance, which will also help support their inclusion into ethical frameworks.[67]

Business for Social Responsibility, a nonprofit organization supporting social responsibility initiatives and reporting, has defined *verification* as an independent assessment of the quality, accuracy, and completeness of a company's social report. Independent verification offers a measure of assurance that the company has reported its performance fairly and honestly, as well as providing an assessment of its social and environmental reporting systems.[68] As such, verification by an independent party gives stakeholders confidence in a company's audit and lends the audit report credibility and objectivity.[69]

Although independent validation of social audits is not required, many companies choose to have their social auditing efforts verified, much as they have their financial reports certified by a reputable auditing firm. Many financial auditors believe that an independent, objective assessment of an audit can be provided only if the auditor has played no role in the reporting process; in other words, consulting and auditing should be distinctly separate roles. The subject of auditor independence has been controversial. The Sarbanes-Oxley Act established a requirement for preventing conflicts of interest by financial auditors, prohibiting most consulting work being done by the same firm that conducts the audit.[70]

The process of verifying the results of an audit should involve standard procedures that control the reliability and validity of the information. As with a financial audit, auditors can apply substantive tests to detect material misstatements in the social audit data and analysis. The tests commonly used in financial audits—confirmation, observation, tracing, vouching, analytical procedures, inquiry, and recomputing—can be used in social audits as well. For example, positive confirmations can be sent to the participants of a stakeholder focus group to affirm that the reported results are consistent with those of the focus group. Likewise, a social auditor can observe the actual working conditions in a company's manufacturing plant to verify statements made in the report. And just as a financial auditor traces from the supporting documents to the financial statements to test their completeness, a social auditor or verifier may examine customer complaints to attest to the completeness of the reporting of such complaints. The auditor can examine canceled checks paid to local charities to vouch for the stated amounts of donations. A social auditor can employ analytical procedures by examining plausible relationships, such as the prior year's employee turnover ratio or the related ratio that is commonly reported within the industry. With the reporting firm's permission, an auditor can contact the company's legal counsel to inquire about pending environmental or civil rights litigation. Finally, a social auditor can recompute salaries reported to attest to the equal pay assertion that companies report.[71]

Additionally, the financial auditor may be asked to provide a letter to the company's management to highlight inconsistencies in the reporting process. The auditor may request a reply from management regarding particular points raised in the letter, indicating actions that management intends to take to address problems or weaknesses. The financial auditor is required to report to the internal audit committee (or equivalent) any significant adjustments found during the audit, disagreements with management, and difficulties encountered during the audit. In reference to the social guidelines on reportable conditions, it seems unlikely that a social auditor would be requested by the company's management to highlight reporting inconsistencies if they had any true consequence on the auditor's report. Therefore, social auditors should be required to report to the company's audit committee the same issues that a financial auditor would report.[72]

Report the Findings

The final step in our framework is issuing the social audit report. This involves reporting the audit findings to the relevant internal parties and, if approved, to external stakeholders in a formal report. Although some companies prefer not to release the results of their auditing efforts to the public, more companies are choosing to make their reports available to a broad group of stakeholders. Some companies, including U.K.-based Co-operative Bank, integrate the results of the social audit with their annual report of financial documents and other important information. Other companies, including The Body Shop, Shell, and VanCity, also make their social audit reports available on the World Wide Web.[73] Based on the guidelines established by the

FIGURE 12.7   Standard Independent Auditor's Disclaimer

To the Board of Directors and Stockholders of XYZ Company:

We have audited the accompanying balance sheet of XYZ Company as of December 31, 2004, and the related statements of income, retained earnings, and cash flows for the year then ended. These financial statements are the responsibility of the company's management. Our responsibility is to express an opinion on these financial statements based on our audit.

We conducted our audit in accordance with generally accepted auditing standards. Those standards require that we plan and perform the audit to obtain reasonable assurance about whether the financial statements are free of material misstatement. An audit includes examining, on a test basis, evidence supporting the amounts and disclosures in the financial statements. An audit also includes assessing the accounting principles used and significant estimates made by management, as well as evaluating the overall financial statement presentation. We believe that our audit provides a reasonable basis for our opinion.

In our opinion, the financial statements referred to above present fairly, in all material respects, the financial position of XYZ Company as of December 31, 2004, and the results of its operations and its cash flows for the year then ended in conformity with generally accepted accounting principles.

Firm's Signature and Report Date

Global Reporting Initiative and AccountAbility, the social report should spell out the purpose and scope of the audit, the methods used in the audit process (evidence gathering and evaluation), the role of the (preferably independent) auditor, any auditing guidelines followed by the auditor, and any reporting guidelines followed by the company.[74]

As mentioned earlier, the social audit may be similar to a financial audit, but their forms are quite different. In a financial audit, the statement of auditing standards dictates literally every word of a financial audit report in terms of content and placement. Based on the auditor's findings, the report issued can be, among other modifications, an unqualified opinion (i.e., the financial statements are fairly stated), a qualified opinion (i.e., although the auditor believes the financial statements are fairly stated, an unqualified opinion is not possible because of limitations placed on the auditor or minor issues with disclosure or accounting principles), an adverse opinion (i.e., the financial statements are not fairly stated), or a disclaimer of opinion (i.e., the auditor didn't have full access to records or discovered a conflict of interest). The technicality of these various opinions has enormous consequences to the company.

Figure 12.7 depicts the standard (unqualified opinion) independent auditor's disclaimer issued at the end of a financial audit report. Every word has significant meaning. Notice, for example, that the introductory paragraph explicitly states the responsibilities: Management is responsible for the financial statements, and the auditors are responsible only for offering an opinion as to their veracity and validity.

| **FIGURE 12.8** | Ideal Independent Auditor's Disclaimer |

To the Board of Directors and Stakeholders of XYZ Company:

We have audited the social responsibility assertions of XYZ Company as of December 31, 2004. These assertions are the responsibility of the company's management. Our responsibility is to express an opinion on these assertions based on our audit.

We conducted our audit in accordance with *generally accepted social auditing standards.* Those standards require that we plan and perform the audit to obtain reasonable assurance about whether the social assertions, relating to the economic, legal, ethical, and philanthropic responsibilities of the company, are free of material misstatement. An audit includes examining, on a test basis, evidence supporting the social responsibility assertions of the company. An audit also includes an independent assessment of the stakeholders' perspectives, as well as the methods used by management to report on such perspectives. We believe that our audit provides a reasonable basis for our opinion.

In our opinion, the social responsibility assertions referred to above present fairly, in all material respects, the position of social responsibility of XYZ Company as of December 31, 2004, in conformity with *generally accepted social responsibility principles.*

Firm's Signature and Report Date

Another paragraph discusses the generally accepted auditing standards and states that the auditors can provide only "reasonable assurance" with regard to the financial statement assertions. Such disclaimers never express absolute assurance due to the many limiting factors such as collusion, error, and cost. The last paragraph of the disclaimer begins, "In our opinion." Here, the auditors acknowledge the risks associated with an audit. They simply state their opinion, but they do not say, "We guarantee," "The fact is," or "We have no reason to believe." The end of the report includes the firm's signature and the date of the report. Social audit reports have not yet reached even this level of scrutiny, but it is desirable to move toward more objective social audits, using the standards typically applied to financial audits. Figure 12.8 provides an example of an ideal standard social audit report.

THE STRATEGIC IMPORTANCE OF SOCIAL AUDITING

The social audit, like the financial audit, should be conducted regularly instead of only when there are problems or questions about a firm's priorities and conduct. In other words, the social audit is not a control process to be used during a crisis, although it can pinpoint potential problem areas and generate solutions. A social audit may be comprehensive and encompass all of the social impact areas of a business, or it can be specific and focus on one or two areas. One specialized audit could be an environmental-impact audit in which specific environmental issues, such as proper waste disposal, are analyzed. Other areas for specialized audits include diversity, ethical conduct, employee benefits, and workplace conditions.

Social audits can present several problems. They can be expensive and time-consuming, and selecting the auditors may be difficult if objective, qualified personnel are not available. Employees sometimes fear comprehensive evaluations, especially by outsiders, and in such cases, social audits can be extremely disruptive. Although the concept of auditing implies an official examination of ethical performance, many organizations audit their performance informally. Any attempt to verify outcomes and to compare them with standards can be considered an auditing activity. Many smaller firms probably would not use the word *audit*, but they do perform auditing activities. Organizations such as the Better Business Bureau provide awards and assessment tools to help any organization evaluate their ethical performance. Companies with fewer resources may wish to use the judging criteria from the Better Business Bureau's Torch Award Criteria for Ethical Companies (Table 12.6) as benchmarks for their informal self-audits. Past winners of this award include large companies such as IBM, Sony, and Niagara Mohawk. The award criteria even provide a category for companies with fewer than ten employees.

All kinds of organizations analyze and report on their social responsibility activities, including the Planned Lifetime Advocacy Network (PLAN), a nonprofit based in Canada. Reprinted with permission of Planned Lifetime Advocacy Network (PLAN).

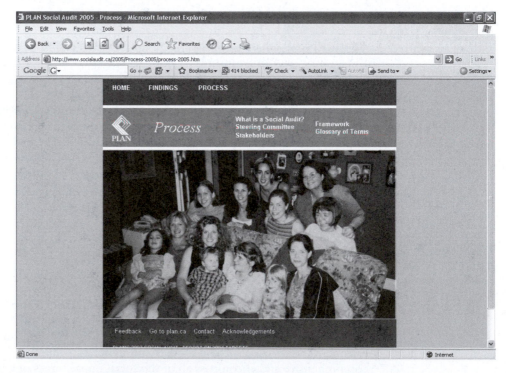

TABLE 12.6	The Better Business Bureau's Torch Award Criteria for Ethical Companies

1. **Management Practices.** *(If you are the owner of the company, with no employees, explain how ethics are used in everyday business practices.)*

   - Pertinent sections from an employee handbook, company manual or training program (formal or informal) showing how ethics policies are communicated to and implemented by employees.

   - Formal training and/or procedures used to address concerns an employee may have in dealing with an ethical dilemma.

   - The existence of an Ethics Officer, Compliance Officer or Ombudsman should be noted, along with information concerning the responsibilities and authority of this position.

   - Formal or informal management practices and policies that foster positive employee relations.

   - Employee benefits and/or workplace practices which contribute to the quality of family life.

   - Actions by the business to assess risks and take appropriate actions to prevent workplace injury.

   - Examples of sound environmental practices.

2. **Customer/Vendor/Supplier/Shareholder Relations.**

   - Examples of how your business has prospered because of your belief in honesty, integrity and doing the right thing.

   - Complimentary feedback from customers, vendors and/or suppliers.

   - Company policies and practices that assure excellence in quality products and/or services, and demonstrate accountability to customers, vendors and suppliers.

   - Actions taken by your company showing that it went "beyond the call of duty."

   - Examples of cases where your company had to make tough decisions that had negative short-term consequences and led to long-term benefits.

   - If your company is publicly traded, discuss how the corporation demonstrates accountability to shareholders and adheres to good governance practices.

3. **Marketing/Advertising/Communications/Sales Practices.**

   - Descriptions of the methods your company uses to assure all sales, promotional materials and advertisements are truthful and accurate.

   - Examples of efforts by your company to improve communications, advertising, marketing and sales practices which benefit your industry as a whole.

   - Sales training policies and/or codes of ethics used by sales personnel that ensure all transactions are made in an upfront and ethical manner.

4. **Reputation within Industry and Community.**

   - Articles in trade, industry publications and news media that reflect your reputation in your industry and community as an ethical business.

   - Awards, recognition and/or complimentary letters from others within your industry or trade group.

   - Recognition for charitable and/or community service projects.

Source: "International Torch Award Judging Criteria," Better Business Bureau, www.bbb.org/BizEthics/criteria.asp, accessed March 30, 2006. Reprinted with permission of the Council of Better Business Bureaus, Inc. Copyright 2003. Council of Better Business Bureaus, Inc. 4200 Wilson Blvd., Arlington, VA 22203. http://www.bbb.org

An example of a specialized audit could be an environmental-impact audit in which specific environmental issues, such as sustainability, could be investigated. According to the KPMG International Survey of Corporate Sustainability Reporting, 52 percent of the top 250 companies in the Global *Fortune* 500 issued environmental, social, or sustainability reports, up from 35 percent four years before.[75] Examples of other specialized audits include diversity, employee benefits, and conflicts of interest. For example, Nestlé has its own set of business principles for its social audit. It believes that principles only make a difference when they are followed. As a result, Nestlé's corporate auditors not only audit the company's financial records, but they also apply a checklist derived from the business principles to every Nestlé location in every country on a rotating basis. Reports are presented to the appropriate Nestlé managers, and any significant finding is also reported to the audit committee. Nestlé has initiated an external audit program called CARE, through which independent outside auditors certify the application of the company's standards in the area of human resources, workplace health and safety, and environmental practices throughout its global manufacturing network. In addition, Nestlé commissions special audits by outside social auditors in particular areas of concern.[76]

Auditing social responsibility performance can generate many benefits, as we have seen throughout this chapter. Hundreds of companies all over the world have been issuing social responsibility reports since the 1970s to accrue these benefits.[77] The social audit provides an assessment of a company's overall social performance compared to its core values, ethics policy, internal operating practices, management systems, and most important, the expectations of key stakeholders.[78] As such, social responsibility reports are a useful management tool to help companies identify and define their social impacts and facilitate improvements in vital areas.[79] This assessment can be used to reallocate resources and activities as well as to focus on new opportunities for social contributions. The audit process can also help companies fulfill their mission statements in ways that boost profits and reduce risks.[80] More specifically, a company may seek continual improvement in its employment practices, environmental responsibilities, customer and community relations, and ethical behavior in its general business practices.[81] Thus, the audit can pinpoint areas where improving operating practices can improve both bottom-line profits and stakeholder relationships.[82]

Most managers view profitability and social responsibility as a trade-off, which prevents them from moving from an "either–or" mind-set to a more proactive "both–and" approach.[83] However, the auditing process can demonstrate the positive impact of social responsibility efforts on the firm's bottom line, convincing managers—and other primary stakeholders—of the value of more socially responsible business practices.[84]

SUMMARY

Social auditing is the process of assessing and reporting a business's performance in fulfilling the economic, legal, ethical, and philanthropic social responsibilities expected of it by its stakeholders. The social audit provides an objective approach for an organization to demonstrate its commitment to improving strategic planning, including social accountability. There are many reasons companies choose to understand, report on, and improve their social responsibility performance.

A social audit can satisfy stakeholder demands for increased transparency and greater disclosure; this can help amend and advance relationships with investors, customers, suppliers, regulators, the media, and the community while helping these stakeholders better understand the firm's goals and operations. Dialogs established with stakeholders during the audit process may contribute insight about a firm's current situation, how various stakeholders perceive it, issues that could create threats for the company in the future, and opportunities (or weaknesses) of which the company is not yet aware. The process of social auditing can also help an organization identify potential risks and liabilities and improve its compliance with the law. A significant benefit of social auditing is that it may help prevent public relations crises associated with ethical or legal misconduct.

Although social audits provide many benefits for companies and their stakeholders, they do have the potential to create risks. In particular, the process of auditing cannot guarantee that the firm will not face challenges related to its efforts. Nonetheless, a core of minimum standards for corporate social performance is evolving.

Whereas a financial audit is concerned primarily with a company's claims about its financial performance, the social audit is interested in a company's assertions about its social responsibility. Unlike financial audits, social auditing is voluntary. Both social auditing and financial auditing employ the same procedures and processes to create a system of integrity and objective reporting. Both types of audits begin with collecting information to understand the company's industry, determining the scope of the audit, and documenting the details of the audit program. This information must be of high quality, consistent, complete, material, segregated, and collected in a controlled environment.

A social audit entails an individualized process and individualized outcomes for each firm, as it requires the careful consideration of the unique issues that face a particular organization. The first step in this process is securing the commitment of the firm's top management and/or its board of directors. The second step involves establishing a committee to oversee the audit process. In the third step, the audit committee, or an outside consultant, defines the scope of the audit process, including important subject matter areas. The scope depends on the type of business, the risks faced by the business, and available opportunities to manage social responsibility. The fourth step involves a review of the current mission statement, strategic objectives, and organizational policies, goals, and objectives. The fifth step defines the organization's social priorities. These should be articulated as a set of measurable parameters or performance indicators.

The sixth step identifies the tools or methods that can be employed to measure the firm's achievement of social objectives. The seventh step involves collecting relevant information for each designated subject matter area. Collection techniques might include examination of internal and external documents, observation of the data-collection process, and confirmation of information in the organization's accounting records. Social audits typically include interviews and focus groups with stakeholders to gain an understanding of their perceptions of the company. The eighth step compares the company's internal perceptions to those discovered during the stakeholder assessment stage and then summarizes these findings. This analysis may also include benchmarking, or comparing organizational performance in designated subject matter areas to other organizations or industry standards.

The ninth step is verification by an independent party. Verification offers a measure of assurance that the company has reported its social performance fairly and honestly as well as an assessment of its social and environmental reporting systems. The process of verifying the results of an audit should involve standard procedures that control the reliability and validity of the information. The final step in the auditing process is issuing the social audit report.

Although the concept of auditing implies an official examination of social performance, many organizations audit their performance informally. The social audit should be conducted regularly. Although social auditing may present problems, it can generate many benefits. Through the auditing process, a firm can demonstrate the positive impact of social responsibility efforts on its bottom line, convincing stakeholders of the value of more socially responsible business practices.

KEY TERM

social auditing (p. 395)

DISCUSSION QUESTIONS

1. What is a social audit? Should a firm conduct an audit before or after developing a social responsibility initiative?
2. Name some benefits and limitations of reporting the social audit. How should a company address negative issues that are discovered in an audit?
3. What are the major differences between a financial audit and a social audit? How are they similar? Should financial audit rules always be applied to a social audit?
4. Why should top management be involved in and committed to developing a social audit?
5. How should the scope of the social audit be defined?
6. Why should social priorities be translated from abstract principles and values into performance indicators that offer a minimum of objectivity?
7. What types of data should be collected during a social audit? Where can a company obtain this information?
8. What is the difference between a qualified opinion, an unqualified opinion, an adverse opinion, and a disclaimer of opinion in a financial audit? How are these opinions relevant to a social audit?
9. Should the organization or individual who verifies the results of the audit be independent? Why or why not?
10. Should a company release audit results that disclose negative information?

EXPERIENTIAL EXERCISE

Visit Vancouver City Savings Credit Union's (VanCity) website (https://www.vancity.com) and find its most recent social audit. Review the audit document. What reasons for conducting the audit are given? Where are VanCity's strengths and opportunities for growth with stakeholders? Provide three recommendations on how VanCity could improve its auditing process and report.

WHAT WOULD YOU DO?

The situation seemed crystal clear to Karey Ponds. Why, then, was the rest of the department willing to look the other way? Karey worked for United Foods, a company that owns and operates 142 restaurants in sixteen states. The restaurants use one name, specialize in pizza and Italian food, and are themed according to local culture. The restaurant's primary target markets are families and large groups, so they are located in cities that attract conventions and tourists.

United Foods was participating in a new program advocated by the National Food and Restaurant Association. An industry council organized through the association was focused on social responsibility and recently completed a position paper on the importance of social auditing. United Foods was very active in the association and agreed to participate in a pilot program for social auditing in the food and restaurant industry. Top managers selected a consulting firm to perform the external audit. The audit team was visiting the company this week to meet with various departments and individuals. The audit team was determining successes and problems that existed with primary stakeholders, including customers, employees, and suppliers.

As a quality manager, Karey's job was to monitor the quality, freshness, and taste of food prepared and served at the restaurants. Karey was in charge of restaurants in five states. The company recently implemented formal and standardized guidelines for all aspects of restaurant operations, including designated suppliers, kitchen equipment, recipes, plate presentations, employee training, electronic systems, and so forth. Two assistant managers, who reported to Karey, traveled to restaurants and conducted both scheduled and nonscheduled site visits.

After their latest trips, the assistant managers shared their informal reports and were surprised to learn that a trend was developing with a new product being served at the restaurants. The entrée was not meeting sales projections, so many kitchens had "expired" entrees in their freezers. The expired entrées were supposed to be discarded within two days. Restaurant managers were slowing their wholesale orders of the entrée through the electronic system, but retail sales figures did not mesh with the situation. Karey and the assistant managers assumed that some restaurants were serving expired entrées instead of ordering new ones. Unsold entrées were a drain on restaurant profitability. In Karey's mind, this was the only explanation for the discrepancies between retail sales and wholesale orders.

At a weekly meeting of all quality managers, Karey expressed concerns about this new finding. Other managers felt that, at this point, it was conjecture and recommended multiple, unannounced site visits before the violation became "official." Karey was firm in her belief but valued her colleagues' insights and experiences. They went on to discuss the importance of documentation and verification. They reminded Karey that the information technology group was still working out problems with the electronic procurement and sales reporting system. Karey was scheduled to meet with two people from the social audit team this afternoon. What would you do?

Home Depot Implements Stakeholder Orientation

When Bernie Marcus and Arthur Blank opened the first Home Depot store in Atlanta in 1979, they forever changed the hardware and home-improvement retailing industry. Marcus and Blank envisioned huge warehouse-style stores stocked with an extensive selection of products offered at the lowest prices. Today, do-it-yourselfers and building contractors can browse from among 40,000 different products for the home and yard, from kitchen and bathroom fixtures to carpeting, lumber, paint, tools, and plants and landscaping items. If there is a product not provided in one of the stores, Home Depot offers 250,000 other products that can be special ordered. Some Home Depot stores are open twenty-four hours a day, but customers can also order products online and pick them up from their local Home Depot stores or have them delivered. The company also offers free home-improvement clinics to teach customers how to tackle everyday projects like tiling a bathroom. For those customers who prefer not to "do it yourself," most stores offer installation services. Trained employees, recognizable by their orange aprons, are on hand to help customers find the right item or demonstrate the proper use of a particular tool.

Today, Home Depot employs 345,000 people and operates approximately 2042 Home Depot stores, EXPO Design Centers, and Villager's Hardware stores in the United States, Canada, and Mexico. It also operates four wholly owned subsidiaries: Apex Supply Company, Georgia Lighting, Maintenance Warehouse, and National Blinds and WallpaperCompany sales are over $81 billion annually, making it the largest home-improvement retailer in the United States. Home Depot continues to do things on a grand scale, including putting its corporate muscle behind a tightly focused social responsibility agenda. Every week 22 million customers visit Home Depot, and that means some conflict associated with providing services in a retail environment will occur.

MANAGING CUSTOMER RELATIONSHIPS

In 2006 John Costello was the chief marketing officer or, as he states, chief customer officer. Costello consolidated marketing and merchandising functions to help consumers achieve their goals in home improvement projects more effectively and efficiently.

According to Costello, "Above all else, a brand is a promise. It says here's what you can expect if you do business with us. Our mission is to empower our customers to achieve the home or condo of their dreams." When he arrived in 2002, Home Depot's reputation was faltering. His plan called for overhauling the Home Depot website as well as integrating mass

---

We appreciate the work of Gwyneth Walters, who helped draft the previous edition of this case, and Melanie Drever, who assisted in this edition. This case was prepared for classroom discussion rather than to illustrate either effective or ineffective handling of an administrative, ethical, or legal decision by management. All sources used for this case were obtained through publicly available material and the Home Depot website.

marketing and direct marketing with the in-store experience. It was all integrated with the new Home Depot mantra: "You can do it. We can help." Teams of people from merchandising, marketing, visual merchandising, and operations attempted to provide the very best shopping experience at Home Depot. The philosophy was simple: Home Depot believed that customers should be able to read why one ceiling fan is better than another, while associates (employees) should be able to offer installation and design advice.

Unfortunately, Home Depot has to deal with negative publicity associated with customer-satisfaction measures provided by outside sources. The University of Michigan's annual American Customer Satisfaction Index in 2006 showed Home Depot slipping to last among major U.S. retailers. With a score of 67, down from 73 in 2004, Home Depot scored 11 points behind Lowe's and 3 points lower than Kmart. "This is not competitive and too low to be sustainable. It's very serious," wrote Claes Fornell, professor of business at the University of Michigan. Fornell believes that the drop in satisfaction is one reason why Home Depot's stock was stagnant.

On the other hand, CEO Robert Nardelli said that the survey was a "sham." Nardelli points out that Fornell created his own ethical concerns when he shorted (purchased options that would profit from Home Depot's stock price decreasing) his personal portfolio before the survey came out in 2003. Fornell says the trades were part of his research into a correlation between companies' customer-satisfaction scores and stock price performance, but the University of Michigan banned the practice, indicating there were concerns about the practice.

Some former managers at Home Depot blame service issues on a culture that focused on military principles for execution. Some employees felt paranoid about being terminated unless they followed directions in a required manner. But Harris Interactive's 2005 Reputation Quotient survey ranked Home Depot number twelve among major companies and said that customers appreciated Home Depot's quality services. In 2006 Home Depot ranked thirteenth in *Fortune's* "America's Most Admired Companies."

A good example of a socially responsible activity to connect with customers is Home Depot's program, called the Kids Workshop, to teach children the skills related to home improvements. The workshops are free, with how-to clinics designed for ages 5 to 12 years old. Children, accompanied by an adult, use their skills to create objects that can be used in and around their homes or communities. Useful projects have included the creation of toolboxes, fire trucks, and mail organizers, as well as more educational projects such as window birdhouses and Declaration of Independence frame kits. Since 1997 more than 12 million projects have been built at Kids Workshops with more than 650,000 children building their first toolbox at Home Depot. Home Depot also provides workshops specially designed for women or people who have recently bought a new home. These workshops are free of charge, and anyone can attend.

ENVIRONMENTAL INITIATIVES

Cofounders Marcus and Blank nurtured a corporate culture that emphasizes social responsibility, especially with regard to the company's impact on the environment. Home Depot began its environmental program in 1990 on the twentieth anniversary of Earth Day by adopting a set of environmental principles (Table C1.1). These principles have since been adopted by the National Retail Hardware Association and Home Center Institute, which represent more than forty-six thousand retail hardware stores and home centers.

Guided by these environmental principles, Home Depot has initiated a number of programs to minimize the firm's—and its customers'—impact on the environment. In 1991 the retailer began using recycled content materials for store and office supplies, advertising, signs, and shopping bags. It also established a process for evaluating the environmental claims made by suppliers. The following year, the firm launched a program to recycle wallboard-shipping packaging, which became the industry's first reverse-distribution program. It also opened the first drive-through recycling center, in Duluth, Georgia. Home Depot became the first home-improvement retailer to offer wood products from tropical and temperate forests certified as well managed by the Scientific Certification System's Forest Conservation Program. The company also began to replace wooden shipping pallets with reusable slip sheets to minimize waste and energy use and to reduce pressure on hardwood resources used to make wood pallets.

In 1999 Home Depot announced that it would endorse independent, third-party forest certification and wood from certified forests. The company joined

TABLE C1.1   Home Depot's Environmental Principles

Home Depot acknowledges the importance of conservation. The following principles are Home Depot's response:

- We are committed to improving the environment by selling products that are manufactured, packaged and labeled in a responsible manner, that take the environment into consideration and that provide greater value to our customers.

- We will support efforts to provide accurate, informative product labeling of environmental marketing claims.

- We will strive to eliminate unnecessary packaging.

- We will recycle and encourage the use of materials and products with recycled content.

- We will conserve natural resources by using energy and water wisely and seek further opportunities to improve the resource efficiency of our stores.

- We will comply with environmental laws and will maintain programs and procedures to ensure compliance.

- We are committed to minimizing the environmental health and safety risk for our associates and our customers.

- We will train our employees to enhance understanding of environmental issues and policies and to promote excellence in job performance and all environmental matters.

- We will encourage our customers to become environmentally conscious shoppers.

Source: "The Home Depot Environmental Principles," Home Depot, www.homedepot.com/HDUS/EN_US/corporate/corp_respon/environ_principles.shtml (accessed May 16, 2006). Reprinted by permission from the Home Depot Headquarters, Homer TLC.

the Certified Forests Products Council, a nonprofit organization that promotes responsible forest product–buying practices and the sale of wood from Certified Well-Managed Forests. But environmentalists believed that the company was only being politically correct and had no real intent, so they picketed company stores in protest of Home Depot's practice of selling wood products from old-growth forests. Led by the Rainforest Action Network, environmentalists have picketed Home Depot and other home center stores for years to stop the destruction of the world's old-growth forests. On our planet, only 20 percent of the old-growth forests survive. Later that year, during Home Depot's twentieth anniversary celebration, Arthur Blank announced,

> Our pledge to our customers, associates, and stockholders is that Home Depot will stop selling wood products from environmentally sensitive areas. . . . Home Depot embraces its responsibility as a global leader to help protect endangered forests. In 2002, Home Depot eliminated . . . wood from endangered areas—including lauan, redwood, and cedar products—and gave preference to "certified" wood.

To be certified by the Forest Stewardship Council, a supplier's wood products must be tracked from the forest, through manufacturing and distribution, to the customer, and harvesting, manufacturing, and distribution practices must ensure a balance of social, economic, and environmental factors. Blank also challenged competitors to follow Home Depot's lead, and within two years, Lowe's (the number-two home-

improvement retailer), Wickes (a lumber company), and Andersen Corporation (a window manufacturer) had met that challenge. By 2003 Home Depot reported that it had reduced its purchases of Indonesian lauan, a tropical rain-forest hardwood used in door components, by 70 percent, and continues to increase its purchases of certified sustainable wood products.

Home Depot has also donated $25 million in 2005 to nonprofit groups like Keep America Beautiful, the Tampa Audubon Society, the World Wildlife Fund Canada, and the Nature Conservancy. In 2002 the company founded the Home Depot Foundation, which provides resources to assist nonprofit organizations throughout the United States and Canada. The foundation awards grants to eligible nonprofits three times per year and partners with successful, innovative nonprofits across the country that are working to increase awareness and successfully demonstrate the connection between housing, the urban forest, and the overall health and economic success of their communities. The company has established a carpooling program for more than three thousand employees in the Atlanta area and remains the only North American home-improvement retailer with a full-time staff dedicated to environmental issues. These efforts have yielded many rewards such as improved relations with environmental stakeholders. Home Depot's environmental programs earned the company an A on the Council on Economic Priorities Corporate Report Card, a Vision of America Award from Keep America Beautiful, and, along with Scientific Certification Systems and Collin Pine, a President's Council for

Sustainable Development Award. The company was also voted *Fortune* magazine's "America's Most Admired Specialty Retailer" in 2005 and 2006. It was also recognized by the U.S. Environmental Protection Agency with its Energy Star Retail Commitment Award.

CORPORATE PHILANTHROPY

In addition to its environmental initiatives, Home Depot focuses corporate social responsibility efforts on disaster relief, affordable housing, and at-risk youth. In 2005 the company supported thousands of nonprofit organizations with nearly $40.6 million in material and financial contributions. The company also posts a Social Responsibility Report on its website, detailing its annual charitable contributions and the community programs in which it has become involved over the years.

Home Depot works with more than 350 affiliates of Habitat for Humanity, a nonprofit organization that constructs and repairs homes for qualified low-income families. In 2005 it helped build twenty-one Habitat for Humanity homes, with over 160 homes built since its partnership began. The company also works with Christmas in April, a nonprofit organization that rehabilitates housing for the elderly and disabled. Home Depot has renovated more than 20,000 homes for the elderly and disabled in more than 230 communities as part of Rebuilding Together with Christmas in April. Through such programs, thousands of Home Depot associates volunteer, using products supplied by the company, to help build or refurbish affordable housing for their communities, thereby reinforcing their own skills and familiarity with the company's products. Home Depot also provides support to dozens of local housing groups around the country, as well as specific community events, like Hands on San Francisco Day.

Home Depot also supports YouthBuildUSA, a nonprofit organization that provides training and skill development for young people. YouthBuildUSA gives students the opportunity to help rehabilitate housing for homeless and low-income families. Home Depot contributes to many at-risk youth programs, including Big Brothers/Big Sisters, KaBOOM!, and the National Center for Missing and Exploited Children. Home Depot believes that every child should have a safe and fun place to play. In 2005 Home Depot partnered with KaBOOM! on 248 projects in the United States, Canada, and Mexico and also pledged $25 million to build one thousand playgrounds in one thousand days. It has been a partner with KaBOOM! for over ten years and has helped build and refurbish more than four hundred playgrounds.

Home Depot has also addressed the growing need for relief from disasters such as hurricanes, tornadoes, and earthquakes. When Hurricane Floyd devastated parts of North Carolina, the company donated nearly $100,000 in cleanup and rebuilding supplies to relief agencies, sent more than fifty thousand gallons of water to storm victims, extended credit to more than fifty communities, and sponsored clinics on how to repair damage resulting from the storm. After the 911 terrorist attacks, the company set up three command centers with more than two hundred associates to help coordinate relief supplies such as dust masks, gloves, batteries, and tools to victims and rescue workers. When a deadly tornado struck Oklahoma City, Home Depot helped by rebuilding roofs, planting trees, and clearing roads. After Hurricanes Katrina, Rita, and Wilma, Home Depot, the Home Depot Foundation, their suppliers, and The Homer Fund contributed $9.3 million in cash and materials to support recovery. Their rebuilding Hope & Homes program will provide more than $1.25 million to rebuild lives and communities on the U.S. Gulf Coast. Home Depot also donated $500,000 to support the American Red Cross's tsunami relief efforts in Southeast Asia. They also hosted more than twenty hurricane-preparation events in eight states, educating the public on necessary steps and precautions. The National Hurricane Conference awarded them the 2004 award for hurricane-awareness efforts. The company has contributed emergency relief funds, supplies, and labor to American Red Cross relief efforts. Home Depot also partners with the Weather Channel in Project SafeSide, a national severe weather public awareness program.

EMPLOYEE RELATIONS

Home Depot encourages employees to become involved in their communities through volunteer and civic activities. In 2005 employees volunteered 795,558 hours to community causes. The Home Depot devoted a week to community service in 2004, with associates throughout the United States, Canada, Mexico, and China donating more than 260,000 volunteer-hours and an additional 17,000 family members helping. These hours led to the completion of more than sixteen hundred projects in a week. In 2005 Home Depot took part in the Corporate Month of Service, which with the nonprofit Hands On Network allowed more than

40,000 volunteers from the Home Depot to help their own communities logging more than 320,000 hours on thirteen hundred neighborhood projects.

Home Depot also strives to apply social responsibility to its employment practices, with the goal of assembling a diverse workforce; however, the company settled a class-action lawsuit brought by female employees who claimed they were paid less than male employees, awarded fewer pay raises, and promoted less often. The $87.5 million settlement represented one of the largest settlements of a gender discrimination lawsuit in U.S. history at the time. In announcing the settlement, the company emphasized that it was not admitting to wrongdoing and defended its record, saying it "provides opportunities for all of its associates to develop successful professional careers and is proud of its strong track record of having successful women involved in all areas of the company."

The settlement required Home Depot to establish a formal system to ensure that employees can notify managers of their interest in advancing to a management or sales position. The company's Job Preference Program (JPP), an automated hiring and promotion computer program, opens all jobs and applicants to the company-wide network, eliminates unqualified applications, and helps managers to learn employee aspirations and skills in a more effective manner. The JPP brought changes for many women and minority managers working at Home Depot. Despite these efforts, the company faced a new sexual discrimination lawsuit brought by the U.S. Equal Employment Opportunity Commission in 2002 on behalf of a woman who claimed that she had been rejected for several positions at a Los Angeles–area store in favor of less-qualified men. Denying the accusations, a spokesperson for Home Depot declared, "The company has a zero tolerance for discrimination of any kind." The company is still in litigation.

A STRATEGIC COMMITMENT TO SOCIAL RESPONSIBILITY

Knowing that stakeholders, especially customers, feel good about a company that actively commits resources to environmental and social issues, company executives believe that social responsibility can and should be a strategic component of Home Depot's business operations. The company remains committed to its focused strategy of philanthropy and volunteerism. This commitment extends throughout the company, fueled by

top-level support from the cofounders and reinforced by a corporate culture that places great value on playing a responsible role within the communities it serves.

Questions

1. Rank the relative power of Home Depot's various stakeholders. Defend why you have ranked the first three as most important.

2. Evaluate Home Depot's philanthropic activities as a link to its overall corporate strategy.

3. How do you think Home Depot has handled ethical issues such as gender discrimination and other human resource issues over the last ten years?

Sources

1999 Annual Report, Home Depot, 2000 http://www.buck .com/10k?tenkyear=99&idx=h&co=HD&nam=DEMO&pw= DEMO (accessed July 25, 2006); *2005 Annual Report,* Home Depot 2005, http://ir.homedepot.com/reports.cfm (accessed July 25, 2006); Jim Carlton, "How Home Depot and Activists Joined to Cut Logging Abuse," *Wall Street Journal,* September 26, 2000, A1ff.; John Caulfield, "Social Responsibility: Retailer's Community Affairs Agenda Includes Disaster Relief, Housing, Youth and the Environment," *National Home Center News,* December 17, 2001, via www.findarticles.com; Cora Daniels, "To Hire a Lumber Expert, Click Here," *Fortune,* April 3, 2000, 267–270; John Galvin, "Chief Customer Officer," *Point,* April 2005, 21–25; Kirstin Downey Grimsley, "Home Depot Settles Gender Bias Lawsuit," *Washington Post,* September 20, 1997, D1; Brian Grow, "Renovating Home Depot," *BusinessWeek* online, March 6, 2006, http://www .businessweek.com/magazine/content/06_10/b3974001.htm (accessed July 25, 2006); "Hands on San Francisco Announces Fifth Annual Citywide Day of Volunteerism on May Tenth," *Business Wire,* April 30, 2003, www.businesswire.com; "Home Depot Faces Federal Sex Discrimination Suit," *USA Today* online, September 6, 2002, www.usatoday.com/money/ industries/retail/2002-09-06-home-depot-sued_x.htm; "Home Depot Lambasted for Attempt to Go Green," Environmental News Network, March 15, 1999, www.enn.com/; "The Home Depot Launches Environmental Wood Purchasing Policy," Rainforest Action Network, August 26, 1999, www.ran.org/ ran_campaigns/old_growth/news/hd_pr.html; "Home Depot Retools Timber Policy," *Memphis Business Journal* online, January 2, 2003, www.bizjournals.com/memphis/stories/ 2002/12/30/daily12.html; Home Depot website, www .homedepot.com (accessed May 5, 2003); Susan Jackson and Tim Smart, "Mom and Pop Fight Back," *BusinessWeek,* April 14, 1997, 46; Janice Revell, "Can Home Depot Get Its Groove Back?" *Fortune* online, February 3, 2003, www.fortune.com/ fortune/investing/articles/0,15114,409691,00.html.

Texas Instruments Creates a Model Ethics and Compliance Program

For Texas Instruments (TI), there are many reasons to develop the most effective organizational ethics and compliance program possible. There is a need to identify potential risks and uncover the existence of activities or events that relate to misconduct. There must be a plan and infrastructure to deal with issues or events, including a rapid response system when there are specific concerns. There is a need to maintain the values, the culture, and the expectations for conduct that employees hold about daily life within the firm. This is achieved explicitly through codes of conduct and statements of values/ethics documented in organizational communication. This is also accomplished implicitly through stories about ethical decisions, treatment of customer complaints, treatment of employee complaints, how meetings are conducted, and which behaviors and accomplishments get rewarded and recognized compared with behaviors that are criticized, ignored, or punished.

Texas Instruments Inc. is headquartered in Dallas, Texas, and has manufacturing, design, or sales operations in more than twenty-five countries. TI has three separate business segments: (1) semiconductors (85 percent of revenue); (2) sensors and controls (10 percent of revenue); and (3) educational and productivity solutions (5 percent of revenue). Their largest geographic sources of revenue, in order, are Asia (excluding Japan), Europe, the United States, and Japan. Their vision is world leadership in digital solutions for the networked society. TI's vision is operationalized with excellence in everything they do: by producing products and technologies that make them and their customers substantially different from the competition, by competing in high-growth markets, and by providing consistently good financial performance.

BACKGROUND AND HISTORY

The company was founded in 1930 as Geophysical Service Inc. (GSI), a pioneering provider of seismic exploration services. In December 1941, as the United States entered World War II, four GSI managers purchased the company. During the war, the company began manufacturing submarine detection equipment for the U.S. Navy, and following the war, became a supplier of defense systems and launched a strategy that would completely change the company. In 1951 the company changed its name to Texas Instruments to reflect the change in its business strategy and entered the semiconductor business in 1952.

TI designed the first transistor radio in 1954, the handheld calculator in 1967, and the single-chip microcomputer in 1971, and it was assigned the first patent on a single-chip microprocessor in 1973. TI is usually given credit with Intel for the almost-simultaneous invention of the microprocessor.

This case was prepared by Melanie Drever, University of Wyoming, under the direction of O. C. Ferrell, for classroom discussion rather than to illustrate either effective or ineffective handling of an administrative, ethical, or legal decision by management. All sources used for this case were obtained through publicly available material and the Texas Instruments website.

TI also created the first commercial silicon transistor and invented the integrated circuit. It continued to manufacture equipment for use in the seismic industry, as well as providing seismic services. TI sold its GSI subsidiary to Halliburton in 1988 and, in the early 1990s, began a strategic process of focusing on its semiconductor business, primarily digital signal processors and analog semiconductors. Few companies can match the 75-year record of innovations from TI. Today TI continues to work in processing and interpreting signals, and its products are used in many items that are an integral part of our daily lives—from the single-chip mobile phone solution to cable modems, home theaters, wireless Internet, digital cameras, and advanced automotive systems. TI is also working on new signal-processing innovations that will help create cars that drive themselves and allow the blind to see, as well as much more.

THE BUSINESS OF TEXAS INSTRUMENTS

Semiconductors are the electronic building blocks used to create modern electronic systems and equipment. Semiconductors come in two basic forms: individual transistors and integrated circuits (generally known as "chips") that combine different transistors on a single piece of material to form a complete electronic circuit. The TI semiconductor segment designs, manufactures, and sells integrated circuits.

Constant, though generally incremental, advances in product designs and manufacturing methods characterize the global semiconductor market. Typically, new chips are produced in limited quantities at first and then ramp to high-volume production over time. Chip prices and manufacturing costs tend to decline over time as manufacturing methods and product life cycles mature.

The *semiconductor cycle* is an important concept that refers to the ebb and flow of supply and demand. The semiconductor market is characterized by periods of tight supply caused by strong demand and/or insufficient manufacturing capacity, followed by periods of surplus products caused by declining demand and/or excess manufacturing capacity. This cycle is affected by the significant time and capital required to build and maintain semiconductor manufacturing facilities.

TI was the world's third-largest semiconductor company in 2004 in terms of revenue. Historically, their semiconductor segment averages a significantly higher growth rate than their other two business segments. About 75 percent of semiconductor revenue comes from their core products, which are analog semiconductors and digital signal processors. These products enhance and often make possible a variety of applications that serve the communications, computer, consumer, automotive, and industrial markets. TI believes that virtually all of today's digital electronic equipment requires some form of analog or digital signal processing.

TI also designs and manufactures other types of semiconductors, such as Digital Light Processing™ devices that enable exceptionally clear video and microprocessors that serve as the brains of high-end computer servers. Knowledge about the systems that their products go into is becoming increasingly important because it enables TI to differentiate their product offerings for their customers. Where a customer may previously have required multiple chips for a system to operate, TI is using their system-level knowledge to allow them to integrate the functionality of those multiple chips onto a few chips or even a single chip. An example is TI's single-chip cell phone, which combines the functionality of many separate chips onto a single chip. The digitization of electronics also requires more high-performance analog functionality. With expertise in both digital signal processing and analog at the system level, TI believes they are one of a very few semiconductor companies capable of integrating both technologies onto a single chip.

In addition, TI enables their customers, particularly original design manufacturers (ODMs), to take advantage of their system-level knowledge and thereby speed their time to market by making available to them standard chipsets and reference designs. (An ODM designs and manufactures products for other companies to sell under their brands. A *chipset* is a group of integrated circuits designed to work together for a specific application and are therefore packaged and sold as a unit. *Reference designs* are technical blueprints that contain all the essential elements in a system.) Customers using TI's reference designs, such as cell-phone ODMs, may enhance or modify the design as required. TI's ability to deliver integrated solutions and system-level knowledge allows their customers to create more advanced systems and products.

In each of their product categories, TI faces significant competition. TI believes that competitive performance in the semiconductor market depends on several factors, including the breadth of a company's product line as well as technological innovation, quality, reliability, price, customer service, and technical support and economies of scale.

EMPLOYEE STAKEHOLDERS

TI employs approximately 35,200 people worldwide with about 16,100 in the United States. In 2005 TI's job growth was a negative 6 percent, or a reduction of 1076 people, and their voluntary turnover was 5 percent. TI's workforce is made up of 34 percent minorities and 25 percent women. They support diversity through thirty employee-networking groups. Among them are a lesbian and gay employee network, a Christian Values Initiative, and a Muslim Initiative, as well as other affinity groups. TI has also been noted as one of nine companies that have a "Best 401 (K) Match"; they offer a 100 percent match up to 4 percent of total compensation. In addition to financial incentives, the company offers employees ancillary benefits such as flexible work options, a trip reduction program, an onsite concierge, a day spa, elder care, a summer camp for children, and special-interest clubs (for example, a flying club).

TI's flexible work arrangements include flextime, part time, compressed workweek schedules, and telecommuting. They have New Mother's Rooms for nursing mothers in all major facilities. They have an online parent's network for employees to share information on issues related to children and parenting. They have onsite seminars on topics such as parenting, child care, elder care, and other work–life balance issues. TI also has corporate wellness programs, services, and recreation associations, which include a child-care room at the onsite Dallas fitness center. Their wellness programs include tobacco-cessation programs, travel-well programs for worldwide employees, and immunizations and preventive screenings for employees. TI also offers onsite walking and weight management programs as well as nutrition resources to ensure that their employees can be as healthy as possible. Their benefits include discount programs at day-care centers, education assistance, life insurance options, pretax reimbursement accounts for dependent care and health care, an employee assistance program (which offers confidential counseling for employees and their family members), and adoption benefits. TI also offers a time-bank program that allows accrued time off to be used for any reason.

In 2005 TI was listed in the "Best Employers for Healthy Lifestyles" from the National Business Group on Health's Institute on the Costs and Health Effects of Obesity, and it was given the "Healthcare Heroes Award" by the *Dallas Business Journal*. In 1998 they also received the C. Everett Koop National Health Award for excellence in health-risk reduction and cost-reduction programs, which is part of The Health Project at the Stanford University.

TI is ranked eighty-third on the *Fortune* list of "100 Best Companies to Work For" in 2006, up three positions from eighty-sixth in 2005. It is the sixth year that TI has been on the list. The *Fortune* list of "Best Companies to Work For" is based on two criteria: an evaluation of the policies and culture of each company and the opinions of the company's employees. The opinions of employees are given a weight of two-thirds of the total score and are based on responses to a fifty-seven-question survey of 350 randomly selected employees. The remaining one-third of the score is based on an evaluation of each company's demographic makeup, pay, and benefits programs, and culture. Companies are scored in four areas: credibility (communication to employees), respect (opportunities and benefits), fairness (compensation, diversity), and pride/camaraderie (philanthropy, celebrations).

TI also ranked tenth on the *Business Ethics* magazine's "100 Best Corporate Citizens" in 2006. The aim of the list is to identify firms that excel at serving a variety of stakeholders with excellence and integrity. For each company, the list rates eight categories: shareholders, community, minorities and women, employees, environment, human rights, customers, and governance. For each area, strengths and concerns are matched against each other to arrive at the final score. TI is also a member of the Domini 400 Social Index and has won numerous awards for corporate citizenship, ethics, being a good employer, and diversity.

TI is concerned with the environment, safety, and health. It is a "Sony Green Partner" for supplying components, devices, and materials to ensure the production of environmentally friendly products. TI is also building a "green" chip factory in Richardson, near Dallas. Although China, Taiwan, and Singapore were all tempting alternatives, TI proposed a challenge to the design team: If the TI design team and community leaders could find a way to build the new factory for $180 million less than the last Dallas factory built in the late 1990s, then TI would locate in Dallas. They managed it. Instead of three floors, the new design has just two, and it is expected to cut utility costs by 20 percent and water usage by 35 percent. Creative design and engineering will eliminate waste and reduce energy usage. Almost all waste from the building construction is being recycled, and all the urinals are waterless.

TEXAS INSTRUMENTS' ETHICS PROGRAM

TI has always been concerned about ethics in its company. They believe that maintaining the highest ethical standards requires a partnership between employees and employers. It proactively supports employees by communicating values and giving individual guidance, and empowered employees participate actively in problem solving. In 1987, TI decided to actively support employees by establishing a TI Ethics Office and appointing a TI Ethics Director. The TI Ethics Office has three primary functions:

- To ensure that business policies and practices continue to be aligned with ethical principles

- To clearly communicate ethical expectations

- To provide multiple channels for feedback through which people can ask questions, voice concerns, and seek resolution to ethical issues

TI has strong documented requirements for ethical business practices, which include the TI Standard Policies and Procedures, The TI Commitment, and "The Values and Ethics of TI" booklet. The TI values and principles are

Integrity—respect and value people; be honest

Innovation—learn and create; act boldly

Commitment—take responsibility; commit to winning

The TI Ethics Quick Test is an integral part of everything that TI does. It is included in the code of ethics booklet as a punch-out card to put in a wallet or purse and is printed on the TI mouse pads given to employees. The test asks the following questions:

Is the action legal?

Does it comply with our values?

If you do it, will you feel bad?

How will it look in the newspaper?

If you know its wrong, don't do it!

If you're not sure, ask.

Keep asking until you get an answer.

There are many resources and alternative communication channels available to help ensure compliance, whether as an individual or as a company. The compliance procedures are the following:

- *Take Direct Action.* The best and most effective approach is to fix problems on the spot. If employees are considering an action or see a proposed action that raises ethical concerns, they should raise the ethical concerns right away. Frequently—perhaps usually—merely highlighting and discussing the issue will result in actions that achieve the desired goal in full compliance with TI's Values and Ethics Statement and the Code of Business Conduct. Employees should use available resources, including the Code of Ethics, the Values and Ethics Statement, the Code of Business Conduct, the Ethics Quick Test, Policies, Business Rules, Chart of Accounts, and other guidance.

- *Consult Your Supervisor.* TI supervisors know their employees' assignments and circumstances better than anyone else. TI supervisors can often help employees find answers and solutions if the one that is being tried just doesn't seem to fit.

- *Talk with Human Resources.* If for any reason employees cannot communicate with their supervisor or local managers, they should contact their site Human Resources Department. The TI HR staff is there to help employees resolve many issues. Employees may counsel with them at any time.

- *Call the TI Law Department.* For questions regarding contracts, pricing practices, or anything with a legal orientation, the TI Law Department can help employees find the answers. There are attorneys assigned to assist each business group, as well as attorneys who specialize in the areas of law that TI most frequently encounters.

- *Get Online*. TI is an information-rich company. There are many sites on the Internet where TI-specific information can be found.

- *Contact the TI Ethics Office*. At any time, for any reason, employees can contact the TI Ethics Office for answers to their questions, including any concerns about accounting, internal accounting controls, or auditing matters. They may even remain anonymous.

THE TEXAS INSTRUMENTS CODE OF ETHICS

The TI code of ethics resembles that of many organizations. It addresses issues relating to policies and procedures; government laws and regulations; relationships with customers, suppliers, and competitors; accepting gifts, travel, and entertainment; political contributions; expense reporting; business payments; conflicts of interest; investing in TI stock; handling proprietary information and trade secrets; using TI employees and assets to perform personal work; relationships with government officials and agencies; and enforcing the code. TI's code emphasizes that ethical behavior is critical to maintaining long-term success and that each individual is responsible for upholding the integrity of the company:

> Our reputation at TI depends upon all of the decisions we make and all the actions we take personally each day. Our values define how we will evaluate our decisions and actions . . . and how we will conduct our business. We are working in a difficult and demanding, ever-changing business environment. Together we are building a work environment on the foundation of Integrity, Innovation, and Commitment. Together we are moving our company into a new century . . . one good decision at a time. We are prepared to make the tough decisions or take the critical actions . . . and do it right. Our high standards have rewarded us with an enviable reputation in today's marketplace . . . a reputation of integrity, honesty, and trustworthiness. That strong ethical reputation is a vital asset . . . and each of us shares a personal responsibility to protect, to preserve, and to enhance it. Our reputation is a strong but silent partner in all business relationships. By understanding and applying the values presented on the following pages, each of us can say to ourselves and to others, "TI is a good company, and one reason is that I am part of it." Know what's right. Value what's right. Do what's right.

Like most codes of ethics, TI requires employees to obey the law. In many instances, however, TI expects its employees to abide by ethical standards that are more demanding than the law. For example, although some local laws permit companies to contribute to political candidates or elected officials, TI's code states that "no company funds may be used for making political contributions of any kind to any political candidate or holder of any office of any government—national, state or local. This is so even where permitted by local law." TI also goes beyond the federal law prohibiting discrimination against minorities and expects its employees to treat all fellow workers with dignity and respect: "The hours we spend at work are more satisfying and rewarding when we demonstrate respect for all associates regardless of gender, age, creed, racial background, religion, handicap, national origin, or status in TI's organization."

TI's code of ethics is not just lip service paid to social concerns about business ethics; the company enforces the code through audits and disciplinary action where necessary. TI's corporate internal audit function measures several aspects of business ethics, including compliance with policies, procedures, and regulations; the economical and efficient use of resources; and the internal controls of management systems. In addition, the code states that "any employee who violates TI's ethical standards is subject to disciplinary action which can include oral reprimand, written reprimand, probation, suspension, or immediate termination." The TI Ethics Committee, established in 1987, oversees all activities of the ethics office. The committee consists of five high-level TI managers, who review and approve policy, procedures, and publications; monitor compliance initiatives; review any major ethical issues; and approve appropriate corrective actions.

TI explicitly states what it expects of its employees and what behaviors are unacceptable. By enforcing the codes wholeheartedly, TI has taken logical steps to safeguard its excellent reputation for ethical and responsible behavior. When such standards of behavior are not made explicit, employees sometimes base ethical decisions on their observations of the behavior of peers and management. The use of rewards and punishments to enforce codes and policies enables TI to control the opportunities employees have to behave unethically and to increase employees' acceptance of ethical standards.

COMMUNICATING VALUES AND ETHICS

"The Values and Ethics of TI" booklet has been in publication for over forty-five years. First published in 1961, it is in its sixth revision, is available in eleven languages, and is given to every TI employee. The booklet contains principles that have long been part of TI's values and ethics statements. TI believes that their reputation depends on all the decisions that employees make and all their daily actions. TI tries to build a work environment on the foundation of integrity, innovation, and commitment. Their high standards have ensured that TI has an enviable reputation in today's marketplace. It is a strong reputation of integrity, honesty, and trustworthiness. Each person in TI is responsible for ensuring that he or she protects, enhances, and preserves the reputation that has been built. Every decision made should be done keeping the Ethics Quick Test in mind: "Know what's right. Value what's right. Do what's right."

The code of ethics is divided into sections: integrity, innovation, commitment, and the code of business conduct. TI is very concerned that employees know and understand that every one of their actions will impact the company and ensures that the employees are aware of this by instilling in them the importance of integrity, innovation, and commitment. In the integrity section of the code of ethics, TI stresses the importance of the basic virtues of respect, dignity, kindness, courtesy, and manners in all work relationships, as well as recognizing and avoiding behaviors that others may find offensive. In the innovation section, TI mentions that they work together with trust to achieve superior results; they encourage open, honest, and candid communications; and they respect all coworkers without regard to their position or level within the organization. By using the word *we,* TI instills a sense of community and belonging in their employees; in this way, they recognize that "we succeed or fail together."

Employees are encouraged to know not only what is right according to the law, rules, and regulations but also what is right according to the ethical aspects of decisions. There is a series of brochures that keep employees abreast of the legal and ethical aspects of their jobs. TI has an open-door policy so that any employee has access to anyone in the management structure. There are plenty of experts, throughout the company, ready to assist in ethical and legal issues covering a variety of areas. Employees are encouraged to discuss any issue they feel is important, without fear of retribution. It is fundamental to TI's philosophy that good ethics and good business are synonymous when viewed from moral, legal, and practical standpoints.

TEXAS INSTRUMENTS' SOCIAL RESPONSIBILITY

TI's focus on integrity, innovation, and commitment is not just words but the spirit enmeshed in every facet of their operations—as a business and as a corporate citizen. The company provides support and leadership to a wide range of efforts. Its highest priority is education, and it is focused on improving the quality of life in the community by providing knowledge, skills, and programs that increase the percentage of high school graduates who are math and science capable. They give to education through calculator donations, university equipment donations, and grants. However, although TI's focus is on education, they also give generously to arts and culture, civic and business organizations, and health and human services.

TI is focused on global economic development; they achieve this through investment and philanthropy in their plant-site communities. Because they have locations in thirty countries, they continue to make capital investments as well as investments in their employees through training and career development. They also support the need of the communities in which they operate through donations. In 2005, for example, they built nine hundred homes in India following the devastating typhoon there and provided funds that led to teacher development.

TI is concerned with protecting the environment, and their policy is to have zero wasted resources—recycling everything from water to paper and scrap wafers—and to preserve natural resources.

ASSESSING THE BENEFITS OF AN ETHICS AND COMPLIANCE PROGRAM

TI is a leader and is a member of a small elite group of companies that have sustained an effective ethics program over a long period of time. The benefits of an ethics program go beyond preventing misconduct to creating a corporate culture that is more productive and effective in the marketplace. An Open Compliance Ethics Group study indicates that among companies with an ethics program in place for ten years or more, none has experienced damage to their reputation in the last five years. The U.S. Sentencing Commission reports no firm with an effective ethics and compliance program was sentenced between 2000 and 2004.

Communication by the firm's leadership helps keep the firm on its ethical course, and these executives must ensure that the ethical climate is consistent with the company's overall mission and objectives. Developing a values-based orientation fosters a system that provides a core of ideals such as respect, honesty, trust, and responsibility. In a values-centered program, employees become more open, are willing to deliver necessary information to supervisors, and generally begin to feel comfortable about how to make decisions in situations where there are no defined rules. Although TI has developed an effective program, they have to remain vigilant and continually revise and update their program to improve and maintain their desired ethical standards.

Questions for Discussion

1. How effectively has TI managed its ethical and legal environment?

2. What are the ethical and legal risks of competing in the defense industry?

3. How would you describe the ethical culture that has been developed at TI?

Sources

"100 Best Corporate Citizens 2006," *Business Ethics,* Spring 2006, 22; "Ethics is the Cornerstone of TI," Texas Instruments, www.ti.com/corp/docs/company/citizen/ethics/benchmark.shtml (accessed February 25, 2003); Thomas L. Friedman, "A Green Dream in Texas," *New York Times* online, January 18, 2006, http://topics.nytimes.com/top/opinion/editorialsandoped/oped/columnists/thomaslfriedman/index.html?inline=nyt-per (accessed February 2, 2006); "Texas Instruments Annual Report 10-K," Texas Instruments, www.ti.com (accessed February 8, 2006); "Texas Instruments Corporate Social Responsibility," Texas Instruments, http://www.ti.com/corp/docs/csr/index.shtml (accessed February 8, 2006); "Texas Instruments Ethics," Texas Instruments, http://www.ti.com/corp/docs/company/citizen/ethics/index.shtml (accessed February 6, 2006); Texas Instruments training materials available for employees in brochure format titled "Designing for the Environment," "Working with Suppliers," "Workplace Safety," "TI, the Law and You. A Survival Guide for Changing Times"; "The TI Code of Ethics," Texas Instruments, http://www.ti.com/corp/docs/investor/corpgov/valuesethicsconduct.pdf (accessed February 6, 2006); "TI Named to 'Fortune' Magazine's 100 Best Companies to Work For List," via http://infolinknews.ti.com/tinews/storydetail.tsp?storyId=106225 (accessed February 2, 2006).

New Belgium Brewing: Ethical and Environmental Responsibility

Most of the companies frequently cited as examples of ethical and socially responsible firms are large corporations, but it is the social responsibility initiatives of small businesses that often have the greatest impact on local communities and neighborhoods. These businesses create jobs and provide goods and services for customers in smaller markets that larger corporations often are not interested in serving. Moreover, they also contribute money, resources, and volunteer time to local causes. Their owners often serve as community and neighborhood leaders, and many choose to apply their skills and some of the fruits of their success to tackling local problems and issues that benefit everyone in the community. Managers and employees become role models for ethical and socially responsible actions. One such small business is the New Belgium Brewing Company, Inc., based in Fort Collins, Colorado.

HISTORY OF THE NEW BELGIUM BREWING COMPANY

The idea for the New Belgium Brewing Company began with a bicycling trip through Belgium. Belgium is arguably the home of some of the world's finest ales, some of which have been brewed for centuries in that country's monasteries. As Jeff Lebesch, an American electrical engineer, cruised around that country on his fat-tired mountain bike, he wondered if he could produce such high-quality beers back home in Colorado. After acquiring the special strain of yeast used to brew Belgian-style ales, Lebesch returned home and began to experiment in his Colorado basement. When his beers earned thumbs up from friends, Lebesch decided to market them.

The New Belgium Brewing Company (NBB) opened for business in 1991 as a tiny basement operation in Lebesch's home in Fort Collins. Lebesch's wife, Kim Jordan, became the firm's marketing director. They named their first brew Fat Tire Amber Ale in honor of Lebesch's bike ride through Belgium. New Belgium beers quickly developed a small but devoted customer base, first in Fort Collins and then throughout Colorado. The brewery soon outgrew the couple's basement and moved into an old railroad depot before settling into its present custom-built facility in 1995. The brewery includes an automated brewhouse, two quality-assurance labs, and numerous technological innovations for which NBB has become nationally recognized as a "paradigm of environmental efficiencies."

The craft brewing market is the only major segment of the beer market that is growing. Figure C3.1 shows craft brewing's share of the U.S. market. Many of the craft brewers engage in reserve bottling and

We appreciate the work of Nikole Haiar, who helped draft the previous edition of this case, and Melanie Drever, who assisted in this edition. This case was prepared for classroom discussion rather than to illustrate either effective or ineffective handling of an administrative, ethical, or legal decision by management. All sources used for this case were obtained through publicly available material and the New Belgium Brewing website.

FIGURE C3.1   Craft Brewing's Share of the U.S. Beer Market

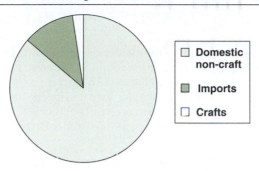

- ☐ Domestic non-craft
- ☑ Imports
- ☐ Crafts

Source: Craft Brewers Association 2005.

special seasonal brands. Craft brew sales grew 9 percent to 7.1 million barrels in 2005, following a 7 percent increase in 2004. This makes craft beers the fastest-growing segment of the U.S. alcoholic-beverage market. As a part of this fast-growing craft market, NBB competes with companies such as Wyoming-based Grand Teton brewing company, Chicago's Goose Island brewing company, and San Diego–based Stone brewing company. Coors is attempting to enter this market with Bluemoon wheat-beer brand, and Anheuser Busch has acquired Red Hook brewing company. NBB has positioned itself based on the quality of its products and its concern for stakeholders.

Today, NBB offers a variety of permanent and seasonal ales and pilsners. The company's standard line includes Sunshine Wheat, Blue Paddle Pilsner, Abbey Ale, Trippel Ale, 1554 Black Ale, and the original Fat Tire Amber Ale, still the firm's best seller. Some customers even refer to the company as the Fat Tire Brewery. The brewery also markets two types of specialty beers on a seasonal basis. Seasonal ales include Frambozen and Abbey Grand Cru, which are released at Thanksgiving and Christmas, and Farmhouse Ale, which is sold during the early fall months. The firm occasionally offers one-time-only brews, such as LaFolie, a wood-aged beer, which are sold only until the batch runs out.

Until 2005 NBB's most effective form of advertising has been its customers' word of mouth. Indeed, before New Belgium beers were widely distributed throughout Colorado, one liquor store owner in Telluride is purported to have offered people gas money if they would stop by and pick up New Belgium beer on

their way through Fort Collins. Although New Belgium beers are distributed in just one-third of the United States, the brewery receives numerous e-mails and phone calls every day inquiring when its beers will be available elsewhere.

With expanding distribution, however, the brewery recognized a need to increase its opportunities for reaching its far-flung customers. It consulted with David Holt, an Oxford professor and branding expert. After studying the young company, Holt, together with Marketing Director Greg Owsley, drafted a seventy-page "manifesto" describing the brand's attributes, character, cultural relevancy, and promise. In particular, Holt identified in New Belgium an ethos of pursuing creative activities simply for the joy of doing them well and in harmony with the natural environment. With the brand thus defined, New Belgium went in search of an advertising agency to help communicate that brand identity; it soon found Amalgamated, an equally young, independent New York advertising agency. Amalgamated created a $10 million advertising campaign for New Belgium that targets high-end beer drinkers, men ages 25 to 44, and highlights the brewery's image as being down to earth. The grainy ads focus on a man rebuilding a cruiser bike out of used parts and then riding it along pastoral country roads. The product appears in just five seconds of each ad between the tag lines, "Follow Your Folly . . . Ours Is Beer." The ads helped position the growing brand as whimsical, thoughtful, and reflective. In addition to the ad campaign, the company maintained its strategy of promotion through event sponsorships.

NEW BELGIUM ETHICAL CULTURE

According to Owsley, beyond a desire for advertising and promotion ethics, there is a fundamental focus on the ethical culture of the brand. Although consumers often view business with suspicion, those in good standing—as opposed to those trading on hype—are eyed with iconic-like adoration. From this polarization comes a new paradigm in which businesses that fully embrace citizenship in the community they serve can forge enduring bonds with customers. Meanwhile, these are precarious times for businesses that choose to ignore consumers looking at brands from an ethical perspective. More than ever before, what the brand says and what the company does must be synchronized. NBB believes the mandate for corporate social responsibility gains momentum beyond the courtroom to the far more powerful marketplace. Any current and future manager of business must realize that business ethics are not so much about the installation of compliance codes and standards as they are about the spirit in which they are integrated. Thus, the modern-day brand steward—usually the most externally focused member of the business management team—must prepare to be the internal champion of the bottom-line necessity for ethical, values-driven company behavior.

At NBB a synergy of brand and values developed naturally into the firm's ethical culture, in the form of core values and beliefs, and was in place long before NBB had a marketing department. Back in early 1991, NBB was just a home-brewed business plan of Jeff Lebesch, an electrical engineer, and his social worker wife, Kim Jordan. Before they signed any business paperwork, the two took a hike into Rocky Mountain National Park. Armed with a pen and a notebook, they took their first stab at what the fledgling company's core purpose would be. If they were going forward with this venture, what were their aspirations beyond profitability? What was the real root cause of their dream? What they wrote down that spring day, give or take a little wordsmithing, was the core values and beliefs that you can read on the NBB website today. More important, ask just about any New Belgium worker, and she or he can list for you many, if not all, of these shared values and can inform you which are the most personally poignant. For NBB, branding strategies are as rooted in their company values as in other business practices.

NEW BELGIUM'S PURPOSE AND CORE BELIEFS

NBB's dedication to quality, the environment, and its employees and customers is expressed in its mission statement: "To operate a profitable brewery which makes our love and talent manifest." The company's stated core values and beliefs about its role as an environmentally concerned and socially responsible brewer include

- Producing world-class beers
- Promoting beer culture and the responsible enjoyment of beer
- Continuous, innovative quality and efficiency improvements
- Transcending customers' expectations
- Environmental stewardship: minimizing resource consumption, maximizing energy efficiency, and recycling
- Kindling social, environmental, and cultural change as a business role model
- Cultivating potential through learning, participative management, and the pursuit of opportunities
- Balancing the myriad needs of the company, staff, and their families
- Committing ourselves to authentic relationships, communications, and promises
- Having fun

Employees believe that these statements help communicate to customers and other stakeholders what NBB, as a company, is about. These simple values developed over fifteen years ago are still meaningful to the company and its customers today, even though there has been much growth.

EMPLOYEE CONCERNS

Recognizing employees' role in the company's success, NBB provides many generous benefits. In addition to the usual paid health and dental insurance and retirement plans, employees get a free lunch every other week and a free massage once a year; they can bring their children and dogs to work. Employees who stay with the company for five years earn an all-expenses paid trip to Belgium to "study beer culture." Perhaps most important, employees can also earn stock in the privately held corporation, which grants them a vote in company decisions. NBB's employees now own one-third of the growing brewery. Open-book management lets employees see the financial costs and performance.

ENVIRONMENTAL CONCERNS

NBB's marketing strategy involves linking the quality of its products, as well as their brand, with the company's philosophy toward affecting the planet. From leading-edge environmental gadgets and high-tech industry advancements to employee-ownership programs and a strong belief in giving back to the community, NBB demonstrates its desire to create a living, learning community.

NBB strives for cost-efficient energy-saving alternatives to conducting its business and reducing its impact on the environment. In staying true to the company's core values and beliefs, the brewery's employee-owners unanimously agreed to invest in a wind turbine, making NBB the first fully wind-powered brewery in the United States. Since the switch from coal power, NBB has been able to reduce its carbon dioxide emissions by 1800 metric tons per year. The company further reduces its energy use by employing a steam condenser that captures and reuses the hot water that boils the barley and hops in the production process to start the next brew. The steam is redirected to heat the floor tiles and de-ice the loading docks in cold weather. Another way that NBB conserves energy is by using "sun tubes," which provide natural daytime lighting throughout the brewhouse all year long.

NBB also takes pride in reducing waste through recycling and creative reuse strategies. The company strives to recycle as many supplies as possible, including cardboard boxes, keg caps, office materials, and the amber glass used in bottling. The brewery also stores spent barley and hop grains in an on-premise silo and invites local farmers to pick up the grains, free of charge, to feed their pigs. NBB even encourages its employees to reduce air pollution by using alternative transportation. As an incentive, NBB gives its employees "cruiser bikes"—like the one pictured on its Fat Tire Amber Ale label—after one year of employment and encourages them to ride to work.

NBB has been a long-time participant in green building techniques. With each expansion of the facility, they have incorporated new technologies and learned a few lessons along the way. In 2002 NBB agreed to participate in the U.S. Green Building Council's Leadership in Energy and Environment Design for Existing Buildings pilot program. From sun tubes and day lighting throughout the facility to reusing heat in the brewhouse, they continue to search for new ways to close loops and conserve resources.

Reduce, Reuse, Recycle are the three Rs of being an environmental steward. The reuse program includes heat for the brewing process, cleaning chemicals, water, and much more. Recycling at NBB takes on many forms, from turning waste products into something new and useful (like spent grain to pig feed) to supporting the recycling market in creative ways (like turning their keg caps into table surfaces). They also buy recycled whenever they can, from paper to office furniture. Reduction surrounds them—from motion sensors on the lights throughout the building to induction fans that pull in cool winter air to chill their beer—because offsetting their energy needs is the cornerstone to being environmentally efficient.

SOCIAL CONCERNS

Beyond its use of environment-friendly technologies and innovations, NBB strives to improve communities and enhance people's lives through corporate giving, event sponsorship, and philanthropic involvement.

Since its inception, NBB has donated more than $1.6 million to organizations in the communities in which they do business. For every barrel of beer sold the prior year, NBB donates $1 to philanthropic causes within their distribution territory. The donations are divided among states in proportion to their percentage of overall sales. This is their way of staying local and giving back to the communities who support and purchase NBB products. In 2006 Arkansas, Arizona, California, Colorado, Idaho, Kansas, Missouri, Montana, Nebraska, Nevada, New Mexico, Oregon, Texas, Washington, and Wyoming received funding.

Funding decisions are made by the NBB Philanthropy Committee, which is composed of employees throughout the brewery, including owners, employee-owners, area leaders, and production workers. NBB looks for nonprofit organizations that demonstrate creativity, diversity, and an innovative approach to their mission and objectives. The committee also looks for groups that involve the community to reach their goals.

NBB maintains a community bulletin board in its facility where it posts an array of community involvement activities and proposals. This community board allows tourists and employees to see the different ways they can help out the community, and it gives nonprofit organizations a chance to make their needs known. Organizations can apply for grants through the NBB website, which has a link designated for this purpose.

NBB sponsors a number of events, with a special focus on those that involve "human-powered" sports that cause minimal damage to the natural environment. Through event sponsorships, such as the Tour de Fat, NBB supports various environmental, social, and cycling nonprofit organizations. New Belgium sponsored the MS 150 "Best Damn Bike Tour," a two-day, fully catered bike tour, from which all proceeds went to benefit more than five thousand local people with multiple sclerosis. NBB also sponsored the Ride the Rockies bike tour, which donated the proceeds from beer sales to local nonprofit groups. The money raised from this annual event funds local projects such as improving parks and bike trails. In the course of one year, NBB can be found at anywhere from 150 to 200 festivals and events, across all fifteen western states.

ORGANIZATIONAL SUCCESS

NBB's efforts to live up to its own high standards have paid off with numerous awards and a very loyal following. It was one of three winners of *Business Ethics* magazine's Business Ethics Awards for its "dedication to environmental excellence in every part of its innovative brewing process." It also won an honorable mention in the Better Business Bureau's 2002 Torch Award for Outstanding Marketplace Ethics competition. Jordan and Lebesch were named the recipients of the Rocky Mountain Region Entrepreneur of the Year Award for manufacturing. The company also captured the award for best mid-sized brewing company of the year and best mid-sized brewmaster at the Great American Beer Festival. In addition, New Belgium took home medals for three different brews, Abbey Belgian Style Ale, Blue Paddle Pilsner, and LaFolie specialty ale.

According to David Edgar, director of the Institute for Brewing Studies, "They've created a very positive image for their company in the beer-consuming public

with smart decision-making." Although some members of society do not believe that a company whose major product is alcohol can be socially responsible, NBB has set out to prove that, for those who make a choice to drink responsibly, the company can do everything possible to contribute to society. Its efforts to promote beer culture and the connoisseurship of beer has even led it to design a special "Worthy Glass," the shape of which is intended to retain foam, show off color, enhance the visual presentation, and release aroma. NBB also promotes the responsible appreciation of beer through its participation in and support of the culinary arts. For instance, it frequently hosts New Belgium Beer Dinners, in which every course of the meal is served with a complementary culinary treat.

According to Owsley, although the Fat Tire brand has a bloodline straight from the enterprise's ethical beliefs and practices, the firm's work is not done. They must continually reexamine ethical, social, and environmental responsibilities. In 2004 NBB received the Environmental Protection Agency's regional Environmental Achievement Award.

There are still many ways for NBB to improve as a corporate citizen. They still don't produce an organic beer. The manufacturing process is a fair distance from being zero waste or emission free. There will always be a need for more public dialogue on avoiding alcohol abuse. Practically speaking, they have a never-ending to-do list. NBB also must acknowledge that as their annual sales increase, the challenges for the brand to remain on a human scale and culturally authentic will increase too. How to boldly grow the brand while maintaining its humble feel has always been a challenge.

Every six-pack of New Belgium Beer displays the phrase, "In this box is our labor of love, we feel incredibly lucky to be creating something fine that enhances people's lives." Although Lebesch has semi-retired from the company to focus on other interests, the founders of NBB hope that this statement captures the spirit of the company. According to employee Dave Kemp, NBB's environmental concern and social responsibility give it a competitive advantage because consumers want to believe in and feel good about the products they purchase. NBB's most important asset is its image—a corporate brand that stands for quality, responsibility, and concern for society. Defining itself as more than just a beer company, NBB also sees itself as a caring organization that is concerned with all stakeholders, including the community, the environment, and employees.

Questions

1. What environmental issues does the New Belgium Brewing Company work to address? How has NBB taken a strategic approach to addressing these issues? Why do you think the company has chosen to focus on environmental issues?

2. Are NBB's social initiatives indicative of strategic philanthropy? Why or why not?

3. Some segments of society vigorously contend that companies that sell alcoholic beverages and tobacco products cannot be socially responsible organizations because of the nature of their primary products. Do you believe that NBB's actions and initiatives are indicative of an ethical and socially responsible corporation? Why or why not?

4. What else could NBB do to foster ethical and responsible conduct?

Sources

Peter Asmus, "Goodbye Coal, Hello Wind," *Business Ethics* 13 (1999): 10–11; Robert Baun, "What's in a Name? Ask the Makers of Fat Tire," *[Fort Collins] Coloradoan,* October 8, 2000, E1, E3; Rachel Brand, "Colorado Breweries Bring Home 12 Medals in Festival," *Rocky Mountain News,* via www.insidedenver.com/news/1008beer6.shtml (accessed November 6, 2000); Stevi Deter, "Fat Tire Amber Ale," The Net Net, www.thenetnet.com/reviews/fat.html (accessed April 29, 2003); DirtWorld, www.dirtworld.com/races/Colorado_race745.htm (accessed November 6, 2000); Robert F. Dwyer and John F. Tanner, Jr., *Business Marketing* (Columbus, OH: Irwin/McGraw-Hill, 1999), 104; "Fat Tire Amber Ale," *Achwiegut* (The Guide to Austrian Beer), www.austrianbeer.com/beer/b000688.shtml (accessed January 19, 2001); "Four Businesses Honored with Prestigious International Award for Outstanding Marketplace Ethics," Better Business Bureau press release, September 23, 2002, www.bbb.org/alerts/2002torchwinners.asp; Julie Gordon, "Lebesch Balances Interests in Business, Community," *[Fort Collins] Coloradoan,* February 26, 2003; Del I. Hawkins, Roger J. Best, and Kenneth A. Coney, *Consumer Behavior: Building Marketing Strategy,* 8th ed. (Columbus, OH: Irwin/McGraw-Hill, 2001); David Kemp, Tour Connoisseur, New Belgium Brewing Company, personal interview by Nikole Haiar, November 21, 2000, 1:00 P.M.; New Belgium Brewing Company, Fort Collins, CO, www.newbelgium.com (accessed April 29, 2003); New Belgium Brewing Company Tour by Nikole Haiar, November 20, 2000, 2:00 P.M.; "New Belgium Brewing Wins Ethics Award," *Denver Business Journal* online, January 2, 2003, http://denver.bizjournals.com/denver/stories/2002/12/30/daily21.html; New Belgium Brewing Company, http://www.newbelgium.com/sustainability.php and http://www.newbelgium.com/philanthropy.php (accessed May 17, 2006); Greg Owsley, "The Necessity for Aligning Brand with Corporate Ethics," in *Fulfilling Our Obligation, Perspectives on Teaching Business Ethics,* ed. Sheb L. True, Linda Ferrell, and O. C. Ferrell (Kennesaw, GA: Kennesaw State University Press, 2005), 128–132; Dan Rabin, "New Belgium Pours It on for Bike Riders," *Celebrator Beer News* online, August/September 1998, www.celebrator.com/9808/rabin.html.

Starbucks' Mission: Responsibility and Growth

Three partners founded Starbucks in 1971, with the first store opening in Seattle's open-air Pike Place Market. The company is named after the first mate in Herman Melville's *Moby Dick*. In 1982 Howard Schultz joined Starbucks as director of retail operations and marketing. After visiting Milan, Italy, with its fifteen hundred coffee bars, Schultz saw the opportunity to develop a similar retail coffee-bar culture in Seattle. In 1985 the first downtown Seattle coffeehouse was tested, and the first Starbucks café latte was served. Since then Starbucks has been expanding across the United States where it operates eight thousand stores and over thirty-two hundred stores in thirty-seven countries. It opens about five new stores a day and serves over 30 million customers a week. Of its customers, 24 percent visit sixteen times per month. No other fast-food chain can post numbers even close to this. Its goal is to have thirty thousand stores globally, which compares to thirty-one thousand operated by McDonald's.

Starbucks purchases and roasts high-quality whole-bean coffees and sells them, along with fresh-brewed coffees, Italian-style espresso beverages, cold blended beverages, a variety of complementary food items, coffee-related accessories and equipment, a selection of premium teas, and a line of compact discs. Starbucks also sells coffee and tea products and licenses its trademark through other channels; through certain of its equity investors, Starbucks produces and sells bottled Frappuccino® coffee drinks and Starbucks DoubleShot® espresso drink and a line of super-premium ice creams.

The company's objective is to establish Starbucks as the most recognized and respected brand in the world. To achieve this goal, Starbucks plans to continue rapid expansion of its retail operations, to grow its specialty operations, and to selectively pursue other opportunities to leverage the Starbucks brand through the introduction of new products and the development of new channels of distribution. Starbucks manages successful growth through careful consideration of stakeholder interests and its corporate social responsibility.

STARBUCKS' CULTURE

In 1990 Starbucks' senior executive team created a mission statement that laid out the guiding principles behind the company. They hoped that the principles included in the mission statement would help their partners (employees) determine the appropriateness of later decisions and actions. As Orin Smith explained, "Those guidelines are part of our culture and we try to live by them every day." After drafting the mission statement, the executive team asked all Starbucks partners to review and comment on the document. Based on their feedback, the final statement put "people first and profits last." In fact, the number-one guiding

This case was prepared by Ben Siltman, University of Wyoming, and Melanie Drever, University of Wyoming, under the direction of Linda Ferrell for classroom discussion rather than to illustrate either effective or ineffective handling of an administrative, ethical, or legal decision by management. All sources used for this case were obtained through publicly available material and the Starbucks website.

principle in Starbucks' mission statement was to "provide a great work environment and treat each other with respect and dignity."

Starbucks does three things to keep the mission and guiding principles alive. First, it distributes a copy of the mission statement and comment cards for feedback during orientation to all new partners. Second, when presentations are made, Starbucks continually relates decisions back to the guiding principle(s) that they support. Third, the company formed a "Mission Review" system so that any partner could comment on a decision or action relative to its consistency with one of the six principles. The partner with the most knowledge pertaining to the comment had to respond directly within two weeks, or if it was anonymous, the response would appear in the monthly report. This continual emphasis on the guiding principles and the underlying values has become the cornerstone of Starbucks.

The efforts have fostered a strong organizational culture that employs a predominately young, educated workforce who are proud to work for Starbucks. According to Smith, "It's extremely valuable to have people proud to work for [the company] and we make decisions that are consistent with what our partners expect of us."

In 2006 Starbucks ranked seventeenth on the *Business Ethics* "100 Best Corporate Citizens" list (2005: forty-fifth; 2004: forty-fifth; 2003: twenty-first; 2002: twenty-first) and on the *Fortune* "100 Best Companies to Work For" list for eight years (2006: twenty-ninth). However, being a great employer comes at a high cost. In 2005 Starbucks spent more on health insurance for its employees than on raw materials to brew its coffee. Starbucks provides health-care coverage to employees who work at least twenty hours a week and has faced double-digit increases in insurance costs each of the last four years. In 2005 Starbucks spent $200 million on health care for its eighty thousand U.S. employees. But the benefits policy is the key reason for low employee turnover and high productivity.

QUESTIONING STARBUCKS' MISSION AND IMPACT

Starbucks has flourished in thirty-eight countries, but this success has also attracted harsh criticism on issues such as fair-trade coffee, bovine growth hormone (BGH) milk, Schultz's alleged financial links to the Israeli government, and the accusations that Starbucks' growth is forcing locally run coffee shops out of business. A survey by Global Marketing Institute found that even Starbucks' customers view the company as "arrogant, intrusive, and self-centered." As a result Starbucks has invested significantly in corporate social responsibility (CSR) activities. They offer grants to charities and produce an annual CSR report. Starbucks was one of the first major coffeehouse brands to introduce "ethical" coffee in 2002 when it began offering a "fair-trade coffee of the week" and shortly after permanently added it to the main menu. Although a fine gesture, many competitors followed suit and switched to 100 percent fair-trade coffee, leaving Starbucks as an ethical trailer instead of a pioneer.

Criticism extends far beyond fair-trade policies in that accusations have centered on Starbucks' clustering strategy that saturates areas with branches, forcing many local coffee shops out of business. *Ethical Consumer* magazine researcher Ruth Rosselson says, "Starbucks has a number of useful policies in how it sources coffee, and its dialogue with Oxfam is progress. However, we would recommend consumers choose non-chain shops that offer fair-trade coffee. Starbucks operates like the supermarkets: it puts local companies out of businesses and with this policy can never be 100 percent ethical." Corporate Watch researcher Chris Grimshaw feels that Starbucks' CSR program is being used as a "smokescreen to create the illusion of ethics," adding that the company is committed solely to making money for shareholders.

CORPORATE SOCIAL MISSION

Just as treating partners well is one of the pillars of Starbucks, so is contributing to the communities it serves and to the environment. As a result of their pillars, Starbucks supports causes in both the communities where stores are located and the countries where Starbucks coffee is grown.

In 1991 Starbucks began contributing to CARE, a worldwide relief and development foundation, as a way to give back to coffee-origin countries. By 1995 Starbucks was CARE's largest corporate donor, pledging more than $100,000 a year and specifying that its support go to coffee-producing countries. The company's donations helped with such projects as clean-water systems, health and sanitation training, and literacy. In that year, Starbucks contributed more than $1.8 million to CARE.

In 1998 Starbucks partnered with Conservation International, a nonprofit organization that helps promote biodiversity in coffee-growing regions and supports producers of shade-grown coffee. Conservation International coffee came from cooperatives in Chiapas, Mexico, and was introduced as a limited edition in 1999. The cooperatives' land bordered the El Triunfo Biosphere Reserve, an area designated by Conservation International as one of twenty-five "hot spots" that is home to over half of the world's known plants and animals. Since 1999 Starbucks has funded seasonal promotions of this coffee every year, with the hope of adding it to its lineup of year-round offerings. The results of the partnership have proven positive for both the environment and Mexican farmers. Shade acreage has increased by 220 percent, while farmers receive a price premium of 65 percent above market price and have increased their exports by 50 percent. Finally, through this partnership, Starbucks made loan guarantees that helped provide over $750,000 to farmers. This financial support enabled farmers to nearly double their income.

Although Starbucks has supported responsible business practices virtually since its inception, as the company has grown, so has the importance of defending its image. At the end of 1999, Starbucks created a CSR department, and Dave Olsen was named the department's first senior vice president. According to Sue Mecklenburg, "Dave really is the heart and soul of the company and is acknowledged by others as a leader. By having Dave as the first Corporate Responsibility SVP, the department had instant credibility within the company." Between 1994 and 2001, Starbucks' CSR department had grown from only one person to fourteen. Starbucks is concerned about the environment and its employees, suppliers, customers, and communities.

The Environment

In 1992 Starbucks developed an environmental mission statement to articulate more clearly how the company interacted with the environment, eventually creating an Environmental Starbucks Coffee Company Affairs team tasked with developing environmentally responsible policies and minimizing the company's "footprint." Additionally, Starbucks was active in using environmental purchasing guidelines, reducing waste through recycling and energy conservation, and continually educating partners through the company's "Green Team" initiatives.

Employees

Schultz proved that businesses can still make money while maintaining fair labor practices and a social conscience. The son of a blue-collar worker, Schultz grew up in Brooklyn, New York, and lost faith in the American dream after his father suffered a tragic injury that left him unemployed with no benefits. "I watched what would happen to the plight of working class families when society and companies turned their back on the worker," Schultz said. "I wanted to build the kind of company my father never got to work for." The result of this is that all Starbucks employees, including part-time workers, are entitled to receive health benefits (including health, medical, dental, and vision benefits) and individuals who work more than twenty hours a week can receive stock options, known as Bean Stock. Schultz's key to maintaining a strong business is by "creating an environment where everyone believes they're part of something larger than themselves but believes they also have a voice." Understanding how vital employees are, Schultz is first to admit that his company focuses on personal interactions. "We are not in the coffee business serving people, but in the people business serving coffee."

Starbucks embraces diversity as an essential component in the way they do business. The company has 91,056 employees with 11,444 outside the United States. Of these, 28 percent are minorities, and 64 percent are women. This has proved successful: Starbucks has a partner turnover rate of 60 percent compared to the restaurant industry average of 200 percent. Furthermore, 82 percent of the partners reported being "very satisfied" and 15 percent as "satisfied" with their jobs when asked by outside audit agencies. Satisfaction rates this high are usually only found in small companies and are practically unheard of for large, publicly traded corporations.

Suppliers

While striving to meet its goal to establish Starbucks as the most recognized and respected brand of coffee in the world, the company maintains an excellent reputation for social responsibility and business ethics throughout the coffee community. It builds relationships with the farmers who supply the coffee, while working with governments in the various countries in which it operates. Starbucks also practices conservation by using Starbucks Coffee and Farmer Equity Practices, a set of socially responsible coffee-buying guidelines, and by offering preferential buying status for participants who score the highest on verified reports. Starbucks pays coffee farmers premium prices that help support their families instead of other illegal crops. The company also invests in social development programs that help build schools, health clinics, and other projects that benefit coffee-growing communities.

Starbucks collaborates with farmers through the Farmer Support Center, located in Costa Rica, to provide technical support and training that promotes high-quality coffee for the future. They are also involved in purchasing conservation and certified coffees—including Fair Trade Certified, shade-grown, and certified organic coffee—to promote responsible environmental and economic efforts.

Social responsibility, fair trade, and support for the environment are a part of the total product for consumers who are concerned about these social issues.

Customers

Starbucks continually works to grow their business by diversifying. The Hear Music platform includes media bars in stores where customers can download music; as of 2006, forty-one music media bars were in service. Starbucks also has more than three hundred drive-through stores. They also provide wireless Internet access with T1 speeds in more than forty-three hundred U.S. and European stores. At Starbucks.com, one can find the closest "Wireless Hotspot Available" by simply using a store locator.

Communities

Starbucks firmly believes that opening a store adds immediate value to the community because the store becomes a gathering spot, drawing people together. Additionally, store managers are granted discretion to donate to local causes and provide coffee for local fundraisers. One Seattle store donated more than $500,000 to Zion Preparatory Academy, an African American school for inner-city youth. In 1998 Starbucks and Erwin "Magic" Johnson's company, Johnson Development Corporation, formed a joint partnership and created Urban Coffee Opportunities.

Subsequently, twenty-eight stores opened in urban communities, providing new employment and revitalization to several U.S. cities.

Schultz personally believes that literacy has the power to change lives and foster hope for young children who live in underserved neighborhoods. Accordingly, Schultz used the advance and ongoing royalties from his book, *Pour Your Heart Into It*, to create the Starbucks Foundation, which provides "opportunity grants" to nonprofit literacy groups, sponsors young writers' programs, and partners with Jumpstart, an organization helping Headstart children.

SUCCESS AND CHALLENGE

Starbucks is trying to change pop culture: what we eat and drink, when we work and play, and how we spend our time and money. Some people call it the "Starbuckization" of society. Starbucks is not only the kingpin of expensive coffee but also among the top trendsetters of our time. Starbucks thinks that "if you love the taste of our coffee, you will love our taste in pop culture."

There are some negative aspects of this new pop culture. Starbucks is changing what we eat (but it is not always healthy). Portions are too big, and the drinks are full of calories and fat. It is possible that healthier food is in their future, but success has made them a target for people who are concerned about a healthy lifestyle.

On the positive side, Starbucks has added more than a teaspoon of social responsibility into its coffee, and there is a cost for social responsibility. Employee benefits and socially responsible actions come with a cost. Starbucks has made the $4 coffee drink acceptable and opened the door for other competitors to charge similar prices.

Psychologist Joyce Brothers says Starbucks has a positive effect in that "there is a sense of security when you go there." On the other hand, Starbucks is changing urban streetscapes; it is impossible in many cities to go more than a few blocks without seeing the familiar Starbucks logo. Even advertisements for apartments for rent point out that they are near a Starbucks. All of this is helping Starbucks become a cultural curator.

Starbucks has achieved amazing growth, creating financial success for shareholders while positioning itself as socially responsible. Its reputation has been built on product quality, stakeholder concerns, and a balanced approach to its business activities. Starbucks receives criticism for its ability to beat the competition, putting other coffee shops out of business, and creating a uniform retail culture in many cities, but it excels in its relationship with its employees and is a role model for the fast-food industry in employee benefits. In addition, in an age of shifts in supply chain power, Starbucks is as concerned about their suppliers and meeting their needs as they are about any other primary stakeholder. One of the areas where the company faces challenges is catching up with some of its competition in providing fair-trade coffee. The future looks bright for Starbucks, but the company must continue to focus on a balanced stakeholder orientation that has been so key to its success.

Questions

1. Why do you think Starbucks has been so concerned with social responsibility in its overall corporate strategy?

2. Is Starbucks unique in being able to provide a high level of benefits to its employees?

3. Do you think that Starbucks has grown rapidly because of its ethical and socially responsible activities or because it provides products and an environment that customers want?

Sources

"Brewing Up a Strong Starbucks Alternative," MSNBC, February 5, 2006, http://www.msnbc.msn.com/id/4163701/; "Coca-Cola May Take on Starbucks," MSNBC, January 30, 2006, http://www.msnbc.msn.com/id/11101825/; Anne Fifield, "Starbucks and Global Exchange," *Tuck Today,* Summer 2003, online, via http://mba.tuck.dartmouth.edu/pdf/2002-1-0023.pdf (accessed May 18, 2006); "'Fortune' Magazine's 100 Best Companies to Work For List 2006," Money/CNN, http://money.cnn.com/magazines/fortune/bestcompanies/full_list/ (accessed July 24, 2006); "Health Care Takes Its Toll on Starbucks," MSNBC, September 14, 2005, http://www.msnbc.msn.com/id/9344634; Adam Horowitz, David Jacobson, Mark Lasswell, and Owen Thomas, "101 Dumbest Moments in Business," *Business 2.0,* February 1, 2006, via http://money.cnn.com/magazines/business2/101dumbest/full_list/page6.html; Bruce Horovitz, "Starbucks Aims Beyond Lattes to Extend Brand to Films, Music and Books," *USA Today,* May 19, 2006, A1, A2; "In Rare Flop, Starbucks Scraps Chocolate Drink," MSNBC, February 10, 2006, http://www.msnbc.msn.com/id/11274445/; "100 Best Corporate Citizens 2006," *Business Ethics* online, Spring 2006, http://www.business-ethics.com/media/Chart%20of%20100%20Best%20Corp%20Citizens%20for%202006.pdf (accessed July 24, 2006); Starbucks, http://www.starbucks.com/retail/thewayiseeit_default.asp (accessed July 24, 2006); Starbucks, http://www.starbuckseverywhere.net/ (accessed July 24, 2006); "Starbucks Annual Report 10-K," Starbucks, www.starbucks.com (July 24, 2006); "Starbucks Company Fact Sheet," Starbucks, http://www.starbucks.com/aboutus/Company_Fact_Sheet_Feb06.pdf (accessed July 24, 2006); "Starbucks: Selling the American Bean," *BusinessWeek* online, December 1, 2005, http://www.businessweek.com/print/innovate/content/dec2005/id20051201_506349.htm (accessed July 24, 2006); Mariam Subjally, "Starbucks Creator Recounts Company's Rise, Emphasizes Importance of Ethical Approach," Emory Wheel, http://www.emorywheel.com (accessed February 8, 2005).

The Healthcare Company: Learning from Past Mistakes?

In 1968 Dr. Thomas Frist, Sr., Jack C. Massey, and Dr. Thomas Frist, Jr., founded the Hospital Corporation of America (HCA) to manage Park View Hospital in Nashville, Tennessee. The firm grew rapidly over the next two decades by acquiring and building new hospitals and contracting to manage additional facilities for their owners. The firm merged with Columbia Hospital Corporation to become Columbia/HCA Healthcare Corporation in 1994, and Columbia founder Richard Scott became chairman and CEO of the combined companies. By 1997 Columbia/HCA Healthcare Corporation had grown to become one of the largest health-care services companies in the United States, operating 343 hospitals, 136 outpatient surgery centers, and approximately 550 home-health locations. It also provided extensive outpatient and ancillary services in thirty-seven states, as well as in the United Kingdom and Switzerland. The firm's comprehensive network included more than 285,000 employees and used economies of scale to increase profits.

Columbia/HCA's stated mission was "to work with our employees, affiliated physicians and volunteers to provide a continuum of quality healthcare, cost-effectively for the people in the communities we serve." Its vision was "to work with employees and physicians, to build a company that is focused on the well-being of people, that is patient-oriented, that offers the most advanced technology and information systems, that is financially sound, and that is synonymous with quality, cost-effective healthcare." Columbia/HCA's goals included measuring and improving clinical outcome and patient satisfaction as well as reducing costs and providing services with compassion. With these goals, the company built the nation's largest chain of hospitals based on cost effectiveness and financial performance. It competed by capitalizing on its size and creating economies of scale in the internal control of its costs and sales activities. The focus was bottom-line performance and new business acquisitions.

However, a number of critics charged that health-care services and staffing at Columbia/HCA often took a back seat to the focus on profits. For example, the company employed shorter training periods than competing hospitals provided. One former administrator reported that training that typically should take six months was sometimes accomplished in as little as two weeks at a Columbia/HCA hospital. In addition, the company was accused of "patient dumping"— discharging emergency-room patients or transferring them to other hospitals when they were not yet in stable condition. In 1997 officials at the Department of Health and Human Services Inspector General's Office indicated that they were considering imposing fines on Columbia/HCA for an unspecified number of patient-dumping cases. Additionally, the corporate watchdog INFACT publicly challenged the company's

We appreciate the work of Mike Thomas, who helped draft this edition of the case. This case is for classroom discussion rather than to illustrate either effective or ineffective handling of an administrative, ethical, or legal decision by management. All sources used for this case were obtained through publicly available material and the HCA website.

459

practices, inducting Columbia/HCA into its "Hall of Shame" for corporations that manipulate public policy to the detriment of public health.

ETHICAL AND LEGAL PROBLEMS BEGIN

In late July 1997, Fawcett Memorial Hospital in Port Charlotte, Florida, a Columbia/HCA hospital, became the focal point of the biggest case of health-care fraud in the industry. A government investigation resulted in the indictment of three mid-level Columbia/HCA Healthcare Corporation executives for filing false cost reports for Fawcett, which resulted in losses of more than $4.4 million from government programs. The government alleged that Columbia/HCA had gained at least part of its profit by overcharging for Medicare and other federal health programs; that is, executives had billed the government for nonreimbursable interest expenses. Other concerns were alleged illegal incentives to physicians and the possible overuse of home-health services. Federal investigators accused Columbia/HCA of engaging in a "systematic effort to defraud government health care programs." In a seventy-four-page document, federal investigators quoted confidential witnesses who stated that Columbia/HCA's former CEO, Richard Scott, and former president, David Vandewater, were briefed routinely on issues relating to Medicare reimbursement claims that the government charged were fraudulent. Samuel Greco, Columbia/HCA's former chief of operations, was also implicated in the scandal.

One of the issues was whether Columbia/HCA had fraudulently overstated home-health care laboratory-test expenses and knowingly miscategorized other expenditures so as to inflate the amounts for which it sought reimbursement. For example, Columbia/HCA's Southwest Florida Regional Medical Center in Fort Myers reportedly claimed $68,000 more in property taxes than it paid. Moreover, documents showed that the hospital had set aside money to return to the government in case auditors caught the inflated figure. Technically, expenses claimed on cost reports must be related to patient care and fall within the realm of allowable Medicare reimbursements. However, medical billing can be confusing, chaotic, imprecise, and subject to interpretation. Hence, it is not unusual for

hospitals to keep two sets of accounting books. One set is provided to Medicare, and the other set, which includes records for set-aside money, is held in case auditors interpret the Medicare cost report differently than the hospital does. Some believe it is appropriate for a hospital to set aside money to return to the government if the hospital in good faith believes the Medicare cost claims are legitimate. However, if administrators believe strongly or know that certain claims are not allowable yet still file the claims and note them in the second set of books, charges of fraud may result.

Confidential witnesses said that Columbia/HCA had made an effort to hide from federal regulators internal documents that could have disclosed the alleged fraud. In addition, Columbia/HCA's top executive in charge of internal audits had instructed employees to soften the language used in internal financial audits that were critical of Columbia/HCA's practices. According to FBI agent Joseph Ford, "investigation by the [Federal Bureau of Investigation] and the [Defense Criminal Investigative Service] has uncovered a systematic corporate scheme perpetrated by corporate officers and managers of Columbia/HCA's hospitals, home health agencies, and other facilities in the states of Tennessee, Florida, Georgia, Texas, and elsewhere to defraud Medicare, Medicaid, and the [Civilian Health and Medical Program of the Uniformed Services]." Indicted Columbia/HCA officials pleaded not guilty, and defense lawyers for Columbia/HCA tried to diminish the importance of the allegations contained in the government's affidavits.

DEVELOPING A NEW ETHICAL CLIMATE AT COLUMBIA/HCA

Soon after the investigation was launched, Dr. Thomas Frist, Jr., was hired as chairman and CEO of Columbia/HCA. Frist, who had been president of HCA before it merged with Columbia, vowed to cooperate fully with the government and to develop a one-hundred-day plan to change the troubled firm's corporate culture. Under the Federal Sentencing Guidelines for Organizations (FSGO), companies that have effective due diligence compliance programs can reduce their fines if they are convicted of fraud. For penalties to be reduced, however, an effective compliance program must be in place before misconduct occurs. Although the FSGO requires that a senior executive be in charge of the due diligence compliance program, Columbia/HCA's general counsel had been designated to take charge of the program.

After a hundred days as chairman and CEO of Columbia/HCA, Frist outlined changes that would reshape the company. His reforms included a new mission statement as well as plans to create a new senior executive position to oversee ethical compliance and quality issues. Columbia/HCA's new mission statement emphasized a commitment to quality medical care and honesty in business practices. It did not, however, mention financial performance. "We have to take the company in a new direction," Frist said. "The days when Columbia/HCA was seen as an adversarial or in your face, a behind-closed-doors kind of place, is a thing of the past." (It has been claimed that some managers viewed Columbia/HCA's corporate culture as so unethical that they resigned before the fraud investigation had even started.)

Columbia/HCA hired Alan Yuspeh as the senior executive to oversee ethical compliance and quality issues. Yuspeh, senior vice president of ethics, compliance, and corporate responsibility, was given a staff of twelve at the corporate headquarters and assigned to work with group, division, and facility presidents to create a "corporate culture where Columbia workers feel compelled to do what is right." Yuspeh's first initiatives were to refine monitoring techniques, boost workers' ethics and compliance training, develop a code of conduct for employees, and create an internal mechanism for workers to report any wrongdoing.

Because of the investigation, consumers, doctors, and the general public lost confidence in Columbia/HCA, and its stock price dropped more than 50 percent from its all-time high. The new management seemed more concerned about developing the corporation's ethical compliance program than about its growth and profits. For instance, at a conference in Phoenix, Arizona, twenty Columbia managers were asked to indicate by a show of hands how many of them had escaped taunts from friends that they were crooks. Not a single hand went up. The discussion that followed that question did not focus on surgery profit margins. It focused on resolving the investigation and on the importance of the corporation's intangible image and values.

COLUMBIA/HCA LAUNCHES AN ETHICS, COMPLIANCE, AND CORPORATE RESPONSIBILITY PROGRAM

Columbia/HCA released a press statement indicating that it was taking a critical step in developing a company-wide ethics, compliance, and corporate responsibility program. To initiate the program, the company designated more than five hundred employees as facility ethics and compliance officers (ECOs). The new ECOs began their roles with a two-day training session in Nashville. The local leadership provided by these facility ECOs was thought to be the key link in ensuring that the company continued to develop a culture of ethical conduct and corporate responsibility.

As part of the program, Yuspeh made a fifteen-minute videotape that was sent to managers throughout the Columbia/HCA system. The tape announced the launching of the compliance-training program and the unveiling of a code of ethics that was designed to effectively communicate Columbia/HCA's new emphasis on compliance, integrity, and social responsibility. Frist stated that "we are making a substantial investment in our ethics and compliance program in order to ensure its success" and that "instituting a values-based culture throughout this company is something our employees have told us is critical to forming our future. The ethics and compliance initiative is a key part of that effort."

Training seminars for all employees, conducted by each facility's ECO, included introductions to the training program, the Columbia/HCA code of conduct, and the company's overall ethics and compliance program. The training seminars also included presentations by members of senior management and small-group discussions in which participants discussed how to apply the new Columbia/HCA code of conduct in ethics-related scenarios.

Although the company wanted individuals to bring their highest sense of personal values to work each day, the purpose of the program was to help employees understand the company's strict definition of ethical behavior rather than to change their personal values. Columbia/HCA's ethical guidelines tackled basic issues such as whether nurses can accept $100 tips— they cannot—as well as complicated topics such as what constitutes Medicare fraud. In addition, the company developed certification tests for the employees who determine billing codes. In 1998 a forty-minute training video was shown to all the firm's employees; it featured three ethical scenarios for employees to examine. Columbia/HCA apparently recognized the importance of ethical conduct and quality service to all of its constituents.

RESOLVING THE CHARGES

In 1997–1998, Columbia/HCA Healthcare settled with the Internal Revenue Service (IRS) for $71 million over allegations that it had made excessive compensation and "golden parachute" payments to some one hundred executives. As a result of the settlement, the IRS, which had sought $276 million in taxes and interest, agreed to drop its charges that Columbia/HCA had awarded excessive compensation by allowing the executives to exercise stock options after a new public offering of Columbia/HCA stock. Frist had reportedly earned about $125 million by exercising stock options after that public offering, and seventeen other top executives each made millions on the deals.

In August 2000, Columbia/HCA became the first corporation ever to be removed from INFACT's Hall of Shame. The executive director of INFACT announced that Columbia/HCA had drastically reduced its political activity and influence. For example, the corporation has no active federal lobbyists and has a registered lobbying presence in only twelve states. According to INFACT's executive director, "This response to grassroots pressure constitutes a landmark development in business ethics overall and challenges prevailing practices among for-profit health care corporations."

In December 2000, Columbia/HCA announced that it would pay the federal government more than $840 million in criminal fines and civil penalties. The company agreed in June 2003 to pay $631 million to settle the last of the government's charges that it had filed false Medicare claims, paid kickbacks to doctors, and overcharged at wound-care centers. No senior executives of the company have ever been charged with a crime. However, the company has paid out a total of $1.7 billion in fines, refunds, and lawsuit settlements after admitting that it had, through two subsidiaries, offered financial incentives to doctors in violation of antikickback laws, falsified records to generate higher payments for minor treatments or treatments that

never occurred, charged for laboratory tests that were never ordered, charged for home-health care for patients who did not qualify for it, and falsely labeled ads as "community education." KPMG, the firm's auditor, denied any wrongdoing on its part but agreed to pay $9 million to settle a whistle-blower lawsuit related to the charges. Columbia/HCA also signed a "Corporate Integrity Agreement" in 2000 that subjected the firm to intense scrutiny until 2009. In the same year, the company was officially renamed HCA—The Healthcare Company.

In January 2001, Frist relinquished the title of CEO to focus on other interests but remained involved in corporate strategy as chairman of HCA's board of directors. Jack Bovender, Jr. (formerly CFO) replaced him. Of the fraud investigation, Bovender said, "We think the major issues have been settled," although the company still has some "physician relations issues and cost report issues" to resolve in civil actions involving individual hospitals. Since 1997 the company has closed or consolidated more than one hundred hospitals. It is currently composed of locally managed facilities that include 175 hospitals and 80 outpatient surgery centers in twenty-four states, England, and Switzerland.

HCA'S COMPLIANCE PROGRAM AT WORK

Today, HCA spends $4 million a year on its ethics program, which includes an ethics and compliance committee of independent board directors, two separate corporate committees that draft ethics policy and monitor its use, and a twenty-member department that implements the program. In all, twenty-six executives oversee ethics and compliance for a variety of issues, ranging from taxes to pollution to the Americans with Disabilities Act.

The ethics compliance program set up by Yuspeh includes seven components: (1) articulating ethics through a code of conduct and a series of company policies and procedures; (2) creating awareness of these standards of compliance and promoting ethical conduct among everyone in the company through ethics training, compliance training, and other ongoing communication efforts; (3) providing a twenty-four-hour, toll-free telephone hot line to report possible misconduct; (4) monitoring and auditing employees' performance in areas of compliance risk to ensure that established policies and procedures are being followed and are effective; (5) establishing organizational supports for the ethics compliance effort; (6) overseeing the company's implementation of and adherence to the Corporate Integrity Agreement; and (7) undertaking other efforts such as clinical ethics and pastoral services.

Training continues to play a major role in helping employees understand HCA's new focus on ethics and legal compliance. Every new employee is required to undergo two hours of "orientation" on the firm's code of conduct within thirty days of employment. At that time, new employees receive a copy of the code of conduct, participate in training using videotapes and games, and sign an acknowledgment card. All employees complete one hour of refresher training on the firm's code of conduct every year.

HCA's new ethics hot line helps the firm identify misconduct and take corrective action where necessary. For example, in the spring of 2002, an anonymous caller to the toll-free line accused a hospital supply clerk of stealing medical gear and reselling it online through eBay. After investigators verified the complaint, the clerk was fired. Since its inception, the ethics program has fielded hundreds of such ethics-related complaints.

The effort to change HCA's corporate culture quickly and become the model corporate citizen in the health-care industry was a real challenge. This health-care provider learned the hard way that maintaining an organizational ethical climate is the responsibility of top management. As Bovender says, "Internal controls can always be corrupted. We've tried to come up with a system that would require a lot of people to conspire. It would be very hard for Tyco-type things to happen here." HCA seems to have recovered well from all of its problems, and at the time of writing this case, a number of companies were trying to acquire it, an indication that they view it as a great business opportunity.

Questions

1. What were the organizational ethical leadership problems that resulted in Columbia/HCA's misconduct?

2. Discuss the strengths and weaknesses of HCA's current ethics program. Does this program appear to satisfy the provisions of the Federal Sentencing Guidelines for Organizations and the Sarbanes–Oxley Act?

3. What other suggestions could Columbia/HCA have implemented to sensitize its employees to ethical issues?

Sources

Columbia/HCA Healthcare Corporation, *1996 Annual Report to Stockholders*; "Columbia/HCA Launches Ethics and Compliance Training Program," AOL News, February 12, 1998, http://cbs.aol.com; "Columbia/HCA to Sell Part of Business," *Commercial Appeal*, June 3, 1998, B8; "Corporate Influence Curtailed," *PR Newswire*, August 2, 2000; Kurt Eichenwald, "Reshaping the Culture at Columbia/HCA," *New York Times*, November 4, 1997, C2; Kurt Eichenwald and N. R. Kleinfield, "At Columbia/HCA, Scandal Hurts," *Commercial Appeal*, December 21, 1997, C1, C3; "Ethics, Compliance, and Corporate Responsibility: Introduction," HCA, http://ec.hcahealthcare.com/ (accessed April 24, 2003); "HCA Tentatively Agrees to Multimillion Fraud Settlement," American Medical News, January 27, 2003, www.ama-assn.org/sci-pubs/amnews/pick_03/gvbf0127.htm; "History," HCA, http://hca.hcahealthcare.com/CustomPage.asp?guidCustomContentID=C2E6928A-D8B1-42AF-BA44-6C2B591282D5 (accessed April 24, 2003); "INFACT Urges Columbia/HCA to Remove Itself from the Hall of Shame," *PR Newswire*, www.prnewswire.com (accessed May 27, 1999); Lucette Lagnado, "Columbia Taps Lawyer for Ethics Post: Yuspeh Led Defense Initiative of 1980s," *Wall Street Journal*, October 14, 1997, B6; Tom Lowry, "Columbia/HCA Hires Ethics Expert," *USA Today*, October 14, 1997, 4B; Tom Lowry, "Loss Warning Hits Columbia/HCA Stock," *USA Today*, February 9, 1998, 2B; Duncan Mansfield, "HCA Names Bovender Chief Executive," January 8, 2001, Yahoo! News, http://biz.yahoo.com/apf/010108/hca_change_ 2.html (accessed January 16, 2001); Charles Ornstein, "Columbia/HCA Prescribes Employee Ethics Program," *Tampa Tribune*, February 20, 1998, 4; Eva M. Rodriguez, "Columbia/HCA Probe Turns to Marketing Billing," *Wall Street Journal*, August 21, 1997, A2; Neil Weinberg, "Healing Thyself," *Forbes* online, March 17, 2003, www.forbes.com/forbes/2003/0317/064.html; Chris Woodyard, "FBI Alleges Systemic Fraud at Columbia," *USA Today*, October 7, 1997, 1B.

PETCO Develops Successful Stakeholder Relationships

BACKGROUND AND HISTORY

PETCO Animal Supplies Inc. is the nation's number-two pet supply specialty retailer of premium pet food, supplies, and services with over 750 stores in forty-eight states and the District of Columbia. Their pet-related products include pet food, pet supplies, grooming products, toys, novelty items, vitamins, veterinary supplies, and small pets such as fish, birds, and other small animals (excluding cats and dogs). PETCO's strategy is to offer their customers a complete assortment of pet-related products and services at competitive prices, with superior levels of customer service at convenient locations and through their e-commerce site, www.petco.com.

PETCO stores offer the broad merchandise selection, convenient location, and knowledgeable customer service of a neighborhood pet-supply store. PETCO believes that this combination differentiates their stores and provides them with a competitive advantage. Their principal format is a 12,000- to 15,000-square-foot store, conveniently located near local neighborhood shopping destinations, including supermarkets, bookstores, coffee shops, dry cleaners, and video stores, where their target "pet parent" customer makes regular weekly shopping trips. PETCO believes that their stores are well positioned, both in terms of product offerings and location, to benefit from favorable long-term demographic trends: a growing pet population and an increasing willingness of pet owners to spend on their pets.

Since mid-2001, all new stores have been opened in their new formats, which incorporate a more dramatic presentation of their companion animals and emphasize higher-margin supplies categories. Each store has approximately ten thousand pet-related items, including premium cat and dog foods, collars, leashes, grooming products, toys, and animal habitats. The stores also offer grooming, obedience training, and veterinary services, and they sponsor pet adoption for cats and dogs with local animal-welfare organizations. PETCO has 16,900 employees, 9,000 of which are full time.

Walter Evan founded PETCO in 1965 as a mail-order veterinary-supplies store. The original name was UPCO, United Pharmacal Company. In 1976 they opened their first retail store in La Mesa, California, buying quality pet and veterinary supplies and selling them directly to animal professionals and the public at discount prices. In 1979 UPCO became PETCO. PETCO's vision is to promote the highest level of well-being for companion animals and to support the human–animal bond. Their aim is to provide a broad array of premium products, companion animals, and services and a fun and exciting shopping experience. Their value proposition to the pet parent/customer is provided through friendly, knowledgeable associates (employees) in convenient, community-based locations.

This case was prepared by Melanie Drever, University of Wyoming, under the direction of O. C. Ferrell, for classroom discussion rather than to illustrate either effective or ineffective handling of an administrative, ethical, or legal decision by management. All sources used for this case were obtained through publicly available material and the PETCO website.

The pet food, supplies, and services industry is benefiting from a number of favorable demographic trends that are continuing to support a steadily growing pet population. The U.S. pet population has now reached 378 million companion animals, including 143 million cats and dogs, with an estimated 62 percent of all U.S. households owning at least one pet, and three-quarters of those households owning two or more pets. It is widely believed that the trend for more pets and for more pet-owning households will continue, driven by an increasing number of children under 18 years of age and a growing number of empty nesters whose pets have become their new "children." Estimates have suggested that U.S. retail sales of pet food, supplies, small animals (excluding cats and dogs), and services increased to approximately $34 billion in 2004. PETCO believes they are well positioned to benefit from several key growth trends within the industry.

THE PET INDUSTRY

The pet industry is growing and getting stronger. Harley Davidson has a line of leather dog jackets, and Paul Mitchell has a line of pet shampoos. Hotels are offering pet-friendly rooms, and Japanese pet-toy company Takara has introduced Bow-Lingual, a device that translates dog barks. Pet owners continue to treat their pet as part of their families. They often lavish as much care and attention on the pet as they do on other family members; this means that many pet owners are prepared to spend considerable sums of money on pet products. However, not all the trends affect the industry in a positive way; for example, pet owners are moving away from dogs toward cats, which means that volumes of pet food will decrease.

PETCO does business in a highly competitive industry and competes against such names as diverse as PetSmart and Wal-Mart. This competition can be categorized into three different segments: (1) supermarkets, warehouse clubs, and mass merchants; (2) specialty pet store chains; and (3) traditional pet stores and independent service providers. The principal competitive factors influencing PETCO are product selection and quality, convenient store locations, customer service, and price. PETCO believes that they compete effectively within their various geographic areas. However, some of their competitors are much larger in terms of sales volume and have access to greater capital and management resources than PETCO does.

THE RISKS ASSOCIATED WITH THE PET INDUSTRY

Most organizations' greatest fear is not discovering risk associated with operating their business. Regardless of the industry, there is concern that the public or a special-interest group can uncover some activity that can immediately be used by critics and the mass media, competitors, or simply skeptical stakeholders to undermine a firm's reputation. Therefore, an ethical risk assessment is an important activity that is included in most companies' ethics initiatives. A single negative incident can influence perceptions of a corporation's image and reputation instantly and possibly continue for years afterwards.

Not all ethical concerns are of a company's making, and there are certainly those disgruntled antagonists who will distort the truth for their own self-interest. Because pets are such a strong emotional attachment for many, assessing risk of accusations in this industry is especially important. For all companies who sell pets, the question is not if there will be accusations, but when the accusations are made, can there be a rapid enough response to explain or correct activities that are in question to mitigate possible negative perceptions. The important focus should be on a commitment to make the right decisions and to constantly assess and deal with the risk of operating a business.

PETCO is committed to pets and animals in general. However, any company selling animals faces inherent risks. Between 2000 and 2005, People for the Ethical Treatment of Animals (PETA) alleged questionable conditions at PETCO. PETA, a special-interest group that makes strong demands not always supported by the general public, is highly critical of most organizations that sell or use animals for commercial purposes.

PETA made complaints regarding cruelty and neglect to animals in PETCO's care, and they filed a complaint against PETCO with the Securities and Exchange Commission (SEC). PETA had concerns about the handling of their animals for sale. PETCO responded and made changes. In particular, PETA was concerned about the sale of large birds; specifically, such birds need plenty of space to move around and exercise. Also, when kept as "companions," large birds need a great deal of socialization and attention—at least eight hours a day. Most parrots die from diseases caused by the same conditions that adversely affect humans—for example, obesity, high-stress environments, and too-little exercise. Many large birds also have multiple guardians in their lifetimes because they tend to outlive one human family after another; their lifespan is typically between forty and seventy years. Adding further to the problem is that about 70 percent of parrots suffer from "miner's lung" disease (pneumoconiosis) because of living in dry, stuffy, indoor environments.

On April 12, 2005, PETA and PETCO announced an agreement that would advance animal welfare across the country. PETA agreed to end its campaign against the national pet food and supply retailer, to take down all references to "PETNO," and dismantle its "PETCOCruelty" website. PETCO agreed to end the sale of large birds in its stores upon completion of the sale of the limited number they had in stock. It also would continue to work with its shelter partners to help those groups adopt not only dogs and cats but also homeless birds of all sizes, as part of PETCO's established "Think Adoption First" program. PETCO also agreed to make some changes to benefit rats and mice; these changes included separating the animals by gender to prevent breeding. Although not required to answer to PETA, PETCO decided to respond to indicate its desire to cooperate, resolve issues and misunderstandings, and improve operations.

Another incident occurred in May 2004 when PETCO paid nearly $1 million in precedent-setting settlements of two California lawsuits involving the mistreatment of animals in PETCO stores in five California counties. After PETA released undercover footage of extreme neglect at North American Pet Distributor, Inc. (NAPD), which supplied at least fifty-five PETCO stores, PETCO halted its business with NAPD because it had established a response system to deal quickly with any knowledge about supplier abuse of animals. Resolving any activity that is not in compliance with an organization's standards of conduct is easy once they have been developed.

Other problems have also plagued PETCO. In 2002 inspectors and customers found sick finches, a moldy dead turtle, dead birds, and a toad "cooked to death" at two San Francisco PETCO stores that were also overcharging customers on sale items. PETCO settled this case in 2004, agreeing to pay more than $900,000—most of which would be spent on new scanners in its stores. PETCO also agreed it would increase training for its managers and employees in regard to caring and looking after animals. Again, this demonstrated the desire to do the right thing and respond to mistakes made by employees. With over sixteen thousand employees, individuals will step outside the bounds of PETCO's desired conduct, but the ability to expose and correct these situations illustrates an effective ethics program.

In 2004 PETCO agreed to settle a Federal Trade Commission charge that it did not take reasonable or appropriate measures to prevent commonly known attacks by hackers to obtain customer information. The settlement required PETCO to implement a comprehensive information security program for its website.

Another worry that PETCO has addressed is pet owners' concerns over pet food-portion control; this concern has been addressed by selling the Electronic Portion Control Le Bistro by Petmate. This product dispenses food at certain times throughout the day. PETCO has also started a PetHotel, a form of kenneling called Best Friends Pet Care, Inc., which includes TV sets tuned to animal shows and special ventilation systems. PETCO is trying hard to find the issues that concern their customers and address them. One issue that might affect PETCO in the future could include concerns about avian flu; this particularly concerns people who buy their bird feed from PETCO.

Managing risk is an important aspect of any business but especially for companies that sell animals. PETCO has tried to limit its risk by selling only a few types of animals and not selling large animals such as dogs or cats. This has limited the extent to which it is at risk and avoided the negative effect of the risk. Animal sales make up only 5 percent of PETCO's revenues; pet supplies and services make up the rest. By avoiding this risk, PETCO ensures not only that it keeps its customers and investors happy but also the animals in its care protected from abuse.

THE PETCO ETHICS PROGRAM

PETCO has a comprehensive code of ethics. Its main emphasis is that animals always come first, and PETCO wants to ensure that all the employees adhere to this code. One of their most important missions is to promote the health, well-being, and humane treatment of animals. They do this through their vendor selection programs, pet adoption programs, and their partnerships with animal-welfare organizations. PETCO was founded on the principle of "connecting with the community."

In 1999 PETCO established the PETCO Foundation to help them promote charitable, educational, and other philanthropic activities for the betterment of animals everywhere. The PETCO Foundation is dedicated to serving the "Four Rs": Reduce, Rescue, Rehabilitate, Rejoice. The PETCO Foundation promotes the welfare of companion animals and the importance of the person–animal bond. The foundation raises funds for animal-welfare groups and promotes pet adoption to all their customers. The PETCO Foundation, a nonprofit organization, has raised more than $28 million since its inception. Through a combination of programs and fundraisers—"Round Up," "Think Adoption First," "Spring a Pet," "Tree of Hope," "National Pet Adoption Days," and "Kind News"—more than thirty-three hundred nonprofit grassroots animal-welfare organizations have received support. They are also responsible for the donation of in-kind goods and services to worthwhile organizations with the same mission of strengthening the bond between people and pets. With an exclusive long-term agreement with Petfinder.com, they also support over seven thousand additional animal welfare agencies.

The code of ethics also has a section relating to dealing with customers and others. It emphasizes that employees should treat customers with the utmost care and that their privacy should be respected at all times. PETCO also ensures that its selling practices, advertising policies, and pricing and buying practices are mentioned in its code. It is against the code to promote one brand over any other brand; associates are expected to interact honestly with each customer and to clearly explain the purpose and benefits of the products and services. PETCO makes efforts to ensure that their advertising is not misleading and that pricing decisions are made without influence from vendors, contractors, or competitors.

The matter of courtesy, dignity, and respect among associates is taken very seriously. The code of ethics addresses concerns about sexual and other types of harassment that could occur in the workplace. If any employee makes a complaint about harassment, it will be treated with confidentiality and appropriate corrective action. Discipline will be directed at offending parties, which may include dismissal. Drug abuse, asset protection, and violence in the workplace are also concerns for PETCO and are addressed in the code. PETCO has implemented measures that aim to increase associate, vendor, and customer protection with the goal of providing a safe working environment.

PETCO associates are to avoid conflicts of interest or what appear to be conflicts of interest. This means that PETCO associates must not place themselves in situations that might force them to choose between their own personal or financial interests and the interests of PETCO. Associates are encouraged to communicate any conflicts of interest to management to determine whether a conflict actually exists.

The code of ethics addresses the acceptance of gifts and entertainment. PETCO associates are prohibited from accepting gifts or gratuities from vendors or potential vendors, whether it is money, merchandise, services, lavish entertainment, travel, or any other good. Associates who receive such gifts are asked to contact their supervisor or the PETCO hot line for guidance and ask vendors to refrain from giving gifts in the future. Acceptance of reasonable entertainment in accordance with customary practice is allowed, as long as it is kept within reasonable limits.

Employment with suppliers, vendors, or others doing business with PETCO is expected to be done at the discretion of associates, and their supervisors are expected to be contacted. Investments in vendors made by associates or their immediate families are not permitted without prior approval from the Ethics Committee. PETCO discourages workplace romances when there is a direct or indirect reporting relationship because undue pressure may occur. Outside interests are allowed; however, they should not be endorsed, funded, or sponsored by PETCO. It is considered inappropriate for associates to publicly make negative remarks about PETCO. If associates have a grievance or concern, they are asked to work with the company to obtain a mutually satisfactory resolution.

Associates must also agree to not interfere with PETCO's business by directly or indirectly soliciting the business of any persons or entities who were customers of PETCO, or soliciting an associate of PETCO to terminate his or her position for a period of six months immediately after the termination of her or his employment. Trade secrets and other proprietary information must also be kept in strict confidence both during employment and forever following separation.

After the scandals of Enron and other publicly traded companies, PETCO strived for and explicitly called for accurate accounting records of all its assets, liabilities, expenses, and other transactions. No unrecorded or undisclosed fund or asset of PETCO or its subsidiaries may be established or maintained for any purpose. Furthermore, PETCO insists that no confidential or proprietary information relating to PETCO, its suppliers, vendors, or customers can be disclosed at any time. All PETCO property and information systems can only be used for conducting company business. Occasional personal use is permitted as long as it does not interfere with or impedes PETCO's business. Knowingly duplicating copyrighted computer software is also prohibited.

All associates are encouraged to comply with accounting laws including the Sarbanes-Oxley Act and the generally accepted accounting principles. Internal controls and procedures are designed to ensure that PETCO's financial records are accurately and completely maintained. It is also against PETCO policy to buy or sell PETCO stock while in possession of important information not publicly available.

The code of ethics also addresses other concerns such as workplace safety, wage and hour laws, and reporting time worked. Political contributions from PETCO funds are not allowed; neither are payments to government personnel. PETCO also respects the environment and strives to conserve natural resources as much as possible.

A section concerning managers and supervisors encourages them to be role models when dealing with employment decisions. When dealing with the media, managers and supervisors are asked to discuss any situations with all parties to determine an appropriate media response if necessary. An associate may also at no time submit or knowingly accept false or misleading information, documents, or proposals. When in doubt, associates are encouraged to phone the code of ethics hot line or ask a supervisor about the appropriate course of action to take.

The code of ethics also presents a chain of command to follow in case an employee is faced with an ethical dilemma. There is also an anonymous 24-hour hotline for associates to call if they do not feel that their immediate supervisor is being responsive or if it involves their immediate supervisor. The code of ethics is reviewed on an annual basis. The company also has an internal Ethics Committee, which oversees compliance with the code and continually monitors related best practices.

PETCO FOUNDATION FUNDRAISERS

The "Round Up" Program

Every year between 5 and 10 million pets are euthanized in the United States. PETCO launched an annual "Spay Today" initiative in 2000 to address the significant and growing problem of pet overpopulation. Overpopulation due to unwanted litters sends millions of animals to animal shelters each year. The "Spay Today" funds come from customer donations at PETCO stores where customers are encouraged to round up their purchases to the nearest dollar or more. Each PETCO store selects one or more spay/neuter–focused charitable partners to which the funds are donated. In addition, 10 percent of all funds raised are donated to the Petfinder.com Foundation to assist their spay/neuter efforts. In 2000 PETCO allowed pet owners to purchase a voucher at PETCO stores to have a cat spayed or neutered for $10 and a dog spayed or neutered for $20 (compared to the regular price of more than $100). In 2004 this program raised $817,000 for local animal-welfare organizations across the country.

The "Think Adoption First" Program

"Think Adoption First," launched in 2005, supports and promotes the person–animal bond. It is a program that sets the standard for responsibility and community involvement for the industry. Each year, 8 to 12 million pets are relinquished to shelters and rescue groups. PETCO, the PETCO Foundation, and Petfinder.com offer a second chance for those orphaned companion animals. "Think Adoption First" recommends the adoption of companion animals beyond dogs and cats as an alternative first choice to consider. They provide access to rescued animals through their partnership network of rescue groups and then work with their partners to make companion animals available for in-store adoption. They have strengthened their relationship with Petfinder.com, and together they have found homes for over 2 million animals. This program reinforces PETCO's commitment to both social responsibility and financial success.

The "Spring a Pet" Program

The "Spring a Pet" fundraiser encourages pet lovers to donate $1, $5, $10, or $20 to animal-welfare causes. Donors receive a personalized cutout bunny to display in their neighborhood store or take home as a reminder of their generosity. Each PETCO store selects an animal-welfare organization to be the recipient of the money raised at its location. In the past, the money has provided veterinary care for homeless and abused animals and outreach programs to help handicapped and disadvantaged individuals adequately care for their companion animals. In 2005 this program raised $1.51 million.

The "Tree of Hope" Program

Customers visiting one of PETCO's 760 stores during the Christmas season can purchase card ornaments for $1, $5, $10, or $20. They can also choose from red or blue "Making a Difference" wristbands or a 2006 PETCO Foundation calendar loaded with coupons. All funds go toward the "Tree of Hope." Anyone donating $20 or more receives a PETCO Foundation hand-painted globe ornament. In 2005, this program raised $2.1 million.

The "National Pet Adoption Days" Program

More than fourteen thousand animals were adopted during "National Pet Adoption Days" on April 2–3, 2005. Not only did dogs and cats find new homes but also hundreds of birds, reptiles, and small mammals.

The "Kind News" Program

"Kind News" is a Humane Education Program that educates children about the humane treatment of companion animals and fellow human beings. It features stories about responsible pet owners' environmental concerns and issues as well as information on all types of animals. It contains many learning tools to reinforce the concept of compassion and concern for all living things.

PETCO'S CHALLENGES AND ACCOMPLISHMENTS

Most companies focus on customers to help establish their reputation and success, but PETCO has adopted a stakeholder orientation and is concerned about its impact on society. Although PETCO wants quality products for its customers, with information and advice for caring for pets, it is also concerned about important issues related to the existence and role of animals in our society. For example, the "Think Adoption First" and the "Round Up" program to encourage spaying/neutering of pets illustrate important

contributions to society. Especially important is the PETCO Foundation support of "Kind News" to educate children about proper humane treatment of animals and fellow human beings. PETCO, like any organization, experiences risk associated with doing business and has developed a comprehensive ethics program to manage relationships with stakeholders. For example, PETCO addressed the concerns of PETA and has taken a proactive approach to answering any accusations or concerns about its operations.

All organizations in the retail area are subject to criticisms and have to work hard to maintain internal controls that provide assurance that employees follow ethical codes. PETCO accomplishes this through an ethics office and by developing an ethical corporate culture. PETCO's code of ethics addresses all organizational risk related to human resources, conflicts of interests, and appropriate behavior in the workplace. All large organizations know that misconduct will occur somewhere in the organization, so discovering, exposing, and addressing any event before it can cause reputation damage are important. For PETCO, the desire to do the right thing and to train all organizational members to make ethical decisions ensures success in the marketplace and a significant contribution to society.

Discussion Questions

1. What are the ethical risks associated with selling pets and pet products in a retail environment?

2. How has PETCO managed the various ethical concerns that have been expressed by stakeholders?

3. Assess the ethical culture of PETCO.

Sources

All websites were accessed between January 23 and July 5, 2006. "Animal Abuse Case Details. PETCO Lawsuit—Mistreating Animals San Diego, CA," May 28, 2004—Pet-Abuse, http://www.pet-abuse.com/cases/2373/CA/US; Catherine Colbert "PETCO Animal Supplies, Inc.," *Hoovers* online, http://www.hoovers.com/petco-(holding)/ID__17256--/free-co-factsheet.xhtml; "*Fortune* 500 2006: Our Annual Ranking of America's Largest Corporations," CNN/Money, http://money.cnn.com/magazines/fortune/fortune500/snapshots/2154.html; Michelle Higgins, "When the Dog's Hotel Is Better Than Yours," *Wall Street Journal*, June 30, 2004, D1; "Just Say

No! Petco—The Place Where Pets Die," Kind Planet, http://www.kindplanet.org/petno.html (accessed July 5, 2006); Melissa Kaplan, "PETCO Settles Suit Alleging Abuse, Overcharging," May 27, 2004, CBS News online, http://www.anapsid.org/pettrade/petocit2.html; Ilene Lelchuk, "San Francisco Alleges Cruelty at 2 PETCOs," *San Francisco Chronicle,* via June 19, 2002, http://www.anapsid.org/pettrade/petcocit2.html; "Lifestyle Trends Affect Pet Markets," *Pet Age* online, January 2006, http://www.petage.com/News010607.asp; Robert McMillan, "PETCO Settles Charge It Left Customer Data Exposed," IDG News Service, November 17, 2004, http://www.networkworld.com/news/2004/1117petcosettl.html; Chris Penttila, "Magic Markets" *Entrepreneur's StartUps* online, September 2004, http://www.entrepreneur.com/article/0,4621,316866-2,00.html; "PETA and PETCO Announce Agreement," PETA, April 2005, http://www.peta.org/feat/PETCOAgreement/default.asp; "Petco Animal Supplies Inc. (PETC)," Yahoo! Finance, http://finance.yahoo.com/q?s=PETC; "PETCO Annual Report to Shareholders" and "PETCO 10-K Annual Report," www.petco.com; "PETCO's Bad Business Is Bad for Animals," PETA, Spring 2003, http://www.peta.org/living/at-spring2003/comp2.html; "PETCO Code of Ethics," http://ir.petco.com/phoenix.zhtml?c=93935&p=irol-govConduct; "PETCO Foundation to 'Round-Up' Support for Spay/Neuter Programs," *Forbes,* online, July 13, 2005, http://www.forbes.com/prnewswire/feeds/prnewswire/2005/07/13/prnewswire200507131335PR_NEWS_B_WES_LA_LAW067.html; "PETCO Looks to the Web to Enhance Multi-Channel Marketing," *Internet Retailer,* January 16, 2006; "PETCO Pays Fine to Settle Lawsuit," PETA, Annual Review 2004, http://www.peta.org/feat/annual_review04/notToAbuse.asp; "PETCO Settles FTC Charges," Federal Trade Commission, November 17, 2004, http://www.ftc.gov/opa/2004/11/petco.htm; "PETCO 'Spring a Pet' Campaign Blossoms for Animals Nationwide," Corporate Social Responsibility press release, Citizenship at Boston College, May 11, 2005, http://www.csrwire.com/ccc/article.cgi/3910.html; "The Pet Market—Market Assessment 2005," Research and Markets, http://www.researchandmarkets.com/reports/c26485/; "Pet Portion Control," *Prevention,* February 2006, 201; "Pet Store Secrets: PETA Uncovers Shocking Back-Room Secrets," PETA, Summer 2000, http://www.peta.org/living/at-summer2000/petco.html; "Say No to PETCO," PETA, Spring 2002, http://www.peta.org/living/at-spring2002/specialrep/; Julie Schmidt, "Pet Bird Buyers Asking Sellers About Avian Flu," *USA Today,* November 28, 2005, via http://www.citizen-times.com/apps/pbcs.dll/article?AID=/20051129/HEALTH/511290304/1008/HEALTH (accessed July 5, 2006); Jessica Stannard-Freil, "Corporate Philanthropy: PR or Legitimate News?" *On Philanthropy* online, May 5, 2005 http://www.onphilanthropy.com/tren_comm/tc2005-05-20.html.

Nike: From Sweatshops to Leadership in Employment Practices

The Nike product has become synonymous with slave wages, forced overtime and arbitrary abuse.—Nike chairman Phil Knight at a speech to the National Press Club, May 12, 1998

The biography of Phil Knight, the driving force behind Nike, has been recounted repeatedly as an example depicting a "self-made billionaire." Philip H. Knight, seventieth on the *Forbes* ranking of the world's richest people in 2006 and now worth $7.3 billion, has come a long way from selling shoes out of his car trunk in 1964. In contrast to the era of its meteoric rise in the 1980s after going public, the late 1990s for Nike was a period composed of combating allegations about subcontractor labor and human rights violations in third-world countries. Nike's response was considered by its critics to be more of a public relations, damage-control stunt rather than a sincere attempt at labor reform.

Knight founded Nike in 1964 under the name "Blue Ribbon Sports." The idea, born as a result of a paper written by Knight during his MBA program at Stanford, was to import athletic shoes from Japan into the U.S. market, which was otherwise dominated by German competitors. The Nike brand was created in 1972 ("Nike" after the Greek goddess of victory), the company went public in 1980, and today Nike is one of the largest manufacturers of athletic goods in the world.

THE SCANDAL

Sweatshops and product origin permeated the public consciousness when Kathy Lee Gifford discovered that her endorsed clothing line was actually made in Honduran sweatshops. Nike is known as a footwear company, but approximately one-third of its revenue comes from apparel, and that manufacturing takes place mostly in factories located in Asia. Contracts with suppliers from Korea and Taiwan replaced Nike's original contracts with Japanese producers. The company's increasing scope and size of operations, along with increasing costs, have meant that these suppliers have had subcontracts with cheaper labor markets in other third-world countries such as Indonesia, China, and Vietnam.

Nike employees were assigned to the new manufacturing facilities in these countries in order to monitor operations. According to Nike's Corporate Responsibility Report (2001), the pool of suppliers came from over seven hundred factories in fifty countries. The lower costs of production coupled with innovative advertising and marketing were the main reasons for Nike's growth.

Since the mid-1990s, Nike has faced a barrage of criticism from labor rights activists, the media, and others for human rights violations in their factories in third-world countries. The accusations include

We appreciate the work of Deepa Pillai, Alexi Sherrill, and Melanie Drever who assisted in this edition of the case. This case was prepared for classroom discussion rather than to illustrate either effective or ineffective handling of an administrative, ethical, or legal decision by management. All sources used for this case were obtained through publicly available material and the Nike website.

deficiencies in health and safety conditions, extremely low wages, and indiscriminate hiring and firing practices. The attention given to this issue by the national media is evident in the number of reports and editorials in leading newspapers as well as programs on television—all lending support to the cause of labor activists campaigning against Nike's unfair labor practices.

In Indonesia, where Korean suppliers owned a majority of Nike factories, several cases of human rights abuses were revealed by nongovernment organizations—for example, Roberta Baskin's CBS report on the conditions in Nike's manufacturing facilities in Indonesia in 1993 and Bob Herbert's op-ed article in the *New York Times* in 1996.

Another of Nike's problems was factory conditions in Vietnam, which became public knowledge. Ernst and Young, commissioned by Nike to audit one of the factories, reported extreme, unacceptable standards of chemicals in the factory and cases of employee health problems caused as a result of this and other infringements of the established code of conduct. Unfortunately for Nike, it was leaked to the press, resulting in the *New York Times* running it as a front-page article.

THE FALLOUT AND RESPONSE

Public protests against Nike took the forms of boycotts and picketing of Nike stores, and universities began canceling their deals with Nike to produce branded athletic goods. In 1998 Nike revenues and stock prices decreased by approximately 50 percent, leading to the laying off of sixteen hundred workers.

Nike had already established its code of conduct in 1992 in the wake of increasing public interest in the operations of multinational corporations in developing countries; Nike was following suit with other companies operating in these areas. In theory, suppliers were required to sign the code of conduct and display it in their factories, but this was not enforced. More recent efforts to enforce standards have been made in the form of monitoring, both through Nike's own production department and by independent consultants; the objective is the dual goal of retaining cost effectiveness while honoring the cost of labor and human rights issues.

The initial reactions of Nike officials to specific criticisms was to ignore them, the rationale being that they did not own the factories and were therefore not responsible for labor and human rights violations. They claimed to be marketers and designers lacking knowledge about manufacturing. However, in 1996 Knight claimed full responsibility for working conditions wherever its products were produced. But in his speech on May 12, 1998, Knight denied that Nike had a sweatshop problem and claimed the problems had to do with public relations rather than actual factory conditions.

During this time, Nike sought to counter the allegations about labor and human rights violations through an extensive public relations campaign. A workplace code of conduct was established to regulate working conditions in foreign factories. In the mid-1990s, Nike finally intervened in the wage policy of its factories in Indonesia and announced wage raises above the legal minimum wage in 1999. In 1998 a statement of corporate responsibility addressing the various allegations against Nike was issued and included several specific steps that Nike intended to implement in its factories.

Nike used a number of other tactics in attempting to repair its tarnished image. Michael Jordan was recruited as a Nike spokesperson. Because universities formed a core segment of Nike's market and repercussions had already been felt in this area with several deals being canceled, letters detailing the acceptable conditions in the factories and stressing Nike's commitment to corporate responsibility were sent to U.S. universities. Representatives from Nike also visited campuses and spoke to students, assuring them of Nike's intention toward responsible corporate citizenship. A key event in this context was Knight's visit to the University of North Carolina at Chapel Hill; numerous press conferences were also held with college newspapers across the United States.

MORE PROBLEMS: *NIKE VS. KASKY*

Nike hired Andrew Young, a former UN ambassador, to visit and report on conditions in its third-world factories. The 1997 report stated that a survey of twenty factories in several Asian countries had revealed that (1) there were no infringements of health and labor codes of conduct and (2) the pay in Nike-controlled factories was substantially higher than the required minimum wage. The report claimed that Nike typically subsidized meals and medical treatment of factory employees. As part of its intensive public relations campaign, Nike used press releases in newspapers and ran full-page advertisements based on parts of Young's report, mentioning that Nike was doing a good job but could do better.

In 1998 Marc Kasky, a self-styled corporate critic, responded to the conflict between Nike's claims and the content of the Ernst and Young report by filing a lawsuit against Nike. The case was to be a landmark one not only from Nike's perspective but also from the perspective of commercial speech laws. Among other allegations, it was claimed that Nike was consciously misleading the public when it claimed that workers in its factories were being paid in accordance with minimum wage laws, that they were being paid substantially more than the minimum wage, and that they received free/subsidized meals and health services. The decision of the California Supreme Court in 2002 went against Nike, and the company was held accountable for its deceptive public statements regarding its labor practices. Nike appealed to the U.S. Supreme Court, but the case was sent back to the San Francisco District Court of Appeals. Faced with the prospect of extended litigation, Nike agreed to settle with Kasky. The settlement included $1.5 million to be paid over three years to the Fair Labor Association—a worker rights–monitoring group in Washington, DC—and $500,000 a year to subsidize entrepreneurial ventures of foreign employees and forums in Nike's factories. Nike officials stated that settling was the correct choice because the focus was on benefits to workers and to Nike's commitment of corporate responsibility.

Nike Recovers and Excels in Managing Social Responsibility

The company has been making numerous changes, learning that an open-minded approach to the issues facing its industry is better than denial. As part of this evolution, Nike has moved away from focusing on its own code of conduct and toward creating a standard code of conduct throughout the industry.

As part of the new Nike, they have moved beyond its old monitoring systems and employ three different types in its factories. First, it uses the SHAPE inspection to determine basic compliance to regulations regarding environment, safety, and health. Nike's field-based production staff generally performs this inspection. The second method is the Management Audit (M-Audit). Nike hired twenty-one staff members and trained them in labor-auditing practices. The M-Audit, an in-depth inspection, is designed to uncover problems that may not be readily obvious. Finally, Nike encourages independent monitoring by the Fair Labor Association. Nike now has a compliance team composed of over ninety people in twenty-one countries.

Nike has also opened the doors of a number of its contract factories to research groups from the Sloan School of Management at the Massachusetts Institute of Technology who are studying the business drivers and outcomes. The company hopes that through this research it can learn more about the business process and how to better manage production flow and work hours in its factories. Nike has also implemented the balanced scorecard, a lettered grading system, to better assess factory compliance with the code of conduct. This system gives the company a reliable method for rewarding high-performance, compliant factories. The balanced scorecard is also used to help Nike avoid pushing factories in one direction to the detriment of others; for example, the card measures cost, delivery, and quality, and all need to be addressed equally for production to flow smoothly.

In addition to building up its monitoring processes, Nike is now disclosing its contract factory base. Doing so is part of the corporate movement toward transparency. By disclosing its supply chain, Nike believes it can be more successful at monitoring and at making changes, not only in its own factories but also industrywide, once issues have been uncovered. Nike hopes that by disclosing its own supply chain it can encourage other companies to do the same. It hopes to standardize a code of conduct followed by all companies and factories in the industry. Nike also feels that transparency should work as a motivator for contract factories. Those with high compliance rankings can be confident that business will come their way.

Another part of Nike's evolution is finding new production methods to avoid the toxic chemicals typically used to make their products. It is also coming up with innovative ways to recycle old shoes and to create products made of recycled polyester or organic cotton. Nike has become more aware of its impact on the environment and is taking steps to make this impact a better one.

Although challenging, putting corporate responsibility at the forefront of Nike's business is a positive move. The company is learning to deliver equal value to its five different stakeholder groups: consumers, shareholders, business partners, employees, and the community. With a focus on corporate responsibility, Nike hopes to build and improve its relationships with consumers, achieve a high-quality supply chain, and create top quality, innovative products. Although this evolution is a difficult one filled with lessons learned along the way, employees worldwide and the company itself are reaping the benefits.

As part of a movement toward corporate responsibility, Knight stepped down as CEO in 2004 although he still is chairman of the board. His reason was to put someone in who was an expert in corporate responsibility. Bill Perez was hired as the new CEO, based on his track record in this area and a belief that companies must invest in and improve the communities in which they coexist. In 2006 Nike veteran Mark Parker, formerly copresident, took over as CEO and director. Parker, who has been with Nike for twenty-seven years, has been part of most of Nike's top innovative plans and is recognized as a product visionary.

As a result of the changes, Nike appeared in *Business Ethics* magazine's "100 Best Corporate Citizens" list for 2005 and 2006. It entered the list in 2005 at number thirty-one and climbed to number thirteen in 2006. *Business Ethics* cites its reasons for listing Nike as the strength of Nike's commitment to community and environment. Nike was actually ranked number one in the magazine's environmental category due to its efforts to eliminate waste and toxic substances from production processes. Nike also made *Fortune* magazine's "100 Best Companies to Work For" list for the first time in 2006, coming in at number 100 and has received a perfect score on the Human Rights Campaign Foundation's Corporate Equality Index two years in a row. Although Nike admits that it has a long way to go, it is being rewarded for its efforts along the way, both by positive results and industry response.

Questions

1. What were Nike's mistakes in handling the negative publicity?

2. Discuss the intent of their public relations tactics.

3. Do you think Nike is doing enough to improve conditions in its contract factories? What might they do differently or better?

4. How would you rank Nike's improvements?

Sources

Academics Studying the Athletic and Campus Apparel Industry, "Academics Studying Nike," maintained by David M. Boje, PhD, updated January 2006, http://business.nmsu.edu/~dboje/nike/nikemain1.html (accessed May 17, 2006); "Business Ethics Magazine Lists "100 Best Corporate Citizens for 2006," Nike, http://www.nike.com/nikebiz/nikebiz.jhtml?page=59&item=tppr&year=2006&release=05a (accessed May 16, 2006); James Ciment, ed., "The Promise and Perils of Globalization: The Case of Nike," in *Social Issues in America: An Encyclopedia* (Armonk, NY: Sharpe, 2006); Ronald K. L. Collins and David M. Skover, "Symposium: *Nike v. Kasky* and the Modern Commercial Speech," June 2004, via http://www.law.seattleu.edu/fachome/skover/articles/nike/ (accessed May 17, 2006); Tim Connor, "Still Waiting for Nike to Do It; Nike's Labor Practices in the Three Years Since CEO Phil Knight's Speech to the National Press Club," Global Exchange, 2001, via http://www.cleanclothes.org/ftp/01-05NikeReport.pdf (accessed July 14, 2006); John H. Cushman, Jr., "Nike Pledges to End Child Labor and Apply U.S. Rules Abroad," *New York Times,* May 13, 1998, via http://www.corpwatch.org/article.php?id=12965 (accessed July 14, 2006); Tony Emerson, "Swoosh Wars: In an Operation Modeled on the Clinton Campaign Machine, Nike Takes on Its Enemies," *Newsweek International,* March 12, 2001, http://www.msu.edu/~jdowell/pdf/SwooshWars.pdf (accessed July 14, 2006); "Evolution: Shifting Our Approach to Labor Compliance," Nike website, updated April 2005, http://www.nike.com/nikebiz/nikebiz.jhtml?page=25&cat=approach (accessed May 16, 2006); Bob Herbert, "In America: Nike's Pyramid Scheme," *New York Times,* June 10, 1996, via http://www.geocities.com/Athens/Acropolis/5232/NYT061096.htm (accessed July 14, 2006); Holman W. Jenkins, Jr., "The Rise and Stumble of Nike," *Wall Street Journal,* June 3, 1998, A6; Jackie Krentzman, "The Force Behind the Nike Empire," *Stanford Magazine* online, http://www.stanfordalumni.org/news/magazine/1997/janfeb/articles/knight.html (accessed May 17, 2006); "Labors' Pains," PBS online, April 14, 1997, http://www.pbs.org/newshour/bb/business/jan-june97/sweatshops_4-14.html (accessed May 17, 2006); "A Letter from Nike Brand's Presidents: Three Areas of Focus for the Future," Nike website, updated April 2005, http://www.nike.com/nikebiz/nikebiz.jhtml?page=54&item=direction (accessed May 16, 2006); "A Message from Phil Knight," Nike website, updated April 2005, http://www.nike.com/nikebiz/nikebiz.jhtml?page=54&item=letter (accessed May 16, 2006);

"Nike-Funded Study Claims Workers at Nike's Indonesian Factories Are Subject to Abuse and Harassment," Institute for Global Ethics, *Ethics Newsline,* February 26, 2001, http://www.globalethics.org/newsline/members/issue.tmpl?articleid=02260116252837 (accessed May 17, 2006); "Nike, Inc. Names Mark Parker CEO, William D. Perez Resigns," Nike press release, January 23, 2006, http://www.nike.com/nikebiz/news/pressrelease.jhtml?year=2006&month=01&letter=d (accessed May 17, 2006); "Niketimeline" and "Highlights," Nike website, http://www.nike.com/nikebiz/media/nike_timeline/nike_timeline.pdf (accessed May 17, 2006); "Workers in Contract Factories," Corporate Responsibility Report 2004, Nike website, http://www.nike.com/nikebiz/gc/r/fy04/docs/workers_factories.pdf (accessed May 16, 2006); "The World's Billionaires, 2006: "#70 Philip Knight," *Forbes* online, March 9, 2006, http://www.forbes.com/lists/2006/10/2KZ5.html (accessed May 17, 2006); Matt Zwolinski, "In the News: International (Global) Business Ethics," *BizEd* online, April 15, 2005, http://www.bized.ac.uk/dataserv/chron/news/2331.htm (accessed May 17, 2006).

Wal-Mart: The Challenge of Managing Relationships with Stakeholders

Wal-Mart Stores Inc.—the world's largest corporation—is possibly the most controversial business in America. With sales over $312 billion in 2006 and approximately 1.7 million employees worldwide (of these, 1.3 million are U.S. employees), managing stakeholder relationships is a major challenge. The Wal-Mart that saves the average family an estimated $2329 per year has its critics. There are concerns about Wal-Mart's treatment of employees, suppliers, the environment, and the overall economic impact on communities. Feminists, human rights activists, antisprawl activists, and labor unions believe that Wal-Mart has engaged in misconduct to provide low prices to consumers. The company that banishes magazines with racy covers and CDs with edgy lyrics is seen as attempting to dictate its vision of American culture.

Wal-Mart claims that it is committed to improving the standard of living for their customers throughout the world. The key strategy is a broad assortment of quality merchandise and services at everyday low prices (EDLP) while fostering a culture that claims to reward and embrace mutual respect, integrity, and diversity. Wal-Mart has three basic beliefs: respect for the individual, service to their customers, and striving for excellence. How well the firm implements these beliefs is the focus of this case.

Wal-Mart, one of the most amazing success stories in the history of American business, has also shaped debate over the relationships between corporations and their stakeholders. Wal-Mart has excelled at market orientation, which is focusing on consumers, defeating competitors, and increasing shareholder value. Only recently has shareholder value lagged behind the major stock market–index performance. Other stakeholders such as employees, suppliers, and communities have been viewed as secondary to low prices for consumers. For example, the *Fortune* 100 best companies to work for does not include Wal-Mart. Number one in 2005 and number two in 2006 on the *Fortune* list was Wegmans Food Markets, with the very unusual motto of employees first and customers second. Starbucks with its generous employee benefits, even for part timers, was number two in 2005 but dropped to twenty-ninth in 2006.

The story of Wal-Mart and its low prices shows both good and bad outcomes for society. The company has grown from a small chain to over five thousand stores in ten countries, making its early investors and some employees financially successful. It has been estimated that Wal-Mart saves consumers $100,000 billion a year. Wal-Mart's entrance into some markets lowers food prices 25 percent, including savings from competitors' price cuts. As competing supermarkets close, their union employees sometimes lose their jobs. One study found that total payroll wages per person declined by almost 5 percent where Wal-Mart stores are located due to Wal-Mart driving down wages. In

This case was prepared by Melanie Drever, University of Wyoming, under the direction of O. C. Ferrell, for classroom discussion rather than to illustrate either effective or ineffective handling of an administrative, ethical, or legal decision by management. All sources used for this case were obtained through publicly available material and the Wal-Mart website.

2005 an internal document made public by Wal-Mart Watch showed that 46 percent of Wal-Mart employees' children were on Medicaid or uninsured. Michael Hicks, an economist at the Air Force Institute of Technology found that Wal-Mart increased Medicaid costs an average of $1,898 per worker. Armed with these alleged facts, the Maryland General Assembly passed the "Wal-Mart Bill" requiring employers with more than 10,000 workers to spend at least 8 percent of their payroll on employee health care or pay into a fund for the uninsured. Wal-Mart is challenging the law, which goes into effect in 2007. Sarah Clark, a Wal-Mart spokesperson, was quoted in *USA Today:* "Wal-Mart does believe that everyone should have access to affordable healthcare, and this legislation adds nothing to accomplish this goal." The debate goes on with the question of the real costs to society for low prices.

HISTORY AND GROWTH OF WAL-MART

Wal-Mart's principal offices are in Bentonville, Arkansas. In 1945 in Newport, Arkansas, Sam Walton, the store's founder, opened a franchise Ben Franklin variety store. In 1946 his brother opened a similar store in Versailles, Missouri. Until 1962 the business was devoted entirely to the operation of variety stores. In 1962 the first Wal-Mart Discount City was opened, which was the first Wal-Mart discount store. In 1984 the first three Sam's Clubs were opened, and in 1988 the first supercenter opened. In 1999 the first neighborhood market was opened. Today the family of Wal-Mart founder Sam Walton has a combined fortune estimated at $90 billion.

The Wal-Mart business model includes two main segments: Wal-Mart Stores and Sam's Clubs. The Wal-Mart Stores come in three sizes: discount stores, which are about 100,000 square feet; supercenters, which are about 187,000 square feet; and the neighborhood markets, which are about 43,000 square feet in size. Sam's Clubs are membership warehouse clubs, which average 128,000 square feet and aim to provide exceptional value on brand-name merchandise at "members only" prices for both small businesses, nonprofit organizations, and personal use, especially large families.

Wal-Mart has continued to expand from its small roots in Arkansas, opening new stores at an accelerated rate. At present, Wal-Mart operates 2,640 discount stores, 2,396 supercenters, 670 Sam's Clubs, and 435 neighborhood markets in the United States. It has continued to open new stores every year, not only in the United States but also abroad. Much of the expansion overseas has been through acquisitions of existing operations in other countries.

Over 138 million people visit Wal-Mart every week, and 84 percent of Americans have shopped at Wal-Mart in the past year. People living in households with incomes of less than $30,000 a year give Wal-Mart its highest marks, proving that those who value Wal-Mart most need Wal-Mart's low prices the most.

Wal-Mart's first international initiative started in 1992 with a 50 percent joint venture in Mexico with Cifera discount stores. In 1998 they acquired control of Cifera and changed its name to Wal-Mart de Mexico. The first international venture was so successful that today Wal-Mart has 774 stores in Mexico. In addition, the company operates stores in Argentina (11), Brazil (295), Canada (278), Germany (88), South Korea (16), Puerto Rico (54), and the United Kingdom (315). Their joint ventures in China and Japan provide Wal-Mart with over 450 stores.

Wal-Mart became the largest grocery chain in 2002 with revenue larger than Safeway and Albertson's combined. It became the first retailer to be number one on the *Fortune* 500 list as the largest company in the United States with sales over $300 billion; in 2006 it topped the *Fortune* 500 list again. Sales climbed 10 percent in 2005, and profits rose 13 percent to more than $10 billion. In addition to being number one on the *Fortune* 500, Wal-Mart was also named the "most admired company in America" in 2003 and 2004; in 2005, however, it slipped and ranked fourth on the list behind Dell, General Electric, and Starbucks; in 2006 it was ranked twelfth. Wal-Mart is the world's largest retailer as well as the largest employer.

RELATIONSHIPS WITH SUPPLIER STAKEHOLDERS

Wal-Mart is focused on keeping its costs low for its EDLP. It does this by streamlining its company and insisting its suppliers do the same. Wal-Mart is well known for its operational excellence in its ability to handle, move, and track merchandise, and it expects its suppliers to continually improve their systems too. It demands that its suppliers consistently lower prices of products from one year to the next by at least 5 percent; if a supplier is unwilling or unable to do so, Wal-Mart will no longer carry the product or will find another supplier for the product at the price they want.

Technology is a driving force in operational efficiency that lowers costs. The merchandise-tracking system—radio-frequency identification (RFID)—ensures that a product can be tracked from the time it leaves the supplier's warehouse to the time it enters and leaves a Wal-Mart store. In 2004 Wal-Mart insisted that its top 100 suppliers ensure that all their pallets and products being shipped to Wal-Mart had RFID by January 2005. The cost to suppliers was much larger than the cost to Wal-Mart because suppliers needed to continually buy the RFID tags while all Wal-Mart needed was a system to read the tags. It has been estimated that the cost to one supplier could be $9 million to install and implement the RFID technology. Smaller Wal-Mart suppliers also have to install the tags, but they had until 2006 to comply.

RFID tags help Wal-Mart keep their shelves stocked and curbs the loss of retail products as they travel through the supply chain. RFID at Wal-Mart has directly resulted in a 16 percent reduction in stock-outs and a 67 percent drop in replenishment times. As customers go through checkout, the RFID system swiftly combines point-of-sale data on their purchases with RFID-generated data on what's available in the stockroom to produce pick lists that are automatically created in real time, based on sales. It also ensures that suppliers are notified when products are sold and can ensure that enough of a product is always at a particular store. This strategy also results in time and labor savings because associates (as employees are called at Wal-Mart) no longer need to scan store shelves to determine what is out of stock, nor do they have to scan cartons and cases arriving at the stockroom. The scanners tag incoming pallets and translate the data into supply chain–management database-forecasting models to address out-of-stock items and reduce stock–restocking mix-ups.

The power Wal-Mart has over its suppliers has more to do with its size and the volume of products it needs than anything else. For example, Dial Corporation does 28 percent of its business with Wal-Mart. If it lost that one account, it would have to double its sales to its next nine customers just to stay even. Other companies that depend on Wal-Mart for sales are Clorox, which does 23 percent of its business with Wal-Mart;

Revlon, 22 percent; Proctor & Gamble, 17 percent; Kraft Foods, 12 percent; General Mills, 12 percent; and Kellogg, 12 percent. This ensures that Wal-Mart can dictate terms to its vendors rather than the other way around. However, there are benefits to suppliers because they become more efficient and streamlined, which helps their other customers too, as they improve their system for Wal-Mart.

Many companies believe that supplying Wal-Mart is the best thing for their business; there are the few, however, who believe that Wal-Mart is hurting their business and decide to no longer do business with them. An example of this is Snapper, a company with a 50-year heritage of making high-quality residential and commercial lawn equipment. CEO Jim Weir believed that Wal-Mart was incompatible with the company's strategy of high quality and, compared to Wal-Mart's typical lawn mowers, high prices. He felt that the long-term survival of the company meant that he should no longer sell to Wal-Mart. Wal-Mart tried to convince him that making a low-cost version of Snapper mowers specifically for Wal-Mart would be a good compromise, as Levi's did with their Levi's Signature brand made specifically for the Wal-Mart market. However, Weir would have none of it.

Weir said no to Wal-Mart and told his other customers about the decision. Wal-Mart accounted for 20 percent of his business, but he wanted to focus more on the other 80 percent of the independent dealers. The other dealers were happy with Weir's decision, and Snapper recouped much of the lost business from the independent dealers by winning their hearts.

The constant drive by Wal-Mart for lower prices affects its suppliers in a more ominous way too. Many suppliers have had to move production from the United States to cheaper locations, such as China, to remain suppliers to Wal-Mart and maintain their business. Wal-Mart imports over $18 billion dollars worth of goods from China and encourages its suppliers to move their production operations to China to systematically lower cost. China and Wal-Mart have developed a unique partnership, and Wal-Mart accounts for 10 percent of the U.S. trade deficit with China. China's annual exports amount to $583 billion, and Wal-Mart ranks as China's eighth-largest trading partner, ahead of Australia, Canada, and Russia. Rubbermaid, once *Fortune*'s most admired company, has gone out of business, and much of its manufacturing equipment was sold to a Chinese company. Although the Rubbermaid brand name lives on, former Rubbermaid managers claim that the low prices that Wal-Mart demanded, including their reluctance to allow Rubbermaid to increase prices when the cost of raw materials increased, caused them to close and sell to a competitor. Companies such as Master Lock, Fruit of the Loom, and Levi's—as well as many other Wal-Mart suppliers—have all moved production overseas at the expense of U.S. jobs and all in the name of low prices for consumers.

ETHICAL ISSUES INVOLVING WAL-MART STAKEHOLDERS

Employee Stakeholders

DISCRIMINATION The U.S. Equal Employment Opportunity Commission (EEOC) has filed fifteen lawsuits against Wal-Mart since 1994. Of these, ten are still pending, and five have been resolved.

FEMALE EMPLOYEES Although women account for more than 67 percent of all Wal-Mart employees, women make up less than 10 percent of top-store managers. Wal-Mart insists that it adequately trains and promotes women, but in 2001 a Wal-Mart executive conducted an internal study that showed the company paid female store managers less than men in the same position.

In June 2004, a federal judge in San Francisco granted class-action status to a sex-discrimination lawsuit against Wal-Mart. It is the largest class-action lawsuit and involves 1.6 million current and former female employees at Wal-Mart. It claims that Wal-Mart discriminated against women in promotions, pay, training, and job assignments. Even Wal-Mart concludes in its annual report that if the company is not successful in its appeal of the class-action certification of the case, the resulting liability could be material to the company.

DISABLED EMPLOYEES In January 2000, Wal-Mart agreed to pay two deaf applicants $132,500. The two applied to work at a Wal-Mart in Tucson, Arizona, but were denied employment because of their disabilities. Wal-Mart agreed to hire the two men as part of the settlement and to make corporate-wide changes in the hiring and training of new employees who are deaf or hearing impaired. However, in June 2001, for failure to comply with the original court order, Wal-Mart

was fined $750,200, ordered to produce and air a TV ad stating that it had violated the Americans with Disabilities Act (ADA), reinstate William Darnell (one of the disabled workers), and create computer-based learning modules in American Sign Language and provide ADA training.

Another EEOC case took place in December 2001. The lawsuit alleged that Wal-Mart's preemployment questionnaire "Matrix of Essential Job Functions" violated the ADA, and the EEOC resolved the suit with a $6.8 million consent decree. In 2002 Wal-Mart agreed to pay $220,000 for rejecting a pregnant applicant. In February 2005, Wal-Mart paid a $7.5-million jury-verdict fine to a disabled former employee in a class-action lawsuit.

SWEATSHOP WORKERS Another class-action lawsuit accuses Wal-Mart Stores Inc. of failing to monitor labor conditions at overseas factories that allegedly maintained sweatshop conditions. The plaintiffs are fifteen workers in Bangladesh, Swaziland, Indonesia, China, and Nicaragua who claim they were paid below minimum wage in their country, forced to work unpaid overtime, and in some cases even endured beatings by supervisors. It also includes four California workers who claim that Wal-Mart's entry into southern California forced their employers to reduce pay and benefits. The lawsuit could cover a class of anywhere from one hundred thousand to five hundred thousand workers.

ILLEGAL IMMIGRANTS In October 2003, federal officials raided Wal-Mart stores across the United States and arrested 250 illegal immigrants working on cleaning crews at sixty-one stores in twenty-one states. The undocumented workers were from Mexico, eastern Europe, and other countries and were employed by several contractors used by Wal-Mart.

The investigation by the U.S. Immigration and Customs Enforcement evolved out of two earlier immigration probes in 1988 and 2001 and ended in March 2005 with a landmark $11 million civil settlement. Twelve corporations that provided janitorial services to Wal-Mart stores agreed to forfeit an additional $4 million and to enter corporate guilty pleas to criminal immigration charges.

However, according to a *Wall Street Journal* article in November 2005, three top Wal-Mart executives knew that its cleaning contractors used illegal immigrants who worked as many as seven days a week for less than the minimum wage. The executives allegedly encouraged the cleaning contractor to make "shells" of the company so that they could continue to hire the contractor if one of the companies was closed for hiring illegal workers. (Shell companies are created for hiding something either illegal or unethical. The company is called a shell because outsiders see it as a company, but in reality, many are just mail drops.)

Even after agreeing to make sure that no people working for Wal-Mart were illegal immigrants, another raid by federal, state, and local authorities in November 2005 netted 125 illegal immigrants. The illegal immigrants were arrested at a Wal-Mart construction site. The workers had been building a 1 million-square-foot distribution center in eastern Pennsylvania. In December 2005, another 14 illegal immigrants were arrested while installing shelves at one of Wal-Mart's distribution centers in Nebraska.

LOW BENEFITS To work full time at Wal-Mart, an employee works a minimum of just 28 hours. Although wages tend to be higher than minimum wage, the few hours that employees are allowed to work ensures that associates can barely cover living expenses. This means that the taxpayer has to pay the difference. According to "The Case Against Wal-Mart," a typical Wal-Mart store with two hundred employees costs federal taxpayers $420,750 per year— about $2103 per employee. This pays for free and reduced lunches for Wal-Mart families, housing assistance, federal tax credits and deductions for low-income families, additional child tax credits, federal health-care costs of moving into state children's health insurance programs, and low-income energy assistance (electric and gas bills).

Wal-Mart fails to provide health insurance to more than 60 percent of its employees. Part-time employees are excluded from Wal-Mart's health program, and the company has an extra-long waiting period before employees become eligible for its health-care program. Even then, many are not eligible if they work part-time, and those who are covered are underinsured. For employees who can get coverage, the deductibles can be prohibitively high for such low-income families, who then have to pay for most of the expenses themselves.

In a leaked Wal-Mart memo to the board of directors, Susan Chambers, Wal-Mart's executive vice president for benefits, described how 46 percent of Wal-Mart employees are uninsured or on Medicaid.

The memo detailed how Wal-Mart's health plan requires such high out-of-pocket payments that the small number of employees hit by a very costly illness "almost certainly end up declaring personal bankruptcy." The memo also proposed that Wal-Mart rewrite job descriptions to involve more physical activity, in part to "dissuade unhealthy people from coming to work at Wal-Mart."

Another influence of Wal-Mart is the downward pressure on wages and benefits in towns when Wal-Mart enters the area. To compete against the retail giant, other stores in the area reduce their wages by about 3.5 percent. Overall payroll wages including Wal-Mart wages are reduced by 5 percent. But even with the decrease in wages, many stores still go out of business, causing many local residents to lose their jobs. According to the advocacy group Good Jobs First, Wal-Mart has received more than $1 billion in public subsidies just for building its stores (not counting the cost to state and local governments of picking up health-care costs of Wal-Mart employees).

WORKING CONDITIONS In December 2005, Wal-Mart was ordered to pay $172 million to more than one hundred thousand California employees in a class-action lawsuit that claimed that Wal-Mart routinely denied workers meal breaks. California has a law that requires a thirty-minute meal break within the first five hours of a shift or an extra hour's pay. The employees also allege that they were denied rest breaks and that Wal-Mart managers deliberately altered timecards to keep people from earning overtime. Hours were regularly deleted from time records, and employees were reprimanded for claiming overtime. Another similar case in New Mexico and Colorado in 2000 ended with Wal-Mart reportedly paying $50 million to sixty-seven thousand employees.

According to www.WalMartFacts.com, forty pending wage-and-hour cases are currently seeking class certification. Wal-Mart states that any manager who requires or even tolerates "off-the-clock" work would be violating policy and labor laws.

UNIONS Germany is the only place where Wal-Mart employees currently are unionized. Employees in German Wal-Mart stores have thirty-six days of vacation a year and are paid overtime. Wal-Mart has, according to some sources, spent a considerable amount of money and resources on ensuring that Wal-Mart employees in the United States and the other fifteen countries in which it does business do not unionize. It has been alleged that when the word *union* surfaces in a Wal-Mart, the top dogs in Bentonville are called and action is taken immediately to thwart any union movements:

- In a Wal-Mart store in Loveland, Colorado, some employees in the Tire and Lube Express wanted to unionize. Wal-Mart found ways, according to some workers, to intimidate and brainwash its employees to pressure the few pro-union employees. Wal-Mart also hired more workers for the Tire and Lube Express to dilute the numbers who would vote for the union. The pressure ensured that once again Wal-Mart did not become unionized.

- In 2000, when seven of ten butchers in a store in Jacksonville, Texas, voted to join the United Food Workers Union, Wal-Mart responded by announcing that henceforth it would sell only precut meat in all of its supercenters, fired four of the union supporters, and transferred the rest into other divisions.

- In Canada, the United Food and Commercial Workers organized a Jonquiere, Quebec, Wal-Mart in 2004. In 2005 the retailer closed the store, claiming it was losing money and that union demands would prevent it from becoming profitable.

Wal-Mart is now facing a tough decision in China. If it wants to continue its growth into China, it might have to accept a union. According to some reports, employees in Chinese Wal-Marts were warned against speaking with trade-union officials during working hours. Poor working conditions in China and low wages are generating social unrest, and the government is trying to craft a new set of labor laws that give workers greater protection. These laws are likely to give greater power to the All-China Federation of Trade Unions. Whether Wal-Mart is forced to accept a union remains to be seen. As for Sam Walton, Wal-Mart's founder, he believed that unions were a divisive force and would make the company uncompetitive.

ETHICAL LEADERSHIP ISSUES: THOMAS COUGHLIN In January 2005, Thomas Coughlin, vice chairman of Wal-Mart Stores Inc., resigned but remained on the Wal-Mart board of directors. At one time as vice chairman—the second-highest-ranking executive at Wal-Mart—he was a candidate to become CEO. Coughlin was a legend at Wal-Mart—a protégé and hunting buddy of Sam Walton. Coughlin would often spend a week on the road with Walton as they expanded Sam's Clubs. His compensation was over $6 million in 2004.

In March 2005, Coughlin was forced to resign from the board of directors for stealing as much as $500,000 from Wal-Mart in the form of bogus expenses and reimbursements, along with the unauthorized use of gift cards. Coughlin had worked at Wal-Mart for twenty-seven years, five of them as the second-most-powerful executive at the company. The case created new concerns about leadership, corporate governance, and the ethical culture of Wal-Mart.

In January 2006, Coughlin pled guilty to federal wire-fraud and tax-evasion charges. Although Coughlin took home millions of dollars in compensation, he secretly had Wal-Mart pay for some of his personal expenses, including hunting vacations, a $2590 dog enclosure at his home, and a $1359 pair of handmade alligator boots.

Coughlin's deceit was discovered when he asked a lieutenant to approve $2000 in expense payments without any receipts. Jared Bowen, a Wal-Mart vice president, says Coughlin mentioned that the money was for the union project. Coughlin claims that he told the Wal-Mart board of directors that he was using money for anti-union activities, including paying union staffers to identify pro-union workers in Wal-Mart stores. Wal-Mart issued statements that there were no anti-union activities and the funds were misappropriated for Coughlin's personal use. Paying union staffers to identify pro-union workers would be a criminal offense under the Taft-Hartley Act. The following day after Bowen reported the alleged misconduct, Wal-Mart fired him. As a whistle-blower on the expense-payment abuses, he could not understand why he was fired. He said that Wal-Mart officials indicated that "he wasn't forthcoming" and there was "a general lack of confidence." Bowen has asked federal prosecutors to investigate whether the company violated corporate whistle-blowing laws in his firing. In the meantime, Wal-Mart has rescinded Coughlin's retirement agreement, worth more than $10 million. Coughlin faces up to twenty-eight years in prison after pleading guilty to five counts of wire fraud and one count of filing a false tax return. He could also be fined $1.35 million. Wal-Mart spokesperson Mona Williams says the experience has been "embarrassing and painful.

Someone we expected to operate with the highest integrity let us down in a very public way."

Environmental Stakeholders

The Environmental Protection Agency (EPA) and the states of Tennessee and Utah allege that Wal-Mart and some of its construction contractors violated the EPA's stormwater regulations at specified sites around the country. Wal-Mart settled the dispute without admitting any wrongdoing or violations of the regulations by paying a $3.1 million civil penalty and agreeing to implement a Supplemental Environmental Project valued at $250,000.

In 2001 the state of Connecticut filed suit against Wal-Mart for violations of state environmental laws and for failing to obtain the appropriate permits or to maintain the required records relating to stormwater-management practices at twelve stores. In 2003 the state also filed an amended complaint alleging that Wal-Mart also discharged wastewater associated with vehicle maintenance activities and photo-processing activities without proper permits. The company settled these suits without admitting any wrongdoing or violations of the regulations by paying $1.5 million and implementing new compliance procedures.

The EPA has alleged that Wal-Mart violated certain air-quality restrictions at various locations in Massachusetts and Connecticut, including state and local restrictions on the amount of time that truck engines are allowed to idle. Wal-Mart settled those allegations by agreeing to pay a $50,000 civil penalty, to implement new compliance procedures, and to implement a Supplemental Environmental Project valued at $100,000.

The district attorneys for Solano County and Orange County, California, allege that the Wal-Mart store in Vacaville failed to comply with certain California statutes regulating hazardous waste– and hazardous materials–handling practices: specifically, that Wal-Mart improperly disposed of a limited amount of damaged or returned product containing dry granular fertilizer and pesticides on or about April 3, 2002, and January 24, 2005. The cases have not yet been settled.

In another environmental case, the EPA alleges that Wal-Mart and one of its construction contractors violated EPA stormwater regulations at a site in Caguas, Puerto Rico. The administrative complaint filed by the agency proposes an administrative penalty in the amount of $157,500. The parties are currently negotiating toward a resolution of this matter.

In November 2005, Wal-Mart received a grand jury subpoena from the U.S. Attorney's Office in Los Angeles seeking documents and information relating to the company's receipt, transportation, handling, identification, recycling, treatment, storage, and disposal of certain merchandise that constitutes hazardous materials or hazardous waste. Wal-Mart also received administrative document requests from the California Department of Toxic Substances Control requesting similar documents and information with respect to two of the company's distribution facilities. California local government authorities and the state of Nevada have also initiated investigations into this matter. The company is cooperating fully with the respective authorities.

Many activists are concerned about urban sprawl created by Wal-Mart stores. The construction of a Wal-Mart supercenter can stress a city's infrastructure of roads, parking, and traffic flows. In addition, there are concerns about the number of acres of green space in a city that can be devoured by Wal-Mart's construction of a new store. Another issue is the number of stores that Wal-Mart deserts after it outgrows the small discount stores and moves to a new supercenter location. There are over 26 million square feet of empty Wal-Marts, enough empty space to fill 534 football fields. The annual number of empty Wal-Marts is between 350 and 400 per year. It has been alleged that Wal-Mart goes out of its way to prevent other retail stores from buying its abandoned stores, especially competitors like Target.

WHAT IS WAL-MART DOING TO IMPROVE ITS REPUTATION?

Global Ethics Office

The Global Ethics Office was established on June 1, 2004. On June 4, 2004, Wal-Mart released a revised "Global Statement of Ethics" to communicate their ethical standards to all Wal-Mart facilities and stakeholders. The Global Ethics Office provides guidance in making ethical decisions based on the "Global Statement of Ethics" and a process for anonymous reporting of suspected ethics violation by calling the Ethics Helpline. The Ethics Helpline provides an anonymous and confidential way for associates to contact the company regarding ethical issues. Wal-Mart's "Guiding

Ethical Principles," added to the revised "Global State-ment of Ethics," were designed to assist Wal-Mart associates and suppliers with making the right decision and doing the right thing:

1. Follow the law at all times.

2. Be honest and fair.

3. Never manipulate, misrepresent, abuse, or conceal information.

4. Avoid conflicts of interest between work and personal affairs.

5. Never discriminate against anyone.

6. Never act unethically—even if someone else instructs you to do so.

7. Never ask someone to act unethically.

8. Seek assistance if you have questions about the "Statement of Ethics" or if you face an ethical dilemma.

9. Cooperate with any investigation of a possible ethics violation.

10. Report ethics violations or suspected violations.

Environment

Although Wal-Mart has recycling locations at each of its stores, it has tied itself to other initiatives over the past couple of years to improve its environmental impact.

EXPERIMENTAL STORES Wal-Mart opened two environmentally friendly stores—one in McKinney, Texas, and the other in Aurora, Colorado. The two locations were chosen because they have different weather and climate considerations. The stores should provide examples of the way that building owners, scientists, engineers, architects, contractors, and land-scape designers can work together to create stores that save energy, conserve natural resources, and reduce pollution. The stores are living laboratories, testing experimental technologies and products. Wal-Mart hopes to take what is learned at these two stores and use that at future stores.

The new stores include pervious pavement, experimental urban forest, water conservation, wildflower meadows, wind turbines, solar energy, recycling efforts, climate control, xeriscape and bioswale

(proenvironmental landscaping methods), and internal lighting and construction experiments.

WAL-MART ACRES FOR AMERICA In 2005 Wal-Mart partnered with the National Fish and Wildlife Foundation to conserve critical wildlife habitats for future generations. It has committed $35 million for the next ten years to conserve at least one acre of priority wildlife habitat for every acre developed for company use. This puts the minimum total acres to be protected at 138,000.

ENERGY CONSERVATION MEASURES There are three main ways that Wal-Mart is conserving energy:

- *Daylighting* (skylights/dimming): Most new stores include this feature, which enables the stores to dim or turn off lights as daylight increases and enters through the skylights, thereby reducing the demand for electricity during peak hours.

- *Heating* and *cooling:* The heating and cooling of Wal-Mart stores in the contiguous fory-eight states is centrally controlled in Bentonville, Arkansas, enabling Wal-Mart to actively control and manage energy consumption.

LIGHTING EFFICIENCY PROGRAM All new Wal-Mart stores and supercenters use T-8 low-mercury fluorescent lamps and electronic ballasts, a very efficient lighting system. By retrofitting older stores with T-8 lighting rather than the T-12 systems, the amount of energy used by each store will be reduced by approximately 15 percent. Wal-Mart started retrofitting its older stores in 2000 and plans to have completed the process by 2007.

PLASTIC SANDWICH BALE Wal-Mart partnered with Rocky Mountain Recycling in 2005 and introduced an innovation in the solid-waste and recycling industry. The Plastic Sandwich Bale is a new way to use existing equipment to reduce store waste. Plastic shopping bags, film from apparel bags, and shrink-wrap are "sandwiched" between layers of cardboard and then compacted for ease of plastic recovery within the store and transportation to end markets. From 2001 to 2006, Wal-Mart facilities in the United States recycled 36,378 tons of plastic. In 2004 it launched a pilot program in 326 stores in Arizona, California, Colorado,

Idaho, Montana, Nevada, New Mexico, Oregon, Utah, and Wyoming. It is proving to be a huge success and is keeping 5,376 tons of plastic out of landfills per year.

KIDS RECYCLING CHALLENGE Wal-Mart introduced a recycling challenge for schools and children, which ran until May 2005. Over thirty-five schools participated, and for each sixty-gallon bag of plastic bags, schools received $5 from Wal-Mart. In the first six months of the program, over two thousand bags of bags were collected, and Wal-Mart gave over $28,000 to schools. The program was such a success that Wal-Mart has extended it, hoping to do it every school year.

2005 WASTE NEWS ENVIRONMENTAL AWARD Wal-Mart won the 2005 *Waste News* Environmental Award. The *Waste News* editor stated that Wal-Mart had made the most significant environmental progress of any business in 2005.

IMPROVING ITS IMAGE AMONG CUSTOMERS

In 2005 Wal-Mart introduced a website (www. Wal-MartFacts.com) to counter claims made by its critics. The website has information about the litigation that Wal-Mart faces and what it thinks about the claims and lawsuits as well as information about the actions it is taking to help the environment. There are sections on community impact, an associate center, key topics, "Do You Know?" and "Talk with Us," as well as a list of all the awards and recognition that Wal-Mart has received. All of this is aimed at reducing misperceptions about Wal-Mart and ensuring that customers are better informed about all the "misleading" news that they hear about the retail giant.

In 2005 Wal-Mart also launched a full-page ad in more than one hundred newspapers across the country. The ad was a direct letter from Wal-Mart CEO H. Lee Scott, which said it was time for the public to hear the "unfiltered truth" about Wal-Mart and time for the company to stand up on behalf of a workforce that includes 1.2 million Americans. Scott called for Congress to increase the minimum wage and said that Wal-Mart has increased spending on health insurance for its workers. The firm says it insures six hundred thousand associates and more than three-fourths of Wal-Mart associates have health insurance.

Wal-Mart has also hired the public relations firm Hill and Knowlton and dozens of communications specialists to help it improve its overall image. This was combined with an aggressive advertising campaign publicizing the millions of dollars that Wal-Mart contributes to local community organizations, as well as focusing on other key concerns such as how Wal-Mart treats its employees and its employee diversity. Wal-mart has one of the most diverse workforces in the United States and is a leading employer of senior citizens in the United States, employing 164,000 workers aged 55 years or older. Of the fifteen board of director members, two Latinos sit alongside two women. It also employs 139,000 Hispanic associates, 208,000 African American associates, and 775,000 women. More than 76 percent of the management team at Wal-Mart started as hourly associates, and as of 2006, the Wal-Mart website reports that more than 40 percent of Wal-Mart store management are women.

WAL-MART AND THE ECONOMY

Wal-Mart is a driving force in the U.S. economy. Wal-Mart saves working families $2329 a year, on average, according to a study analyzing the national and regional economic impact of Wal-Mart. The consumer savings continue to be especially meaningful to lower-income and retired consumers. Low prices are due to Wal-Mart's higher levels of capital investment in distribution and inventory-control assets, operational excellence, advanced information technology, low import prices from China, and greater efficiency in its whole supply chain.

The study by Global Insight, an independent economic analysis firm, concluded that the efficiencies that Wal-Mart has fostered in the retail sector have led to lower prices for the U.S. consumer. The expansion of Wal-Mart over the 1985–2004 period can be associated with a cumulative decline of 9.1 percent in food-at-home prices, a 4.2 percent decline in commodities prices, and a 3.1 percent decline in overall consumer prices as measured by the Consumer Price Index. The 3.1 percent decline in prices was partially offset by a 2.2 percent decline in nominal wages, but there was still a net increase in real disposable income of 0.9 percent. Wal-Mart also created 210,000 jobs nationwide.

In Dallas, Fort Worth, and Arlington, Texas, Wal-Mart's effect has been considerable. The cost savings have been 4 percent, and Wal-Mart has provided sixty-three hundred more jobs and a 2.6 percent increase in real disposable income in the Dallas–Fort Worth area.

For a new store with about 150 to 350 employees in an area, Wal-Mart typically increases employment in the area by 137 jobs in the short term, which levels off in the long term to an increase of 97 jobs. This is due to the net job decline in food, apparel, and accessory stores but an increase in building materials, garden supply, and general merchandise store jobs. Although Wal-Mart displaces other retail establishments in the short term, it stimulates the overall development of the retail sector, which leads to an overall positive impact (in terms of retail employment) for the countries in which Wal-Mart has expanded. Wal-Mart has contributed modestly to lower import prices because it has been able to purchase imported goods for 5 percent less than traditional retailers due to the high volume and distribution efficiencies.

HURRICANE KATRINA

Wal-Mart's response to Hurricane Katrina was fast, efficient, and significant. Wal-Mart contributed $17 million in cash to the hurricane relief effort, more than $3 million in merchandise, $15 million to the Bush–Clinton Katrina Fund, $1 million to the Salvation Army, and $1 million to the American Red Cross. Wal-Mart also provided more than $8.5 million in cash assistance to impacted associates through Wal-Mart's Associate Disaster Relief Fund. They gave $20,000 in cash donations to assist various animal shelters and organizations taking in lost animals in hurricane-impacted areas. In addition, they also dispatched 2,450 Wal-Mart truckloads, donated 70 pallets of clothes to help evacuees, and set up donation centers in various shelters to help arriving evacuees needing personal health and beauty products, clothing, food, and water. For example, at the Houston Astrodome, Wal-Mart provided five trucks of relief supplies, forty-five associate volunteers, and a computer, fax machine, TV, VCR, and children's movies.

Wal-Mart donated one hundred truckloads of water and other supplies to the afflicted area. They also donated food for one hundred thousand meals and the promise of a job for every one of its displaced workers. Cliff Brumfield, executive vice president of the Brookhaven–Lincoln County Chamber of Commerce, said he was impressed with Wal-Mart's preparations: "They were ready before FEMA was." Scott, Wal-Mart's CEO, appeared on *Larry King Live* to discuss the chain's response to the storm and was singled out and praised by former Presidents George H. W. Bush and Bill Clinton.

These measures have attempted to stem the tide of negative publicity that has focused on the company. Although it has tried to address all the major concerns of its various stakeholders, only time will tell whether these measures prove effective and whether Wal-Mart can overcome the negative publicity. Consumers always vote with their money.

THE FUTURE

Wal-Mart indicates it is willing to accept the challenge of improving stakeholder relationships. The firm claims that it is being singled out because of its large size. Moves by the company to enter into the banking industry were rejected due to the banking industry's fears that the retailer would quickly dominate the field.

Wal-Mart has also faced criticism for encouraging suppliers to join a group called Working Families for America, an organization that has more than one hundred thousand members and is helping Wal-Mart counter the wave of negative publicity. But because the group is funded in part by Wal-Mart, its suppliers are worried that if they don't join they will face repercussions. Wal-Mart has denied these claims and says that suppliers who do not join will not face any adverse consequences.

There is no doubt that Wal-Mart's size and rapid growth have put it at the center of a debate about its impact on workers, unions, suppliers, local communities, competition, and the environment. Wal-Mart's push to import most of its products from China and to force its suppliers to manufacture in China creates an issue that significantly affects the U.S. economy. However, Wal-Mart is continuing to move into new areas, increasing its focus on organic foods and even moving into more expensive products for upscale clientele.

Wal-Mart remains controversial and there are different points of view. Consider these quotes:

> Some well-meaning critics believe that Wal-Mart Stores today, because of our size, should, in fact, play the role that is believed that General Motors played after World

War II. And that is to establish this post–World War middle class that the country is so proud of. . . . The facts are that retail does not perform that role in the economy.
—Wal-Mart CEO H. Lee Scott

This is one of our nation's great companies. . . . The story of Wal-Mart exemplifies some of the very best qualities in our country—hard work, the spirit of enterprise, fair dealing and integrity.
—Vice President Dick Cheney

It is extremely troubling when the vice president . . . praises a company that pays low wages and benefits, discriminates on the basis of gender, locks its own workers into stores at night, busts unions and violates child-labor laws.
—Representative George Miller (D., Calif.)

It's time for Wal-Mart to understand that their company practices run counter to the very values that make this country great—fairness, opportunity and equality.
—Senator Edward Kennedy (D., Mass.)

Questions

1. Evaluate how Wal-Mart has ranked and responded to various stakeholders.

2. Why do you think Wal-Mart has recently had a number of ethical issues that have been in the news almost constantly?

3. What do you think Wal-Mart could do to develop an improved ethical culture and respond more positively to its diverse stakeholders?

Sources

Stephanie Armour, "Maryland First to OK 'Wal-Mart Bill,'" *USA Today,* January 13, 2005, 1B; Associated Press, "Ex-Wal-Mart Vice Chairman Pleads Guilty in Fraud Case," *Wall Street Journal* online, January 31, 2006, www.online.wsj.com; James Bandler, "Former No. 2 at Wal-Mart Set to Plead Guilty," *Wall Street Journal,* January 7, 2006, A1; James Bandler and Ann Zimmerman, "A Wal-Mart Legend's Trail of Deceit," *Wall Street Journal,* April 8, 2005, A10; Michael Barbaro, "Image Effort by Wal-Mart Takes a Turn," *New York Times,* May 12, 2006, C1, C4; Michael Barbaro and Justin Gillis, "Wal-Mart at Forefront of Hurricane Relief," *Washington Post* online, September 6, 2005, www.WashingtonPost.com (accessed January 10, 2006); Matthew Boyle, "Wal-Mart Keeps the Change," *Fortune,* November 10, 2003, 46; "Buy Blue: Wal-Mart," Buy Blue, http://www.buyblue.org/node/2137/view/summary (accessed January 10, 2006); Lauren Coleman-Lochner, "Independent Look at Wal-Mart Shows Both Good and Bad. With Savings and Jobs Come Falling Wages and Rising Medicaid Costs," *[San Antonio] Express-News,* November 5, 2005, 4D; Cora Daniels, "Class Act: Women Scorned? He's on the Case," *Fortune,* September 20, 2004, 52; Kathleen Day, "Critics Fear a Wal-Mart Move into Banking Would Dominate the Industry," *Washington Post* in *The Branding Iron,* February 15, 2006, 6; "Dell Beats Wal-Mart as Most-Admired," *Fortune,* February 22, 2005, via http://money.cnn.com/2005/02/21/news/ fortune500/most_admired/index.htm; "EEOC: Wal-Mart," Equal Employment Opportunity Commission, http://search .access.gpo.gov/eeoc/SearchRight.asp?ct=eeoc&q1=wal-mart (accessed January 2005); Lauren Etter, "China: Engagement or Containment," *Wall Street Journal,* November 19–20, 2005, A5; Lauren Etter, "Gauging the Wal-Mart Effect," *Wall Street Journal,* December 3–4, 2005, A9; "Event Highlights the Wal-Mart Health Care Crisis: New Study Declares Wal-Mart in Critical Condition," WalMartWatch, November 16, 2005, http:// walmartwatch.com (accessed January 18, 2006); Jack Ewing, "Germany: Wal-Mart. Local Pipsqueek. The U.S. Giant Is Struggling in Germany Where Discounters Already Dominate," *BusinessWeek,* April 11, 2005, 54; Liza Featherstone, "Wal-Mart to the Rescue!" *The Nation* online, September 13, 2005, http://www.thenation.com/doc/20050926/featherstone (accessed January 2005); Teri Finneman, "When Wal-Mart Comes to Town; Supercenters Push into Western Minnesota, N.D.," *Forum,* August 7, 2005, via www.wakeupwalmart.com; Charles Fishman, "The Wal-Mart You Don't Know; Why Low Prices Have a High Cost," *Fast Company,* December 2003, 68–80; Charles Fishman, "The Man That Said No to Wal-Mart," *Fast Company,* January/February 2006, 66–71; Mei Fong and Ann Zimmerman, "China's Union Push Leaves Wal-Mart with Hard Choice," *Wall Street Journal,* May 13–14, 2006, A1, A6; "Global Insight Releases New Study on the Impact of Wal-Mart on the U.S. Economy," Global Insight, http://www.globalinsight.com/MultiClientStudy/ MultiClientStudyDetail2438.htm (accessed January 23, 2005); Russell Gold and Ann Zimmerman, "Papers Suggest Wal-Mart Knew of Illegal Workers," *Wall Street Journal,* November 5, 2005, A3; Marcy Gordon, "Wal-Mart's Banking Bid Opposed, Critics Worried About Safety of Local Banks," *USA Today,* April 11, 2006, B2; Lorrie Grant, "Wal-Mart Faces a New Class Action," *USA Today,* September 14, 2005, 63; Lorrie Grant, "Wal-Mart Prepares for 2nd Hurricane," *USA Today* online, September 23, 2005, http://www.usatoday.com/money/ industries/retail/2005-09-22-walmart-preparation_x .htm?csp=34; Robert Greenwald, *Wal-Mart—The High Cost of Low Price,* a film by Robert Greenwald and Brave New Films, November 4, 2005, www.walmartmovie.com; Thomas A. Hemphill, "Rejuvenating Wal-Mart's Business," Indiana University Kelley School of Business, *Business Horizons* 48 (2005): 48, 11–21; Candace Hoke, www.walmartsurvivor.com; John Johnson, "RFid Watch: Transmissions from the RFid Front Lines: How They Did It," DC Velocity, January 2006, www.DCVelocity.com (accessed January 10, 2006); Del Jones, "Corporate Giving for Katrina Reaches $547 million," *USA Today* online, September 13, 2005, http://www.usatoday.com/money/companies/2005-09-12-katrina-corporate-giving_x.htm; Marcus Kabel, "Wal-Mart at War: Retailer Faces Bruised Image, Makes Fixes," *Marketing News,* January 15, 2006, 25; David Koenig, "Wal-Mart Wants to Be Where You Go for $500 Wine; New Texas Store Stocks Posh Products for Upscale Clientele," *USA Today,* March 23, 2006, B2; Robert Levering and Milton Moskowitz, "The 100 Best Companies to Work For," *Fortune,* January 24, 2005, 61–88; Daniel McGinn, "Wal-Mart Hits the Wall," *Newsweek,* November 14, 2005, 44–46; Ylan Q. Mui, "Wal-Mart List Racially Offensive," *Washington Post/Denver Post,* January 8, 2006, 14A; Harold Meyerson, "Open Doors, Closed Minds. How One Wal-Mart True Believer Was Excommunicated for His Faith in Doing What He Thought the Company Expected of Him: Crying Foul," Prospect, November 11, 2005, www.prospect.org (accessed January 20, 2006); Al Norman, "The Case Against Wal-Mart." Raphel Marketing, 2004; Zena Olijnyk, "The Wal-Mart Effect," *Canadian Business* 77, no. 8 (2004): 67–68; Karen Olsson, "Up Against Wal-Mart," *Mother Jones* online, March/April 2003, http://www.motherjones.com/news/feature/2003/03/ma_276_01.html (accessed January 10, 2006); Steve Quinn, "Wal-Mart Green with Energy," *[Fort Collins] Coloradoan,* July 24, 2005, E1–E2; "The Real Facts About Wal-Mart," Wakeupwalmart.com, http://www.wakeupwalmart.com/facts/; Jim Renden "Wal-Mart Touts RFid Results," Search CIO, January 18, 2005, http://searchcio.techtarget.com/originalContent/

0,289142,sid19_gci1045698,00.html?bucket=NEWS (accessed January 10, 2006); Andy Serwer, "Bruised in Bentonville," *Fortune,* April 18, 2005, 84–89; "Statement on Poll Showing Americans Believe Wal-Mart Is a Good Place to Shop," Wal-Martfacts.com, http://www.walmartfacts.com/newsdesk/article.aspx?id=1557 (accessed January 2005); "Statements Regarding Union-Funded 'Where Would Jesus Shop Campaign,'" WalMartfacts.com, http://www.walmartfacts.com/newsdesk/article. aspx?id=1539 (accessed January 2005); Laurie Sullivan, "Wal-Mart CEO: Hurricane Charlie Paved Way for Katrina Response," *Information Week* online, September 19, 2005, www.informationweek.com; Jim Wagner, "Wal-Mart RFID Tests Underway," *Wireless,* April 30, 2004, via www.internetnews.com (accessed January 10, 2006); "Wal-Mart Annual Report 10-K"; "Wal-Mart Annual Report to Shareholders 2006"; "Wal-Mart and the Environment," WalMartfacts.com, walmartfacts.com, http://www.walmartfacts.com/eytopics/environment.aspx; "Wal-Mart Urged to 'Clean Up Act,'" BBC online, June 3, 2005, http://news.bbc.co.uk/2/hi/business/4605733.stm; www.WalMartfacts.com; Ann Zimmerman, "Federal Officials Asked to Probe Wal-Mart Firing," *Wall Street Journal,* April 28, 2005, via www.wakeupwalmart.com; Ann Zimmerman, "In Wal-Mart's Case, Its Enemies Aren't Terribly Good Friends," *Wall Street Journal,* January 11, 2006, A1, A10; Ann Zimmerman and James Bandler, "How Gift Cards Helped Trip Up Wal-Mart Aide," *Business News/Wall Street Journal,* July 15, 2005, via http://www.post-gazette.com/pg/05196/538565.stm.

The Coca-Cola Company Struggles with Ethical Crises

Coca-Cola has the most valuable brand name in the world and, as one of the most visible companies worldwide, has a tremendous opportunity to excel in all dimensions of business performance. However, over the last ten years, the firm has struggled to reach its financial objectives and has been associated with a number of ethical crises. Warren Buffet served as a member of the board of directors and was a strong supporter and investor in Coca-Cola but resigned from the board in 2006 after several years of frustration with Coca-Cola's failure to overcome many challenges.

Many issues were facing Doug Ivester when he took over the reins at Coca-Cola in 1997. Ivester was heralded for his ability to handle the financial flows and details of the soft-drink giant. Former-CEO Roberto Goizueta had carefully groomed Ivester for the top position, which he assumed in October 1997 after Goizueta's untimely death. However, Ivester seemed to lack leadership in handling a series of ethical crises, causing some to doubt "Big Red's" reputation and its prospects for the future. For a company with a rich history of marketing prowess and financial performance, Ivester's departure in 1999 represented a high-profile glitch on a relatively clean record in one hundred years of business. In 2000 Doug Daft, the company's former president and chief operating officer, replaced Ivester as the new CEO. Daft's tenure was rocky, and the company continued to have a series of negative events in the early 2000s. For example, the company was allegedly involved in racial discrimination, misrepresenting market tests, manipulating earnings, and disrupting long-term contractual arrangements with distributors. By 2004 Daft was out and Neville Isdell had become president and worked to improve Coca-Cola's reputation.

HISTORY OF THE COCA-COLA COMPANY

The Coca-Cola Company is the world's largest beverage company, and markets four of the world's top five leading soft drinks: Coke, Diet Coke, Fanta, and Sprite. It also sells other brands including Powerade, Minute Maid, and Dansani bottled water. The company operates the largest distribution system in the world, which enables it to serve customers and businesses in more than two hundred countries. Coca-Cola estimates that more than 1 billion servings of its products are consumed every day. For much of its early history, Coca-Cola focused on cultivating markets within the United States.

Coca-Cola and its archrival, PepsiCo, have long fought the "cola wars" in the United States, but Coca-Cola, recognizing additional market potential, pursued international opportunities in an effort to dominate the global soft-drink industry. By 1993 Coca-Cola controlled 45 percent of the global soft-drink market,

We appreciate the work of Kevin Sample, who helped draft the previous edition of this case, and Melanie Drever, who assisted in this edition. This case was prepared for classroom discussion rather than to illustrate either effective or ineffective handling of an administrative, ethical, or legal decision by management. All sources used for this case were obtained through publicly available material and the Coca-Cola website.

while PepsiCo received just 15 percent of its profits from international sales. By the late 1990s, Coca-Cola had gained more than 50 percent of the global market in the soft-drink industry. Pepsi continued to target select international markets to gain a greater foothold in international markets. Since 1996 Coca-Cola has focused on traditional soft drinks, and PepsiCo has gained a strong foothold on new-age drinks, has signed a partnership with Starbucks, and has expanded rapidly into the snack-food business. PepsiCo's Frito-Lay division has 60 percent of the U.S. snack-food market. Coca-Cola, on the other hand, does much of its business outside of the United States, and 85 percent of its sales now come from outside the United States. As the late Roberto Goizueta once said, "Coca-Cola used to be an American company with a large international business. Now we are a large international company with a sizable American business."

Coca-Cola has been a successful company since its inception in the late 1800s. PepsiCo, although founded about the same time as Coca-Cola, did not become a strong competitor until after World War II when it began to gain market share. The rivalry intensified in the mid-1960s, and the "cola wars" began in earnest. Today, the duopoly wages war primarily on several international fronts. The companies are engaged in an extremely competitive—and sometimes personal—rivalry, with occasional accusations of false market-share reports, anticompetitive behavior, and other questionable business conduct, but without this fierce competition, neither would be as good a company as it is today.

By January 2006, PepsiCo had a market value greater than Coca-Cola for the first time ever. Its strategy of focusing on snack foods and innovative strategies in the non-cola beverage market helped the company gain market share and surpass Coca-Cola in overall performance.

COCA-COLA'S REPUTATION

Coca-Cola is the most recognized trademark and brand name in the world today with a trademark value estimated to be about $25 billion. The company has always demonstrated a strong market orientation, making strategic decisions and taking actions to attract, satisfy, and retain customers. During World War II, for example, company president Robert Woodruff committed to selling Coke to members of the armed services for just a nickel a bottle. As one analyst said

later, "Customer loyalty never came cheaper." This philosophy helped make Coke a truly global brand, with its trademark brands and colors recognizable on cans, bottles, and advertisements around the world. The advance of Coca-Cola products into almost every country in the world demonstrated the company's international market orientation and improved its ability to gain brand recognition. These efforts contributed to the company's strong reputation.

However, in 2000 Coca-Cola failed to make the top ten of *Fortune*'s annual "America's Most Admired Companies" list for the first time in a decade. Problems at the company were leadership issues, poor economic performance, and other upheavals. The company also dropped out of the top one hundred in *Business Ethics*' annual list of "100 Best Corporate Citizens" in 2001. For a company that spent years on both lists, this was disappointing, but perhaps not unexpected, given several ethical crises.

Coca-Cola's promise is that the company exists "to benefit and refresh everyone who is touched by our business." It has successfully done this by continually increasing market share and profits, with Coca-Cola being the most recognized brand in the world. Because the company is so well known, the industry so pervasive, and the market orientation of Coca-Cola so strong, the company has developed a number of social responsibility initiatives to enhance its trademarks. These initiatives are guided by the company's core beliefs in the marketplace, workplace, community, and environment. For example, Coke wants to inspire moments of optimum through their brands and their actions, as well as creating value and making a difference everywhere they do business. Their vision for sustainable growth is fostered by being a great place to work where people are inspired to be the best they can be, by bringing the world a portfolio of beverage brands that anticipate and satisfy peoples' desires and needs, by being a responsible global citizen that makes a difference, and by maximizing return to shareowners while being mindful of their overall responsibilities.

SOCIAL RESPONSIBILITY FOCUS

Coca-Cola has made local education and community improvement programs a top priority for its philanthropic initiatives. Coca-Cola foundations "support the promise of a better life for people and their communities." For example, Coca-Cola is involved in a program called "Education on Wheels" in Singapore where history is brought to life in an interactive discovery adventure for children. In an interactive classroom bus, children are engaged in a three-hour drama specially written for the program. It challenges creativity and initiative while enhancing communication skills as children discover new insights into life in the city.

Coca-Cola also offers grants to various colleges and universities in more than half of the United States, as well as numerous international grants. In addition to grants, Coca-Cola provides scholarships to more than 170 colleges, and this number is expected to grow to 287 over the next four years. It includes 30 tribal colleges belonging to the American Indian College Fund. Coca-Cola is also involved with the Hispanic Scholarship Fund. Such initiatives help enhance the Coca-Cola name and trademark and thus ultimately benefit shareholders. Each year 250 new Coca-Cola Scholars are designated and invited to Atlanta for personal interviews. Fifty students are then designated as National Scholars and receive awards of $20,000 for college; the remaining 200 are designated as Regional Scholars and receive $4000 awards. Since the program's inception in 1986, a total of over twenty-five hundred Coca-Cola scholars have benefited from nearly $22 million for education. The program is open to all high school seniors in the United States.

The company recognizes its responsibilities on a global scale and continues to take action to uphold this responsibility, such as taking steps not to harm the environment while acquiring goods and setting up facilities. The company is proactive on local issues, such as HIV/AIDS in Africa, and has partnered with UNAIDS and other nongovernment organizations to put into place important initiatives and programs to help combat the threat of the HIV/AIDS epidemic.

Because consumers trust its products, and develop strong attachments through brand recognition and product loyalty, Coca-Cola's actions also foster relationship marketing. For these reasons, problems at a firm like Coca-Cola can stir the emotions of many stakeholders.

CRISIS SITUATIONS

The following documents a series of alleged misconduct and questionable behavior affecting Coca-Cola stakeholders. These ethical and legal problems appear to have had an impact on Coca-Cola's financial performance, with its stock trading today at the same price it did ten years ago. The various ethical crises have been associated with turnover in top management, departure of key investors, and the loss of reputation. There seems to be no end to these events as major crises continue to develop. It is important to try to understand why Coca-Cola has not been able to eliminate these events that have been so destructive to the company.

Contamination Scare

Perhaps the most damaging of Coca-Cola's crises—and the situation that every company dreads—began in June 1999, when about thirty Belgian children became ill after consuming Coca-Cola products. Although the company recalled the product, the problem soon escalated. The Belgian government eventually ordered the recall of all Coca-Cola products, leading officials in Luxembourg and the Netherlands to recall all Coca-Cola products as well. The company eventually determined that the illnesses were the result of a poorly processed batch of carbon dioxide. Coca-Cola took several days to comment formally on the problem, which the media quickly labeled a slow response. Coca-Cola initially judged the situation to be minor and not a health hazard, but by that time a public relations nightmare had begun. France soon reported more than one hundred people sick and banned all Coca-Cola products until the problem was resolved. Soon after, a shipment of Bonaqua, a new Coca-Cola water product, arrived in Poland, contaminated with mold. In each instance, the company's slow response and failure to acknowledge the severity of the situation harmed its reputation.

The contamination crisis was exacerbated in December 1999 when Belgium ordered Coca-Cola to halt its "Restore" marketing campaign in order to regain consumer trust and sales in Belgium. A rival firm claimed that the campaign strategy that included free cases of the product, discounts to wholesalers and retailers, and extra promotion personnel was intended to illegally strengthen Coca-Cola's market share. Under Belgium's strict antitrust laws, the claim was upheld, and Coca-Cola abandoned the campaign. This decision, along with the others, reduced Coca-Cola's market standing in Europe.

Competitive Issues

Questions about Coca-Cola's market dominance started government inquiries into its marketing tactics. Because most European countries have very strict antitrust laws, all firms must pay close attention to market share and position when considering joint ventures, mergers, and acquisitions. During the summer of 1999, Coca-Cola became very aggressive in the French market. As a result, the French government responded by refusing to approve Coca-Cola's bid to purchase Orangina, a French beverage company. French authorities also forced Coca-Cola to scale back its acquisition of Cadbury Schweppes, another beverage maker. Moreover, Italy successfully won a court case against Coca-Cola over anticompetitive prices in 1999, prompting the European Commission to launch a full-scale probe of the company's competitive practices. PepsiCo and Virgin accused Coca-Cola of using rebates and discounts to crowd their products off shelves, thereby gaining greater market share. Coca-Cola's strong-arm tactics proved to be in violation of European laws and once again demonstrated the company's lack of awareness of European culture and laws.

Despite these legal tangles, Coca-Cola products, along with many other U.S. products, dominate foreign markets throughout the world. According to some European officials, the pain that U.S. automakers felt in the 1970s because of Japanese imports is the same pain that U.S. firms are meting out in Europe. The growing omnipresence of U.S. products, especially in highly competitive markets, is the reason why corporate reputation—both perceived and actual—is so important to relationships with business partners, government officials, and other stakeholders.

Racial Discrimination Allegations

In the spring of 1999, initially fifteen hundred African American employees sued Coca-Cola for racial discrimination but eventually grew to include two thousand current and former employees. Coca-Cola was accused of discriminating against them in pay, promotions, and performance evaluations. Plaintiffs charged that the company grouped African American workers at the bottom of the pay scale, where they typically earned $26,000 a year less than Caucasian employees in comparable jobs. The suit also alleged that top management had known of the discrimination since 1995 but had done nothing. Although in 1992 Coca-Cola had pledged to spend $1 billion on goods and services from minority vendors, it did not seem to apply to their workers.

Although Coca-Cola strongly denied the allegations, the lawsuit evoked strong reactions. To reduce collateral damage, Coca-Cola created a diversity council and paid $193 million to settle the racial discrimination lawsuit.

Problems with the Burger King Market Test

In 2002 Coca-Cola ran into more troubles when Matthew Whitley, a mid-level Coca-Cola executive, filed a whistle-blowing suit, alleging retaliation for revealing fraud in a market study performed on behalf of Burger King. To increase sales, Coca-Cola suggested that Burger King invest in and promote frozen Coke as a child's snack. The fast-food chain arranged to test market the product for three weeks in Richmond, Virginia, and evaluate the results before agreeing to roll out the new product nationally. The test market involved customers receiving a coupon for a free frozen Coke when they purchased a Value Meal (sandwich, fries, and drink). Burger King executives wanted to be cautious about the new product because of the enormous investment that each restaurant would require to distribute and promote the product. Restaurants would need to purchase equipment to make the frozen drink, buy extra syrup, and spend a percentage of their advertising funds to promote the new product.

When results of the test marketing began coming in to Coca-Cola, sales of frozen Coke were grim. Coca-Cola countered the bad statistics by giving at least one individual $10,000 to take hundreds of children to Burger King to purchase Value Meals including the frozen Coke. Coca-Cola's action netted seven hundred additional Value Meals out of nearly one hundred thousand sold during the entire promotion. But when the U.S. attorney general for the North District of Georgia discovered and investigated the fraud, the company had to pay $21 million to Burger King, $540,000 to the whistle-blower, and a $9 million pretax write-off had to be taken. Although Coca-Cola disputes the allegations, the cost of manipulating the frozen Coke research cost the company considerably in negative publicity, criminal investigations, a soured relationship with a major customer, and a loss of stakeholder trust.

Inflated Earnings Related to Channel Stuffing

Another problem that Coca-Cola faced during this period was accusations of channel stuffing. *Channel stuffing* is the practice of shipping extra inventory to wholesalers and retailers at an excessive rate, typically before the end of a quarter. Essentially, a company counts the shipments as sales although the products often remain in warehouses or are later returned to the manufacturer. Channel stuffing tends to create the appearance of strong demand (or conceals declining demand) for a product, which may result in inflated financial statement earnings, thus misleading investors.

Coke was accused of sending extra concentrate to Japanese bottlers from 1997 through 1999 in an effort to inflate profits. In 2004 Coca-Cola reported finding statements of inflated earnings due to the company's shipping extra concentrate to Japan. Although the company settled the allegations, the Securities and Exchange Commission (SEC) did find that channel stuffing had occurred. Coca-Cola had pressured bottlers into buying additional concentrate in exchange for extended credit, which is technically considered legitimate.

To settle with the SEC, Coca-Cola agreed to avoid engaging in channel stuffing in the future. The company also created an ethics and compliance office and is required to verify quarterly that it has not altered the terms of payment or extended special credit. The company further agreed to work on reducing the amount of concentrate held by international bottlers. Although it settled with the SEC and the Justice Department, it still faces a shareholder lawsuit regarding channel stuffing in Japan, North America, Europe, and South Africa.

Trouble with Distributors

In early 2006, Coca-Cola faced problems with its bottlers, after fifty-four of them filed lawsuits seeking to block Coca-Cola from expanding delivery of Powerade sports drinks directly to Wal-Mart warehouses beyond the limited Texas test area. Bottlers alleged that the Powerade bottler contract did not permit warehouse delivery except for commissaries and that Coca-Cola had materially breached the agreement by committing to provide warehouse delivery of Powerade to Wal-Mart and by proposing to use a subsidiary, CCE, as its agent for warehouse delivery.

The problem was that Coca-Cola was trying to step away from the century-old tradition of direct-store delivery, known as DSD, wherein bottlers drop off product at individual stores, stock shelves, and build merchandising displays. Coca-Cola and CCE assert they were simply trying to accommodate a request from Wal-Mart for warehouse delivery, which is how PepsiCo distributes its Gatorade brand. CCE had also proposed making payments to some other bottlers in return for taking over Powerade distribution in their exclusive territories. But the bottlers had concerns that such an arrangement would violate antitrust laws and claimed that if Coca-Cola and CCE went forward with their warehouse delivery, it would greatly diminish the value of the bottlers' businesses.

The problems faced by Coca-Cola were reported negatively by the media and had a negative effect on Coca-Cola's reputation. When the reputation of one company within a channel structure suffers, all firms within the supply chain suffer in some way or another. This was especially true because Coca-Cola adopted an enterprise resource system that linked Coca-Cola's once almost classified information to a host of partners. Thus, the company's less-than-stellar handling of the ethical crises introduced a lack of integrity in its partnerships. Although some of the crises had nothing to do with the information shared across the new system, the partners still assume greater risk because of their relationships with Coca-Cola. The interdependence between Coca-Cola and its partners requires a diplomatic and considerate view of the business and its effects on various stakeholders. Thus, these crises harmed Coco-Cola's partner companies, their stakeholders, and eventually, their bottom lines.

International Problems Related to Unions

Around the same time, Coca-Cola also faced intense criticism in Colombia where unions were making progress inside Cokes plants. Coincidently, at the same time, eight Coca-Cola workers died, forty-eight went into hiding, and sixty-five received death threats. The union alleges that Coca-Cola and its local bottler were complicit in these cases and is seeking reparations to the families of the slain and displaced workers. Coca-Cola denies the allegations, noting that only one of the eight workers was killed on the premises of the bottling plant. Also, the other deaths all occurred off premises and could have been the result of Colombia's four-decade-long civil war.

Coke Employees Offer to Sell Trade Secrets

A Coca-Cola administrative secretary and two accomplices were arrested in 2006 and charged in a criminal complaint with wire fraud and unlawfully stealing and selling trade secrets from the Coca-Cola Company. The accused contacted PepsiCo executives and indicated that an individual identifying himself as "Dirk," who claimed to be employed at a high level with Coca-Cola, offered "very detailed and confidential information." When Coca-Cola received a letter from PepsiCo about the offer, the FBI was contacted, and an undercover FBI investigation began. The FBI determined that "Dirk" was Ibrahim Dimson of Bronx, New York. Dirk provided an FBI undercover agent with fourteen pages of Coca-Cola logo-marked "Classified—Confidential" and "CLASSIFIED—Highly Restricted" material. In addition, Dirk also provided samples of Coca-Cola top-secret products. The source of the information was Joya Williams, an executive administrative assistant for Coca-Cola's global brand director in Atlanta, who had access to some information and materials described by "Dirk." Employees should be held responsible for protecting intellectual property, and this breach of confidence by a Coca-Cola employee was a serious ethical issue.

ETHICAL RECOVERY?

Despite Coca-Cola's problems, consumers surveyed after the European contamination indicated they felt that Coca-Cola would still behave correctly during times of crises. The company also ranked third globally in a PricewaterhouseCoopers survey of most-respected companies. Coca-Cola managed to retain its strong ranking while other companies facing setbacks, including Colgate-Palmolive and Procter & Gamble, were dropped or fell substantially in the rankings.

Coca-Cola has taken the initiative to counter diversity protests. The racial discrimination lawsuit, along with the threat of a boycott by the NAACP, led to Daft's plan to counter racial discrimination. The plan was designed to help Coca-Cola improve employment of minorities.

When Coca-Cola settled the racial discrimination lawsuit, the agreement stipulated that the company (1) donate $50 million to a foundation to support programs in minority communities, (2) hire an ombudsman who would report directly to CEO Daft, (3) investigate complaints of discrimination and harassment, and (4) set aside $36 million for a seven-person task force and authorize it to oversee the company's employment practices. The task force includes business and civil rights experts and is to have unprecedented power to dictate company policy with regard to hiring, compensating, and promoting women and minorities. Despite the unusual provision to grant such power to an outside panel, Daft said, "We need to have outside people helping us. We would be foolish to cut ourselves off from the outside world."

Belgian officials closed their investigation of the health scare involving Coca-Cola and announced that no charges would be filed against the company. A Belgian health report indicated that no toxic contamination had been found in Coke bottles, even though the bottles were found to have contained tiny traces of carbonyl sulfide, which produces a rotten-egg smell; the amount of carbonyl sulfide would have to have been a thousand times higher to be toxic. Officials also reported that they found no structural problems with Coca-Cola's production plant and that the company had cooperated fully throughout the investigation.

CURRENT SITUATION AT COCA-COLA

While Coca-Cola's financial performance continues to lag, one issue that may have great impact on the success of the company is its relationship with distributors. Lawsuits that distributors have launched against Coca-Cola for its attempt to bypass them with Powerade have the potential of destroying trust and cooperation in the future. Other issues related to channel stuffing and falsifying market tests to customers indicate a willingness by management to bend the rules to increase the bottom line.

Although Coca-Cola seems to be trying to establish its reputation based on quality products and socially responsible activities, it has failed to manage ethical decision making in dealing with various stakeholders. An important question to consider is whether Coca-Cola's strong emphasis on social responsibility, especially philanthropic and environmental concerns, can help the company maintain its reputation in the face of highly public ethical conflict and crises.

CEO Isdell developed a two-year turnaround plan focused on new products, and the company created one thousand new products, including coffee-flavored Coca-Cola Blak to be marketed as an energy beverage and soft drink. The company is also adopting new-age drinks such as lower-calorie Powerade sports drink and flavored Dasani water. These moves are an attempt to catch up with PepsiCo, which has become the noncarbonated-beverage leader. Coca-Cola continues developing products such as bottled coffee called Far Coast, and black and green tea drinks called Gold Peak. Although PepsiCo has outexecuted Coca-Cola since 1996, Coca-Cola still has a 50 percent market share; but PepsiCo has become the larger company in 2006, and Coca-Cola's long-term earnings and sales have been lowered. If so many ethical issues had not distracted Coca-Cola, would its financial performance have been much better?

Questions

1. Why do you think Coca-Cola has had one ethical issue after another to resolve over the last decade or so?

2. A news analyst said that Coca-Cola could become the next Enron. Do you think this is possible? Defend your answer.

3. What should Coca-Cola do to restore its reputation and eliminate future ethical dilemmas with stakeholders?

Sources

Elise Ackerman, "It's the Real Thing: A Crisis at Coca-Cola," *U.S. News & World Report,* October 4, 1999, 40–41; Ronald Alsop, "Corporate Reputations Are Earned with Trust, Reliability, Study Shows," *Wall Street Journal* online, September 23, 1999, http://interactive.wsj.com; "America's Most Admired Companies," *Fortune,* February 8, 2000, via www.pathfinder.com/fortune; "America's Most Admired Companies," *Fortune* online, www.fortune.com/fortune/mostadmired/ (accessed December 17, 2002); Paul Ames, "Case Closed on Coke Health Scare," Associated Press, April 22, 2000; Dan Beucke, "Coke Promises a Probe in Colombia," *BusinessWeek,* February 6, 2006, 11; James Bone, "Three Charged with Stealing Coca-Cola Trade Secrets," *Times Online,* July 6, 2006, http://www.timesonline.co.uk/printfriendly/0,,1-3-2259092-3,00.html

(accessed July 7, 2006); Katrina Brooker, "The Pepsi Machine," *Fortune,* February 6, 2006, 68–72; Mary Jane Credeur, "Coke Poured Out 1000 New Products in 2005, Two-Year Turnaround Plan on Track, CEO Says," *USA Today,* December 8, 2005, B5; Coca-Cola Company, www2.coca-cola.com (accessed August 21, 2003); "Coca-Cola Introduces 'Real' Marketing Platform," *PR Newswire,* January 9, 2003, accessed via Lexis Nexis; "Coca-Cola Names E. Neville Isdell Chairman and Chief Executive Officer Elect," Coca-Cola press release, May 4, 2004, http://www2.coca-cola.com/presscenter/pc_include/nr_20040504 (accessed May 17, 2006); "Coke Rapped for Restore," *The Grocer,* December 4, 1999, 14; "Corporate Reputation in the Hands of Chief Executive," *Westchester County Business Journal,* May 18, 1998, 17; Patrick Crosby, "DOJ Statement, Evidence In Coke Trade-Secrets Case," *Wall Street Journal* online, July 5, 2006, http://online.wsj.com/article_print/SB115213927958898855.html (accessed July 7, 2006); T. C. Doyle, "Channel Stuffing Rears Its Ugly Head," *VARBusiness* online, May 6, 2003, www.varbusiness.com/showArticle.jhtml;jsessionid=PCVHTC511CHQ0QSNDBCSKHSCJUMEKJVN?articleID=18823602; James Faier, "The Name Is the Game," *Retail Traffic* online, http://retailtrafficmag.com/mag/retail_name_game/index.html (accessed May 15, 2006); Sharon Foley, "Cola Wars Continue: Coke vs. Pepsi in the 1990s," Harvard Business School Press, April 10, 1995, Case 9-794-055; Dean Foust and Geri Smith, "'Killer Coke' or Innocent Abroad? Controversy over Anti-Union Violence in Colombia Has Colleges Banning Coca-Cola," *Business Week,* January 23, 2006, 46–48; "FYI," *Incentive* 176 (2002): 67; "Grand Jury to Investigate Coke on Channel Stuffing Allegations," *Atlanta Business Chronicle* online, May 3, 2004, http://atlanta.bizjournals.com/atlanta.stories/2004/05/03/daily2.html; Ann Harrington, "Prevention Is the Best Defense," *Fortune,* July 10, 2000, 188; Constance Hays, "Coca-Cola to Cut Fifth of Workers in a Big Pullback," *New York Times,* January 27, 2000, A1; Ernest Holsendolph, "Facing Suit, Coca-Cola Steps Up Diversity Efforts," *Atlanta Journal and Constitution,* May 27, 1999, F1; Anita Howarth, "Coca-Cola Struggles to Refurbish Image After Recent European Troubles," *Daily Mail,* January 16, 2000, accessed via Lexis Nexis Academic Universe; Tammy Joyner, "Generous Severance Packages," *Atlanta Journal and Constitution,* January 27, 2000, E1; Jeremy Kahn, "The World's Most Admired Companies," *Fortune,* October 11, 1999, 267–275; Marjorie Kelly, "100 Best Corporate Citizens," *Business Ethics* (Spring 2006): 23–24; Scott Leith, "Where Has Daft Been?" *Atlanta Journal and Constitution,* December 1, 2002, 1Q; Betty Lui, "Think of Us as a Local Company," *Financial Times,* January 20, 2003, 6; Betsy McKay and Chad Terhune, "Coca-Cola Settles Regulatory Probe; Deal Resolves Allegations by SEC That Firm Padded Profit by Channel Stuffing," *Wall Street Journal,* via http://proquest.umi.com/pqweb?did=823831501&sid=1&Fmt=3&clientId=2945&RQT=309&Vname=PQD (accessed November 8, 2005); Betsy Morris and Patricia Sellers, "What Really Happened at Coke," *Fortune,* January 10, 2000, 114–116; Dan

Morse and Ann Carrns, "Coke Rated 'Acceptable' on Diversity," *Wall Street Journal,* September 26, 2002, A9; Jon Pepper, "Europe Resents That Europeans Much Prefer to Buy American," *Detroit News* online, November 10, 1999, http://detnews .com/1999/business/9911/10/11100025.htm; Jordan T. Pine, "Coke Counters Protests with New Diversity Commitment," *Diversity Inc.* online, March 13, 2000, www.diversityinc .com/; V. L. Ramsey, "$1 Billion Pledged to Vendors," *Black Enterprise,* July 1992, 22; Maria Saporta, "Transition at Coca-Cola: Ivester Paid a Price for Going It Alone," *Atlanta Journal and Constitution,* December 8, 1999, E1; "Second Annual List of '100 Best Corporate Citizens' Quantifies Stakeholder Service," *Business Ethics* online, www.businessethics.com/ newpage24.htm (accessed December 17, 2002); Patricia Sellers, "Coke's CEO Doug Daft Has to Clean Up the Big Spill," *Fortune,* March 6, 2000, 58–59; Christopher Seward, "Company Forewarned: Meaning of Goizueta's '96 Letter Echoes Today," *Atlanta Journal and Constitution,* January 27, 2000, E4; Chad Terhune, "Bottlers' Suit Challenge Coke Distribution Plan," *Wall Street Journal,* February 18–19, 2006, A5; Chad Terhune, "A Suit by Coke Bottlers Exposes Cracks in a Century-Old System," *Wall Street Journal,* March 13, 2006, A1; "Top 75: The Greatest Management Decisions Ever Made," *Management Review,* November 1998, 20–23; Henry Unger, "Revised Suit Cites Coca-Cola Execs," *Atlanta Journal and Constitution,* December 21, 1999, D1; Greg Winter, "Bias Suit Ends in Changes for Coke," *Austin American-Statesman* online, November 17, 2000, http://austin360.com/statesman.

The Fall of Enron: A Stakeholder Failure

Once upon a time, there was a gleaming head-quarters office tower in Houston, with a giant tilted "E" in front, slowly revolving in the Texas sun. The Enron Corporation, which once ranked among the top *Fortune* 500 companies, collapsed in 2001 under a mountain of debt that had been concealed through a complex scheme of off-balance-sheet partnerships and investor loss of confidence. Forced to declare bankruptcy, the energy firm laid off five thousand employees; thousands more lost their retirement savings, which had been invested in Enron stock. The company's shareholders lost tens of billions of dollars after the stock price plummeted. The scandal surrounding Enron's demise engendered a global loss of confidence in corporate integrity that continues to plague markets, and eventually it triggered tough new scrutiny of financial reporting practices such as the Sarbanes-Oxley Act in 2002. To understand what went wrong, let's examine the history, culture, and major players in the Enron scandal.

HISTORY

The Enron Corporation was created out of the merger of two major gas pipeline companies in 1985. Through its subsidiaries and numerous affiliates, the company provided products and services related to natural gas, electricity, and communications for its wholesale and retail customers. Enron transported natural gas through pipelines to customers all over the United States. It generated, transmitted, and distributed electricity to the northwestern United States and marketed natural gas, electricity, and other commodities globally. It was also involved in the development, construction, and operation of power plants, pipelines, and other energy-related projects all over the world, including the delivery and management of energy to retail customers in both the industrial and commercial business sectors.

Throughout the 1990s, Chairman Kenneth Lay, chief executive officer (CEO) Jeffrey Skilling, and chief financial officer (CFO) Andrew Fastow transformed Enron from an old-style electricity and gas company into a $150 billion energy company and Wall Street favorite that traded power contracts in the investment markets. From 1998 to 2000 alone, Enron's revenues grew from about $31 billion to more than $100 billion, making it the seventh-largest company of the *Fortune* 500. Enron's wholesale energy income represented about 93 percent of 2000 revenues, with another 4 percent derived from natural gas and electricity. The remaining 3 percent came from broadband services and exploration. Enron-Online—the company's worldwide Internet trading platform—completed on average over five thousand transactions per day, buying and selling over eighteen hundred separate products

We appreciate the work of Neil Herndon, who wrote the previous edition of this case under the direction of O. C. Ferrell, and Melanie Drever, who assisted in this edition. This case is for classroom discussion rather than to illustrate either effective or ineffective handling of an administrative, ethical, or legal decision by management. All sources used for this case were obtained through publicly available material and the Enron website.

A Timeline of the Enron Scandal

1985   Houston Natural Gas merges with Omaha-based InterNorth; the resulting company is eventually named Enron Corporation. Ken Lay, who had been CEO of Houston Natural Gas, becomes chairman and CEO the following year.

2000   Annual revenues reach $100 billion, and the Energy Financial Group ranks Enron as the sixth-largest energy company in the world, based on market capitalization.

February 2001   Jeff Skilling takes over as CEO. Lay remains chairman.

August 2001   Skilling unexpectedly resigns for "personal reasons," and Lay steps back into the CEO job. That same month, a letter from an Enron executive raises serious questions about the company's business and accounting practices.

October 2001   Enron releases third-quarter earnings, showing $1 billion in charges, including $35 million related to investment partnerships headed by Andrew Fastow, Enron's former CFO. Fastow is replaced as CFO.

October 22, 2001   Enron announces that the Securities and Exchange Commission (SEC) has launched a formal investigation into its "related party transactions."

November 8, 2001   Enron restates earnings for 1997 through 2000 and the first three quarters of 2001.

December 2, 2001   Enron files for protection from creditors in a New York bankruptcy court.

December 3, 2001   Enron announces that it is laying off four thousand employees.

January 9, 2002   The Justice Department announces that it is pursuing a criminal investigation of Enron.

January 14, 2002   U.S. House and Senate lawmakers return campaign contributions from Enron.

January 24, 2002   Lay resigns as chairman and CEO of Enron. The first of at least eight congressional hearings on Enron begins.

January 30, 2002   Enron names Stephen Cooper, a restructuring specialist, as acting CEO.

February 4, 2002   A report by a special committee of Enron's board investigating the energy trader's collapse portrays a company riddled with improper financial transactions and extensive self-dealing by company officials.

May 2, 2002   Enron announces plans to reorganize as a small company with a new name.

October 2, 2002   Fastow voluntarily surrenders to federal authorities after prosecutors indicate they will file charges for his role in the company's collapse.

October 31, 2002   Fastow is indicted on seventy-eight counts of masterminding a scheme to artificially inflate the energy company's profits.

February 3, 2003   Creditors of Enron sue Lay and his wife, Linda, to recover more than $70 million in transfers.

July 11, 2003   Enron finally announces a plan to restructure and pay off creditors after five deadline extensions.

July 2003   J. P. Morgan Chase and Citigroup pay nearly $300 million to settle allegations from the SEC, New York state, and New York City that they helped Enron manipulate its financial statements and mislead investors.

September 2003   Merrill Lynch avoids prosecution related to the barge deal by acknowledging that some employees may have broken the law and by implementing reforms.

October 2003   Wesley Colwell, former chief accounting officer for Enron's trading unit, agrees to pay $500,000 to settle SEC allegations of manipulating earnings by using trading profits to offset massive losses in Enron's retail energy unit. He is still cooperating with the Justice Department but faces no criminal charges.

December 2003   Canadian Imperial Bank of Commerce avoids prosecution by accepting responsibility for crimes committed by employees who knowingly participated in complicated transactions that wrongly moved assets off of Enron's balance sheet so that the energy company could inflate earnings.

April 30, 2003   Fastow's wife, Lea, is charged with tax crimes and conspiracy for participating in husband's deals.

September 10, 2003   Former Enron treasurer Ben Glisan pleads guilty to conspiracy and is sentenced to five years in prison.

January 14, 2004   Andrew Fastow pleads guilty to two counts of conspiracy and agrees to serve ten years in prison.

January 22, 2004   Richard Causey pleads innocent to conspiracy and fraud charges.

(*continued*)

A Timeline of the Enron Scandal (*continued*)

February 19, 2004   Skilling, added to the Causey indictment, pleads innocent to more than thirty criminal counts including conspiracy, fraud, and inside trading.

May 6, 2004   Lea Fastow pleads guilty to filing a false tax form and is sentenced to the maximum sentence of one year in prison.

July 8, 2004   Lay surrenders after being indicted. He pleads innocent.

July 15, 2004   Bankruptcy judge confirms Enron's reorganization plan in which most creditors will receive about one-fifth of the about $63 billion they're owed in cash and stock.

October 19, 2004   Federal judge grants Lay a separate bank fraud trial but rules that Lay, Skilling, and Causey will be tried together on other charges.

February 2005   Raymond Bowen, Jr., finance chief at Enron from the aftermath of its failure through his resignation in October 2004, agrees to pay $500,000 to settle SEC allegations that he knew or should have known some assets were grossly overvalued to falsely inflate profits. Bowen did not admit or deny the allegations and faces no criminal charges.

May 31, 2005   The Supreme Court overturns the Arthur Andersen conviction.

December 28, 2005   Causey pleads guilty to securities fraud and agrees to serve seven years in prison in exchange for cooperating with the government.

January 30, 2006   The Lay and Skilling trial begins.

May 25, 2006   Lay and Skilling are convicted of conspiracy to commit securities and wire fraud. Lay is convicted in a separate bank fraud case.

July 5, 2006   Lay dies of a heart attack, erasing his conviction. A person who dies before an appeal is not considered convicted.

Sources: "A Chronology of Enron's Woes: The Accounting Debacle," *Wall Street Journal* online, March 20, 2003, http://online.wsj.com; "A Chronology of Enron's Woes: The Investigation," *Wall Street Journal* online, March 20, 2003, http://online.wsj.com; "Enron Timeline," *Houston Chronicle* online, January 17, 2002, http://www.chron.com/cs/CDA/story.hts/special/enron/1127125; Kristen Hays, "16 Cents on $1 for Enron Creditors," *Austin American-Statesman* online, July 12, 2003, http://statesman.com; "Key Dates Leading to Convictions of Lay, Skilling," *USA Today,* May 26, 2006, 3B; Associated Press; "Enron Who's Who," *USA Today* online, http://www.usatoday.com/money/industries/energy/2006-01-26-enron-whos-who_x.htm (accessed June 1, 2006).

online that generated over $2.5 billion in business every day.

There was every reason to believe that Enron was still financially sound in the third quarter of 2001, even though a bankruptcy examiner later reported a discrepancy in Enron's claimed net income and cash flow. This was done under certain accounting assumptions after the bankruptcy. For the third quarter of 2001, Enron's wholesale business generated a potential $754 million of earnings (before interest and taxes), an increase of 35 percent from the previous year. This represented over 80 percent of Enron's worldwide earnings. It was acknowledged by all parties that Enron's wholesale business was highly profitable and growing at a rapid rate. Even in the fourth quarter of 2001, Lay believed that Enron was still a growing, viable company for the long run, based on physical volume moving through the pipelines.

ENRON'S CORPORATE CULTURE

When describing Enron's corporate culture, people like to use the words *arrogant* or *prideful*, perhaps justifiably. The firm employed competent, creative, and hard-working employees and recruited the best and brightest graduates from top universities. In 2001 *Fortune* magazine ranked Enron the twenty-second best company to work for in America. A large banner in the lobby at corporate headquarters proclaimed Enron "The World's Leading Company," and Enron executives blithely believed that competitors had no chance against it. Skilling even went so far as to tell utility executives at a conference that he was going to "eat their lunch." There was an overwhelming aura of pride, carrying with it the deep-seated belief that

Enron's people could handle increasing risk without danger.

The culture also was about a focus on how much money could be made for many executives, at many levels, that shared in a stock option incentive program. For example, after the Enron collapse, it was alleged that Enron's compensation plans seemed less concerned with generating profits for shareholders than with enriching employee wealth. This may have been the result of the highly competent and aggressive employee workforce that was motivated by the desire to improve their financial position. Enron's corporate culture reportedly encouraged risky behavior, if not breaking the rules.

Skilling appears to be the executive who created a system in which Enron's employees were rated every six months, with those ranked in the bottom 20 percent forced out. This "rank-and-yank" system helped create a fierce environment in which employees competed against rivals not only outside the company but also at the next desk. Delivering bad news could result in the "death" of the messenger, so problems in the trading operation, for example, were covered up rather than being communicated to management.

Lay once said that he felt that one of the great successes at Enron was the creation of a corporate culture in which people could reach their full potential. He said that he wanted it to be a highly moral and ethical culture and that he tried to ensure that people did in fact honor the values of respect, integrity, and excellence. On his desk was an Enron paperweight with the slogan "Vision and Values." Lay maintained that he was always concerned about ethics, and he continued to discuss the ethical and legal ramifications of the Enron disaster even after his conviction. The business ethics issue involved in his indictment was that he lied about the financial condition of Enron, but he continued to maintain that he had openly dealt with all issues that were brought to his attention. Some of the people inside Enron believed that nearly anything could be turned into a financial product and, with the aid of complex statistical modeling, traded for profit. Short on assets and heavily reliant on intellectual capital, Enron's corporate culture rewarded innovation and punished employees deemed weak. An important question is, How much does a CEO know about misconduct in a corporation?

Aggressive and highly intelligent Enron employees, in many divisions, were "pushing the limits" and bending the rules to achieve success. This highly competitive risk culture existed in a corporation that was trying to redefine how the energy industry did business. Lawyers, accountants, and the board of directors approved key decisions. As intelligent and creative as Enron's executives were, no one person, under Enron's organizational system of checks and balances, could orchestrate the schemes that created the demise of a company that large. The downfall took many layers of "pushing the envelope" and a great deal of complacency on the part of employees who, at many levels in the organization, saw wrongdoing and ignored it. To some extent, the Enron failure was the result of a free-enterprise system that rewarded risk taking and a corporate culture that pushed complex financial decisions to the edge. In addition, the right environmental conditions evolved in the financial markets, especially the dot-com bubble, contributing to Enron's stock collapse. Enron was the perfect corporate storm (or disaster) that required many failures by multiple stakeholders.

ENRON'S ACCOUNTING PROBLEMS

Enron's bankruptcy in December 2001 was the largest in U.S. corporate history at the time. The bankruptcy filing came after a series of revelations that the giant energy trader had been using partnerships, also called special-purpose entities (SPEs). These off-balance-sheet financing approaches are the heart of losses and write-offs that turned Enron into a disaster. In a meeting with Enron's lawyers in August 2001, the company's then CFO, Fastow, stated that Enron had established the SPEs to move assets and debt off its balance sheet and to increase cash flow by showing that funds were flowing through its books when it sold assets. Although these practices produced a very favorable financial picture, outside observers believed they might constitute fraudulent financial reporting because they did not accurately represent the company's true financial condition.

According to John C. Coffee, Columbia University law professor, once formed by Enron, the SPEs would then borrow debt from banks, and Enron would typically guarantee that debt. Although such guarantees are not unusual when SPEs are used, far less common (and indeed unique) was the fact that the principal asset of many Enron SPEs was Enron restricted stock. Thus, if Enron's stock price declined, the SPEs assets would be insufficient to cover the bank debt, and Enron would have to assume it.

In reality, these SPEs were legal entities, and many investment banks were involved as third-party investors becoming partners in these entities. Most companies engage in third-party transactions to move debt off the balance sheet. For example, a company builds its own plant or office building, sells it to a group of investors, and then leases back the property for its business purposes but still maintains some ownership. In other words, SPEs can be an asset that helps facilitate daily business operations.

Most of the SPEs at Enron were alleged to be entities in name only, and Enron funded them with its own stock and maintained control over them. This is not too different from leasing back property that can be used for storage, transportation, or other energy-related activities. After the crash of Enron's stock price, any assets associated with the SPE system had to be written off. Enron had to take a $1.2 billion reduction in equity in late 2001 because of the SPE write-off.

After Enron restated its financial statements for fiscal 2000 and the first nine months of 2001, its cash flow from operations dropped from a positive $127 million in 2000 to a negative $753 million in 2001. In 2001, with its stock price falling, Enron faced a critical cash shortage. Already shaken by questions about lack of disclosure in Enron's financial statements and by reports that executives had profited personally from the partnership deals, investor confidence collapsed, taking Enron's stock price with it.

For a time, it appeared that Dynegy might save the day by providing $1.5 billion in cash, secured by Enron's premier pipeline Northern Natural Gas, and then purchasing Enron for about $10 billion. But when Standard & Poor downgraded Enron's debt below investment grade on November 28, some $4 billion in off-balance-sheet debt came due, and Enron didn't have the resources to pay. Dynegy terminated the deal. On December 2, 2001, Enron filed for bankruptcy. Enron faced twenty-two thousand claims totaling about $400 billion.

Many complex accounting issues contributed to determining the value of Enron. For example, sometimes accounting rules changed, and different opinions emerged on which rules applied, such as the accounting rules governing goodwill. *Goodwill* is the difference between what a company pays for an entity and the book value of that company's net assets. For example, changes to the accounting rules governing goodwill required Enron to disclose impairments to certain

of its assets including interests in Wessex Water, a business located in Bath, England. Companies such as Enron depend on accounting firms to determine what rules apply to valuing goodwill as well as other assets. The government alleged that Enron's claim of being committed to a water-growth strategy was flawed because it would require Enron to disclose impairments in certain of its assets related to goodwill. According to Lay, Enron's accounting firm, Arthur Andersen, communicated that the company was in compliance with the goodwill accounting rules and the government's claims of flawed disclosures were wrong.

THE WHISTLE-BLOWER

Assigned to work directly with Fastow in June 2001, Enron vice president Sherron Watkins, an eight-year Enron veteran, was given the task of finding some assets to sell off. With the high-tech bubble bursting and Enron's stock price slipping, Watkins was troubled to find unclear, off-the-books arrangements backed only by Enron's deflating stock. No one could explain to her what was going on. Knowing that she faced difficult consequences if she confronted then-CEO Skilling, she began looking for another job, planning to confront Skilling just as she left for a new position. Skilling, however, suddenly quit on August 14, saying he wanted to spend more time with his family. Chairman Lay stepped back in as CEO and began inviting employees to express their concerns and put them into a box for later collection. Watkins prepared an anonymous memo and placed it into the box. When Lay held a companywide meeting shortly thereafter and did not mention her memo, however, she arranged a personal meeting with him.

On August 22, Watkins handed Lay a seven-page letter that she had prepared outlining her concerns. She told him that Enron would "implode in a wave of accounting scandals" if nothing was done. On the other hand, Watkins continued to perform her duties at Enron and participate in all business matters. Lay arranged to have Enron's law firm, Vinson & Elkins, look into the questionable deals. There is evidence that Lay followed up on Watkin's concerns with appropriate action. Watkins sold $30,000 worth of stock in August 2001 and some options in late September. She claimed that she was panicked by the 9/11 terrorist attacks and about the company. She sold another block and netted about $17,000. She had more information than most people, and it is possible the government could have charged her for insider trading if she truly believed Enron was going to become bankrupt.

Watkins alleges that her computer's hard drive was confiscated and she was moved from her plush executive office suite on the top floors of the Houston headquarters tower to a lower-level plain office with a metal desk. That desk was no longer filled with the high-level projects that had once taken her all over the world on Enron business. Instead, now a vice president in name only, she claimed she faced meaningless "make-work" projects. In February 2002, she testified before Congress about Enron's partnerships and resigned from Enron in November. Although Watkins claims to be a whistle-blower, most of her statements were made after Enron filed for bankruptcy and was a financial disaster. In addition, there is no factual evidence that her earlier claims and concerns had any merit.

THE CHIEF FINANCIAL OFFICER

CFO Fastow was indicted in October 2002 by the U.S. Department of Justice on ninety-eight federal counts for his alleged efforts to inflate Enron's profits. These charges included fraud, money laundering, conspiracy, and one count of obstruction of justice. Fastow pled guilty to two counts of conspiracy, admitting to orchestrating a myriad of schemes to hide Enron debt and inflate profits while enriching himself with millions. He surrendered nearly $30 million in cash and property and agreed to serve up to ten years in prison once prosecutors no longer needed his cooperation. He was a key government witness against Lay and Skilling. His wife, Lea Fastow, former assistant treasurer, who quit Enron in 1997, first pled guilty to a felony tax crime, admitting to helping hide from the government ill-gotten gains from her husband's schemes. Withdrawing her plea, she then pled guilty to a newly filed misdemeanor tax crime. In July 2005, she was released from a year-long prison sentence, followed by a year of supervised release.

Federal prosecutors argued that Enron's case is not about exotic accounting practices but fraud and theft. They contend that Fastow was the brain behind the partnerships used to conceal some $1 billion in Enron debt and that this led directly to Enron's bankruptcy. The federal complaints allege that Fastow defrauded Enron and its shareholders through the off-the-balance-sheet partnerships that made Enron appear to be more profitable than it actually was. They also allege that Fastow made about $30 million both by using these partnerships to get kickbacks that were disguised as gifts from family members who invested in them and by taking income himself that should have gone to other entities. Lay maintained that Enron found no visible flaws in Fastow's ethical background before hiring him as CFO and was taken by surprise when Fastow's personal gains from the off-balance-sheet partnerships were discovered. Lay believed that Fastow's manipulations of the off-balance-sheet partnerships were a key factor in the Enron disaster.

Fastow alleges that he was hired to arrange the off-balance-sheet financing and that Enron's board of directors, chairman, and CEO directed and praised his work. He also claims that both lawyers and accountants reviewed his work and approved what was being done and that "at no time did he do anything he believed was a crime." Skilling, chief operating officer (COO) from 1997 to 2000 before becoming CEO, reportedly championed Fastow's rise at Enron and supported his efforts to keep up Enron's stock prices.

The case against Fastow was largely based on information provided by the managing director, Michael Kopper, a key player in the establishment and operation of several of the off-the-balance-sheet partnerships. Kopper, a chief aide to Fastow, pled guilty to money laundering and wire fraud. He agreed to serve ten years in prison and to surrender some $12 million that he earned from his dealings with the partnerships. Others charged in the Enron affair were Timothy Belden, Enron's former top energy trader, who pled guilty to one count of conspiring to commit wire fraud, and three British bankers—David Bermingham, Giles Darby, and Gary Mulgrew—who were indicted in Houston on wire-fraud charges related to a deal at Enron. They used secret investments to take $7.3 million in income that belonged to their employer, according to the Justice Department. The three, employed by the finance group Greenwich National Westminster Bank, were arrested in 2004, faced extradition, and pled innocent.

THE CHIEF EXECUTIVE OFFICER

Former CEO Skilling is widely seen as Enron's mastermind. He was so sure that he had committed no crime that he waived his right to self-incrimination and testified before Congress that "I was not aware of any inappropriate financial arrangements." However, Jeffrey McMahon, who took over as Enron's president and COO in February 2002, told a congressional subcommittee that he had informed Skilling about the company's off-the-balance-sheet partnerships in March 2000, when he was Enron's treasurer. McMahon said that Skilling had told him "he would remedy the situation."

Calling the Enron collapse a "run on the bank" and a "liquidity crisis," Skilling said that he did not understand how Enron went from where it was to bankruptcy so quickly. He also said that the off-the-balance-sheet partnerships were Fastow's creation. Skilling is also reported to have sold 39 percent of his Enron holdings before the company disclosed its financial troubles.

THE CHAIRMAN

Lay became chairman and CEO of the company that was to become Enron in February 1986. A decade later, Lay promoted Skilling to president and COO and then, as expected, stepped down as CEO in February 2001, to make way for Skilling. Lay remained as chairman of the board. When Skilling resigned in August 2001, Lay resumed the role of CEO.

Lay, who held a doctorate in economics from the University of Houston, contended that he knew little of what was going on even though he had participated in the board meetings that allowed the off-the-balance-sheet partnerships to be created. He said he believed the transactions were legal because attorneys and accountants approved them. In the late summer of 2001, he was reassuring employees and investors that all was well at Enron, based on strong wholesale sales and physical volume being delivered through the Enron marketing channel. Although cash flow does not always follow sales, there was every reason to believe that Enron was still a company with much potential. On February 12, 2002, on the advice of his attorney, Lay told the Senate Commerce Committee that he was invoking his Fifth Amendment rights not to answer questions that could be incriminating.

Prosecutors looked into why Lay began selling about $80 million of his own stock beginning in late 2000, even while he encouraged employees to buy more shares of the company. It appears that Lay drew down his $4 million Enron credit line repeatedly and then repaid the company with Enron shares. These transactions, unlike usual stock sales, do not have to be reported to investors. Lay said that he sold the stock because of margin calls on loans that he had secured with Enron stock and that he had no other source of liquidity.

VINSON & ELKINS

Enron was Houston law firm Vinson & Elkins' top client, accounting for about 7 percent of its $450 million revenue. Enron's general counsel and a number of members of Enron's legal department came from Vinson & Elkins. Vinson & Elkins seems to have dismissed Watkins' allegations of accounting fraud after making some inquiries, but this does not appear to leave it open to civil or criminal liability. Of greater concern are allegations that Vinson & Elkins helped structure some of Enron's special-purpose partnerships. Watkins, in her letter to CEO Lay, indicated that the law firm had written opinion letters supporting the legality of the deals. In fact, Enron could not have done many of the transactions without such opinion letters. Although the law firm denies that it has done anything wrong, legal experts say the key question is whether or not Vinson & Elkins approved deals that it knew were fraudulent.

Documents reviewed by *Business Week* indicate that their experts felt that Vinson & Elkins had concerns about the legitimacy of Enron's business practices. So far, the law firm has yet to pay any damages nor have any of its lawyers faced professional misconduct charges by the Texas bar. Enron's bankruptcy trustee is attempting to settle with Vinson & Elkins for $30 million. The Securities and Exchange Commission (SEC) continues to investigate the advice provided to Enron by the firm. In addition, there is an attempt to hold Vinson & Elkins liable for the $40 billion in investor losses resulting from the Enron collapse.

MERRILL LYNCH

The prestigious brokerage and investment banking firm of Merrill Lynch faced scrutiny by federal prosecutors and the SEC for its role in Enron's 1999 sale of Nigerian barges. Merrill Lynch allegedly bought the barges for $28 million, of which Enron financed $21 million through Fastow's oral assurance that

Enron would buy Merrill Lynch's investment out in six months with a 15 percent guaranteed rate of return. Merrill Lynch went ahead with the deal despite an internal Merrill Lynch document that suggested that the transaction might not be appropriate. Merrill Lynch denies that the transaction was a sham and said that it never knowingly helped Enron to falsify its financial reports.

The barge deal was not among the financial blunders that pushed Enron into bankruptcy in 2001. However, prosecutors claimed that it showed Enron was willing to employ suspect financial practices to meet lofty earnings targets. Four former Merrill Lynch executives and two former mid-level Enron executives were charged with conspiracy and fraud related to the transaction. The defense attorneys disputed the government's claims. Enforcement Director Stephen Cutler said,

> Even if you don't have direct responsibility for a company's financial statements, you cannot turn a blind eye when you have reason to know what you are doing will help make those statements false and misleading. At the end of 1999, Merrill Lynch and the executives we are suing today did exactly that: They helped Enron defraud its investors through two deals that were created with one purpose in mind—to make Enron's financial statements look better than they actually were.

ARTHUR ANDERSEN LLP

In its role as Enron's auditor, Arthur Andersen was responsible for ensuring the accuracy of Enron's financial statements and internal bookkeeping. Andersen's reports were used by potential investors to judge Enron's financial soundness and future potential before they decided whether to invest and by current investors to decide if their funds should remain invested there. These investors would expect that Andersen's certifications of accuracy and application of proper accounting procedures were independent and without any conflict of interest. If Andersen's reports were in error, investors could be seriously misled. However, Andersen's independence has been called into question. The accounting firm was a major business partner of Enron, with more than one hundred employees dedicated to its account, and it sold about $50 million a year in consulting services to Enron. Some Andersen executives even accepted jobs with the energy trader.

Andersen was found guilty of obstruction of justice in March 2002 for destroying Enron-related auditing documents during an SEC investigation of Enron. As a result, Andersen has gone out of business. The U.S. Supreme Court overturned the obstruction-of-justice decision, but Andersen had closed its doors.

It is still not clear why Andersen auditors failed to ask Enron to better explain its complex partnerships before certifying Enron's financial statements. Some observers believe that the large consulting fees received from Enron unduly influenced Andersen. However, an Andersen spokesperson said that the firm had looked hard at all available information from Enron at the time. But shortly after she spoke to Enron CEO Lay, Watkins had taken her concerns to an Andersen audit partner, who reportedly conveyed her questions to senior Andersen management responsible for the Enron account. It is not clear what action, if any, Andersen took.

THE BREAKUP OF ENRON'S ASSETS

Enron's demise caused tens of billions of dollars of investor losses, triggered a collapse of electricity-trading markets, and ushered in an era of accounting scandals that precipitated a global loss of confidence in corporate integrity. Now companies must defend legitimate but complicated financing arrangements, even legitimate financing tools tainted by association with Enron. On a more personal level, thousands of former Enron employees struggle to find jobs, while many retirees have been forced to return to work in a bleak job market because their Enron-heavy retirement portfolios were wiped out. One senior Enron executive committed suicide.

In July 2003, Enron announced its intention to restructure and a plan to pay off its creditors. Pending creditor and court approval of the plan, most creditors would receive between 14.4 cents and 18.3 cents for each dollar they were owed—more than most expected. Under the plan, creditors would receive about two-thirds of the amount in cash and the rest in equity in three new companies, neither of which would carry the tainted Enron name. The three companies were CrossCountry Energy Corporation, Prisma Energy International Inc., and Portland General Electric.

CrossCountry Energy would retain Enron's interests in three North American natural gas pipelines. CrossCountry Energy, formed from Enron's domestic gas pipeline assets, was immediately placed on the market for creditor compensation. On September 1, 2004, Enron announced an agreement to sell CrossCountry Energy to CCE Holdings LLC (a joint venture between Southern Union Company and a unit of General Electric) for $2.45 billion. The money would be used for debt repayment and represented a substantial increase over the previous offer made by NuCoastal LLC earlier in 2004.

Prisma Energy International would take over Enron's nineteen international power and pipeline holdings. Prisma Energy International, formed out of Enron's remaining overseas assets, emerged from bankruptcy as a main-line descendant of Enron through a stock offering to Enron creditors. Currently, many of Prisma's assets remain under direct Enron ownership with Prisma operating in a management capacity.

The third company, Portland General Electric (PGE), was founded in 1889 and ranks as Oregon's largest utility. PGE was acquired by Enron during the 1990s and emerged from bankruptcy as an independent company through a private stock offering to Enron creditors.

All remaining assets not related to CrossCountry, Prisma, or PGE were liquidated. As of 2006, CrossCountry was under CCE Holdings ownership, while the PGE and Prisma deals remained to be consummated. Enron emerged from Chapter 11 bankruptcy protection in November 2004 but will likely be wound down once the recovery plan is carried out. Enron's remaining assets are grouped under two main subsidiary companies, Prisma Energy International and PGE, both of which will likely be spun off.

On November 14, 2004, all of Enron's outstanding common stock and preferred stock was canceled. Each person who was the record holder of Enron Corporation stock on that day was allocated an uncertificated, nontransferable interest in one of two trusts that held new shares of Enron Corporation. In the very unlikely event that the value of Enron's assets exceeds the amount of its allowed claims, distributions would be made to the holders of these trust interests in the same order of priority of the stock that they previously held.

According to the Enron website in 2006, it was in the midst of liquidating its remaining operations and distributing its assets to its creditors. Even with the conviction of Enron executives, the justice system will not reform the way that corporate America runs businesses. Many businesspeople see this as an event outside their lives and businesses, very much like passing the traffic accident and thinking it can never happen to them. To prevent future Enron-type failures, the corporate culture, corporate governance, and reward systems will have to change in many organizations. In most cases, a CEO acting alone cannot "sink the ship," and many of the structural, cultural, and corporate governance conditions that caused the collapse of Enron haven't been removed from corporate America.

THE LAY AND SKILLING TRIAL

On May 25, 2006, a Houston jury found Kenneth Lay and Jeffrey Skilling guilty on all counts of conspiring to hide the company's financial condition in 2000 and 2001. During the case, the judge dealt a blow to the two defendants when he told the jury that they could find the defendants guilty of consciously avoiding knowing about wrongdoing at the company. Many former Enron employees refused to testify because they were not guaranteed that their testimony would not be used against them at future trials to convict them. Many questions about the accounting fraud remained after the trial. The verdict was a total victory for federal prosecutors who had spent four years building a criminal case against the two men who had played a key role in building Enron as a role model for the energy industry. Sean M. Berkowitz, director of the Justice Department's Enron Task Force, said "You can't lie to shareholders, you can't put yourself in front of your employees' interests, and no matter how rich and powerful you are you have to play by the rules." The verdict was a blow to Lay and Skilling who testified that "Enron was a fundamentally sound company brought low in a market panic spurred by short sellers and negative media reports." On the other hand, the government maintained that Enron used deceptive accounting and bogus claims of the growth potential of new business units.

The jury found Lay, 64 years old, guilty of six counts of conspiracy and fraud. Skilling, 52 years old, was convicted on eighteen counts of conspiracy and securities fraud but acquitted on nine out of ten counts of illegal insider trading. On the way out of the courtroom, Lay said he was "shocked" by the verdict. "I firmly believe I am innocent of the charges against me as I've said from day one." Then juror Wendy Vaughan said, "I felt it was their duty to know what was going on." Outside the courthouse, prosecutors said the trial should send a message to executives who manipulate their companies' earnings.

Many people don't feel much sympathy for Skilling and Lay because so many people lost a lot of money, but there is an alternative viewpoint. A number of law professors and lawyers have concerns about the Enron Task Force's prosecution of Lay and Skilling, accusing the government of "criminalizing corporate agency costs." In other words, the government is accused of misusing criminal laws to punish questionable business transactions and bad management decisions. In a civilized society, do we imprison people for the rest of their lives because they may have made some bad business decisions?

No doubt, this was a very complex case, and even the most hard-core antibusiness types are queasy with the conclusion of this tragedy. There was not conclusive evidence that there was intent to defraud investors, although investor losses were massive. The important question is, Was there complacency at all managerial levels about rule bending among some employees or was there massive corruption at all levels? One of the key prosecution elements was complacent negligence, that Skilling and Lay just turned a blind eye.

The truth is that the jury would have had to understand the entire corporate culture as well as many systemic embedded business decisions at Enron to know for sure that Lay and Skilling were guilty of their charges. Bad business decisions were made, but there is uncertainty as to the true involvement and intent of many of the CEO's decisions. Society and the courts tend to simplify events and blame all that goes wrong on just a few individuals. At this stage of understanding, there are few people who understand how an organizational culture can evolve with complacency and constant reinforcement from coworkers driving bad decisions. In our society, we are taught that the opinion of trusted professionals such as accountants and lawyers can be followed in business decisions. In this case, the accounting firm Arthur Andersen, internal and external attorneys, as well as the board of directors approved the key decisions at Enron.

Lay said he never intended to harm anyone; in fact, he came back as CEO after Skilling stepped down and at the insistence of the Enron board of directors to provide leadership and attempt to save the company—a decision that he and his wife both regretted. As CEO, Lay was responsible for thirty thousand employees operating in thirty countries. He managed an exceptional group of employees, as alluded to in the film *Enron: The Smartest Men in the Room.* Great leaders are often given accolades for their accomplishments, and Lay was no exception in the "heyday" of Enron. But most will acknowledge that the heart of their success, or in this case, ultimate failure, is the people with whom they surround themselves and place in positions of authority. The people who Lay trusted, such as Fastow (convicted former CFO), were key operatives in the day-to-day decision making at Enron. It was a complex maze of events that caused the failure of Enron.

On July 5, 2006, Ken Lay died of a heart attack in Aspen, Colorado. He was awaiting sentencing and still maintained his innocence. Lay had endured a five-month trial but was working hard to develop an appeal of his conviction. He did not feel that it was possible to get a fair trial in Houston and indicated that the jury had not even read his indictment. He thought he was convicted because as CEO he was charged with responsibility for what happened at Enron, even if he was unaware of wrongdoing. The heart of the case against Lay was that he allegedly lied about the financial condition at Enron. Federal courts, including the Fifth Court of Appeals, hold that a defendant's death erases a conviction. Lay stated that he wanted to be of use to society and would continue to do that in any way possible. In the five weeks before his death, he read several drafts of this case and tried to provide insights about what happened at Enron. He wanted to share his knowledge and perspective about Enron with future business leaders.

Questions

1. How did the corporate culture of Enron contribute to its bankruptcy?

2. Did Enron's bankers, auditors, and attorneys contribute to Enron's demise? If so, what was their contribution?

3. What role did the CFO play in creating the problems that led to Enron's financial problems?

Sources

Personal conversations with Ken Lay between May 27, 2006, and June 20, 2006, by O. C. Ferrell and Linda Ferrell; Associated Press, "Enron Who's Who," *USA Today* online, http://www.usatoday.com/money/industries/energy/2006-01-26-enron-whos-who_x.htm (accessed June 1, 2006);

Mark Banineck and Mary Flood, "Enron's Top Execs Are Guilty, Guilty," *San Antonio Express News,* May 26, 2006, 1A; Alexei Barrionuevo, Jonathan Weil, and John R. Wilke, "Enron's Fastow Charged with Fraud," *Wall Street Journal,* October 3, 2002, A3–A4; Eric Berger, "Report Details Enron's Deception," *Houston Chronicle,* March 6, 2003, 1B, 11B; Maria Bartiromo, "The Ones Who Got Away," *BusinessWeek* online, June 12 2006, http://www.businessweek.com/magazine/content/06_24/b3988122.htm?campaign_id=search (accessed June 7, 2006); Christine Y. Chen, "When Good Firms Get Bad Chi," *Fortune,* November 11, 2002, 56; Andrew Dunn and Laurel Brubaker Calkins, "Death to Hinder Feds," *Denver Post,* July 6, 2006, C1; Peter Elkind and Bethany McLean, "Feds Move Up Enron Food Chain," *Fortune,* December 30, 2002, 43–44; John R. Emshwiller, "Enron's Kenneth Lay is Dead at 64," *Wall Street Journal* online, July 6, 2006, A1, http://online.wsj.com/article_print/SB115210822917098397.html (accessed July 6, 2006); "Enron's Last Mystery," *BusinessWeek* online, June 12 2006, http://www.businessweek.com/magazine/content/06_24/b3988056.htm?campaign_id=search (accessed June 7, 2006); Enron website, for facts about Enron, www.enron.com (accessed May 18, 2006); "Enron Whistle-Blower Resigns," MSNBC News, www.msnbc.com/news/835432.asp (accessed December 2, 2002); Greg Farrell, "Lay, Skilling Found Guilty," *USA Today,* May 26, 2006, A1, B1; Greg Farrell, "Former Enron CFO Charged," *USA Today,* October 3, 2002, B1; Greg Farrell, Edward Iwata, and Thor Valdmanis, "Prosecutors Are Far from Finished," *USA Today,* October 3, 2002, 1B–2B; "Fastow Indicted on 78 Counts," MSNBC News, www.msnbc.com/news/828217.asp (accessed November 6, 2002); O. C. Ferrell, "Ethics," *BizEd,* May/June 2002, 43–45; Jeffrey A. Fick, "Report: Merrill Replaced Enron Analyst," *USA Today,* July 30, 2002, B1; "Finger-Pointing Starts as Congress Examines Enron's Fast Collapse," *Investor's Business Daily,* February 8, 2002, A1; Daren Fonda, "Enron: Picking over the Carcass," *Fortune,* December 30, 2002, 56; Mike France, "One Big Client, One Big Hassle," *BusinessWeek,* January 28, 2002, 38–39; Bryan Gruley and Rebecca Smith, "Keys to Success Left Kenneth Lay Open to Disaster," *Wall Street Journal,* April 26, 2002, A1, A5; Tom Hamburger, "Enron CEO Declines to Testify at Hearing," *Wall Street Journal,* December 12, 2001, B2; Kristen Hays, "16 Cents on $1 for Enron Creditors," *Austin American-Statesman* online, July 12, 2003, http://statesman.com; Kristen Hays, "Conspiracy with Merrill Lynch Charged in Enron Trial," *Washington Post* online, http://www.washingtonpost.com/wp-dyn/articles/A39044-2004Sep21.html (accessed June 7, 2006); Edward Iwata, "Merrill Lynch Will Pay $80M to Settle Enron Case," *USA Today* online, February 20, 2003, www.usatoday.com; Jeremy Kahn, "The Chief Freaked Out Officer," *Fortune,* December 9, 2002, 197–198, 202; Kenneth Lay Speech, Houston Forum,

December 13, 2005, www.kenlayinfo.com/public/pag142.aspx (accessed June 7, 2006); Kathryn Kranhold and Rebecca Smith, "Two Other Firms in Enron Scheme, Documents Say," *Wall Street Journal,* May 9, 2002, C1, C12; Peter Lattman, "Enron: Two Very Different Views from the Peanut Gallery," *Wall Street Journal* online, May 26, 2006, http://blogs.wsj.com/law/2006/05/26/enron-two-very-different-views-from-the-peanut-gallery (accessed May 31, 2006); Bethany McLean, "Why Enron Went Bust," *Fortune,* December 24, 2001, 58, 60–62, 66, 68; Jodie Morse and Amanda Bower, "The Party Crasher," *Fortune,* December 30, 2002, 53–56; Belverd E. Needles, Jr., and Marian Powers, "Accounting for Enron," in *Houghton Mifflin's Guide to the Enron Crisis* (Boston: Houghton Mifflin, 2003), 3–6; *New York Times* coverage of the Enron trial, http://www.nytimes.com/business/businessspecial3/index.html?adxnnl=1&adxnnlx=1147986237-z56Vd16RUkp6e HnHTXBHw (accessed May 18, 2006); Michael Orey, "Lawyers: Enron's Last Mystery?" *BusinessWeek* online, June 1, 2006, www.businessweek.com/investor/content/may2006/pi20060 531_972686.htm; Mitchell Pacelle, "Enron's Creditors to Get Peanuts," *Wall Street Journal* online, July 11, 2003, http://online.wsj.com; "Primer: Accounting Industry and Andersen," *Washington Post* online, www.washingtonpost.com (accessed October 2, 2002); Miriam Schulman, "Enron: What Ever Happened to Going Down with the Ship?" Markkula Center for Applied Ethics, www.scu.edu/ethics/publications/ethicalperspectives/schulman0302.html (accessed September 11, 2002); Chris H. Sieroty, "3 Ex-Bankers Charged in Enron Scandal," *Washington Times* online, www.washtimes.com (accessed October 2, 2002); William Sigismond, "The Enron Case from a Legal Perspective," in *Houghton Mifflin's Guide to the Enron Crisis* (Boston: Houghton Mifflin, 2003), 11–13; Elliot Blair Smith, "Panel Blasts Enron Tax Deals," *USA Today* online, February 13, 2003, www.usatoday.com; Rebecca Smith and Kathryn Kranhold, "Enron Knew Portfolio's Value," *Wall Street Journal,* May 6, 2002, C1, C20; Rebecca Smith and Mitchell Pacelle, "Enron Plans Return to Its Roots," *Wall Street Journal,* May 2, 2002, A1; Jake Ulick, "Enron: A Year Later," CNN/Money, www.money.cnn.com/2002/11/26/news/companies/enron_anniversary/index.htm (accessed December 2, 2002); U.S. Securities and Exchange Commission, "SEC Charges Merrill Lynch, Four Merrill Lynch Executives with Aiding and Abetting Enron Accounting Fraud," 2003, http://www.sec.gov/news/press/2003-32.htm (accessed June 7, 2006); Joseph Weber, "Can Andersen Survive?" *BusinessWeek,* January 28, 2002, 39–40; Wikipedia, http://en.wikipedia.org/wiki/Enron (accessed May 18, 2006); Winthrop Corporation, "Epigraph," in *Houghton Mifflin's Guide to the Enron Crisis* (Boston: Houghton Mifflin, 2003), 1; Wendy Zellner, "A Hero—and a Smoking-Gun Letter," *BusinessWeek,* January 28, 2002, 34–35.

Verizon: The Legacy of WorldCom and MCI

The story of Verizon starts with WorldCom in 1983 when businessmen Murray Waldron and William Rector sketched out a plan to create a long-distance telephone service provider on a napkin in a coffee shop in Hattiesburg, Mississippi. Their new company, Long Distance Discount Service (LDDS), began operating as a long-distance reseller in 1984. Early investor Bernard Ebbers was named CEO the following year. Through acquisitions and mergers, LDDS grew quickly over the next fifteen years. It changed its name to WorldCom, achieved a worldwide presence, acquired telecommunications giant MCI, and eventually expanded beyond long-distance service to offer the whole range of telecommunications services. It seemed poised to become one of the largest telecommunications corporations in the world. Instead, it became the largest bankruptcy filing in U.S. history and another name on a long list of those disgraced by the accounting scandals of the early twenty-first century.

CUTTING EDGE BOOKKEEPING OR ACCOUNTING FRAUD?

Today we can say that WorldCom used questionable accounting practices and improperly recorded $3.8 billion in capital expenditures that boosted cash flows and profit in 2001 as well as the first quarter of 2002. This disguised the firm's actual net losses for five quarters because capital expenditures can be deducted over a longer period of time, whereas expenses must be immediately subtracted from revenue. Investors, unaware of the fraud, continued to buy the company's stock, which accelerated the stock's price. Internal investigations uncovered questionable accounting practices stretching as far back as 1999.

Even before the improper accounting practices were disclosed, WorldCom was already in financial turmoil. Declining rates and revenues and an ambitious buying spree had pushed the company deeper into debt. In addition, CEO Ebbers received a controversial $408 million loan to cover margin calls on loans that were secured by company stock. In July 2001, WorldCom signed a credit agreement with multiple banks, including Citigroup, to borrow up to $2.65 billion and repay it within a year. According to the banks, WorldCom used the entire amount six weeks before the accounting irregularities were disclosed. The banks contended that if they had known WorldCom's true financial picture, they would not have extended the financing without demanding additional collateral.

In 2002 the Securities and Exchange Commission (SEC) directed WorldCom to detail the facts underlying the events that the company had described in a June 25, 2002, press release. That press release stated that

We appreciate the work of Nichole Scheele, University of Wyoming, and Renee Galvin, Colorado State University, in helping draft the previous edition of this case. This case was prepared for classroom discussion rather than to illustrate either effective or ineffective handling of an administrative, ethical, or legal decision by management. All sources used for this case were obtained through publicly available material and the company website.

WorldCom intended to restate its 2001 and first-quarter 2002 financial statements and that Scott Sullivan—who reported to Ebbers until he resigned in April 2002—had prepared the financial statements for 2001 and the first quarter of 2002. On February 6, 2002, a meeting was held between the board's audit committee and Arthur Andersen, the firm's outside auditor, to discuss the audit for fiscal year 2001. Andersen assessed WorldCom's accounting practices to determine whether it had adequate controls to prevent material errors in its financial statements and attested that WorldCom's processes were in fact effective. When the committee asked Andersen whether its auditors had any disagreements with WorldCom's management, Andersen replied that they had not; they were comfortable with the accounting positions that WorldCom had taken.

As the primary outside auditor, Arthur Andersen was faulted for failing to uncover the accounting irregularities. In its defense, Andersen claimed that it could not have known about the improper accounting because former CFO Scott Sullivan never informed Andersen's auditors about the firm's questionable accounting practices. But, in WorldCom's statement to the SEC, the company claimed that Andersen did know about these accounting practices, had no disagreement with WorldCom's management, and was not uncomfortable with any accounting positions taken by World-Com. WorldCom took expenses that should have been directly attributed to the balance sheet and attributed them to specific assets. For example, by claiming that general maintenance of a building actually increased its asset value, it allowed for a longer write-off time for the depreciation. The formula, assets = liabilities + stockholders equity, is the basic accounting equation that states that what you have as an asset—for example, land, cash, and buildings—has to equal what you owe plus how much the company is worth to investors.

Generally, when a company pays cash for an expense, it comes off assets and then out of stockholders' equity, which lowers net income. However, WorldCom was taking the expense and, instead of applying it to stockholders' equity, was attributing it to another asset. They were hiding the expense and making it look as though they had no decrease in asset and no decrease in net income. Generally, attributing an expense to an asset to increase its value is possible but only at the time of acquisition. WorldCom was doing this all the time and at any given time, which was where they got into trouble.

WorldCom did not have the cash needed to pay $7.7 billion in debt and therefore filed for Chapter 11 bankruptcy protection on July 21, 2002. In its bankruptcy filing, the firm listed $107 billion in assets and $41 billion in debt. WorldCom's bankruptcy filing allowed it to pay current employees, continue service to customers, retain possession of assets, and gain breathing room to reorganize. However, the telecommunications giant lost credibility along with the business of many large corporate and government clients, organizations that typically do not do business with companies in Chapter 11 proceedings.

Several former WorldCom finance and accounting executives, including David Myers, Buford Yates, Betty Vinson, and Troy Normand, pleaded guilty to securities-fraud charges (see Table C11.1). They claimed that

TABLE C11.1   Former WorldCom and MCI Executives: Convictions

Bernard Ebbers, CEO	25 years in prison
Scott Sullivan, finance CEO	5 years in prison
David Myers, controller	1 year and 1 day in prison
Buford Yates, accounting	1 year and 1 day in prison
Betty Vinson, accounting department manager	5 months in prison
Troy Normand, accounting	3 years probation
John Sidgmore, CEO before and after Ebbers	Deceased
Jack Grubman, broker	Resigned

Board of Directors Ordered to Pay $54 Million

James C. Allen; Judith Areen; Carl J. Aycock; Max E. Bobbitt; C. L. Alexander, Jr.; Stiles A. Kellett, Jr.; Gordon S. Macklin; John A. Porter; Lawrence C. Tucker they were directed by top managers to cover up World-Com's worsening financial situation. Although they claim to have protested that what they were told to do was improper, they say they agreed to follow orders after their superiors told them it was the only way to save the company.

Sullivan, who worked above many of these employees, pleaded not guilty. CEO Ebbers stated that he did nothing fraudulent and had nothing to hide. WorldCom's lawyers said that Ebbers did not know of the money that had shifted into the capital expenditure accounts. However, the *Wall Street Journal* reported that an internal WorldCom report identified an e-mail and a voice mail that suggested otherwise. The issue was solved when the jury found Ebbers guilty of securities fraud, conspiracy, and filing false documents with regulators. In July 2005, Ebbers was sentenced to twenty-five years in a federal prison in Mississippi. To date it was the toughest sentence given in recent corporate scandals. In 2006 the 68-year-old Ebbers was still out on bail while he appealed his conviction. If sentenced in 2007, Ebbers will be eligible for parole in 2029; he will be over 88 years old.

John Sidgmore, who briefly replaced Ebbers as CEO, blamed WorldCom's former management for the company's woes. Richard Thornburgh, the independent investigator appointed by WorldCom's bankruptcy court, asserted that there was a "cause for substantial concern" regarding WorldCom's board of directors and independent auditors. The board was accused of lax oversight, and the board's compensation committee was attacked for approving Ebbers' generous compensation package. Moreover, Thornburgh's report claimed that Ebbers and Sullivan ran WorldCom "with virtually no checks or restraints placed on their actions by the board of directors or other management." Another report, prepared for the firm's new board of directors, also criticized Ebbers for bucking efforts to develop a code of conduct, which Ebbers was said to have called a "colossal waste of time."

Additionally, Jack Grubman, a Wall Street analyst specializing in the telecommunications industry who rated WorldCom's stock highly, admitted he did so for too long. He insisted he was unaware of the company's true financial shape. Grubman was later fired by Salomon Smith Barney because of accusations that he hyped telecommunications stocks, including Global Crossing and WorldCom, even after it became public knowledge that the stocks were poor investments.

Many people have blamed the rising number of telecommunication company failures and scandals on neophytes who had no experience in the telecommunication industry. Among these telecommunication outsiders were a junk bond financier (Gary Winnick of Global Crossing), a railroad baron (Phil Anschutz, who founded Qwest), and Ebbers, who operated a motel before he took the helm of WorldCom. They tried to transform their start-ups into gigantic full-service providers like AT&T, but in an increasingly competitive industry it was unlikely that so many large companies could survive.

A Chapter 11 reorganization bankruptcy filing means different things to different investor groups, but the reality is that in the end, few investors will get back what they put into WorldCom. In a bankruptcy proceeding, shareholders have a legal right to some money, but because they essentially sit at the bottom of the list of creditors, they will likely receive nothing.

MCI BECOMES WORLDCOM

In 2001 WorldCom created a separate "tracking" stock for its declining MCI consumer long-distance business in the hopes of isolating MCI from WorldCom's Internet and international operations, which were seemingly stronger. WorldCom announced the elimination of the MCI tracking stock and suspended its dividend in May 2002 in the hopes of saving $284 million a year. The actual savings was just $71 million. The S&P 500 cut WorldCom's long-term and short-term corporate credit rating to "junk" status on May 10, 2002, and the NASDAQ delisted WorldCom's stock on June 28, 2002, when the price dropped to 9 cents a share. Likewise, holders of WorldCom's bonds, which included banks' investment departments, insurance companies, and pension funds, did not really expect to receive interest and principal payments on those bonds. Although they have received new stock and bonds in exchange for the bonds they held, the new stock is not worth nearly as much as investors lost. Various state funds alone lost $277 million when WorldCom's stock tanked.

MCI, the long-distance giant acquired by WorldCom years ago, continued service during WorldCom's Chapter 11 bankruptcy reorganization and has stayed afloat because of Citigroup. Citigroup denies any wrongdoing in relation to WorldCom. Instead, Citigroup's CEO Charles Prince agreed to pay out

$2.65 billion "solely to eliminate the uncertainties, burden and expense of further protracted litigation" and praised ex-CEO Weill for his leadership in reforming Citigroup even though he was presiding over the structures that led to the conflicts of interest and subsequent litigations. But, in 2005 Prince sent out an internal memo describing a five-point ethics and compliance strategy. Citigroup would create an Independent Global Compliance function and tighten rules on stock ownership, insisting some three thousand senior managers hold at least 25 percent of the company shares they receive. Finally, Citigroup would offer guidance and perhaps a moral compass by creating an ethics hot line for staff issues.

In 2005 Qwest and Verizon were courting MCI. Finally, in the spring of 2006, Verizon bought MCI for approximately $8 billion including dividends. A term of the deal was that Michael Capellas be let go (fired) as MCI's CEO. His severance package was $39.2 million. Why did Qwest, which was billions in debt, and Verizon want MCI? MCI barely made a profit, and its sales were down in 2005. Also in that year, MCI settled dozens of lawsuits, paid World-Com's back taxes, but they also began to see a little light at the end of the tunnel. Was this the reason that Qwest and Verizon wanted MCI?

It seems that everyone has wanted MCI. For example, in 1997 GTE Corporation wanted to buy MCI. They didn't because, maybe, in part there were questions about the implications for phone consumers if GTE took over MCI, that such a merger would stifle competition.

VERIZON AND THE FUTURE

To understand Verizon's future, one must first understand the past. In 1984 AT&T was broken up into smaller independent companies because it had a monopoly on telecommunications. The seven "Baby Bells" that were created were not allowed to offer such things as manufacturing telecommunications products or customer-premise equipment and provide long-distance, information, and cable services. With the passage of the Telecommunications Act of 1996, however, everything was up for grabs as long as a company

could convince the courts that competition was being preserved. Today there are only five major players that provide phone service: Verizon, Qwest, AT&T, Sprint, and a new company called Vonage. But Vonage has reason to fear Verizon: Verizon publicly stated that it would slice the price of its Web-calling plan by $10, to $24.95, below the price of Vonage's comparable package. This could be the start of a price battle among providers of so-called voice-over Internet protocol phone services. Vonage may try to offset price pressure by differentiating its offering through features, but do they have the resources to outlast Verizon?

In the meantime, Verizon appears to be consolidating their power base by attempting to buy out Vodaphone's stake in the U.S. market. At the time of the writing of this case, Vodaphone believed that the buyout should be $50 billion, whereas Verizon wanted to pay only $38 billion.

Verizon's future is by no means secure. For example, it appears that in certain areas such as Rhode Island, the company is losing so much money that although sales are increasing, profits are declining. Verizon also has been named in a $5 billion civil lawsuit arguing that Verizon gave customer data to the National Security Agency.

In addition to the large, pending lawsuit, some Verizon employees initiated a small lawsuit concerning fair compensation. According to the suit, the company's pay plans penalized sales employees by automatically deducting sales commissions when they failed to persuade directory advertisers to renew accounts. It also deducted workers' wages when the company was forced to give credits to advertisers even though employees had no control over the renewal or the issuance of the credit. Verizon Information Services spokeswoman Mary De La Garza said the company doesn't comment on existing litigation but added, "We believe the lawsuit is without merit."

Questions

1. What are the factors that caused WorldCom to crumble?

2. Why did MCI bail out WorldCom?

3. Why did Verizon and Qwest go after MCI?

4. Are there any ethical concerns in the future for Verizon, Qwest, and others?

Sources

"02 CV 8083 (JSR) Complaint (Securities Fraud)," Securities and Exchange Commission, October 31, 2002, www.sec.gov/litigation/complaints/comp17783.htm; "Accounting Fraud," WorldCom News, http://Worldcomnews. com/accountingfraud.html (accessed April 3, 2003); Andrew Backover, "Overseer Confident WorldCom Will Come Back," *USA Today,* December 31, 2002, 8A; "Bankruptcy," WorldCom News, http://Worldcomnews.com/bankruptcy.html (accessed April 3, 2003); Andrew Barakat, "Reports Detail How Ebbers, Officers Ran Wild at WorldCom," *Austin American-Statesman* online, June 10, 2003, http://statesman.com; Timothy C. Barmann, "For 3rd Consecutive Year, Verizon Losing Money in R.I.," *Providence [RI] Journal,* May 28, 2006; Ken Belson, "Profit Falls as Sales Rise at Verizon," *New York Times,* May 3, 2006, C3; Rebecca Blumenstein and Ken Brown, "Scrapped WorldCom Merger Sparked Sprint Tax Shelter," Yahoo! News, February 27, 2003, http://story.news.yahoo.com/news?tmpl=story&u=/dowjones/20030207/bs_dowjones/200302070218000057; "Capellas Close to Leading WorldCom," CNN/Money online, November 13, 2002, http://cnnmoney.printthis.clickability.com/pt/cpt?action=cpt&expire=&urlID=4597701&fb; "Corporate Scandals: WorldCom," MSNBC, www.msnbc.com/news/corpscandal_front. asp?odm=C2ORB (accessed April 4, 2003); Nora Devine, "WorldCom to Write Off $45B Goodwill, Adjust Intangibles," Dow Jones Newswires, March 13, 2003, http://story.news.yahoo.com/news?tmpl=story&u=/dowjones/20030313/bs_dowjones/200303131736001097; "Ebbers Reportedly Knew of Fraud," MSNBC, March 12, 2003, www.msnbc.com/news/884175.asp; "Effect on Consumer," WorldCom News, http://Worldcomnews.com/effectonconsumer.html (accessed April 3, 2003); "Effect on Investors," WorldCom News, http://Worldcomnews.com/effectoninvestors.html (accessed April 3, 2003); Janet Elliott, "AG Would Have More Investigative Power—Bill Focuses on Integrity in Business," *Houston Chronicle* online, March 11, 2003, www.chron.com/cs/CDA/story.hts/metropolitan/1812842; "Enron & WorldCom Scandals Inspire Movie and National Ethics Scholarship for Students," Yahoo! News, March 12, 2003, http://biz.yahoo.com/prnews/030312/daw022_1.html; Faces of the Week: February 14–18, "Trump Bankruptcy Plan Wins Court OK," *Forbes* online, http://www.forbes.com/fdc/welcome.html (accessed June 27, 2006); "Former WorldCom CEO, CFO Take the Fifth," *eWeek,* July 8, 2002, www.eweek.com/article2/0,3959,362703,00.asp; Charles Gasparino, "Grubman Informed Weill of AT&T Meetings," *Wall Street Journal,* November 15, 2002, C1, C13; Mark Harrington, "Workers Sue Verizon for Wages: Sales Employees Say Commission Payment Practices Unlawful," *Newsday [Melville, NY],* April 26, 2006; "Investment and Litigation," WorldCom News, http://Worldcomnews.com/investmentandlitigation.html (accessed April 3, 2003); Carrie Johnson, "More Guilty Pleas from WorldCom Managers," *Washington Post* online, October 11, 2002, via http://nl12.newsbank.com/nlsearch/we/Archives?p_action=list&p_topdoc=126; "Judge Outlines Budget Plan for WorldCom," Yahoo! News, March 6, 2003, http://story.news.yahoo.com/news?tmpl=story2&cid=509&ncid=509&e=41&u=/ap/20030306/ap_on_bi_ge/worldcom_budget_1; Olga Kharif, "Verizon's VoIP Offensive," *BusinessWeek* online, May 5, 2006, 6-6; Gina Keating, "U. of Calif. Files $353 Million WorldCom Lawsuit," Yahoo! News, February 13, 2003, http://story.news.yahoo.com/news?tmpl=story&u=/nm/20030213/tc_nm/telecoms_worldcom_lawsuit_dc_1; Peter Kennedy, "WorldCom Puts Ebbers' B.C. Ranch Up for Sale," *Globe and Mail* online, January 28, 2003, http://www.globeandmail.com/servlet/ArticleNews/PEstory/TGAM/20030128/RANCH/Headlines/headdex/headdexBusiness_temp/52/52/58/; Stephanie Kirchgaessner, "WorldCom Mulls Further $16 Billion Write-off," Yahoo! News, January 30, 2003, http://story.news. yahoo.com/news? tmpl=story2&cid=1106&ncid=1106&e= 5&u=/ft/20030130/bs_ft/1042491347715; Matt Krantz, "Capitalizing on the Oldest Trick in Book: How WorldCom, and Others, Fudged Results," *USA Today* online, June 27, 2002, www.usatoday.com/tech/techinvestor/2002/06/27/worldcom whatdo.htm; Adam Lahinsky, "WorldCom: Picking Up the Pieces," *Business 2.0* online, May 2, 2002, www.business2.com/articles/web/print/0,1650,40140,FF.html; Joseph McCafferty, "Scott Sullivan," *CFO Magazine,* September 1998, via www. findarticles.com/cf_0/m3870/n9_v14/21119225/print. jhtml; Jack McCarthy, "WorldCom Woes," *InfoWorld* online, August 2, 2002, www.infoworld.com/article/02/08/02/020805 cttelco_1.html; Stephanie Mehata, "Birds of a Feather," *Fortune,* October 2002, via www.business2.com/articles/mag/print/0,1643,43957,00.html; Adrian Michaels, "SEC Extends Charges Against WorldCom," *Financial Times* online, November 6, 2002, http://news.ft.com/servlet/ContentServer?pagename=Synd/StoryFT/FTFull&artid=10358730; Arshad Mohammed, "Verizon Says It Did Not Give Customer Records to NSA," *Washington Post,* May 17, 2006; Susan Pulliam, "Ordered to Commit Fraud, A Staffer Balked, Then Caved," *Wall Street Journal* online, June 23, 2003, http://online.wsj.com; "Qwest Eyes MCI Again," *Forbes* online, http://www.forbes.com/fdc/welcome.shtml (accessed June 27, 2006); Amanda Ripley, "The Night Detective," *Time* online, December 22, 2002, www.time.com/time/personoftheyear/2002/poycooper.html; Simon Romero, "WorldCom to Write Down $79.8 Billion of Good Will," *New York Times* online, March 14, 2003, www.nytimes.com/2003/03/14/technology/14TELE. html; Mathew Secker, "WorldCom (Company Operations)," *Telecommunications,* March 2001, via www.mobilepaymentforum.org/pdfs/TelecommunicationsIntlEd.pdf; Ben Silverman, "WorldCom Waits for Blame Game,"

New York Post online, March 10, 2003, www.nypost.com/
business/70283.htm; Christopher Stern, "6 Resign from World-
Com Board," *Washington Post* online, December 18, 2002,
E04, http://www.washingtonpost.com/ac2/wp-dyn?pagename=
article& node=&contentId=A3966-2002Dec17&notFound=
true; Christopher Stern, "Cost-Cutting WorldCom Considers
More Layoffs," *Washington Post* online, February 2, 2003,
p. A02, www.washingtonpost.com/ac2/wp-dyn?pagename=
article&node=&contentId=A16324-2003Feb2&notFound=
true; David Teather, "Former WorldCom Controller Admits
Fraudulent Entries," *The Guardian,* September 27, 2002;
David Teather, "To Ebber's Wedding, on Expenses," *The
Guardian,* August 30, 2002; Steven Titch, "Deconstructing
WorldCom: A Revealing Autopsy of the 1998 Mega-Merger,"
America's Network, May 1, 2001, via www.findarticles
.com/cf_0/m0DUJ/6_105/74651470/print.jhtml; John Van
and Michael Oneal, "$750 Million WorldCom Settlement Is
Approved," *Austin American-Statesman* online, July 8, 2003,
http://statesman.com; Jon Van and Bob Secter, "Experts Say
Phone Firm's at Law's Edge: Verizon Hit with $5 Billion Law-
suit," *Chicago Tribune,* May 13, 2006; "Verizon Buyout Runs
into Hitch," *London Times,* May 9, 2006, and BBC News
online, http://news.bbc.co.uk/1/hi/business/4977016.stm
(accessed June 27, 2006); Lingling Wei, "More WorldCom
Restatements?" *Wall Street Journal,* November 4, 2002, via
http://www.msnbc.com/news/83048.asp; "Who Is to
Blame?" WorldCom News, http://Worldcomnews.com/
whoistoblame.html (accessed April 3, 2003); "WorldCom Announces Its Post-Restructuring Management Plan," WorldCom
press release, September 10, 2002, www1.worldcom. com/
infodesk/news/news2.xml?newsid=4392&mode=long&lang=e;
"WorldCom to Cut 2,000 Jobs," CNN online, September 16,
2002, www.cnn.com/2002/BUSINESS/09/16/worldcom/
index.html; "WorldCom Finances," WorldCom News, http://
Worldcomnews.com/worldcom finances.html (accessed April 3,
2003); "WorldCom Issues July and August 2002 Operating
Results," WorldCom press release, October 22, 2002, www
.worldcom.com/global/about/news/news2 .xml?newsid=4870
&mode=long&lang=en&width =530&root=global/about/;
"WorldCom's Latest Development," CNN/Money online,
November 11, 2002, www.cnnmoney.printthis.clickability
.com/pt/cpt?action=cpt&expire= urlID=4580252&fb; "World-
Com Milestones," *Washington Post* online, August 9, 2002,
www.washingtonpost.com/ac2/wp-dyn/A49156-2002Jun26?
language=printer; "WorldCom Report Suggests Ebbers Knew
of Accounting Fraud," Quicken Brokerage online, March 12,
2003, www.quicken.com/investments/news_center/story/?
story=NewsStory/dowJones/20030312/ON20030312040600
0594.var& column =P0DFP; "World Com Report Suggests
Ebbers Knew of Fraud," *Forbes* online, March 12, 2003,
www.forbes.com/technology/newswire/2003/03/12
/rtr 904375.html; "WorldCom Revised Statement Pursuant to
Section 21 (a)(1) of the Securities Exchange Act of 1934,"
Securities and Exchange Commission, July 8, 2002,
www.sec.gov/news/extra/wcresponserv. htm; "WorldCom,
SEC to Settle Charges," CNN online, November 5, 2002,
www.cnn.com/2002/BUSINESS/11/05/worldcom
.reut/index.html.

Martha Stewart: A Brand in Crisis

Martha Stewart was one of the most visible CEOs to become embroiled in a widening series of corporate scandals in the early 2000s. She founded Martha Stewart Living Omnimedia Inc. (MSLO), a company with interests in publishing, television, merchandising, e-commerce, and related international partnerships. Along the way, she became America's most famous homemaker and one of its richest women executives. But in late 2001 she became the center of headlines, speculations, a federal investigation, indictment, trial, and guilty verdict on charges related to her sale of four thousand shares of ImClone stock one day before that firm's stock price plummeted. The question for many is why?

EVOLUTION OF A MEDIA EMPIRE

Born in 1941 as Martha Kostyra in Nutley, New Jersey, in a Polish American family with six children, Martha developed a passion for cooking, gardening, and homemaking. She learned the basics of cooking, baking, canning, and sewing from her mother, and her father introduced her to gardening.

While earning a bachelor's degree in history and architectural history at Barnard College, she worked as a model to pay her tuition. It was there that she became Martha Stewart, when she married in her sophomore year. Although a successful stockbroker on Wall Street, she left to pursue her passions and opened a gourmet-food shop that later became a catering business in Westport, Connecticut. She used the distinct visual presentations and stylish recipes that she developed in her catering business as a source for her first book, *Entertaining,* which was first published in 1982.

Stewart's natural business instincts and leadership skills helped her make smart choices as she transformed her small business into a media empire. Martha Stewart's name had now become a well-recognized brand. As such she joined Kmart as an image and product consultant in 1987 and persuaded the retailer to sell her growing line of products. She eventually became partners with the firm that helped her gain the capital necessary to break free of Time Warner, publisher of her highly successful *Martha Stewart Living* magazine.

When Stewart and Time Warner disagreed over her plan to cross-sell and market her publishing, television, merchandising, and Web interests, she used everything she owned to buy back the brand rights of her products and publishing for an estimated $75 million. In 1999 she took her rapidly growing business public. MSLO, the company she created, now owns three magazines, a TV and cable program, thirty-four books, a newspaper column, a radio program, a website, and a merchandising line, as well as the "Martha by Mail"

We appreciate the work of Leyla Baykal in helping draft the previous edition of this case. This case was prepared for classroom discussion rather than to illustrate either effective or ineffective handling of an administrative, ethical, or legal decision by management. All sources used for this case were obtained through publicly available material and the Martha Stewart website.

catalog business. The company earns 65 percent of its revenues from publishing, and its media properties reach 88 million people a month around the world, allowing MSLO to command top advertising rates.

Stewart's successes have been widely recognized. Her television show won an Emmy, and *Adweek* named her "Publishing Executive of the Year" in 1996. She has been named one of "New York's 100 Most Influential Women in Business" by *Forbes* 400, one of the "50 Most Powerful Women" by *Fortune,* and one of "America's 25 Most Influential People" by *Time*. In 1998 she was the recipient of an Edison Achievement Award from the American Marketing Association as well as many other national awards and honors.

MSLO is a classic success story: the small catering business transformed into a well-known brand, in the process making its founder synonymous with stylish living and good taste. Even those who ridiculed Stewart's cheery perfect-housewife image acknowledge her confidence and business acumen. One author commented, "To the degree that her business partners were prepared to help advance the success of Martha Stewart, she was prepared to work with them. To the degree that they got in her way, she was willing to roll right over them." Another admired her hard-working nature by saying, "Anyone who spends more than a few minutes with America's most famous homemaker learns that she is one heck of a juggler."

THE INSIDER-TRADING SCANDAL

Despite her reputation and business successes, Stewart was indicted in 2003 on criminal charges and faced several civil lawsuits related to her sale of ImClone stock. Stewart sold the stock on December 27, 2001, one day before the Food and Drug Administration (FDA) refused to review ImClone System's cancer drug Erbitux; the company's stock tumbled following the FDA's announcement. The scandal also touched a number of other ImClone insiders, including the company's counsel, John Landes, who dumped $2.5 million worth of the company's stock on December 6; Ronald Martell, ImClone's vice president of marketing, who sold $2.1 million worth of company stock on December 11; and four other company executives who cashed in shares between December 12 and December 21.

Developments in the Scandal

After learning that the FDA was going to refuse to review Erbitux, Sam Waksal, the CEO of ImClone and a close friend of Stewart's, instructed his broker Peter Bacanovic, who was also Stewart's broker, to transfer $4.9 million in ImClone stock to the account of his daughter, Aliza Waksal. His daughter also requested that Bacanovic sell $2.5 million of her own ImClone stock. Sam Waksal then tried to sell the shares he had transferred to his daughter but was blocked by brokerage firm Merrill Lynch. Phone records indicate that Bacanovic called Stewart's office on December 27 shortly after Waksal's daughter dumped her shares. Stewart's stock was sold ten minutes later.

Sam Waksal was arrested on June 12, 2002, on charges of insider trading, obstruction of justice, and bank fraud, in addition to previously filed securities fraud and perjury charges. Although he pled innocent for nine months, Waksal eventually pled guilty to insider trading and another six charges. In his plea, Waksal said, "I am aware that my conduct, while I was in possession of material non-public information, was wrong. I've made some terrible mistakes and I deeply regret what has happened." He was later sentenced to more than seven years in prison—the maximum allowed by federal sentencing guidelines—and ordered to pay a $3 million fine. Prosecutors continue to investigate whether he tipped off others, including family members and an individual who sold $30 million of the biotechnology company's shares. Sam Waksal's father and daughter also faced a criminal investigation and the possible forfeiture of nearly $10 million that the government contended was obtained from illegal insider trading. In 2006 Waksal agreed to pay a $3 million penalty, and his father returned $2 million in profits.

Stewart denied that she engaged in any improper trading when she sold her shares of ImClone stock. On December 27, Stewart says she was flying in her private jet to Mexico for a vacation with two friends. En route, she called her office to check her messages, which included one from her broker Peter Bacanovic, with news that her ImClone stock had dropped below $60 per share. Stewart claimed she had previously issued a "stop-loss" order to sell the stock if it fell below $60 per share. She called Bacanovic and asked him to sell her 3,928 shares; she also called her friend Sam Waksal, but could not reach him. Stewart's assistant left a message for Waksal saying, "Something's going on with ImClone, and she wants to know what it is. She's staying at Los Ventanos." Waksal did not call her back. Investigators also looked into the sale of another ten thousand shares of ImClone stock by Bart Pasternak, a close friend of Stewart. At about the time Stewart made her sale, she was on her way to Mexico with Pasternak's estranged wife, Mariana.

However, Stewart's explanation that she unloaded her stock because of a prearranged sell order collapsed when Douglas Faneuil, the broker's assistant who handled the sale of the ImClone stock for Stewart, told Merrill Lynch lawyers that his boss, Peter Bacanovic, had pressured him to lie about a stop-loss order. Although Faneuil initially backed Stewart's story, he later told prosecutors that Bacanovic prompted him to advise Stewart that Waksal family members were dumping their stock and that she should consider doing the same. During the trial, Faneuil said, "I did not truthfully reveal everything I knew about the actions of my immediate supervisor and the true reason for the sales. There came a point in time where I just couldn't continue to lie. I felt that the coverup was part of my daily existence, and I just couldn't take it anymore." He also acknowledged that Bacanovic never "explicitly" directed him to lie. Faneuil pled guilty to a misdemeanor and received a $2000 fine. Merrill Lynch fired Faneuil. Bacanovic was also fired for declining to cooperate with investigators looking into trading activity of ImClone's shares and served five months in prison.

The Probe

In August 2002, investigators requested Stewart's phone and e-mail records on the ImClone stock trade and her Merrill Lynch account as well as those of her business manager. Congressional investigators for the U.S. House of Representatives' Energy and Commerce Committee could not find any credible record of such an order between Stewart and her broker. However, portions of the documents presented to the committee were unreadable because they were blacked out. Stewart's lawyers later agreed to return to Capitol Hill with unedited documents. The committee did not call Stewart to testify because her lawyers had made it clear that she would invoke her Fifth Amendment right to remain silent.

Investigators, who had been negotiating unsuccessfully with Stewart's lawyers to arrange for her voluntary testimony, came to believe that Stewart was "stonewalling" and would not cooperate. Many wondered, "If Ms. Stewart has been straight about her story, then why wouldn't she tell it under oath?" After the scandal broke, however, Stewart and her spokespeople declined to comment or could not be reached. The House Energy and Commerce Committee ultimately handed the Martha Stewart/ImClone investigation over to the U.S. Justice Department, with a strong suggestion that it investigate whether Stewart had lied to the committee.

Additionally, the Securities and Exchange Commission (SEC) indicated that it was ready to file civil securities fraud charges against Stewart for her alleged role in the insider-trading scandal and her public statement about the stop-loss arrangement with her broker. Federal prosecutors soon widened their investigation to include determining whether Stewart had tampered with a computerized phone log to delete a message from her broker as well as whether she had made her public statements about why she sold ImClone shares in order to maintain the price of her own company's stock. Federal law bars officers of public corporations from knowingly making false statements that are material in effect—meaning they have the potential to shape a reasonable investor's decision to buy or sell stock in a particular company.

The Charges

On June 4, 2003, a federal grand jury indicted Stewart on charges of securities fraud, conspiracy (together with Bacanovic), making false statements, and obstruction of justice. Although the forty-one page indictment did not specifically charge Stewart with insider trading, it alleged that she lied to federal investigators about the stock sale, attempted to cover up her activities, and defrauded MSLO shareholders by misleading them about the gravity of the situation and thereby keeping the stock price from falling. The indictment further accused Stewart of deleting a computer log of the telephone message from Bacanovic informing her that he thought ImClone's stock "was going to start trading downward." Bacanovic was also indicted on charges of making false statements, making and using false documents, perjury, and obstruction of justice. The indictment stated that Bacanovic had altered his personal notes to create the impression of a prior agreement to sell Stewart's ImClone shares if the price fell below $60 per share. Both Stewart and Bacanovic pled "not guilty" to all charges.

Additionally, the SEC filed a civil lawsuit accusing both Stewart and Bacanovic of insider trading, demanding more than $45,000 in recompensation, and seeking to bar Stewart from being an officer or director of a public company. Although Stewart denied the charges, she resigned her positions as CEO and chairman of the board of MSLO just hours after the indictment, avowing, "I love this company, its people and everything it stands for, and I am stepping aside as chairman and CEO because it is the right thing to do." She retained a seat on the firm's board of directors and remained its chief shareholder. Sharon Patrick, the company's president and CFO, replaced Stewart as CEO, and Jeffrey Ubben, the founder of an investment group that owns MSLO stock, was named chairman.

Ironically, Stewart could have sold her ImClone stock on December 31 instead of December 27 and collected $180,000 in profit without raising any concerns. That's just $48,000 less than what she gained through the earlier sale. The $48,000 gain cost Stewart $261,371,672 plus legal fees and five months in prison.

Despite Stewart's denials of any wrongdoing, the scandal sliced more than 70 percent off the stock price of MSLO and according to one estimate, washed away more than a quarter of her net worth. Before the scandal, Stewart had an estimated net worth of $650 million.

After the indictment and Stewart's resignation, she took out a full-page newspaper ad in which she reiterated her innocence and appealed to her customers to remain loyal. Stewart insisted in the ad that "I simply returned a call from my stockbroker. . . . Based in large part on prior discussions with my broker about price, I authorized a sale of my remaining shares in a biotech company called ImClone. I later denied any wrongdoing in public statements and voluntary interviews with prosecutors. The government's attempt to criminalize these actions makes no sense to me." Stewart also retained a public relations firm to help her firm weather the crisis and set up a website, www.marthatalks.com, to update her customers and fans about the case.

After the scandal became public, Stewart began a campaign to detach herself from the events. However, she couldn't escape questions about the insider-trading scandal. Even in her regular weekly cooking segment on CBS's *The Early Show,* host Jane Clayson attempted to ask about the scandal, but Stewart responded, "I

want to focus on my salad. . . ." Her appearances on the morning program were put on hold, pending the trial.

MARTHA STEWART IS CONVICTED AND SENTENCED TO PRISON

At her trial, the indictments for securities fraud were dropped, but the other indictments were prosecuted. In February 2004, the judge threw out the most serious of the charges against Stewart—securities fraud. However, just one week later, a jury convicted Stewart on four remaining charges of making false statements and conspiracy to obstruct justice. She was sentenced to serve five months in prison and five months in home detention. She finished her prison time in March 2005.

Shortly after her prison release, Stewart decided to fight rather than settle civil insider-trading charges from the SEC. In June 2003, the SEC civil complaint was stayed until criminal proceedings were completed. In a response to the SEC complaint filed in May 2006 with the U.S. District Court in Manhattan, Stewart denied the allegations that she used nonpublic information when she sold 3,928 shares of ImClone stock in December 2001. Instead, she said she "acted in good faith." Fighting the charges offers Stewart the chance to reclaim her CEO and chairman titles. Another public trial, however, could deal a blow to the company and reverse the turnaround that it has made so far since her release.

MARTHA STEWART RECOVERS AND MAKES A COMEBACK

There are few companies so closely identified with their founders as Martha Stewart Living Omnimedia. Her most important role in the company is as its highly recognizable spokesperson, brand, and television personality. Finding someone to replace her in that role would be far more difficult than finding a replacement chairperson and CEO. Although many companies have survived scandals and the exit of their founders, Stewart has a one-of-a-kind relationship with her company, its brands, and products. Many wondered whether the firm could truly recover. She branded herself as the ultimate last word on perfect living, but her image had been a media spectacle.

The scandal occurred at an unfortunate time for MSLO. The company's publishing arm was in its mature stage, its television show was suffering declining ratings, and the Internet operation was taking heavy losses. Moreover, some market analysts expressed concern that the company depended too heavily on the name and image of its celebrated founder. One shareholder voiced the concern felt by many: "Without Martha, the company is only a shell. She's it." Stewart personifies the brand that is associated with her credibility and honesty—traits that the public and investigators questioned. In this case, the strength of the brand also becomes its weakness because it is hard to tell where the person ends and the brand begins.

Market analysts agree that Stewart needs to take steps to ensure that the brand can go beyond the person. With the tremendous growth of her company, Stewart has surrounded herself with a group of trustworthy professionals, who are as detail oriented as she is, to deal with the fine points. Although Stewart took strides to make the brand more independent, there are lingering doubts about the long-term effects of the scandal.

Others, however, believe that Stewart's drive and spirit will help her overcome this setback. Jerry Della Femina, an advertising executive, said, "The brand will survive because Martha has gone beyond being a person who represents a brand." She built an empire and became famous by making the most discouraging circumstances seem neat and elegant. The question now is whether the billionaire "diva of domesticity" can survive the scandal. Before the scandal broke, Stewart was asked about her close ties with her brand. She replied, "I think that my role is Walt Disney. There are very few brands that were really started by a person, with a person's name, that have survived as nicely as that. Estee Lauder has certainly survived beautifully, despite Mrs. Lauder's absence from the business in the last, maybe, 15 years. I would like to engender that same kind of spirit and same kind of high quality."

In the fall of 2005, Stewart launched a prime-time NBC TV show, *The Apprentice: Martha Stewart,* with lackluster ratings and ultimate cancellation. The blame, as she sees it, was not with her performance or her personal brand being overexposed but the overexposure of *The Apprentice* itself. Also, six weeks after being released from federal prison, Stewart reached a deal with Sirius Satellite Radio Inc. to create a twenty-four-hour channel featuring cooking, gardening, and entertaining programming for women. The four-year agreement was a move to rebuild her business.

Shares of MSLO surged since the company reported better-than-expected 2005 results. *Martha Stewart Living* magazine also had strong ad sale gains. Additionally in 2006 the company started a new magazine, *Blueprint,* a publication targeted at 25- to 45-year-old women. In 2005 MSLO announced a deal with homebuilder KB Home to build "Martha Stewart–inspired" homes in the Southeast; due to the success of the first community in Cary, North Carolina, the companies announced that they were expanding the partnership across the country.

In 2007 MSLO and Federated Department Stores, specifically Macy's stores, will sell an exclusive line of Martha Stewart–branded home merchandise such as bedding, dinnerware, and cookware. Also search engine Yahoo! has a site that features content from MSLO's various publications and TV and radio shows.

Stewart appears to be on the road to recovery with many contractual relationships and ongoing media deals. Most of the jokes and late-night TV comments about Stewart's prison time are gone. Her stock is recovering, and her future once again looks bright even though she lost her appeal.

Stewart serves as a classic example of what can happen to a CEO who forgets that she or he is in the spotlight and that an ethical transgression can quickly damage or halt progress and success. Only time will tell if Stewart makes a complete recovery or if she will ever be as successful as she could have been without these events.

Questions

1. Stewart repeatedly denied any wrongdoing, despite the conviction and failed appeal, yet she still says she did nothing wrong. Is this the right strategy?

2. Did Stewart's actions justify the subsequent sentence given to her and those around her?

3. Compare other executives' wrongdoings versus Stewart's. Discuss why MSLO's case is or is not different from what happened at companies such as Enron and Tyco.

Sources

Diane Brady, "Martha Inc.: Inside the Growing Empire of America's Lifestyle Queen," *BusinessWeek,* January 17, 2000; Christopher M. Byron, *Martha Inc.: The Incredible Story of Martha Stewart Living Omnimedia* (New York: Wiley, 2002); Julie Creswell, "Will Martha Walk?" *Fortune,* November 25, 2002, 121–124; Anne D'Innocenzio, "Charges Imperil Stewart Company," *[Fort Collins] Coloradoan,* June 5, 2003, D1, D7; Mike Duff, "Martha Scandal Raises Questions, What's in Store for Kmart?" *DSN Retailing Today,* July 8, 2002, 1, 45; Shelley Emling, "Martha Stewart Indicted on Fraud," *Austin American-Statesman* online, June 5, 2003, www.statesman.com; Shelley Emling, "Stewart Defends Her Name with Ad," *Austin American-Statesman* online, June 6, 2003, www.statesman.com; "Feds Tighten Noose on Martha," CNN/Money, February 6, 2003, http://money.cnn.com/2003/02/06/news/companies/martha/index.htm; Charles Gasparino and Kara Scannell, "Probe of Martha Stewart's Sale of Stock Enters Its Final Phase," *Wall Street Journal,* January 24, 2003, C7; Constance L. Hays, "Stiff Sentence for ImClone Founder," *Austin American-Statesman* online, June 11, 2003, http://www.statesman.com; "ImClone Founder Pleads Guilty," CBS News online, October 15, 2002, www.cbsnews.com/stories/2002/08/12/national/main518354.shtml; "ImClone Probe Costly for Martha Stewart," MSNBC, January 27, 2003, http://stacks.msnbc.com/news/864675.asp; Paul R. La Monica, "Momentum for Martha," CNN/Money, April 24, 2006; Charles M. Madigan, "Woman Behaving Badly," *Across the Board,* July/August 2002, 75; Jerry Markon, "Martha Stewart Could Be Charged as 'Tippee,'" *Wall Street Journal,* October 3, 2002, C1, C9; "Martha Stewart Enters Not Guilty Plea to Charges," *Wall Street Journal* online, June 4, 2003, http://online.wsj.com; "Martha's Mouthpiece: We'll Deliver," CBS News online, August 20, 2002, www.cbsnews.com/stories/2002/08/20/national/main519320.shtml; "Martha Stewart Living Slides into Red, Expects More Losses," *Wall Street Journal* online, March 4, 2003, http://online.wsj.com/article/0,,SB1046721988332486840,00.html; Erin McClam, "Martha Stewart Indicted in Stock Scandal," *[Fort Collins] Coloradoan,* June 5, 2003, A1; Amy Merrick, "Can Martha Deliver Merry?" *Wall Street Journal,* October 8, 2002, B1, B3; Keith Naughton, "Martha's Tabloid Dish," *Newsweek,* June 24, 2002, 36; Keith Naughton and Mark Hosenball, "Setting the Table," *Newsweek,* September 23, 2002, 7; "New Witness in Martha Probe," CBS News online, August 9, 2002, www.cbsnews.com/stories/2002/08/12/national/main518448.shtml; Marc Peyser, "The Insiders," *Newsweek,* July 1, 2002, 38–53; Patricia Sellers, "Remodeling Martha," *Fortune,* November 14, 2005, 101; Thomas A. Stewart, "Martha Stewart's Recipe for Disaster," Business2.com, July 3, 2002; Seth Sutel, "Martha Stewart Gets Own Channel on Sirius," Yahoo! Finance, April 18, 2005, http://biz.yahoo.com/ap/050418/sirius_martha_stewart.html?.v=15; Jeffrey Toobin, "Lunch at Martha's," *New Yorker,* February 3, 2003, 38–44; Thor Valdmanis, "Martha Stewart Leaves NYSE Post," *USA Today,* October 4, 2002, 3B.

Tyco International: Leadership Crisis

On September 12, 2002, Tyco International's former chief executive officer, L. Dennis Kozlowski, and former chief financial officer, Mark H. Swartz, were seen in handcuffs on national television after they were arrested and charged with misappropriating more than $170 million from the company. They were also accused of stealing more than $430 million through fraudulent sales of Tyco stock and concealing the information from shareholders. The two executives were charged in a Manhattan federal court with numerous counts of grand larceny, enterprise corruption, and falsifying business records. Another executive, former general counsel Mark A. Belnick, was also charged with concealing $14 million in personal loans. Months after the initial arrests, charges and lawsuits were still being filed in a growing scandal that threatened to eclipse the notoriety of other companies facing accounting fraud charges in the early 2000s.

TYCO'S HISTORY

Tyco, Inc., was founded by Arthur J. Rosenberg in 1960, in Waltham, Massachusetts, as an investment and holding company focusing on solid-state science and energy conversion. It developed the first laser with a sustained beam for medical procedures. With a shifting of focus to the commercial sector, Tyco became a publicly traded company in 1964. It also began a pattern of acquisitions—sixteen different companies by 1968—that would continue through 1982 as the company sought to fill gaps in its development and distribution network. The rapidly growing and diversifying firm grew from $34 million in sales in 1973 to $500 million in 1982.

In 1982 Tyco reorganized into three business segments (fire protection, electronics, and packaging) to strengthen itself from within. By 1986 Tyco had returned to a growth-through-acquisitions mode. In the 1990s Tyco maintained four core segments: electrical and electronic components, health-care and specialty products, fire and security services, and flow control. The company changed its name to Tyco International in 1993 to signal its global presence to the financial community. By 2000 the firm had acquired more than thirty major companies, including well-known firms such as ADT, Raychem, and the CIT Group.

THE RISE OF DENNIS KOZLOWSKI

Leo Dennis Kozlowski was born in Newark, New Jersey, in 1946. His parents, Leo Kelly and Agnes Kozlowski, were second-generation Polish Americans. His father worked for Public Service Transport (later the New Jersey Transport), and his mother was a

We appreciate the work of Linda G. Mullen in helping draft the previous edition of this case. This case was prepared for classroom discussion rather than to illustrate either effective or ineffective handling of an administrative, ethical, or legal decision by management. All sources used for this case were obtained through publicly available material and the Tyco website.

school crossing guard in Newark's predominantly Polish neighborhood. Kozlowski attended public school and graduated from West Side High in 1964. He lived at home while he studied accounting at Seton Hall University in South Orange, New Jersey.

After brief stints at SCM Corp. and Nashua Corporation, Kozlowski went to work for Tyco in 1976. He soon found a friend and mentor in CEO Joseph Gaziano, whose lavish style—including company jets, extravagant vacations, company cars, and country club memberships—impressed Kozlowski. However, the luxurious lifestyle came to an end when Gaziano died of cancer in 1982. Fellow MIT graduate John F. Fort III, who differed sharply in management style, replaced Gaziano. Where Gaziano had been extravagant, Fort was analytical and thrifty, and Wall Street responded approvingly to his new course and direction for Tyco. Fort's goal was to increase profits for the shareholders of Tyco and cut out extravagant spending that had characterized Gaziano's tenure.

Kozlowski, who had thrived under Gaziano, had to shift gears to adapt to the abrupt change in leadership. However, Kozlowski's accounting background helped push him up the ranks at Tyco. He was very adept at crunching numbers and helping achieve Fort's vision of taking care of shareholders first. Fort soon noticed Kozlowski's talents.

Kozlowski's first major promotion within Tyco was to president of Grinnell Fire Protection Systems Co., Tyco's largest division. At Grinnell, Kozlowski cut out extras and reduced overhead, eliminated 98 percent of the paperwork, and reworked compensation programs. Although he slashed managers' salaries, he also set up a bonus compensation package that gave them greater control over the money they could earn. He gave public recognition to high achievers at a yearly banquet, but he also recognized the underachievers, giving out an award for the worst-producing unit as well as the best. Perhaps most important, Kozlowski systematically began to buy out and acquire each of the fire protection division's competitors. As described in a *BusinessWeek* article, he gained a reputation as a "corporate tough guy, respected and feared in roughly equal measure."

Over the next few years, Kozlowski continued his rise up Tyco's corporate ladder, becoming the company's president in 1987, before rising to CFO and eventually CEO in 1992. However, his aggressive approach to acquisitions and mergers during this period became a concern for then-CEO Fort, who wanted to slow the rate of activity in Kozlowski's division. His largest acquisition was Wormald International, a $360 million global fire-protection concern. However, integrating Wormald proved problematic, and Fort was reportedly not happy with so large a purchase. Fort and Kozlowski also disagreed over the rapid changes that Kozlowski made in the fire-protection division. Kozlowski responded by lobbying to convince Tyco's board of directors that the problems with Wormald were a "bump in the road" and the firm should continue its strategy of acquiring profitable companies that met its guidelines. The board sided with Kozlowski, and Fort resigned as CEO and later as chairman of the board, although he remained a member of Tyco's board of directors until 2003.

KOZLOWSKI'S TYCO EMPIRE

At the age of 46, Kozlowski found himself at the helm of Tyco International in 1992. He eventually moved out of his North Hampton home, leaving his wife and two daughters for a waitress, Karen Lee Mayo Locke, whom he eventually married in 2000. Before 2000 Kozlowski's lifestyle was comparatively ordinary for a person of such rank; however, some subtle changes in lifestyle did occur after the Hampton move but before his second marriage. His new lifestyle—which included parties that were regular gossip-column fodder and homes in Boca Raton, Nantucket, Beaver Creek, and New York City—appeared to emulate that of Kozlowski's mentor, former CEO Joseph Gaziano. Indeed, Kozlowski's aggressive strategy of mergers and acquisitions made Tyco look more like the company it had been under Gaziano.

Kozlowski had learned Tyco and its businesses from the bottom up, giving him an advantage in his determination to make Tyco the greatest company of the new century. Among other things, he recognized that one of the conglomerate's major shortcomings was its reliance on cyclical industries. Thus, he decided to diversify into more noncyclical industries. His first major acquisition toward that objective was the Kendall Company, a manufacturer of medical supplies, which had emerged from bankruptcy just two years before. Kozlowski quickly revived the business, which became very profitable and doubled Tyco's earnings. Although Tyco's board of directors had initially balked at the

Kendall acquisition, the directors were pleased with the subsidiary's turnaround and contribution to profits. Kozlowski made Kendall the core of his new Tyco Healthcare Group, which quickly grew to become the second-largest producer of medical devices behind Johnson & Johnson. The board rewarded Kozlowski's performance by increasing his salary to $2.1 million and giving him shares of the company's stock.

Kozlowski's next strategic move was the acquisition of ADT Security Services, a British-owned company located in Bermuda, in 1997. By structuring the deal as a "reverse takeover," Tyco acquired a global presence as well as ADT's Bermuda registration, which allowed the firm to create a network of offshore subsidiaries to shelter its foreign earnings from U.S. taxes.

While Kozlowski continued to acquire new companies to build his vision of Tyco, he handpicked a few trusted people and placed them in key positions. One of these individuals was Mark Swartz, who was promoted from director of Mergers and Acquisitions to CFO. Swartz, who had developed a strong financial background as an auditor for Deloitte & Touche and a reputation for being more approachable than Kozlowski, was aware of Kozlowski's business practices. Kozlowski also recruited Mark Belnick to become Tyco's general counsel.

By this time, Tyco's corporate governance system was composed of Kozlowski as CEO and the firm's board of directors, which had eleven members, including Joshua Berman, a vice president of Tyco and former outside counsel; Mark Swartz, CFO; Lord Michael Ashcroft, a British dignitary who came with the ADT merger; James S. Pasman, Jr., also from ADT; W. Peter Slusser, also from ADT; Richard S. Bodman, a venture capitalist; Stephen W. Foss, CEO of a textile concern; Joseph F. Welch, CEO of snack-food maker Bachman Co.; Wendy Lane, a private equity investor; John F. Fort III, former CEO and chairman of Tyco; and Frank E. Walsh, Jr., director of the board. Kozlowski particularly liked the prestige of Lord Ashcroft being associated with his company. The majority of the directors had been on the board for ten to twenty years, and they were very familiar with Tyco's strategies and Kozlowski's management style. As directors, they were responsible for protecting Tyco's shareholders by disclosing any questionable situations or issues that might seem unethical or inappropriate, such as conflicts of interest. However, after the arrests of Kozlowski and Swartz, investigations subsequently uncovered the following troubling relationships among the board's members:

- Swartz participated in loan-forgiveness programs.

- Bodman invested $5 million for Kozlowski in a private stock fund managed by Bodman.

- Walsh received $20 million for helping arrange the acquisition of CIT Group without the knowledge of the rest of the board of directors.

- Walsh also held controlling interest in two firms that received more than $3.5 million for leasing an aircraft and providing pilot services to Tyco between 1996 and 2002.

- Foss received $751,101 for supplying a Cessna Citation aircraft and pilot services.

- Ashcroft used $2.5 million in Tyco funds to purchase a home.

With his handpicked board in place, Kozlowski decided to open a Manhattan office overlooking Central Park. However, the firm maintained its humble Exeter, New Hampshire, office, where Kozlowski preferred to be interviewed. According to *BusinessWeek,* he bragged to a guest, "We don't believe in perks, not even executive parking spots." The unpublicized Manhattan office essentially became the firm's unofficial headquarters, and Kozlowski lavished it with every imaginable perk. He used Tyco funds to purchase and furnish apartments for key executives and employees in New York's pricey Upper East Side as well.

Meanwhile, Jeanne Terrile, an analyst for Tyco at Merrill Lynch, was not so impressed with Kozlowski's activities and Tyco's performance. Stock analysts like those at Merrill Lynch make recommendations to investors whether to buy, hold, or sell a particular stock. After Terrile wrote a less than favorable review of Tyco's rapid acquisitions and mergers and refused to upgrade Merrill's position on Tyco's stock, Kozlowski met with David Komansky, the CEO of Merrill Lynch. Although the subject of the meeting was never confirmed, shortly thereafter, Terrile was replaced by Phua Young, who immediately upgraded Merrill's recommendation for Tyco to "buy" from "accumulate." Merrill Lynch continued to be one of Tyco's top underwriters as well as one of its primary advisers for mergers and acquisitions.

Between 1997 and 2001, Tyco's revenues climbed 48.7 percent a year, and its pretax operating margins increased to 22.1 percent. The pace of mergers and acquisitions escalated with the assistance of Swartz, Tyco's CFO. In February 2002, Tyco announced that it had spent more than $8 billion on more than seven hundred acquisitions in the last three years. Among these were AMP Inc., an electronics maker for $11.3 billion in stock, and CIT Group, a commercial finance company. However, some of the merged companies were less than satisfied with the arrangement. Kozlowski forced acquired companies to scale back sharply and eliminate anything—and anyone—that did not produce revenue. The toll on human capital was enormous. Tyco shareholders and directors, however, were very happy with Kozlowski's performance, as demonstrated by his rapid salary increases from $8 million in 1997, to $67 million in 1998, to $170 million in 1999, which made him the second-highest paid CEO in the United States. A transaction that would be considered somewhat pivotal in Kozlowski's personal life was his 1997 purchase of a four-acre, three-bedroom, 7,000-square-foot house in Nantucket, Massachusetts, for $5 million.

During 1997–2002, Kozlowski's charismatic leadership style together with the firm's decentralized corporate structure meant that few people, including members of the board of directors, had a true picture of the firm's activities and finances. The company was organized into four distinct divisions—fire protection (53 percent); valves, pipes, and other "flow-control" devices (23 percent); electrical and electronic components (13 percent); and packaging materials (11 percent) —and there was little interaction among them. Each division's president reported directly to Kozlowski, who in turn reported to the board.

Those who saw red flags at Tyco International were shot down, including Jeanne Terrile at Merrill Lynch and David W. Tice, a short seller who questioned whether Tyco's use of large reserves in connection with its acquisitions was obscuring its results. A nonpublic investigation by the Securities and Exchange Commission (SEC) resulted only in Tyco amending its earnings per share for 1999.

THE FALL OF DENNIS KOZLOWSKI

At the beginning of 2002, Kozlowski announced that Tyco would split into four independent, publicly traded companies: security and electronics, health care, fire protection and flow control, and financial services. Tyco believed these actions would increase shareholder value. Kozlowski stated that

> I am extremely proud of Tyco's performance. We have built a great portfolio of businesses and over the five years ended September 30, 2001, we have delivered earnings per share growth at a compounded annual rate of over 40% and industry-leading operating profit margins in each of our businesses. During this same period, we have increased annual free cash flow from $240 million in 1996 to $4.8 billion in fiscal 2001. Nonetheless, even with this performance, Tyco is trading at a 2002 P/E multiple of 12.0x, a discount of almost 50% to the S&P 500.

But then everything began to fall apart, especially when the board of directors learned that one of its members, Walsh, had received a $20 million bonus for his part in securing and aiding in the CIT merger. Walsh promptly resigned from the board. Troubled by the idea that Kozlowski had made such a major payment without their knowledge, the remaining board members launched an investigation to determine whether other board members had earned such "commissions." The probe uncovered numerous expense abuses. Finally, after learning that he was about to be indicted for tax evasion, Kozlowski agreed to resign as CEO of Tyco on June 2, 2002.

Months earlier, the New York State Bank Department had observed large sums of money going into and out of Tyco's accounts. This would not have been unusual except that the funds were being transferred into Kozlowski's personal accounts. Eventually, authorities discovered that Kozlowski had allegedly avoided $3.1 million in New York state taxes by appearing to ship rare artwork to New Hampshire when in fact it was sent to New York. On June 3, Kozlowski was arrested for tax evasion, but the scandal was only just beginning.

On September 12, 2002, Kozlowski and Swartz, who had also resigned from Tyco, were indicted on thirty-eight felony counts for allegedly stealing $170 million from Tyco and fraudulently selling an additional $430 million in stock options. Among other allegations, Kozlowski was accused of taking $242 million from a program intended to help Tyco employees buy company stock, so that he could buy yachts, fine art, and luxury homes. Together with former legal counsel Mark Belnick, the three face criminal charges and a civil complaint from the SEC. Kozlowski was also accused of granting $106 million to various employees through "loan forgiveness" and relocation programs. Swartz was also charged with falsifying documents in this loan program in the amount of $14 million. Belnick was charged with larceny and trying to steer a federal investigation, as well as taking more than $26 million from Tyco.

In addition, several former board members were cited for conflict-of-interest issues. Walsh, a former board member who received a $20 million bonus for the CIT merger, pled guilty and agreed to repay the $20 million plus an additional $2 million in court costs. Moreover, Jerry Boggess, the president of Tyco Fire and Security Division, was fired and accused of creating a number of "bookkeeping issues" that had a negative impact on earnings to shareholders. Richard Scalzo, the PricewaterhouseCoopers auditor who signed off on Tyco's 2002 audit, was removed. Tyco's stock plunged from $60 per share in January 2002 to $18 per share by December, and investors lost millions of dollars. Many of the firm's 260,000 employees were also shareholders and watched their savings dwindle. Tyco's retirees found that their savings and retirement plans, which were tied up in company shares, plummeted with the company's stock price.

REBUILDING AN EMPIRE

After Kozlowski's resignation, he was replaced as CEO by Edward Breen (see Table C13.1). The company filed suit against Kozlowski and Swartz for more than $100 million. The SEC allows companies to sue for profits made by "insiders" who are profiting by buying and selling company stock within a six-month period. The company stated that "to hold him accountable for his misconduct, we seek not only full payment for the funds he misappropriated but also punitive damages for the serious harm he did to Tyco and its shareholders." Additionally, Tyco is suing for monies paid by Kozlowski to keep some of those closest to him from testifying against him.

Breen launched a review of the company's accounting and corporate governance practices to determine whether any other fraud had occurred. Although the probe uncovered no fraud, the firm announced in late 2002 that it would restate its 2002 financial results by $382.2 million. Tyco's new management declared in a regulatory filing that the firm's previous management had "engaged in a pattern of aggressive accounting which, even when in accordance with Generally Accepted Accounting Principles, was intended to increase reported earnings above what they would have been if more conservative accounting had been employed." Although Tyco's investigations found no further fraud, the company repeatedly restated its financial results or took accounting charges totaling more than $2 billion over the next six months.

In 2004 Kozlowski and Swartz went before a jury that ended in a mistrial. However, in 2005 both were found guilty on twenty-two of twenty-three counts of grand larceny and conspiracy, falsifying business records, and violating business law. The judge also ordered both to pay $134 million to Tyco. Kozlowski also must pay a $70 million fine and Swartz a $35 million fine. Kozlowski's total bill came to $167 million in fines and restitution. The prison time for both appears to be a little less than seven years in a state facility. Both are appealing their sentences while incarcerated. Kozlowski has so far raised over $105.8 million by selling off a Monet, a Renoir, his three-bedroom condominium in Beaver Creek, Colorado, and his Nantucket home.

To restore investors' faith in the company, Tyco's new management team worked hard to reorganize the company and recover some of the funds taken by Kozlowski. At its annual meeting, shareholders elected a completely new board of directors and voted to make future executive severance agreements subject to shareholder approval and to require the board chairman to be an independent person, rather than a Tyco CEO. However, the shareholders elected to keep the company incorporated in Bermuda. In 2006 Breen announced that Tyco would be splitting into three entities: Tyco Healthcare ($10 billion, 40,000 employees), one of the world's leading diversified health-care companies; Tyco Electronics ($12 billion, 88,000 employees), the world's largest passive electronic components manufacturer; and the combination of Tyco Fire & Security and Engineered Products & Services (TFS/TEPS) ($18 billion, 118,000 employees), a global business with leading positions in residential and commercial security, fire protection, and industrial products and services. Tyco has survived the doomsday predictions with over $40 billion in revenue, and their employees have sighed a breath of relief for their jobs and pensions.

| **TABLE C13.1** | Tyco Timeline and Statements from Tyco Press Releases |

June 3, 2002   Dennis Kozlowski resigns as chairman of the board and CEO for personal reasons. Kozlowski also steps down from the board of directors. At the request of Tyco's board, John Fort agrees to assume primary executive responsibilities during an interim period while a search for a permanent replacement is completed.

June 10, 2002   Tyco replaces its general counsel, Mark Belnick, with Irving Gutin. Gutin previously served as general counsel of Tyco.

June 17, 2002   Tyco files suit against Belnick for a broad pattern of misconduct, including using company funds for personal gain.

June 17, 2002   Tyco files suit against Frank Walsh, former member of the board of directors, for breaching his fiduciary obligations in the company's CIT Group acquisition.

July 25, 2002   The board of directors appoints Edward Breen, former president and COO of Motorola, Inc., as chairman of the board and CEO.

August 6, 2002   Tyco appoints Eric Pillmore as senior vice president of corporate governance. Breen, chairman and CEO, said, "I have made an absolute commitment to establishing the highest standards of corporate governance in every aspect of this company's financial reporting, operations and management."

September 11, 2002   David FitzPatrick is appointed executive vice president and CFO and succeeds Mark Swartz, who has resigned from the company.

September 12, 2002   Tyco board of directors nominates five business leaders to fill expected vacancies:

- Jerome York is chairman, president, and CEO of Micro Warehouse, Inc. Before joining Micro Warehouse, York was the vice chairman of Tracinda Corporation from 1995 to 1999, was CFO of IBM Corporation from 1993 to 1995, and held various positions at Chrysler Corporations from 1979 to 1993. York graduated from the U.S. Military Academy and received an MS from the Massachusetts Institute of Technology and an MBA from the University of Michigan.

- Mackey McDonald served as the chairman, president, and CEO of VF Corporation. McDonald began his tenure at VF Corporation in 1982 and was named chairman, president, and CEO in 1998. He also was a director of operations at Hanes Corporation. McDonald graduated from Davidson College and received an MBA in marketing from Georgia State University.

- George Buckley is the chairman and CEO of Brunswick Corporation. Formerly serving as the chief technology officer and president of two divisions throughout his career at Emerson Electric Company from 1993 to 1997, Buckley joined Brunswick in 1997 and has held the role of chairman and CEO for over two years. Buckley combined postgraduate work at Huddersfield and Southampton Universities and received a doctorate at the University of Huddersfield in 1977.

- Bruce Gordon is the president of retail markets at Verizon Communications, Inc. Gordon fulfilled a variety of positions at Bell Atlantic Corporation, including group president, vice president of marketing and sales, and vice president of sales. Gordon graduated from Gettysburg College and received an MS from Massachusetts Institute of Technology.

- Sandra Wijnberg is a senior vice president and CFO at Marsh & McLennan Companies, Inc. Before joining Marsh & McLennan in January 2000, Wijnberg served as a senior vice president and treasurer of Tricon Global Restaurants, Inc., and held various positions at PepsiCo, Inc.; Morgan Stanley Group, Inc.; and American Express Company. Wijnberg is a graduate of the University of California, Los Angeles, and received an MBA from the University of Southern California.

November 8, 2002   The board of directors nominates Admiral Dennis C. Blair (U.S. Navy, Ret.) to be on the board. Blair retired as commander in chief of the U.S. Pacific Fleet in 1999 after more than thirty years of service in the armed forces. Previously, Blair served as vice admiral and director of the Joint Staff and member of the Reserve Forces Policy Board for the Department of Defense. During his career, he had also worked closely with the White House, the National Security Council, and the Central Intelligence Agency and served as rear admiral and commander of the *Kitty Hawk* Battle Group. Blair graduated from the U.S. Naval Academy and holds a master's degree from Oxford University.

November 18, 2002   Jerome York, chairman, president, and CEO of Micro Warehouse, Inc., and Mackey McDonald, chairman, president, and CEO of VF Corporation, are appointed to the board of directors. York fills the seat vacated by Ashcroft, and McDonald serves in place of Pasman. Ashcroft and Pasman, who submitted letters of resignation to Tyco chairman and CEO Breen, were the first Tyco directors to resign following the board's unanimous decision not to nominate or support for reelection at the company's 2003 annual meeting any of the nine current directors who were members of the board prior to July 2002.

| **TABLE C13.1** | Tyco Timeline and Statements from Tyco Press Releases (*continued*) |

Ashcroft said, "After 18 years of service on the Board, it was time for me to move on and allow the company's new management team to do its job. I am pleased that the Board agreed with my suggestion of appointing as advisors to the Board two current directors. I have, however, told the Board that I do not wish to serve in this capacity because there are others more suitable than I for this role. Looking ahead, I wish the company well in successfully meeting the challenges of rebuilding Tyco." Pasman said, "I believe that a new Board will help propel Tyco to the levels of operating performance, shareholder value and investor confidence that the company deserves. Even though I am leaving my position as director, I will always remain a staunch supporter of this business and the people of Tyco."

January 30, 2003   H. Carl McCall, former comptroller of the state of New York, is nominated to join the board of directors. He began his term as New York state comptroller in May 1993, was reelected to his second term as comptroller in November 1998, and served until November 2002 when he became the Democratic nominee for governor of the state of New York. Previous to his position as comptroller, McCall was a vice president of Citicorp for eight years. He has also served as the president of the New York City Board of Education, ambassador to the United Nations, commissioner of the Port Authority of New York and New Jersey, and commissioner of the New York State Division of Human Rights, and he was elected to three terms as New York state senator. He received a bachelor's degree from Dartmouth College and a master's of divinity degree from Andover-Newton Theological School in Andover, Massachusetts, and is an ordained minister of the United Church of Christ. He is a member of the New York Stock Exchange board of directors where he serves as chairman of the board's Audit and Finance Committee. He also cochaired the board's Committee on Corporate Accountability.

March 29, 2004   The board of directors approves stock option and restricted-stock awards for the company's chairman and CEO Breen. The awards consist of 200,000 restricted shares, which vest on the third anniversary of the grant date, and 600,000 premium-priced stock options with strike prices ranging from $33 to $40, which vest in equal annual installments over a three-year period beginning immediately after the grant date.

January 18, 2005   Tyco nominates Raj Gupta, chairman and CEO of Rohm and Haas Company, for election to Tyco's board of directors. Gupta, age 59, would become Tyco's twelfth director and its eleventh independent director. Gupta also serves on the board of trustees for Drexel University and is a board member of The Vanguard Group.

March 14, 2005   The board of directors approves stock option and restricted-stock awards for the company's chairman and CEO Breen. The awards consist of 160,000 restricted shares, which vest on the third anniversary of the grant date, and 600,000 premium-priced stock options with strike prices ranging from $37 to $45, which vest in three equal annual installments beginning on the first anniversary of the grant date. The board feels that premium-priced stock options provide an effective vehicle to align Breen's incentives with shareholder interests.

Questions

1. What are the ethical and legal issues in this case?

2. What role did Tyco's corporate culture play in the scandal?

3. What roles did the board of directors, CEO, CFO, and legal counsel play?

4. Have Tyco's recent actions been sufficient to restore confidence in the company?

5. What other actions should the company take to demonstrate that it intends to play by the rules?

6. How will the implementation of the Sarbanes-Oxley Act of 2002 prevent future dilemmas in Tyco?

7. Can the SEC trust Tyco's new board?

Sources

Bud Angst, "The Continuing Tyco Saga: December 2002," *[Valley View, PA] Citizen Standard,* January 1, 2003, via http://budangst.com/news/News763.htm; James Bandler and Jerry Guidera, "Tyco Ex-CEO's Party for Wife Cost $2.1 Million, but Had Elvis," *Wall Street Journal,* September 17, 2002, A1; Anthony Bianco, William Symonds, and Nanette Byrnes, "The Rise and Fall of Dennis Kozlowski," *BusinessWeek,* December 23, 2002, 64–77; Laurie P. Cohen, "Tyco Ex-Counsel Claims Auditors Knew of Loans," *Wall Street Journal* online, October 22, 2002, http://online.wsj.com/article_print0,, SB103524176089398951,00.html; Laurie P. Cohen and John Hechinger, "Tyco Suits Say Clandestine Pacts Led to Payments," *Wall Street Journal,* June 18, 2002, A3, A10; Laurie P. Cohen and Mark Maremont, "Tyco Ex-Director Faces Possible Criminal Charges," *Wall Street Journal,* September 9, 2002, A3, A11; Laurie P. Cohen and Mark Maremont, "Tyco Relocations to

Florida Are Probed," *Wall Street Journal,* June 10, 2002, A3, A6; "Corporate Scandals: Tyco, International," MSNBC, www.msnbc.com/news/corpscandal_front.asp?odm=C2ORB (accessed April 4, 2003); "Former Tyco Execs Face Fraud Charges," Canadian Broadcasting Corporation online, September 12, 2002, www.cbc.ca/stories/2002/09/12/tyco020912; Charles Gasparino, "Merrill Replaced Its Tyco Analyst After Meeting," *Wall Street Journal,* September 17, 2002, C1, C13; Jerry Guidera, "Veteran Tyco Director Steps Down," *Wall Street Journal,* November 12, 2002, A8; "History," Tyco International, www.tyco.com/tyco/history.asp (accessed April 25, 2003); Arianna Huffington, "Pigs at the Trough Sidebars," Arianna Online, www.ariannaonline.com/books/pigs_updown.html (accessed April 25, 2003); Louis Lavelle, "Rebuilding Trust in Tyco," *BusinessWeek,* November 25, 2002, 94–96; Robin Londner, "Tyco to Consider Reincorporation, Auditor Removed," *[South Florida] Business Journal* online, March 10, 2003, http://southflorida.bizjournal.com/southflorida/stories/2003/03/10/daily2.html; Loann Lublin and Jerry Guidera, "Tyco Board Criticized on Kozlowski," *Wall Street Journal,* June 7, 2002, A5; Mark Maremont, "Tyco May Report $1.2 Billion in Fresh Accounting Problems" *Wall Street Journal* online, April 30, 2003, http://online.wsj.com/article/0,,SB105166908562976400,00.html?mod=home_whats_news_us; Mark Maremont, "Tyco Seeks Hefty Repayments from Former Financial Officer," *Wall Street Journal,* October 7, 2002, A6; Mark Maremont and Laurie P. Cohen, "Ex-Tyco CEO Is Likely to Face Charges over Unauthorized Pay," *Wall Street Journal,* September 12, 2002, A1, A8; Mark Maremont and John Hechinger, "Tyco's Ex-CEO Invested in Fund Run by Director," *Wall Street Journal* online, October 23, 2002, http://online.wsj.com/article_print0,,SB1035329530787240111,00.html; Mark Maremont and Jerry Markon, "Former Tyco Chief, Two Others Face New Charges and Lawsuits," *Wall Street Journal,* September 13, 2002, A3, A6; Mark Maremont and Jerry Markon, "Former Tyco Executives Are Charged," *Wall Street Journal* online, September 13, 2002, http://online.wsj.com/article_print0,SB1031836600798528755,00.html; Mark Maremont and Jerry Markon, "Tyco's Kozlowski Is Indicted on Charges of Tax Evasion," *Wall Street Journal,* June 5, 2002, A1, A7; Samuel Maull, "Kozlowski Claims Tyco Owes Him Millions," *Real Cities* online, March 14, 2003, www.realcities.com/mld/realcities/business/financial_markets/5395148.htm; Kevin McCoy, "Tyco Acknowledges More Accounting Tricks," *USA Today,* December 31, 2002, 3B; Kevin McCoy, "Investigators Scrutinize $20M Tyco Fee," *USA Today,* September 16, 2002, 1B; Kevin McCoy, "Directors' Firms on Payroll at Tyco," *USA Today,* September 18, 2002, 1B; Gary Panter, "The Big Kozlowski," *Fortune,* November 18, 2002, 123–126; Stephen Taub, "Tyco on Tyco: Errors Made, but No Fraud," CFO.com, December 31, 2002, www.cfo.com/article/1,5309,8596,00.html?f=related; "Tyco's History Under Kozlowski, *Washington Post* online, June 3, 2002, www.washingtonpost.com; "Tyco's Shareholders Defeat Proposal to Leave Bermuda," *USA Today* online, March 6, 2003, www.usatoday.com/money/industries/retail/2003-03-06-tyco_x.htm; "Tyco Smells Smoke at Fire Unit," TheStreet.com, March 12, 2003,www.thestreet.com/_yahoo/tech/earnings.10073763.html., 2006 http://www.tyco.com/livesite.

Global Crossing: Inflated Sales Lead to Bankruptcy

Global Crossing began in 1997 as a grand idea. It was to become the fourth-largest bankruptcy in U.S. history just five years later. The road to that bankruptcy is a story of revenues inflated by what appears to be fraudulent accounting, in which senior executives enriched themselves while Arthur Andersen served as auditor and consultant. Global Crossing employees and shareholders seem to have been left holding the bag, much as in the Enron bankruptcy filed just two months earlier.

THE GLOBAL CROSSING BUSINESS CONCEPT

Global Crossing was Gary Winnick's brainchild. Winnick was a former junk bond financier who worked with Michael Milken at Drexel Burnham Lambert but escaped untarnished from a 1990s scandal at that firm. Together with a group of financial gurus and CEOs, he envisioned a global broadband network that would link continents with undersea fiber-optic cables. This was a risky proposition in 1997 because no such network existed and no one knew exactly how profitable, or unprofitable, such a network would be. It has always been extremely difficult to forecast the profitability of new services or new technologies, and the Global Crossing proposal was no exception.

Demand for high-speed data services that could span continents exploded in the middle of the 1990s. Sprint, AT&T, and MCI owned the fiber-optic networks in the United States, with a few other relatively small players. None of these firms seemed able to keep up with growing business demand for broadband capacity. Level 3, Qwest Communications International, and Williams Communications stepped in to add capacity by building fiber-optic networks that spanned the country, expecting that many businesses would pay extra just to have access to this service. The creators of Global Crossing, as its name implies, envisioned a fiber-optic network that extended globally rather than just domestically.

Global Crossing faced one, not-so-small obstacle to executing its business plan: It effectively had no assets, and building such a high-tech, undersea network would be tremendously expensive, on the order of $2.7 billion. Fortunately, Wall Street investors valued the Global Crossing concept highly and offered Winnick and his management team about $40 billion in equity financing and $10 billion in debt financing. Investment analysts gave the stock a "strong buy" rating.

If demand for the services that Global Crossing offered continued to exceed supply—in other words, creating a "seller's market"—then Global Crossing's plan to create additional fiber-optic broadband capacity had great profit potential because the company could set a high price for its service. However, if supply began

We appreciate the work of Neil Herndon, who wrote the previous edition of this case under the direction of O. C. Ferrell. This case was prepared for classroom discussion rather than to illustrate either effective or ineffective handling of an administrative, ethical, or legal decision by management. All sources used for this case were obtained through publicly available material and the Global Crossing website.

Global Crossing Timeline

1997   Global Crossing is created.

1999   Two years after its founding, Global Crossing's stock hits a high of $64 a share.

2001   Global Crossing starts selling off assets.

January 28, 2002   Global Crossing declares Chapter 11 bankruptcy.

January 31, 2002   Hutchinson Whampoa Limited and Singapore Technologies Telemedia plan to invest $750 million in the company.

March 2002   Twenty-four hundred layoffs are announced.

May 2002   Global Crossing says it has more than sixty potential investors. Bids must be made before June 20, 2002.

August 9, 2002   Hutchinson Telecommunications and ST Telemedia sign a definitive agreement to invest $250 million for a 61.5 percent majority interest in a newly constituted Global Crossing.

September 2003   Global Crossing receives approval from the Committee for Foreign Investment in the United States for Singapore Technologies Telemedia's proposition of investment in Global Crossing.

December 2003   Global Crossing completes its restructuring and emerges from bankruptcy after Singapore Technologies Telemedia buys a two-thirds stake in the business.

October 2004   Global Crossing announces a large business-restructuring plan, de-emphasizing lower-margin products and eliminating activities considered as noncore business.

March 2005   Global Crossing announces it expects to be cash-positive in the second half of 2006. Losses were $129 million in 2004 and $85 million in 2003.

July 2005   The U.S. Supreme Court approves a settlement between the plaintiffs (investors, creditors, and so on) and Arthur Andersen LLP. The settlement (1) partially resolves a lawsuit over whether the prices of common stock and convertible preferred stock and bonds of Global Crossing and Asia Global Crossing were artificially inflated as a result of alleged fraudulent misrepresentations and nondisclosures and violations of federal securities laws; and (2) provides for a settlement fund of approximately $25 million, less fees and costs.

---

to outstrip demand and prices dropped accordingly— a "buyer's market"—then Global Crossing's profits would drop, possibly taking profits into negative territory. In fact, the race to build fiber-optic networks quickly created excess capacity in the industry, which ultimately resulted in customers paying a lower price for broadband service rather than the premium price executives had hoped for. The bottom line was that Global Crossing's profits could no longer pay the interest on its debt.

At its peak, Global Crossing had a market valuation of more than $50 billion, larger than General Motors on paper, and its fiber-optic telecommunications (telecom) network connected two hundred cities in twenty-seven countries. However, it amassed about $12.4 billion in debt establishing its global fiber-optic telecom network. So when Global Crossing's revenues dropped to $2.4 billion in the first three quarters of 2001, down from about $3.8 billion for the same period in 2000, the writing was on the wall. After finishing 2000 with a

loss of some $1.67 billion, Global Crossing was forced to declare bankruptcy on January 28, 2002.

THE TELECOMMUNICATIONS STOCK ANALYST

Jack Grubman, a telecom stock analyst for investment house Salomon Smith Barney (owned by Citigroup, Inc.), was consistently "bullish" on Global Crossing after the company went public in August 1998. His support continued until November 2001 when it became clear that demand for broadband capacity was falling short of the demand that Grubman and other telecom stock analysts had predicted in 1998 and 1999. Although he lowered his price target for Global Crossing stock in May 2001 by $40 per share, from $70 to $30, he also labeled the stock a "core holding" and maintained his "buy" recommendation.

It later emerged that Grubman, though employed by Salomon Smith Barney, helped Global Crossing make key business and management decisions for about two years after the company's initial public offering (IPO). In fact, Global Crossing Chairman Winnick and Grubman reportedly communicated almost daily for some time after Global Crossing's debut. Grubman allegedly advised Winnick on his personal stock sales and was reported to be involved in the recommendation to hire Robert Annunziata as Global Crossing's CEO. Grubman also allegedly helped to negotiate mergers with U.S. West, Inc. and Frontier Corporation on Global Crossing's behalf.

Grubman's extensive activities with Global Crossing were unusual given the traditional role of stock analysts, who are generally expected to provide only impartial advice to investors and shareholders. Although Grubman's activities do not appear to violate federal securities law, investigators from the New York State Attorney General's Office are looking into the source of Grubman's bonuses. Was he being rewarded for his role as a telecom stock analyst or for his role as an advisor to Global Crossing's management?

Grubman was certainly not the only Wall Street analyst enthusiastic about the prospects of the telecom industry, but he seems to have had more influence over the telecom sector than any of his peers. One former telecom CEO was quoted as saying that if Grubman didn't endorse a deal, the deal didn't happen. But, to get his endorsement, Salomon Smith Barney had to secure a major part of the investment business.

CONCERNS ABOUT INSIDER TRADING

The laws regulating business in the United States emphasize fairness to all involved in commerce, regardless of wealth, fame, position of power, or role, such as consumer, producer, or investor. Some refer to these protections as "maintaining a level playing field," a metaphor that suggests that one team should not have to struggle to move the ball uphill while the other moves the ball easily downhill—aided by gravity. This fairness philosophy, enshrined in many facets of U.S. business law and associated regulations, is especially evident in the laws regarding insider trading.

Insider trading generally occurs when a person has nonpublic information that is material about a security or the company that issues it and then buys or sells that security based on that information. The Securities and Exchange Commission (SEC) requires that an individual who is privy to inside information that might affect a stock's price must not trade in that company's securities unless he or she discloses what is known before buying or selling the stock. The SEC and the courts use three sets of rules to determine whether insider trading has occurred:

1. All partners and employees of a firm, including people whose professional activities put them in a relationship of trust or confidence with the firm or its shareholders, must not trade in the securities of the company in which they hold material, nonpublic information.

2. They are not permitted to disclose this information to others if they expect to profit in any way whatsoever from that disclosure. A person who receives a tip from an insider and then trades in that company's securities is generally guilty of insider trading.

3. The misappropriation rule effectively extends insider liability to people who receive nonpublic, material information from insiders who have a duty to keep that information confidential, including people with whom the insider habitually shares confidential information, such as a spouse. Under tender-offer rules, traditional insiders and any others who obtain material information about the tender offer may not legally trade in that company's securities.

Penalties for insider trading are stiff. Making just over $10,000 in an illegal insider trade would draw a mandatory eight- to fourteen-month jail sentence if convicted. The combined maximum civil and criminal penalties for insider trading are even harsher. Civil penalties assessed to violators may be up to three times the amount of illegal profits gained or losses avoided by the act of insider trading. In addition, the maximum criminal penalties for individuals are twenty years in prison and a $5 million fine. Private parties may also sue the inside trader for damages.

There is evidence that top officials at Global Crossing knew that the company's business future appeared bleak before they sold company stock. These transactions resulted in millions of dollars of income for those involved. Winnick is reported to have sold stock valued at $123 million on May 23, 2001, but a witness told a congressional committee investigating

Global Crossing that he had seen an April forecast projecting a revenue fall of $300 million. A much earlier June 5, 2000, e-mail from then-CEO Leo Hindery, Jr., encouraged Winnick to offer the assets of Global Crossing for sale to other telecom companies. Winnick denies that he sold stock based on his inside information that the company was in financial trouble. Winnick's lawyer, Gary Naftalis, insists the stock sales were proper and had been approved by Global Crossing's counsel. Altogether, it appears that Winnick sold some $734 million in Global Crossing stock before the company filed for bankruptcy.

Other Global Crossing executives also profited from the sale of company stock. Between 1999 and the end of December 2001, they are reported to have sold some $1.3 billion worth. David Walsh, formerly the COO, sold stock worth $8.7 million on May 31, 2001; Global Crossing cochairman Lodwrick Cook sold stock worth $9.8 million on May 16, 2001. Cook said that he sold his shares to satisfy a margin call—that is, he had borrowed money to pay for Global Crossing shares, and when share prices dropped, he needed to sell some of his shares to repay the margin loans.

THE CAPACITY SWAPS

During the "gold rush" fever of the telecom boom, start-up fiber-optic telecom companies like Global Crossing and Qwest would swap network capacity. In other words, the two companies would simultaneously sell each other the right to use some part of their respective fiber-optic networks, creating in effect a long-term lease that allowed one company to take control of part of the other company's network. The companies would then declare in their quarterly and annual reports the income from selling the rights to use a portion of the network but would not declare the expense of purchasing the rights. This consequently "boosted" their revenues and overstated their profits, sending their stock price higher. This transaction, called a *capacity swap*, or *swap*, would have the effect of making the balance sheets of the two companies appear stronger than they actually were. Such deals added about $375 million to Global Crossing's bottom line in the first quarter of 2001.

Signing contracts to gain access to each firm's networks appears to be legal. The issue with such swaps is that one asset is replaced with another, virtually identical asset. It does not appear that any real economic value

is created in the transaction, even though the financial statements of the telecom firms involved do not reflect this fact. This procedure tended to mislead shareholders and potential investors about the financial health of the company in which they were investing.

Global Crossing senior operations executive Carl Grivner commissioned an internal review of fiber-optic capacity that reported most of the company's capacity purchases were of limited or no value. Less than 20 percent of the swapped assets could be cost effectively added to Global Crossing's existing network. In some swaps, the assets were hundreds of miles from a Global Crossing connection point, making interconnection prohibitively expensive. It appears that engineers were sometimes consulted about the swaps and sometimes not, especially when the deals were being made in a quarter's closing minutes. Reportedly, the study was presented to the company's executive vice president of finance, Joseph Perrone, in September 2001.

The SEC looked into Global Crossing's accounting practices after it filed for bankruptcy protection and said that Global Crossing's accounting for these swaps did not comply with generally accepted accounting principles (GAAP). It ordered Global Crossing to change its financial statements to reflect adherence to these principles, a ruling that would likely apply to other telecom companies that had adopted the practice of swapping capacity. Global Crossing indicated that restating its earnings from such capacity swaps to comply with the SEC order for the first nine months of 2001 would cost it about $19 million in revenue. This would lower the $2.44 billion booked in revenue for this period and thereby increase the company's net loss of $4.77 billion by about $13 million. Global Crossing also said that when it accounted for the swaps, it had acted in accordance with information provided by Arthur Andersen, its accounting firm. Arthur Andersen reportedly had told Global Crossing that it did not agree with the SEC's interpretation of the accounting rule that Global Crossing used for the swaps.

THE CONGRESSIONAL INVESTIGATION

The House of Representatives' Energy and Commerce Committee looked into insider trading by Global Crossing executives. It also investigated possible efforts by Global Crossing to increase revenues by acquiring other businesses and capacity swaps, which effectively misled investors. The probe was triggered by a former Global Crossing vice president of finance, Roy Olofson, who claimed publicly that the company had improperly increased revenues and underreported costs to improve earnings so it could meet Wall Street expectations and support its stock price. Olofson later lost his job and sued Global Crossing and key executives.

The committee released documents showing that Global Crossing bought 360networks, Inc. in something of a rush during March 2001. Some board members and top company officials objected, but Winnick reportedly rammed the deal through even though there were limited opportunities for due diligence before the deal was consummated. It appears that the main reason for the rush purchase was to use 360networks' revenue to enhance Global Crossing's financial statements to avoid disappointing Wall Street investors' earnings expectations for Global Crossing.

Some members of Congress expressed concern that capacity swaps were used to inflate Global Crossing's revenue. Its CFO, Dan Cohrs, told the House Financial Services Subcommittee on Oversight and Investigations that his company had not set out to inflate revenue by entering into some twenty-four deals or capacity swaps with other telecom companies. Rather, Cohrs said that Global Crossing wanted to expand the capacity and the reach of its global network. But committee members noted that many of these deals dated from 2000 and 2001, a time when there was already overcapacity in the global telecom market. Qwest Communications International, also involved in deals for network capacity, said it was reversing some $950 million in revenue from capacity swaps and may have to make adjustments of another $531 million in revenue from other sales.

AFTER THE FALL

The U.S. Justice Department and the Enforcement Division of the SEC had hearings on Global Crossing and Qwest.

The committee also investigated alleged illegal insider trading. Winnick denied that he sold stock based on inside information that Global Crossing was in financial trouble and said that all of his stock transactions were appropriate. However, witnesses claim that top officials knew that Global Crossing's business outlook was weak before they sold company stock.

The subcommittee expressed concern that Global Crossing relied on nonstandard, pro forma numbers in reports circulated to investors but used GAAP in its public filings with the SEC. These pro forma reports claimed a 50 percent increase, about $531 million, over the statements filed by Global Crossing under generally accepted accounting rules.

There is also evidence that Global Crossing executives deliberately misled investors about the strength of the organization's finances. One report indicates that Winnick learned on February 26, 2001, that Global Crossing would fall some $200 million short of the first-quarter financial targets expected by Wall Street investors. However, in April, then-CEO Tom Casey told top stock analysts during a conference call that there were "record results in cash revenue" and that Global Crossing's results exceeded the estimates of the stock analysts themselves. This report led analysts to encourage investors to buy Global Crossing stock, sparking a surge in stock prices just before Winnick sold some $123 million of his shares. Winnick's lawyer, Gary Naftalis, said that Global Crossing did not mislead investors, but that it believed it would make its first-quarter financial targets legitimately.

Grubman, the telecom stock analyst for investment house Salomon Smith Barney, was also of interest to the committee for his ties between Global Crossing and Salomon Smith Barney and for the positive research reports that Grubman wrote about telecom firms that later crashed. The reports of inappropriate conduct were found to be true, and Grubman, under the terms of his settlement with the SEC/NASD/NYSE/NYAG, is barred from the securities business and is consulting on telecom issues.

Global Crossing hoped to emerge from bankruptcy protection in 2003. The rationale for their optimism was the argument that its restatements of financial results related to its capacity swaps would have very limited impact on its continuing operations because it would use so-called fresh-start accounting procedures, which do not include any previous financial results. The company also indicated that its use of nonstandard, pro forma numbers in reports to investors should have been disregarded. In 2002 the company listed debt of $12.4 billion. In 2005 it left bankruptcy, and Temasek Holdings Ltd., Singapore's state-owned investment company, acquired the majority of debt. In 2005 regulators ended a three-year inquiry into whether Global Crossing inflated revenue using swaps of fiber-optic network capacity with phone carriers such as Qwest Communications International Inc. Global Crossing agreed to cease and desist from any future violations, and three executives paid $100,000 fines. They didn't admit or deny any wrongdoing.

Global Crossing investors lost a total of about $54 billion. Some fourteen thousand employees lost 401(k) funds and pension funds, as well as health and severance benefits. The employees' 401(k) funds alone declined in value from about $191 million to $8.9 million in 2001. Leo Hindery, Global Crossing's CEO from March to October 2000, asked U.S. Bankruptcy Judge Robert Gerber to order Global Crossing to treat him as an administrative creditor. This would have given his claims precedent over other creditors in the bankruptcy proceeding. Hindery claimed $821,714 dollars in unpaid severance benefits, which include $22,378 a month rent on his apartment in the Waldorf-Astoria Towers on Manhattan's Park Avenue.

Global Crossing founder and chairman Winnick resigned from the board on December 31, 2002, under pressure from investor groups. All together, it appears that Winnick profited by about $734 million from his sales of Global Crossing stock before the company filed bankruptcy. However, he and more than twenty Global Crossing executives and directors faced lawsuits filed in the Federal District Court in Manhattan that consolidated several class-action complaints on behalf of investors who lost billions of dollars on Global Crossing stocks and bonds.

The scandal took a new twist when Richard N. Perle, who the firm retained to help overcome Defense Department concerns about the proposed sale to two Asian firms, was forced to resign as chairman of the Defense Policy Board after the press suggested that the two roles created a conflict of interest, perhaps violating ethics rules. Although Perle remained a member of the Defense Policy Board that advises the Pentagon and secretary of defense on war matters, including the conflict in Iraq, he withdrew from his role as advisor to Global Crossing.

Interestingly, Global Crossing shareholders were not the greatest beneficiaries of their risk taking; they will lose almost all of their investment. The real beneficiaries are the customers of the telecom services market. They will have more fiber-optic broadband capacity connected to more locations at a lower price than would have been possible if Global Crossing and other telecom companies had not invested in the creation of these networks.

In April 2005, Global Crossing settled a three-year investigation launched by the SEC into the telecom company's business practices and those of its top three executives: former CEO Thomas Case, former accounting officer Joseph Perrone, and former CFO Dan Cohrs. No monetary penalty was assessed against the company, which neither admitted nor denied the allegations that it failed to disclose the extent to which its results depended on swaps of fiber-optic network capacity with other telecom companies. The SEC decided in December 2004 not to charge or fine Winnick in the investigation, but he was accused of having played a much more active role in this affair; he is still under investigation. Stock analyst Grubman is banned for life from the securities industry and must pay a fine of $15 million. Until October 2004, Hindery was chairman of The YES Network, the nation's premier regional sports network that he formed in the summer of 2001 as the television home of the New York Yankees. He is now an active board member for a wide range of AIDS, political, and philanthropic organizations.

Questions

1. How did the pressure to meet earnings forecasts for Wall Street investors contribute to unethical conduct at Global Crossing?

2. Was there some unacceptable level of greed at Global Crossing that contributed to its bankruptcy? Support your position with facts from the case.

3. Are there similarities between the bankruptcy at Global Crossing and the bankruptcy at Enron (Case 10)? If so, what are they?

4. Who were the stakeholders in Global Crossing, and which one lost the most and why?

Sources

Andrew Backover, "Telecom Executives Deny Wrongdoing," *USA Today,* October 2, 2002, B1; Andrew Backover, "Global Crossing Plans Bold End to Chapter 11," *USA Today* online, October 16, 2002, www.usatoday.com/money/industries/telecom/2002-10-16-global_x.htm; Andrew Backover, "Spring CEO Says Strong Will Survive," *USA Today* online, October 21, 2002, www.usatoday.com/money/industries/telecom/2002-10-21-sprint_x.htm; Dennis K. Berman, "Global Crossing Faces More Accusations," *Wall Street Journal,* February 6, 2002,

B6; Dennis K. Berman, "Study Questioned Global Crossing Deals," *Wall Street Journal,* February 19, 2002, B6; Dennis K. Berman, "Hindery Wants Global Crossing to Give Him Pay," *Wall Street Journal,* October 14, 2002, B6; Dennis K. Berman, "Global Crossing's Accounting for 'Swap' Trades to Be Amended," *Wall Street Journal,* October 22, 2002, A10; Dennis K. Berman and Laurie P. Cohen, "SEC to Investigate Insiders' Trades at Global Crossing," *Wall Street Journal,* June 3, 2002, A1, A8; Laurie P. Cohen and Dennis K. Berman, "How Analyst Grubman Helped Call Shots at Global Crossing," *Wall Street Journal,* May 31, 2002, A1, A6; Julie Creswell, "The Emperor of Greed," *Fortune,* June 24, 2002, 106–116; "Ex-Global Crossing CEO Seeks $821,714 in Severance Benefits," *Boston Globe,* October 15, 2002, D4; Harold Furchtgott-Roth, "Manager's Journal: Global Crossing's Bankruptcy Is a Success Story," *Wall Street Journal,* February 5, 2002, A18; "Global Crossing Exec Denies Insider Trading," *USA Today* online, October 1, 2002, www.usatoday.com/money/industries/telecom/2002-10-01-global-crossing-hearing_x.htm; "Global Crossing Probe Eyes 2001 Accounts," InfoWorld Media Group, Inc. online, October 14, 2002, http://staging.infoworld.com/articles; "A Guide to Corporate Scandals," *The Economist Newspaper,* July 10, 2002, 1; Tom Hamburger and Dennis K. Berman, "U.S. Adviser Perle Resigns as Head of Defense Board," *Wall Street Journal* online, March 28, 2003, http://online.wsj.com; Jim Hopkins, "Winnick Quits Board at Global Crossing," *USA Today,* December 31, 2002, B03; Susan Ivancevich, Lucian C. Jones, and Thomas Keaveney, "Don't Run the Risk," *Journal of Accountancy* 194 (2002): 47–51; Siobhan Kennedy, "Global Crossing Restates Earnings," Reuters online, October 21, 2002, http://reuters.com; Jonathan Krim, "Panel Widens Probe of Global Crossing," *Washington Post* online, August 30, 2002, www.washingtonpost.com; Stephen Labaton, "Pentagon Adviser Is Also Advising Global Crossing," *New York Times* online, March 21, 2003, www.nytimes.com/2003/03/21/business/21GLOB.html; Stephanie N. Mehta, "Birds of a Feather," *Fortune,* October 14, 2002, 197–202; Jeremy Pelofsky, "Ex-Global Crossing CEO Demands Rent Paid," Reuters online, October 14, 2002, www.reuters.com; Simon Romero, "Adding to Claims Against Global Crossing," *New York Times,* January 30, 2003, C4; Simon Romero, "Technology; IDT Offers $255 Million to Control Global Crossing," *New York Times* online, February 25, 2003, www.nytimes.com; Christopher Stern, "At Global Crossing, 'No Enron,'" *Washington Post,* March 22, 2002, E04; James Toedtman, "Telecom Head Pledges $25M," *Newsday,* October 2, 2002, www.newsday.com; "Under Fire: These Execs, Too, Are Embroiled in a Range of Investigations," *BusinessWeek,* January 13, 2003, 87, 89; Michael Weisskopf, "Global Crossing: What Did Winnick Know?" *Time,* October 7, 2002, 28; "Winnick Was Told of Telecom Risks," *Washington Post,* October 1, 2002, E03.

Notes

CHAPTER 1

1. Tricia Bisoux, "Playing by the Rules," *BizEd* (September–October 2005): 18–25; Huntsman LLC, www.huntsman.com, accessed May 30, 2006; Jon M. Huntsman, *Winners Never Cheat* (Philadelphia: Wharton School Publishing, 2005).

2. "How Business Rates: By the Numbers," *Business Week,* September 11, 2000, pp. 148–149.

3. "Conseco Seeks Protection," http://money.cnn.com/2002/12/18/news/companies/conseco/, accessed September 25, 2003; Janet Adamy, "Conseco Names Interim CEO; Says Net Fell 21% in First Quarter," *Wall Street Journal,* May 5, 2006, p. B5.

4. Milton Friedman, *Capitalism and Freedom* (Chicago: University of Chicago Press, 1962).

5. Clive Crook, "Why Good Corporate Citizens Are a Public Menace," *National Journal,* April 24, 1999, p. 1087; Charles Handy, "What's a Business For?" *Harvard Business Review* 80 (December 2002): 49–55.

6. Nancy J. Miller and Terry L. Besser, "The Importance of Community Values in Small Business Strategy Formation: Evidence from Rural Iowa," *Journal of Small Business Management* 38 (January 2000): 68–85; James Knight and Mary Kate O'Riley, "Local Heroes," *Director* 55 (February 2002): 28.

7. "The Small Business Economy: A Report to the President 2005," U.S. Small Business Administration, www.sba.gov/advo/research/sb_econ2005.pdf, accessed June 11, 2006.

8. Shimizu Corporation, http://www.shimz.co.jp/english/index.html, accessed June 11, 2006.

9. "Corporate Awards and Recognition," Herman Miller Inc., http://www.hermanmiller.com/CDA/SSA/Awards/0,1582,a10-c21,00.html, accessed May 30, 2006"; Journey Toward Sustainability," Herman Miller, http://www.hermanmiller.com/CDA/SSA/Category/0,1564,a10-c605,00.html, accessed June 11, 2006.

10. "The 1997 Cone/Roper Cause-Related Marketing Trends Report," *Business Ethics* 11 (March–April 1997): 14–16; Ronald Alsop, "Corporate Reputations Are Earned with Trust, Reliability, Study Shows," *Wall Street Journal,* September 23, 1999; http://interactive.wsj.com; Dale Kurschner, "5 Ways Ethical Busine$$ Creates Fatter Profit$," *Business Ethics* 10 (March–April 1996): 21.

11. Jim Carlton, "New Leaf: Once Targeted by Protestors, Home Depot Plays Green Role," *Wall Street Journal,* August 6, 2004, p. A1.

12. Ann E. Tenbrunsel, Zoe I. Barsness, and Paul M. Hirsch, "Sara Lee Corporation and Corporate Citizenship: Unity in Diversity," in *Corporate Global Citizenship,* ed. Noel M. Tichy, Andrew R. McGill, and Lynda St. Clair (San Francisco: New Lexington Press, 1997), pp. 197–213.

13. "Overview: Message from the President," http://www.toto.co.jp/company/kankyo_en/management/message.htm, accessed June 11, 2006.

14. Archie Carroll, "The Four Faces of Corporate Citizenship," *Business and Society Review,* January 1, 1998, p. 1; Naomi Gardberg and Charles Fombrun, "Corporate Citizenship: Creating Intangible Assets Across Institutional Environments," *Academy of Management Review* 31 (April 2006): 329–336.

15. "Corruption Perceptions Index 2005," Transparency International, http://www.transparency.org/policy_research/surveys_indices/cpi/2005, accessed May 31, 2006.

16. "Judge Rules That Microsoft Violated U.S. Antitrust Laws," *Wall Street Journal,* April 3, 2000, http://interactive.wsj.com; Steven Levy, "Look, Ma, No Breaks," *Newsweek,* September 17, 2001, pp. 52–54; "Microsoft Begins Implementing Antitrust Settlement," *Computer & Online Industry Litigation Reporter,* November 19, 2002, p. 1.

17. "Code of Ethics," Direct Selling Association, http://www.dsa.org/ethics/, accessed May 31, 2006; "World Codes of Conduct for Direct Selling," World Federation of Direct Selling Associations, http://www.wfdsa.org/world_codes/, accessed June 1, 2006.

18. The Hitachi Foundation, http://www.hitachifoundation.org/, accessed June 11, 2006.

19. Altman, "Transformed Corporate Community Relations," p. 43; Carroll, "The Four Faces of Corporate Citizenship," p. 1.

20. Feliza Mirasol, "Pfizer, Merck Point to Pharma's Fate," *Chemical Market Reporter,* January 9–15, 2006, p. 26.

21. Malcolm McIntosh, Deborah Leipziger, Keith Jones, and Gill Coleman, *Corporate Citizenship: Successful Strategies for Responsible Companies* (London: Financial Times Management, 2000); Linda S. Munilla and Morgan P. Miles, "The Corporate Social Responsibility Continuum as a Component of Stakeholder Theory," *Business and Society Review* 110 (December 2005): 371–387.

22. Betsy Morris and Patricia Sellers, "What Really Happened at Coke," *Fortune,* January 10, 2000, pp. 114–116; "America's Most Admired Companies," www.fortune.com/fortune/mostadmired/, accessed December 17, 2002; "The 100 Best

Corporate Citizens for 2001," http://www.business-ethics.com/whats_new/2001-100b.html, accessed July 30, 2006; "Global Most Admired Companies 2006," http://money.cnn.com/magazines/fortune/globalmostadmired/top50/, accessed June 1, 2006.

23. Charles Handy, "What's a Business For?" *Harvard Business Review* 80 (December 2002): 49–55.

24. R. E. Freeman, *Strategic Management: A Stakeholder Approach* (Boston: Pitman, 1984).

25. "Steps to Responsible Growth: Social Responsibility Report 2005," http://www.kingfisher.com/socialresponsibility/files/pdf/SR_report_summary_2005.pdf, accessed June 10, 2006.

26. Edward S. Mason, Introduction, in *The Corporation in Modern Society*, ed. Edward S. Mason (Cambridge, MA: Harvard University Press, 1959), pp. 1–24.

27. "About Benetton: Our Campaigns," http://press.benettongroup.com/ben_en/about/campaigns/list/, accessed June 11, 2006; Michael McCarthy and Lorrie Grant, "Sears Drops Benetton After Controversial Death Row Ads," *USA Today,* February 18, 2000, www.usatoday.com.

28. Isabelle Maignan and O. C. Ferrell, "Measuring Corporate Citizenship in Two Countries: The Case of the United States and France," *Journal of Business Ethics* 23 (February 2000): 283; Robert J. Samuelson, "R.I.P.: The Good Corporation," *Newsweek,* July 5, 1993, p. 41.

29. Charles W. Wootton and Christie L. Roszkowski, "Legal Aspects of Corporate Governance in Early American Railroads," *Business and Economic History* 28 (Winter 1999): 325–326.

30. Ralph Estes, *Tyranny of the Bottom Line* (San Francisco: Berrett-Koehler, 1996); David Finn, *The Corporate Oligarch* (New York: Simon & Schuster, 1969).

31. Marina v. N. Whitman, *New World, New Rules* (Boston: Harvard Business School Press, 1999).

32. Edward S. Mason, Introduction, in *The Corporation in Modern Society,* ed. Mason, pp. 1–24.

33. Carl Kaysen, "The Corporation: How Much Power? What Scope?" in *The Corporation in Modern Society,* ed. Mason, pp. 85–105.

34. Whitman, *New World, New Rules.*

35. Ibid.

36. David M. Gordon, *Fat and Mean: The Corporate Squeeze of Working Americans and the Myth of Managerial "Downsizing"* (New York: Free Press, 1996).

37. Richard Leider, *The Power of Purpose: Creating Meaning in Your Life and Work* (San Francisco: Barrett-Koehler, 1997).

38. Mark Lilla, "The Big Extract: Does Anyone Remember '68?" *Guardian Editor* (London), August 29, 1998, p. 12; Mark Lilla, "Still Living with '68," *New York Times Magazine,* August 16, 1998, p. 34.

39. Marjorie Kelly, "The Next Step for CSR: Economic Democracy," *Business Ethics* 16 (May–August 2002): 3–4.

40. Martin Wolf, "Comment and Analysis: The Big Lie of Global Inequality," *Financial Times,* February 9, 2000, p. 25.

41. Aaron Bernstein, "Too Much Corporate Power?" *Business Week,* September 11, 2000, pp. 144–158.

42. Bruce Horovitz, "Scandals Shake Public," *USA Today,* July 16, 2002, p. 1A.

43. "Public Trust Is Recovering," GlobeScan, Inc., http://www.globescan.com/news_archives/wef_trust_release .pdf, accessed June 12, 2006.

44. "Top 200: The Rise of Global Corporate Power," http://www.corpwatch.org/article.php?id=377, accessed May 31, 2006; Paul Magnusson, "Making a Federal Case Out of Overseas Abuses," *Business Week,* November 25, 2002, p. 78; "Unocal to Settle Rights Claims," www.corpwatch.com, accessed June 2, 2006.

45. M. N. Graham Dukes, "Accountability of the Pharmaceutical Industry," *The Lancet,* November 23, 2002, pp. 1682–1684; Elizabeth Olson, "Global Trade Negotiations Are Making Little Progress," *New York Times,* December 7, 2002, p. C3; Robert Pear, "Investigators Find Repeated Deception in Ads for Drugs," *New York Times,* December 4, 2002, p. A22.

46. John Dalla Costa, *The Ethical Imperative: Why Moral Leadership Is Good Business* (Reading, MA: Addison-Wesley, 1998).

47. "All About Nestlé: Business Principles," Nestlé, http://www.nestle.com/All_About/Business_Principles/Business+Principles.htm, accessed June 12, 2006.

48. Lynda St. Clair, "Compaq Computer Corporation: Maximizing Environmental Conscientiousness Around the Globe," in *Corporate Global Citizenship,* ed. Tichy, McGill, and St. Clair, pp. 230–244.

49. S. A. Anwar, "APEC: Evidence and Policy Scenarios," *Journal of International Marketing and Marketing Research* 27 (October 2002): 141–153; Richard Feinberg, "Two Leading Lights of Humane Globalisation," *Singapore Straits Times,* February 21, 2000, p. 50.

50. Jonathan Levine, "Fear, Loathing and Opportunity: The Pollster's View of Global Citizenship," *The Voice of Corporate Citizenship,* May–June 2003, http://www.imakenews.com/cccbc/e_article000153082.cfm, accessed July 30, 2006.

51. Frederick Reichheld, *The Loyalty Effect* (Cambridge, MA: Harvard Business School, 1996); Jeffrey S. Harrison and R. Edward Freeman, "Stakeholders, Social Responsibility, and Performance: Empirical Evidence and Theoretical Perspectives," *Academy of Management Journal* 42 (October 1999): 479.

52. Stephen R. Covey, "Is Your Company's Bottom Line Taking a Hit?" *PR Newswire,* June 4, 1998, www.prnewswire.com; Terry W. Loe, "The Role of Ethical Climate in Developing Trust, Market Orientation and Commitment to Quality," unpublished Ph.D. dissertation, University of Memphis, 1996.

53. Ethics Resource Center, *2005 National Business Ethics Survey* (Washington, DC: Ethics Resource Center, 2005).

54. "The 1997 Cone/Roper Cause-Related Marketing Trends Report," *Business Ethics* 11 (March–April 1997): 14–16.

55. Rebecca Gardyn, "Philanthropy Post-Sept 11," *American Demographics* 24 (February 2002): 16–17; "The 1997 Cone/Roper Cause-Related Marketing Trends Report," p. 14.

56. Ronald Alsop, "Corporate Reputations Are Earned with Trust, Reliability, Study Shows," http://interactive.wsj.com.

57. Bernard J. Jaworski and Ajay K. Kohli, "Market Orientation: Antecedents and Consequences," *Journal of Marketing* 57 (July 1993): 10.

58. "About Hershey Foods," http://www.thehersheycompany.com/about/, accessed July 30, 2006; "Hershey Foods Philosophy and Values," Hershey Foods Corporation Videotape, 1990.

59. "2005 Loyalty in the Workplace," Walker Information, press release, November 21, 2005, http://walkerinfo.com/what/loyaltyreports/studies/employee05/newsrelease.cfm, accessed July 30, 2006.

60. John Galvin, "The New Business Ethics," *SmartBusinessMag .com,* June 2000, p. 97.

61. John A. Byrne, "Chainsaw," *Business Week,* October 18, 1999, pp. 128–149.

62. "Mutual Funds to Boycott Mitsubishi over Proposed Mexican Salt Plant," CNN, October 25, 1999, www.cnn.com.

63. David Rynecki, "Here Are 8 Easy Ways to Lose Your Shirt in Stocks," *USA Today,* June 26, 1998, p. 3B.

64. "Investment Club Numbers Decline; Crisis of Confidence Caused Many to Take Their Money and Run," *Investor Relations Business,* September 23, 2002, p. 1; Charles Jaffe, "Securities Industry Aims to Renew Trust; Leaders Face Challenge of Rebuilding Investor Confidence Amid Slump," *Boston Globe,* November 8, 2002, p. E1.

65. Isabelle Maignan, O. C. Ferrell, and G. Thomas Hult, "Corporate Citizenship: Antecedents and Business Benefits," *Journal of the Academy of Marketing Science* 24, no. 4 (1999): 455–469.

66. S. B. Graves and S. A. Waddock, "Institutional Owners and Corporate Social Performance: Maybe Not So Myopic After All," *Proceedings of the International Association for Business and Society,* San Diego, CA, 1993; Ronald M. Roman, Sefa Hayibor, and Bradley R. Agle, "The Relationship Between Social and Financial Performance," *Business and Society* 38 (March 1999); W. Gary Simpson and Theodor Kohers, "The Link Between Corporate Social and Financial Performance: Evidence from the Banking Industry," *Journal of Business Ethics* 35 (January 2002): 97–109; Curtis Verschoor and Elizabeth A. Murphy, "The Financial Performance of U.S. Firms and Those with Global Prominence: How Do the Best Corporate Citizens Rate?" *Business and Society Review* 107 (Fall 2002): 371–380; S. Waddock and S. Graves, "The Corporate Social Performance–Financial Performance Link," *Strategic Management Journal* 18 (1997): 303–319.

67. Chris C. Verschoor, "A Study of the Link Between a Corporation's Financial Performance and Its Commitment to Ethics," *Journal of Business Ethics* 31 (October 1998): 1509.

68. Shawn L. Berman, Andrew C. Wicks, Suresh Kotha, and Thomas M. Jones, "Does Stakeholder Orientation Matter? The Relationship Between Stakeholder Management Models and Firm Financial Performance," *Academy of Management Journal* 42 (October 1999): 502–503.

69. Roman, Hayibor, and Agle, "The Relationship Between Social and Financial Performance."

70. Melissa A. Baucus and David A. Baucus, "Paying the Payer: An Empirical Examination of Longer Term Financial Consequences of Illegal Corporate Behavior," *Academy of Management Journal* 40 (1997): 129–151.

71. K. J. Arrow, *The Limits of Organization* (New York: W. W. Norton, 1974), pp. 23, 26; D. C. North, *Institutions: Institutional Change, and Economic Performance* (Cambridge: Cambridge University Press, 1990).

72. Shelby D. Hunt, "Resource-Advantage Theory and the Wealth of Nations: Developing the Socio-Economic Research Tradition," *Journal of Socio-Economics* 26 (1997).

73. North, *Institutions,* p. 9.

74. L. E. Harrison, *Who Prospers? How Cultural Values Shape Economic and Political Success* (New York: Basic Books, 1992), p. 16.

75. Hunt, "Resource-Advantage Theory and the Wealth of Nations."

76. Ibid., pp. 351–352.

77. "Global Corruption Report 2006," Transparency International, http://www.transparency.org/publications/gcr, accessed June 12, 2006.

78. Cummins, Inc., www.cummins.com/, accessed May 31, 2006; Cummins Sustainability Report, http://www.cummins .com/cmi/attachments/public/About%20Cummins/ Sustainability%20Report/ SustainabilityReport2005FINALWEBVERSION.pdf, accessed June 8, 2006.

79. Jennifer Rewick, "Connecticut Attorney General Launches Probe of Priceline.com After Complaints," *Wall Street Journal,* October 2, 2000, p. E16.

80. "19th Annual Technical Excellence Awards," *PC Magazine,* November 19, 2002, www.pcmag.com, accessed December 20, 2002; Glenn R. Simpson, "Raytheon Offers Office Software for Snooping," *Wall Street Journal,* June 14, 2000, p. B1.

81. Bernstein, "Too Much Corporate Power?" p. 153.

82. Julia Angwin, "Credit-Card Scams: The Devil E-stores," *Wall Street Journal,* September 19, 2000, pp. B1, B4; Michelle Delio, "Cops Bust Massive ID Theft Ring," Wired.com, November 25, 2002, www.wired.com/news/privacy/ 0,1848,56567,00.html, accessed December 20, 2002.

83. William B. Werther and David Chandler, "Strategic Corporate Social Responsibility as Global Brand Insurance," *Business Horizons* 48 (July–August 2005): 317–324.

CHAPTER 2

1. Sarah Ellison and Janet Adamy, "Panel Faults Food Packaging for Kid Obesity," *Dow Jones Reprints,* December, 7, 2005, http://online.wsj.com/article/SB113387976454515095 .html, accessed December 7, 2005; "Kaiser Family Foundation Releases New Report on Role of Media in Childhood Obesity," Washington Panel Discussion to Explore Role of Media/Policy Options, www.kff.org, February 24, 2004, http://www.kff.org/entmedia/entmedia022404nr.cfm, accessed December 12, 2005; "Supersizing Europeans," from William M. Pride and O. C. Ferrell, *Marketing* (Houghton Mifflin Company, 2006), p. 122; David Kiley, "Senate Bill Seeks to Shine a Brighter Light on Marketing to Children," *Business Week Online,* November 10, 2005, http://www .businessweek.com/the_thread/brandnewday/archives/2005/ 11/senate_bill_see.html?campaign_id=search, accessed April 15, 2006; "More 'Healthy' Junk Food on the Horizon?" CNNMoney.com, September 16, 2005, http://money.cnn .com/2005/09/16/news/fortune500/healthy_food/ index.htm, accessed April 15, 2006; "A Ban on Soft Drinks in Schools?" CNNMoney.com, December 7, 2005, http:// money.cnn.com/2005/12/07/news/fortune500/soda_ schools/index.htm, accessed April 15, 2006; "Study Finds More Fast-Food Ads on Black-Oriented Television," *Wall Street Journal Online,* April 3, 2006, http://online.wsj.com/ article/sb114409477653015625-search.html?keywords= obesity&collection=wsjie/6month, accessed April 15, 2006; Pallavi Gogoi, "McDonald's New Wrap," *Business Week Online,* February 17, 2006, http://online.wsj.com/article/ sb114409477653015625-search.html?keywords= obesity& collection=wsjie/6month, accessed April 15, 2006.

2. Scott J. Reynolds, Frank C. Schultz, and David R. Hekman, "Stakeholder Theory and Managerial Decision-Making: Constraints and Implications of Balancing Stakeholder Interests," *Journal of Business Ethics* 64, no. 3 (March 2006): 285–301.

3. Vikas Anand, Blake E. Ashforth, and Mahendra Joshi, "Business as Usual: The Acceptance and Perpetuation of Corruption in Organizations," *Academy of Management Executive* 18, no. 2 (2004): 39–53.

4. D. L. Swanson and W. C. Frederick, "Denial and Leadership in Business Ethics Education," in *Business Ethics: New Challenges for Business Schools and Corporate Leaders,* ed. R. A. Peterson and O. C. Ferrell (New York: M. E. Sharpe, 2004).

5. American Productivity & Quality Center, *Community Relations: Unleashing the Power of Corporate Citizenship* (Houston, TX: American Productivity & Quality Center, 1998); Thomas Donaldson and Lee E. Preston, "The Stakeholder Theory of the Corporation: Concepts, Evidence and Implications," *Academy of Management Review* 29 (January 1995): 65–91; Jaan Elias and J. Gregory Dees, "The Normative Foundations of Business," Harvard Business School Publishing, June 10, 1997.

6. G. A. Steiner and J. F. Steiner, *Business, Government, and Society* (New York: Random House, 1988).

7. Milton Friedman, "Social Responsibility of Business Is to Increase Its Profits," *New York Times Magazine,* September 13, 1970, pp. 122–126.

8. "Business Leaders, Politicians and Academics Dub Corporate Irresponsibility 'An Attack on America from Within'," Business Wire, November 7, 2002, via America Online.

9. Adam Smith, *The Theory of Moral Sentiments*, Vol. 2 (New York: Prometheus, 2000).

10. Theodore Levitt, *The Marketing Imagination* (New York: Free Press, 1983).

11. Norman Bowie, "Empowering People as an End for Business," in *People in Corporations: Ethical Responsibilities and Corporate Effectiveness*, ed. Georges Enderle, Brenda Almond, and Antonio Argandona (Dordrecht, The Netherlands: Kluwer Academic Press, 1990), pp. 105–112.

12. Chris Marsden, "The New Corporate Citizenship of Big Business: Part of the Solution to Sustainability?" *Business and Society Review* 105 (Spring 2000): 9–25; James E. Post, Lee E. Preston, and Sybille Sachs, *Redefining the Corporation: Stakeholder Management and Organizational Wealth* (Stanford, CA: Stanford University Press, 2002).

13. 1997 Cone/Roper Cause-Related Marketing Trends, in "Does It Pay to Be Ethical?" *Business Ethics,* March–April 1997, p. 15.

14. Isabelle Maignan, "Antecedents and Benefits of Corporate Citizenship: A Comparison of U.S. and French Businesses," unpublished Ph.D. dissertation, University of Memphis, 1997.

15. Adapted from Isabelle Maignan, O .C. Ferrell, and Linda Ferrell, "A Stakeholder Model for Implementing Social Responsibility in Marketing," *European Journal of Marketing* 39 (September–October 2005), pp. 956–977.

16. Ibid.

17. Ibid.

18. Isabelle Maignan and O. C. Ferrell, "Corporate Social Responsibility: Toward a Marketing Conceptualization," *Journal of the Academy of Marketing Science* 32 (2004): 3–19.

19. Ibid.

20. David L. Schwartzkopf, "Stakeholder Perspectives and Business Risk Perception," *Journal of Business Ethics* 64, no. 4 (April 2006): 327–342.

21. Maignan and Ferrell, "Corporate Social Responsibility."

22. Amy Merrick, "Gap Report Says Factory Inspections Are Getting Better," *The Wall Street Journal*, July 13, 2005, p. B10.

23. Maignan and Ferrell, "Corporate Social Responsibility."

24. This section is adapted from Isabelle Maignan, Bas Hillebrand, and Debbie Thorne McAlister, "Managing Socially Responsible Buying: How to Integrate Non-economic Criteria into the Purchasing Process," *European Management Journal* 20 (December 2002): 641–648.

25. Andrew L. Friedman and Samantha Miles, "Developing Stakeholder Theory," *Journal of Management Studies* 39 (January 2002): 1–21; Ronald K. Mitchell, Bradley R. Agle, and Donna J. Wood, "Toward a Theory of Stakeholder Identification and Salience: Defining the Principle of Who and What Really Counts," *Academy of Management Review* 22 (October 1997): 853–886.

26. Dana Frank, *Buy American: The Untold Story of Economic Nationalism* (Boston: Beacon Press, 1999); David Kaplan, "U.S. Goods Are Preferred, Says Poll," *Adweek,* June 24, 2002, p. 1.

27. Amitai Etzioni, *Modern Organizations* (Upper Saddle River, NJ: Prentice Hall, 1964).

28. Aaron Bernstein, "Too Much Corporate Power?" *Business Week,* September 11, 2000, pp. 144–158.

29. Treasury Advisory Committee on International Child Labor Enforcement, "Notices," *Federal Register,* March 6, 2000, 65 FR 11831.

30. Andrew Ward, "McDonald's Eager for Talks with Critics," *Financial Times* (London), May 3, 2000, p. 3.

31. Mark C. Suchman, "Managing Legitimacy: Strategic and Institutional Approaches," *Academy of Management Review* 20 (July 1995): 571–610.

32. Brad Knickerbock, "Activists Step Up War to 'Liberate' Nature," *Christian Science Monitor,* January 20, 1999, p. 4.

33. Elliott Choueka, "Big Mac Fights Back," BBC Money Programme, July 8, 2005, http://news.bbc.co.uk/2/hi/business/4665205.stm, accessed April 27, 2006.

34. Joshua Kurlantzick, "Protestors Form Human Chain Outside ADB Meeting," *Agence France Presse,* May 8, 2000, via LEXIS®-NEXIS® Academic Universe.

35. "Diamond Trade Funding Wars," *African Business* 248 (November 1999): 28; James E. Post and Shawn L. Berman, "Global Corporate Citizenship in a Dot.com World," in *Perspectives on Corporate Citizenship,* ed. Jörg Andriof and Malcolm McIntosh (Sheffield, UK: Greenleaf Publishing, 2001): 66–82; "Shaming the Sanctions-Busters," *Economist,* March 18, 2000, p. 47.

36. Ronald Alsop, "Corporate Reputations Are Earned with Trust, Reliability, Study Shows," *Wall Street Journal,* September 23, 1999, http://interactive.wsj.com; John F. Mahon, "Corporate Reputation: A Research Agenda Using Strategy and Stakeholder Literature," *Business and Society* 41 (December 2002): 415–445.

37. Ronald Alsop, "Ranking Corporate Reputation," *Wall Street Journal,* December 6, 2005, p. B1.

38. Manto Gotsi and Alan Wilson, "Corporate Reputation Management: 'Living the Brand,'" *Management Decision* 39, no. 2 (2001): 99–105; Jim Kartalia, "Technology Safeguards for a

Good Corporate Reputation," *Information Executive* 3 (September 1999): 4; Prema Nakra, "Corporate Reputation Management: 'CRM' with a Strategic Twist?" *Public Relations Quarterly* 45 (Summer 2000): 35–42.

39. Jeanne Logsdon and Donna J. Wood, "Reputation as an Emerging Construct in the Business and Society Field: An Introduction," *Business and Society* 41 (December 2002): 265–270; "Putting a Price Tag to Reputation," Council of Public Relations Firms, www.prfirms.org, accessed December 20, 2002; Allen M. Weiss, Erin Anderson, and Deborah J. MacInnis, "Reputation Management as a Motivation for Sales Structure Decisions," *Journal of Marketing* 63 (October 1999): 74–89.

40. Christy Eidson and Melissa Master, "Who Makes the Call?" *Across the Board* 37 (March 2000): 16; Logsdon and Wood, "Reputation as an Emerging Construct in the Business and Society Field."

41. Alison Rankin Frost, "Brand vs. Reputation," *Communication World* 16 (February–March 1999): 22–25.

42. Glen Peters, *Waltzing with the Raptors: A Practical Roadmap to Protecting Your Company's Reputation* (New York: Wiley, 1999).

43. Green Mountain Coffee Annual Report 10-K, 2005, www.greenmountaincoffee.com, accessed April 27, 2006; Hoover Fact Sheet About Green Mountain Coffee, http://www. hoovers.com/green-mountain-coffee-roasters, -inc./--ID__45721--/free-co-factsheet.xhtml, accessed April 27, 2006; "200 Best Small Companies in America," *Forbes Magazine*, October 14, 2005, http://www.forbes.com/ 200best/, accessed April 27, 2006; "100 Best Corporate Citizens 2005," *Business Ethics*, Spring 2005, pp. 22–23.

44. Much of this section is adapted from Lisa A. Mainiero, "Action or Reaction? Handling Businesses in Crisis After September 11," *Business Horizons* 45 (September–October 2002): 2–10; Robert R. Ulmer and Timothy L. Sellnow, "Consistent Questions of Ambiguity in Organizational Crisis Communication: Jack in the Box as a Case Study," *Journal of Business Ethics* 25 (May 2000): 143–155; Robert R. Ulmer and Timothy L. Sellnow, "Strategic Ambiguity and the Ethic of Significant Choices in the Tobacco Industry's Crisis Communication," *Communication Studies* 48, no. 3 (1997): 215–233; Timothy L. Sellnow and Robert R. Ulmer, "Ambiguous Argument as Advocacy in Organizational Crisis Communication," *Argumentation and Advocacy* 31, no. 3 (1995): 138–150; Peter V. Stanton, "Ten Communication Mistakes You Can Avoid When Managing a Crisis," *Public Relations Quarterly* 47 (Summer 2002): 19–22.

45. "Crisis Survival Tactics for HR," *HR Focus* 79 (April 2002): 1, 13; "Boss of IBM's Disaster Recovery Center Tells What He Learned from Last Week's Crisis," *InfoWorld.com*, http://www .infoworld.com/articles/hn/xml/01/09/19/010919hngordon .xml, accessed August 28, 2003.

46. Lynn Brewer, Robert Chandler, and O. C. Ferrell, "Managing Risks for Corporate Integrity: How to Survive an Ethical Misconduct Disaster" (Mason, OH: Texere/Thomson, 2006), pp. 2–3.

47. HealthSouth, http://www.healthsouth.com/medinfo/home/ app/frame?2+article.jsp,0,091505_Scrushy_Press, accessed July 13, 2006.

48. Helen Shaw and Dave Cook, "Scrushy Acquitted on All Counts," *CFO.com*, June 28, 2005, www.cfo.com/

article.cfm/4076776/c_4125234?f=todayinfinance_inside, accessed July 13, 2006.

49. HealthSouth Statement Regarding Scrushy Press Conference, http://www.healthsouth.com/medinfo/home/app/ frame?2=article.jsp,0,091505_Scrushy_Press, accessed March 7, 2006.

50. Caroline E. Mayer, "Blockbuster Sued over Return Policy," *Washington Post,* February 19, 2005, www.washingtonpost .com/wp-dyn/articles/A36767-2005Feb18.html, accessed July 13, 2006.

51. Paul Argenti, "Crisis Communication: Lessons from 9/11," *Harvard Business Review* 80 (December 2002): 103–109; L. Paul Bremer, "Corporate Governance and Crisis Management," *Directors and Boards* 26 (Winter 2002): 16–20; Christine M. Pearson and Judith A. Clair, "Reframing Crisis Management," *Academy of Management Review* 23 (January 1998): 59–76.

52. "Disney World Ride Reopened," CBS News, July 14, 2005, www.cbsnews.com/stories/2005/07/13/national/main708906 .shtml, accessed July 13, 2006.

53. Ibid.

54. Michael John Harker, "Relationship Marketing Defined?" *Marketing Intelligence and Planning* 17 (January 1999): 13–20; Robert M. Morgan and Shelby D. Hunt, "The Commitment-Trust Theory of Relationship Marketing," *Journal of Marketing* 58 (July 1994): 20–38.

55. "Hormel Plans Ahead with Oracle Internet Procurement," *Fortune,* May 1, 2000, p. S12.

56. Jörg Andriof and Sandra Waddock, "Unfolding Stakeholder Engagement," in *Unfolding Stakeholder Thinking: Theory, Responsibility and Engagement,* ed. Jörg Andriof, Sandra Waddock, Bryan Husted, and Sandra S. Rahman (Sheffield, UK: Greenleaf Publishing, 2002): 19–42; James Coleman, "Social Capital in the Creation of Human Capital," *American Journal of Sociology* 94 (1988): S95–S120; Carrie R. Leana and Harry J. Van Buren III, "Organizational Social Capital and Employment Practices," *Academy of Management Review* 24 (July 1999): 538–555.

57. Chemical Manufacturers Association, *Improving Responsible Care Implementation, Enhancing Performance and Credibility* (Washington, DC: Chemical Manufacturers Association, 1993); "Details of Revamped *Responsible Care* Take Shape," *Chemical Week,* November 20, 2002, pp. 33–39; Jennifer Howard, Jennifer Nash, and John Ehrenfeld, "Standard or Smokescreen? Implementation of a Voluntary Environmental Code," *California Management Review* 42 (Winter 2000): 63–82.

58. Adapted from Maignan, Ferrell, and Ferrell, "A Stakeholder Model for Implementing Social Responsibility in Marketing," pp. 956–977.

59. Marjorie Kelly, "*Business Ethics* 100 Best Corporate Citizens 2006," *Business Ethics*, Spring 2006, pp. 20–25.

60. "Obesity Becomes Political Issue as Well as Cultural Obsession," Washington Wire, *Wall Street Journal*, March 3, 2006, www.wsj.com, accessed March 21, 2006.

61. Corporate Social Responsibility at Starbucks, http://www .starbucks.com/aboutus/csr.asp, accessed March 21, 2006.

62. Stephanie Armour, "Maryland First to OK 'Wal-Mart Bill' Law Requires More Health Care Spending," *USA Today*, January 13, 2006, p. B1.

63. Kris Hudson. "Wal-Mart to Offer Improved Health-Care Benefits," *Wall Street Journal*, February 24, 2006, p. A2.

64. Jon Entine, "The Body Shop: Truth and Consequences," *Drug & Cosmetics Industry* 156 (February 1995): 54; Jon Entine, "Body Shop's Packaging Starts to Unravel," *Australian Financial Review,* December 18, 2002, p. 52.

65. Matthew Gitsham, "Cleaner, but Not Sparkling," *Ethical Corporation,* December 2005, pp. 48–49.

66. M. B. Clarkson, "A Stakeholder Framework for Analyzing and Evaluating Corporate Social Performance," *Academy of Management Review* 20 (January 1995): 92–117.

67. Ibid., p. 109.

68. Ibid.

69. Ibid.

70. Ibid.

71. Jörg Andriof, "Managing Social Risk Through Stakeholder Partnership Building," unpublished Ph.D. dissertation, Warwick Business School, 2000; Jörg Andriof, "Patterns of Stakeholder Partnership Building," in *Perspectives on Corporate Citizenship,* ed. Andriof and McIntosh, pp. 215–238.

72. Nick Chaloner and David Brontzen, "How SABMiller Protects Its Biggest Asset—Its Reputation," *Strategic Communication Management* 6 (October–November 2002): 12–15.

CHAPTER 3

1. "2002 Developments in the Field of Risk Management," *Business Insurance,* January 6, 2003, p. 16; "Adelphia Suing Deloitte & Touche," *Business Insurance,* November 11, 2002, p. 1; "Adelphia Files Lawsuit Against John Rigas and Other Former Executives and Board Members of Adelphia," July 24, 2002, http://www.adelphia.com/invest/pdf/7_24_02.pdf; "Adelphia Statement Regarding the Federal Indictment of the Rigas Family Members," September 23, 2002, http://www.adelphia.com/invest/pdf/09_23_02.pdf; "Century/ML Cable Venture Files Petition for Chapter 11 Reorganization," press release, September 30, 2002, http://www.adelphia.com/invest/pdf/CMLCV_CH11_93002.pdf; "Sabres File for Bankruptcy Protection," *CNN Sports Illustrated,* January 15, 2003, http://sportsillustrated.cnn.com/hockey/news/2003/01/13/sabres_bankruptcy_ap/, accessed July 21, 2006; Mike Farrell, "Adelphia's Numbers Aren't All Bad," *Multichannel News,* December 2, 2002, pp. 6–7; Ronald Grover, "Adelphia's Fall Will Bruise a Crowd," *Business Week,* July 8, 2002, p. 44; Avital Louria Hahn, "The Jailed, the Probed, the Embarrassed: A New Who's Who of the Afflicted in the Business and Street Worlds," *Investment Dealers' Digest,* September 16, 2002, p. 4; Devin Leonard, "The Adelphia Story," *Fortune,* August 12, 2002, pp. 136–148. "Adelphia Founder Sentenced to 15 Years," CNNMoney.com, June 20, 2005, http://money.cnn.com/2005/06/20/news/newsmakers/rigas_sentencing/, accessed April 26, 2006; Mike Farrell, "Rigas, Son Guilty," Multichannel.com, July 12, 2004, http://www.multichannel.com/article/CA435394.html, accessed April 26, 2006; Stephen Taub, "Probation for Adelphia's Michael Rigas," CFO.com, March 7, 2006, http://www.cfo.com/article.cfm/5598021/c_5598677?f=home_todayinfinance, accessed April 26, 2006; "John Rigas, Son to Remain Free Pending Appeal," *Associated Press,* MSNBC.com, July 13, 2005, http://www.msnbc.msn.com/id/8567249/, accessed April 26, 2006; Adelphia History, company website, http://www.adelphia.com/about/history.cfm, accessed April 26, 2006.

2. Rafael LaPorta and Florencio Lopez-de-Silanes, "Investor Protection and Corporate Governance," *Journal of Financial Economics* 58 (October–November 2000): 3–38.

3. James McRitchie, "Ending the Wall Street Walk: Why Corporate Governance Now?" www.corpgov.net/forums/commentary/ending.html, accessed September 16, 2003.

4. "The 2020 Vision Project," Institute of Chartered Accountants in England & Wales, www.icaew.co.uk/, accessed October 29, 2001.

5. "In Plain Sight, in Plain English," *Across the Board* 39 (November–December 2002): 24–27.

6. *Dodge v. Ford Motor Co.,* 204 Mich. 459, 179 N.W. 668, 3 A.L.R. 413 (1919).

7. Alfred Marcus and Sheryl Kaiser, *Managing Beyond Compliance: The Ethical and Legal Dimensions of Corporate Responsibility* (Garfield Heights, OH: North Coast Publishers, 2006), p. 79.

8. Ben W. Heineman Jr., "Are You a Good Corporate Citizen?" *Wall Street Journal,* June 28, 2005, p. B2.

9. "John Rigas," Wikipedia, http://en.wikipedia.org/wiki/John_Rigas, accessed August 2, 2006.

10. Darryl Reed, "Corporate Governance Reforms in Developing Countries," *Journal of Business Ethics* 37 (May 2002): 223–247.

11. Bryan W. Husted and Carlos Serrano, "Corporate Governance in Mexico," *Journal of Business Ethics* 37 (May 2002): 337–348.

12. Robert A. G. Monks, *Corporate Governance in the Twenty-First Century: A Preliminary Outline* (Portland, ME: LENS, 1996), available at www.lens-library.com/info/cg21.html.

13. McRitchie, "Ending the Wall Street Walk."

14. David A. Cifrino and Garrison R. Smith, "NYSE and NASDAQ Propose to Review Corporate Governance Listing Standards," *Corporate Governance Advisor* 10 (November–December 2002): 18–25.

15. Maria Maher and Thomas Anderson, *Corporate Governance: Effects on Firm Performance and Economic Growth* (Paris: Organisation for Economic Co-operation and Development, 1999).

16. A. Demb and F. F. Neubauer, *The Corporate Board: Confronting the Paradoxes* (Oxford: Oxford University Press, 1992).

17. Sandy Shore, "Ex-Qwest Exec Settlement Said Collapsed," *Associated Press,* January 20, 2006, http://accounting.smartpros.com/x51431.xml, accessed March 15, 2006.

18. Maher and Anderson, *Corporate Governance.*

19. Organisation for Economic Co-operation and Development, *The OECD Principles of Corporate Governance* (Paris: Organisation for Economic Co-operation and Development, 1999).

20. Edward A. Stolzenberg, "Governance Change for Public Hospitals," *Journal of Healthcare Management* 45 (September–October 2000): 347–350; Jeffrey A. Alexander, Bryan J. Weiner, and Richard J. Bogue, "Changes in the Structure, Composition, and Activity of Hospital Governing Boards, 1989–1997: Evidence from Two National Surveys," *Milbank Quarterly* 79 (May 2001): 253–279.

21. World Bank Group, "About Corporate Governance," http://www.worldbank.org/html/fpd/privatesector/cg/, accessed January 16, 2003.

22. Clive Crook, "Why Good Corporate Citizens Are a Public Menace," *National Journal,* April 24, 1999, p. 1087.

23. "Why Outsourcing Succeeds or Not," *HR Focus* 82 (July 2005), pp. 1–3; Anita Hawser, "Gaining Ground," *Global Finance* 19 (September 2005), pp. 16–18; Murray Weidenbaum, "Outsourcing: Pros and Cons," *Business Horizons* 48 (July–August 2005), pp. 311–315; James Cox, "As Economy Expands, India on Verge of Something Big," *USA Today,* February 9, 2004, pp. 1B–2B; Joanna Slater and Jay Soloman, "With a Small Car, India Takes Big Step onto Global Stage," *Wall Street Journal,* February 5, 2004, pp. 1A, 9A.

24. Andrew Backover, "Overseer Confident WorldCom Will Come Back," *USA Today,* December 31, 2002, p. 8A.

25. Melvin A. Eisenberg, "Corporate Governance: The Board of Directors and Internal Control," *Cordoza Law Review* 19 (September–November 1997): 237.

26. "TD Bank Splits CEO and Chairman Roles," *Toronto Star,* December 21, 2002, p. D3; John A. Byrne, "This Corporate Reform Lacks Spine," *Business Week Online,* January 13, 2003, http://www.businessweek.com/bwdaily/dnflash/jan2003/nf20030110_4900.htm, accessed January 17, 2003; Joann Lublin, "Splitting Posts of Chairman, CEO Catches On," *Wall Street Journal,* November 11, 2002, pp. B1, B3.

27. Norfolk Southern Corporation Annual Report 2005.

28. Louis Lavelle, "The Best and Worst Boards," *Business Week,* October 7, 2002, p. 104; McKinsey & Company, *McKinsey Director Opinion Survey on Corporate Governance, 2002,* http://www.mckinsey.com/practices/corporategovernance/PDF/DirectorOpinion.pdf, accessed January 17, 2003.

29. Lavelle, "The Best and Worst Boards," p. 104; Gretchen Morgenson, "Shares of Corporate Nice Guys Can Finish First," *New York Times,* April 27, 2003, p. 1; Peter Stanwick and Sarah Stanwick, "The Relationship Between Corporate Governance and Financial Performance: An Empirical Study," *Journal of Corporate Citizenship* 8 (Winter 2002): 35–48.

30. Geoffrey Colvin, "CEO Knockdown," *Fortune,* April 4, 2005.

31. "Billionaire Warren Buffett Leaving Coca-Cola Board," *Atlanta Business Chronicle,* February 14, 2006, http://atlanta.bizjournals.com/atlanta/stories/2006/02/13/daily10.html.

32. Matt Krantz, "Web of Board Members Ties Together Corporate America," *USA Today,* November 24, 2002, http://www.usatoday.com/money/companies/management/2002-11-24-interlock_x.htm, accessed August 2, 2006.

33. James Covert. "Wal-Mart Urged to Review Controls," *Wall Street Journal,* June 2, 2005.

34. Adrian Cadbury, "What Are the Trends in Corporate Governance? How Will They Impact Your Company?" *Long Range Planning* 32 (January 1999): 12–19.

35. "How Shareholder Proposals Work," The Equality Project, http://www.equalityproject.org/how.htm#do, accessed January 14, 2003; Barry Burr, "Shareholder Activism Hot in Poor Business Climate," *Pensions & Investments,* July 8, 2002, pp. 4, 32; Jake Ulick, "Anger Rising over CEO Pay,"

CNN/Money, April 21, 2003, http://money.cnn.com/2003/04/21/news/proxy_season/, accessed August 7, 2003.

36. Amy Borrus, "Should Directors Be Nervous," *Businessweek-online,* March 6, 2006, http://www.businessweek.com/magazine/content/06_10/b3974062.htm, accessed March 8, 2006.

37. Peter D. Kinder, Steven D. Lyndenberg, and Amy L. Domini, *The Social Investment Almanac* (New York: Holt, 1992).

38. "Companies Fail Social Investors, Most Investors Value Corporate Responsibility, Few Are Satisfied," *Investor Relations Business,* August 6, 2001, pp. 1, 13; SocialFunds.com/Motley Fool, "Investor Survey on Corporate Responsibility," http://www.socialfunds.com/page.cgi/fool_results.html, accessed September 16, 2003.

39. Susan Scherreik, "Following Your Conscience Is Just a Few Clicks Away," *Business Week,* May 13, 2002, pp. 116–118.

40. B. Langtry, "The Ethics of Shareholding," *Journal of Business Ethics* 37 (May 2002): 175–185.

41. R. Bruce Hutton, Louis D'Antonio, and Tommi Johnsen, "Socially Responsible Investing: Growing Issues and New Opportunities," *Business and Society* 37 (September 1998): 281–305.

42. William Baue, "Corporate Responsibility Ratings and SRI Screens Sometimes Differ," SocialFunds.com, http://www.socialfunds.com/news/article.cgi?sfArticleId=1007, accessed August 13, 2003.

43. Social Investment Forum, 2005 Report on Socially Responsible Investing Trends in the United States, http://www.socialinvest.org/areas/research/trends/sri_trends_report_2005.pdf, accessed April 24, 2006.

44. Robert A. G. Monks, "What Will Be the Impact of Active Shareholders? A Practical Recipe for Constructive Change," *Long Range Planning* 32 (January 1999): 20–27.

45. "Proposal for Socially Responsible Investment by Colleges and Universities," Student Alliance to Reform Corporations, http://www.starcalliance.org/assets/sri/starcsri.doc, accessed August 7, 2003. Reprinted with permission from the STARC Alliance.

46. "Annual Eaton Vance Investor Survey Shows Unshaken Faith in Capitalism; Confidence in Corporate Management and Wall Street Dips," *Business Wire,* January 7, 2003, accessed via LexisNexis; David Schepp, "US Urged to Lift Investor Confidence," *BBC News Online,* September 27, 2002, http://news.bbc.co.uk/2/hi/business/2285847.stm, accessed January 14, 2003.

47. "Internal Auditors: Integral to Good Corporate Governance," *Internal Auditor* 59 (August 2002): 44–49.

48. Eisenberg, "Corporate Governance."

49. Kathy Hoke, "Eyes Wide Open," *Business First–Columbus,* August 27, 1999, pp. 27–28.

50. Lynn Brewer, Robert Chandler, and O. C. Ferrell, *Managing Risks for Corporate Integrity: How to Survive an Ethical Misconduct Disaster* (Mason OH: Texere/Thomson, 2006), p. 72.

51. Ray A. Goldberg, *Kraft General Foods: Risk Management Philosophy* (Boston: Harvard Business School Press, 1994).

52. Brewer, Chandler, and Ferrell, *Managing Risks for Corporate Integrity,* p. 75.

53. Ibid.

54. Jim Billington, "A Few Things Every Manager Ought to Know About Risk," *Harvard Management Update,* March 1997,

pp. 10–11; Lee Puschaver and Robert G. Eccles, "In Pursuit of the Upside: The New Opportunity in Risk Management," *PW Review,* December 1996.

55. Scott Alexander, "Achieving Enterprisewide Privacy Compliance," *Insurance & Technology* 25 (November 2000): 53; M. Joseph Sirgy and Chenting Su, "The Ethics of Consumer Sovereignty in an Age of High Tech," *Journal of Business Ethics* 28 (November 2000): 1–14.

56. "How to Pay Bosses," *Economist,* November 16, 2002, p. 60; Charles Elson, "What's Wrong with Executive Compensation?" *Harvard Business Review* 81 (January 2003): 5–12; Roger L. Martin, "Taking Stock," *Harvard Business Review* 81 (January 2003): 19.

57. John A. Byrne, with Louis Lavelle, Nanette Byrnes, Marcia Vickers, and Amy Borrus, "How to Fix Corporate Governance," *Business Week,* May 6, 2002, pp. 69–78.

58. "How Business Rates: By the Numbers," *Business Week,* September 11, 2000, pp. 148–149.

59. Kaja Whitehouse. "Investors Sue H-P over Size of Fiorina Severance Package," *Wall Street Journal,* March 8, 2006.

60. Lucian Bebchuk, "The Disney Verdict Shuts Out Investors," *FT.com* August 12, 2005.

61. Elliot Blair Smith, "New Rule to Expose Pay Packages," *USA Today,* July 27, 2006, p. B1.

62. "What We Learned in 2002," *Business Week,* December 30, 2002, p. 170.

63. Sarah Anderson, John Cavanagh, Ralph Estes, Chuck Collins, and Chris Hartman, *A Decade of Executive Excess: The 1990s Sixth Annual Executive Compensation Survey* (Boston: United for a Fair Economy, 1999).

64. Sarah Anderson, John Cavanagh, Scott Klinger, and Liz Stanton, "Executive Excess 2005. Defense Contractors Get More Bucks for the Bang. 12th Annual CEO Compensation Survey," *Institute for Policy Studies, United for a Fair Economy,* August 30, 2005, http://www.faireconomy.org/press/2005/EE2005_pr.html, accessed March 15, 2006.

65. Ibid.

66. Louis Lavelle, "CEO Pay, The More Things Change . . . ," *Business Week,* October 16, 2000, pp. 106–108.

67. Scott DeCarlo. "CEO Compensation: Special Report," *Forbes.com.,* April 21, 2005.

68. Gary Strauss and Barbara Hansen, "Companies Think They're Worth $100,000,000. Median Pay for CEOs of 100 Largest Companies Rose 25%," *USA Today,* April 10, 2006, p. B1.

69. Joann S. Lublin, "Boards Tie CEO Pay More Tightly to Performance," *Wall Street Journal,* February 21, 2006, p. A1.

70. Ibid.

71. Gary Strauss, "America's Corporate Meltdown," *USA Today,* June 27, 2002, pp. 1A, 2A.

72. Conference Board Commission on Public Trust and Private Enterprise, *Findings and Recommendations, Part 1: Executive Compensation* (New York: Conference Board, 2002), http://www.conference-board.org/pdf_free/756.pdf, accessed January 16, 2003; Lucian Bebchuk and Jesse Fried, "Improving Executive Compensation," *TIAA-CREF Investment Forum* (June 2003): 11–12.

73. Stephen M. Davis, "Global Governance: How Nations Compare," *Corporate Board* 20 (September–October 1999): 5–9.

74. "Measuring Corporate Governance Standards," *Asiamoney* 11 (December 2000–January 2001): 94–95.

75. Edward Iwata, "Investors Globally Want Better Corporate Governance," *USA Today,* April 17, 2006, p. B1.

76. Barbara Crutchfield George, Kathleen A. Lacey, and Jotta Birmele, "The 1998 OECD Convention," *American Business Law Journal* 37 (Spring 2000): 485–525; Ira Millstein, "Corporate Governance: The Role of Market Forces," *OECD Observer* (Summer 2000): 27–28; "What Is OECD," Organisation for Economic Co-operation and Development, http://www.oecd.org/pdf/M00008000/M00008299.pdf, accessed January 10, 2003.

77. Davis Global Advisors, *Leading Corporate Governance Indicators™ 2002: An International Comparison,* Newton, MA, November 2002.

78. "Asian Capitalism: The End of Tycoons," *Economist,* April 29, 2000, pp. 67–69; "The Importance of Corporate Governance," *Asiamoney* 10 (December 1999–January 2000): 92–94; "The Lost (Half) Decade—East Asian Economies," *Economist,* July 6, 2002, via LexisNexis.

79. "Cost of Workplace Regulation," *USA Today,* October 24, 2001, p. 1B.

80. Adam M. Brandenburger and Barry J. Nalebuff, *Co-opetition: 1. A Revolutionary Mindset That Redefines Competition and Cooperation; 2. The Game Theory Strategy That's Changing the Game of Business* (New York: Doubleday, 1997).

81. Maher and Anderson, *Corporate Governance.*

82. Monks, *Corporate Governance in the Twenty-First Century.*

83. "Three Skills for Today's Leaders," *Harvard Management Update* 4 (November 1999): 11.

84. Catherine M. Daily, Dan R. Dalton, and Albert A. Cannella Jr., "Corporate Governance: A Decade of Dialogue and Data," *Academy of Management Review* 28 (July 2003): 371–382.

85. "The Way We Govern Now—Corporate Boards," *Economist,* January 11, 2003, pp. 59–61; Carol Hymowitz, "How to Fix a Broken System," *Wall Street Journal,* February 24, 2003, pp. R1–R3.

86. Monks, *Corporate Governance in the Twenty-First Century.*

CHAPTER 4

1. Better Business Bureau, "About Us," http://www.bbb.org/about/index.asp, accessed June 10, 2006. "BBB Advises Caution When Dealing with Talent/Modeling Agencies," http://www.bbb.org/alerts/article.asp?ID=477, accessed June 10, 2006; Coreen Bailor, "A BBB Sees Bigger Business," *Customer Relationship Management* 10 (May 2006): 42.

2. George J. Siedel, "Six Forces and the Legal Environment of Business," *American Business Law Journal* 37 (Summer 2000): 717–742.

3. Paul Starr, "Liberalism After Clinton," *American Prospect,* August 28, 2000; Amy Borrus and Paula Dwyer, "Surprise: Bush Is Emerging as a Fighter for Privacy on the Net," *Business Week,* June 5, 2000, p. 63.

4. Julia Appleby, "Columbia Agrees to $745 Million Penalty," *USA Today,* May 19, 2000, p. B1.

5. G. Meirovich and A. Reichel, "Illegal but Ethical: An Inquiry into the Roots of Illegal Corporate Behavior in Russia," *Business Ethics: A European Review* 9 (July 2000): 126–135; M. Vaadi and K. Jaakson, "The Importance of Valuing

Honesty: Determining Factors and Some Hints to Ethics," University of Tartu–Faculty of Economics & Business Administration Working Paper Series 43 (2006): 3–33, accessed via Business Source Complete.

6. Pam King, Mountain States Better Business Bureau, February 2003.

7. Better Business Bureau, BBBOnLine: Reliability Program Requirements, http://www.bbbonline.org/reliability/requirement.asp, accessed June 16, 2006.

8. "Need to Pay to Claim a Prize? It Could Be a Scam!" Competition Bureau Canada, http://www.competitionbureau.gc.ca/, accessed June 16, 2006.

9. "Drug Firms Agree to Settle Lawsuit over Cardizem," *Wall Street Journal,* January 28, 2003, p. A1.

10. "Execs Go to Jail; Companies Fined for Environmental Crimes," *Industrial Safety and Hygiene News* 40 (May 2006): 8.

11. David A. Vise, "AOL, Microsoft Team Up, Ask Government to Help Stop Spam," *Commercial Appeal,* February 21, 2003, p. C2.

12. S. Bono, A. Rubin, A. Stubblefield, and M. Green, "Security Through Legality," *Communications of the ACM* 49 (June 2006): 41–43.

13. "Warning Signs," *Business Ethics* 15 (September–October 2001): 11.

14. Federal Trade Commission, "Consumer Fraud and Identity Theft Complaint Data," http://www.consumer.gov/sentinel/pubs/Top10Fraud2005.pdf, accessed June 15, 2006.

15. Jim Carlton and Pui-Wing Tam, "Online Auctioneers Face Growing Fraud Problem," *Wall Street Journal,* May 12, 2000, p. B2.

16. "The Sherman Antitrust Act," Antitrust Case Browser, http://www.stolaf.edu/people/becker/antitrust/statutes/sherman.html, accessed June 10, 2006.

17. Ibid.

18. Jennifer Jones, "Government Drops Breakup Bid," *InfoWorld,* September 10, 2001, http://www.findartices.com, accessed October 20, 2001; U.S. Department of Justice, "Joint Status Report on Microsoft's Compliance with the Final Judgments," http://www.usdoj.gov/atr/cases/f216100/216127.htm, accessed June 18, 2006.

19. U.S. Department of Justice, "Antitrust Enforcement and the Consumer," http://www.usdoj.gov/atr/public/div_stats/211491.pdf, accessed June 15, 2006.

20. U.S. Federal Trade Commission, "FTC Alleges Stanley Made False Made in the USA Claims About Its Tools," http://www.ftc.gov/opa/2006/06/stanley.htm, accessed June 10, 2006.

21. "Appeals Court Upholds FTC Ruling: Doan's Must Include Corrective Message in Future Advertising and Labeling," Federal Trade Commission press release, August 21, 2000, http://www.ftc.gov/opa/2000/08/doans.htm, accessed June 10, 2006.

22. "FTC Sues Failed Website, Toysmart.com, for Deceptively Offering for Sale Personal Information of Website Visitors," Federal Trade Commission, http://www.ftc.gov/opa/2000/07/toysmart.htm, accessed June 18, 2006.

23. "Nine West Settles State and Federal Price Fixing Charges," Federal Trade Commission, http://www.ftc.gov/os/2000/04/ninewest.do.htm, accessed June 10, 2006.

24. Harry First, "The Vitamins Case," *Antitrust Law Journal* 68, no. 3 (2001): 711–734.

25. Albert A. Foer and Robert H. Lande, "The Evolution of United States Antitrust Law: The Past, Present & (Possible) Future," *American Antitrust Institute,* October 20, 1999, http://www.antitrustinstitute.org/recent/64.cfm, accessed July 30, 2006.

26. Richard Waddington, "World Health Body Warns That Mad Cow Still a Risk," Reuters Newswire, January 30, 2003.

27. Ernest Beck, "Stores Told to Lift Prices in Germany," *Wall Street Journal,* September 11, 2000, p. A27; Debbie Garbato, "Producing Results," *Retail Merchandiser* 46 (May 2006): 6–10.

28. Brandon Mitchener, "Global Antitrust Process May Get Simpler," *Wall Street Journal,* October 27, 2000, p. A17; Debbie Thorne LeClair, O. C. Ferrell, and Linda Ferrell, "Federal Sentencing Guidelines for Organizations: Legal, Ethical, and Public Policy Issues for International Marketing," *Journal of Public Policy and Marketing* 16 (Spring 1997): 30.

29. Ibid., p. 31.

30. European Union, "Key Facts and Figures about Europe and the Europeans," http://europa.eu/abc/keyfigures/index_en.htm, accessed July 30, 2006.

31. LeClair, Ferrell, and Ferrell, "Federal Sentencing Guidelines for Organizations," p. 31.

32. "Today's Briefing," *Commercial Appeal,* February 12, 2003, p. C1.

33. Ted Bridis, "Computer-Crime Treaty," *Wall Street Journal,* October 26, 2000, p. B8.

34. "Administrative Costs of Federal Regulation," via http://wc.wustl.edu/Reg_Report/Press_Release2005.pdf, accessed June 15, 2006.

35. "Youth Smoking Prevention," Philip Morris website, http://www.philipmorrisusa.com/en/our_initiatives/ysp.asp, accessed June 15, 2006.

36. U.S. Department of Justice, "Antitrust Enforcement and the Consumer," http://www.usdoj.gov/atr/public/div_stats/211491.pdf, accessed June 15, 2006.

37. Mark Wigfield, "FCC to Diminish Role in Monitoring Phone Equipment," *Wall Street Journal,* May 15, 2000, p. B12.

38. Shawn Tully, "Friendly Skies Aren't Out of the Picture," *Fortune,* December 18, 2002, http://www.fortune.com/fortune/articles/0,15114,400967,00.html, accessed March 1, 2003.

39. William M. Pride and O. C. Ferrell, *Marketing: Concepts and Strategies,* 12th ed. (Boston: Houghton Mifflin, 2003), pp. 54–55.

40. "The Better Business Bureau System," http://www.bbb.org/about/aboutCouncil.asp, accessed June 10, 2006.

41. Jennifer Rewick, "Connecticut Attorney General Launches Probe of Priceline.com After Complaints," *Wall Street Journal,* October 2, 2000, p. B16.

42. Pride and Ferrell, *Marketing: Concepts and Strategies,* pp. 54–55.

43. "Electronic Signatures in Global and National Commerce Act," http://www.ftc.gov/os/2001/06/esign7.htm, accessed July 28, 2006.

44. "Image Is Everything," *Business China,* June 5, 2006, pp. 6–7.

45. Daniel Malan, "Corporate Citizens, Colonialists, Tourists or Activists? Ethical Challenges Facing South African Corporations in Africa," *Journal of Corporate Citizenship* 18 (Summer 2005): 49–60.

46. Joint Committee on the Organization of Congress, "Historical Overview," Organization of the Congress, December 1993, www.house.gov/rules/jcoc2c.htm#b, accessed July 22, 2006; Joint Committee on the Organization of Congress, "Reorganization in the Modern Congress," Organization of the Congress, December 1993, www.house.gov/rules/jcoc2o.htm; Marc A. Triebwasser, "Congressional Leadership and Reform: The Trends Toward Centralization and Decentralization," *American Politics,* www.polisci.ccsu.edu/trieb/Cong-9.html, accessed October 21, 2001; "Driving Mr. Gephardt," *Newsweek,* August 21, 2000, p. 48.

47. "About the FEC," Federal Election Commission, http://www.fec.gov/about.shtml, accessed June 10, 2005.

48. "Common Cause Victories," Common Cause, www.commoncause.org/, accessed June 12, 2006.

49. Don Corney, Amy Borrus, and Jay Greene, "Microsoft's All Out Counterattack," *Business Week,* May 15, 2000, pp. 103–106.

50. Declan McCullagh, "Cable Operators Pledge to Keep Net Open," C/Net news.com, February 24, 2003.

51. "Corporate Lobbying Becoming a Key Business Risk," Lifeworth.com press release, February 11, 2003, via America Online.

52. Corney, Borrus, and Greene, "Microsoft's All Out Counterattack."

53. "Election Regulators Seek Scrutiny of Presidential Hopefuls PACs," http://www.cnn.com/2003/ALLPOLITICS/02/26/political.pacs.ap/index.html, accessed August 14, 2003.

54. "High Court Declines Ex-Governor's Appeal," http://www.nola.com/news/t-p/washington/index.ssf?/base/news-1/1151389761142370.xml&coll=1, accessed July 30, 2006.

55. Win Swenson, "The Organizational Guidelines Carrot and Stick Philosophy and Their Focus on Effective Compliance," in *Corporate Crime in America: Strengthening the Good Citizen Corporation* (Washington, DC: U.S. Sentencing Commission, 1993), p. 17.

56. Lynn Brewer, Robert Chandler, and O. C. Ferrell, *Managing Risks for Corporate Integrity: How to Survive an Ethical Misconduct Disaster* (Mason, OH: Texere/Thomson, 2006); United States Code Service (Lawyers Addition), 18 U.S.S.C. Appendix, Sentencing Guidelines for the United States Courts (Rochester, NY: Lawyers Cooperative Publishing, 1995), § 8A.1.

57. "Corporate Criminals Strike Out in 2005," *Information Management Journal* 40 (March–April): 10.

58. Elliot Blair Smith, "Probe: Former Kmart CEO 'Grossly Derelict,'" *USA Today,* January 27, 2003, p. B1.

59. Stephen Taub, "SEC: 1,300 'Whistles' Blown Each Day: Most Tips Concerning Accounting Problems at Public Companies; 'a Tremendous Source of Leads,'" CFO.com, August 3, 2004, http://www.cfo.com/article.cfm/3015607, accessed March 15, 2006.

60. Julie Homer. "Overblown: In the Wake of Sarbanes-Oxley, Some Serious Misconceptions Have Arisen About What Blowing the Whistle Actually Means," CFO.com, October 1, 2003.

61. Amy Borrus, "Learning to Love Sarbanes-Oxley," *Business Week,* November 21, 2005, pp. 126–128.

CHAPTER 5

1. "About Allstate," "The Allstate Corporation at a Glance," Allstate Insurance Company, www.allstate.com/about/pagerender.asp?page=allstate_at_a_glance.htm, accessed January 19, 2006; "Allstate CEO: Firms Should Be Politically Active," *USA Today,* July 18, 2005; "Community Commitment," "The Allstate Foundation," Allstate Insurance Company, www.allstate.com/Community/PageRender.asp?Page=foundation.html, accessed January 19, 2006; "Years Like 2004 Bring Out the Best in Allstate," The Allstate Corporation Summary Annual Report 2004, pp. 5–9.

2. Amy Joyce, "Wal-Mart Bias Case Moves Forward: 1.6 Million Women May Join Class-Action Suit," *Washington Post,* June 23, 2004, p. A01, http://www.washingtonpost.com/ac2/wp-dyn/A62004-2004Jun22?language=printer, accessed May 1, 2006.

3. Wendy Zellner, "No Way to Treat a Lady?" *Business Week,* March 3, 2003, pp. 63, 66.

4. "Privacy for Sale," *Business Ethics* 13 (July–August 1999): 8.

5. Andrew Singer, "CEO's Focus on 'Reputation' Buoys Unisys' Ethics Program," *Ethikos* 13 (November–December 1999): 1–3, 8, 16.

6. "Obesity Becomes Political Issue as Well as Cultural Obsession," Washington Wire, *Wall Street Journal,* March 3, 2006, www.wsj.com, accessed March 21, 2006.

7. "Readers on Health Care," *Wall Street Journal,* January 9, 2006, p. R3, www.wsj.com, accessed March 21, 2006.

8. "SEC Chief Donaldson Pushes Ethics," MSNBC News, February 28, 2003, www.msnbc.com/news/878994.asp, accessed March 1, 2003.

9. "Full Survey: Trust in Governments, Corporations and Global Institutions Continues to Decline," World Economic Forum, December 15, 2005, Geneva, Switzerland.

10. "Eye on Europe," *Business Ethics* 16 (January–February 2002): 9.

11. "Andrea Jung," in Wikipedia, http://en.wikipedia.org/wiki/Andrea_Jung, accessed April 25, 2006.

12. Oliver Ryan, "Avon Looks Ripe for a Rebound," *Fortune,* March 15, 2006, http://money.cnn.com/magazines/fortune/fortune_archive/2006/03/20/8371795/index.htm, accessed April 25, 2006.

13. Greg Farrell, "Hunt Is on for Notebook That Scrushy Denies Exists," *USA Today,* June 12, 2003, p. B1.

14. Jay Reeves, "HealthSouth Reports Continuing Problems," Associated Press, March 17, 2006, http://www.forbes.com/feeds/ap/2006/03/17/ap2603529.html, accessed May 1, 2006.

15. "State Supreme Court Rules Scrushy Must Repay Bonus," WVTM-TV, April 12, 2006, http://www.msnbc.msn.com/id/12290791/, accessed May 1, 2006.

16. Greg Farrell, "Scrushy Guilty of Bribery in Case Involving Ex-Governor," *USA Today,* June 30, 2006, p. B1.

17. Debbie Thorne McAlister and Robert Erffmeyer, "A Content Analysis of Outcomes and Responsibilities for Consumer Complaints to Third Party Organizations," *Journal of Business Research* 56 (April 2003): 341–352.

18. http://money.cnn.com/news/specials/corruption, accessed January 31, 2003.

19. Lisa Roner, "Words Ahead of Substance: Public Faith in the Integrity of Big Business Remains Extremely Low," *Ethical Corporation,* January 2006, pp. 21–22.

20. Barry Newman, "An Ad Professor Huffs Against Puffs, but It's a Quixotic Enterprise," *Wall Street Journal,* January 24, 2003, p. A1.

21. Andrew Adam Newman, "If the Children Can Drink Uncola, What About Unbeer?" *New York Times,* September 19, 2005, www.nytimes.com; "Drink That Looks Like Beer Getting Popular with Kids," JapanToday.com, September 28, 2005, http://www.tomomasu.co.jp/tomomasu/company.htm, accessed December 10, 2005.

22. Peter Lattman, "Boeing's Top Lawyer Spotlights Company's Ethical Lapses," *Wall Street Journal,* Law Blog, January 30, 2006, http://blogs.wsj.com/law/2006/01/31/boeings-top-lawyer-rips-into-his-company, accessed March 31, 2006.

23. David Whelan, "Only the Paranoid Resurge," *Forbes,* April 10, 2006.

24. O. C. Ferrell, John Fraedrich, and Linda Ferrell, *Business Ethics,* 7th ed. (Boston: Houghton Mifflin).

25. Ibid.

26. Ibid.

27. Janet Guyon, "Jack Grubman Is Back. Just Ask Him," *Fortune,* May 16, 2005, pp. 119–126.

28. "Arthur Andersen," in Wikipedia, http://en.wikipedia.org/wiki/Arthur_Andersen, accessed April 25, 2006.

29. Jenny Summerour, "Bribery Game," *Progressive Grocer,* January 2000, pp. 2–5, 43.

30. "Warning Signs," *Business Ethics* 16 (September–December 2002): 8.

31. "What Is Fraud: What Every CEO or Business Owner Should Know," *The Fraud Detectives Consultant Network,* http://www.frauddetectives.com/what.shtml, accessed May 1, 2006.

32. "Insurance Fraud Costs the Average American Family $200–$300 Annually," Michigan Agent, http://www.michagent.org/publications/magazine/sept00/fraud.htm, accessed May 1, 2006.

33. Bob Sullivan, "Online Fraud Costs $2.6 Billion This Year," *MSNBC,* November 11, 2004, http://www.msnbc.msn.com/id/6463545/, accessed May 1, 2006.

34. "Co-workers Reporting Fraud," *USA Today,* Snapshot, October 3, 2002, p. 1D.

35. Kara Scannell, "Tyco to Pay $50 Million to Settle SEC Accounting-Fraud Charges," *Wall Street Journal,* April 18, 2006, p. C2.

36. "Krispy Kreme Problems," *Coloradoan,* August 11, 2005, p. D7.

37. Ronald Alsop, "Scandal-Filled Year Takes Toll on Firms' Good Names," *Wall Street Journal,* February 12, 2003, http://online.wsj.com.

38. Greg Farrell, "Sullivan Gets 5-year Prison Sentence," *USA Today,* August 12, 2005, p. B1.

39. Archie B. Carroll, *Business and Society: Ethics and Stakeholder Management* (Cincinnati, OH: South-Western, 1989), pp. 228–230.

40. Sara Nathan, "Phony Jobs," *USA Today,* March 7, 2000, p. B1.

41. Russell Mokhiber, "Warning Signs," *Business Ethics* 13 (May–June 1999): 8.

42. "Mott's Will Rewrite Some Labels Blamed for Misleading People," *Wall Street Journal,* August 2, 2000, p. B7.

43. Heather Won Tesoriero, "Merck Is Handed Another Loss over Vioxx," *Wall Street Journal,* April 22–23, 2006, p. A1.

44. Lisa Roner, "Drug-makers' Spoonful of Sugar," *Ethical Corporation,* October 2005, p. 27.

45. Consumer Fraud and Identity Theft Complaint Data January–December 2005, Federal Trade Commission 2006; Data from Consumer Sentinel and the Identity Theft Data Clearinghouse, http://www.consumer.gov/sentinel/pubs/Top10Fraud2005.pdf, accessed April 25, 2006.

46. "Newsletter; Federal Trade Commission Report: ID Theft #1 Complaint," February 2005, http://www.machine-solution.com/_Article+FTC+ID+Theft.html, accessed July 23, 2006.

47. "Retail Theft and Inventory Shrinkage," *What You Need to Know About . . . Retail Industry,* http://retailindustry.about.com/library/weekly/02/aa021126a.htm, accessed February 6, 2003.

48. Daryl Koehn, "Consumer Fraud: The Hidden Threat," University of St. Thomas, www.stthom.edu/cbes/commentary/HBJCONFRAUD.html, accessed February 6, 2003.

49. Annie Finnigan, "Different Strokes," *Working Woman,* April 2001, p. 44.

50. O. C. Ferrell and Geoffrey Hirt, *Business: A Changing World,* 4th ed. (Boston: McGraw-Hill Irwin, 2003), pp. 312–316.

51. See pp. 164–165 of this text.

52. Ferrell and Hirt, *Business,* pp. 298–301.

53. "$3.5 Million Settlement in Woolworth Age Discrimination Case," CNN.com, November 15, 2002, www.cnn.com.

54. Sue Shellenberger, "Work & Family," *Wall Street Journal,* May 23, 2001, p. B1.

55. "What Is Affirmative Action?" HR Content Library, October 12, 2001, www.hrnext.com/content/view.cfm?articles_id=2007&subs_id=32.

56. Ibid.

57. "What Affirmative Action Is (and What It Is Not)," National Partnership for Women and Families, www.nationalpartnership.org/content.cfm?L1=202&DBT=Documents&NewsItemID=289&HeaderTitle=Affirmative%20Action, accessed December 4, 2002.

58. Ibid.

59. *U.S. Equal Employment Opportunity Commission: An Overview* (Washington, DC: U.S. Equal Employment Opportunity Commission, 1997), www.eeoc.gov/overview.html.

60. Mary Miller, "Warning Signs," *Business Ethics* 16 (January–February 2002): 8.

61. *The U.S. Equal Employment Opportunity Commission,* "Retaliation," http://www.eeoc.gov/types/retaliation.html, accessed May 1, 2006.

62. Joann S. Lublin, "Retaliation over Harassment Claims Takes Focus," *Wall Street Journal,* April 17, 2006, p. B4.

63. Jefferson Graham, "College Students Face Lawsuits on File Sharing," *USA Today,* April 13, 2005, p. 5B.

64. Michael Josephson, "The Biennial Report Card: The Ethics of American Youth," Josephson Institute of Ethics, press release, www.josephsoninstitute.org/survey2004/, accessed August 11, 2005.

65. "Teens Respect Good Business Ethics," *USA Today,* Snapshots, December 12, 2005, p. 13-1.

66. Marianne Jennings, "An Ethical Breach by Any Other Name . . ." *Financial Engineering News,* January–February 2006.

67. Kirk O. Hanson, "A Nation of Cheaters," Markula Center for Applied Ethics website, http://www.scu.edu/ethics/publications/ethicalperspectives/cheating.html, January 19, 2003, accessed January 28, 2003.

68. "Company Watch," *Business Ethics* 16 (Fall 2002): 7.

69. This section was adapted from O. C. Ferrell, John Fraedrich, and Linda Ferrell, *Business Ethics: Ethical Decision Making and Cases,* 5th ed. (Boston: Houghton Mifflin, 2002), pp. 54–68.

70. "Warning Signs," *Business Ethics* 16 (September–December 2002): 8.

71. "Police Warn of Phone Scam," *Inside Tucson Business,* November 11, 1999, p. 3.

72. "Prize Offers: You Don't Have to Pay to Play!" *Federal Trade Commission: Facts for Consumers,* http://www.ftc.gov/bcp/conline/pubs/tmarkg/prizes.htm, accessed April 25, 2006.

73. Lawrence J. H. Schulze, "OSHA's Proposed Ergonomics Standard," *Professional Safety* 45 (August 2000): 8.

74. Joanne Silberner, "All Things Considered," National Public Radio, April 11, 2000.

75. Immanuel Kant, "Fundamental Principles of the Metaphysics of Morals," in *Problems of Moral Philosophy: An Introduction,* 2nd ed., ed. Paul W. Taylor (Encino, CA: Dickenson, 1972), p. 229.

76. Stefanie E. Naumann and Nathan Bennett, "A Case for Procedural Justice Climate: Development and Test of a Multilevel Model," *Academy of Management Journal* 43 (October 2000): 881–889.

77. Joel Brockner and P. A. Siegel, "Understanding the Interaction Between Procedural and Distributive Justice: The Role of Trust," in *Trust in Organizations: Frontiers of Theory and Research,* ed. R. M. Kramer and T. R. Tyler (Thousand Oaks, CA: Sage, 1995), pp. 390–413.

78. Ferrell, Fraedrich, and Ferrell, *Business Ethics,* 7th ed., p. 55.

79. John Fraedrich and O. C. Ferrell, "Cognitive Consistency of Marketing Managers in Ethical Situations," *Journal of the Academy of Marketing Science* 20 (Summer 1992): 245–252.

80. Debbie Thorne LeClair, O. C. Ferrell, and John Fraedrich, *Integrity Management: A Guide to Managing Legal and Ethical Issues in the Workplace* (Tampa, FL: University of Tampa Press, 1998), p. 37.

81. This section was adapted from Ferrell, Fraedrich, and Ferrell, *Business Ethics,* pp. 106–109; and LeClair, Ferrell, and Fraedrich, *Integrity Management,* pp. 37–39.

82. Lawrence Kohlberg, "Stage and Sequence: The Cognitive Developmental Approach to Socialization," in *Handbook of Socialization Theory and Research,* ed. D. A. Goslin (Chicago: Rand McNally, 1969), pp. 347–480.

83. Suein L. Hwang, "The Executive Who Told Tobacco's Secrets," *Wall Street Journal,* November 28, 1995, pp. B1, B6.

84. Kohlberg, "Stage and Sequence," pp. 347–480.

85. Rebecca Goodell, *Ethics in American Business: Policies, Programs and Perceptions* (Washington, DC: Ethics Resource Center, 1994), p. 15.

86. David McClelland, "The Urge to Achieve," in *The Great Writings in Management and Organizational Behavior,* ed. Louis E. Boone and Donald D. Bowen (New York: McGraw-Hill, 1987), p. 386.

87. Harriet McLeod, "Home Depot Co-founder Sees Focus on Business," *Reuters,* November 29, 2005, www.reuters.com, accessed December 1, 2005.

88. O. C. Ferrell and Larry G. Gresham, "A Contingency Framework for Understanding Ethical Decision Making in Marketing," *Journal of Marketing* 49 (Summer 1985): 87–96.

89. Joseph W. Weiss, *Business Ethics: A Managerial, Stakeholder Approach* (Belmont, CA: Wadsworth, 1994), p. 13.

90. Chip Cummins, "Shell Trader, Unit Are Fined over Bogus Oil Trades," *Wall Street Journal,* January 5, 2006, p. C3.

91. Thomas L. Friedman. "A Green Dream in Texas," *New York Times,* January 18, 2006. http://topi<<friedman.new.184.jpg>>cs.nytimes.com/top/opinion/editorialsandoped/oped/columnists/thomaslfriedman/index.html?inline=nyt-per, accessed January 19, 2006.

92. White Dog Café website, http://www.whitedog.com/, accessed April 25, 2006.

93. The Ethics Resource Center, *2005 National Business Ethics Survey: How Employees Perceive Ethics at Work* (Washington, DC: Ethics Resource Center, 2005), pp. 4, 28, 29.

94. O. C. Ferrell, Larry G. Gresham, and John Fraedrich, "A Synthesis of Ethical Decision Models for Marketing," *Journal of Macromarketing* 9 (Fall 1989): 58–59.

95. Michael S. James, "What Is Ethical?" ABCNews.com, February 21, 2003.

96. David Oyama, "Mitsubishi Electric Reveals TV Dangers After 8-Year Silence," *Wall Street Journal,* September 13, 2000, p. A21.

97. "Lack of Formal Ethics Program Connected to Workplace Problems: Survey Looks at Why People Sometimes Bend the Rules," PRNewswire, February 3, 1998.

98. Ethics Resource Center, *The Ethics Resource Center's 2005 National Business Ethics Survey,* p. 41.

99. "Fraud a Growing Problem, *Wall Street Journal* Reports," Bloomberg Newswire, November 3, 2000, via America Online.

100. Vault Editors, "Pens and Post-Its Among Most Pilfered Office Supplies, Says New Vault Survey," Vault.com November 16, 2005, http://www.vault.com/nr/newsmain.jsp?nr_page=3&ch_id=420&article_id=25720773, accessed July 23, 2006.

101. Jeffrey L. Seglin, "Forewarned Is Forearmed? Not Always," *New York Times,* February 16, 2003, www.nytimes.com/2003/02/16/business/yourmoney/16ETHI.html; Barbara Ley Toffler, *Final Accounting: Ambition, Greed and the Fall of Arthur Andersen* (New York: Broadway Books, 2003).

102. Rebecca Smith and Alexei Barrionuevo, "Dynegy Ex-Trader Is Indicted on Criminal Fraud Charges," *Wall Street Journal,* January 28, 2003, http://online.wsj.com/article/0,SB1043687255134893064,00.html?mod=home_whats_ne. . . , accessed January 27, 2003.

103. Helen Huntley, "Brokerages Won't Keep Investors Safe From Crooks," St. Petersburg Times Online, March 20, 2005, http://sptimes.com/2005/03/20/Columns/Brokerages_won_t_keep.shtml, accessed August 2, 2006; "Regulators Charge Brokerage Firm Raymond James," *Reuters,* September 30, 2004, Securities Attorneys Shepherd, Smith and Edwards, LLP, http://www.stockbroker-fraud.com/james.htm, accessed August 2, 2006.

104. Ferrell, Gresham, and Fraedrich, "A Synthesis of Ethical Decision Models for Marketing," pp. 58–59.

CHAPTER 6

1. Cate Whitfield, Staff Administrator, Honda Engineering N.A. Inc., "A Small Company Case Study," Ethics and Compliance Officer Association Annual Business Ethics and Compliance Conference, 2005.

2. Bob Hohler, "Palmeiro Remains on Sideline: Suspension Over, He Gets More Rest," *Boston Globe*, August 12, 2005.

3. "62% of Americans Tell CEOs 'You're Not Doing Enough to Restore Trust and Confidence in American Business," Golin/Harris International, press release, June 20, 2002, www.golinharris.com/news/releases.asp?ID=3788.

4. "Ex-Tyco CFO Indicted for Tax Evasion," CNN/Money, February 19, 2003, http://money.cnn.com/; "A Guide to Corporate Scandals," MSNBC.com, www.msnbc.com/news/wld/business/brill/CorporateScandal_DW.asp, accessed February 26, 2003.

5. Gary R. Weaver and Linda K. Trevino, "Compliance and Values Oriented Ethics Programs: Influences on Employees' Attitudes and Behavior," *Business Ethics Quarterly* 9 (April 1999): 315–335.

6. "How Am I Doing?" *Business Ethics*, Fall 2005, p. 11.

7. "The Value and Ethics of TI," http://www.ti.com/corp/docs/company/citizen/ethics/brochure/index.shtml, accessed April 16, 2006. Courtesy Texas Instruments.

8. "The TI Ethics Quick Test," http://www.ti.com/corp/docs/company/citizen/ethics/quicktest.shtml, accessed April 26, 2006.

9. Mark S. Schwartz, "A Code of Ethics for Corporate Code of Ethics," *Journal of Business Ethics* 41 (2002): 37.

10. Ibid.

11. Ethics Resource Center, *The Ethics Resource Center's 2005 National Business Ethics Survey: How Employees Perceive Ethics at Work* (Washington DC: Ethics Resource Center, 2000), p. 12.

12. "Corporate Information," Fidelity Investments, http://www100.fidelity.com/about/world/ethics_code.html, accessed November 20, 2000.

13. Ethics Resource Center, *The Ethics Resource Center's 2005 National Business Ethics Survey*, p. 56.

14. "USSC Commissioner John Steer Joins with Compliance and Ethics Executives from Leading U.S. Companies to Address Key Compliance, Business Conduct and Governance Issues," *Society for Corporate Compliance and Ethics, PR Newswire*, October 31, 2005.

15. Allynda Wheat, "Keeping an Eye on Corporate America," *Fortune*, November 25, 2002, pp. 44–45.

16. About the ECOA. At a Glance, http://www.theecoa.org/AboutEOA.asp.

17. Wheat, "Keeping an Eye on Corporate America," pp. 44–45.

18. Ibid.

19. *PR Newswire*, June 17, 2002.

20. Debbie Thorne LeClair and Linda Ferrell, "Innovation in Experiential Business Ethics Training," *Journal of Business Ethics* 23 (2000): 313–322.

21. Gwendolyn Bounds, "Training Firms Find Niche in Compliance Needs," *Enterprise*, February 22, 2005, p. B10.

22. "Ethics and Business Conduct," www.boeing.com/companyoffices/aboutus/ethics/index.htm, accessed February 25, 2003. Courtesy of Boeing Business Services Company.

23. O. C. Ferrell and Larry G. Gresham, "A Contingency Framework for Understanding Ethical Decision Making in Marketing," *Journal of Marketing* 49 (Summer 1985): 87–96.

24. Diane E. Kirrane, "Managing Values: A Systematic Approach to Business Ethics," *Training and Development Journal* 1 (November 1990): 53–60.

25. "Boeing Ethics Line: 1-888-970-7171," http://www.boeing.com/companyoffices/aboutus/ethics/, accessed April 26, 2006.

26. Janet Wiscombe, "Don't Fear Whistle-blowers: With HR's Help, Principled Whistle-blowers Can Be a Company's Salvation," *Workforce*, July 2002, http://www.findarticles.com, accessed February 7, 2003.

27. Ibid.

28. Mael Kaptein, "Guidelines for the Development of an Ethics Safety Net," *Journal of Business Ethics* 41 (December 2002): 217.

29. Ibid.

30. Richard Lacavo and Amanda Ripley, "Persons of the Year 2002—Cynthia Cooper, Coleen Rowley, and Sherron Watkins," *Time*, December 22, 2002, www.time.com/personoftheyear/2002, accessed July 24, 2006.

31. John W. Schoen, "Split CEO–Chairman Job, Says Panel," MSNBC.com, January 9, 2003, www.msnbc.com/news/857171.asp, accessed July 24, 2006.

32. Jathon Sapsford and Paul Beckett, "The Complex Goals and Unseen Cost of Whistle-blowing," *Wall Street Journal*, November 25, 2002, pp. A1, A10.

33. "Today's Briefing," *Commercial Appeal*, March 2, 2000, p. C1.

34. Shannon Duffy, "Hospital Chain to Pay $265M to Settle Whistleblower Suits," *The Legal Intelligencer*, June 16, 2006, http://www.law.com/jsp/article.jsp?id=1150362319607, accessed August 2, 2006.

35. Darren Dahl, "Learning to Love Whistleblowers," *Inc.*, March 2006, pp. 21–23.

36. National Business Ethics Survey, *How Employees View Ethics in Their Organizations 1994–2005* (Washington, DC: Ethics Resource Center), p. 29.

37. Thomas A. Stewart, Ann Harrington, and Maura Griffin Sol, "America's Most Admired Companies: Why Leadership Matters," *Fortune*, March 3, 1998, pp. 70–71.

38. Daniel J. Brass, Kenneth D. Butterfield, and Bruce C. Skaggs, "Relationship and Unethical Behavior: A Social Science Perspective," *Academy of Management Review* 23, no. 1 (1998): 14–31.

39. J. M. Burns, *Leadership* (New York: Harper & Row, 1985).

40. "WorldCom Chief Outlines Initial Turnaround Strategy," *Wall Street Journal*, January 14, 2003, http://online.wsj.com, accessed July 24, 2007.

41. John R. P. French and Bertram Ravin, "The Bases of Social Power," in *Group Dynamics: Research and Theory*, ed. Dorwin Cartwright (Evanston, IL: Row, Peterson, 1962), pp. 607–623.

42. Lynn Brewer, Robert Chandler, and O. C. Ferrell, *Managing Risks for Corporate Integrity* (Mason, OH: Texere/Thomson, 2006), p. 35.

43. "Ex Worldcom Comptroller Gets Prison Time," "Ex Worldcom CFO Gets Five Years," CNN/Money, August 11, 2005, www.money.cnn.com, accessed August 11, 2005.

44. "Company Recognition," http://www.starbucks.com/aboutus/Company_Recognition_Feb06.pdf, accessed April 26, 2006.

45. Ibid.

46. Ferrell and Gresham, "A Contingency Framework for Understanding Ethical Decision Making in Marketing."
47. Wiscombe, "Don't Fear Whistle-blowers."
48. John Fraedrich and O. C. Ferrell, "Cognitive Consistency of Marketing Managers in Ethical Situations," *Journal of the Academy of Marketing Science* 20 (Summer 1992): 243–252.

CHAPTER 7

1. "About the Shell Group," http://www.shell.com/home/Framework?siteId=royal-en, accessed July 30, 2006; "Invest in Risavika," http://www.energiparken.no/doc/RISAVIKAeng_til_nett.pdf, accessed July 30, 2006; "Shell Announces the Next Stage of its European Refinery Rationalisation Program," http://www.shell.com/home/Framework?siteId=media-en&FC2=/media-en/html/iwgen/leftnavs/zzz_lhn2_9_0.html&FC3=/media-en/html/iwgen/news_and_library/press_releases/1998/dir_1998_pressrelease_index.html, accessed July 30, 2006.
2. Joanne B. Ciulla, *The Working Life: The Promise and Betrayal of Modern Work* (New York: Times Books, 2000).
3. Ciulla, *The Working Life;* Adriano Tilgher, *Work: What It Has Meant to Men Through the Ages,* trans. Dorothy Canfield Fisher (New York: Harcourt, Brace & World, 1958).
4. These facts are derived from Brenda Paik Sunoo, "Relying on Faith to Rebuild a Business," *Workforce* 78 (March 1999): 54–59.
5. Karen Sarkis, "Injured Workers File Claim with Malden Mills," *Occupational Hazards* 62 (February 2000): 16.
6. Sunoo, "Relying on Faith to Rebuild a Business"; Justin Pope, "Malden Mills Emerges from the Bankruptcy, Still Under Financial Cloud," *Houston Chronicle,* August 15, 2003, p. B1. Janet B. Rodie, "Textile World News," *Textile World* 152 (January 2002): 12; Malden Mills, "Corporate News," http://www.polartec.com/about/corporate.php, accessed April 19, 2006
7. "Worldatwork Finds One-Third of Companies Downsized After 9/11," *Report on Salary Surveys* 2 (December 2002): 12; Stephanie Armour, "Companies Chisel Away at Workers' Benefits," *USA Today,* November 18, 2002, pp. 1B–3B; Lynn Gresham, "Winning the Talent War Requires a Fresh Benefits Approach," *Employee Benefit News,* April 15, 2006, p. 9.
8. Neil Conway and Rob B. Briner, *Understanding Psychological Contracts at Work* (London: Oxford University Press, 2006); Denise M. Rousseau, *Psychological Contracts in Organizations: Understanding Written and Unwritten Agreements* (Thousand Oaks, CA: Sage, 1995).
9. Jacqueline Coyle-Shapiro, "A Psychological Contract Perspective on Organizational Citizenship Behavior," *Journal of Organizational Behavior* 23 (December 2002): 927–946; William H. Turnley and Daniel C. Feldman, "The Impact of Psychological Contract Violations on Exit, Voice, Loyalty, and Neglect," *Human Relations* 52 (July 1999): 895–922.
10. Ibid.
11. Kimberly D. Elsbach and Greg Elafson, "How the Packaging of Decision Explanations Affects Perceptions of Trustworthiness," *Academy of Management Journal* 43 (February 2000): 80–89; David E. Guest and Neil Conway, "Communicating the Psychological Contract: An Employer Perspective," *Human Resource Management Journal* 12, no. 2 (2002): 22–38.
12. Gillian Flynn, "Looking Back on 100 Years of Employment Law," *Workforce* 78 (November 1999): 74–77.
13. "A Guru Ahead of Her Time," *Nation's Business* 85 (May 1997): 24.
14. Steve Sayer, "Cleaning Up the Jungle," *Occupational Health & Safety* 66 (May 1997): 22.
15. Flynn, "Looking Back on 100 Years of Employment Law."
16. "Employee Relations in America," *IRS Employment Review* (March 1997): E7–E12; Roger LeRoy Miller and Gaylord A. Jentz, *Business Law Today* (Cincinnati, OH: West Legal Studies in Business, 2000).
17. C. Wright Mills, *White Collar: The American Middle Classes* (New York: Oxford University Press, 1951).
18. Ciulla, *The Working Life;* William H. Whyte, *The Organization Man* (New York: Simon & Schuster, 1956).
19. *Work in America: Report of a Special Task Force to the Secretary of Health, Education, and Welfare* (Cambridge, MA: MIT Press, 1973).
20. Ciulla, *The Working Life.*
21. Taina Savolainen, "Leadership Strategies for Gaining Business Excellence Through Total Quality Management: A Finnish Case Study," *Total Quality Management* 11 (March 2000): 211–226.
22. "Younger Employees Want Security," *USA Today,* October 3, 2001, p. 1B.
23. This section is adapted from Debbie Thorne LeClair, "The Ups and Downs of Rightsizing the Workplace," *ABACA Profile,* November–December 1999, p. 25.
24. Priti Pradhan Shah, "Network Destruction: The Structural Implications of Downsizing," *Academy of Management Journal* 43 (February 2000): 101–112; Steve Lohr, "Cutting Here, but Hiring Over There," *New York Times,* June 24, 2005, p. C3.
25. *New York Times Special Report: The Downsizing of America* (New York: Times Books, 1996); Victor B. Wayhan and Steve Werner, "The Impact of Workforce Reductions on Financial Performance: A Longitudinal Perspective," *Journal of Management* 26 (2000): 341–363.
26. Harry J. Van Buren III, "The Bindingness of Social and Psychological Contracts: Toward a Theory of Social Responsibility in Downsizing," *Journal of Business Ethics* 25 (January 2000): 205–219; David J. Flanagan and K. C. O'Shaughnessy, "The Effects of Layoffs on Firm Reputation," *Journal of Management* (June 2005): 445.
27. Steve Beigbeder, "Easing Workforce Reduction," *Risk Management* 47 (May 2000): 26–30; Matthew Camardella, "Legal Considerations of Workforce Reduction," *Employment Relations Today* 29 (Autumn 2002): 101–106.
28. U.S. Department of Labor, "The Worker Adjustment and Retraining Notification Act," http://www.doleta.gov/programs/factsht/warn.htm, accessed April 19, 2006.
29. Robert A. Nozar, "Nashville's Hot Job Market May Absorb Opryland Cuts," *Hotel and Motel Management* 214 (August 1999): 4, 40.
30. Angelo J. Kinicki, Gregory E. Prussia, and Francis M. McKee-Ryan, "A Panel Study of Coping with Involuntary Job Loss," *Academy of Management Journal* 43 (February 2000): 90–100.

31. Wayhan and Werner, "The Impact of Workforce Reductions on Financial Performance."

32. Nicholas Stein, "Winning the War to Keep Top Talent," *Fortune,* May 29, 2000, pp. 132–138.

33. Kathleen Melymuka, "Showing the Value of Brainpower," *Computerworld,* March 27, 2000, pp. 58–59; Milton Moskowitz and Robert Levering, "Best Companies to Work For: 10 Great Companies in Europe," *Fortune,* February 4, 2002, www.fortune.com/lists/bestcompanies/ten_great.html, accessed November 22, 2002.

34. Carlyn Kolker, "Survivor Blues," *American Lawyer* 24 (October 2002): 116–118; Susan Reynolds Fisher and Margaret A. White, "Downsizing in a Learning Organization," *Academy of Management Review* 25 (January 2000): 244–251.

35. Susan Beck, "What to Do Before You Say 'You're Outta Here,'" *Business Week,* December 8, 1997, p. 6.

36. U.S. Department of Labor, Employment Law Guide, http://www.dol.gov/asp/programs/EmpLawGuideFINAL.pdf, accessed March 30, 2006.

37. "Minimum Wage Laws in the States," U.S. Department of Labor, http://www.dol.gov/esa/minwage/america.htm, accessed March 19, 2006; Miller and Jentz, *Business Law Today.*

38. Flynn, "Looking Back on 100 Years of Employment Law."

39. Robert J. Nobile, "HR's Top 10 Legal Issues," *HR Focus* 74 (April 1997): 19–20.

40. Miller and Jentz, *Business Law Today.*

41. Flynn, "Looking Back on 100 Years of Employment Law."

42. Peter Elstrom, "Needed: A New Union for the New Economy," *Business Week,* September 4, 2000, p. 48; Tim Stentiford and David L. Young, "Case Study: Verizon Wireless Delivers on Its HR Web Site," *Employee Benefit Plan Review* 57 (November 2002): 43.

43. *The New OSHA: Reinventing Worker Safety and Health* (Washington, DC: U.S. Department of Labor, Occupational Safety and Health Administration, 1995), available at http://www.osha.gov/doc/outreachtraining/htmlfiles/newosha.html; Dana E. Corbin, "Speaking Their Language," *Occupational Health & Safety* 71 (July 2002): 32.

44. Judith N. Mottl, "Industry Fights OSHA's Proposed Ergonomic Rule," *Informationweek,* June 19, 2000, p. 122; Daniel R. Miller, "OSHA Goes Too Far with Ergonomics Rules," *National Underwriter,* May 8, 2000, p. 59; John D. Schulz, "Trucking Wants Out," *Traffic World,* May 29, 2000, pp. 21–22; Robin Suttell, "Healthy Work," *Buildings* 96 (October 2002): 56–58.

45. "Ergonomics Focus Makes Waterloo Ready, Not Reactive," http://www.deere.com/en_US/compinfo/envtsafety/innovation/waterloo_ergo.html, accessed April 19, 2006.

46. "Workplace Violence," Occupational Safety and Health Administration, http://www.osha-slc.gov/SLTC/workplaceviolence/index.html, accessed March 30, 2006.

47. Karen Sarkis, "Workplace Violence Top Concern for Employers," *Occupational Hazards* 62 (June 2000): 23; Sarah J. Smith, "Workplace Violence," *Professional Safety* 47 (November 2002): 34–43.

48. *Fear and Violence in the Workplace: A Survey Documenting the Experiences of American Workers* (Minneapolis, MN: Northwestern National Life Insurance Company, 1993).

49. Cal/OSHA Guidelines for Workplace Security (State of California, 1995), available at http://www.dir.ca.gov/dosh/dosh%5Fpublications/worksecurity.html.

50. Anonymous and Andrew R. Thomas, *Crisis in the Skies* (Amherst, NY: Prometheus, 2001); Irene Korn, "Emergency Training," *Successful Meetings* 51 (November 2002): 35; Steve Rubenstein, "Flight Attendants Fight 'Air Rage,'" *San Francisco Chronicle,* July 7, 2000, p. A2.

51. "Suspect in Honolulu Shooting Spree Faces First-Degree Murder Charges," CNN, November 3, 1999, www.cnn.com; "Xerox Hawaii Cited Unsafe in Connection with Mass Shooting," CNN, November 7, 2000, www.cnn.com.

52. Richard V. Denenberg and Mark Braverman, *The Violence-Prone Workplace: A New Approach to Dealing with Hostile, Threatening, and Uncivil Behavior* (Ithaca, NY: Cornell University Press, 1999); Robert Grossman, "Bulletproof Practices," *HR Magazine* 47 (November 2002): 34–42; Bill Merrick, "Make Work a Safe Place," *Credit Union Magazine* 66 (June 2000): 19.

53. Carrie Coolidge, "Risky Business," *Forbes,* January 6, 2003, p. 54; Todd Henneman, "Ignoring Signs of Violence Can Be Fatal, Costly Mistake," *Workforce Management,* February 27, 2006, p.10; John Leming, "New Product Covers Losses Related to Workplace Violence," *Journal of Commerce,* April 6, 2000, p. 15.

54. John Kohl, Milton Mayfield, and Jacqueline Mayfield, "Recent Trends in Pregnancy Discrimination Law," *Business Horizons* (September–October 2005): 48–50.

55. Judy Greenwald, "Employers Confront AIDS in Africa," *Business Insurance* 35 (July 23, 2001): 15; Michael T. Parker, "Fighting AIDS Stigma in the Workplace," *Business Mexico* 15 (August 2005): 43–44.

56. "What Affirmative Action Is (and What It Is Not)," National Partnership for Women & Families, http://www.nationalpartnership.org/portals/p3/library/CivilRightsAffAction/AffirmativeActionFacts.pdf, accessed April 21, 2006.

57. Julio Faundez, *Affirmative Action: International Perspectives* (Geneva, Switzerland: International Labour Office, 1994).

58. "Facts About Sexual Harassment," U.S. Equal Employment Opportunity Commission, www.eeoc.gov/facts/fs-sex.html, accessed April 21, 2006.

59. Donald J. Petersen and Douglas P. Massengill, "Sexual Harassment Cases Five Years After *Meritor Savings Bank v. Vinson,*" *Employee Relations Law Journal* 18 (Winter 1992–1993): 489–516.

60. Maria E. Conway, "Sexual Harassment Abroad," *Workforce* 77 (September 1998): 8–9.

61. "EU Tightens Rules on Sexual Harassment at Work," European Commission, http://www.eubusiness.com/archive/Employment/78499/view?searchterm=sexual%20harassment, accessed July 30,2006.

62. Robert D. Lee and Paul S. Greenlaw, "The Legal Evolution of Sexual Harassment," *Public Administration Review* 55 (July 1995): 357–364.

63. Ibid.

64. George D. Mesritz, "Hostile Environment Sexual Harassment Claims: When Once Is Enough," *Employee Relations Law Journal* 22 (Spring 1997): 79–85; Laura Hoffman Roppe, "*Harris v. Forklift Systems, Inc.:* Victory or Defeat?" *San Diego Law Review* 32 (Winter 1996): 321–342.

65. Joann Muller, "Ford: The High Cost of Harassment," *Business Week,* November 15, 1999, pp. 94–96.

66. "Mitsubishi Agrees to $34 Million Sexual Harassment Settlement," *Business Week,* June 15, 1998, pp. 1–3; Samuel Greengard, "Zero Tolerance: Making It Work," *Workforce* 78 (May 1999): 28–34.

67. Jonathan W. Dion, "Putting Employers on the Defense: The Supreme Court Develops a Consistent Standard Regarding an Employer's Liability for a Supervisor's Hostile Work Environment Sexual Harassment," *Wake Forest Law Review* 34 (Spring 1999): 199–227; Darlene Orlov and Michael T. Roumell, *What Every Manager Needs to Know About Sexual Harassment* (New York: AMACOM, 1999).

68. Joann Lublin, "Retaliation over Harassment Claims Takes Focus," *Wall Street Journal,* April 17, 2006, p. B4.

69. This section is adapted from Randy Chiu, Richard Tansey, Debbie Thorne, and Michael. White, "Is Procedural Justice the Dominant Whistleblowing Motive Among Employees?" unpublished manuscript.

70. J. P. Near and M. P. Miceli, "Organizational Dissidence: The Case of Whistleblowing," *Journal of Business Ethics* 4 (January 1985): 1–16.

71. Greg Palast, *The Best Democracy Money Can Buy* (New York: Penguin Plume, 2004).

72. Ron Ruggles, "Education, Training Is Beneficial to Employees 'Knowing It All' About Industry," *Nation's Restaurant News,* October 16, 2000, pp. 80, 162; Rose French, "Cracker Barrel Launches Programs to Rebuild Image," *Marketing News,* July 15, 2005, p. 31.

73. Jill Schachner Chanen, "You Rang, Sir?" *ABA Journal* 86 (October 2000): 82–84.

74. Scott Westcott, "Good Bye and Good Luck," *Inc* 28 (April 2006): 40–41.

75. Betsy Cummings, "Training's Top Five," *Successful Meetings* 49 (October 2000): 67–73; Adam J. Grossberg, "The Effect of Formal Training on Employment Duration," *Industrial Relations* 39 (October 2000): 578–599; Kathryn Tyler, "Extending the Olive Branch," *HR Magazine* 47 (November 2002): 85–89.

76. "ASTD Highlights International Training Trends in Its 2002 International Comparisons Report," American Society for Training and Development, http://www1.astd.org/pressRoom/pdf/ICRreport.pdf, accessed April 23, 2006.

77. "Diversity: A 'New' Tool for Retention," *HR Focus* 77 (June 2000): 1, 14.

78. David Pollitt, "Diversity Is About More Than Observing the Letter of the Law," *Human Resource Management International Digest* 13 (2005): 37–40.

79. David P. Schulz, "Different Approaches to Approaching Differences," *Stores* 87 (April 2005): 98.

80. Marilyn Loden and Judith B. Rosener, *Workforce America! Managing Employee Diversity as a Vital Resource* (Burr Ridge, IL: Irwin/McGraw-Hill, 1991).

81. "Diversity Low Priority Reaps Low Numbers," *Editor & Publisher,* April 17, 2000, p. 16; Maryann Hammers, "Scripps Funds Media Diversity," *Workforce* 81 (December 2002): 16; Joe Strupp, "NAA: Diversity Under Review," *Editor & Publisher,* December 2, 2002, p. 6.

82. Ira Teinowitz, "Courting Change," *Advertising Age* 72 (May 14, 2001): 16–20.

83. New York Life, Diversity brochure, http://www.newyorklife.com/NYL2/pdf/diversity_broch.pdf, accessed April 20, 2006.

84. Rebecca Herwick, "Entrepreneurs, Hire the Disabled," http://www.usatoday.com/money/smallbusiness/2004-04-15-entre-3-apr_x.htm, accessed April 23, 2006.

85. "Verizon Named Private-Sector Employer of the Year By 'CAREERS & the disABLED' Magazine," news release, April 8, 2005, http://newscenter.verizon.com/, accessed April 20, 2006.

86. Phil Gorman, Teresa Nelson, and Alan Glassman, "The Millennial Generation: A Strategic Opportunity," *Organizational Analysis* 12, no. 3 (2004): 255–270; Ron Zemke, Claire Raines, and Bob Filipczak, *Generations at Work: Managing the Clash of Veterans, Boomers, Xers, and Nexters in Your Workplace* (New York: AMACOM, 2000).

87. Arthur P. Brief, Elizabeth Umphress, Joerg Dietz, Rebecca Butz, John Burrows, and Lotte Scholten, "Community Matters: Realistic Group Conflict Theory and the Impact of Diversity, *Academy of Management Journal* 48 (October 2005): 830–844.

88. Cora Daniels, "To Hire a Lumber Expert, Click Here," *Fortune,* April 3, 2000, pp. 267–270; Faye Wilson, "Implementing a Successful Corporate Diversity Plan," http://www.bna.com/bnabooks/ababna/eeo/2001/wilson.doc, accessed April 23, 2006.

89. Tyrone A. Holmes, "How to Connect Diversity to Performance," *Performance Improvement* 44 (May–June 2005): 13–17.

90. Robert D. Winsor and Ellen A. Ensher, "Choices Made in Balancing Work and Family: Following Two Women on a 16-Year Journey," *Journal of Management Inquiry* 9 (June 2000): 218–231.

91. Jeffrey R. Edwards and Nancy P. Rothbard, "Mechanisms Linking Work and Family," *Academy of Management Review* 25 (January 2000): 178–199.

92. Douglas M. McCracken, "Winning the Talent War for Women: Sometimes It Takes a Revolution," *Harvard Business Review* 78 (November–December 2000): 159–167; Sally Roberts, "Work/Life Programs No Longer a 'Woman's Issue,'" *Business Insurance,* August 8, 2005, pp. 3–4.

93. "DuPont," *Working Mother,* http://www.workingmother.com/dupont.html, accessed April 19, 2006.

94. Daniel Griffiths, "Japan's Workaholic Culture," *BBC News Online,* http://news.bbc.co.uk/1/low/world/asia-pacific/701458.stm, accessed March 21, 2006; Nik Paton, "Japan Cracks Down on Workaholic Culture," http://www.management-issues.com/display_page.asp?section=research&id=2939, accessed March 25, 2006; Rebecca Segall, "Japanese Killer," *Psychology Today* 33 (September–October 2000): 10–11.

95. Charles R. Stoner, Jennifer Robin, and Lori Russell-Chapin, "On the Edge: Perceptions and Responses to Life Imbalance," *Business Horizons* (July–August 2005): 48–54.

96. SAS, Annual Report, http://www.sas.com/corporate/report03/culture.html, accessed April 20, 2006; Thomas Watson, "Goodnight, Sweet Prince," *Canadian Business,* May 27, 2002, pp. 77–78.

97. E. Jeffrey Hill, Andrea Jackson, and Giuseppe Martinengo, "Twenty Years of Work and Family at International Business Machines Corporation," *American Behavioral Scientist* 49 (May 2006): 1165–1183.

98. Michael A. Verespej, "Balancing Act," *Industry Week,* May 15, 2000, pp. 81–85.

99. Debby Scheinholtz, "Work/Life Professionals Discuss Trends for the 21st Century," DiversityInc., March 16, 2000, www.diversityinc.com/.

100. Texas Instruments, Work/Life Effectiveness, http://www.ti .com/recruit/docs/worklife.shtml, accessed April 19, 2006.

101. "The State of Knowledge Surrounding Employee Volunteering in the United States," Points of Light Foundation, http://www.pointsoflight.org/downloads/pdf/resources/ research/StateOfKnowledge.pdf, accessed April 24, 2006.

102. William C. Symonds, "Sweating for Dollars," *Business Week,* September 19, 2005, pp. 88–90.

103. Alan J. Liddle, "McD Franchisees Make Online McStatement to Workers, Communities," *Nation's Restaurant News,* September 18, 2000, pp. 19, 94; McDonald's USA Corporate Responsibility Report 2004, http://www.mcdonalds.com/ usa/good/report.html, accessed March 21, 2006.

104. "Small Dog Gives Pet Perk," CNNfn, July 10, 2000, www .cnnfn.com; T3, The Think Tank, http://www.t-3.com/ company/prog_t3under.aspx, accessed April 20, 2006.

105. ENSR, "An Employer of Choice," http://www.ensr.aecom .com/Careers/48/27/index.jsp, accessed April 20, 2006; Roger E. Herman and Joyce L. Gioia, *How to Become an Employer of Choice* (Winchester, VA: Oakhill Press, 2000).

106. Ibid.; Da Joseph Kornik, "The Morale Majority," *Training* 43 (January 2006): 4.

107. "Corporate Performance," ESOP Association, http://www .esopassociation.org/media/media_corporate.asp, accessed December 14, 2006; Dale Kurschner, "5 Ways Ethical Busine$$ Creates Fatter Profit$," *Business Ethics* 10 (March–April 1996): 21; Jacquelyn Yates and Marjorie Kelly, "The Employee Ownership 100," *Business Ethics* 14 (September–October 2000): 12–19.

108. Kris Frieswick, "ESOPs: Split Personality," *CFO,* July 7, 2003, p. 1; Ronald Mano and E. Devon Deppe, "We Told You So: ESOPs Are Risky," *Ohio CPA Journal* 61 (July–September 2002): 67–68; Matthew Mouritsen, Ronald Mano, and E. Devon Deppe, "The ESOP Fable Revisited: Employees' Exposure to ESOPs and Enron's Exit," *Personal Financial Planning Monthly* 2 (May 2002): 27–31.

109. "The Nike Case and Corporate Self-Censorship," *Business & the Environment with ISO 14000 Updates* 15 (March 2004): 6–7; Isabelle Maignan, Bas Hillebrand, and Debbie Thorne McAlister, "Managing Socially Responsible Buying: How to Integrate Non-economic Criteria into the Purchasing Process," *European Management Journal* 20 (December 2002): 641–648.

CHAPTER 8

1. "Winners and Losers," *Latin Trade* 13 (September 2005): 34; Banco Azteca, http://www.grupoelektra.com.mx/elektra/ English/Units/Financial/Brands/Banco/default.asp, accessed May 8, 2006; Theresa Braine, "Courting the Unbanked," *Business Mexico* 14–15, no. 12–1 (2005): 40–41; Lucy Conger, "A Bank for Mexico's Working Families," *New York Times,* December 31, 2002, p. W1; Geri Smith, "Buy a Toaster, Open a Bank Account," *Business Week,* January 13, 2003, p. 54.

2. "Whole Foods Market Reminds Consumers That How Their Food Tastes Has Everything to Do with How It Is Grown," *CSR Newswire,* January 3, 2003, http://www.csrwire.com/ article.cgi/1494.html, accessed May 8, 2006; "The Whole Philosophy," Whole Foods Market, http://www .wholefoodsmarket.com/company/philosophy.html, accessed May 6, 2006.

3. "International Buy Nothing Day," http://ecoplan.org/ibnd/, accessed May 8, 2006.

4. Consumers International, www.consumersinternational.org/, accessed May 2, 2006.

5. "World Consumer Rights Day," Consumers International, www.consumersinternational.org/, accessed May 8, 2006.

6. "Consumer Charter for Global Business," Consumers International, www.consumersinternational.org/, accessed May 2, 2006.

7. "The Aggro of the Agora," *Economist,* January 14, 2006, p. 76; F. Knox, "The Doctrine of Consumer Sovereignty," *Review of Social Economy* 63 (September 2005): 383–394.

8. S. M. Solaiman, "Protection Through Administrative Enforcement of Disclosure Requirements in Prospectuses: Bangladeshi Laws Compared with Their Equivalents in India and Malaysia," *Journal of Financial Crime* 12 (August 2005): 260–293.

9. Lee E. Norrgard and Julia M. Norrgard, *Consumer Fraud: A Reference Handbook* (New York: ABC-Clio, 1998).

10. David M. Gardner, Jim Harris, and Junyong Kim, "The Fraudulent Consumer," in *Marketing and Public Policy Conference Proceedings,* ed. Gregory Gundlach, William Wilkie, and Patrick Murphy (Chicago: American Marketing Association, 1999), pp. 48–54.

11. Richard C. Hollinger, *2004 National Retail Security Survey,* 13th ed. (Gainesville: University of Florida, 2004); Merchant Risk Council, "Online Fraud Rates Approaching Fraud Rates at Card-Present Retail According to 5th Annual Survey by Merchant Risk Council," press release, April 18, 2006, www.merchantriskcouncil.org.

12. "ASA Bans Boots Anti-Cellulite Ads," *Soap, Perfumery & Cosmetics* 78 (October 2005): 5; Lisa McLaughlin, "Cloaking Cellulite," *Time,* May 24, 2004, p. 90; Christine Doyle, "How to Beat Cellulite—Part Two: Do Anti-Cellulite Creams, Lotions and Massage Really Work, or Do Women Just Like to Think They Do?" *Ottawa Citizen,* May 23, 2000, p. D8.

13. "Department of Consumers Affairs ID's Five Hot Issues Facing California Consumers in Today's Marketplace," California Department of Consumer Affairs, http://www.dca.ca.gov/ press_releases/2006/0206_cpw.htm, accessed May 8, 2006.

14. "Bureau of Consumer Protection," Federal Trade Commission, www.ftc.gov/bcp/bcp.htm, accessed May 2, 2006.

15. "Debt Management Operation Settle FTC Charges," U.S. Federal Trade Commission, http://www.ftc.gov/opa/2006/ 05/lighthouse.htm, accessed May 2, 2006.

16. "Consumer Affairs and Outreach Division," Federal Communications Commission, http://www.fcc.gov/cgb/ cgb_offices.html#CPD, accessed May 3, 2006.

17. "Consumer Brochures," Iowa Attorney General, http:// www.state.ia.us/government/ag/consumer/consumer_info .html, accessed May 8, 2006.

18. State of Texas, Business & Commerce Code, "Chapter 17: Deceptive Trade Practices," http://www.capitol.state.tx.us/ statutes/bc.toc.htm, accessed April 28, 2006.

19. Robert B. Downs, "Afterword," in Upton Sinclair, *The Jungle* (New York: New American Library, 1960).

20. "Manufacturers Pay $460,000 in Civil Penalties," *Consumer Product Litigation Reporter* 11 (June 2000): 15.

21. "2006 Fair Housing Month Statement from Assistant Secretary Kim Kendrick," U.S. Department of Housing and Urban Development, http://www.hud.gov/offices/fheo/FHMonth/fhm2006.cfm, accessed May 2, 2006; "The State of Fair Housing, U.S. Department of Housing and Urban Development, http://www.hud.gov/offices/fheo/library/FY2005_Annual_Report.pdf, accessed April 28, 2006.

22. Charles Fleming, "Politics & Economics: Financial Bias Simmers in Europe," *Wall Street Journal*, May 8, 2006, p. A8; Justin Hibbard, "The Fed Eyes Subprime Loans," *Business Week*, April 11, 2005, p. 87.

23. "Sweepstakes Giant Agrees to $34 Million Settlement," CNN.com, June 27, 2001, http://www.cnn.com/2001/LAW/06/26/sweepstakes.lawsuit/index.html, accessed May 18, 2006; Helen Rothschild and Roberta Ewald, "'You're a Guaranteed Winner': Composing 'You' in a Consumer Culture," *Journal of Business Communication* 40 (April 2003): 98–117.

24. John Eggerton, "FTC Declares Diet Claims Have No Weight," *Broadcasting & Cable*, November 25, 2002, p. 7; Federal Trade Commission, "A Reference Guide for Media on Bogus Weight Loss Claims," http://www.ftc.gov/bcp/conline/pubs/buspubs/redflag.pdf, accessed May 9, 2006.

25. Wine Institute, "Direct Wine Shipments," http://www.wineinstitute.org/programs/shipwine/main.htm, accessed May 29, 2006.

26. "Lemon Law Information and Sites," http://autopedia.com/html/HotLinks_LemonLaw.html, accessed May 20, 2006.

27. Michael Bradford, "New South Korean Law May Bring Increased Product Liability Claims," *Business Insurance*, April 22, 2002, pp. 29–30; Tom Chung, "When Products Cause User Damages," *Korea Herald*, January 12, 2005, p. 1.

28. "Roche Diagnostics Issues Worldwide Voluntary Recall," U.S. Food and Drug Administration, http://www.fda.gov/oc/po/firmrecalls/roche01_06.html, accessed May 9, 2006; Christine Gorman, "Diabetes Recall," *Time*, April 3, 2000, p. 94.

29. "17th, 18th and 19th Product Liability Lawsuits Dismissed Against TASER International," http://www.taser.com/press/index.htm, May 22, 2006, press release; Alex Berenson, "The Safety of Tasers Is Questioned Again," *New York Times*, May 25, 2006, p. C3.

30. "Regulatory Watch," *Business China*, February 27, 2006, p. 11.

31. Sandra N. Hurd, Peter Shears, and Frances E. Zollers, "Consumer Law," *Journal of Business Law* (May 2000): 262–277.

32. Irene M. Kunii, "Stand Up and Fight," *Business Week*, September 11, 2000, pp. 54–55.

33. Suk-ching Ho, "Executive Insights: Growing Consumer Power in China," *Journal of International Marketing* 9 (Spring 2001): 64–84.

34. Nigel Davis, "REACH Readiness Is Thrown into Focus," *Chemical News & Intelligence*, May 16, 2006, p. 1.

35. Kenneth J. Meier, E. Thomas Garman, and Lael R. Keiser, *Regulation and Consumer Protection: Politics, Bureaucracy and Economics* (Houston, TX: Dame Publications, 1998).

36. Allan Asher, "Going Global: A New Paradigm for Consumer Protection," *Journal of Consumer Affairs* 32 (Winter 1998): 183–203; Benet Middleton, "Consumerism: A Pragmatic Ideology," *Consumer Policy Review* 8 (November–December 1998): 213–217; Audhesh Paswan and Jhinuk Chowdhury, "Consumer Protection Issues and Non-governmental Organizations in a Developing Market," in *Developments in Marketing Science*, ed. Harlan E. Spotts and H. Lee Meadow (Coral Gables, FL: Academy of Marketing Science, 2000), pp. 171–176.

37. "On the Left: What Makes Ralph Run," *Business Week*, September 25, 2000, pp. 82, 86.

38. Paul N. Bloom and Stephen A. Greyser, "The Maturing of Consumerism," *Harvard Business Review* 59 (November–December 1981): 130–139.

39. Consumers Union, www.consumersunion.org/, accessed July 29, 2006; Rhoda H. Karpatkin, "Toward a Fair and Just Marketplace for All Consumers: The Responsibilities of Marketing Professionals," *Journal of Public Policy and Marketing* 18 (Spring 1999): 118–123.

40. "Empowerment to the Consumer," *Marketing Week*, October 21, 1999, p. 3; Pierre M. Loewe and Mark S. Bonchek, "The Retail Revolution," *Management Review* 88 (April 1999): 38–44.

41. Jim Guest, "Grassroots Advocacy Is Still in Style," *Consumer Reports* 70 (August 2005): 5.

42. "Consumer Bill of Rights and Responsibilities: Report to the President of the United States," Advisory Commission on Consumer Protection and Quality in the Health Care Industry, November 1997, www.hcqualitycommission.gov/cborr/, accessed July 25, 2006; Mary Jane Fisher, "Pressure Mounts for Patient Rights Agreement," *National Underwriter/Life & Health Financial Services*, May 22, 2000, pp. 3–4; Michael Pretzer, "New Mind 'Patient Relations': Get Ready for 'Consumer Rights,'" *Medical Economics*, February 23, 1998, pp. 47–55.

43. "Comprehensive Consumer Rights Bill Addresses Bank Fees, Identity Theft," *Consumer Financial Services Law Report*, May 15, 2000, p. 2.

44. Nichole Christian, "Domino's Reaches Deal on Accusations of Bias," *New York Times*, June 7, 2000, p. A28; T. J. Degroat, "Domino's Revises Delivery Policy," DiversityInc., June 6, 2000, www.diversityinc.com.

45. Marianne Lavelle, "The States Take the Lead on Gun Control," *U.S. News & World Report*, April 17, 2000, p. 24.

46. Steve Jarvis, "They're Not Quitting," *Marketing News*, November 20, 2000, pp. 1, 9; Marianne Lavelle, "Big Tobacco Rises from the Ashes," *U.S. News & World Report*, November 13, 2000, p. 50; Nancy Shute, "Building a Better Butt," *U.S. News & World Report*, September 18, 2000, p. 66.

47. www.diversityinc.com; "Pirate's Booty: Too Good to Be True," *Washington Post*, February 19, 2002, p. F3; Paige Smoron, "Is Booty-licious Diet Food Part of a Large Conspiracy?" *Chicago Sun-Times*, April 18, 2002, p. 42.

48. A. Ben Oumlil and Alvin J. Williams, "Consumer Education Programs for Mature Consumers," *Journal of Services Marketing* 14, no. 3 (2000): 232–243; Lauren Paetsch, "URAC Accreditation Provides Benchmark for Health Information Web Sites," *Employee Benefit Plan Review* 56 (June 2002): 10–18.

49. Lyuba Pronina, "Top Firms Team Up to Create Consumer Telephone Hot Line," *Moscow Times*, November 29, 2000.

50. "Dispute Resolution," Better Business Bureau, http://www.dr.bbb.org/, accessed January 6, 2003.

51. Federal Trade Commission, *Privacy Online: Fair Information Practices in the Electronic Marketplace: A Federal Trade Commission Report to Congress* (Washington, DC: FTC, May 2000), also available at www.ftc.gov/reports/privacy2000/privacy2000.pdf.

52. "CMC Properties," Better Business Bureau International Torch Award, http://www.bbb.org/torchaward/cmc.asp, accessed May 30, 2006; "Four Businesses Honored with Prestigious International Award for Outstanding Marketplace Ethics," *PR Newswire,* September 23, 2002, via LexisNexis.

53. Southwest Airlines, "Customer Service Commitment," http://www.southwest.com/about_swa/customer_service_commitment/customer_service_commitment.html, accessed May 1, 2006.

54. "Wal-Mart Bucks for Education," *Home Textiles Today,* June 5, 2000, p. 11; Mike France and Joann Muller, "A Site for Soreheads," *Business Week,* April 12, 1999, p. 86; Wendy Zellner, "Wal-Mart: Why an Apology Made Sense," *Business Week,* July 3, 2000, pp. 65–66; Wendy Zellner and Aaron Bernstein, "Up Against the Wal-Mart," *Business Week,* March 13, 2000, p. 76.

55. Damien McElroy, "Chinese Shun Toshiba in Anti-Japan Protests," *Sunday Telegraph* (London), June 4, 2000, p. 27.

56. Andy Altman-Ohr, "World Boycott of Transamerica Launched," *Jewish Bulletin News of Northern California,* January 21, 2000, www.angelfire.com/biz4/consumerama/transam.htm, accessed May 9, 2006.

57. "Home of the Casino Royale Boycott," http://www.craignotbond.com/, accessed May 30, 2006; Jamie Wienman, "Everything Old Is Young Again," *Maclean's,* May 8, 2006, p. 56.

58. "The 1997 Cone/Roper Cause-Related Marketing Trends Report," *Business Ethics* 12 (March–April 1997): 14–16.

59. Edwin R. Stafford and Cathy L. Hartman, "Environmentalist-Business Collaborations: Social Responsibility, Green Alliances, and Beyond," in *Advertising Research: The Internet, Consumer Behavior and Strategy,* ed. George Zinkhan (Chicago: American Marketing Association, 2000), pp. 170–192.

60. "David Lansky to Join the Markle Foundation," Markle Foundation, http://www.markle.org/resources/press_center/press_releases/2004/press_release_09282004.php, accessed May 9, 2006; Foundation for Accountability, "FACCT Legacy Documents," www.facct.org, accessed August 19, 2003.

61. Lauren Gibbons Paul, "Charitable Impulses," *Electronic Business* 32 (January 2006): 14.

62. D'Arcy Doran, "Village Women Paralyze Oil Giant in Nigeria," *Associated Press Worldstream,* July 12, 2002, via LexisNexis.

63. James L. Creighton, "The Utility as Civic Partner," *Public Utilities Fortnightly,* June 15, 2000, pp. 32–38.

CHAPTER 9

1. Howard Rothman and Mary Scott, *Companies with a Conscience,* 3rd ed. (Denver, CO: MyersTempleton, 2004); "Chiefs Recognized Nationally for Their Community Commitment," Kansas City Chiefs, http://www.kcchiefs.com/news_article.asp?ID=Y8NTDBHEJFDYXR8NQH759NDS72, accessed October 10, 2005; "The Chiefs Way," Kansas City Chiefs, http://www.kcchiefs.com/chiefsway/, accessed October 11, 2005.

2. Merlino's Family Steakhouse, http://www.merlinossteakhouse.com/, accessed May 10, 2006.

3. American Productivity and Quality Center, *Community Relations: Unleashing the Power of Corporate Citizenship* (Houston, TX: American Productivity and Quality Center, 1998); Edmund M. Burke, *Corporate Community Relations: The Principle of the Neighbor of Choice* (Westport, CT: Praeger, 1999).

4. Bradley K. Googins, "Why Community Relations Is a Strategic Imperative," *Strategy & Business* (Third Quarter 1997): 14–16.

5. "We Build CommUnity," http://corporate.homedepot.com/wps/portal/!ut/p/.cmd/cs/.ce/7_0_A/.s/7_0_11N/_s.7_0_A/7_0_11N, accessed April 22, 2006.

6. "FedEx Community," http://www.fedex.com/us/about/responsibility/community/index.html, accessed April 22, 2006.

7. Business for Social Responsibility, "Community Involvement," www.bsr.org/resourcecenter/, accessed December 4, 2000; Sandra A. Waddock and Mary-Ellen Boyle, "The Dynamics of Change in Corporate Community Relations," *California Management Review* 37 (Summer 1995): 125–138; Barron Wells and Nelda Spinks, "Communicating with the Community," *Career Development International* 4, no. 2 (1999): 108–116.

8. "Cisco Systems, Grand Circle, and KaBOO! Win CECP Awards Honoring 'Excellence in Corporate Philanthropy,'" *Business Wire,* February 27, 2006, http://80-web.lexis-nexis.com.proxy.uwlib.uwyo.edu/universe/document?_m=ca22850a03, accessed April 22, 2006.

9. Kenneth D. Lewis, "Saving the Best for Philanthropy," *Boston Globe,* February 27, 2006, www.80-web.lexis-nexis.com, accessed April 20, 2006.

10. Business for Social Responsibility, "Community Involvement"; Janelia Moreno, "More Casas for the Workers," *Houston Chronicle,* March 4, 2001, p. Business 1.

11. "Community Needs Assessment Survey Guide," Utah State University Extension, http://extension.usu.edu/coop/comm/survey/survey.htm, accessed January 6, 2003.

12. Thomas A. Klein and Robert W. Nason, "Marketing and Development: Macromarketing Perspectives," in *Handbook of Marketing and Society,* ed. Paul N. Bloom and Gregory T. Gunlach (Thousand Oaks, CA: Sage, 2001), pp. 263–297.

13. BP Global, http://www.bp.com/sectiongenericarticle.do?categoryId=9007608&contentId=7014452, accessed May 10, 2006.

14. FedEx St. Jude Classic, http://www.pgatour.com/tournaments/r025/charity, accessed April 22, 2006.

15. John Welbes, "Ford Layoffs Likely in July," www.twincities.com, March 1, 2006, www.twincities.com/mld.twincities/14034757.htm.

16. Robert Jablon, "Squid Boat Companies Charged with Dumping," *Business Week Online,* May 9, 2006, www.businessweek.com/ap/financial news/d8hgii509.htm?campaign_id=search, accessed May 11, 2006.

17. Zellner and Bernstein, "Up Against the Wal-Mart," *BusinessWeek,* March 13, 2000, pp. 76–78.

18. David Kaplan, "Plant for Recycling Food Waste Planned," *Houston Chronicle,* February 13, 2001, p. Business 2; Rebecca Mowbray, "Turning Trash into Profits: An Entrepreneur's Plans to Turn Waste into Animal Feed Take the Community into Consideration," *Houston Chronicle,* August 1, 1999, p. 4D.

19. Janicca Lee, "Daniels Fund Supporting Integrity and Ethics in Business," *UWYO Magazine,* 7, no. 4 (Spring 2006): 6.

20. New Belgium Brewing Company, Inc., www.newbelgium.com, accessed May 11, 2006.

21. "Volunteer Trends: Statistics," Sigma Theta Tau International Honor Society of Nursing, 2004,

22. Diane E. Lewis, "Volunteering Is a Way of Life for Some and at Some Firms, It Is Something That Is Expected," *Minneapolis Star Tribune,* April 26, 1999, p. D8.

23. "About Employee Volunteering," National Centre for Volunteering, http://www.employeevolunteering.org.uk/about/essentials.htm, accessed August 19, 2003.

24. Bill Leonard, "Supporting Volunteerism as Individual Americans Invest More Hours into Volunteer Activities," *HR Magazine,* June 6, 1998, p. 4.

25. Lewis, "Volunteering Is a Way of Life for Some."

26. "Vanderbilt Targets 100% Volunteerism," *Business Ethics,* Winter 2005, p. 10.

27. Time Warner Cable, http://www.timewarnercable.com/CustomerService/FAQ/TWCFaqs.ashx?faqID=621&MarketID=25&CatID=239, accessed May 17, 2006.

28. Ingrid Murro Botero, "Charitable Giving Has 4 Big Benefits," *Business Journal of Phoenix,* January 1, 1999, www.bizjournals.com/phoenix/stories/1999/01/04/smallb3.html, accessed August 6, 2006.

29. "The Gift Shift," *Wall Street Journal,* November 25, 2005, pp. W1, W10.

30. Paul Sullivan, "U.S. Corporate Donations Decrease," FinancialTimes.com, May 12, 2006, https://registration.ft.com/registration/barrier?referer=http://www.google.com/search?q=%22corporate+donations%22&hl=en&lr=&ie=UTF-8&start=10&sa=N&location=http%3A//news.ft.com/cms/s/703c3b22-e200-11da-bf4c-0000779e2340.html, accessed May 16, 2006.

31. "2004 Contributions: $248.52 Billion by Source of Contributions," Giving USA Foundation—American Association of Fundraising Counsel (AAFRC) Trust for Philanthropy/Giving USA 2005, http://www.aafrc.org/gusa/chartbysource.html.

32. Marjorie Kelly. "100 Best Corporate Citizens 2005," *Business Ethics,* Spring 2005, p. 25.

33. Steve Stecklow, "How Companies Help Charities and Cut Inventory," *Wall Street Journal,* December 10–11, 2005, p. 1.

34. Wal-Mart Giving, Walmartfacts.com, http://www.walmartfacts.com/community/walmart-foundation.aspx, accessed March 17, 2006.

35. "Charity Holds Its Own in Tough Times: Giving in 2002 Nears $241 Billion, 1 Percent Above New Figures for 2001," AAFRC Trust for Philanthropy/Giving USA 2003, http://aafrc.org/press_releases/trustreleases/charityholds.html, accessed August 22, 2003.

36. "Money Woes May Close Russian Museum," *Associated Press Online,* November 24, 2000, via Comtex; "Our Partners," Moscow Center for Prison Reform, http://www.prison.org/english/mcprpart.htm, accessed August 22, 2003.

37. Diane Lindquist, "Drug Companies' Rx for the Bottom Line," *Industry Week,* September 7, 1998, p. 25.

38. Noel M. Tichy, Andrew R. McGill, and Lynda St. Clair, *Corporate Global Citizenship: Doing Business in the Public Eye* (San Francisco: New Lexington Press, 1997).

39. Michael E. Porter and Mark R. Kramer, "The Competitive Advantage of Corporate Philanthropy," *Harvard Business Review* 80 (December 2002): 56–68; Robbie Shell, "Breaking the Stereotypes of Corporate Philanthropy," *Wall Street Journal,* November 26, 2002, p. B2.

40. Reynold Levy, *Give and Take: A Candid Account of Corporate Philanthropy* (Boston: Harvard Business School Press, 1999); Noah's Bagels, www.noahs.com, accessed August 22, 2003.

41. Tichy, McGill, and St. Clair, *Corporate Global Citizenship.*

42. Jessica Stannard and Tamara Backer, "How Employee Volunteers Multiply Your Community Impact PART 2," *OnPhilanthropy.com,* December 29, 2005, http://www.onphilanthropy.com/articles/print.aspx?cid=760, accessed May 11, 2006.

43. "Corporate Citizen," Fuji Bank, www.fujibank.co.jp/eng/fb/topics/philan.html, accessed January 4, 2001.

44. Curt Weeden, "Leave-Based Donation Programs," Contributions Academy, www.contributionsacademy.com/html/news.html, accessed November 5, 2001.

45. http://benjerry.custhelp.com/cgi-bin/benjerry.cfg/php/enduser/std_adp.php?p_sid=oTybnf7i&p_lva=&p_faqid=136&p_created=955568704&p_sp=cF9zcmNoPSZwX2dyaWRzb3J0PSZwX3Jvd19jbnQ9MjI4JnBfcGFnZT0x&p_li=, accessed May 11, 2006.

46. Curt Weeden, *Corporate Social Investing* (San Francisco: Berrett-Koehler, 1998), pp. 116–123.

47. Avon, "Avon Breast Cancer Crusade," www.avoncompany.com/women/avoncrusade, accessed May 11, 2006.

48. Tichy, McGill, and St. Clair, *Corporate Global Citizenship.*

49. Daniel Kadlec and Bruce Voorst, "The New World of Giving: Companies Are Doing More Good, and Demanding More Back," *Time,* May 5, 1997, pp. 62–66.

50. Kevin T. Higgins, "Marketing with a Conscience," *Marketing Management* 11 (July–August 2002): 12–15; P. Rajan Varadarajan and Anil Menon, "Cause-Related Marketing: A Coalignment of Marketing Strategy and Corporate Philanthropy," *Journal of Marketing* 52 (July 1988): 58–74.

51. Allyson L. Stewart-Allen, "Europe Ready for Cause-Related Campaigns," *Marketing News,* July 6, 1998, p. 9.

52. "Business in the Community, Awards for Excellence," http://www.bitc.org.uk/awards/index.html, accessed January 27, 2003; Sue Adkins, "Why Cause-Related Marketing Is a Winning Business Formula," *Marketing,* July 20, 2000, p. 18.

53. Steve Hoeffler and Kevin Lane Keller, "Building Brand Equity Through Corporate Societal Marketing," *Journal of Public Policy & Marketing* 21 (Spring 2002): 78–89; Sue Adkins and Nina Kowalska, "Consumers Put 'Causes' on the Shopping List," *M2 PressWire,* November 17, 1997.

54. Jennifer Mullen, "Performance-Based Corporate Philanthropy: How 'Giving Smart' Can Further Corporate Goals," *Public Relations Quarterly,* June 22, 1997, p. 42; Michal Strahilevitz, "The Effects of Prior Impressions of a Firm's Ethics on the Success of a Cause-Related Marketing Campaign," *Journal of Nonprofit & Public Sector Marketing* 11, no. 1: 77–92.

55. Stan Friedman and Charles Kouns, "Charitable Contribution: Reinventing Cause Marketing," *Brand Week,* October 27, 1997.

56. Bob Nelson, *1001 Ways to Energize Employees.* (New York: Workman Publishing, 1997).

57. "How Strategic Philanthropy Builds Brands," Letter to *Harvard Business Review* responding to Michael Porter and Mark Kramer's article, "The Strategic Advantage of Corporate Philanthropy," available through *HBS Publishing,* http://www.holding.com/articles/philanthropy.html, accessed May 16, 2006.

58. "Corporate Philanthropy: Sony in America-Working Together to Make a Difference," http://www.sony.com/SCA/philanthropy.shtml, accessed May 16, 2006.

59. United Airlines, "Volunteerism," http://www.united.com/page/article/0,,1364,00.html, accessed May 17, 2006.

60. Rosenbluth and Peters, *Good Company.*

61. BE & K, "BE & K Awards," www.BEK.com/awards.html, accessed January 28, 2003.

62. "The Home Depot Announces $57 Million Investment to Support Gulf Coast Rebuilding Efforts," http://ir.homedepot.com/releasedetail.cfm?releaseid=195363, accessed May 17, 2006.

63. "BT Bolsters Wealth of Responsibility Program," *Private Asset Management,* January 24, 2000, p. 7; "Wealth with Responsibility," Deutsche Bank, http://www.pwm.db.com/com_en_philan_wealth.html, accessed January 27, 2003.

64. Verizon Literacy Network, http://www.verizonreads.net/, accessed May 17, 2006.

65. "Take Charge of Education," http://sites.target.com/site/en/corporate/page.jsp?contentId=PRD03-001825, accessed May 17, 2006.

66. Richard Cree, "Cover Story: Rory Stear," *Director* 56 (November): 64–67; Cheryl Dahle, "Social Justice: The Freeplay Group," *Fast Company,* April 1999, pp. 166–182.

67. Don Babwin, "Gateway to Good Health," *Hospital and Health Networks,* November 20, 1998, p. 20.

68. Coca-Cola Company, "Environment," http://www2.coca-cola.com/citizenship/environment.html, accessed May 17, 2006.

69. Alan Reder, *75 Best Business Practices for Socially Responsible Companies* (New York: Putnam, 1995); Merck, "The Merck Mectizan Donation Program," http://www.merck.com/cr/enabling_access/developing_world/mectizan/home.html, accessed May 17, 2006.

70. "Glasses Drive a Big Success," *Florida Times-Union,* May 10, 2003, p. K4; Marianne Williams, "More Than Just Causes," *Chain Store Age* 76 (August 2000): 37–40.

71. American Apparel and Footwear Association, http://www.apparelandfootwear.org/4col.cfm?pageID=127&textID=donate.html, accessed May 17, 2006.

72. Reder, *75 Best Business Practices for Socially Responsible Companies.*

73. "3M Earns Second Place in Eco-Ranking of Major Companies," 3M, www.3M.com/us/about3M/innovation/eco/index/html, accessed January 28, 2003.

74. Walker Information, *Corporate Philanthropy National Benchmark Study, Employee Report* (Chicago: Walker Information, 2002).

75. "For All Kids Foundation," http://www.4allkids.com/, accessed August 22, 2003.

76. Robert J. Williams and J. Douglas Barrett, "Corporate Philanthropy, Criminal Activity, and Firm Reputation: Is There a Link?" *Journal of Business Ethics* 26 (2000): 341–350.

77. Roger Bennett, "Corporate Philanthropy in France, Germany, and the UK," *International Marketing Review* 15 (June 1998): 469.

78. American Productivity and Quality Center, *Community Relations: Unleashing the Power of Corporate Citizenship* (Houston, TX: American Productivity and Quality Center, 1998).

79. John A. Byrne, "Chainsaw," *Business Week,* October 18, 1999, pp. 128–149.

80. Levy, *Give and Take.*

81. Weeden, *Corporate Social Investing.*

82. Reprinted with permission of the publisher. From *Corporate Social Investing,* copyright ©1998 by Curt Weeden, Berrett-Koehler Publishers, Inc., San Francisco, CA. All rights reserved. www.bkconnection.com.

83. Walter W. Wymer Jr. and Sridhar Samu, "Dimensions of Business and Nonprofit Collaborative Relationships," *Journal of Nonprofit & Public Sector Marketing* 11, no. 1: 3–22.

84. John A. Byrne, "The New Face of Philanthropy," *Business Week,* December 2, 2002, pp. 82–86; Stephanie Strom, "Ground Zero: Charity; a Flood of Money, Then a Deluge of Scrutiny for Those Handing It Out," *New York Times,* September 11, 2002, p. B5; Cheryl Wetzstein, "Americans' Generosity Runs Deep; $1.4 Billion Released, but Process Has Created Skepticism," *Washington Times,* September 9, 2002, p. A1.

85. Cathy Brisbois, "Ranking Disclosure: VanCity Savings & Credit Union, Canada," in *Building Corporate Accountability: The Emerging Practices in Social and Ethical Accounting, Auditing and Reporting,* ed. Simon Zadek, Peter Pruzan, and Richard Evans (London: Earthscan Publications, 1997).

CHAPTER 10

1. "Interface Recognized for Green Initiatives," *Textile World* 154 (December 2004): 11; Ray C. Anderson, "Shared Air Summit Speech," http://www.interfacesustainability.com/pdf/SharedAirSummitSpeech.pdf, accessed June 21, 2006; Environmental Protection Agency, "2004 Green Power Leadership Award Winners," http://www.epa.gov/greenpower/winners/2004_awards.htm#interface, accessed June 21, 2006; Connie Hensler, "Carpet Maker Closes the Loop," *In Business* 28 (May–June 2006): 25–26; Paul Teague, "From Green to Greenbacks," *Purchasing,* March 2, 2006, p. 13; Interface Sustainability, http://www.interfacesustainability.com/, accessed June 21, 2006.

2. "Gallup Poll: Public Supports Environmental Movement, but Not as a Priority," CNN, April 17, 2000, www.cnn.com/nature/specials/earthday, accessed September 10, 2003.

3. Alan K. Reichert, Marion S. Webb, and Edward G. Thomas, "Corporate Support for Ethical and Environmental Policies: A Financial Management Perspective," *Journal of Business Ethics* 25 (2000): 53–64.

4. "Air Quality," Office of Air Quality Planning and Standards, Environmental Protection Agency, February 20, 2003, www.epa.gov/oar/oaqps/cleanair.html, accessed June 10, 2006.

5. "The Plain English Guide to the Clean Air Act," Office of Air Quality Planning and Standards, Environmental Protection Agency, http://www.epa.gov/oar/oaqps/peg_caa/pegcaain.html, accessed June 10, 2006.

6. "Effects of Acid Rain," Environmental Protection Agency, www.epa.gov/airmarkets/acidrain/effects/index.html, accessed June 10, 2006.

7. "Texaco Quits Global Warming Group," CNN, March 1, 2000, http://edition.cnn.com/2000/NATURE/03/01/tex.climate/, accessed September 10, 2003.

8. "Climate Change," http://www.newscientist.com/channel/earth/climate-change/, accessed June 20, 2006.

9. Ibid.

10. "Study: Growth of 'Greenhouse Emissions' Slowing," http://archives.cnn.com/2002/TECH/science/01/14/greenhouse.emissions/index.html, accessed August 9, 2006.

11. "Global Warming FAQ: All You Ever Wanted to Know About Climate Change," http://www.newscientist.com/channel/earth/climate-change/, accessed June 10, 2006.

12. "Texaco Quits Global Warming Group."

13. Mark Alpert, "Protections for the Earth's Climate," *Scientific American*, 293 (December 2005): 55; PricewaterhouseCoopers, "Pricing Energy for Sustainability: Experience of Emissions Trading in the EU," http://www.pwcglobal.com, accessed June 20, 2006.

14. David Rothbard and Craig Rucker, "Global Shifts on Global Warming," www.cfact.org, accessed June 20, 2006.

15. Joe Kamalick, "Canada Abandons the Kyoto Treaty," *Chemical Market Reporter*, May 29–June 4, 2006, p. 10.

16. Ibid.

17. Erin Kelly, "States Foul Out on Clean Water Act," *Coloradoan*, April 6, 2000, p. B1.

18. Ibid.

19. "Water Quality," http://www.sierraclub.org/cleanwater/waterquality/, accessed June 9, 2006.

20. Kathleen Fackelmann, "Teen Discovers Antibiotics in Public Supplies; Scientists Fear 'Superbugs,'" *USA Today*, November 8, 2000, pp. 1D, 2D.

21. *Seattle Times*, December 17, 2002.

22. Kelly, "States Foul Out on Clean Water Act."

23. "Clean Water Act," www.sierraclub.org/cleanwater/cleanwater_act/, accessed June 10, 2006.

24. Peter Jahrling, PRIMEDIA Business Magazines & Media Inc., January 8, 2003.

25. Mark H. Hunter, "Water, Harvest Cuts Urged at Conference: San Luis Valley Assesses Drought," *Denver Post*, January 20, 2003.

26. Robert Rosenblatt, "Man and Nature: All the Days of the Earth," *Time Earth Day 2000* 155 (Spring 2000): 12.

27. Gerald Urquhart, Walter Chomentowski, David Skole, and Chris Barber, "Tropical Deforestation," earthobservatory.nasa.gov/Library/Deforestation/, accessed June 9, 2006.

28. James Howard Kunstler, *The Geography of Nowhere: The Rise and Decline of America's Man-Made Landscape* (New York: Simon & Schuster, 1994).

29. Mark Walters, "Current Regulatory Environment and Impediments to the Establishment of a Compact City," directed research project, Southwest Texas University, San Marcos, Texas, November 1, 2001.

30. Sierra Club, "Roads and Highways," in *Sprawl Costs Us All: How Your Taxes Fuel Suburban Sprawl* (Sierra Club, 2000), www.sierraclub.org/sprawl/report00/roads.asp, accessed June 11, 2006.

31. Eugene Linden, "State of the Planet: Condition Critical," *Time Earth Day 2000* 155 (Spring 2000): 24.

32. "Tropical Forest Species Richness," World Resources Institute, http://pubs.wri.org/pubs_content_text.cfm?ContentID=515, accessed August 9, 2006.

33. G. T. Miller, "Deforestation and Loss of Diversity," in *Living in the Environment: Principles, Connections and Solutions,* 8th ed. (Belmont, CA: Wadsworth, 1994).

34. "Monkey's Extinction May Be a Sign," CNN, September 13, 2000, www.cnn.com, accessed September 10, 2003.

35. Laura Tangley, "Keeping the Delicate Balance of Nature," *U.S. News & World Report,* November 15, 1999, p. 95.

36. "Earth Matters: Pollinator Decline Puts World Food Supply at Risk, Experts Warn," CNN, http://www.cnn.com/2000/NATURE/05/05/pollinators.peril/, accessed June 19, 2006.

37. "Overcutting Costs More Timber Jobs Than Owl, Study Says," *Idaho Statesman*, February 16, 1997.

38. Paul Magnusson, Ann Therese, and Kerry Capell, "Furor over Frankenfood," *Business Week,* October 18, 1999, pp. 50, 51.

39. "Biotech Food Safe, but More Tests Needed, Study Suggests," *Coloradoan*, April 6, 2000, p. B3.

40. Ellen Licking, "Tinkering with Genes: Time for a National Debate," *Business Week,* November 8, 1999, p. 44.

41. Jack Lewis, "The Birth of EPA," *EPA Journal,* November 1985, www.epa.gov/history/topics/epa/15c.htm, accessed August 9, 2006.

42. "EPA's Mission, Goals, and Principles," *EPA Strategic Plan,* Office of the Chief Financial Officer, Environmental Protection Agency, www.epa.gov/ocfo/plan/plan.htm, accessed August 9, 2006.

43. Peter Eisler, "EPA to Phase Out Popular Insecticide Diazinon," *USA Today,* December 5, 2000, p. 1A.

44. "EPA's Mission, Goals, and Principles," http://www.epa.gov/epahome/aboutepa.htm, accessed May 10, 2006.

45. John J. Fialka, "Koch Industries' $30 Million Fine Is Biggest-Ever Pollution Penalty," *Wall Street Journal,* January 14, 2000, p. A10.

46. O. C. Ferrell, John Fraedrich, and Gwyneth Vaughn, "The Wreck of the *Exxon Valdez*," in *Business Ethics: Ethical Decision Making and Cases,* 6th ed., ed. O. C. Ferrell, John Fraedrich, and Linda Ferrell (Boston: Houghton Mifflin, 2005).

47. "Major Environmental Laws: Clean Air Act," Environmental Protection Agency, www.epa.gov/region5/defs/html/caa.htm, accessed May 10, 2006.

48. Lewis, "The Birth of EPA"; "Major Environmental Laws: Clean Air Act," http://www.epa.gov/history/topics/epa/15c.htm, accessed May 10, 2006.

49. "Major Environmental Laws: Clean Air Act."

50. "Major Environmental Laws: Federal Insecticide, Fungicide, and Rodenticide Act," Environmental Protection Agency, http://www.epa.gov/region5/defs/html/fifra.htm, accessed June 20, 2006.

51. "Major Environmental Laws: Endangered Species Act," Environmental Protection Agency, www.epa.gov/region5/defs/html/esa.htm, accessed June 20, 2006.

52. Ibid.

53. "How Has the ESA Impacted America?" National Endangered Species Act Reform Coalition, www.nesarc.org/stories.htm, accessed June 21, 2006.

54. "Major Environmental Laws: Toxic Substances Control Act," Environmental Protection Agency, http://www.epa.gov/region5/defs/html/tsca.htm, accessed June 10, 2006.

55. "Major Environmental Laws: Clean Water Act," Environmental Protection Agency, http://www.epa.gov/region5/water/cwa.htm, accessed May 31, 2006.

56. Michael McLaughlin, "One Big Problem—Save the Waves," *Fast Company,* http://www.fastcompany.com/online/32/waves.html, accessed August 9, 2006.

57. "What Is the Toxics Release Inventory (TRI) Program," Environmental Protection Agency, http://www.epa.gov/tri/whatis.htm, accessed May 31, 2006; Scorecard: The Pollution Information Site, "Facilities Releasing TRI Chemicals to the Environment," http://www.scorecard.org/env-releases/us-map.tcl, accessed June 20, 2006.

58. "Major Environmental Laws: Pollution Prevention Act," Environmental Protection Agency, http://www.epa.gov/region5/defs/html/ppa.htm, accessed June 20, 2006.

59. "Food Quality Protection Act (FQPA) of 1996," Office of Pesticide Programs, Environmental Protection Agency, http://www.epa.gov/pesticides/regulating/laws/fqpa, accessed May 31, 2006.

60. "The Food Quality Protection Act (FQPA) Background," Office of Pesticide Programs, Environmental Protection Agency, http://www.epa.gov/pesticides/regulating/laws/fqpa, accessed June 1, 2006.

61. "Sustainability (Environment)," http://www.fujifilm.com/about/sustainability/index.html, accessed June 21, 2006; Scott Medintz, "Point, Shoot, Toss," *Money* 28 (July 1999): 143–145.

62. Jeffrey Ball, "GM to Produce Hybrid Trucks, Buses in Scramble to Build 'Green' Vehicles," *Wall Street Journal,* August 3, 2000, p. A4, online.wsj.com, accessed September 11, 2003.

63. "Park Support," Parks Company, http://www.theparksco.com/, accessed June 19, 2006.

64. Nikki Sameshima, "Natural Born 'Burbs," *Coloradobiz* 27 (April 2000): 72, 74.

65. "The EU Eco-label," http://www.eco-label.com/default.htm, accessed June 20, 2006.

66. "Saving the Forest for the Trees," *Business Week,* November 20, 2000, pp. 62–63, www.businessweek.com, accessed January 27, 2003.

67. Jim Carlton, "Chiquita to Take Part in Environmental Program," *Wall Street Journal,* November 16, 2000, p. A3, online.wsj.com; Sarah Murray, "Small Farmers Struggle with Rapid Change," *FT.com,* October 7, 2005, p. 1.

68. Jason Hopps, "Study Finds 'Green' Product Labeling Misleading," Reuters Newswire, www.ac-reunion.fr/pedagogie/anglaislp/Teaching_aids/readymade/environmentally_friendly.htm, accessed September 11, 2003.

69. Paul Hawken and William McDonough, "Seven Steps to Doing Good Business," *Inc.,* November 1993, pp. 79–90, www.inc.com/magazine/19931101/3770.html, accessed December 14, 2006.

70. Business and Sustainable Development, "Case Studies: Caeran," http://www.bsdglobal.com/viewcasestudy.asp?id=48, accessed June 20, 2006.

71. "Tire Recycling Gains Traction with Help from Business," CNN, April 25, 2000, www.cnn.com.

72. "Environment & Recycling," American Forest and Paper Association, http://www.afandpa.org/Template.cfm?section=Environment_and_Recycling, accessed June 20, 2006.

73. "Starbucks Serves Up Coffee Grounds for Compost: Great Coffee Is Also Good for the Garden," *Business Wire,* March 20, 2000.

74. "Doing What It Takes to Be Wastewise," Environmental Protection Agency, www.epa.gov/wastewise/about/id-bev.htm, accessed June 20, 2006.

75. Eric Peterson, "The Wal-Mart of Recycling," *Coloradobiz* 26 (October 1999): 66.

76. "Complete Recycling of Water Will Protect Environment, Resources at DaimlerChrysler Plant in Mexico," *PR Newsletter,* March 29, 2000, via America Online.

77. Sharon Begley, "The Battle for Planet Earth," *Newsweek,* April 24, 2000, pp. 50–53.

78. Duncan Austin and Craig Hanson, "Corporate Guide to Green Power Markets," World Resources Institute, http://pubs.wri.org/pubs_description.cfm?PubID=3771, accessed June 20, 2006.

79. Begley, "The Battle for Planet Earth."

80. John J. Fialka, "An Environment-Business Global-Warming Link," *Wall Street Journal,* November 22, 2000, p. A2.

81. Minette E. Drumwright, "Socially Responsible Organizational Buying: Environmental Concern as a Noneconomic Buying Criterion," *Journal of Marketing* 58 (July 1994): 1.

82. "It's On the Shelf, and Here To Stay," *The Grocer,* July 22, 2006, p. 34.

83. Isabelle Maignan and Debbie Thorne McAlister, "Socially Responsible Organizational Buying: Can Stakeholders Dictate Purchasing Policies?" *Journal of Macromarketing* 23 (December 2003): 78.

84. A Guide to World Resources 2002–2004: Decisions for the Earth: Balance, Voice, and Power, World Resources Institute, http://pubs.wri.org/pubs_description.cfm?PubID=3764, accessed May 30, 2006.

85. William M. Pride and O. C. Ferrell, eds., *Marketing: Concepts and Strategies,* 12th ed. (Boston: Houghton Mifflin, 2003), p. 89.

86. Jan Collins, "Being Green," *Business and Economic Review* 52 (January–March 2006): 3–7; "WasteWise Awards," *Business and the Environment* 17 (January 2006): 12–13; Herman Miller, "The Environment," http://www.hermanmiller.com/CDA/SSA/Category/0,1564,a10-c382,00.html, accessed May 10, 2006.

87. "Gregory Conko, "The Benefits of Biotech," Biotech Knowledge Center, www.biotechknowledge.com, accessed June 20, 2006.

88. Begley, "The Battle for Planet Earth."

89. "International Standard ISO 14000," Quality Network, www.quality.co.uk/iso14000.htm, accessed May 31, 2006.

90. Tim O'Brien, *Ford & ISO 14001: The Synergy Between Preserving the Environment and Rewarding Shareholders* (New York: McGraw-Hill, 2001).

CHAPTER 11

1. Lucas Mearian, "System Break-in Nets Hackers 8 Million Credit Card Numbers," *ComputerWorld,* www.computerworld.com/securitytopics/security/story/0,10801,78747,00.html, accessed March 6, 2003; PriceWaterhouseCoopers, *Information Security Breaches Survey 2006,* http://www.pwc.com/uk/eng/ins-sol/publ/pwc_dti-fullsurveyresults06.pdf,

accessed August 24, 2006; Jon Swartz, "Firms' Hacking-related Insurance Costs Soar," *USA Today,* February 9, 2003; Andrew Conry-Murray, "Strategies & Issues: Security Spending," *Network Magazine,* March 1, 2003.

2. Jesse Ellison, "Cute Little Censors," *Newsweek,* April 17, 2006, p. 34; David Ketchum, "Framing the China Internet Debate Will Be the Battle to Win," *Media,* February 24, 2006, p. 17.

3. Kevin Bonsor, "How Electronic Ink Will Work," www.howstuffworks.com/e-ink1.htm, accessed June 11, 2006.

4. Dana James, "Broadband Horizons," *Marketing News,* March 13, 2000, pp. 1, 9.

5. Edward Taylor, "Supercomputers Speed Up Game," *Wall Street Journal,* April 14, 2006, p. C1.

6. Bill Saporito, "Get Ready for Class Warfare," January 13, 2003, www.cnn.com/2003/ALLPOLITICS/01/13/timep.classware.tm/index.html, accessed August 24, 2006.

7. Stacey Wells, "Across the Divide," Business2.com, December 12, 2000, pp. 186–204, www.business2.com/search?qt=Across+the+Divide&business2=on&expanded=, accessed September 11, 2003.

8. Gateway Computers, "Hispanic Association of Colleges and Universities," http://www.gateway.com/work/ed/hi-ed/hacu.shtml, accessed August 25, 2006.

9. "Charting the Future of the Net," MSNBC, July 7, 2000, www.msnbc.com, accessed August 8, 2006.

10. Leslie Walker, "The Lord of the Webs," *Washington Post,* January 30, 2003, p. E1.

11. "Supporting Research and Development to Promote Economic Growth: The Federal Government's Role," Council of Economic Advisers, Washington, DC, October 1995.

12. Alan Greenspan, Remarks to the Economic Club of New York, Federal Reserve Board, New York, January 13, 2000.

13. Elana Varon, "The ABCs of B2B," The E-Business Research Center, www.cio.com/research/ec/edit/b2babc.html, accessed August 23, 2006.

14. Greenspan, Remarks to the Economic Club of New York.

15. "Covisint Parts Exchange Officially Opens for Business," *Bloomberg Newswire,* December 11, 2000, via AOL.

16. Greenspan, Remarks to the Economic Club of New York.

17. Richard Karpinski, "Web Delivers Big Results for Staples," *B to B,* November 11, 2002, p. 14.

18. Kimberly Hill, "Next Stop: Free Wireless Broadband?" Wireless News Factor, January 24, 2002, www.wirelessnewsfactor.com/perl/sotry/20557.html, accessed September 16, 2003.

19. Mark Hall, "Opinion: The Problem with Wireless Interoperability," *ComputerWorld,* December 16, 2002, www.computerworld.com/mobiletopics/mobile/story/0,10801,76667,00.html, accessed August 24, 2006.

20. John Cox, "Navy Set to Navigate with Wireless LANS," *Network World,* January 29, 2003, www.nwfusion.com/news/2003/0127navywireless.html, accessed December 14, 2006.

21. David Lieberman, "America's Digital Divide," *USA Today,* October 11, 1999, p. 1B.

22. David Ho, "Broadband Access Is on the Rise, Study Says," *Austin American-Statesman,* May 29, 2006, p. D1.

23. Arbitron Radio Studies, "Broadband Revolution 2: The Media World of Speedies," http://www.arbitron.com/study_h/broadband2.asp, accessed August 26, 2006.

24. Anick Jesdanun, "Wiring Rural America," MSNBC, September 5, 2000, www.msnbc.com, accessed September 11, 2003.

25. Greenspan, Remarks to the Economic Club of New York.

26. Kyle Stock, "Internet Tax Ban Efforts Resume," PC World.com, www.computerworld.com/managementtopics/ebusiness/story/0,10801,77563,00.html?f=x010, accessed June 9, 2006.

27. Center for Advanced Purchasing Studies, "The Future of Purchasing and Supply: A Five and Ten Year Forecast," http://www.capsresearch.org/publications/pdfs-public/capsnapm1998es.pdf, accessed August 26, 2006.

28. Karen Thomas, "An Early Education in Tech Toys," *USA Today,* December 6, 2000, pp. 1D, 2D.

29. David Field, "Some E-ticket Fliers Can Print Boarding Passes on PC," *USA Today,* December 5, 2000, p. 12B.

30. Glenda Chui, "Mapping Goes Deep: Technology Points the Way to a Revolution in Cartography," *San Jose Mercury News,* September 12, 2000, p. 1F.

31. "Active Home Web Use by Country, May 2006," http://www.clickz.com/stats/sectors/geographics/article.php/3613876, accessed June 19, 2006.

32. Elizabeth Weise, "Web Users to Get More Places to Visit," *USA Today,* December 5, 2000, p. 3D.

33. William M. Pride and O. C. Ferrell, *Marketing: Concepts and Strategies,* 12th ed. (Boston: Houghton Mifflin, 2003), p. 493.

34. Julia Angwin, "Credit-Card Scams: The Devil E-stores," *Wall Street Journal,* September 19, 2000, pp. B1, B4.

35. Michael Pastore, "Fraud Continues to Haunt Online Retail," http://www.internetnews.com/ec-news/article.php/984441, accessed August 20, 2006.

36. Jim Carlton and Pui Wing Tam, "Online Auctioneers Face Growing Fraud Problem," *Wall Street Journal,* May 12, 2000, p. B2.

37. Michael Pastore, "Consumers Remain Confident in Online Auctions," http://www.clickz.com/showPage.html?page=578201, accessed August 26, 2006.

38. David H. Freedman, "Sleaze Bay," *Forbes ASAP,* November 27, 2000, pp. 134–140.

39. eBay Business, "Capital Equipment," http://pages.ebay.com/ebaybusiness/Capital.html, accessed August 26, 2006; Steve Ulfelder, "Online Auctions Offer IT Bargains, Risks," *ComputerWorld,* www.computerworld.com/hardwaretopic/hardware/story/0,10801,76944,00.html, accessed August 25, 2006.

40. Carlton and Tam, "Online Auctioneers Face Growing Fraud Problem."

41. Eve M. Caudill and Patrick E. Murphy, "Consumer Online Privacy: Legal and Ethical Issues," *Journal of Public Policy & Marketing* 19 (Spring 2000): 7–12.

42. "Survey Shows Security and Privacy Remain Major Concerns for Online Shoppers; Third Annual Internet Report Also Reveals That the Internet Has Become Internet Users' Most Important Source of Information," *M2 Presswire,* January 31, 2003, accessed via Lexis-Nexis Academic Database.

43. www.peoplesearch.com, www.UsSearch.com, accessed June 10, 2006.

44. "Internet Peaks as America's Most Important Source of Information, Reports Year Three of UCLA Internet Project; but Study Finds Doubts About Credibility, Privacy, Security,"

AScribe Newswire, January 30, 2003, accessed via Lexis-Nexis Academic Database.

45. "Privacy Initiatives," Federal Trade Commission, www.ftc.gov/privacy/index.html, accessed May 31, 2006.

46. "interMute Launches SpamSubtract to Bring an End to the Spam Epidemic; Maker of AdSubtract Introduces Family-Friendly Tool to Stop Junk E-mail," *Business Wire,* January 27, 2003, accessed via Lexis-Nexis Academic Database.

47. Pride and Ferrell, *Marketing: Concepts and Strategies,* pp. 600–601.

48. "Identity Theft Nightmare," *ABA Bank Compliance,* 23 (December 2002): 1.

49. Scott Wooley, "We Know Where You Live," *Forbes,* November 13, 2000, p. 332.

50. Nancy Weil, "Report Prompts Investigation of Health-Oriented Web Sites," CNN, April 3, 2000, www.cnn.com, accessed September 11, 2003.

51. "FTC Gets Complaints About Amazon.com's New Privacy Policy," *Wall Street Journal,* December 5, 2000, p. A10.

52. Edward C. Baig, "Progress in Online Privacy, but Critics Say Not Enough," *Business Week Online,* May 13, 1999, www.businessweek.com.

53. Heather Green, "Commentary: Privacy—Don't Ask Technology to Do the Job," *Business Week Online,* June 26, 2000, www.businessweek.com.

54. "Federal Web Sites Fail FTC Privacy Test," *USA Today,* September 12, 2000, www.usatoday.com.

55. "Survey: Kids Disclose Private Details Online," CNN, May 17, 2000, www.cnn.com.

56. Anne Reeks, "Electronic Sitters Evolve, but Some Still Beat Others," *Houston Chronicle,* January 23, 2003, p. 3.

57. Federal Trade Commission, "FTC Releases Top 10 Consumer Fraud Complaint Categories," http://www.ftc.gov/opa/2006/01/topten.htm, accessed August 20, 2006.

58. Jack McCarthy, "National Fraud Center: Internet Is Driving Identity Theft," CNN, March 20, 2000, www.cnn.com.

59. "Technology Briefing Internet: Senators Introduce Bill on Identity Theft," *New York Times,* January 28, 2003, p. C4.

60. "Georgetown Internet Privacy Policy Survey," E-Center for Business Ethics, www.e-businessethics.com/, accessed June 10, 2006.

61. "Verizon Earns Top Telecom Ranking in Study of Online Services by *Fortune* 100 Companies, *PR Newswire,* January 30, 2003, accessed by Lexis-Nexis Academic Database.

62. Marcia Stepanek, "The Privacy Penalty on Dot-Coms," *Business Week Online,* June 13, 2000, www.businessweek.com.

63. "Internet Site Agrees to Settle FTC Charges of Deceptively Collecting Personal Information in Agency's First Internet Privacy Case," Federal Trade Commission, press release, August 13, 1998, http://www.ftc.gov/opa/1998/08/geocitie.htm, accessed June 9, 2006.

64. "European Union Directive on Privacy," Banking & Financial Services Policy Report, December 2002.

65. Thomas E. Weber, "Views on Protecting Privacy Diverse in U.S. and Europe," *Wall Street Journal Interactive,* June 19, 2000, http://interactive.wsj.com, accessed September 11, 2003.

66. "A Private Sector Privacy Law," Privacy Commissioner of Canada, http://www.privcom.gc.ca/, accessed June 18, 2006.

67. "Privacy in Japan," E-Center for Business Ethics, www.e-businessethics.com/privacyJA.htm, accessed June 10, 2006.

68. Lorrie Cranor, "No Quick Fixes for Protecting Online Privacy," *Business Week Online,* March 14, 2000, www.businessweek.com.

69. "Privacy in Russia," E-Center for Business Ethics, www.e-businessethics.com/privacyRU.htm, accessed June 11, 2006.

70. "Customer Database Piracy Common in Russia," *Communications Today,* January 27, 2003, accessed via Lexis-Nexis Academic Database.

71. Guy Chazan, "A High-Tech Folk Hero Challenges Russia's Right to Snoop," *Wall Street Journal,* November 27, 2000, p. A28.

72. "Russia Regulators Clamp Down on Vodka Ads on the Internet," Agence France Presse, December 16, 2002, accessed via Lexis-Nexis Academic Database; Anna Bowles, "RuNet: A Cyberian Adventure," *Russian Life* 48 (March–April 2005): 41–47.

73. Catherine Siskos, "In the Service of Guarding Secrets," *Kiplinger's Personal Finance,* February 2003, www.kiplinger.com/magazine.

74. "TRUSTe.com," www.truste.com, accessed June 19, 2006.

75. "American Education Services Sends One Million Trusted Sender Messages: Major Milestone in War Against Spam," *PR Newswire,* February 4, 2003, accessed via Lexis-Nexis Academic Database.

76. "Better Business Bureau Online," www.bbbonline.org, accessed June 11, 2006.

77. "Better Business Bureau and PlanetFeedback Will Help Companies Meet 'Whistleblower' Provision of Recent Corporate Reform Legislation: Two Trusted Organizations Agree to Create System for Confidential Reporting of Alleged Misconduct," *PR Newswire,* December 11, 2002, accessed via Lexis-Nexis Academic Database.

78. Federal Trade Commission, "FTC Announces Settlement with Bankrupt Website, Toysmart.com, Regarding Alleged Privacy Policy Violations," http://www.ftc.gov/opa/2000/07/toysmart2.htm, accessed June 10, 2006.

79. David G. McDonough, "But Can the WTO Really Sock It to Software Pirates?" *Business Week Online,* March 9, 1999, www.businessweek.com, accessed September 11, 2003.

80. "Study Finds PC Software Piracy Declining in Emerging Markets," *Computer & Internet Lawyer* 23 (September 2006): 37–38.

81. McDonough, "But Can the WTO Really Sock It to Software Pirates?"

82. Jim Duffy, "Cisco Sues Huawei over Intellectual Property," *Network World,* January 23, 2003, IDGNews Service, accessed via Lexis-Nexis Academic Database.

83. Rebecca Buckman, "Microsoft Steps Up Software Piracy War," *Wall Street Journal,* August 2, 2000, p. B6.

84. "Microsoft Missing Out Unnecessarily on Billion Dollar Revenues Due to Piracy," *Business Wire,* November 5, 2002, accessed via Lexis-Nexis Academic Database.

85. Stephen Wildstrom, "Can Microsoft Stamp Out Piracy?" *Business Week Online,* October 2, 2000, www.businessweek.com.

86. Rebecca Edelson and Adrienne D. Herman, "The Digital Millennium Copyright Act: A Tool to Limit Liability for Copyright Infringement and to Protect and Enforce Copyrights on the Internet," Alschuler, Grossman, Stein, and Kahan LLP, www.agsk.com/print/index.html, accessed September 11, 2003.

87. Elijah Cocks, "Internet Ruling: Hypertext Linking Does Not Violate Copyright," Intellectual Property and Technology Forum, Boston College Law School, Newton, MA, April 4, 2000.

88. William T. Neese and Charles R. McManis, "Summary Brief: Law, Ethics and the Internet: How Recent Federal Trademark Law Prohibits a Remedy Against 'Cyber-Squatters,'" *Proceedings from the Society of Marketing Advances*, November 4–7, 1998.

89. Linda Rosencrance, "Ways to Verify Accuracy of Domain Name Data Sought," *Computer World*, December 9, 2002, www.computerworld.com.

90. Neese and McManis, "Summary Brief: Law, Ethics and the Internet."

91. Martyn Williams, "Update: ICANN President Calls for Major Overhaul," IDG News Service, February 25, 2002, accessed via Lexis-Nexis Academic Database.

92. Thomas A. Guida and Gerald J. Ferguson, "Strategy ICANN Arbitration vs. Federal Court: Choosing the Right Forum for Trademark Disputes," *Internet Newsletter*, November 7, 2002.

93. Rana Foorohar, "The Internet Splits Up; The Web Changed the World. Politics Is Now Changing It Back," *Newsweek*, May 15, 2006, p. 1.

94. Arthur L. Caplan and Glenn McGee, "An Introduction to Bioethics," Bioethics.net, http://www.bioethics.net/articles.php?viewCat=3&articleId=1, accessed June 18, 2006.

95. Lucette Lagundo, "Drug Companies Face Assault on Prices," *Wall Street Journal*, May 11, 2000, p. B1.

96. Lisa Stansky, "Drug Makers Could Face Wave of Cases," *Connecticut Law Tribune*, January 24, 2003, pp. 123–128.

97. Lagundo, "Drug Companies Face Assault on Prices."

98. Christopher Oster, "Cracking the Code on Biotech Investing," *Wall Street Journal*, June 9, 2000, p. C1.

99. "Attention Business, Technology, Biotechnology, Health Care, Financial Services, Mutual Fund and Investing Special Report," *Canada NewsWire*, January 14, 2003, www.newswire.ca.

100. Mike Jensen, "A Modern Goldrush in Genetics," MSNBC, www.msnbc.com, accessed July 18, 2000.

101. GeneWatch UK, "Research Agendas and Patenting," http://www.genewatch.org/sub.shtml?als[cid]=396424, accessed August 20, 2006.

102. "Avon Foundation Continues Commitment to Breast Cancer Cause; Awards Nearly $30 Million in Grants to Thirteen Organizations," *PR Newswire*, September 24, 2002, www.prnewswire.com.

103. Marilynn Marchione, "Study Suggests Setback in Effort to Morph Stem Cells into Insulin-Producing Pancreas Cells," *Milwaukee Journal Sentinel*, January 17, 2003, p. B8.

104. John Leavitt, "What Will Human Clones Be Like?" *Connecticut Law Tribune*, January 24, 2003, p. 5.

105. Andy Coghlan, "Cloning Special Report: Cloning Without Embryos," *New Scientist*, January 29, 2000, p. 4.

106. Natasha McDowell, "Mini-pig Clone Raises Transplant Hope," http://www.newscientist.com/article/dn3257.html, accessed June 10, 2006.

107. Rachel Nowak, "Australia OKs Human Embryo Research," http://www.newscientist.com/article/dn3149.html, accessed June 11, 2006.

108. Jacqueline Stensen, "Gene Patents Raise Concerns," MSNBC, www.msnbc.com, accessed September 11, 2003.

109. Rebecca S. Eisenberg, "How Can You Patent Genes?" *American Journal of Bioethics* 2 (Summer 2002): 3–11.

110. Sarah Lueck, "New Kits Let You Test Your Own Genes, but Interpreting Results Can Be Tricky," *Wall Street Journal*, May 24, 2005, p. D1.

111. "Conservation Ecology: Risks and Benefits of Genetically Modified Crops," http://www.ecologyandsociety.org/vol4/iss1/art13/, accessed August 26, 2006.

112. Bill Gates, "Will Frankenfood Feed the World?" June 11, 2000, http://www.microsoft.com/presspass/ofnote/06-11time.mspx, accessed June 19, 2006.

113. "Weighing the Future of Biotech Food," MSNBC, www.msnbc.com, accessed July 18, 2000.

114. Julia A. Moore and Gilbert Winham, "Let's Not Escalate the 'Frankenfood' War," www.csmonitor.com/2002/1220/p13s02-coop.html, accessed June 19, 2006.

115. "Green Groups Target Campbell Soup in GM Food Fight," CNN, July 20, 2000, www.cnn.com.

116. "Conservation Ecology: Risks and Benefits of Genetically Modified Crops," http://www.ecologyandsociety.org/vol4/iss1/art13, accessed August 26, 2006.

117. Paul Magnusson, Ann Therese, and Kerry Capell, "Furor over Frankenfood," *Business Week*, October 18, 1999, pp. 50, 51; "Japan Asks That Imports of Corn Be StarLink-Free," *Wall Street Journal*, October 30, 2000, p. A26.

118. Peter Tyson, "Should We Grow GM Crops?" http://www.pbs.org/wgbh/harvest/exist/, accessed August 26, 2006.

119. Magnusson, Therese, and Capell, "Furor over Frankenfood."

120. "McDonald's to Bar GMO Fries," CNNfn, April 28, 2000, www.cnnfn.com.

121. "EU's Anti-GM Stance Under Threat," January 10, 2003, www.cnn.com/2003/WORLD/europe/01/10/biotech.us.europe/index.html; "Conservation Ecology: Risks and Benefits of Genetically Modified Crops," http://www.ecologyandsociety.org/vol4/iss1/art13, accessed August 26, 2006.

122. "'Terminator' Victory a Small Step in Long War," CNN, October 7, 1999, www.cnn.com/NATURE/9910/07/terminator.victory.enn/index.html, accessed August 24, 2006.

123. Francesca Lyman, "Biotech Battle of Seattle, and Beyond," MSNBC, www.msnbc.com, accessed September 11, 2003.

124. Fred Guterl, "The Fear of Food," *Newsweek International*, January 27, 2003, accessed via Lexis-Nexis Academic Database.

125. Greg Farrell, "Police Have Few Weapons Against Cyber-Criminals," *USA Today*, December 6, 2000, p. 5B; Edward Iwata and Kevin Johnson, "Computer Crime Outpacing Cybercops," *USA Today*, June 7, 2000, pp. 1A.

126. Kevin Poulsen, "Feds Seek Public Input on Hacker Sentencing," *SecurityFocus*, January 13, 2003, online.securityfocus.com/news/2028, accessed August 15, 2006.

127. Patrick Thibodeau, "DMCA," *ComputerWorld*, December 2, 2002, www.computerworld.com/governmenttopics/government/legalissues/story/0,10801,76301,00.html, accessed August 26, 2006.

128. "Websense," http://www.websense.com/global/en/, accessed June 10, 2006.

129. Mathis Thurman, "Proxy Server Serves to Block Slacker," *ComputerWorld*, April 29, 2002, www.computerworld.com.

130. PriceWaterhouseCoopers, *Information Security Breaches Survey 2006*, http://www.pwc.com/uk/eng/ins-sol/publ/pwc_dti-fullsurveyresults06.pdf, accessed August 24, 2006.

131. Lindsey Gerdes, "You Have 20 Minutes to Surf. Go," *Business Week,* December 26, 2005, p. 16.

132. Michael J. McCarthy, "Keystroke Loggers Save E-mail Rants, Raising Workplace Privacy Concerns," *Wall Street Journal,* March 7, 2000, http://interactive.wsj.com.

133. Julene Snyder, "Should Overworked Employees Be Allowed to Surf the Web on the Job?" CNN online, May 11, 2000, www.cnn.com/2000/TECH/computing/05/11/job.surf .idg/, accessed August 23, 2006.

134. Roberta Fusaro, "Chief Privacy Officer: A Conversation with Richard Purcell," *Harvard Business Review* 78 (November–December 2000): 20–22.

135. Sheila M. J. Bonini, Lenny T. Mendonca, and Jeremy M. Oppenheim, "When Social Issues Become Strategic," *The McKinsey Quarterly* 2 (2006): 20.

CHAPTER 12

1. David Magee, *The John Deere Way: Performance That Endures* (New York: John Wiley, 2005); http://www.deere.com/ en_US/compinfo/index.html, accessed February 14, 2006; http://www.deere.com/en_US/compinfo/reports/ehs/ index.html, accessed February 15, 2006.

2. "Why Count Social Performance," in *Building Corporate Accountability: The Emerging Practices in Social and Ethical Accounting, Auditing and Reporting,* ed. Simon Zadek, Peter Pruzan, and Richard Evans (London: Earthscan Publications, 1997), pp. 12–34.

3. Business for Social Responsibility, "Accountability," www.bsr .org/BSRResources/WhitePaperDetail.cfm?DocumentID=259, accessed September 9, 2003.

4. Ibid.

5. Sandra Waddock and Neil Smith, "Corporate Responsibility Audits: Doing Well by Doing Good," *Sloan Management Review* 41 (Winter 2000): 75–83.

6. "Why Count Social Performance."

7. John Pearce, "Measuring Social Wealth" (London: New Economics Foundation, 1996) as reported in Warren Dow and Roy Crowe, *What Social Auditing Can Do for Voluntary Organizations* (Vancouver, WA: Volunteer Vancouver, 1999), p. 8.

8. Mark Maremont, "Tyco Delayed Some Bonuses, Likely Boosting Cash Flows," *Wall Street Journal Online,* January 21, 2003, http://online.wsj.com, accessed August 8, 2006.

9. Business for Social Responsibility, "Accountability."

10. Ibid.

11. Anne Fisher, "America's Most Admired Companies," *Fortune,* March 6, 2006, p. 65.

12. Wendy Zellner, "No Way to Treat a Lady?" *Business Week,* March 3, 2003, pp. 63–66.

13. Fisher, "America's Most Admired Companies," p. 72.

14. Business for Social Responsibility, "Verification," www.bsr.org/ BSRResources/WhitePaperDetail.cfm?DocumentID=440, accessed September 9, 2003.

15. Business for Social Responsibility, "Accountability."

16. Trey Buchholz, "Auditing Social Responsibility Reports: The Application of Financial Auditing Standards," Colorado State University, professional paper, November 28, 2000, p. 3.

17. Business for Social Responsibility, "Accountability."

18. Ibid.

19. Louise Gordon, "An Update on Smith O'Brien's CSR Audit—A Tool to Help Companies Measure Progress and Its Value," *Executive Citizen,* September–October 1996, p. 38.

20. "Social Audits and Accountability," Business for Social Responsibility, www.bsr.org/BSRresources/whitepaperdetail .cfm, accessed December 12, 2006.

21. Buchholz, "Auditing Social Responsibility Reports," pp. 2–3.

22. "Results of the DJSI Review 2002," Dow-Jones Sustainability Indexes, www.sustainability-indexes.com/news/pdf/ press_releases/DJSI_PR_020904_Review2002.pdf, accessed March 27, 2003.

23. Dow and Crowe, *What Social Auditing Can Do for Voluntary Organizations,* pp. 15–18.

24. Peter Raynard, "Coming Together: A Review of Contemporary Approaches to Social Accounting, Auditing and Reporting in Non-Profit Organizations," *Journal of Business Ethics* 17 (October 1998): 1471–1479.

25. Tracy Swift and Nicole Dando, "From Methods to Ideologies: Closing the Assurance Gap in Social and Ethical Accounting," *Journal of Corporate Citizenship* (Winter 2002): 81–90.

26. "U.S. Companies Risk Reputations and Finances Due to Broadening Public Concern with All Forms of Corporate Behavior," *PR Newswire,* August 19, 2002, www .findarticles.com.

27. Penelope Patsuris, "The Corporate Accounting Scandal Sheet," *Forbes,* August 26, 2002, www.forbes.com/ 2002/07/25/accountingtracker.html.

28. "What Is Corporate Social Responsibility?" Vasin, Heyn & Company, www.vhcoaudit.com/SRAarticles/WhatIsCSR.htm, accessed February 13, 2003.

29. Nick Crossley, "Global Anti-Corporate Struggle: A Preliminary Analysis," *British Journal of Sociology* 53, no. 4 (2002): 667–691; John Giuffo, "Smoke Gets in Your Eyes," *Columbia Journalism Review* 40, no. 3 (2001): 14–18; Stan Sutter, "What Are You Afraid Of?" *Marketing* 109, no. 31 (2004): 3; Laura Tucker and T. C. Melewar, "Corporate Reputation and Crisis Management: The Threat and Manageability of Anti-Corporatism," *Corporate Reputation Review* 7, no. 4 (2005): 337–387; http://www.sustainability-index.com/ accessed April 17, 2006.

30. Tobias Webb, James Rose, and Peter Davis, "ISO 26000 Indicates Immaturity: If Corporate Responsibility Is to Be Effective, Prominence Has to Be Given to Both Quantitative and Qualitative Analyses," *Ethical Corporation,* December 2005, p. 9.

31. Paul Hohnen and Tom Rotherham, "The ISO and Social Responsibility: Breakdown or Breakthrough in Bangkok," *Ethical Corporation,* October 2005, p. 40–41.

32. "Social Balance Sheet," www.eurofound.eu.int/emire/SPAIN/ SOCIALBALANCESHEET-ES.html, accessed March 3, 2003.

33. Six Sigma, http://en.wikipedia.org/wiki/Six_Sigma, accessed April 4, 2006.

34. The Balanced Scorecard, http://en.wikipedia.org/wiki/ Balanced_scorecard, accessed April 4, 2006.

35. The Triple Bottom Line, http://en.wikipedia.org/wiki/ Triple_bottom_line, accessed April 4, 2006.

36. Lynn Brewer, "Capitalizing on the Value of Integrity: An Integrated Model to Standardize the Measure of Non-Financial Performance as an Assessment of Corporate Integrity," Appendix B in Lynn Brewer, Robert Chandler, and O. C. Ferrell, *Managing Risks for Corporate Integrity: How to Survive an Ethical Misconduct Disaster* (Mason, OH: Texere/Thomson, 2006).

37. Brewer, Chandler, and Ferrell, *Managing Risks for Corporate Integrity,* pp. 49–50.
38. *Journal of Corporate Citizenship,* December 2002, p. 81.
39. "CSR Governance Structures," www.bsr.org/BSRResources/IssueBriefDetail.cfm?DocumentID=190, accessed November 11, 2003. Copyright © 2003 by Business for Social Responsibility. Reprinted with permission.
40. Lauren Coleman-Lochner, "Independent Look at Wal-Mart Shows Both Good and Bad," *San Antonio Express-News,* November 5, 2005, p. 4D.
41. Business for Social Responsibility, "Accountability."
42. Johann Mouton, "Chris Hani Baragwanath Hospital Ethics Audit," Ethics Institute of South Africa, 2001, available at www.ethicsa.org/report_CHB.html.
43. "Who We Are and What Our Values Are," www.furnitureresourcesentre.com, accessed March 27, 2003. Copyright © 2003 by Furniture Resource Centre Ltd. Reprinted with permission.
44. "Ethical Statement," SocialAudit.org, www.socialaudit.org/pages/ethical.htm, accessed March 4, 2003.
45. Business for Social Responsibility, "Verification."
46. Ibid.
47. "Ethical Statement."
48. "Wells Fargo's Community Reinvestment Leadership Commitment," Wells Fargo, www.wellsfargo.com/wfcra/index.jhtml, accessed March 5, 2003.
49. Community Involvement, www.homedepot.com, accessed March 5, 2003.
50. Business for Social Responsibility, "Community Involvement," www.bsr.org/BSRResources/WhitePaperDetail.cfm?DocumentID=264, accessed March 5, 2003.
51. Anil Hira and Jared Ferrie, "Fair Trade: Three Key Challenges for Reaching the Mainstream," *Journal of Business Ethics* 63, no. 2 (January 2006), pp. 107–118.
52. Matthew Gitsham, "Cleaner But Not Sparkling," *Ethical Corporation,* December 2005, pp. 48–49.
53. Business for Social Responsibility, "Verification."
54. Buchholz, "Auditing Social Responsibility Reports," p. 15.
55. Ibid., p. 16.
56. Business for Social Responsibility, "Verification."
57. Chad Terhune, "A Suit by Coke Bottlers Exposes Cracks in a Century-Old System," *Wall Street Journal,* March 13, 2006, p. A1.
58. Business for Social Responsibility, "Introduction to Corporate Social Responsibility," www.bsr.org/BSRResources/White Paper Detail.cfm?DocumentID=138, accessed March 5, 2003.
59. Ibid.
60. Ibid.
61. Helen Shaw and Dave Cook, "Scrushy Acquitted on All Counts," CFO.com, June 28, 2005, www.cfo.com/article.cfm/4076776/c_4125234?f=TodayInFinance_inside, accessed August 8. 2006; Andrew Countryman, "SEC: HealthSouth Earnings Overstated by $1.4 Billion," *Austin American-Statesman,* March 20, 2003, http://austin360.com/statesman/.
62. Brewer, Chandler, and Ferrell, *Managing Risks for Corporate Integrity,* p. 91.
63. Business for Social Responsibility, "Accountability."
64. Ibid.
65. Ethics and Compliance Officer Association, www.theecoa.org, accessed March 5, 2003.
66. Business for Social Responsibility, "Accountability."
67. Harriett Ryan, "Non-financial Reporting More Essential Than Ever, Finds New Survey by Arup," *M2 Presswire,* February 27, 2003.
68. Business for Social Responsibility, "Verification."
69. Ibid.
70. Buchholz, "Auditing Social Responsibility Reports," pp. 18–19; "SEC Approves Conflict-of-Interest Limits for Auditors," Bloomberg LP, aol://4344:30.bloomberg.389091.602536905, accessed November 17, 2000.
71. Buchholz, "Auditing Social Responsibility Reports," pp. 16–18.
72. Ibid., pp. 19–20.
73. Business for Social Responsibility, "Accountability."
74. Buchholz, "Auditing Social Responsibility Reports," pp. 19–20.
75. *KPMG International Survey of Corporate Sustainability Reporting 2005* (Amsterdam: University Amsterdam, 2005), http://www.kpmg.com/news/index.asp?cid=1040, accessed March 28, 2006.
76. "The Nestlé Concept of Social Responsibility," March 2006, Nestlé S.A. Public Affairs, p. 7.
77. Ibid., p. 1.
78. Waddock and Smith, "Corporate Responsibility Audits."
79. Buchholz, "Auditing Social Responsibility Reports," p. 1.
80. Waddock and Smith, "Corporate Responsibility Audits."
81. Buchholz, "Auditing Social Responsibility Reports," p. 1.
82. Waddock and Smith, "Corporate Responsibility Audits."
83. J. C. Collins and J. I. Porras, *Built to Last: Successful Habits of Visionary Companies* (New York: HarperCollins, 1997).
84. Waddock and Smith, "Corporate Responsibility Audits."

Index